DICTIONARY OF
ACCOUNTING

THIRD EDITION

Dictionary Titles in the Series

Specialist Dictionaries:

Dictionary of Banking and Finance	0 7475 6685 2
Dictionary of Business	0 7475 9680 0
Dictionary of Computing	0 7475 6622 4
Dictionary of Economics	0 7475 6632 1
Dictionary of Environment and Ecology	0 7475 7201 1
Dictionary of Hotels, Tourism and Catering Management	1 9016 5999 2
Dictionary of Human Resources and Personnel Management	0 7475 6623 2
Dictionary of ICT	0 7475 6990 8
Dictionary of Marketing	0 7475 6621 6
Dictionary of Medical Terms	0 7475 6987 8
Dictionary of Military Terms	1 9038 5620 5
Dictionary of Nursing	0 7475 6634 8
Dictionary of Science and Technology	0 7475 6620 8

English Language:

Easier English Basic Dictionary	0 7475 6644 5
Easier English Basic Synonyms	0 7475 6979 7
English Study Dictionary	1 9016 5963 1
Easier English Student Dictionary	0 7475 6624 0
English Thesaurus for Students	1 9016 5931 3

Check your English Vocabulary Workbooks:

Business	0 7475 6626 7
Computing	1 9016 5928 3
English for Academic Purposes	0 7475 6691 7
PET	0 7475 6627 5
FCE +	0 7475 6981 9
IELTS	0 7475 6982 7
TOEFL®	0 7475 6984 3

Visit our website for full details of all our books
http://www.bloomsbury.com/reference

DICTIONARY OF
ACCOUNTING

THIRD EDITION

S.M.H. Collin

BLOOMSBURY

A BLOOMSBURY REFERENCE BOOK

www.bloomsbury.com

Originally published by Peter Collin Publishing

Third edition published 2004
Second edition published 2001
First published in Great Britain 1992

Bloomsbury Publishing Plc
38 Soho Square, London W1D 3HB
© Copyright S.M.H. Collin, 1992, 2001
This edition © copyright Bloomsbury Publishing Plc 2004

British Library Cataloguing-in-Publication Data

A catalogue record for this book is available from the British Library

ISBN 0 7475 6991 6

Text processing and computer typesetting by Bloomsbury
Printed and bound in Italy by Legoprint

Text Production and Proofreading
Katy McAdam, Stephen Curtis, Heather Bateman

All papers used by Bloomsbury Publishing are natural, recyclable products made from wood
grown in well-managed forests. The manufacturing processes conform to the environmental
regulations of the country of origin.

Preface

This dictionary provides a basic vocabulary of terms used in accounting, from personal finance and investments to company accounts, balance sheets and stock valuations. It is ideal for students of accounting and for anyone who needs to check the meaning of an accountancy term, from people working in businesses who may not be professional accountants to translators or those for whom English is an additional language.

Each headword is explained in clear, straightforward English and examples are given to show how the word may be used in context. There are also quotations from newspapers and specialist magazines. Sample documents and financial statements are also provided.

Thanks are due to Jeremy Kourdi for his help and advice during the production of this new edition.

Symbols

■	before a new part of speech
○	before examples
□	before a phrase or collocation
◇	before an idiom
◊	a definition of the word will be found at the place indicated
♦	extra information will be found at the place indicated

Pronunciation

The following symbols have been used to show the pronunciation of the main words in the dictionary.
Stress has been indicated by a main stress mark (') and a secondary stress mark (ˌ). Note that these are only guides, as the stress of the word changes according to its position in the sentence.

Vowels		*Consonants*	
æ	back	b	buck
ɑː	harm	d	dead
ɒ	stop	ð	other
aɪ	type	dʒ	jump
aʊ	how	f	fare
aɪə	hire	g	gold
aʊə	hour	h	head
ɔː	course	j	yellow
ɔɪ	annoy	k	cab
e	head	l	leave
eə	fair	m	mix
eɪ	make	n	nil
eʊ	go	ŋ	sing
ɜː	word	p	print
iː	keep	r	rest
i	happy	s	save
ə	about	ʃ	shop
ɪ	fit	t	take
ɪə	near	tʃ	change
u	annual	θ	theft
uː	pool	v	value
ʊ	book	w	work
ʊə	tour	x	loch
ʌ	shut	ʒ	measure
		z	zone

A

AAA *abbr* American Accounting Association

AARF *abbr* Australian Accounting Research Foundation

AAT *abbr* Accounting of Accounting Technicians

abacus /ˈæbəkəs/ *noun* a counting device consisting of parallel rods strung with beads, still widely used for business and accounting in China and Japan

abandonment /əˈbændənmənt/ *noun* an act of giving up voluntarily something that you own, such as an option or the right to a property □ **abandonment of a claim** giving up a claim in a civil action

abatement /əˈbeɪtmənt/ *noun* **1.** an act of reducing **2.** a reduction in a payment, e.g., if a company's or individual's total assets are insufficient to cover their debts or legacies

ABB *abbr* activity-based budgeting

abbreviated accounts /əˌbriːvieɪtɪd ə ˈkaʊnts/ *noun* a shortened version of a company's annual accounts that a small or medium sized company can file with the Registrar of Companies, instead of a full version

ab initio /ˌæb ɪ ˈnɪʃiəʊ/ *Latin phrase meaning* 'from the beginning'

abnormal /æbˈnɔːm(ə)l/ *adjective* not normal, atypical

abnormal gain /æbˌnɔːm(ə)l ˈɡeɪn/ *noun* any reduction in the volume of process loss below that set by the normal loss allowance. Abnormal gains are generally costed as though they were completed products.

abnormal loss /æbˌnɔːm(ə)l ˈlɒs/ *noun* any losses which exceed the normal loss allowance. Abnormal losses are generally costed as though they were completed products.

above par /əˌbʌv ˈpɑː/ *adjective* referring to a share with a market price higher than its par value

above the line /əˌbʌv ðə ˈlaɪn/ *adjective, adverb* **1.** used to describe entries in a company's profit and loss accounts that appear above the line separating entries showing the origin of the funds that have contributed to the profit or loss from those that relate to its distribution. Exceptional and extraordinary items appear above the line. ○ *Exceptional items are noted above the line in company accounts.* **2.** relating to revenue items in a government budget **3.** relating to advertising for which payment is made (such as an ad in a magazine or a stand at a trade fair) and for which a commission is paid to an advertising agency. Compare **below the line**

abridged accounts /əˌbrɪdʒd əˈkaʊnts/ *noun* financial statements produced by a company that fall outside the requirements stipulated in the Companies Act

absorb /əbˈzɔːb/ *verb* **1.** to take in a small item so that it forms part of a larger one □ **a business which has been absorbed by a competitor** a small business which has been made part of a larger one **2.** to assign an overhead to a particular cost centre in a company's production accounts so that its identity becomes lost. ◊ **absorption costing**

absorbed overhead /əbˌzɔːbd ˈəʊvəhed/ *noun* an overhead attached to products or services by means of **overhead absorption rates**

absorption /əbˈzɔːpʃən/ *noun* the process of making a smaller business part of a larger one, so that the smaller company in effect no longer exists

absorption costing /əbˈzɔːpʃən ˌkɒstɪŋ/ *noun* **1.** a form of costing for a product that includes both the direct costs of production and the indirect overhead costs as well **2.** an accounting practice in which fixed and variable costs of production are absorbed by different cost centres. Providing all the products or services can be sold at a price that covers the allocated costs, this method ensures that both fixed and variable costs are recovered in full. ◊ **marginal costing**

absorption rate /əbˈzɔːpʃən ˌreɪt/ *noun* a rate at which overhead costs are absorbed into each unit of production

abstract /ˈæbstrækt/ *noun* a short form of a report or document ○ *to make an abstract of the company accounts*

Academy of Accounting Historians /əˌkædəmi əv əˈkaʊntɪŋ/ *noun* a US organisation, founded in 1973, that promotes the study of the history of accounting

ACAUS /ˈeɪkæs/ *abbr* Association of Chartered Accountants in the United States

ACCA *abbr* Association of Chartered Certified Accountants

accelerate /əkˈseləreɪt/ *verb* to reduce the amount of time before a maturity date

acceleration /əkˌseləˈreɪʃ(ə)n/ *noun* the speeding up of debt repayment

acceleration clause /əkˌseləˈreɪʃən ˌklɔːz/ *noun US* a clause in a contract providing for immediate payment of the total balance if there is a breach of contract

accept /əkˈsept/ *verb* **1.** to take something which is being offered **2.** to say 'yes' or to agree to something ○ *She accepted the offer of a job in Australia.* ○ *He accepted £2000 in lieu of notice.*

acceptance /əkˈsept(ə)ns/ *noun* **1.** the act of signing a bill of exchange to show that you agree to pay it □ **to present a bill for acceptance** to present a bill for payment by the person who has accepted it **2.** a bill which has been accepted **3.** the act of accepting an offer of new shares for which you have applied

acceptance credit /əkˈsept(ə)ns ˌkredɪt/ *noun* an arrangement of credit from a bank, where the bank accepts bills of exchange drawn on the bank by the debtor: the bank then discounts the bills and is responsible for paying them when they mature. The debtor owes the bank for the bills but these are covered by letters of credit.

acceptance sampling /əkˈsept(ə)ns ˌsɑːmplɪŋ/ *noun* the process of testing a small sample of a batch to see if the whole batch is good enough to be accepted

accepting house /əkˈseptɪŋ ˈhaʊs/, **acceptance house** /əkˈsept(ə)ns ˈhaʊs/ *noun* a firm, usually a merchant bank, which accepts bills of exchange at a discount, in return for immediate payment to the issuer, in this case the Bank of England

Accepting Houses Committee /ək ˌseptɪŋ ˌhaʊzɪz kəˈmɪti/ *noun* the main London merchant banks, which organise the lending of money with the Bank of England. They receive slightly better discount rates from the Bank.

acceptor /əkˈseptə/ *noun* a person who accepts a bill of exchange by signing it, thus making a commitment to pay it by a specified date

accident insurance /ˌæksɪd(ə)nt ɪn ˈʃʊərəns/ *noun* insurance which will pay the insured person when an accident takes place

accommodation /əˌkɒməˈdeɪʃ(ə)n/ *noun* money lent for a short time

accommodation address /əˌkɒmə ˈdeɪʃ(ə)n əˌdres/ *noun* an address used for receiving messages, but which is not the real address of the company

accommodation bill /əˌkɒməˈdeɪʃ(ə)n ˌbɪl/ *noun* a bill of exchange where the person signing (the 'drawee') is helping another company (the 'drawer') to raise a loan

account /əˈkaʊnt/ *noun* **1.** a record of financial transactions over a period of time, such as money paid, received, borrowed or owed ○ *Please send me your account* or *a detailed* or *an itemised account.* **2.** (*in a shop*) an arrangement which a customer has to buy goods and pay for them at a later date, usually the end of the month ○ *to have an account* or *a charge account* or *a credit account with Harrods* ○ *Put it on my account* or *charge it to my account.* ○ *They are one of our largest accounts.* **3.** a customer who does a large amount of business with a firm and has an account with it ○ *Smith Brothers is one of our largest accounts.* ○ *Our sales people call on their best accounts twice a month.* **4.** a period during which shares are traded for credit, and at the end of which the shares bought must be paid for (NOTE: On the London Stock Exchange, there are twenty-four accounts during the year, each running usually for ten working days.) **5.** a structured record of financial transactions that may be maintained as a list or in a more formal structured credit and debit basis

accountability /əˌkaʊntəˈbɪlɪti/ *noun* the fact of being responsible to someone for something, e.g. the accountability of directors to the shareholders

accountable /əˈkaʊntəb(ə)l/ *adjective* referring to a person who has to explain what has taken place or who is responsible for something (NOTE: you are accountable **to** someone **for** something)

accountancy /əˈkaʊntənsi/ *noun* the work of an accountant ○ *They are studying accountancy* or *They are accountancy students.* (NOTE: The US term is **accounting** in this meaning.)

accountancy bodies /əˈkaʊntənsi ˌbɒdiːz/ *noun* professional institutions and associations for accountants

accountancy profession /ə,kaʊntənsi prə'feʃ(ə)n/ *noun* the professional bodies that establish entry standards, organise professional examinations, and draw up ethical and technical guidelines for accountants

accountant /ə'kaʊntənt/ *noun* a person who keeps a company's accounts or deals with an individual person's tax affairs ○ *The chief accountant of a manufacturing group.* ○ *The accountant has shown that there is a sharp variance in our labour costs.*

Accountants' International Study Group /ə,kaʊntənts ,ɪntənæʃ(ə)nəl 'stʌdi ,gruːp/ *noun* a body of professional accounting bodies from the United States, Canada, and the United Kingdom that was established in 1966 to research accounting practices in the three member countries. After publishing 20 reports, it was disbanded in 1977 with the foundation of the International Federation of Accountants.

accountant's opinion /ə,kaʊntənts ə 'pɪnjən/ *noun* a report of the audit of a company's books, carried out by a certified public accountant (NOTE: The US term is **audit opinion**.)

accountants' report /ə,kaʊntənts rɪ 'pɔːt/ *noun* in the United Kingdom, a report written by accountants that is required by the London Stock Exchange to be included in the prospectus of a company seeking a listing on the Exchange

account code /ə'kaʊnt kəʊd/ *noun* a number assigned to a particular account in a numerical accounting system, e.g., a chart of accounts

account end /ə,kaʊnt 'end/ *noun* the end of an accounting period

account executive /ə'kaʊnt ɪg ,zekjʊtɪv/ *noun* 1. an employee who looks after customers or who is the link between customers and the company 2. an employee of an organisation such as a bank, public relations firm or advertising agency who is responsible for looking after particular clients and handling their business with the organisation

account form /ə'kaʊnt fɔːm/ *noun* a balance sheet laid out in horizontal form. It is the opposite of 'report' or 'vertical' form.

accounting /ə'kaʊntɪŋ/ *noun* 1. the work of recording money paid, received, borrowed or owed ○ *accounting methods* ○ *accounting procedures* ○ *an accounting machine* 2. accountancy, the work of an accountant as a course of study

'...applicants will be professionally qualified and have a degree in Commerce or Accounting' [*Australian Financial Review*]

Accounting and Finance Association of Australia and New Zealand /ə ,kaʊntɪŋ ən ,faɪnæns ə,səʊsi,eɪʃ(ə)n əv ɒs 'treɪliə njuː/ *noun* an organisation for accounting and finance academics, researchers, and professionals working in Australia and New Zealand. Abbreviation **AFAANZ**

accounting bases /ə,kaʊntɪŋ 'beɪsiːz/ *plural noun* the possible ways in which accounting concepts may be applied to financial transactions, e.g. the methods used to depreciate assets, how intangible assets or work in progress are dealt with

accounting concept /ə'kaʊntɪŋ ,kɒnsept/ *noun* a general assumption on which accounts are prepared. The main concepts are: that the business is a going concern, that revenue and costs are noted when they are incurred and not when cash is received or paid, that the present accounts are drawn up following the same principles as the previous accounts, that the revenue or costs are only recorded if it is certain that they will be incurred.

accounting conventions /ə'kaʊntɪŋ kən,venʃ(ə)nz/ *noun* the fundamental assumptions that govern the practice of accounting, e.g., consistency and **prudence**. Also called **accounting concepts**. ◊ **conceptual framework**

accounting date /ə'kaʊntɪŋ ,deɪt/ *noun* the date on which an accounting period ends, usually 31st December for annual accounts but it can in fact be any date

accounting entity /ə'kaʊntɪŋ ,entəti/ *noun* the unit for which financial statements and accounting records are prepared, e.g., a limited company or a partnership. ◊ **reporting entity**

accounting equation /ə,kaʊntɪŋ ɪ 'kweɪʒ(ə)n/ *noun* the basic formula that underpins double-entry bookkeeping. It can be expressed most simply as 'assets + expenses = liabilities + capital + revenue' where the debit amounts to the left of the equals sign must be equivalent to the credit amounts to the right. Also called **balance sheet equation**

accounting event /ə,kaʊntɪŋ ɪ'vent/ *noun* a transaction recorded in a business's books of account

accounting fees /ə'kaʊntɪŋ ,fiːz/ *plural noun* fees paid to an accountant for preparing accounts, which are deductible against tax

accounting manual /ə,kaʊntɪŋ 'mænjuəl/ *noun* a handbook or set of instructions that set out all procedures and responsibilities of those engaged in an entity's accounting systems

accounting period /ə'kaʊntɪŋ ,pɪəriəd/ *noun* a period of time at the end of which the firm's accounts are made up

accounting policies /ə'kaʊntɪŋ ,pɒlɪsiz/ *noun* the accounting bases used by a company when preparing its financial statements

Accounting Principles Board /ə ,kaʊntɪŋ 'prɪnsɪp(ə)z ,bɔːd/ *noun* the US body which issued Opinions that formed much of US Generally Accepted Accounting Principles up to 1973 when the Financial Accounting Standards Board (FASB) took over that role. Abbreviation **APB**

accounting procedure /ə'kaʊntɪŋ prə ,siːdʒə/ *noun* an accounting method developed by an individual or organisation to deal with routine accounting tasks

accounting rate of return /ə,kaʊntɪŋ reɪt əv rɪ'tɜːn/ *noun* a method of valuing shares in a company where the company's estimated future profits are divided by the rate of return required by investors. Abbreviation **ARR**

accounting reference date /ə,kaʊntɪŋ 'ref(ə)rəns ,deɪt/ *noun* the last day of a company's accounting reference period

accounting reference period /ə ,kaʊntɪŋ 'ref(ə)rəns ,pɪəriəd/ *noun* **1.** the period for which a company makes up its accounts. In most, but not all, cases, the period is 12 months. **2.** the period for which corporation tax is calculated

accounting software /ə,kaʊntɪŋ 'sɒftweə/ *noun* programs used to enter and process accounts information on an office computer

accounting standard /ə,kaʊntɪŋ 'stændəd/ *noun* an authoritative statement of how particular types of transaction and other events should be reflected in financial statements. Compliance with accounting standards will normally be necessary for financial statements to give a true and fair view.

accounting standards /ə,kaʊntɪŋ 'stændədz/ *plural noun* rules of accounting practice recommended by the Accounting Standards Board (or FASB in the USA)

Accounting Standards Board /ə ,kaʊntɪŋ 'stændədz bɔːd/ *noun* a committee set up by British accounting institutions to monitor methods used in accounting. Abbreviation **ASB**

Accounting Standards Committee /ə,kaʊntɪŋ 'stændədz kə,mɪti/ *noun* a UK accounting standards issuing body whose functions were taken over by the ASB in 1990. Abbreviation **ASC**

accounting technician /ə,kaʊntɪŋ tek 'nɪʃ(ə)n/ *noun* a person who assists in the preparation of accounts but who is not a fully qualified accountant

account payee /ə,kaʊnt peɪ'iː/ *noun* the words printed on most UK cheques indicating that the cheque can only be paid into the account of the person or business to whom the cheque is written, or be cashed for a fee at an agency offering a cheque cashing service

accounts department /ə'kaʊnts dɪ ,pɑːtmənt/ *noun* a department in a company which deals with money paid, received, borrowed or owed

accounts manager /ə'kaʊnts ,mænɪdʒə/ *noun* the manager of an accounts department

accounts payable /ə,kaʊnts 'peɪəb(ə)l/ *noun* money owed by a company

accounts receivable /ə,kaʊnts rɪ 'siːvəb(ə)l/ *noun* money owed to a company. Abbreviation **AR**

accrete /ə'kriːt/ *verb* to have something added to it, especially of a fund to have interest added to it

accretion /ə'kriːʃ(ə)n/ *noun* the process of adding interest to a fund over a period of time

accrual /ə'kruːəl/ *noun* **1.** the act of noting financial transactions when they take place, and not when payment is made **2.** a gradual increase by addition

accruals concept /ə'kruːəlz ,kɒnsept/ *noun* the concept that accounts are prepared with financial transactions accrued. Revenue and costs are both reported during the accounting period to which they refer.

accrue /ə'kruː/ *verb* **1.** to record a financial transaction in accounts when it takes place, and not when payment is made or received **2.** to increase and be due for payment at a later date ○ *Interest accrues from the beginning of the month.*

accrued dividend /ə,kruːd ,dɪvɪ'dend/ *noun* a dividend earned since the last dividend was paid

accrued expense /ə,kruːd ɪk'spens/ *noun* an expense that has been incurred within in a given accounting period but not yet paid

accrued income /əˌkruːd 'ɪnkʌm/ *noun* revenue entered in accounts, although payment has not yet been received

accrued interest /əˌkruːd 'ɪntrəst/ *noun* interest which has been earned by an interest-bearing investment ○ *Accrued interest is added quarterly.*

accrued liabilities /əˌkruːd ˌlaɪə'bɪlɪtiz/ *noun* liabilities which are recorded in an accounting period, although payment has not yet been made. This refers to liabilities such as rent, electricity, etc.

accumulate /ə'kjuːmjʊleɪt/ *verb* to grow in quantity by being added to, or to get more of something over a period of time ○ *We allow dividends to accumulate in the fund.*

accumulated depreciation /əˌkjuːmjʊleɪtɪd dɪˌpriːʃi'eɪʃ(ə)n/ *noun* the total amount by which an asset has been depreciated since it was purchased

accumulated earnings tax /əˌkjuːmjʊˌleɪtd 'ɜːnɪŋz tæks/, **accumulated profits tax** /əˌkjuːmjʊˌleɪtd 'prɒfɪts tæks/ *noun US* a tax on earnings above a specified limit which are unjustifiably retained in a business to avoid paying higher personal income tax

accumulated profit /əˌkjuːmjʊleɪtɪd 'prɒfɪt/ *noun* a profit which is not paid as dividend but is taken over into the accounts of the following year

accumulated reserves /əˌkjuːmjʊleɪtɪd rɪ'zɜːvz/ *plural noun* reserves which a company has put aside over a period of years

accumulation /əˌkjuːmjʊ'leɪʃ(ə)n/ *noun* the process of growing larger by being added to, or of getting more and more of something

ACH /ˌeɪ siː 'eɪtʃ/ *abbr US* Automated Clearing House

acid test /ˌæsɪd 'test/ *noun* an accounting ratio used to measure an organisation's liquidity. It is calculated by taking the business's current assets, minus its stocks, divided by its current liabilities. The higher the ratio, the better: a low ratio is usually a sign that a company is overstretched.

acid test ratio /ˈæsɪd 'test 'reɪʃɪəʊ/ *noun* same as **liquidity ratio**

acquire /ə'kwaɪə/ *verb* to buy ○ *to acquire a company* ○ *We have acquired a new office building in the centre of town.*

acquirer /ə'kwaɪərə/ *noun* a person or company which buys something

acquisition /ˌækwɪ'zɪʃ(ə)n/ *noun* **1.** something bought ○ *The chocolate factory is our latest acquisition.* **2.** the takeover of a company. The results and cash flows of the

acquired company are brought into the group accounts only from the date of acquisition: the figures for the previous period for the reporting entity should not be adjusted. The difference between the fair value of the net identifiable assets acquired and the fair value of the purchase consideration is goodwill. **3.** the act of getting or buying something

acquisition accounting /ˌækwɪ'zɪʃ(ə)n əˌkaʊntɪŋ/ *noun* a full consolidation, where the assets of a subsidiary company which has been purchased are included in the parent company's balance sheet, and the premium paid for the goodwill is written off against the year's earnings

across-the-board /əˌkrɒs ðə 'bɔːd/ *adjective* applying to everything or everyone ○ *an across-the-board price increase* or *wage increase*

act /ækt/ *noun* a law passed by parliament which must be obeyed by the people

ACT *abbr* Advance Corporation Tax

active /'æktɪv/ *adjective* involving many transactions or activities ○ *an active demand for oil shares* ○ *an active day on the Stock Exchange* ○ *Computer shares are very active.*

active account /ˌæktɪv ə'kaʊnt/ *noun* an account, such as a bank account or investment account, which is used to deposit and withdraw money frequently

active partner /ˌæktɪv 'pɑːtnə/ *noun* a partner who works in a company that is a partnership

activity-based budgeting /æk,tɪvɪti ˌbeɪst 'bʌdʒɪtɪŋ/ *noun* the allocation of resources to individual activities. Activity-based budgeting involves determining which activities incur costs within an organisation, establishing the relationships between them, and then deciding how much of the total budget should be allocated to each activity. Abbreviation **ABB**

activity-based management /æk,tɪvɪti ˌbeɪst 'mænɪdʒmənt/ *noun* a system of management that uses activity-based cost information for a variety of purposes including cost reduction, cost modelling, and customer profitability analysis. Abbreviation **ABM**

activity chart /æk'tɪvɪti tʃɑːt/ *noun* a plan showing work which has been done, made so that it can be compared to a previous plan showing how much work should be done

activity cost pool /æk,tɪvɪti 'kɒst ˌpuːl/ *noun* a grouping of all cost elements associated with an activity

activity driver analysis /æk͵tɪvɪti ͵draɪvə ə'næləsɪs/ *noun* the identification and evaluation of the activity drivers used to trace the cost of activities to cost objects. It may also involve selecting activity drivers with potential to contribute to the cost management function with particular reference to cost reduction.

act of God /͵ækt əv 'gɒd/ *noun* something you do not expect to happen and which cannot be avoided, e.g. a storm or a flood (NOTE: Acts of God are not usually covered by insurance policies.)

actual /'æktʃuəl/ *adjective* real or correct ○ *What is the actual cost of one unit?* ○ *The actual figures for directors' expenses are not shown to the shareholders.*

actual cash value /͵æktʃuəl kæʃ 'væljuː/ *noun* the amount of money, less depreciation, that it would cost to replace something damaged beyond repair with a comparable item

actual price /͵æktʃuəl 'praɪs/ *noun* a price for a commodity which is for immediate delivery

actuals /'æktʃuəlz/ *plural noun* real figures ○ *These figures are the actuals for last year.*

actuarial /͵æktʃu'eəriəl/ *adjective* calculated by an actuary ○ *The premiums are worked out according to actuarial calculations.*

actuarial tables /͵æktʃueəriəl 'teɪb(ə)lz/ *noun* lists showing how long people are likely to live, used to calculate life assurance premiums and annuities

actuary /'æktʃuəri/ *noun* a person employed by an insurance company or other organisation to calculate the risk involved in an insurance, and therefore the premiums payable by people taking out insurance

ACU *abbr* Asian Currency Unit

add /æd/ *verb* to put figures together to make a total ○ *If you add the interest to the capital you will get quite a large sum.* ○ *Interest is added monthly.*

added value /͵ædɪd 'væljuː/ *noun* an amount added to the value of a product or service, equal to the difference between its cost and the amount received when it is sold. Wages, taxes, etc. are deducted from the added value to give the profit.

addend /'ædend/ *noun* a number added to the augend in an addition

addition /ə'dɪʃ(ə)n/ *noun* **1.** a thing or person added ○ *The management has stopped all additions to the staff.* ○ *We are exhibiting*

several additions to our product line. ○ *The marketing director is the latest addition to the board.* **2.** an arithmetical operation consisting of adding together two or more numbers to make a sum ○ *You don't need a calculator to do simple addition.*

additional /ə'dɪʃ(ə)nəl/ *adjective* extra which is added ○ *additional costs* ○ *They sent us a list of additional charges.* ○ *Some additional clauses were added to the contract.* ○ *Additional duty will have to be paid.*

additional personal allowance /ə ͵dɪʃ(ə)nəl ͵pɜːs(ə)n(ə)l ə'lauəns/ *noun* a tax allowance which can be claimed by a single person who has a child of school age living with them, formerly called the 'single-parent allowance'

additional premium /ə͵dɪʃ(ə)nəl 'priːmiəm/ *noun* a payment made to cover extra items in an existing insurance

additional voluntary contributions /ə͵dɪʃ(ə)n(ə)l ͵vɒlənt(ə)ri ͵kɒntrɪ 'bjuːʃ(ə)nz/ *plural noun* extra payments made voluntarily by an employee to a pension scheme on top of the normal contributions, up to a maximum of 15% of gross earnings. Abbreviation **AVCs**

address /ə'dres/ *verb* to write the details of an address on an envelope or package ○ *a letter addressed to the managing director* ○ *an incorrectly addressed package* ○ *Please address your enquiries to the manager.*

addressee /ædre'siː/ *noun* a person to whom a letter or package is addressed

address list /ə'dres lɪst/ *noun* a list of names and addresses of people and companies

add up /͵æd 'ʌp/ *verb* to put several figures together to make a total ○ *He made a mistake in adding up the column of figures.*

add up to /͵æd 'ʌp tʊ/ *verb* to make a total of ○ *The total expenditure adds up to more than £1,000.*

adequacy /'ædɪkwəsi/ *noun* the fact of being large enough or good enough for something

adjudicate /ə'dʒuːdɪkeɪt/ *verb* to give a judgement between two parties in law or to decide a legal problem ○ *to adjudicate a claim* ○ *to adjudicate in a dispute*

adjudication /ə͵dʒuːdɪ'keɪʃ(ə)n/ *noun* the act of giving a judgement or of deciding a legal problem

adjudication of bankruptcy /ə ͵dʒuːdɪkeɪʃ(ə)n əv 'bæŋkrʌptsi/ *noun* a legal order making someone bankrupt

adjudication tribunal /ə,dʒuːdɪ'keɪʃ(ə)n traɪ,bjuːn(ə)l/ *noun* a group which adjudicates in industrial disputes

adjudicator /ə'dʒuːdɪkeɪtə/ *noun* a person who gives a decision on a problem ○ *an adjudicator in an industrial dispute*

adjust /ə'dʒʌst/ *verb* to change something to fit new conditions ○ *Prices are adjusted for inflation.*

'…inflation-adjusted GNP moved up at a 1.3% annual rate' [*Fortune*]

'Saudi Arabia will no longer adjust its production to match short-term supply with demand' [*Economist*]

'…on a seasonally-adjusted basis, output of trucks, electric power, steel and paper decreased' [*Business Week*]

adjustable rate mortgage /ə,dʒʌstəb(ə)l reɪt 'mɔːgɪdʒ/ *noun* a mortgage where the interest rate changes according to the current market rates. Abbreviation **ARM**

adjustable rate preferred stock /ə,dʒʌstəb(ə)l reɪt prɪ,fɜːd 'stɒk/ *noun* a preference shares on which dividends are paid in line with the interest rate on Treasury bills. Abbreviation **ARPS**

adjusted gross income /ə,dʒʌstɪd grəʊs 'ɪnkʌm/ *noun US* a person's total annual income less expenses, pension contributions, capital losses, etc., used as a basis to calculate federal income tax. Abbreviation **AGI**

adjuster /ə'dʒʌstə/ *noun* a person who calculates losses for an insurance company

adjusting entry /ə,dʒʌstɪŋ 'entri/ *noun* an entry in accounts which is made to correct a mistake in the accounts

adjustment /ə'dʒʌstmənt/ *noun* **1.** the act of adjusting ○ *to make an adjustment to salaries* ○ *an adjustment of prices to take account of rising costs* **2.** a slight change ○ *Details of tax adjustments are set out in the enclosed document.* **3.** an entry in accounts which does not represent a receipt or payment, but which is made to make the accounts correct **4.** a change in the exchange rates, made to correct a balance of payment deficit

administer /əd'mɪnɪstə/ *verb* to organise, manage or direct the whole of an organisation or part of one ○ *She administers a large pension fund.* ○ *It will be the HR manager's job to administer the induction programme.*

administered price /əd'mɪnɪstəd praɪs/ *noun US* a price fixed by a manufacturer which cannot be varied by a retailer (NOTE: The UK term is **resale price maintenance**.)

administration /əd,mɪnɪ'streɪʃ(ə)n/ *noun* **1.** the action of organising, controlling or managing a company **2.** an appointment by a court of a person to manage the affairs of a company

administration costs /əd,mɪnɪ 'streɪʃ(ə)n ,kɒsts/, **administration expenses** /əd,mɪnɪ'streɪʃ(ə)n ɪk,spensɪz/ *plural noun* the costs of management, not including production, marketing or distribution costs

administrative /əd'mɪnɪstrətɪv/ *adjective* referring to administration ○ *administrative details* ○ *administrative expenses*

administrative expenses /əd ,mɪnɪstrətɪv ɪk'spensɪz/ *plural noun* costs of administration

administrative receiver /əd ,mɪnɪstrətɪv rɪ'siːvə/ *noun* a person appointed by a court to administer the affairs of a company

administrative receivership /əd ,mɪnɪstrətɪv rɪ'siːvəʃɪp/ *noun* the appointment of an administrative receiver by a debenture holder

administrator /əd'mɪnɪstreɪtə/ *noun* **1.** a person who directs the work of other employees in a business ○ *After several years as a college teacher, she hopes to become an administrator.* **2.** a person appointed by a court to manage the affairs of someone who dies without leaving a will

ADR *abbr* American Depositary Receipt

ad valorem /,æd və'lɔːrəm/ *adjective* used to describe a tax or commission, e.g., Value Added Tax, that is calculated on the value of the goods or services provided, rather than on their number or size ○ *ad valorem duty* ○ *ad valorem tax*

ad valorem duty /,æd və'lɔːrəm ,djuːti/ *noun* the duty calculated on the sales value of the goods

ad valorem tax /,æd və'lɔːrem tæks/ *noun* a tax calculated according to the value of the goods taxed

advance /əd'vɑːns/ *noun* money paid as a loan or as a part of a payment to be made later ○ *She asked if she could have a cash advance.* ○ *We paid her an advance on account.* ○ *Can I have an advance of £100 against next month's salary?* ■ *adjective* early, or taking place before something else happens ○ *advance payment* ○ *Advance holiday bookings are up on last year.* ○ *You must give seven days' advance notice of withdrawals from the account.* ■ *verb* **1.** to pay an amount of money to someone as a loan or as a part of a payment to be made later ○ *The bank ad-*

vanced him £100,000 against the security of his house. **2.** to make something happen earlier ○ *The date of the AGM has been advanced to May 10th.* ○ *The meeting with the German distributors has been advanced from 11.00 to 09.30.*

Advance Corporation Tax /əd₁vɑːns ₁kɔːpə'reɪʃ(ə)n tæks/ *noun* a tax which was abolished in 1999, paid by a company in advance of its main corporation tax payments. It was paid when dividends were paid to shareholders and was deducted from the main tax payment when that fell due. It appeared on the tax voucher attached to a dividend warrant. Abbreviation **ACT**

advance payment guarantee /əd ₁vɑːns ₁peɪmənt ₁gærən'tiː/, **advance payment bond** /əd₁vɑːns 'peɪmənt bɒnd/ *noun* a guarantee that enables a buyer to recover an advance payment made under a contract or order if the supplier fails to fulfil its contractual obligations

adverse /'ædvɜːs/ *adjective* unfavourable

adverse balance /₁ædvɜːs 'bæləns/ *noun* the deficit on an account, especially a nation's balance of payments account

adverse opinion /₁ædvɜːs ə'pɪnjən/ *noun US* an auditor's report that a company's financial statement is not a fair representation of the company's actual financial position

adverse variance /₁ædvɜːs 'veəriəns/ *noun* variance which shows that the actual result is worse than expected

advice /əd'vaɪs/ *noun* a notification telling someone what has happened

adviser /əd'vaɪzə/, **advisor** *noun* a person who suggests what should be done ○ *He is consulting the company's legal adviser.*

advisory /əd'vaɪz(ə)ri/ *adjective* as an adviser ○ *She is acting in an advisory capacity.*

advisory board /əd'vaɪz(ə)ri ₁bɔːd/ *noun* a group of advisors

advisory funds /əd'vaɪz(ə)ri ₁fʌndz/ *plural noun* funds placed with a financial institution to invest on behalf of a client, the institution investing them at its own discretion

AFBD *abbr* Association of Futures Brokers and Dealers

affiliated /ə'fɪlieɪtɪd/ *adjective* connected with or owned by another company ○ *Smiths Ltd is one of our affiliated companies.*

affiliated enterprise /ə₁fɪlieɪtɪd 'entəpraɪz/, **affiliated company** /ə ₁fɪlieɪtɪd 'kʌmp(ə)ni/ *noun* company which is partly owned by another (though less than 50%), and where the share-owning company exerts some management control or has a close trading relationship with the associate ○ *one of our affiliated companies*

aftermarket /'ɑːftə₁mɑːkɪt/ *noun* a market in new shares, which starts immediately after trading in the shares begins

after tax /₁ɑːftər 'tæks/ *adverb* after tax has been paid

after-tax profit /₁ɑːftə 'tæks ₁prɒfɪt/ *noun* a profit after tax has been deducted

age analysis of debtors /eɪdʒ ə ₁nælɪsɪs əv 'detəs/ *noun* the amount owed by debtors, classified by age of debt

aged debtors analysis /'eɪdʒd 'detəz ə 'nælɪsɪs/, **ageing schedule** /'eɪdʒɪŋ 'ʃedjuːl/ *noun* a list which analyses a company's debtors, showing the number of days their payments are outstanding

agency /'eɪdʒənsi/ *noun* **1.** an office or job of representing another company in an area ○ *They signed an agency agreement* or *an agency contract.* **2.** an office or business which arranges things for other companies

agency bank /'eɪdʒənsi bæŋk/ *noun* a bank which does not accept deposits, but acts as an agent for another, usually foreign, bank

agency bill /'eɪdʒənsi bɪl/ *noun* a bill of exchange drawn on the local branch of a foreign bank

agency broker /'eɪdʒənsi ₁brəʊkə/ *noun* a dealer who acts as the agent for an investor, buying and selling for a commission

agency worker /₁eɪdʒənsi 'wɜːkə/ *noun* a person who is employed by an agency to work for another company. He or she is taxed as an employee of the agency, not of the company where he or she actually works.

agenda /ə'dʒendə/ *noun* a list of things to be discussed at a meeting ○ *The conference agenda* or *the agenda of* ○ *After two hours we were still discussing the first item on the agenda.* ○ *We usually put finance at the top of the agenda.* ○ *The chair wants two items removed from* or *taken off the agenda.*

agent /'eɪdʒənt/ *noun* **1.** a person who represents a company or another person in an area ○ *to be the agent for BMW cars* ○ *to be the agent for IBM* **2.** a person in charge of an agency ○ *an advertising agent* ○ *The estate agent sent me a list of properties for sale* ○ *Our trip was organised through our local travel agent.*

agent bank /'eɪdʒənt bæŋk/ *noun* a bank which uses the credit card system set up by another bank

agent's commission /₁eɪdʒənts kə 'mɪʃ(ə)n/ *noun* money, often a percentage of sales, paid to an agent

age-related /ˈeɪdʒ rɪˌleɪtɪd/ *adjective* connected with a person's age

age-related allowance /eɪdʒ rɪˌleɪtɪd ə ˈlaʊəns/ *noun* an extra tax allowance which a person over 65 may be entitled to

aggregate /ˈægrɪgət/ *adjective* total, with everything added together ○ *aggregate output*

aggregate demand /ˌægrɪgət dɪ ˈmɑːnd/ *noun* the total demand for goods and services from all sectors of the economy including individuals, companies and the government ○ *Economists are studying the recent fall in aggregate demand.* ○ *As incomes have risen, so has aggregate demand.*

aggregate risk /ˌægrɪgət ˈrɪsk/ *noun* the risk which a bank runs in lending to a customer

aggregate supply /ˌægrɪgət səˈplaɪ/ *noun* all goods and services on the market ○ *Is aggregate supply meeting aggregate demand?*

AGI *abbr US* adjusted gross income

agio /ˈædʒɪəʊ/ *noun* **1.** a charge made for changing money of one currency into another, or for changing banknotes into cash **2.** the difference between two values, such as between the interest charged on loans made by a bank and the interest paid by the bank on deposits, or the difference between the values of two currencies

AGM /ˌeɪ dʒiː ˈem/ *abbr* Annual General Meeting

agreed /əˈɡriːd/ *adjective* having been accepted by everyone ○ *We pay an agreed amount each month.* ○ *The agreed terms of employment are laid down in the contract.*

agreed price /əˌɡriːd ˈpraɪs/ *noun* a price which has been accepted by both the buyer and seller

agree with /əˈɡriː wɪð/ *verb* **1.** to say that your opinions are the same as someone else's ○ *I agree with the chairman that the figures are lower than normal.* **2.** to be the same as ○ *The auditors' figures do not agree with those of the accounts department.*

AICPA *abbr* American Institute of Certified Public Accountants

airmail transfer /ˈeəmeɪl ˌtrænsfɜː/ *noun* an act of sending money from one bank to another by airmail

alien corporation /ˌeɪliən ˌkɔːpə ˈreɪʃ(ə)n/ *noun US* a company which is incorporated in a foreign country

A list /ˈeɪ lɪst/ *noun* a list of members of a company at the time it is wound up who may be liable for the company's unpaid debts

all-in price /ˌɔːl ɪn ˈpraɪs/ *noun* a price which covers all items in a purchase such as goods, delivery, tax or insurance

all-in rate /ˌɔːl ɪn ˈreɪt/ *noun* **1.** a price which covers all the costs connected with a purchase, such as delivery, tax and insurance, as well as the cost of the goods themselves **2.** a wage which includes all extra payments such as bonuses and merit pay

allocate /ˈæləkeɪt/ *verb* to divide something in various ways and share it out ○ *How are we going to allocate the available office space?* ■ *noun* to assign a whole item of cost, or of revenue, to a single cost unit, centre, account, or time period

allocated costs /ˈæləˌkeɪtd kɒsts/ *plural noun* overhead costs which have been allocated to a specific cost centre

allocation /ˌæləˈkeɪʃ(ə)n/ *noun* the process of providing sums of money for particular purposes, or a sum provided for a purpose ○ *the allocation of funds to a project*

allot /əˈlɒt/ *verb* to share out

allotment /əˈlɒtmənt/ *noun* **1.** the process of sharing out something, especially money between various departments, projects or people ○ *The allotment of funds to each project is the responsibility of the finance director.* **2.** the act of giving shares in a new company to people who have applied for them ○ *share allotment* ○ *payment in full on allotment*

allow /əˈlaʊ/ *verb* **1.** to say that someone can do something ○ *Junior members of staff are not allowed to use the chairman's lift.* ○ *The company allows all members of staff to take six days' holiday at Christmas.* **2.** to give ○ *to allow 5% discount to members of staff* **3.** to agree to or accept legally ○ *to allow a claim* or *an appeal*

allowable /əˈlaʊəb(ə)l/ *adjective* legally accepted. Opposite **disallowable**

allowable deductions /əˌlaʊəb(ə)l dɪ ˈdʌkʃ(ə)ns/ *plural noun* deductions from income which are allowed by the Inland Revenue, and which reduce the tax payable

allowable expenses /əˌlaʊəb(ə)l ɪk ˈspensɪz/ *plural noun* business expenses which can be claimed against tax

allowable losses /əˌlaʊəb(ə)l ˈlɒsɪz/ *plural noun* losses, e.g. on the sale of assets, which are allowed to be set off against gains

allowance /əˈlaʊəns/ *noun* **1.** money which is given for a special reason ○ *a travel allowance* or *a travelling allowance* **2.** a part of an income which is not taxed ○ *allowances against tax* or *tax allowances* ○ *personal* *allowances* **3.** money removed in the form of a discount ○ *an allowance for depreciation* ○ *an allowance for exchange loss*

'…the compensation plan includes base, incentive and car allowance totalling $50,000+' [*Globe and Mail (Toronto)*]

allowance for bad debt /ə,laʊəns fə bæd 'det/ *noun* a provision made in a company's accounts for debts which may never be paid

allowances against tax /ə,laʊənss ə 'genst tæks/ *plural noun* part of someone's income which is not taxed

allow for /ə'laʊ fɔː/ *verb* to give a discount for something, or to add an extra sum to cover something ○ *to allow for money paid in advance* ○ *Add on an extra 10% to allow for postage and packing.*

all-risks policy /,ɔːl 'rɪsks ,pɒlɪsi/ *noun* an insurance policy which covers risks of any kind, with no exclusions

amalgamate /ə'mælgəmeɪt/ *verb* to join together with another group ○ *The amalgamated group includes six companies.*

amalgamation /ə,mælgə'meɪʃ(ə)n/ *noun* the joining together of several trade unions to increase their strength

American Accounting Association /ə,merɪkən ə'kaʊntɪŋ ə,səʊsieɪʃ(ə)n/ *noun* a US voluntary organisation for those with an interest in accounting research and best practice, which aims to promote excellence in the creation, dissemination and application of accounting knowledge and skills. Abbreviation **AAA**

American Depositary Receipt /ə 'merɪkən dɪ'pɒzɪtri rɪ'siːt/ *noun* a document issued by an American bank to US citizens, making them unregistered shareholders of companies in foreign countries. The document allows them to receive dividends from their investments, and ADRs can themselves be bought or sold. Abbreviation **ADR**

American Institute of Certified Public Accountants /ə,merɪkən ,ɪnstɪtjuːt əv ,sɜːtɪfaɪd ,pʌblɪk ə'kaʊntənts/ *noun* the national association for certified public accountants in the United States. Abbreviation **AICPA**

amortisable /,æmɔː'taɪzəb(ə)l/ *adjective* being possible to amortise ○ *The capital cost is amortisable over a period of ten years.*

amortisation /ə,mɔːtaɪ'zeɪʃ(ə)n/, **amortising** *noun* an act of amortising ○ *amortisation of a debt*

amortisation period /ə,mɔːtaɪ'zeɪʃ(ə)n ,pɪəriəd/ *noun* the length of a lease, used

when depreciating the value of the asset leased

amortise /ə'mɔːtaɪz/, **amortize** *verb* **1.** to repay a loan by regular payments, most of which pay off the interest on the loan at first, and then reduce the principal as the repayment period progresses ○ *The capital cost is amortised over five years.* **2.** to depreciate or to write down the capital value of an asset over a period of time in a company's accounts

amount /ə'maʊnt/ *noun* a quantity of money ○ *A small amount has been deducted to cover our costs.* ○ *A large amount is still owing.* ○ *What is the amount to be written off?*

amount paid up /ə,maʊnt peɪd 'ʌp/ *noun* an amount paid for a new issue of shares, either the total payment or the first instalment, if the shares are offered with instalment payments

analyse /'ænəlaɪz/, **analyze** *verb* to examine someone or something in detail ○ *to analyse a statement of account* ○ *to analyse the market potential*

analysis /ə'næləsɪs/ *noun* a detailed examination and report ○ *a job analysis* ○ *market analysis* ○ *Her job is to produce a regular sales analysis.* (NOTE: The plural is **analyses.**)

analyst /'ænəlɪst/ *noun* a person who analyses ○ *a market analyst* ○ *a systems analyst*

annual /'ænjuəl/ *adjective* for one year ○ *an annual statement of income* ○ *They have six weeks' annual leave.* ○ *The company has an annual growth of 5%.* ○ *We get an annual bonus.*

'…real wages have risen at an annual rate of only 1% in the last two years' [*Sunday Times*]

'…the remuneration package will include an attractive salary, profit sharing and a company car together with four weeks' annual holiday' [*Times*]

annual accounts /,ænjuəl ə'kaʊnts/ *plural noun* the accounts prepared at the end of a financial year ○ *The annual accounts have been sent to the shareholders.*

annual depreciation /,ænjuəl dɪ,priːʃi 'eɪʃ(ə)n/ *noun* a reduction in the book value of an asset at a particular rate per year. ◊ **straight line depreciation**

annual depreciation provision /,ænjuəl dɪ,priːʃi'eɪʃ(ə)n prə,vɪʒ(ə)n/ *noun* an allocation of the cost of an asset to a single year of the asset's expected year

annual exemptions /,ænjuəl ɪg 'zempʃns/ *plural noun* amount of income which is exempt from tax. For example, the first £7,900 in capital gains in any one year is exempt from tax.

Annual General Meeting /ˌænjuəl ˌdʒen(ə)rəl ˈmiːtɪŋ/ *noun* an annual meeting of all shareholders of a company, when the company's financial situation is presented by and discussed with the directors, when the accounts for the past year are approved and when dividends are declared and audited. Abbreviation **AGM** (NOTE: The US term is **annual meeting** or **annual stockholders' meeting**.)

annual income /ˌænjuəl ˈɪnkʌm/ *noun* money received during a calendar year

annualised /ˈænjuəlaɪzd/, **annualized** *adjective* shown on an annual basis

'…he believes this may have caused the economy to grow at an annualized rate of almost 5 per cent in the final quarter of last year' [*Investors Chronicle*]

annualised percentage rate /ˌænjuəlaɪzd pəˈsentɪdʒ reɪt/ *noun* a yearly percentage rate, calculated by multiplying the monthly rate by twelve. Abbreviation **APR** (NOTE: The annualised percentage rate is not as accurate as the Annual Percentage Rate (APR), which includes fees and other charges.)

annually /ˈænjuəli/ *adverb* each year ○ *The figures are updated annually.*

annual return /ˌænjuəl rɪˈtɜːn/ *noun* an official report which a registered company has to make each year to the Registrar of Companies

annuitant /əˈnjuːɪtənt/ *noun* a person who receives an annuity

annuity /əˈnjuːɪti/ *noun* money paid each year to a retired person, usually in return for a lump-sum payment. The value of the annuity depends on how long the person lives, as it usually cannot be passed on to another person. Annuities are fixed payments, and lose their value with inflation, whereas a pension can be index-linked. ○ *to buy* or *to take out an annuity* ○ *She has a government annuity* or *an annuity from the government.*

annuity certain /əˌnjuːɪti ˈsɜːtən/ *noun* an annuity that provides payments for a specific number of years, regardless of life or death of the annuitant

annuity contract /əˌnjuːɪti kənˈtrækt/ *noun* a contract under which a person is paid a fixed sum regularly for life

antedate /ˌæntɪˈdeɪt/ *verb* to put an earlier date on a document ○ *The invoice was antedated to January 1st.*

anti- /ænti/ *prefix* against

anti-inflationary /ˌænti ɪnˈfleɪʃ(ə)n(ə)ri/ *adjective* restricting or trying to restrict inflation ○ *anti-inflationary measures*

anti-trust /ˌænti ˈtrʌst/ *adjective* attacking monopolies and encouraging competition ○ *anti-trust measures*

anti-trust laws /ˌænti ˈtrʌst lɔːz/, **anti-trust legislation** /ˌledʒɪˈsleɪʃ(ə)n/ *plural noun* laws in the US which prevent the formation of monopolies

APB *abbr* 1. Accounting Principles Board 2. Auditing Principles Board

applicant /ˈæplɪkənt/ *noun* a person who applies for something ○ *an applicant for a job* or *a job applicant* ○ *an applicant to an industrial tribunal* ○ *There were thousands of applicants for shares in the new company.*

application /ˌæplɪˈkeɪʃ(ə)n/ *noun* 1. the act of asking for something, usually in writing, or a document in which someone asks for something, e.g. a job ○ *shares payable on application* ○ *She sent off six applications for job* or *six job applications.* 2. effort or diligence ○ *She has shown great application in her work on the project.*

application form /ˌæplɪˈkeɪʃ(ə)n ˌfɔːm/ *noun* a form to be filled in when applying for a new issue of shares or for a job

application of funds /ˌæplɪˈkeɪʃ(ə)n əv fʌndz/ *noun* details of the way in which funds have been spent during an accounting period

appointment /əˈpɔɪntmənt/ *noun* 1. an arrangement to meet ○ *to make* or *to fix an appointment with someone for two o'clock* ○ *He was late for his appointment.* ○ *She had to cancel her appointment.* 2. the act of being appointed to a job, or of appointing someone to a job □ **on his appointment as manager** when he was made manager

apportion /əˈpɔːʃ(ə)n/ *verb* to share out something, e.g. costs, funds or blame ○ *Costs are apportioned according to projected revenue.*

apportionment /əˈpɔːʃ(ə)nmənt/ *noun* the sharing out of costs

appraisal /əˈpreɪz(ə)l/ *noun* a calculation of the value of someone or something

'…we are now reaching a stage in industry and commerce where appraisals are becoming part of the management culture. Most managers now take it for granted that they will appraise and be appraised' [*Personnel Management*]

appraise /əˈpreɪz/ *verb* to assess or to calculate the value of something or someone

appreciate /əˈpriːʃieɪt/ *verb* 1. to notice how good something is 2. (*of currency, shares, etc.*) to increase in value

appreciation /əˌpriːʃiˈeɪʃ(ə)n/ *noun* 1. an increase in value. Also called **capital appreciation** 2. the act of valuing something highly ○ *She was given a pay rise in appreciation of her excellent work.*

appropriate *verb* /ə'prəʊprieɪt/ to put a sum of money aside for a special purpose ○ *to appropriate a sum of money for a capital project*

appropriation /ə,prəʊpri'eɪʃ(ə)n/ *noun* the act of putting money aside for a special purpose ○ *appropriation of funds to the reserve*

appropriation account /ə,prəʊpri'eɪʃ(ə)n ə,kaʊnt/ *noun* the part of a profit and loss account which shows how the profit has been dealt with, e.g., how much has been given to the shareholders as dividends and how much is being put into the reserves

approval /ə'pruːv(ə)l/ *noun* the act of saying or thinking that something is good ○ *to submit a budget for approval*

approve /ə'pruːv/ *verb* **1.** □ **to approve of something** to think something is good ○ *The chairman approves of the new company letter heading.* ○ *The sales staff do not approve of interference from the accounts division.* **2.** to agree to something officially ○ *to approve the terms of a contract* ○ *The proposal was approved by the board.*

approved accounts /ə,pruːvd ə'kaʊnts/ *noun* accounts that have been formally accepted by a company's board of directors

approved scheme /ə,pruːvd 'skiːm/ *noun* a pension scheme or share purchase scheme which has been approved by the Inland Revenue

approved securities /ə,pruːvd sɪ'kjʊərɪtiz/ *plural noun* state bonds which can be held by banks to form part of their reserves (NOTE: The list of these bonds is the 'approved list'.)

approximate /ə'prɒksɪmət/ *adjective* not exact, but almost correct ○ *The sales division has made an approximate forecast of expenditure.*

approximately /ə'prɒksɪmətli/ *adverb* not quite exactly, but close to the figure shown ○ *Expenditure on marketing is approximately 10% down on the previous quarter.*

approximation /ə,prɒksɪ'meɪʃ(ə)n/ *noun* a rough calculation ○ *Each department has been asked to provide an approximation of expenditure for next year.* ○ *The final figure is only an approximation.*

APR *abbr* annualised percentage rate

APRA *abbr* Australian Prudential Regulation Authority

AR *abbr* accounts receivable

arbitrage /'ɑːbɪ,trɑːʒ/ *noun* the business of making a profit from the difference in value of various assets, e.g. by selling foreign currencies or commodities on one market and buying on another at almost the same time to profit from different exchange rates, or by buying currencies forward and selling them forward at a later date, to benefit from a difference in prices

arbitrage syndicate /'ɑːbɪtrɑːʒ ,sɪndɪkət/ *noun* a group of people who together raise the capital to invest in arbitrage deals

arbitration /,ɑːbɪ'treɪʃ(ə)n/ *noun* the settling of a dispute by an outside party agreed on by both sides ○ *to take a dispute to arbitration* or *to go to arbitration* ○ *arbitration in an industrial dispute* ○ *The two sides decided to submit the dispute to arbitration* or *to refer the question to arbitration.*

arbitrator /'ɑːbɪtreɪtə/ *noun* a person not concerned with a dispute who is chosen by both sides to try to settle it ○ *an industrial arbitrator* ○ *They refused to accept* or *they rejected the arbitrator's ruling.*

area manager /,eəriə 'mænɪdʒə/ *noun* a manager who is responsible for a company's work in a specific part of the country

arithmetic mean /,ærɪθmetɪk 'miːn/ *noun* a simple average calculated by dividing the sum of two or more items by the number of items

around /ə'raʊnd/ *preposition* **1.** approximately ○ *The office costs around £2,000 a year to heat.* ○ *Her salary is around $85,000.* **2.** with a premium or discount

ARPS *abbr* adjustable rate preferred stock

ARR *abbr* accounting rate of return

arrangement fee /ə'reɪndʒmənt fiː/ *noun* a charge made by a bank to a client for arranging credit facilities

arrears /ə'rɪəz/ *plural noun* money which is owed, but which has not been paid at the right time ○ *a salary with arrears effective from January 1st* ○ *We are pressing the company to pay arrears of interest.* ○ *You must not allow the mortgage payments to fall into arrears.*

article /'ɑːtɪk(ə)l/ *noun* a section of a legal agreement such as a contract or treaty ○ *See article 8 of the contract.*

articles of association /,ɑːtɪk(ə)lz əv ə,səʊsi'eɪʃ(ə)n/ *plural noun* a document which lays down the rules for a company regarding such matters as the issue of shares, the conduct of meetings and the appointment of directors ○ *This procedure is not allowed under the articles of association of the company.*

articles of incorporation /ˌɑːtɪk(ə)lz əv ɪnˌkɔːpəˈreɪʃ(ə)n/ *plural noun US* a document which sets up a company and lays down the relationship between the shareholders and the company (NOTE: The UK term is **Memorandum of Association**.)

ASB *abbr* Accounting Standards Board

ASC *abbr* Accounting Standards Committee

A shares /ˈeɪ ˌʃeəz/ *plural noun* ordinary shares with limited voting rights or no voting rights at all

asked price /ˌɑːskd ˈpraɪs/ *noun* a price at which a commodity or stock is offered for sale by a seller, also called 'offer price' in the UK

asking price /ˈɑːskɪŋ ˌpraɪs/ *noun* a price which the seller is hoping will be paid for the item being sold ○ *the asking price is £24,000*

as per /ˌæz ˈpɜː/ ♦ **per**

assess /əˈses/ *verb* to calculate the value of something or someone ○ *to assess damages at £1,000* ○ *to assess a property for the purposes of insurance*

assessment /əˈsesmənt/ *noun* a calculation of value ○ *a property assessment* ○ *a tax assessment* ○ *They made a complete assessment of each employee's contribution to the organisation.*

asset /ˈæset/ *noun* something which belongs to a company or person, and which has a value ○ *He has an excess of assets over liabilities.* ○ *Her assets are only £640 as against liabilities of £24,000.*

'…many companies are discovering that a well-recognised brand name can be a priceless asset that lessens the risk of introducing a new product' [*Duns Business Month*]

asset-backed securities /ˌæset bækt sɪˈkjʊərɪtiz/ *plural noun* shares which are backed by the security of assets

asset backing /ˈæset ˌbækɪŋ/ *noun* a support for a share price provided by the value of the company's assets

asset-rich company /ˌæset rɪtʃ ˈkʌmp(ə)ni/ *noun* company with valuable tangible assets, such as property, which provide firm backing for its shares

assets /ˈæsets/ *plural noun* liabilities plus owners' equity

asset stripper /ˈæset ˌstrɪpə/ *noun* a person who buys a company to sell its assets

asset stripping /ˈæset ˌstrɪpɪŋ/ *noun* the practice of buying a company at a lower price than its asset value, and then selling its assets

asset turnover ratio /ˌæset ˈtɜːnəʊvə ˌreɪʃiəʊ/ *noun* the number of times assets are turned over by sales during the year, calculated as turnover divided by total assets less current liabilities

asset value /ˌæset ˈvæljuː/ *noun* the value of a company calculated by adding together all its assets

assign /əˈsaɪn/ *verb* **1.** to give something to someone by means of an official legal transfer ○ *to assign a right to someone* ○ *to assign shares to someone* **2.** to give someone a job of work to do and make him or her responsible for doing it ○ *She was assigned the task of checking the sales figures.*

assignation /ˌæsɪɡˈneɪʃ(ə)n/ *noun* a legal transfer ○ *the assignation of shares to someone* ○ *the assignation of a patent*

assignee /ˌæsaɪˈniː/ *noun* a person who receives something which has been assigned to him or her

assignment /əˈsaɪnmənt/ *noun* the legal transfer of a property or right ○ *the assignment of a patent* or *of a copyright* ○ *to sign a deed of assignment*

assignor /ˌæsaɪˈnɔː/ *noun* a person who assigns something to someone

associate /əˈsəʊsiət/ *adjective* linked ■ *noun* **1.** a person who works in the same business as someone ○ *She is a business associate of mine.* **2.** a person or company linked to another in a takeover bid

associate company /əˌsəʊsiət ˈkʌmp(ə)ni/ *noun* a company which is partly owned by another company

associated company /əˌsəʊsieɪtɪd ˈkʌmp(ə)ni/ *noun* a company which is partly owned by another company (though less than 50%), which exerts some management control over it or has a close trading relationship with it ○ *Smith Ltd and its associated company, Jones Brothers*

associate director /əˌsəʊsiət daɪˈrektə/ *noun* a director who attends board meetings, but has not been elected by the shareholders

Association of Accounting Technicians /əˌsəʊsieɪʃ(ə)n əv əˈkaʊntɪŋ ˌteknɪʃ(ə)nz/ *noun* an organisation which groups accounting technicians and grants membership to people who have passed its examinations. Abbreviation **AAT**

Association of Authorized Public Accountants /əˌsəʊsieɪʃ(ə)n əv ˌɔːθəraɪzd ˌpʌblɪk əˈkaʊntənts/ *noun* an organisation which groups accountants who have been authorised by the government to work as auditors

Association of Chartered Accountants in the United States /ə
ˌsəʊsieɪʃ(ə)n əv ˌtʃɑːtəd əˌkaʊntənts ɪn
ði juːˌnaɪtɪd 'steɪts/ *noun* an organisation
representing Chartered Accountants from
Australia, Canada, England and Wales, Ireland, New Zealand, Scotland and South Africa who are based in the United States. Abbreviation **ACAUS**

**Association of Chartered Certified
Accountants** /əˌsəʊsieɪʃ(ə)n əv ˌtʃɑːtəd
ˌsɜːtɪfaɪd ə'kaʊntənts/ *noun* an organisation whose members are certified accountants. Abbreviation **ACCA**

**Association of Corporate Treasur-
ers** /əˌsəʊsieɪʃ(ə)n əv ˌkɔːp(ə)rət
'treʒərəz/ *noun* an organisation which
groups company treasurers and awards membership to those who have passed its examinations

Association of Financial Advisers /ə
ˌsəʊsieɪʃ(ə)n əv faɪˌnænʃ(ə)l əd'vaɪzəz/
noun a trade association that represents the
interests of independent financial advisers

**Association of Futures Brokers and
Dealers** /əˌsəʊsieɪʃ(ə)n əv 'fjuːtʃəz
ˌbrəʊkəz ən ˌdiːləz/ *noun* a self-regulating
organisation which oversees the activities of
dealers in futures and options. Abbreviation
AFBD

assumable mortgage /əˌsjuːməb(ə)l
'mɔːɡɪdʒ/ *noun US* a mortgage which can be
passed to another person

assumption /ə'sʌmpʃən/ *noun* a general
belief ○ *We are working on the assumption
that the exchange rate will stay the same.*

assurance /ə'ʃʊərəns/ *noun* a type of insurance which pays compensation for an
event that is certain to happen at some time,
especially for the death of the insured person.
Also called **life assurance, life insurance**

assure /ə'ʃʊə/ *verb* to insure someone, or
someone's life, so that the insurance company will pay compensation when that person
dies ○ *He has paid the premiums to have his
wife's life assured.* (NOTE: **Assure, assurer**
and **assurance** are used in Britain for insurance policies relating to something which
will certainly happen (such as death); for
other types of policy (i.e. those against
something which may or may not happen,
such as an accident) use the terms **insure,
insurer** and **insurance.**)

assurer /ə'ʃʊərə/, **assuror** *noun* an insurer or a company which insures

AST *abbr* Automated Screen Trading

at best /ˌæt 'best/ *adverb* □ **sell at best** an
instruction to a stockbroker to sell shares at
the best price possible

at call /ˌæt 'kɔːl/ *adverb* immediately available

ATM /ˌeɪ tiː 'em/ *abbr* automated teller machine

'Swiss banks are issuing new cards which will allow
cash withdrawals from ATMs in Belgium, Denmark,
Spain, France, the Netherlands, Portugal and Germany' [*Banking Technology*]

'…the major supermarket operator is planning a new
type of bank that would earn 90% of its revenue from
fees on automated teller machine transactions. With
the bank setting up ATMs at 7,000 group outlets nationwide, it would have a branch network at least 20
times larger than any of the major banks' [*Nikkei
Weekly*]

at par /ˌæt 'pɑː/ *phrase* equal to the face
value

at sight /ˌæt 'saɪt/ *adverb* immediately,
when it is presented ○ *a bill of exchange payable at sight*

attach /ə'tætʃ/ *verb* to fasten or to link ○ *I
am attaching a copy of my previous letter.* ○
*Please find attached a copy of my letter of
June 24th.* ○ *The company attaches great importance to good timekeeping.*

attachment /ə'tætʃmənt/ *noun* the act of
holding a debtor's property to prevent it being sold until debts are paid

attachment of earnings /əˌtætʃmənt
əv 'ɜːnɪŋz/ *noun* legal power to take money
from a person's salary to pay money, which is
owed, to the court

attachment of earnings order /ə
ˌtætʃmənt əv 'ɜːnɪŋz ˌɔːdə/ *noun* a court
order to make an employer pay part of an employee's salary to the court to pay off debts

attachment order /ə'tætʃmənt ˌɔːdə/
noun an order from a court to hold a debtor's
property to prevent it being sold until debts
are paid

attest /ə'test/ *noun* a formal statement, e.g.
a statement by an auditor that a company's financial position is correctly stated in the
company's accounts

attributable profit /əˌtrɪbjʊtəb(ə)l
'prɒfɪt/ *noun* a profit which can be shown to
come from a particular area of the company's
operations

auction /'ɔːkʃən/ *noun* **1.** a method of selling goods where people want to buy compete
with each other by saying how much they
will offer for it, and the item is sold to the
person who makes the highest offer ○ *Their
furniture will be sold in the auction rooms
next week.* ○ *They announced a sale by auction of the fire-damaged stock.* ○ *The equip-*

ment was sold by auction or *at auction.* □ **to put an item up for auction** to offer an item for sale at an auction **2.** a method of selling government stock, where all stock on issue will be sold, and the highest price offered will be accepted, as opposed to tendering ■ *verb* to sell something at an auction ○ *The factory was closed and the machinery was auctioned off.*

auctioneer /ˌɔːkʃəˈnɪə/ *noun* the person who conducts an auction

auction system /ˈɔːkʃən ˌsɪstəm/ *noun* a system where prices are agreed as the result of marketmakers offering stock for sale on the trading floor (as opposed to a quote system, where prices are quoted on a computerised screen)

audit /ˈɔːdɪt/ *noun* the examination of the books and accounts of a company ○ *to carry out the annual audit* ■ *verb* to examine the books and accounts of a company ○ *Messrs Smith have been asked to audit the accounts.* ○ *The books have not yet been audited.* □ **to audit the stock** to carry out a stock control, in front of witnesses, so as to establish the exact quantities and value of stock

Audit Commission /ˌɔːdɪt kəˈmɪʃ(ə)n/ *noun* British government agency whose duty is to audit the accounts of ministries and other government departments (NOTE: The US term is **General Accounting Office**.)

audited accounts /ˌɔːdɪtɪd əˈkaʊnts/ *noun* a set of accounts that have been thoroughly scrutinised, checked, and approved by a team of auditors

audit fee /ˈɔːdɪt fiː/ *noun* a fee charged by an auditor for auditing a company's accounts

auditing /ˈɔːdɪtɪŋ/ *noun* the work of examining the books and accounts of a company

Auditing Practices Board /ˌɔːdɪtɪŋ ˈpræktɪsɪz ˌbɔːd/ *noun* a body responsible for developing and issuing professional auditing standards in the United Kingdom and the Republic of Ireland. The APB was created in 1991 following an agreement between the six members of the Consultative Committee of Accountancy Bodies. Abbreviation **APB**

audit opinion /ˌɔːdɪt əˈpɪnjən/ *noun US* a report of the audit of a company's books, carried out by a certified public accountant (NOTE: The UK term is **accountant's opinion**.)

auditor /ˈɔːdɪtə/ *noun* a person who audits

auditors' fees /ˈɔːdɪtəz fiːz/ *plural noun* fees paid to a company's auditors, which are approved by the shareholders at an AGM

auditors' qualification /ˌɔːdɪtəz ˌkwɒlɪfɪˈkeɪʃ(ə)n/ *noun* a form of words in a report from the auditors of a company's accounts, stating that in their opinion the accounts are not a true reflection of the company's financial position. Also called **qualification of accounts**

auditors' report /ˌɔːdɪtəz rɪˈpɔːt/ *noun* a report written by a company's auditors after they have examined the accounts of the company (NOTE: If the auditors are satisfied, the report certifies that, in their opinion, the accounts give a 'true and fair' view of the company's financial position.)

audit programme /ˌɔːdɪt ˈprəʊɡræm/ *noun* a listing of all the steps to be taken when auditing a company's accounts

audit regulation /ˈɔːdɪt ˌreɡjʊleɪʃ(ə)n/ *noun* the regulating of auditors by government

audit report /ˌɔːdɪt rɪˈpɔːt/ *noun* same as **auditors' report**

audit risk /ˈɔːdɪt rɪsk/ *noun* the risk that auditors may give an inappropriate audit opinion on financial statements

audit trail /ˈɔːdɪt treɪl/ *noun* the records that show all the stages of a transaction, e.g. a purchase, a sale or a customer complaint, in the order in which they happened (NOTE: An audit trail can be a useful tool for problem-solving and, in financial markets, may be used to ensure that the dealers have been fair and accurate in their proceedings.)

augend /ˈɔːɡend/ *noun* the number to which another number (the addend) is added to produce the sum

Australian Prudential Regulation Authority /ɒˌstreɪliən prʊˌdenʃ(ə)l ˌreɡjʊˈleɪʃ(ə)n ɔːˌθɒrəti/ *noun* a federal government body responsible for ensuring that financial institutions are able to meet their commitments. Abbreviation **APRA**

AUT *abbr* authorised unit trust

authenticate /ɔːˈθentɪkeɪt/ *verb* to say that something is true or genuine

authorise /ˈɔːθəraɪz/, **authorize** *verb* **1.** to give permission for something to be done ○ *to authorise payment of £10,000* **2.** to give someone the authority to do something ○ *to authorise someone to act on the company's behalf*

authorised /ˈɔːθəraɪzd/, **authorized** *adjective* permitted

authorised capital /ˌɔːθəˌraɪzd ˈkæpɪt(ə)l/ *noun* an amount of capital which a company is allowed to have, as stated in the memorandum of association

authorised stock /ˌɔːθəraɪzd ˈstɒk/ *noun* same as **authorised capital**

authorised unit trust /ˌɔːθəraɪzd ˈjuːnɪt trʌst/ *noun* the official name for a unit trust which has to be managed according to EU directives. Abbreviation **AUT**

automated /ˈɔːtəmeɪtɪd/ *adjective* worked automatically by machines ○ *a fully automated car assembly plant*

Automated Clearing House /ˌɔːtəmeɪtɪd ˈklɪərɪŋ haʊs/ *noun US* an organisation set up by the federal authorities to settle transactions carried out by computer, such as automatic mortgage payments and trade payments between businesses. Abbreviation **ACH**

Automated Screen Trading /ˌɔːtəmeɪtɪd ˈskriːn ˌtreɪdɪŋ/ *noun* a system where securities are bought, sold and matched automatically by computer. Abbreviation **AST**

automated teller machine /ˌɔːtəmætɪk ˈtelɪŋ məˌʃiːn/ *noun* a machine which gives out money when a special card is inserted and special instructions given. Abbreviation **ATM**

automation /ˌɔːtəˈmeɪʃ(ə)n/ *noun* the use of machines to do work with very little supervision by people

availability /əˌveɪləˈbɪlɪti/ *noun* the fact of being easy to obtain

available capital /əˌveɪləb(ə)l ˈkæpɪt(ə)l/ *noun* capital which is ready to be used

average /ˈæv(ə)rɪdʒ/ *noun* **1.** a number calculated by adding several figures together and dividing by the number of figures added ○ *the average for the last three months* or *the last three months' average* ○ *sales average* or *average of sales* **2.** the sharing of the cost of damage or loss of a ship between the insurers and the owners ■ *adjective* equal to the average of a set of figures ○ *the average increase in salaries* ○ *The average cost per unit is too high.* ○ *The average sales per rep-*

resentative are rising. ■ *verb* to work out an average figure for something

'…a share with an average rating might yield 5 per cent and have a PER of about 10' [*Investors Chronicle*]

'…the average price per kilogram for this season to the end of April has been 300 cents' [*Australian Financial Review*]

average adjuster /ˌæv(ə)rɪdʒ əˈdʒʌstə/ *noun* a person who calculates how much of a maritime insurance is to be paid by the insurer against a claim

average adjustment /ˌæv(ə)rɪdʒ əˈdʒʌstmənt/ *noun* a calculation of the share of the cost of damage or loss of a ship that an insurer has to pay

average due date /ˌæv(ə)rɪdʒ djuː ˈdeɪt/ *noun* the average date when several different payments fall due

average income per capita /ˌæv(ə)rɪdʒ ˈɪnkʌm pə/ *noun* same as **per capita income**

average out /ˌæv(ə)rɪdʒ ˈaʊt/ *verb* to come to a figure as an average ○ *It averages out at 10% per annum.* ○ *Sales increases have averaged out at 15%.*

averager /ˈævərɪdʒə/ *noun* a person who buys the same share at various times and at various prices to get an average value

average-sized /ˌævərɪdʒ ˈsaɪzd/ *adjective* of a similar size to most others, not very large or very small ○ *They are an average-sized company.* ○ *She has an average-sized office.*

averaging /ˈævərɪdʒɪŋ/ *noun* the buying or selling of shares at different times and at different prices to establish an average price

avoidance /əˈvɔɪd(ə)ns/ *noun* the act of trying not to do something or not to pay something ○ *tax avoidance*

award /əˈwɔːd/ *noun* something given by a court, tribunal or other official body, especially when settling a dispute or claim ○ *an award by an industrial tribunal* ○ *The arbitrator's award was set aside on appeal.* ○ *The latest pay award has been announced.*

B

BAA /ˌbiː eɪ ˈeɪ/ *abbr* British Accounting Association

baby bonds /ˈbeɪbi bɒndz/ *plural noun US* bonds in small denominations which the small investor can afford to buy

back /bæk/ *adjective* referring to the past ○ *a back payment* ■ *verb* to help someone, especially financially ○ *The bank is backing us to the tune of £10,000.* ○ *She is looking for someone to back her project.* □ **to back someone** to help someone financially ○ *The bank is backing him to the tune of £100,000.*

'…the businesses we back range from start-up ventures to established companies in need of further capital for expansion' [*Times*]

backdate /bæk'deɪt/ *verb* to put an earlier date on a document such as a cheque or an invoice ○ *Backdate your invoice to April 1st.*

back duty /ˈbæk ˌdjuːti/ *noun* a duty or tax which is due but has not yet been paid

back-end loaded /ˌbæk end ˈləʊdɪd/ *adjective* referring to an insurance or investment scheme where commission is charged when the investor withdraws his or her money from the scheme. Compare **front-end loaded**

backer /ˈbækə/ *noun* **1.** a person or company that backs someone ○ *One of the company's backers has withdrawn.* **2.** □ **the backer of a bill** the person who backs a bill

backing /ˈbækɪŋ/ *noun* support, especially financial support ○ *She has the backing of an Australian bank.* ○ *The company will succeed only if it has sufficient backing.* ○ *She gave her backing to the proposal.*

'…the company has received the backing of a number of oil companies who are willing to pay for the results of the survey' [*Lloyd's List*]

back interest /ˌbæk ˈɪntrəst/ *noun* interest which has not yet been paid

backlog /ˈbæklɒg/ *noun* an amount of work, or of items such as orders or letters, which should have been dealt with earlier but is still waiting to be done ○ *The warehouse is trying to cope with a backlog of orders.* ○

We're finding it hard to cope with the backlog of paperwork.

backlog depreciation /ˈbæklɒg dɪˌpriːʃieɪʃ(ə)n/ *noun* depreciation which has not been provided in previous accounts because of an increase in the value of the asset during the current year due to inflation

back office /ˌbæk ˈɒfɪs/ *noun US* the part of a broking firm where the paperwork involved in buying and selling shares is processed

back out /ˌbæk ˈaʊt/ *verb* to stop being part of a deal or an agreement ○ *The bank backed out of the contract.* ○ *We had to cancel the project when our German partners backed out.*

back payment /ˈbæk ˌpeɪmənt/ *noun* **1.** a payment which is due but has not yet been paid **2.** the act of paying money which is owed

back rent /ˈbæk rent/ *noun* a rent due but not paid ○ *The company owes £100,000 in back rent.*

back tax /ˈbæk tæks/ *noun* tax which is owed

back-to-back loan /ˌbæk tə ˌbæk ˈləʊn/ *noun* a loan from one company to another in one currency arranged against a loan from the second company to the first in another currency. Also called **parallel loan** (NOTE: Back-to-back loans are used by international companies to get round exchange controls.)

backup /ˈbækʌp/ *adjective* supporting or helping ○ *We offer a free backup service to customers.* ○ *After a series of sales tours by representatives, the sales director sends backup letters to all the contacts.*

backup copy /ˈbækʌp ˌkɒpi/ *noun* a copy of a computer disk to be kept in case the original disk is damaged

backup withholding /ˈbækʌp wɪθ ˌhəʊldɪŋ/ *noun US* a tax retained from investment income so that the IRS is sure of getting the tax due

backwardation /ˌbækwəˈdeɪʃ(ə)n/ *noun* **1.** a penalty paid by the seller when postponing delivery of shares to the buyer **2.** a situation where the spot price of a commodity or currency is higher than the futures price

backward integration /ˌbækwəd ɪntɪ ˈɡreɪʃ(ə)n/ *noun* a process of expansion in which a business which deals with the later stages in the production and sale of a product acquires a business that deals with an earlier stage in the same process, usually a supplier ○ *Buying up rubber plantations is part of the tyre company's backward integration policy.* ○ *Backward integration will ensure cheap supplies but forward integration would bring us nearer to the market.* Also called **vertical integration** (NOTE: The opposite is **forward integration**.)

backwards spreading /ˌbækwədz ˈspredɪŋ/ *noun* spacing income over a period of a number of previous years

BACS /bæks/ *noun* a company set up to organise the payment of direct debits, standing orders, salary cheques and other payments generated by computers. It operates for all the British clearing banks and several building societies; it forms part of APACS. Compare **CHAPS**. Full form **Bankers' Automated Clearing Services**

bad bargain /ˌbæd ˈbɑːɡɪn/ *noun* an item which is not worth the price asked

bad buy /ˌbæd ˈbaɪ/ *noun* a thing bought which was not worth the money paid for it

bad cheque /ˌbæd ˈtʃek/ *noun* a cheque which is returned to the drawer for any reason

bad debt /bæd ˈdet/ *noun* a debt which will not be paid, usually because the debtor has gone out of business, and which has to be written off in the accounts ○ *The company has written off £30,000 in bad debts.*

bad debt provision /bæd ˈdet prə ˌvɪʒ(ə)n/ *noun* money put aside in accounts to cover potential bad debts

bad debts recovered /ˌbæd dets rɪ ˈkʌvəd/ *noun* money formerly classified as [bad debt]s and therefore written off that has since been recovered either wholly or in part

badges of trade /ˌbædʒɪz əv ˈtreɪd/ *noun* a collection of principles established by case law to determine whether or not a person is trading. If so, he or she is taxed under different rules from non-traders.

bailment /ˈbeɪlmənt/ *noun* a transfer of goods by someone (the 'bailor') to someone (the 'bailee') who then holds them until they have to be returned to the bailor (NOTE: Putting jewels in a bank's safe deposit box is an example of bailment.)

bail out /ˌbeɪl ˈaʊt/ *verb* to rescue a company which is in financial difficulties

'…the government has decided to bail out the bank which has suffered losses to the extent that its capital has been wiped out' [*South China Morning Post*]

balance /ˈbæləns/ *noun* **1.** the amount which has to be put in one of the columns of an account to make the total debits and credits equal □ **balance brought down** *or* **forward** the closing balance of the previous period used as the opening balance of the current period □ **balance carried down** *or* **forward** the closing balance of the current period **2.** the rest of an amount owed ○ *You can pay £100 deposit and the balance within 60 days.* ■ *verb* **1.** to be equal, i.e. the assets owned must always equal the total liabilities plus capital **2.** to calculate the amount needed to make the two sides of an account equal ○ *I have finished balancing the accounts for March.* **3.** to plan a budget so that expenditure and income are equal ○ *The president is planning for a balanced budget.*

balanced budget /ˌbælənst ˈbʌdʒɪt/ *noun* a budget where expenditure and income are equal

balance off /ˌbæləns ˈɒf/ *verb* to add up and enter the totals for both sides of an account at the end of an accounting period in order to determine the balance

balance of payments /ˌbæləns əv ˈpeɪmənts/ *noun* a comparison between total receipts and payments arising from a country's international trade in goods, services and financial transactions. Abbreviation **BOP** □ **balance of payments current account** record of imports and exports of goods and services and the flows of money between countries arising from investments □ **long-term balance of payments** record of movements of capital relating to overseas investments and the purchase of companies overseas

balance of payments deficit /ˌbæləns əv ˈpeɪmənts ˌdefɪsɪt/ *noun* a situation when a country imports more than it exports

balance of payments surplus /ˌbæləns əv ˈpeɪmənts ˌsɜːpləs/ *noun* a situation where a country sells more to other countries than it buys from them

balance sheet /ˈbæləns ʃiːt/ *noun* a statement of the financial position of a company at a particular time, such as the end of the financial year or the end of a quarter, showing the company's assets and liabilities ○ *Our accountant has prepared the balance* *sheet for the first half-year.* ○ *The company balance sheet for the last financial year shows a worse position than for the previous year.* ○ *The company balance sheet for 1984 shows a substantial loss.* □ **balance sheet asset value** value of a company calculated by adding together all its assets □ **balance sheet date** the date (usually the end of a financial or accounting year) when a balance sheet is drawn up

balance sheet audit /ˌbæləns ʃiːt 'ɔːdɪt/ *noun* a limited audit of the items on a company's balance sheet in order to confirm that it complies with the relevant standards and requirements

balance sheet total /ˌbæləns ʃiːt 'təʊt(ə)l/ *noun* in the United Kingdom, the total of assets shown at the bottom of a balance sheet and used to classify a company according to size

balancing item /ˈbælənsɪŋ ˌaɪtəm/, **balancing figure** /ˈbælənsɪŋ ˌfɪɡə/ *noun* an item introduced into a balance sheet to make the two sides balance

balloon /bəˈluːn/ *noun* a loan where the last repayment is larger than the others

balloon mortgage /bəˌluːn ˈmɔːɡɪdʒ/ *noun US* a mortgage where the final payment (called a 'balloon payment') is larger than the others

BALO *noun* a French government publication that includes financial statements of public companies. Full form **Bulletin des Annonces Légales Obligatoires**

bank /bæŋk/ *noun* a business which holds money for its clients, lends money at interest, and trades generally in money ○ *the First National Bank* ○ *the Royal Bank of Scotland* ○ *She put all her earnings into the bank.* ○ *I have had a letter from my bank telling me my account is overdrawn.* ■ *verb* to deposit money into a bank or to have an account with a bank ○ *He banked the cheque as soon as he received it.*

bankable /ˈbæŋkəb(ə)l/ *adjective* acceptable by a bank as security for a loan

bankable paper /ˌbæŋkəb(ə)l ˈpeɪpə/ *noun* a document which a bank will accept as security for a loan

bank account /ˈbæŋk əˌkaʊnt/ *noun* an account which a customer has with a bank, where the customer can deposit and withdraw money ○ *to open a bank account* ○ *to close a bank account* ○ *How much money do you have in your bank account?* ○ *If you let the balance in your bank account fall below £100, you have to pay bank charges.* (NOTE: The US term is **banking account**.)

bank advance /ˈbæŋk ədˌvɑːns/ *noun* same as **bank loan** ○ *She asked for a bank advance to start her business.*

bank balance /ˈbæŋk ˌbæləns/ *noun* the state of a bank account at any particular time ○ *Our bank balance went into the red last month.*

bank base rate /ˌbæŋk 'beɪs ˌreɪt/ *noun* a basic rate of interest, on which the actual rate a bank charges on loans to its customers is calculated

bank bill /ˈbæŋk bɪl/ *noun* **1.** a bill of exchange by one bank telling another bank, usually in another country, to pay money to someone **2.** *US* same as **banknote**

bank book /ˈbæŋk bʊk/ *noun* a book given by a bank or building society which shows money which you deposit or withdraw from your savings account or building society account. Also called **passbook**

bank borrowing /ˌbæŋk 'bɒrəʊɪŋ/ *noun* money borrowed from a bank ○ *The new factory was financed by bank borrowing.*

bank borrowings /ˈbæŋk ˌbɒrəʊɪŋz/ *noun* money borrowed from banks

bank card /ˈbæŋk kɑːd/ *noun* a credit card or debit card issued to a customer by a bank for use instead of cash when buying goods or services (NOTE: There are internationally recognised rules that govern the authorisation of the use of bank cards and the clearing and settlement of transactions in which they are used.)

bank certificate /ˈbæŋk səˌtɪfɪkət/ *noun* a document, often requested during an audit, that is signed by a bank official and confirms the balances due or from a company on a specific date

bank charges /ˈbæŋk ˌtʃɑːdʒɪz/ *plural noun* charges which a bank makes for carrying out work for a customer (NOTE: The US term is **service charge**.)

bank confirmation /ˈbæŋk ˌkɒnfəˈmeɪʃ(ə)n/ *noun* verification of a company's balances requested by an auditor from a bank

bank credit /ˈbæŋk ˌkredɪt/ *noun* loans or overdrafts from a bank to a customer

bank deposits /ˈbæŋk dɪˈpɒzɪts/ *plural noun* all money placed in banks by private or corporate customers

bank draft /ˈbæŋk drɑːft/ *noun* an order by one bank telling another bank, usually in another country, to pay money to someone

banker /ˈbæŋkə/ *noun* **1.** a person who is in an important position in a bank **2.** a bank ○ *the company's banker is Barclays*

banker's acceptance /ˌbæŋkəz ək
'septəns/ *noun* a bill of exchange guaranteed by a bank

Bankers' Automated Clearing Services /ˌbæŋkəz ˌɔːtəmeɪtɪd 'klɪərɪŋ ˌsɜːvɪsɪz/ *plural noun* full form of **BACS**

banker's credit card /ˌbæŋkəz 'kredɪt ˌkɑːd/ *noun* a credit card issued by a bank, as opposed to cards issued by stores. Typical such cards are Visa, Access, MasterCard, etc.

banker's draft /ˌbæŋkəz 'drɑːft/ *noun* a draft payable by a bank in cash on presentation. Abbreviation **B/D**

banker's lien /ˌbæŋkəz 'liːn/ *noun* the right of a bank to hold some property of a customer as security against payment of a debt

banker's order /'bæŋkəz ˌɔːdə/ *noun* an order written by a customer asking a bank to make a regular payment ○ *He pays his subscription by banker's order.*

banker's reference /ˌbæŋkəz 'ref(ə)rəns/ *noun* a written report issued by a bank regarding a particular customer's creditworthiness

bank giro /'bæŋk ˌdʒaɪrəʊ/ *noun* a method used by clearing banks to transfer money rapidly from one account to another

bank holiday /ˌbæŋk 'hɒlɪdeɪ/ *noun* a weekday which is a public holiday when the banks are closed ○ *New Year's Day is a bank holiday.* ○ *Are we paid for bank holidays in this job?*

bank identification number /ˌbæŋk ˌaɪdentɪfɪ'keɪʃ(ə)n ˌnʌmbə/ *noun* an internationally organised six-digit number which identifies a bank for charge card purposes. Abbreviation **BIN**

banking /'bæŋkɪŋ/ *noun* the business of banks ○ *He is studying banking.* ○ *She has gone into banking.*

banking account /'bæŋkɪŋ əˌkaʊnt/ *noun US* an account which a customer has with a bank

Banking Ombudsman /ˌbæŋkɪŋ 'ɒmbʊdzmən/ *noun* an official whose duty is to investigate complaints by members of the public against banks

banking products /ˌbæŋkɪŋ 'prɒdʌkts/ *plural noun* goods and services produced by banks for customers, e.g. statements, direct debits

bank loan /'bæŋk ləʊn/ *noun* a loan made by a bank to a customer, usually against the security of a property or asset ○ *She asked for a bank loan to start her business.* Also called **bank advance**

bank manager /'bæŋk ˌmænɪdʒə/ *noun* the person in charge of a branch of a bank ○ *They asked their bank manager for a loan.*

bank mandate /'bæŋk ˌmændeɪt/ *noun* a written order to a bank, asking it to open an account and allow someone to sign cheques on behalf of the account holder, and giving specimen signatures and relevant information

banknote /'bæŋknəʊt/ *noun* **1.** a piece of printed paper money ○ *a counterfeit £20 note* ○ *He pulled out a pile of used notes.* (NOTE: The US term is **bill**.) **2.** *US* a non-interest bearing note, issued by a Federal Reserve Bank, which can be used as cash

bank reconciliation /ˌbæŋk ˌrekənsɪli'eɪʃ(ə)n/ *noun* the act of making sure that the bank statements agree with the company's ledgers

bank reserves /ˌbæŋk rɪ'zɜːvz/ *noun* cash and securities held by a bank to cover deposits

bank return /'bæŋk rɪˌtɜːn/ *noun* a regular report from a bank on its financial position

bankrupt /'bæŋkrʌpt/ *noun, adjective* (a person) who has been declared by a court not to be capable of paying his or her debts and whose affairs are put into the hands of a receiver ○ *a bankrupt property developer* ○ *She was adjudicated or declared bankrupt.* ○ *He went bankrupt after two years in business.* ■ *verb* to make someone become bankrupt ○ *The recession bankrupted my father.*

bankruptcy /'bæŋkrʌptsi/ *noun* the state of being bankrupt ○ *The recession has caused thousands of bankruptcies.* (NOTE: The plural is **bankruptcies**.)

bankruptcy order /'bæŋkrʌptsi ˌɔːdə/ *noun* same as **declaration of bankruptcy**

bankruptcy petition /ˌbæŋkrʌptsi pə'tɪʃ(ə)n/ *noun* an application to a court asking for an order making someone bankrupt

bankruptcy proceedings /ˌbæŋkrʌptsi prə'siːdɪŋz/ *plural noun* court case to make someone bankrupt

bank statement /'bæŋk ˌsteɪtmənt/ *noun* a written statement from a bank showing the balance of an account at a specific date

bank syndicate /'bæŋk ˌsɪndɪkət/ *noun* a group of major international banks which group together to underwrite a massive loan

bank transfer /'bæŋk ˌtrænsfɜː/ *noun* an act of moving money from a bank account to another account

bargain /ˈbɑːgɪn/ *noun* **1.** an agreement on the price of something ○ *to strike a bargain* or *to make a bargain* **2.** something which is cheaper than usual ○ *That car is a (real) bargain at £500.* **3.** a sale and purchase of one lot of shares on the Stock Exchange ■ *verb* to try to reach agreement about something, especially a price, usually with each person or group involved putting forward suggestions or offers which are discussed until a compromise is arrived at ○ *You will have to bargain with the dealer if you want a discount.* ○ *They spent two hours bargaining about* or *over the price.* (NOTE: You bargain **with** someone **over** or **about** or **for** something.)

bargain hunting /ˈbɑːgɪn ˌhʌntɪŋ/ *noun* looking for cheap goods or shares, which no one has noticed

bargaining /ˈbɑːgɪnɪŋ/ *noun* the act of trying to reach agreement about something, e.g. a price or a wage increase for workers

bargaining position /ˈbɑːgɪnɪŋ pəˌzɪʃ(ə)n/ *noun* the offers or demands made by one group during negotiations

bargain price /ˌbɑːgɪn ˈpraɪs/ *noun* a cheap price ○ *These carpets are for sale at a bargain price.*

bargain sale /ˌbɑːgɪn ˈseɪl/ *noun* the sale of all goods in a store at cheap prices

barter /ˈbɑːtə/ *noun* a system in which goods are exchanged for other goods and not sold for money

'…under the barter agreements, Nigeria will export 175,000 barrels a day of crude oil in exchange for trucks, food, planes and chemicals' [*Wall Street Journal*]

bartering /ˈbɑːtərɪŋ/ *noun* the act of exchanging goods for other goods and not for money

base /beɪs/ *noun* **1.** the lowest or first position ○ *Turnover increased by 200%, but started from a low base.* **2.** a place where a company has its main office or factory, or a place where a businessperson's office is located ○ *The company has its base in London and branches in all the European countries.* ○ *She has an office in Madrid which he uses as a base while travelling in Southern Europe.* ■ *verb* □ **to base something on something** to calculate something using something as your starting point or basic material for the calculation ○ *We based our calculations on the forecast turnover.* □ **based on** calculating from ○ *based on last year's figures* ○ *based on population forecasts*

'…the base lending rate, or prime rate, is the rate at which banks lend to their top corporate borrowers' [*Wall Street Journal*]

'…other investments include a large stake in the Chicago-based insurance company' [*Lloyd's List*]

base currency /ˈbeɪs ˌkʌrənsi/ *noun* a currency against which exchange rates of other currencies are quoted

base period /ˈbeɪs ˌpɪəriəd/ *noun US* **1.** a period against which comparisons are made **2.** the time that an employee must work before becoming eligible for state unemployment insurance benefits ○ *Because she had not worked for the base period, she had to rely on the support of her family when she lost her job.* ○ *The new government shortened the base period, in order to increase social service spending.*

base-weighted index /ˌbeɪs ˌweɪtɪd ˈɪndeks/ *noun* an index which is weighted according to the base year

base year /ˈbeɪs jɪə/ *noun* the first year of an index, against which changes occurring in later years are measured

basic /ˈbeɪsɪk/ *adjective* **1.** normal **2.** simple, or from which everything starts ○ *She has a basic knowledge of the market.* ○ *To work at the cash desk, you need a basic qualification in maths.*

basic balance /ˌbeɪsɪk ˈbæləns/ *noun* the balance of current account and long-term capital accounts in a country's balance of payments

basic commodities /ˌbeɪsɪk kəˈmɒdɪtiz/ *plural noun* ordinary farm produce, produced in large quantities, e.g. corn, rice or sugar

basic discount /ˌbeɪsɪk ˈdɪskaʊnt/ *noun* a normal discount without extra percentages ○ *Our basic discount is 20%, but we offer 5% extra for rapid settlement.*

basic pay /ˌbeɪsɪk ˈpeɪ/ *noun* a normal salary without extra payments

basic product /ˌbeɪsɪk ˈprɒdʌkt/ *noun* the main product made from a raw material

basic rate /ˌbeɪsɪk ˈreɪt/ *noun* the minimum rate for a job

basic rate tax /ˈbeɪsɪk reɪt ˌtæks/ *noun* the lowest rate of income tax

basic salary /ˌbeɪsɪk ˈsæləri/ *noun* same as **basic pay**

basic wage /ˌbeɪsɪk ˈweɪdʒ/ *noun* same as **basic pay** ○ *The basic wage is £110 a week, but you can expect to earn more than that with overtime.*

basis /ˈbeɪsɪs/ *noun* **1.** a point or number from which calculations are made ○ *We forecast the turnover on the basis of a 6% price increase.* (NOTE: The plural is **bases**.) **2.** the general terms of agreement or general principles on which something is decided or done ○ *This document should form the basis for an agreement.* ○ *We have three people working on a freelance basis.* (NOTE: The plural is **bases**.) □ **on a short-term**, **long-term basis** for a short or long period ○ *He has been appointed on a short-term basis.*

basis of apportionment /ˌbeɪsɪs əv ə'pɔːʃ(ə)nmənt/ *noun* a way in which common overhead costs are shared among various cost centres

basis of assessment /ˌbeɪsɪs əv ə'sesmənt/ *noun* a method of deciding in which year financial transactions should be assessed for taxation

basis period /ˌbeɪsɪs 'pɪərɪəd/ *noun* the period during which transactions occur, used for the purpose of deciding in which they should be assessed for taxation

basis point /ˈbeɪsɪs pɔɪnt/ *noun* an one hundredth of a percentage point (0.01%), the basic unit used in measuring market movements or interest rates

basis swap /ˈbeɪsɪs swɒp/ *noun* the exchange of two financial instruments, each with a variable interest calculated on a different rate

basket of currencies /ˌbɑːskɪt əv 'kʌrənsiz/ *noun* same as **currency basket**

batch /bætʃ/ *noun* **1.** a group of items which are made at one time ○ *This batch of shoes has the serial number 25–02.* **2.** a group of documents which are processed at the same time ○ *Today's batch of invoices is ready to be mailed.* ○ *The factory is working on yesterday's batch of orders.* ○ *The accountant signed a batch of cheques.* ○ *We deal with the orders in batches of fifty at a time.* ■ *verb* to put items together in groups ○ *to batch invoices or cheques*

batch costing /ˌbætʃ 'kɒstɪŋ/ *noun* a method of calculating the price of one item as part of a batch of items made at the same time

batch number /ˈbætʃ ˌnʌmbə/ *noun* a number attached to a batch ○ *When making a complaint always quote the batch number on the packet.*

batch processing /ˈbætʃ ˌprəʊsesɪŋ/ *noun* a system of data processing where information is collected into batches before being loaded into the computer

batch production /ˈbætʃ prə,dʌkʃən/ *noun* production in batches

b/d *abbr* brought down

B/D *abbr* banker's draft

bear /beə/ *noun* a person who sells shares, commodities or currency because he or she

thinks their price will fall and it will be possible to buy them again more cheaply later. Opposite **bull** ■ *verb* **1.** to give interest ○ *government bonds which bear 5% interest* **2.** to have something, especially to have something written on it ○ *an envelope which bears a London postmark* ○ *a letter bearing yesterday's date* ○ *The cheque bears the signature of the company secretary.* ○ *The share certificate bears his name.* **3.** to pay costs ○ *The costs of the exhibition will be borne by the company.* ○ *The company bore the legal costs of both parties.* (NOTE: **bearing – bore – has borne**)

bear covering /ˈbeə ˌkʌvərɪŋ/ *noun* a point in a market where dealers who sold stock short, now buy back at lower prices to cover their positions

bearer /ˈbeərə/ *noun* a person who holds a cheque or certificate

bearer bond /ˈbeərə bɒnd/, **bearer security** *noun* a bond which is payable to the bearer and does not have a name written on it

bearing /ˈbeərɪŋ/ *adjective* producing ○ *certificates bearing interest at 5%* ○ *interest-bearing deposits*

bear market /ˈbeə ˌmɑːkɪt/ *noun* a period when share prices fall because shareholders are selling since they believe the market will fall further. Opposite **bull market**

bear position /ˈbeə pə,zɪʃ(ə)n/ *noun* a short position, that is, selling shares which you do not own with the intention of buying them back later at a lower price, so as to be able to settle

bear raid /ˈbeə reɪd/ *noun* the act of selling large numbers of shares to try to bring down prices

behavioural accounting /bɪˌheɪvjərəl ə'kaʊntɪŋ/ *noun* an approach to the study of accounting that emphasises the psychological and social aspects of the profession in addition to the more technical areas

bellwether /ˈbelweðə/ *noun* a leading share which is thought of as an indicator of market trends as a whole, e.g. Lloyds in the UK

below par /bɪˌləʊ 'pɑː/ *adjective* referring to a share with a market price lower than its par value

below the line /bɪˌləʊ ðə 'laɪn/ *adjective*, *adverb* used to describe entries in a company's profit and loss account that show how the profit is distributed, or where the funds to finance the loss originate

below-the-line expenditure /bɪˌləʊ ðə laɪn ɪk'spendɪtʃə/ *noun* **1.** payments which do not arise from a company's usual activities, e.g. redundancy payments **2.** extraordinary items which are shown in the profit and loss account below net profit after taxation, as opposed to exceptional items which are included in the figure for profit before taxation

benchmark /'bentʃmɑːk/ *noun* a point or level which is important, and can be used as a reference when making evaluations or assessments

benchmark accounting policy /ˌbentʃmɑːk əˈkaʊntɪŋ ˌpɒlɪsi/ *noun* one of a choice of two possible policies within an International Accounting Standard. The other policy is marked as an 'allowed alternative', although there is no indication of preference.

beneficial interest /ˌbenɪfɪʃ(ə)l ˈɪntrəst/ *noun* a situation where someone is allowed to occupy or receive rent from a house without owning it

beneficial occupier /ˌbenɪfɪʃ(ə)l ˈɒkjʊpaɪə/ *noun* a person who occupies a property but does not own it fully

beneficiary /ˌbenɪˈfɪʃəri/ *noun* a person who gains money from something ○ *the beneficiaries of a will*

benefit /'benɪfɪt/ *verb* **1.** to make better or to improve ○ *A fall in inflation benefits the exchange rate.* **2.** □ **to benefit from** *or* **by something** to be improved by something, to gain more money because of something ○ *Exports have benefited from the fall in the exchange rate.* ○ *The employees have benefited from the profit-sharing scheme.*

'…the retail sector will also benefit from the expected influx of tourists' [*Australian Financial Review*]

'…what benefits does the executive derive from his directorship? Compensation has increased sharply in recent years and fringe benefits for directors have proliferated' [*Duns Business Month*]

'…salary is negotiable to £30,000, plus car and a benefits package appropriate to this senior post' [*Financial Times*]

'California is the latest state to enact a program forcing welfare recipients to work for their benefits' [*Fortune*]

'…salary range is $54,957 – $81,189, with a competitive benefits package' [*Washington Post*]

benefit in kind /ˌbenɪfɪt ɪn ˈkaɪnd/ *noun* a benefit other than money received by an employee as part of his or her total compensation package, e.g. a company car or private health insurance. Such benefits are usually subject to tax.

Benford's Law /'benfədz lɔː/ *noun* a law discovered by Dr Benford in 1938, which shows that in sets of random numbers, it is more likely that the set will begin with the number 1 than with any other number

BEP *abbr* breakeven point

bequeath /bɪˈkwiːð/ *verb* to leave property, money, etc. (but not freehold land) to someone in a will

bequest /bɪˈkwest/ *noun* something such as property or money (but not freehold land), given to someone in a will ○ *He made several bequests to his staff.*

beta /'biːtə/ *noun* a measurement of the return on investment in a stock compared against a one percentage point return on the stock market in general: it shows the volatility in the price of the share compared to the FTSE All-Share Index

b/f *abbr* brought forward

BFH *noun* in Germany, the supreme court for issues concerning taxation. Full form **Bundesfinanzhof**

bid /bɪd/ *noun* **1.** an offer to buy something at a specific price. ◊ **takeover bid** □ **to make a bid for something** to offer to buy something ○ *We made a bid for the house.* ○ *The company made a bid for its rival.* □ **to make a cash bid** to offer to pay cash for something □ **to put in** *or* **enter a bid for something** to offer to buy something, usually in writing **2.** an offer to sell something or do a piece of work at a specific price ○ *She made the lowest bid for the job.* ■ *verb* to offer to buy □ **to bid for something** (*at an auction*) to offer to buy something □ **he bid £1,000 for the jewels** he offered to pay £1,000 for the jewels

bidder /'bɪdə/ *noun* a person who makes a bid, usually at an auction ○ *Several bidders made offers for the house.*

bidding /'bɪdɪŋ/ *noun* the act of making offers to buy, usually at an auction □ **the bidding started at £1,000** the first and lowest bid was £1,000 □ **the bidding stopped at £250,000** the last bid, i.e. the successful bid, was for £250,000 □ **the auctioneer started the bidding at £100** the auctioneer suggested that the first bid should be £100

bid market /'bɪd ˌmɑːkɪt/ *noun* a market where there are more bids to buy than offers to sell

bid rate /'bɪd reɪt/ *noun* a rate of interest offered on deposits

big business /ˌbɪg ˈbɪznɪs/ *noun* very large commercial firms

Big Four /ˌbɪg ˈfɔː/ *noun* **1.** the four large British commercial banks: Barclays, LloydsTSB, HSB and Natwest, now joined by several former building societies that have become banks **2.** the four largest Japanese securities houses: Daiwa, Nikko, Nomura and Yamaichi

bilateral /baɪˈlæt(ə)rəl/ *adjective* between two parties or countries ○ *The minister signed a bilateral trade agreement.*

bilateral clearing /baɪˌlæt(ə)rəl ˈklɪərɪŋ/ *noun* the system of annual settlements of accounts between some countries, where accounts are settled by the central banks

bilateral credit /baɪˌlæt(ə)rəl ˈkredɪt/ *noun* credit allowed by banks to other banks in a clearing system, to cover the period while cheques are being cleared

bill /bɪl/ *noun* **1.** a written list of charges to be paid ○ *The sales assistant wrote out the bill.* ○ *Does the bill include VAT?* ○ *The bill is made out to Smith Ltd.* ○ *The builder sent in his bill.* ○ *She left the country without paying her bills.* **2.** a list of charges in a restaurant ○ *Can I have the bill please?* ○ *The bill comes to £20 including service.* ○ *Does the bill include service?* ○ *The waiter has added 10% to the bill for service.* **3.** a written paper promising to pay money □ **bills payable (B or P)** bills, especially bills of exchange, which a company will have to pay to its creditors □ **bills receivable (B or R)** bills, especially bills of exchange, which are due to be paid by a company's debtors **4.** *US* same as **banknote** ○ *a $5 bill* (NOTE: The UK term is **note** or **banknote**.) **5.** a draft of a new law which will be discussed in Parliament ■ *verb* to present a bill to someone so that it can be paid ○ *The plumbers billed us for the repairs.*

bill broker /ˈbɪl ˌbrəʊkə/ *noun* a discount house, a firm which buys and sells bills of exchange for a fee

billing /ˈbɪlɪŋ/ *noun* the work of writing invoices or bills

billion /ˈbɪljən/ *noun* one thousand million (NOTE: In the USA, it has always meant one thousand million, but in UK English it formerly meant one million million, and it is still sometimes used with this meaning. With figures it is usually written **bn: $5bn** say 'five billion dollars'.)

'…gross wool receipts for the selling season to end June 30 appear likely to top $2 billion' [*Australian Financial Review*]

'…at its last traded price the bank was capitalized at around $1.05 billion' [*South China Morning Post*]

bill of exchange /ˌbɪl əv ɪksˈtʃeɪndʒ/ *noun* a document, signed by the person authorising it, which tells another person or a financial institution to pay money unconditionally to a named person on a specific date (NOTE: Bills of exchange are usually used for payments in foreign currency.)

bill of lading /ˌbɪl əv ˈleɪdɪŋ/ *noun* a list of goods being shipped, which the transport-

er gives to the person sending the goods to show that the goods have been loaded

bill of sale /ˌbɪl əv ˈseɪl/ *noun* a document which the seller gives to the buyer to show that the sale has taken place

bill payable /ˌbɪl ˈpeɪəb(ə)l/ *noun* a promissory note or bill of exchange payable

bill receivable /ˌbɪl rɪˈsiːvəb(ə)l/ *noun* a promissory note or bill of exchange receivable

BIN *abbr* bank identification number

bin card /ˈbɪn kɑːd/ *noun* a stock record card in a warehouse

bind /baɪnd/ *verb* to tie or to attach (NOTE: **binding – bound**)

binder /ˈbaɪndə/ *noun* *US* a temporary agreement for insurance sent before the insurance policy is issued (NOTE: The UK term is **cover note**.)

binding /ˈbaɪndɪŋ/ *adjective* being a legal requirement that someone does something ○ *a binding contract* ○ *This document is not legally binding.*

BiRiLiG *noun* the 1985 German accounting directives law. Full form **Bilanzricht-tliniengesetz**

black economy /blæk ɪˈkɒnəmi/ *noun* goods and services which are paid for in cash, and therefore not declared for tax. Also called **hidden economy, parallel economy, shadow economy**

black market /ˌblæk ˈmɑːkɪt/ *noun* the buying and selling of goods or currency in a way which is not allowed by law ○ *There is a flourishing black market in spare parts for cars.*

blank /blæŋk/ *adjective* with nothing written on it

blank cheque /ˌblæŋk ˈtʃek/ *noun* a cheque with the amount of money and the payee left blank, but signed by the drawer

blanket lien /ˌblæŋkɪt ˈliːn/ *noun* *US* a lien on a person's property, including personal effects

blind trust /ˈblaɪnd trʌst/ *noun* a trust set up to run a person's affairs without the details of any transaction being known to the person concerned (NOTE: Blind trusts are set up by politicians to avoid potential conflicts of interest.)

block /blɒk/ *noun* a series of items grouped together ○ *I bought a block of 6,000 shares.* ■ *verb* to stop something taking place ○ *He used his casting vote to block the motion.* ○ *The planning committee blocked the redevelopment plan.*

block booking /ˌblɒk ˈbʊkɪŋ/ *noun* an act of booking of several seats or rooms at the same time ○ *The company has a block booking for twenty seats on the plane* or *for ten rooms at the hotel.*

blocked account /ˌblɒkt əˈkaʊnt/ *noun* a bank account which cannot be used, usually because a government has forbidden its use

blocked currency /ˌblɒkt ˈkʌrənsi/ *noun* a currency which cannot be taken out of a country because of government exchange controls ○ *The company has a large account in blocked roubles.*

blocked funds /ˌblɒkt ˈfʌndz/ *noun* money that cannot be transferred from one place to another, usually because of exchange controls imposed by the government of the country in which the funds are held

block trading /ˌblɒk ˈtreɪdɪŋ/ *noun* trading in very large numbers of shares

blowout /ˈbləʊaʊt/ *noun US* a rapid sale of the whole of a new stock issue (*informal*)

Blue Book /ˌbluː ˈbʊk/ *noun* an annual publication of national statistics of personal incomes and spending patterns

blue chip /ˈbluː tʃɪp/ *noun* a very safe investment, a risk-free share in a good company

Blue list /ˈbluː lɪst/ *noun US* a daily list of municipal bonds and their ratings, issued by Standard & Poor's

blue sky laws /ˌbluː ˈskaɪ ˌlɔːz/ *plural noun US* state laws to protect investors against fraudulent traders in securities

board /bɔːd/ *noun* **1. ♦ board of directors** ○ *He sits on the board as a representative of the bank.* ○ *Two directors were removed from the board at the AGM.* **2.** a group of people who run an organisation, trust or society **3.** □ **on board** on a ship, plane or train ■ *verb* to go on to a ship, plane or train ○ *Customs officials boarded the ship in the harbour.*

'CEOs, with their wealth of practical experience, are in great demand and can pick and choose the boards they want to serve on' [*Duns Business Month*]

board meeting /ˈbɔːd ˌmiːtɪŋ/ *noun* a meeting of the directors of a company

Board of Customs and Excise /bɔːd əv ˌkʌstəmz ən, ɪkˈsaɪz/ *noun* the ruling body of the Customs and Excise

board of directors /ˌbɔːd əv daɪˈrektəz/ *noun* **1.** a group of directors elected by the shareholders to run a company ○ *The bank has two representatives on the board of directors.* **2.** *US* a group of people elected by the shareholders to draw up company policy and to appoint the president and other executive officers who are responsible for managing the company

'…a proxy is the written authorization an investor sends to a stockholder meeting conveying his vote on a corporate resolution or the election of a company's board of directors' [*Barrons*]

Board of Inland Revenue /bɔːd əv ˌɪnlənd ˈrevənjuː/ *noun* the ruling body of the Inland Revenue, appointed by the Treasury

bona fide /ˌbəʊnə ˈfaɪdi/ *adjective* trustworthy, which can be trusted

bond /bɒnd/ *noun* **1.** a contract document promising to repay money borrowed by a company or by the government on a specific date, and paying interest at regular intervals **2.** □ **goods (held) in bond** goods held by customs until duty has been paid □ **entry of goods under bond** bringing goods into a country in bond □ **to take goods out of bond** to pay duty on goods so that they can be released by customs **3.** a form of insurance fund which is linked to a unit trust, but where there is no yield because the income is automatically added to the fund

bond discount /ˌbɒnd dɪsˈkaʊnt/ *noun* the difference between the face value of a bond and the lower price at which it is issued

bonded /ˈbɒndɪd/ *adjective* held in bond

bonded warehouse /ˌbɒndɪd ˈweəhaʊs/ *noun* a warehouse where goods are stored until excise duty has been paid

bondholder /ˈbɒndhəʊldə/ *noun* a person who holds government bonds

bondised /ˈbɒndaɪzd/, **bondized** *adjective* referring to an insurance fund linked to a unit trust

bond market /ˈbɒnd ˌmɑːkɪt/ *noun* a market in which government or municipal bonds are traded

bond premium /ˌbɒnd ˈpriːmiəm/ *noun* the difference between the face value of a bond and a higher price at which it is issued

bond-washing /ˈbɒnd ˌwɒʃɪŋ/ *noun* the act of selling securities cum dividend and buying them back later ex dividend, or selling US Treasury bonds with the interest coupon, and buying them back ex-coupon, so as to reduce tax

bond yield /ˈbɒnd jiːld/ *noun* income produced by a bond, shown as a percentage of its purchase price

bonus /ˈbəʊnəs/ *noun* an extra payment in addition to a normal payment

bonus issue /ˌbəʊnəs ˈɪʃuː/ *noun* a scrip issue or capitalisation issue, where a company transfers money from reserves to share capital and issues free extra shares to the shareholders. The value of the company remains the same, and the total market value of shareholders' shares remains the same, the market price being adjusted to account for the new shares. Also called **share split** (NOTE: The US term is **stock dividend** or **stock split**.)

bonus share /ˈbəʊnəs ʃeə/ *noun* an extra share given to an existing shareholder

book /bʊk/ *noun* **1.** a set of sheets of paper attached together □ **a company's books** the financial records of a company **2.** a statement of a dealer's exposure to the market, i.e. the amount which he or she is due to pay or has borrowed □ **to make a book** to have a list of shares which he or she is prepared to buy or sell on behalf of clients

bookkeeper /ˈbʊkkiːpə/ *noun* a person who keeps the financial records of a company or an organisation

bookkeeping /ˈbʊkkiːpɪŋ/ *noun* the work of keeping the financial records of a company or an organisation

bookkeeping barter /ˌbʊkkiːpɪŋ ˈbɑːtə/ *noun* the direct exchange of goods between two parties without the use of money as a medium, but using monetary measures to record the transaction

bookkeeping transaction /ˈbʊkkiːpɪŋ trænˌzækʃən/ *noun* a transaction which involves changes to a company's books of accounts, but does not alter the value of the company in any way, e.g. the issue of bonus shares

book of account /ˌbʊk əv əˈkaʊnt/ *noun* an account book, a book which records financial transactions

book of prime entry /ˌbʊk əv ˌpraɪm ˈentri/ *noun* a chronological record of a business's transactions arranged according to type, e.g., cash or sales. The books are then used to generate entries in a double-entry bookkeeping system. Also called **book of original entry**

book sales /ˈbʊk seɪlz/ *plural noun* sales as recorded in the sales book

books of prime entry /ˌbʊks əv ˌpraɪm ˈentri/ *plural noun* books of account recording a company's financial transactions

book value /ˈbʊk væljuː/ *noun* the value of an asset as recorded in the company's balance sheet

boom /buːm/ *noun* a time when sales, production or business activity are increasing ○ *a period of economic boom* ○ *the boom of the 1990s*

boom industry /ˈbuːm ˌɪndəstri/ *noun* an industry which is expanding rapidly

booming /ˈbuːmɪŋ/ *adjective* expanding or becoming prosperous ○ *a booming industry* or *company* ○ *Technology is a booming sector of the economy.*

boost /buːst/ *noun* help given to increase something ○ *This publicity will give sales a boost.* ○ *The government hopes to give a boost to industrial development.* ■ *verb* to make something increase ○ *We expect our publicity campaign to boost sales by 25%.* ○ *The company hopes to boost its market share.* ○ *Incentive schemes are boosting production.*

'…the company expects to boost turnover this year to FFr 16bn from FFr 13.6bn last year' [*Financial Times*]

BOP *abbr* balance of payments

border /ˈbɔːdə/ *noun* a frontier between two countries

border tax adjustment /ˈbɔːdə tæks əˌdʒʌstmənt/ *noun* a deduction of indirect tax paid on goods being exported or imposition of local indirect tax on goods being imported

borrow /ˈbɒrəʊ/ *verb* **1.** to take money from someone for a time, possibly paying interest for it, and repaying it at the end of the period ○ *She borrowed £1,000 from the bank.* ○ *The company had to borrow heavily to repay its debts.* ○ *They borrowed £25,000 against the security of the factory.* **2.** to buy at spot prices and sell forward at the same time

borrower /ˈbɒrəʊə/ *noun* a person who borrows ○ *Borrowers from the bank pay 12% interest.*

borrowing /ˈbɒrəʊɪŋ/ *noun* the action of borrowing money ○ *The new factory was financed by bank borrowing.*

'…we tend to think of building societies as having the best borrowing rates and indeed many do offer excellent terms' [*Financial Times*]

borrowing costs /ˈbɒrəʊɪŋ kɒsts/ *plural noun* the interest and other charges paid on money borrowed

borrowing power /ˈbɒrəʊɪŋ ˌpaʊə/ *noun* the amount of money which a company can borrow

borrowings /ˈbɒrəʊɪŋz/ *plural noun* money borrowed ○ *The company's borrowings have doubled.*

bottom /ˈbɒtəm/ *verb* to reach the lowest point □ **the market has bottomed out** the market has reached the lowest point and does not seem likely to fall further

bottom line /ˌbɒtəm ˈlaɪn/ *noun* **1.** the last line on a balance sheet indicating profit or loss □ **the boss is interested only in the bottom line** he is only interested in the final profit **2.** the final decision on a matter ○ *The bottom line was that the work had to completed within budget.*

bottom-up budgeting *noun* same as participative budgeting

bought day book /bɔːt deɪ bʊk/ *noun* a book used to record purchases made on credit

bought ledger /'bɔːt ˌledʒə/ *noun* a book in which purchases are recorded

bought ledger clerk /ˌbɔːt 'ledʒə ˌklɑːk/ *noun* an office employee who deals with the bought ledger or the sales ledger

bounce /baʊns/ *verb* to be returned by the bank to the person who has tried to cash it, because there is not enough money in the payer's account to pay it ○ *She paid for the car with a cheque that bounced.*

bracket /'brækɪt/ *noun* a group of items or people taken together □ **she is in the top tax bracket** she pays the highest level of tax

branch accounts /ˌbrɑːntʃ ə'kaʊnts/ *plural noun* accounts showing transactions belonging to the branches of a large organisation, i.e., between a branch and other branches or its head office, or other companies outside the organisation

branch manager /ˌbrɑːntʃ 'mænɪdʒə/ *noun* a person in charge of a branch of a company

'…a leading manufacturer of business, industrial and commercial products requires a branch manager to head up its mid-western Canada operations based in Winnipeg' [*Globe and Mail (Toronto)*]

branch office /ˌbrɑːntʃ 'ɒfɪs/ *noun* a less important office, usually in a different town or country from the main office

brand /brænd/ *noun* a make of product, which can be recognised by a name or by a design ○ *the top-selling brands of toothpaste* ○ *The company is launching a new brand of soap.*

'…the multiple brought the price down to £2.49 in some stores. We had not agreed to this deal and they sold out very rapidly. When they reordered we would not give it to them. This kind of activity is bad for the brand and we cannot afford it' [*The Grocer*]

'…you have to look much further down the sales league to find a brand which has not been around for what seems like ages' [*Marketing*]

'…major companies are supporting their best existing brands with increased investment' [*Marketing Week*]

brand name /'brænd neɪm/ *noun* a name of a particular make of product

breach /briːtʃ/ *noun* a failure to carry out the terms of an agreement

breach of contract /ˌbriːtʃ əv 'kɒntrækt/ *noun* the failure to do something which has been agreed in a contract

breach of trust /ˌbriːtʃ əv 'trʌst/ *noun* a situation where a person does not act correctly or honestly when people expect him or her to

break /breɪk/ *noun* **1.** a pause between periods of work ○ *She keyboarded for two hours without a break.* ○ *She typed for two hours without a break.* **2.** a sharp fall in share prices ■ *verb* **1.** to fail to carry out the duties of a contract ○ *The company has broken the contract* or *the agreement by selling at a lower price.* **2.** to cancel a contract ○ *The company is hoping to be able to break the contract.* (NOTE: [all verb senses] **breaking – broke – has broken**)

breakages /'breɪkɪdʒɪz/ *plural noun* breaking of items ○ *Customers are expected to pay for breakages.*

break down /ˌbreɪk 'daʊn/ *verb* **1.** to stop working because of mechanical failure ○ *The fax machine has broken down.* **2.** to stop ○ *Negotiations broke down after six hours.* **3.** to show all the items in a total list of costs or expenditure ○ *We broke the expenditure down into fixed and variable costs.*

breakdown /'breɪkdaʊn/ *noun* **1.** an act of stopping working because of mechanical failure ○ *We cannot communicate with our Nigerian office because of the breakdown of the telephone lines.* **2.** an act of stopping talking ○ *a breakdown in wage negotiations* **3.** an act of showing details item by item ○ *Give me a breakdown of investment costs.*

breakeven *verb* to balance costs and receipts, so as to make neither a profit nor a loss ○ *last year the company only just broke even* ○ *we broke even in our first two months of trading* ■ *noun* a situation where there is neither a profit nor a loss

breakeven analysis /breɪk'iːv(ə)n ə ˌnæləsɪs/ *noun* **1.** the analysis of fixed and variable costs and sales that determines at what level of production the breakeven point will be reached ○ *The breakeven analysis showed that the company will only break even if it sells at least 1,000 bicycles a month.* **2.** a method of showing the point at which a company's income from sales will be equal to its production costs so that it neither makes a profit nor makes a loss (NOTE: Breakeven analysis is usually shown in the form of a chart and can be used to help companies make decisions, set prices for their products and work out the effects of changes in production or sales volume on their costs and profits.)

breakeven point /ˌbreɪkˈiːv(ə)n pɔɪnt/ *noun* the point or level of financial activity at which expenditure equals income, or the value of an investment equals its cost so that the result is neither a profit nor a loss. Abbreviation **BEP**

break-out /ˈbreɪk aʊt/ *noun* a movement of a share price above or below its previous trading level

break up /ˌbreɪk ˈʌp/ *verb* to split something large into small sections ○ *The company was broken up and separate divisions sold off.*

break-up value /ˈbreɪk ʌp ˌvæljuː/ *noun* **1.** the value of the material of a fixed asset ○ *What would the break-up value of our old machinery be?* ○ *Scrap merchants were asked to estimate the tractors' break-up value.* **2.** the value of various parts of a company taken separately

bribe /braɪb/ *noun* money given secretly and usually illegally to someone in authority to get them to help ○ *The minister was dismissed for taking a bribe.*

bricks-and-mortar /ˌbrɪks ən ˈmɔːtə/ *adjective* referring to the fixed assets of a company, especially its buildings

bridge finance /ˈbrɪdʒ ˌfaɪnæns/ *noun* loans to cover short-term needs

bridging loan /ˈbrɪdʒɪŋ ləʊn/ *noun* a short-term loan to help someone buy a new house when the old one has not yet been sold (NOTE: The US term is **bridge loan**.)

bring down /ˌbrɪŋ ˈdaʊn/ *verb* to reduce ○ *Petrol companies have brought down the price of oil.*

bring forward /ˌbrɪŋ ˈfɔːwəd/ *verb* **1.** to make something take [place earlier ○ *to bring forward the date of repayment* ○ *The date of the next meeting has been brought forward to March.* **2.** to take an account balance from the end of the previous period as the starting point for the current period ○ *Balance brought forward: £365.15*

bring in /ˌbrɪŋ ˈɪn/ *verb* to earn an amount of interest ○ *The shares bring in a small amount.*

British Accounting Association /ˌbrɪtɪʃ əˈkaʊntɪŋ əˌsəʊsieɪʃ(ə)n/ an organisation whose aim is to promote accounting education and research in the United Kingdom. F. Abbreviation **BAA**

broker /ˈbrəʊkə/ *noun* a dealer who acts as a middleman between a buyer and a seller

brokerage /ˈbrəʊkərɪdʒ/, **broker's commission** /ˌbrəʊkəz kəˈmɪʃ(ə)n/ *noun* **1.** payment to a broker for a deal carried out **2.** same as **broking**

brokerage firm /ˈbrəʊkərɪdʒ fɜːm/, **brokerage house** /ˈbrəʊkərɪdʒ haʊs/ *noun* a firm which buys and sells shares for clients

broker-dealer /ˌbrəʊkə ˈdiːlə/ *noun* a dealer who buys shares and holds them for resale, and also deals on behalf of investor clients

broker's commission /ˌbrəʊkəz kəˈmɪʃ(ə)n/ *noun* the payment to a broker for a deal which he or she has carried out (NOTE: Formerly, the commission charged by brokers on the London Stock Exchange was fixed, but since 1986, commissions have been variable.)

broking /ˈbrəʊkɪŋ/ *noun* the business of dealing in stocks and shares

brought down /ˈbrɔːt ˈdaʊn/, **brought forward** /ˈbrɔːt ˈfɔːwəd/ *noun* balance in an account from the previous period taken as the starting point for the current period ○ *balance brought down* or *forward: £365.15* Abbreviation **b/d, b/f**

B/S *abbr* balance sheet

B shares /ˈbiː ˌʃeəz/ *plural noun* ordinary shares with special voting rights, often owned by the founder of a company and his or her family

buck /bʌk/ *noun* US a dollar (*informal*)

bucket shop /ˈbʌkɪt ʃɒp/ *noun* a firm that sells cheap airline or other travel tickets (*informal*)

'…at last something is being done about the thousands of bucket shops across the nation that sell investment scams by phone' [*Forbes Magazine*]

budget /ˈbʌdʒɪt/ *noun* **1.** a plan of expected spending and income for a period of time ○ *to draw up a budget for salaries for the coming year* ○ *We have agreed the budgets for next year.* **2.** □ **the Budget** the annual plan of taxes and government spending proposed by a finance minister. In the UK, the budget is drawn up by the Chancellor of the Exchequer. ○ *The minister put forward a budget aimed at boosting the economy.* ■ *verb* to plan probable income and expenditure ○ *We are budgeting for £10,000 of sales next year.*

'…he budgeted for further growth of 150,000 jobs (or 2.5 per cent) in the current financial year' [*Sydney Morning Herald*]

'…the Federal government's budget targets for employment and growth are within reach according to the latest figures' [*Australian Financial Review*]

budget account /ˈbʌdʒɪt əˌkaʊnt/ *noun* a bank account where you plan income and expenditure to allow for periods when expenditure is high, by paying a set amount each month

budgetary /'bʌdʒɪt(ə)rɪ/ *adjective* referring to a budget

budgetary control /ˌbʌdʒɪt(ə)rɪ kən 'trəʊl/ *noun* controlled spending according to a planned budget

budgetary policy /ˌbʌdʒɪt(ə)rɪ 'pɒlɪsi/ *noun* the policy of planning income and expenditure

budgetary requirements /ˌbʌdʒɪt(ə)rɪ rɪ'kwaɪəməntz/ *plural noun* the rate of spending or income required to meet the budget forecasts

budget committee /ˌbʌdʒɪt kə'mɪti/ *noun* the group within an organisation responsible for drawing up budgets that meet departmental requirements, ensuring they comply with policy, and then submitting them to the board of directors

Budget Day /'bʌdʒɪt deɪ/ *noun* the day when the Chancellor of the Exchequer presents the budget to Parliament. This is usually in March, but with an advance budget statement in November.

budget deficit /'bʌdʒɪt ˌdefɪsɪt/ *noun* **1.** a deficit in a country's planned budget, where income from taxation will not be sufficient to pay for the government's expenditure **2.** a deficit in personal finances where a household will borrow to finance large purchases which cannot be made out of income alone

budget department /'bʌdʒɪt dɪ ˌpɑːtmənt/ *noun* a department in a large store which sells cheaper goods

budget director /ˌbʌdʒɪt daɪ'rektə/ *noun* the person in an organisation who is responsible for running the budget system

budgeted capacity /ˌbʌdʒɪtɪd kə 'pæsɪti/ *noun* an organisation's available output level for a budget period according to the budget. It may be expressed in different ways, e.g., in machine hours or standard hours.

budgeted revenue /ˌbʌdʒɪtɪd 'revənjuː/ *noun* the income that an organisation expects to receive in a budget period according to the budget

budgeting /'bʌdʒɪtɪŋ/ *noun* the preparation of budgets to help plan expenditure and income

budget lapsing /'bʌdʒɪt ˌlæpsɪŋ/ *noun* withdrawal of unspent budget allowance due to the expiry of the budget period

budget manual /ˌbʌdʒɪt 'mænjuəl/ *noun* a handbook or set of documents that detail budgetary procedure for a company or organisation

budget period /ˌbʌdʒɪt 'pɪəriəd/ *noun* a period of time covered by a budget

budget variance /ˌbʌdʒɪt 'veəriəns/ *noun* the difference between the cost as estimated for a budget and the actual cost

buffer stocks /'bʌfə 'stɒks/ *plural noun* stocks of a commodity bought by an international body when prices are low and held for resale at a time when prices have risen, with the intention of reducing sharp fluctuations in world prices of the commodity

building and loan association /ˌbɪldɪŋ ən 'ləʊn əˌsəʊsieɪʃ(ə)n/ *noun US* same as **savings and loan**

building society /'bɪldɪŋ səˌsaɪəti/ *noun* a financial institution which accepts and pays interest on deposits, and lends money to people who are buying property against the security of the property which is being bought ○ *We put our savings into a building society* or *into a building society account.* ○ *I have an account with the Nationwide Building Society.* ○ *I saw the building society manager to ask for a mortgage.*

build into /'bɪld ˌɪntuː/ *verb* to include something in something which is being set up ○ *You must build all the forecasts into the budget.*

build up /ˌbɪld 'ʌp/ *verb* **1.** to create something by adding pieces together ○ *She bought several shoe shops and gradually built up a chain.* **2.** to expand something gradually ○ *to build up a profitable business* ○ *to build up a team of sales representatives*

buildup /'bɪldʌp/ *noun* a gradual increase ○ *a buildup in sales* or *a sales buildup* ○ *There will be a big publicity buildup before the launch of the new model.* ○ *There has been a buildup of complaints about customer service.*

built-in obsolescence /'bɪlt ɪn ɒbsə ˌles(ə)ns/ *noun* a method of ensuring continuing sales of a product by making it in such a way that it will soon become obsolete

bulk buying /ˌbʌlk 'baɪɪŋ/ *noun* the act of buying large quantities of goods at low prices

bull /bʊl/ *noun* a person who believes the market will rise, and therefore buys shares, commodities or currency to sell at a higher price later. Opposite **bear**

'…lower interest rates are always a bull factor for the stock market' [*Financial Times*]

bullet bond /'bʊlɪt bɒnd/ *noun US* a eurobond which is only redeemed when it is mature (NOTE: Bullet bonds are used in payments between central banks and also act as currency backing.)

bullet loan /'bʊlɪt ləʊn/ *noun US* a loan which is repaid in a single payment

bullion /'bʊliən/ *noun* a gold or silver bars ○ *A shipment of gold bullion was stolen from the security van.* ○ *The price of bullion is fixed daily.*

bull market /'bʊl ˌmɑːkɪt/ *noun* a period when share prices rise because people are optimistic and buy shares. Opposite **bear market**

bull position /'bʊl pəˌzɪʃ(ə)n/ *noun* a strategy of buying shares in the hope that they will rise

bumping /'bʌmpɪŋ/ *noun US* a lay-off procedure that allows an employee with greater seniority to displace a more junior employee ○ *The economic recession led to extensive bumping in companies where only the most qualified were retained for some jobs.* ○ *The trade unions strongly objected to bumping practices since they considered that many employees were being laid off unfairly.*

business /'bɪznɪs/ *noun* **1.** work in buying, selling or doing other things to make a profit ○ *We do a lot of business with Japan.* ○ *Business is expanding.* ○ *Business is slow.* ○ *Repairing cars is 90% of our business.* ○ *We did more business in the week before Christmas than we usually do in a month.* ○ *Strikes are very bad for business.* ○ *What's your line of business?* **2.** a commercial company ○ *He owns a small car repair business.* ○ *She runs a business from her home.* ○ *I set up in business as an insurance broker.* **3.** the affairs discussed ○ *The main business of the meeting was finished by 3 p.m.*

Business Accounting Deliberation Council /ˌbɪznəs əˌkaʊntɪŋ dɪˌlɪbə'reɪʃ(ə)n ˌkaʊns(ə)l/ *noun* in Japan, a committee controlled by the Ministry of Finance that is responsible for drawing up regulations regarding the consolidated financial statements of listed companies

business address /'bɪznɪs əˌdres/ *noun* the details of number, street and town where a company is located

business call /'bɪznɪs kɔːl/ *noun* a visit to talk to someone about business

business card /'bɪznɪs kɑːd/ *noun* a card showing a businessperson's name and the name and address of the company he or she works for

business centre /'bɪznɪs ˌsentə/ *noun* the part of a town where the main banks, shops and offices are located

business combination /ˌbɪznɪs ˌkɒmbɪ'neɪʃ(ə)n/ *noun* an action when one or more businesses become subsidiaries of another business

business computer /'bɪznɪs kəmˌpjuːtə/ *noun* a powerful small computer programmed for special business uses

business correspondence /'bɪznɪs kɒrɪˌspɒndəns/ *noun* letters concerned with a business

business cycle /'bɪznɪs ˌsaɪk(ə)l/ *noun* the period during which trade expands, slows down and then expands again. Also called **trade cycle**

business day /'bɪznɪs deɪ/ *noun* a weekday when banks and stock exchanges are open for business

business expenses /'bɪznɪs ɪkˌspensɪz/ *plural noun* money spent on running a business, not on stock or assets

business hours /'bɪznɪs ˌaʊəz/ *plural noun* the time when a business is open, usually 9.00 a.m. to 5.30 p.m.

businessman /'bɪznɪsmæn/ *noun* a man engaged in business

business name /'bɪznɪs neɪm/ *noun* a name used by a company for trading purposes

business plan /'bɪznɪs plæn/ *noun* a document drawn up to show how a business is planned to work, with cash flow forecasts, sales forecasts, etc., often used when trying to raise a loan, or when setting up a new business

business property relief /ˌbɪznɪs ˌprɒpəti rɪ'liːf/ *noun* in the United Kingdom, a reduction in the amount liable to inheritance tax on certain types of business property

business ratepayer /ˌbɪznəs 'reɪtpeɪə/ *noun* a business which pays local taxes on a shop, office, factory, etc.

business rates /'bɪznɪs reɪts/ *noun* in the United Kingdom, a tax on businesses calculated on the value of the property occupied. Although the rate of tax is set by central government, the tax is collected the local authority.

business review /ˌbɪznɪs rɪ'vjuː/ *noun* a report on business carried out over the past year. It forms part of the directors' report.

business segment /ˌbɪznɪs seg'ment/ *noun* a section of a company which can be distinguished from the rest of the company by its own revenue and expenditure

business transaction /'bɪznɪs trænˌzækʃən/ *noun* an act of buying or selling

business travel /ˌbɪznɪs ˈtræv(ə)l/ *noun* travel costs incurred in the course of work, as opposed to private travel or daily travel to your usual place of work

businesswoman /ˈbɪznɪsmæn/ *noun* a woman engaged in business

buy /baɪ/ *verb* to get something by paying money ○ *to buy wholesale and sell retail* ○ *to buy for cash* ○ *She bought 10,000 shares.* ○ *The company has been bought by its leading supplier.* (NOTE: **buying- bought**) □ **to buy at best** to buy securities at the best price available, even if it is high

buy back /ˌbaɪ ˈbæk/ *verb* to buy something which you sold earlier ○ *She sold the shop last year and is now trying to buy it back.*

buyback /ˈbaɪbæk/ *noun* **1.** a type of loan agreement to repurchase bonds or securities at a later date for the same price as they are being sold **2.** an international trading agreement where a company builds a factory in a foreign country and agrees to buy all its production

'…the corporate sector also continued to return cash to shareholders in the form of buy-backs, while raising little money in the form of new or rights issues' [*Financial Times*]

buyer /ˈbaɪə/ *noun* **1.** a person who buys **2.** a person who buys stock on behalf of a trading organisation for resale or for use in production

buyer's market /ˈbaɪəz ˌmɑːkɪt/ *noun* a market where products are sold cheaply because there are few people who want to buy them. Opposite **seller's market**

buy in /ˌbaɪ ˈɪn/ *verb* **1.** (*of a seller at an auction*) to buy the thing which you are trying to sell because no one will pay the price you want **2.** to buy stock to cover a position **3.** (*of a company*) to buy its own shares

buying /ˈbaɪɪŋ/ *noun* the act of getting something for money

buying department /ˈbaɪɪŋ dɪ ˌpɑːtmənt/ *noun* the department in a company which buys raw materials or goods for use in the company

buying power /ˈbaɪɪŋ ˌpaʊə/ *noun* the ability to buy ○ *The buying power of the pound has fallen over the last five years.*

buyout /ˈbaɪaʊt/ *noun* the purchase of a controlling interest in a company

'…we also invest in companies whose growth and profitability could be improved by a management buyout' [*Times*]

'…in a normal leveraged buyout, the acquirer raises money by borrowing against the assets or cash flow of the target company' [*Fortune*]

bylaws /ˈbaɪlɔːz/ *noun* a rule made by a local authority or organisation, and not by central government

by-product /ˈbaɪ ˌprɒdʌkt/ *noun* a product made as a result of manufacturing a main product

C

c/a *abbr* capital account

C/A *abbr* current account

cage /keɪdʒ/ *noun US* **1.** the part of a broking firm where the paperwork involved in buying and selling shares is processed (NOTE: The UK term is **back office**.) **2.** a section of a bank where a teller works, surrounded by glass windows

calculate /ˈkælkjʊleɪt/ *verb* **1.** to find the answer to a problem using numbers ○ *The bank clerk calculated the rate of exchange for the dollar.* **2.** to estimate ○ *I calculate that we have six months' stock left.*

calculation /ˌkælkjʊˈleɪʃ(ə)n/ *noun* the answer to a problem in mathematics ○ *According to my calculations, we have six months' stock left.* □ **we are £20,000 out in our calculations** we have made a mistake in our calculations and arrived at a figure which is £20,000 too much or too little

calendar variance /ˌkælɪndə ˈveəriəns/ *noun* variance which occurs if a company uses calendar months for the financial accounts but uses the number of actual working days to calculate overhead expenses in the cost accounts

calendar year /ˌkælɪndə ˈjɪə/ *noun* a year from the 1st January to 31st December

call /kɔːl/ *noun* **1.** a demand for repayment of a loan by a lender **2.** a demand to pay for new shares which then become paid up ■ *verb* to ask for a loan to be repaid immediately

callable bond /ˌkɔːləb(ə)l ˈbɒnd/ *noun* a bond which can be redeemed before it matures

callable capital /ˌkɔːləb(ə)l ˈkæpɪt(ə)l/ *noun* the part of a company's capital which has not been called up

call account /ˈkɔːl əˌkaʊnt/ *noun* a type of current account where money can be withdrawn without notice

call-back pay /ˈkɔːl bæk ˌpeɪ/ *noun* pay given to an employee who has been called back to work after their usual working hours

called up capital /ˌkɔːld ʌp ˈkæpɪt(ə)l/ *noun* a share capital in a company which has been called up but not yet paid for

> '…a circular to shareholders highlights that the company's net assets as at August 1, amounted to £47.9 million – less than half the company's called-up share capital of £96.8 million. Accordingly, an EGM has been called for October 7' [*Times*]

call in /ˌkɔːl ˈɪn/ *verb* **1.** to visit ○ *Their sales representative called in twice last week.* **2.** to ask for a debt to be paid

call-in pay /ˈkɔːl ɪn ˌpeɪ/ *noun* payment guaranteed to employees who report for work even if there is no work for them to do ○ *Call-in pay is often necessary to ensure the attendance of employees where there is at least the possibility of work needing to be done.*

call money /ˈkɔːl ˌmʌni/ *noun* money loaned for which repayment can be demanded without notice. Also called **money at call, money on call**

call option /ˈkɔːl ˌɒpʃən/ *noun* an option to buy shares at a future date and at a specific price

call-over price /ˌkɔːl ˈəʊvə praɪs/ *noun* a price which is applied when selling is conducted by a chairman, and not by open outcry

call price /ˈkɔːl praɪs/ *noun* a price to be paid on redemption of a US bond

call purchase /ˈkɔːl ˌpɜːtʃɪs/, **call sale** /ˈkɔːl seɪl/ *noun* a transaction where the seller or purchaser can fix the price for future delivery

calls in arrear /ˌkɔːls ɪn əˈrɪə/ *plural noun* money called up for shares, but not paid at the correct time and a special calls in arrear account is set up to debit the sums owing

call up /ˌkɔːl ˈʌp/ *verb* to ask for share capital to be paid

Canadian Institute of Chartered Accountants /kəˌneɪdiən ˌɪnstɪtjuːt əv ˌtʃɑːtəd əˈkaʊntənts/ *noun* in Canada, the principal professional accountancy body that is responsible for setting accounting standards. Abbreviation **CICA**

cancel /'kænsəl/ *verb* to stop something which has been agreed or planned ○ *to cancel an appointment* or *a meeting* ○ *The government has cancelled the order for a fleet of buses.* ○ *The manager is still ill, so the interviews planned for this week have been cancelled.* (NOTE: **cancelling – cancelled**)

cancellation /ˌkænsə'leɪʃ(ə)n/ *noun* the act of stopping something which has been agreed or planned ○ *the cancellation of an appointment* ○ *the cancellation of an agreement*

cancel out /ˌkænsəl 'aʊt/ *verb* (*of two things*) to balance each other or act against each other so that there is no change in the existing situation ○ *The two clauses cancel each other out.* ○ *Higher costs have cancelled out the increased sales revenue.*

cap /kæp/ *noun* an upper limit placed on something, such as an interest rate. The opposite, i.e. a lower limit, is a 'floor'). ■ *verb* to place an upper limit on something ○ *to cap a local authority's budget* ○ *to cap a department's budget* (NOTE: **capping – capped**)

CAPA *noun* a large association of accountancy bodies that operate in Asia and the Pacific Rim countries. Full form **Confederation of Asian and Pacific Accountants**

capacity /kə'pæsɪti/ *noun* **1.** the amount which can be produced, or the amount of work which can be done ○ *industrial* or *manufacturing* or *production capacity* **2.** the amount of space □ **to use up spare** *or* **excess capacity** to make use of time or space which is not fully used **3.** ability ○ *She has a particular capacity for detailed business deals with overseas companies.*

'…analysts are increasingly convinced that the industry simply has too much capacity' [*Fortune*]

capacity usage variance /kəˌpæsɪti ˌjuːsɪdʒ 'veərɪəns/ *noun* the difference in gain or loss in a given period compared to budgeted expectations, caused because the hours worked were longer or shorter than planned

capacity variance /kəˌpæsɪti 'veərɪəns/ *noun* variance caused by the difference between planned and actual hours worked

Caparo case /kə'pɑːrəʊ ˌkeɪs/ *noun* in England, a court decision taken by the House of Lords in 1990 that auditors owe a duty of care to present (not prospective) shareholders as a body but not as individuals

CAPEX *abbr* capital expenditure

capital /'kæpɪt(ə)l/ *noun* **1.** the money, property and assets used in a business ○ *a company with £10,000 capital* or *with a capital of £10,000* **2.** money owned by individu-

als or companies, which they use for investment

'…issued and fully paid capital is $100 million, comprising 2340 shares of $100 each and 997,660 ordinary shares of $100 each' [*Hongkong Standard*]

capital account /'kæpɪt(ə)l ə,kaʊnt/ *noun* **1.** an account of dealings such as money invested in or taken out of the company by the owners of a company **2.** items in a country's balance of payments which do not refer to the buying and selling merchandise, but refer to investments **3.** the total equity in a business

capital adequacy /ˌkæpɪt(ə)l 'ædɪkwəsi/, **capital adequacy ratio** /ˌkæpɪt(ə)l 'ædɪkwəsi ˌreɪʃiəʊ/ *noun* the amount of money which a bank has to have in the form of shareholders' capital, shown as a percentage of its assets. Also called **capital-to-asset ratio** (NOTE: The amount is internationally agreed at 8%.)

capital allowances /ˌkæpɪt(ə)l ə'laʊənsɪz/ *plural noun* the allowances based on the value of fixed assets which may be deducted from a company's profits and so reduce its tax liability

capital asset pricing model /ˌkæpɪt(ə)l ˌæset 'praɪsɪŋ ˌmɒd(ə)l/ *noun* a method of calculating the expected return on a share, by showing what percentage of future return is dependent on the movements of the stock market taken as a whole. Abbreviation **CAPM**

capital base /ˌkæpɪt(ə)l 'beɪs/ *noun* the capital structure of a company (shareholders' capital plus loans and retained profits) used as a way of assessing the company's worth

capital bonus /ˌkæpɪt(ə)l 'bəʊnəs/ *noun* an extra payment by an insurance company which is produced by a capital gain

capital budget /ˌkæpɪt(ə)l 'bʌdʒɪt/ *noun* a budget for planned purchases of fixed assets during the next budget period

capital commitments /ˌkæpɪt(ə)l kə'mɪtmənts/ *plural noun* expenditure on assets which has been authorised by directors, but not yet spent at the end of a financial period

capital consumption /ˌkæpɪt(ə)l kən'sʌmpʃ(ə)n/ *noun* in a given period, the total depreciation of a national economy's fixed assets based on replacement costs

capital costs /ˌkæpɪt(ə)l 'kɒsts/ *noun* expenses on the purchase of fixed assets

capital employed /ˌkæpɪt(ə)l ɪm'plɔɪd/ *noun* an amount of capital consisting of shareholders' funds plus the long-term debts of a business

capital equipment /ˌkæpɪt(ə)l ɪ
'kwɪpmənt/ *noun* equipment which a factory or office uses to work

capital expenditure /ˌkæpɪt(ə)l ɪk
'spendɪtʃə/ *noun* money spent on fixed assets such as property, machines and furniture.
Also called **capital investment, capital
outlay**. Abbreviation **CAPEX**

capital expenditure budget
/ˌkæpɪt(ə)l ɪkˌspendɪtʃə 'bʌdʒɪt/ *noun* a
budget for planned purchases of fixed assets
during the budget period

capital flight /ˌkæpɪt(ə)l 'flaɪt/ *noun* the
transfer of large sums of money between
countries to seek higher rates of return or to
escape a political or economic disturbance.
Also called **flight of capital**

capital gain /ˌkæpɪt(ə)l 'ɡeɪn/ *noun* an
amount of money made by selling a fixed asset. Opposite **capital loss**

capital gains /ˌkæpɪt(ə)l 'ɡeɪnz/ *plural
noun* money made by selling a fixed asset or
by selling shares (NOTE: If the asset is sold
for less than its purchase price, the result is
a capital loss.)

capital gains expenses /ˌkæpɪt(ə)l
ɡeɪns ɪk'spensɪz/ *plural noun* expenses incurred in buying or selling assets, which can
be deducted when calculating a capital gain
or loss

capital gains tax /ˌkæpɪt(ə)l 'ɡeɪnz
tæks/ *noun* a tax on the difference between
the gross acquisition cost and the net proceeds when an asset is sold. In the United
Kingdom, this tax also applies when assets
are given or exchanged, although each individual has an annual capital gains tax allowance that exempts gains within that tax year
below a stated level. In addition, certain assets may be exempt, e.g., a person's principal
private residence and transfers of assets between spouses. Abbreviation **CGT**

capital goods /'kæpɪt(ə)l ɡʊdz/ *plural
noun* machinery, buildings and raw materials
which are used to make other goods

capital-intensive industry /ˌkæpɪt(ə)l
ɪn'tensɪv ˌɪndʌstri/ *noun* an industry which
needs a large amount of capital investment in
plant to make it work

capital investment appraisal
/ˌkæpɪt(ə)l ɪnˌvestmənt ə'preɪz(ə)l/ *noun*
an analysis of the future profitability of capital purchases as an aid to good management

capitalisation of costs
/ˌkæpɪt(ə)laɪzeɪʃ(ə)n əv 'kɒsts/ *noun* the
act of including costs usually charged to the
profit and loss account in the balance sheet.
The effect is that profits are higher than if

such costs are matched with revenues in the
same accounting period.

capitalise /'kæpɪt(ə)laɪz/, **capitalize** *verb*
1. to invest money in a working company □
the company is capitalised at £10,000 the
company has a working capital of £10,000 **2.**
to convert reserves or assets into capital

'…at its last traded price the bank was capitalized at
around $1.05 billion with 60 per cent in the hands of
the family' [*South China Morning Post*]

capitalise on /'kæpɪt(ə)laɪz ɒn/ *verb* to
make a profit from ○ *We are seeking to capitalise on our market position.*

capitalism /'kæpɪt(ə)lɪz(ə)m/ *noun* the
economic system in which each person has
the right to invest money, to work in business
and to buy and sell, with no restrictions from
the state

capitalist /'kæpɪt(ə)lɪst/ *adjective* working according to the principles of capitalism
○ *the capitalist system* ○ *the capitalist countries* or *world*

capitalist economy /ˌkæpɪt(ə)lɪst ɪ
'kɒnəmi/ *noun* an economy in which each
person has the right to invest money, to work
in business and to buy and sell, with no restrictions from the state

capital levy /ˌkæpɪt(ə)l 'levi/ *noun* a tax
on the value of a person's property and possessions

capital loss /ˌkæpɪt(ə)l 'lɒs/ *noun* a loss
made by selling assets. Opposite **capital
gain**

capital maintenance concept
/ˌkæpɪt(ə)l 'meɪntənəns ˌkɒnsept/ *noun* a
concept used to determine the definition of
profit, that provides the basis for different
systems of inflation accounting

capital market /ˌkæpɪt(ə)l 'mɑːkɪt/ *noun*
an international market where money can be
raised for investment in a business

capital outlay /ˌkæpɪt(ə)l 'aʊtleɪ/ *noun*
same as **capital expenditure**

capital profit /ˌkæpɪt(ə)l 'prɒfɪt/ *noun* a
profit made by selling an asset

capital reconstruction /ˌkæpɪt(ə)l
ˌriːkən'strʌkʃən/ *noun* the act of putting a
company into voluntary liquidation and then
selling its assets to another company with the
same name and same shareholders, but with
a larger capital base

capital redemption reserve
/ˌkæpɪt(ə)l rɪ'dempʃən/ *noun* an account
required to prevent a reduction in capital,
where a company purchases or redeems its
own shares out of distributable profits

capital reorganisation /ˌkæpɪt(ə)l riː
ˌɔːɡənaɪ'zeɪʃ(ə)n/ *noun* the process chang-

ing the capital structure of a company by amalgamating or dividing existing shares to form shares of a higher or lower nominal value

capital reserves /ˌkæpɪt(ə)l rɪˈzɜːvz/ plural noun **1.** money from profits, which forms part of the capital of a company and can be used for distribution to shareholders only when a company is wound up. Also called **undistributable reserves 2.** the share capital of a company which comes from selling assets and not from their usual trading

capital shares /ˌkæpɪt(ə)l ˈʃeəz/ plural noun (on the Stock Exchange) shares in a unit trust which rise in value as the capital value of the units rises, but do not receive any income (NOTE: The other form of shares in a split-level investment trust are income shares, which receive income from the investments, but do not rise in value.)

capital structure /ˌkæpɪt(ə)l ˈstrʌktʃə/ noun the relative proportions of equity capital and debt capital within a company's balance sheet

capital tax /ˈkæpɪt(ə)l tæks/ noun a tax levied on the capital owned by a company, rather than on its spending. ◊ **capital gains tax**

capital to asset ratio /ˌkæpɪt(ə)l tə, tʊ ˈæset/, **capital/asset ratio** noun same as **capital adequacy**

capital transactions /ˌkæpɪt(ə)l trænˈzækʃ(ə)ns/ noun transactions affecting non-current items such as fixed assets, long-term debt, or share capital, rather than revenue transactions

capital transfer tax /ˌkæpɪt(ə)l ˈtrænsfɜː ˌtæks/ noun in the United Kingdom, a tax on the transfer of assets that was replaced in 1986 by inheritance tax

capital turnover ratio /ˌkæpɪt(ə)l ˌtɜːnəʊvə ˈreɪʃiəʊ/ noun turnover divided by average capital during the year

CAPM abbr capital asset pricing model

capped floating rate note /ˌkæpt ˈfləʊtɪŋ reɪt ˌnəʊt/ noun a floating rate note which has an agreed maximum rate

captive market /ˌkæptɪv ˈmɑːkɪt/ noun a market where one supplier has a monopoly and the buyer has no choice over the product which he or she must purchase

carriage /ˈkærɪdʒ/ noun the transporting of goods from one place to another ○ to pay for carriage

carriage forward /ˌkærɪdʒ ˈfɔːwəd/ noun a deal where the customer pays for transporting the goods

carriage free /ˌkærɪdʒ ˈfriː/ adverb the customer does not pay for the shipping

carriage inwards /ˌkærɪdʒ ˈɪnwədz/ noun delivery expenses incurred through the purchase of goods

carriage outwards /ˌkærɪdʒ ˈaʊtwədz/ noun delivery expenses incurred through the sale of goods

carriage paid /ˌkærɪdʒ ˈpeɪd/ noun a deal where the seller has paid for the shipping

carry /ˈkæri/ noun the cost of borrowing to finance a deal (NOTE: **carries – carrying – carried**)

carry back /ˌkæri ˈbæk/ verb to take back to an earlier accounting period

carry down /ˌkæri ˈdaʊn/, **carry forward** /ˌkæri ˈfɔːwəd/ verb to take an account balance at the end of the current period as the starting point for the next period

carry forward /ˌkæri ˈfɔːwəd/ verb to take an account balance at the end of the current period or page as the starting point for the next period or page

carrying cost /ˈkæriɪŋ kɒst/ noun any expense associated with holding stock for a given period, e.g., from the time of delivery to the time of dispatch. Carrying costs will include storage and insurance.

carry-over /ˈkæri ˌəʊvə/ noun the stock of a commodity held at the beginning of a new financial year

cartel /kɑːˈtel/ noun a group of companies which try to fix the price or to regulate the supply of a product so that they can make more profit

cash /kæʃ/ noun **1.** money in the form of coins or notes **2.** the using of money in coins or notes

cashable /ˈkæʃəb(ə)l/ adjective able to be cashed ○ A crossed cheque is not cashable at any bank.

cash account /ˈkæʃ əˌkaʊnt/ noun an account which records the money which is received and spent

cash accounting /ˌkæʃ əˈkaʊntɪŋ/ noun **1.** an accounting method in which receipts and expenses are recorded in the accounting books in the period when they actually occur **2.** in the United Kingdom, a system for Value Added Tax that enables the tax payer to account for tax paid and received during a given period, thus allowing automatic relief for bad debts

cash advance /ˌkæʃ əd'vɑːns/ *noun* a loan in cash against a future payment

cash and carry /ˌkæʃ ən 'kæri/ *noun* **1.** a large store selling goods at low prices, where the customer pays cash and takes the goods away immediately ○ *We get our supplies every morning from the cash and carry.* **2.** the activity of buying a commodity for cash and selling the same commodity on the futures market

> '…the small independent retailer who stocks up using cash and carries could be hit hard by the loss of footfall associated with any increase in smuggled goods' [*The Grocer*]

cash at bank /ˌkæʃ ət 'bæŋk/ *noun* the total amount of money held at the bank by an individual or company

cashback /'kæʃbæk/ *noun* a discount system where a purchaser receives a cash discount on the completion of the purchase

cash balance /'kæʃ ˌbæləns/ *noun* a balance in cash, as opposed to amounts owed

cash basis /'kæʃ ˌbeɪsɪs/ *noun* a method of preparing the accounts of a business, where receipts and payments are shown at the time when they are made, as opposed to showing debts or credits which are outstanding at the end of the accounting period. Also called **receipts and payments basis**

cash budget /'kæʃ ˌbʌdʒɪt/ *noun* a plan of cash income and expenditure

cash card /'kæʃ kɑːd/ *noun* a plastic card used to obtain money from a cash dispenser

cash cow /'kæʃ kaʊ/ *noun* a product or subsidiary company that consistently generates good profits but does not provide growth

cash crop /'kæʃ krɒp/ *noun* an agricultural crop grown for sale to other buyers or to other countries, rather than for domestic consumption

cash deal /ˌkæʃ 'diːl/ *noun* a sale done for cash

cash desk /'kæʃ desk/ *noun* the place in a store where you pay for the goods bought

cash discount /kæʃ 'dɪskaʊnt/ *noun* a discount given for payment in cash. Also called **discount for cash**

cash dispenser /'kæʃ dɪˌspensə/ *noun* a machine which gives out money when a special card is inserted and instructions given

cash dividend /ˌkæʃ 'dɪvɪdend/ *noun* a dividend paid in cash, as opposed to a dividend in the form of bonus shares

cash economy /ˌkæʃ ɪ'kɒnəmi/ *noun* a black economy, where goods and services are paid for in cash, and therefore not declared for tax

cash equivalent /ˌkæʃ ɪ'kwɪvələnt/ *noun* the equivalent in cash terms of an asset which is enjoyed

cash equivalents /ˌkæʃ ɪ'kwɪvələnts/ *noun* short-term investments that can be converted into cash immediately and that are subject to only a limited risk. There is usually a limit on their duration, e.g., three months.

cash float /'kæʃ fləʊt/ *noun* cash put into the cash box at the beginning of the day or week to allow change to be given to customers

cash flow /'kæʃ fləʊ/ *noun* cash which comes into a company from sales (cash inflow) or the money which goes out in purchases or overhead expenditure (cash outflow)

cash-flow accounting /ˌkæʃ fləʊ ə'kaʊntɪŋ/ *noun* the practice of measuring the financial activities of a company in terms of cash receipts and payments, without recording accruals, prepayments, debtors, creditors and stocks

cash flow budget /'kæʃ fləʊ ˌbʌdʒɪt/ *noun* a cash budget, a plan of cash income and expenditure

cash flow forecast /'kæʃ fləʊ ˌfɔːkɑːst/ *noun* a forecast of when cash will be received or paid out

cash-flow risk /'kæʃ fləʊ ˌrɪsk/ *noun* the risk that a company's available cash will not be sufficient to meet its financial obligations

cash flow statement /'kæʃ fləʊ ˌsteɪtmənt/ *noun* a record of a company's cash inflows and cash outflows over a specific period of time, typically a year

cash fraction /ˌkæʃ 'frækʃən/ *noun* a small amount of cash paid to a shareholder to make up the full amount of part of a share which has been allocated in a share split

cash-generating unit /ˌkæʃ ˌdʒenəreɪtɪŋ 'juːnɪt/ *noun* the smallest identifiable group of assets that generates cash inflows and outflows that can be measured

cashier /kæ'ʃɪə/ *noun* **1.** a person who takes money from customers in a shop or who deals with the money that has been paid **2.** a person who deals with customers in a bank and takes or gives cash at the counter

cashier's check /kæˌʃɪəz 'tʃek/ *noun* US a bank's own cheque, drawn on itself and signed by a cashier or other bank official

cash in /ˌkæʃ 'ɪn/ *verb* to sell shares or other property for cash

cash inflow /ˌkæʃ 'ɪnfləʊ/ *noun* receipts of cash or cheques

cash in on /ˌkæʃ 'ɪn ɒn/ *verb* to profit from ○ *The company is cashing in on the interest in computer games.*

cash items /'kæʃ ˌaɪtəmz/ *plural noun* goods sold for cash

cashless society /ˌkæʃləs sə'saɪəti/ *noun* a society where no one uses cash, all purchases being made by credit cards, charge cards, cheques or direct transfer from one account to another

cash limit /kæʃ 'lɪmɪt/ *noun* **1.** a fixed amount of money which can be spent during some period **2.** a maximum amount someone can withdraw from an ATM using a cash card

cash offer /'kæʃ ˌɒfə/ *noun* an offer to pay in cash, especially an offer to pay cash when buying shares in a takeover bid

cash outflow /ˌkæʃ 'aʊtfləʊ/ *noun* expenditure in cash or cheques

cash payment /'kæʃ ˌpeɪmənt/ *noun* payment in cash

cash payments journal /kæʃ ˌpeɪmənts 'dʒɜːn(ə)l/ *noun* a chronological record of all the payments that have been made from a company's bank account

cash position /'kæʃ pəˌzɪʃ(ə)n/ *noun* a state of the cash which a company currently has available

cash price /'kæʃ praɪs/ *noun* a lower price or better terms which apply if the customer pays cash

cash purchase /'kæʃ ˌpɜːtʃɪs/ *noun* a purchase made for cash

cash receipts journal /kæʃ rɪˌsiːts 'dʒɜːn(ə)l/ *noun* a chronological record of all the receipts that have been paid into a company's bank account

cash register /'kæʃ ˌredʒɪstə/ *noun* a machine which shows and adds the prices of items bought, with a drawer for keeping the cash received

cash reserves /'kæʃ rɪˌzɜːvz/ *plural noun* a company's reserves in cash deposits or bills kept in case of urgent need ○ *The company was forced to fall back on its cash reserves.*

cash sale /'kæʃ seɪl/ *noun* a transaction paid for in cash

cash terms /'kæʃ tɜːmz/ *plural noun* lower terms which apply if the customer pays cash

cash transaction /'kæʃ trænˌzækʃən/ *noun* a transaction paid for in cash

cash up /ˌkæʃ 'ʌp/ *verb* to add up the cash in a shop at the end of the day

cash voucher /'kæʃ ˌvaʊtʃə/ *noun* a piece of paper which can be exchanged for cash ○ *With every £20 of purchases, the customer gets a cash voucher to the value of £2.*

casting vote /ˌkɑːstɪŋ 'vəʊt/ *noun* a vote used by the chairman in the case where the votes for and against a proposal are equal ○ *The chairman has the casting vote.* ○ *She used her casting vote to block the motion.*

casual /'kæʒuəl/ *adjective* informal or not serious

casual labour /ˌkæʒuəl 'leɪbə/ *noun* workers who are hired for a short period

casual work /'kæʒuəl wɜːk/ *noun* work where the employees are hired only for a short period

casual worker /ˌkæʒuəl 'wɜːkə/ *noun* an employee who can be hired for a short period

CCA *abbr* current cost accounting

CD /siː'diː/ *abbr* certificate of deposit

ceiling /'siːlɪŋ/ *noun* the highest point that something can reach, e.g. the highest rate of a pay increase ○ *to fix a ceiling for a budget* ○ *There is a ceiling of $100,000 on deposits.* ○ *Output reached its ceiling in June and has since fallen back.* ○ *What ceiling has the government put on wage increases this year?*

central /'sentrəl/ *adjective* organised from one main point

central bank discount rate /ˌsentrəl bæŋk 'dɪskaʊnt reɪt/ *noun* the rate at which a central bank discounts bills such as treasury bills

central bank intervention /ˌsentrəl bæŋk ˌɪntə'venʃ(ə)n/ *noun* an action by a central bank to change base interest rates, to impose exchange controls or to buy or sell the country's own currency in an attempt to influence international money markets

central government /ˌsentrəl 'gʌv(ə)nmənt/ *noun* the main government of a country as opposed to municipal, local, provincial or state governments

centralise /'sentrəlaɪz/, **centralize** *verb* to organise from a central point ○ *All purchasing has been centralised in our main office.* ○ *The group benefits from a highly centralised organisational structure.* ○ *The company has become very centralised, and far more staff work at headquarters.*

central purchasing /ˌsentrəl 'pɜːtʃɪsɪŋ/ *noun* purchasing organised by a central office for all branches of a company

centre /'sentə/ *noun* **1.** an important town ○ *Sheffield is a major industrial centre.* ○ *Nottingham is the centre for the shoe industry.* **2.** a department, area, or function to which costs and/or revenues are charged

(NOTE: [all senses] The US spelling is **center**.)

certain annuity /ˌsɜːt(ə)n əˈnjuːɪtɪ/ *noun* an annuity which will be paid for a specific number of years only

certificate /səˈtɪfɪkət/ *noun* an official document carrying an official declaration by someone, and signed by that person

certificated bankrupt /səˌtɪfɪkeɪtɪd ˈbæŋkrʌpt/ *noun* a bankrupt who has been discharged from bankruptcy with a certificate to show that he or she was not at fault

certificate of approval /səˌtɪfɪkət əv əˈpruːv(ə)l/ *noun* a document showing that an item has been approved officially

certificate of deposit /səˈtɪfɪkət əv dɪˈpɒzɪt/ *noun* a document from a bank showing that money has been deposited at a guaranteed interest rate for a certain period of time. Abbreviation **CD**

'…interest rates on certificates of deposit may have little room to decline in August as demand for funds from major city banks is likely to remain strong. After delaying for months, banks are now expected to issue a large volume of CDs. If banks issue more CDs on the assumption that the official discount rate reduction will be delayed, it is very likely that CD rates will be pegged for a longer period than expected' [*Nikkei Weekly*]

certificate of incorporation /səˌtɪfɪkət əv ɪnˌkɔːpəˈreɪʃ(ə)n/ *noun* a document issued by Companies House to show that a company has been legally set up and officially registered

certificate of origin /səˌtɪfɪkət əv ˈɒrɪdʒɪn/ *noun* a document showing where imported goods come from or were made

certificate of quality /səˌtɪfɪkət əv ˈkwɒlɪtɪ/ *noun* a certificate showing the grade of a soft commodity

certificate of registration /səˌtɪfɪkət əv ˌredʒɪˈstreɪʃ(ə)n/ *noun* a document showing that an item has been registered

certificate to commence business /səˌtɪfɪkət tə kəˌmens ˈbɪznɪs/ *noun* a document issued by the Registrar of Companies which allows a registered company to trade

certified accountant /ˌsɜːtɪfaɪd əˈkaʊntənt/ *noun* an accountant who has passed the professional examinations and is a member of the Chartered Association of Certified Accountants

Certified Accounting Technician /ˌsɜːtɪfaɪd əˌkaʊntɪŋ tekˈnɪʃ(ə)n/ *noun* a person who has passed the first stage course of the Association of Chartered Certified Accountants (ACCA). Abbreviation **CAT**

certified cheque /ˌsɜːtɪfaɪd ˈtʃek/, **certified check** *noun* a cheque which a bank says is good and will be paid out of money put aside from the payer's bank account

certified public accountant /ˌsɜːtɪfaɪd ˌpʌblɪk əˈkaʊntənt/ *noun US* an accountant who has passed the examinations of the AICPA and been given a certificate by a state, allowing him or her to practise in that state. Abbreviation **CPA**

certify /ˈsɜːtɪfaɪ/ *verb* to make an official declaration in writing ○ *I certify that this is a true copy.* ○ *The document is certified as a true copy.* (NOTE: **certifies – certifying – certified**)

cessation /seˈseɪʃ(ə)n/ *noun* the stopping of an activity or work

cession /ˈseʃ(ə)n/ *noun* the act of giving up property to someone, especially a creditor

CGT *abbr* capital gains tax

CH *abbr* Companies House

chairman /ˈtʃeəmən/ *noun* **1.** a person who is in charge of a meeting ○ *Mr Howard was chairman* or *acted as chairman* **2.** a person who presides over the board meetings of a company ○ *the chairman of the board* or *the company chairman* □ **the chairman's report**, **the chairman's statement** an annual report from the chairman of a company to the shareholders

'…the corporation's entrepreneurial chairman seeks a dedicated but part-time president. The new president will work a three-day week' [*Globe and Mail (Toronto)*]

Chamber of Commerce /ˌtʃeɪmbər əv ˈkɒmɜːs/ *noun* a group of local business people who meet to discuss problems which they have in common and to promote commerce in their town

Chancellor of the Exchequer /ˌtʃɑːnsələr əv ðɪ ɪksˈtʃekə/ *noun* the chief finance minister in a government (NOTE: The US term is **Secretary of the Treasury**.)

change /tʃeɪndʒ/ *noun* **1.** money in coins or small notes □ **to give someone change for £10** to give someone coins or notes in exchange for a ten pound note **2.** money given back by the seller, when the buyer can pay only with a larger note or coin than the amount asked ○ *She gave me the wrong change.* ○ *You paid the £5.75 bill with a £10 note, so you should have £4.25 change.* **3.** an alteration of the way something is done or of the way work is carried out □ **change in accounting principles** using a method to state a company's accounts which is different from the method used in the previous accounts. This will have to be agreed with the auditors, and possibly with the Inland Revenue. ■ *verb* **1.** □ **to change a £20 note** to give someone smaller notes or coins in place of a £20 note **2.** to give one type of currency for another ○ *to change £1,000 into dollars* ○ *We want to change some traveller's cheques.*

change machine /ˈtʃeɪndʒ məˌʃiːn/ *noun* a machine which gives small change for a note or larger coin

channel /ˈtʃæn(ə)l/ *noun* a means by which information or goods pass from one place to another ■ *verb* to send in some direction ○ *They are channelling their research funds into developing European communication systems.* (NOTE: **channelling – channelled**)

CHAPS *noun* a computerised system for clearing cheques organised by the banks. Compare **BACS**. Full form **Clearing House Automated Payments System**

Chapter 7 /ˌtʃæptə ˈsevən/ *noun* a section of the US Bankruptcy Reform Act 1978, which sets out the rules for the liquidation of an incorporated company

Chapter 11 /ˌtʃæptə ˈten/ *noun* a section of the US Bankruptcy Reform Act 1978, which allows a corporation to be protected from demands made by its creditors for a period of time, while it is reorganised with a view to paying its debts. The officers of the corporation will negotiate with its creditors as to the best way of reorganising the business.

Chapter 13 /ˌtʃæptə θɜːˈtiːn/ *noun* a section of the Bankruptcy Reform Act 1978, which allows a business to continue trading and to pay off its creditors by regular monthly payments over a period of time

character set /ˈkærɪktə set/ *noun* a list of all the characters which can be printed or displayed

charge /tʃɑːdʒ/ *noun* **1.** money which must be paid, or the price of a service ○ *to make no charge for delivery* ○ *to make a small charge for rental* ○ *There is no charge for this service.* or *No charge is made for this service.* **2.** a guarantee of security for a loan, for which assets are pledged ■ *verb* **1.** to ask someone to pay for services later **2.** to ask for money to be paid ○ *to charge £5 for delivery* ○ *How much does he charge?* □ **he charges £16 an hour** he asks to be paid £16 for an hour's work **3.** to take something as guarantee for a loan

chargeable /ˈtʃɑːdʒəb(ə)l/ *adjective* able to be charged ○ *repairs chargeable to the occupier*

chargeable asset /ˌtʃɑːdʒəb(ə)l ˈæset/ *noun* an asset which will produce a capital gain when sold. Assets which are not charge-

able include your family home, cars, and some types of investments such as government stocks.

chargeable business asset /ˌtʃɑːdʒəb(ə)l ˌbɪznɪs ˈæset/ *noun* an asset which is owned by a business and is liable to capital gains if sold

chargeable gains /ˌtʃɑːdʒəb(ə)l ˈɡeɪnz/ *plural noun* gains made by selling an asset such as shares, on which capital gains will be charged

chargeable transfer /ˌtʃɑːdʒəb(ə)l ˈtrænsfɜː/ *noun* in the United Kingdom, gifts that are liable to inheritance tax. Under UK legislation, individuals may gift assets to a certain value during their lifetime without incurring any liability to inheritance tax. These are regular transfers out of income that do not affect the donor's standard of living. Additionally, individuals may transfer up to £3,000 a year out of capital.

charge account /ˈtʃɑːdʒ əˌkaʊnt/ *noun* an arrangement which a customer has with a store to buy goods and to pay for them at a later date, usually when the invoice is sent at the end of the month (NOTE: The customer will make regular monthly payments into the account and is allowed credit of a multiple of those payments.)

charge and discharge accounting /ˌtʃɑːdʒ ən ˈdɪstʃɑːdʒ əˌkaʊntɪŋ/ *noun* formerly, a bookkeeping system in which a person charges himself or herself with receipts and credits himself or herself with payments. This system was used extensively in medieval times before the advent of double-entry bookkeeping.

charge by way of legal mortgage /ˌtʃɑːdʒ baɪ weɪ əv ˌliːɡ(ə)l ˈmɔːɡɪdʒ/ *noun* a way of borrowing money on the security of a property, where the mortgagor signs a deed which gives the mortgagee an interest in the property

charge card /ˈtʃɑːdʒ kɑːd/ *noun* a type of credit card for which a fee is payable, but which does not allow the user to take out a loan, e.g. American Express. The total sum must be charged at the end of each month.

chargee /tʃɑːˈdʒiː/ *noun* a person who has the right to force a debtor to pay

charges forward /ˌtʃɑːdʒɪz ˈfɔːwəd/ *noun* charges which will be paid by the customer

charitable /ˈtʃærɪtəb(ə)l/ *adjective* benefiting the general public as a charity

charitable deductions /ˌtʃærɪtəb(ə)l dɪˈdʌkʃ(ə)nz/ *plural noun* deductions from taxable income for contributions to charity

charitable purposes /ˌtʃærɪtəb(ə)l ˈpɜːpəs s/ *plural noun* the aims of a charity

charitable trust /ˈtʃærɪtəb(ə)l trʌst/, **charitable corporation** /ˌtʃærɪtəb(ə)l ˌkɔːpəˈreɪʃ(ə)n/ *noun* a trust which benefits the public as a whole, which promotes education or religion, which helps the poor or which does other useful work

charity /ˈtʃærɪti/ *noun* an organisation which offers free help or services to those in need ○ *Because the organisation is a charity it does not have to pay taxes.* ○ *The charity owes its success to clever marketing strategies in its fund-raising.*

charity accounts /ˌtʃærɪti əˈkaʊnts/ *noun* the accounting records of a charitable institution, that include a statement of financial activities rather than a profit and loss account. In the United Kingdom, the accounts should conform to the requirements stipulated in the Charities Act (1993).

Charity Commissioners /ˈtʃærɪti kəˌmɪʃ(ə)nəz/ *plural noun* UK body which governs charities and sees that they follow the law and use their funds for the purposes intended

chart /tʃɑːt/ *noun* a diagram displaying information as a series of lines, blocks, etc.

charter /ˈtʃɑːtə/ *noun* a document giving special legal rights to a group ○ *a shoppers' charter* or *a customers' charter* ■ *verb* to hire for a special purpose ○ *to charter a plane* or *a boat* or *a bus*

chartered /ˈtʃɑːtəd/ *adjective* referring to a company which has been set up by charter, and not registered under the Companies Act ○ *a chartered bank*

chartered accountant /ˌtʃɑːtəd əˈkaʊntənt/ *noun* an accountant who has passed the professional examinations and is a member of the Institute of Chartered Accountants. Abbreviation **CA**

Chartered Association of Certified Accountants /ˌtʃɑːtəd əˌsəʊsieɪʃ(ə)n əv ˌsɜːtɪfaɪd əˈkaʊntənts/ *noun* the former name of the Association of Chartered Certified Accountants

chartered bank /ˌtʃɑːtəd ˈbæŋk/ *noun* a bank which has been set up by government charter, formerly used in England, but now only done in the USA and Canada

chartered company /ˌtʃɑːtəd ˈkʌmp(ə)ni/ *noun* a company which has been set up by royal charter, and not registered under the Companies Act

Chartered Institute of Public Finance and Accountancy /ˌtʃɑːtəd ˌɪnstɪtjuːt əv ˌpʌblɪk ˌfaɪnæns ən əˈkaʊntənsi/ full form of **CIPFA**

Chartered Institute of Taxation /ˌtʃɑːtəd ˌɪnstɪtjuːt əv tækˈseɪʃ(ə)n/ *noun* in the United Kingdom, an organisation for professionals in the field of taxation, formerly the Institute of Taxation

charting /ˈtʃɑːtɪŋ/ *noun* the work of using charts to analyse stock market trends and forecast future rises or falls

chartist /ˈtʃɑːtɪst/ *noun* a person who studies stock market trends and forecasts future rises or falls

chart of accounts /ˌtʃɑːt əv əˈkaʊnts/ *noun* a detailed and ordered list of an organisation's numbered or named accounts. Originally devised in Germany, it provides a standard list of account codes for assets, liabilities, capital, revenue, and expenses. It is still used in Germany on a voluntary basis and was adopted as part of the French general accounting plan after the second world war.

chattel mortgage /ˈtʃæt(ə)l ˌmɔːgɪdʒ/ *noun* money lent against the security of an item purchased, but not against real estate

chattels real /ˌtʃæt(ə)lz ˈrɪəl/ *noun* leaseholds

cheap labour /ˌtʃiːp ˈleɪbə/ *noun* workers who do not earn much money

cheap money /tʃiːp ˈmʌni/ *noun* money which can be borrowed at a low rate of interest

cheat /tʃiːt/ *verb* to trick someone so that he or she loses money ○ *He cheated the Inland Revenue out of thousands of pounds.* ○ *She was accused of cheating clients who came to ask her for advice.*

check /tʃek/ *noun* **1.** a sudden stop **2.** investigation or examination ○ *a routine check of the fire equipment* ○ *The auditors carried out checks on the petty cash book.* **3.** US (*in a restaurant*) a bill **4.** US a mark on paper to show that something is correct ○ *Make a check in the box marked 'R'.* (NOTE: The UK term is **tick**.) ■ *verb* **1.** to stop or delay something ○ *to check the entry of contraband into the country* ○ *to check the flow of money out of a country* **2.** to examine or to investigate something ○ *to check that an invoice is correct* ○ *to check and sign for goods* □ **she checked the computer printout against the invoices** she examined the printout and the invoices to see if the figures were the same **3.** US to mark something with a sign to show that it is correct ○ *check the box marked 'R'* (NOTE: The UK term is **tick**.)

checkable /'tʃekəb(ə)l/ *adjective US* referring to a deposit account on which checks can be drawn

checkbook /'tʃekbʊk/ *noun* US spelling of **cheque book**

check routing symbol /tʃek 'ru:tɪŋ ˌsɪmbəl/ *noun US* a number shown on an American cheque which identifies the Federal Reserve district through which the cheque will be cleared, similar to the British 'bank sort code'

check sample /'tʃek ˌsɑ:mp(ə)l/ *noun* a sample to be used to see if a consignment is acceptable

cheque /tʃek/ *noun* a note to a bank asking them to pay money from your account to the account of the person whose name is written on the note ○ *a cheque for £10* or *a £10 cheque* (NOTE: The US spelling is **check**.)

cheque account /'tʃek əˌkaʊnt/ *noun* same as **current account**

cheque book /'tʃek bʊk/ *noun* a booklet with new blank cheques (NOTE: The usual US term is **checkbook**.)

cheque card /'tʃek kɑ:d/, **cheque guarantee card** /ˌtʃek gærən'ti: kɑ:d/ *noun* a plastic card from a bank which guarantees payment of a cheque up to some amount, even if the user has no money in his account

cheque requisition /'tʃek ˌrekwɪzɪʃ(ə)n/ *noun* an official note from a department to the company accounts staff asking for a cheque to be written

cheque stub /'tʃek stʌb/ *noun* a piece of paper left in a cheque book after a cheque has been written and taken out

cheque to bearer /ˌtʃek tə 'beərə/ *noun* a cheque with no name written on it, so that the person who holds it can cash it

chief /tʃi:f/ *adjective* most important ○ *He is the chief accountant of an Industrial group.* ○ *She is the chief buyer for a department store.*

chief executive /tʃi:f ɪg'zekjʊtɪv/, **chief executive officer** /tʃi:f ɪg'zekjʊtɪv ˌɒfɪsə/ *noun US* the most important director in charge of a company. Abbreviation **CEO**

Chief Secretary to the Treasury /ˌtʃi:f ˌsekrətri tə ðə 'treʒ(ə)ri/ *noun* a government minister responsible to the Chancellor of the Exchequer for the control of public expenditure (NOTE: In the USA, this is the responsibility of the **Director of the Budget**.)

Chinese walls /ˌtʃaɪni:z 'wɔ:lz/ *plural noun* imaginary barriers between departments in the same organisation, set up to avoid insider dealing or conflict of interest.

For example, if a merchant bank is advising on a planned takeover bid, its investment department should not know that the bid is taking place, or they would advise their clients to invest in the company being taken over.

chop /tʃɒp/ *noun* a mark made on a document to show that it has been agreed, acknowledged, paid, or that payment has been received

chose /tʃəʊz/ *French word meaning* 'item' or 'thing' □ **chose in possession** physical thing which can be owned (such as a piece of furniture)

chose in action /ˌtʃəʊz ɪn 'ækʃən/ *noun* the legal term for a personal right which can be enforced or claimed as if it were property, e.g. a patent, copyright or debt

Christmas bonus /ˌkrɪsməs 'bəʊnəs/ *noun* an extra payment made to staff at Christmas

chronological order /ˌkrɒnəlɒdʒɪk(ə)l 'ɔ:də/ *noun* the arrangement of records such as files and invoices in order of their dates

churning /'tʃɜ:nɪŋ/ *noun* **1.** a practice employed by stockbrokers, where they buy and sell on a client's discretionary account in order to earn their commission. The deals are frequently of no advantage to the client. **2.** a practice employed by insurance salesmen where the salesman suggests that a client should change his or her insurance policy solely in order to earn the salesman a commission

'…more small investors lose money through churning than almost any other abuse, yet most people have never heard of it. Churning involves brokers generating income simply by buying and selling investments on behalf of their clients. Constant and needless churning earns them hefty commissions which bites into the investment portfolio' [*Guardian*]

CICA *abbr* Canadian Institute of Chartered Accountants

CIPFA *noun* a leading professional accountancy body in the UK, specialising in the public services. Full form **Chartered Institute of Public Finance and Accountancy**

circularisation of debtors /ˌsɜ:kjʊləraɪzeɪʃ(ə)n əv 'detəz/ *noun* the sending of letters by a company's auditors to debtors in order to verify the existence and extent of the company's assets

circularise /'sɜ:kjʊləraɪz/, **circularize** *verb* to send a circular to ○ *The committee has agreed to circularise the members of the society.* ○ *They circularised all their customers with a new list of prices.*

circular letter /ˌsɜ:kjʊlə 'letə/ *noun* a letter sent to many people

circular letter of credit /ˌsɜːkjʊlə ˌletər əv ˈkredɪt/ *noun* a letter of credit sent to all branches of the bank which issues it

circulate /ˈsɜːkjʊleɪt/ *verb* **1.** to send or to give out without restrictions **2.** to send information to ○ *They circulated a new list of prices to all their customers.* ○ *They circulated information about job vacancies to all colleges in the area.*

circulating capital /ˌsɜːkjʊleɪtɪŋ ˈkæpɪt(ə)l/ *noun* capital in the form of cash or debtors, raw materials, finished products and work in progress which a company requires to carry on its business

circulation /ˌsɜːkjʊˈleɪʃ(ə)n/ *noun* **1.** the act of sending information ○ *The company is trying to improve the circulation of information between departments.* **2.** movement

circulation of capital /ˌsɜːkjʊleɪʃ(ə)n əv ˈkæpɪt(ə)l/ *noun* a movement of capital from one investment to another

civil action /ˌsɪv(ə)l ˈækʃən/ *noun* a court case brought by a person or a company against someone who has done them wrong

claim /kleɪm/ *noun* an act of asking for something that you feel you have a right to ■ *verb* **1.** to ask for money, especially from an insurance company ○ *He claimed £100,000 damages against the cleaning firm.* ○ *She claimed for repairs to the car against her insurance policy.* **2.** to say that you have a right to something or that something is your property ○ *She is claiming possession of the house.* ○ *No one claimed the umbrella found in my office.* **3.** to state that something is a fact ○ *He claims he never received the goods.* ○ *She claims that the shares are her property.*

claimant /ˈkleɪmənt/ *noun* a person who makes a claim against someone in the civil courts (NOTE: This term has now replaced **plaintiff**. The other side in a case is the **defendant**.)

claimer /ˈkleɪmə/ *noun* same as **claimant**

claim form /ˈkleɪm fɔːm/ *noun* a form which has to be filled in when making an insurance claim

claims department /ˈkleɪmz dɪˌpɑːtmənt/ *noun* a department of an insurance company which deals with claims

claims manager /ˈkleɪmz ˌmænɪdʒə/ *noun* the manager of a claims department

classical system of corporation tax /ˌklæsɪk(ə)l ˌsɪstəm əv ˌkɔːpəˈreɪʃ(ə)n ˌtæks/ *noun* a system in which companies and their owners are liable for corporation tax as separate entities. A company's taxed income is therefore paid out to shareholders

who are in turn taxed again. This system operates in the United States and the Netherlands. It was replaced in the United Kingdom in 1973 by an imputation system.

classify /ˈklæsɪfaɪ/ *verb* to put into classes or categories according to specific characteristics (NOTE: **classifies – classifying – classified**)

class of assets /ˌklɑːs əv ˈæsets/ *noun* the grouping of similar assets into categories. This is done because under International Accounting Standards Committee rules, tangible assets and {intangible asset}intangible assets cannot be revalued on an individual basis, only for a class of assets.

clause /klɔːz/ *noun* a section of a contract ○ *There are ten clauses in the contract of employment.* ○ *There is a clause in this contract concerning the employer's right to dismiss an employee.* ■ *verb* to list details of the relevant parties to a bill of exchange

claw back /ˌklɔː ˈbæk/ *verb* to take back money which has been allocated ○ *Income tax claws back 25% of pensions paid out by the government.* ○ *Of the £1m allocated to the project, the government clawed back £100,000 in taxes.*

clawback /ˈklɔːbæk/ *noun* **1.** money taken back, especially money taken back by the government from grants or tax concessions which had previously been made **2.** the allocation of new shares to existing shareholders, so as to maintain the value of their holdings

clean bill of lading /ˌkliːn bɪl əv ˈleɪdɪŋ/ *noun* a bill of lading with no note to say the shipment is faulty or damaged

clean float /ˈkliːn fləʊt/ *noun* an act of floating a currency freely on the international markets, without any interference from the government

clean opinion /kliːn əˈpɪnjən/, **clean report** /kliːn rɪˈpɔːt/ *noun* an auditor's report that is not qualified

clean surplus concept /kliːn ˌsɜːpləs ˈkɒnsept/ *noun* the idea that a company's income statement should show the totality of gains and losses, without any of them being taken directly to equity

clearance certificate /ˈklɪərəns səˌtɪfɪkət/ *noun* a document showing that goods have been passed by customs

clearance sale /ˈklɪərəns seɪl/ *noun* a sale of items at low prices to get rid of stock

clearing /ˈklɪərɪŋ/ *noun* **1.** □ **clearing of goods through customs** passing of goods through customs **2.** □ **clearing of a debt** paying all of a debt **3.** an act of passing of a cheque through the banking system, transferring money from one account to another

clearing agency /ˈklɪərɪŋ ˈeɪdʒənsi/ *noun US* central office where stock exchange or commodity exchange transactions are settled (NOTE: The UK term is **clearing house**.)

clearing bank /ˈklɪərɪŋ bæŋk/ *noun* a bank which clears cheques, especially one of the major British High Street banks, specialising in usual banking business for ordinary customers such as loans, cheques, overdrafts and interest-bearing deposits

clearing house /ˈklɪərɪŋ haʊs/ *noun* a central office where clearing banks exchange cheques, or where stock exchange or commodity exchange transactions are settled

Clearing House Automated Payments System /ˈklɪərɪŋ haʊs ˈɔːtəmeɪtɪd ˈpeɪmənts ˌsɪstəm/ *noun* full form of **CHAPS**

clear profit /ˌklɪə ˈprɒfɪt/ *noun* a profit after all expenses have been paid ○ *We made $6,000 clear profit on the deal.*

clerical error /ˌklerɪk(ə)l ˈerə/ *noun* a mistake made by someone doing office work

client /ˈklaɪənt/ *noun* a person with whom business is done or who pays for a service ○ *One of our major clients has defaulted on her payments.*

client account /ˈklaɪənt əˈkaʊnt/ *noun* a bank account opened by a solicitor or estate agent to hold money on behalf of a client

clientele /ˌkliːɒnˈtel/ *noun* all the clients of a business or all the customers of a shop

close /kləʊs/ *verb* **1.** □ **to close the accounts** to come to the end of an accounting period and make up the profit and loss account **2.** to bring something to an end □ **she closed his building society account** she took all the money out and stopped using the account **3.** to stop doing business for the day ○ *The office closes at 5.30.* ○ *We close early on Saturdays.*

close company /ˌkləʊs ˈkʌmp(ə)ni/ *noun* a privately owned company controlled by a few shareholders (in the UK, fewer than five) where the public may own a small number of the shares (NOTE: The US term is **close corporation** or **closed corporation**.)

closed economy /ˌkləʊzd ɪˈkɒnəmi/ *noun* a type of economy where trade and financial dealings are tightly controlled by the government

closed-end credit /ˌkləʊzd end ˈkredɪt/ *noun* FINANCE, BANKING, AND ACCOUNTING, GENERAL MANAGEMENT a loan, plus any interest and finance charges, that is to be repaid in full by a specified future date. Loans that have property or motor vehicles as collateral are usually closed-end. ◊ **revolving credit** (NOTE: Most loans for the purchase of property or motor vehicles are closed-end credits.)

closed-end fund /ˌkləʊzd end ˈfʌnd/ *noun* an investment company with a fixed capital which investments can only be made by buying shares in the company

closed fund /ˌkləʊzd ˈfʌnd/ *noun* a fund, such as an investment trust, where the investor buys shares in the trust and receives dividends. This is as opposed to an open-ended trust, such as a unit trust, where the investor buys units, and the investment is used to purchase further securities for the trust.

closed market /ˌkləʊzd ˈmɑːkɪt/ *noun* a market where a supplier deals only with one agent or distributor and does not supply any others direct ○ *They signed a closed-market agreement with an Egyptian company.*

close-ended /ˌkləʊs ˈendɪd/, **closed-end** /ˈkləʊzd end/ *adjective* referring to an investment which has a fixed capital, such as an investment trust

closely held /ˌkləʊsli ˈheld/ *adjective* referring to shares in a company which are controlled by only a few shareholders

close off /ˌkləʊz ˈɒf/ *verb* to come to the end of an accounting period and make up the profit and loss account

closing /ˈkləʊzɪŋ/ *adjective* **1.** final or coming at the end **2.** at the end of an accounting period ○ *At the end of the quarter the bookkeeper has to calculate the closing balance.* ■ *noun* **1.** the shutting of a shop or being shut **2.** □ **the closing of an account** the act of stopping supply to a customer on credit

closing balance /ˌkləʊzɪŋ ˈbæləns/ *noun* the balance at the end of an accounting period

closing bid /ˈkləʊzɪŋ bɪd/ *noun* the last bid at an auction, the bid which is successful

closing date /ˈkləʊzɪŋ deɪt/ *noun* the last date ○ *The closing date for tenders to be received is May 1st.*

closing-down sale /ˌkləʊzɪŋ ˈdaʊn ˌseɪl/ *noun* the sale of goods when a shop is closing for ever

closing entries /ˌkləʊzɪŋ ˈentriz/ *noun* in a double-entry bookkeeping system, entries made at the very end of an accounting period to balance the expense and revenue ledgers

closing entry /ˌkləʊzɪŋ ˈentri/ *noun* an entry which closes an account

closing out /ˌkləʊzɪŋ ˈaʊt/ *noun US* the act of selling goods cheaply to try to get rid of them

closing price /ˈkləʊzɪŋ praɪs/ *noun* the price of a share at the end of a day's trading

closing rate /ˈkləʊzɪŋ reɪt/ *noun* the exchange rate of two or more currencies at the close of business of a balance sheet date, e.g. at the end of the financial year

closing-rate method /ˈkləʊzɪŋ reɪt ˌmeθəd/ *noun* a technique for translating the figures from a set of financial statements into a different currency using the closing rate. This method is often used for the accounts of a foreign subsidiary of a parent company.

closing stock /ˌkləʊzɪŋ ˈstɒk/ *noun* a business's remaining stock at the end of an accounting period. It includes finished products, raw materials, or work in progress and is deducted from the period's costs in the balance sheets. ○ *At the end of the month the closing stock was 10% higher than at the end of the previous month.*

closing time /ˈkləʊzɪŋ taɪm/ *noun* the time when a shop or office stops work

closure /ˈkləʊʒə/ *noun* the act of closing

C/N *abbr* credit note

CNCC *abbr* Compagnie Nationale des Commissaires aux Comptes

co- /kəʊ/ *prefix* working or acting together

CoCoA *abbr* continuously contemporary accounting

co-creditor /ˌkəʊ ˈkredɪtə/ *noun* a person who is a creditor of the same company as you are

code /kəʊd/ *noun* **1.** a system of signs, numbers or letters which mean something **2.** a set of rules

code of practice /ˌkəʊd əv ˈpræktɪs/ *noun* **1.** rules drawn up by an association which the members must follow when doing business **2.** the formally established ways in which members of a profession agree to work ○ *Advertisers have agreed to abide by the code of practice set out by the advertising council.*

codicil /ˈkəʊdɪsɪl/ *noun* a document executed in the same way as a will, making additions or changes to an existing will

coding /ˈkəʊdɪŋ/ *noun* the act of putting a code on something ○ *the coding of invoices*

co-director /ˌkəʊ daɪˌrektə/ *noun* a person who is a director of the same company as you

co-financing /ˌkəʊ ˈfaɪnænsɪŋ/ *noun* the act of arranging finance for a project from a series of sources

co-insurance /ˌkəʊ ɪnˈʃʊərəns/ *noun* an insurance policy where the risk is shared among several insurers

cold call /ˌkəʊld ˈkɔːl/ *noun* a telephone call or sales visit where the salesperson has no appointment and the client is not an established customer ■ *verb* to make a cold call

cold start /ˌkəʊld ˈstɑːt/ *noun* the act of beginning a new business or opening a new shop with no previous turnover to base it on

collateral /kəˈlæt(ə)rəl/ *noun* a security, such as negotiable instruments, shares or goods, used to provide a guarantee for a loan

'…examiners have come to inspect the collateral that thrifts may use in borrowing from the Fed' [*Wall Street Journal*]

collateralisation /kəˌlæt(ə)rəlaɪˈzeɪʃ(ə)n/ *noun* the act of securing a debt by selling long-term receivables to another company which secures them on the debts

collateralise /kəˈlæt(ə)rəlaɪz/, **collateralize** *verb* to secure a debt by means of a collateral

collect /kəˈlekt/ *verb* **1.** to get money which is owed to you by making the person who owes it pay **2.** to take things away from a place ○ *We have to collect the stock from the warehouse.* ■ *adverb, adjective* referring to a phone call which the person receiving the call agrees to pay for

collectables /kəˈlektəb(ə)lz/ *plural noun* items which people collect, e.g. stamps, playing cards or matchboxes

collectibility /kəˌlektɪˈbɪlɪti/ *noun* ability of cash owed to be collected

collecting agency /kəˈlektɪŋ ˌeɪdʒənsi/ *noun* an agency which collects money owed to other companies for a commission

collecting bank /kəˈlektɪŋ bæŋk/ *noun* a bank into which a person has deposited a cheque, and which has the duty to collect the money from the account of the writer of the cheque

collection /kəˈlekʃən/ *noun* **1.** the act of getting money together, or of making someone pay money which is owed ○ *tax collection* or *collection of tax* **2.** the fetching of goods ○ *The stock is in the warehouse awaiting collection.*

collection ratio /kəˌlekʃən ˈreɪʃiəʊ/ *noun* the average number of days it takes a firm to convert its accounts receivable into cash. Also known as **days' sales outstanding**

collections /kəˈlekʃənz/ *plural noun* money which has been collected

collector /kəˈlektə/ *noun* a person who makes people pay money which is owed ○ *He works as a debt collector.*

column /ˈkɒləm/ *noun* a series of numbers arranged one underneath the other ○ *to add up a column of figures* ○ *Put the total at the bottom of the column.*

combined financial statement /kəm ˌbaɪnd faɪˌnænʃəl ˈsteɪtmənt/ *noun* a written record covering the assets, liabilities, net worth, and operating statement of two or more related or affiliated companies

commerce /ˈkɒmɜːs/ *noun* the buying and selling of goods and services

commercial /kəˈmɜːʃ(ə)l/ *adjective* 1. referring to business 2. profitable

commercial aircraft /kəˌmɜːʃ(ə)l ˈeəkrɑːft/ *noun* an aircraft used to carry cargo or passengers for payment

commercial bank /kəˈmɜːʃ(ə)l bæŋk/ *noun* a bank which offers banking services to the public, as opposed to a merchant bank

commercial bill /kəˌmɜːʃ(ə)l ˈbɪl/ *noun* a bill of exchange issued by a company (a trade bill) or accepted by a bank (a bank bill) (as opposed to Treasury bills which are issued by the government)

commercial directory /kəˈmɜːʃ(ə)l daɪ ˌrekt(ə)ri/ *noun* a book which lists all the businesses and business people in a town

commercial failure /kəˌmɜːʃ(ə)l ˈfeɪljə/ *noun* a financial collapse or bankruptcy

commercial law /kəˌmɜːʃ(ə)l ˈlɔː/ *noun* the laws regarding business

commercial lawyer /kəˌmɜːʃ(ə)l ˈlɔːjə/ *noun* a person who specialises in company law or who advises companies on legal problems

commercial loan /kəˌmɜːʃ(ə)l ˈləʊn/ *noun* a short-term renewable loan or line of credit used to finance the seasonal or cyclical working capital needs of a company

commercially /kəˈmɜːʃ(ə)li/ *adverb* in a business way

commercial paper /kəˌmɜːʃ(ə)l ˈpeɪpə/ *noun* an IOU issued by a company to raise a short-term loan. Abbreviation **CP**

commercial port /kəˌmɜːʃ(ə)l ˈpɔːt/ *noun* a port which has only goods traffic and no passengers

commercial property /kəˌmɜːʃ(ə)l ˈprɒpəti/ *noun* a building, or buildings, used as offices or shops

commercial report /kəˌmɜːʃ(ə)l rɪˈpɔːt/ *noun* an investigative report made by an organisation such as a credit bureau that specialises in obtaining information regarding a person or organisation applying for something such as credit or employment

commercial substance /kəˌmɜːʃ(ə)l ˈsʌbstəns/ *noun* the economic reality that underlies a transaction or arrangement, regardless of its legal or technical denomination. For example, a company may sell an office block and then immediately lease it back: the commercial substance may be that it has not been sold.

commercial year /kəˌmɜːʃ(ə)l ˈjɪə/ *noun* an artificial year treated as having 12 months of 30 days each, used for calculating such things as monthly sales data and inventory levels

commission /kəˈmɪʃ(ə)n/ *noun* 1. money paid to a salesperson or agent, usually a percentage of the sales made ○ *She gets 10% commission on everything she sells.* ○ *He is paid on a commission basis.* 2. a group of people officially appointed to examine some problem ○ *He is the chairman of the government commission on export subsidies.*

commission agent /kəˈmɪʃ(ə)n ˌeɪdʒənt/ *noun* an agent who is paid a percentage of sales

commission broker /kəˈmɪʃ(ə)n ˌbrəʊkə/ *noun* a stockbroker who works for a commission

commissioner /kəˈmɪʃ(ə)nə/ *noun* an ombudsman

Commissioner of Inland Revenue /kəˌmɪʃ(ə)nə əv ˌɪnlənd ˈrevənjuː/ *noun* a person appointed officially to supervise the collection of taxes, including income tax, capital gains tax and corporation tax, but not VAT

Commissioners of the Inland Revenue /kəˌmɪʃ(ə)nəz əv ðiː ˌɪnlənd ˈrevənjuː/ *noun* in the United Kingdom, officials responsible for hearing appeals by taxpayers against their tax assessment

commission house /kəˈmɪʃ(ə)n haʊs/ *noun* a firm which buys or sells for clients, and charges a commission for this service

commission rep /kəˈmɪʃ(ə)n rep/ *noun* a representative who is not paid a salary but receives a commission on sales

commit /kəˈmɪt/ *verb* □ **to commit yourself to** to guarantee something, especially a loan issue, or to guarantee to do something

commitment /kəˈmɪtmənt/ *noun* something which you have agreed to do ○ *to make a commitment* or *to enter into a commitment* *to do something* ○ *The company has a commitment to provide a cheap service.*

commitment document /kə,mɪtmənt 'dɒkjumənt/ *noun* a contract, change order, purchase order, or letter of intent pertaining to the supply of goods and services that commits an organisation to legal, financial, and other obligations

commitment fee /kə'mɪtmənt fiː/ *noun* a fee paid to a bank which has arranged a line of credit which has not been fully used

commitments basis /kə,mɪtmənts 'beɪsɪs/ *noun* the method of recording the expenditure of a public sector organisation at the time when it commits itself to it rather than when it actually pays for it

commitments for capital expenditure /kə,mɪtmənts fə ,kæpɪt(ə)l ɪk 'spendɪtʃə/ *noun* the amount a company has committed to spend on fixed assets in the future. In the United Kingdom, companies are legally obliged to disclose this amount, and any additional commitments, in their annual report.

Committee on Accounting Procedure /kə,mɪti ɒn ə'kaʊntɪŋ prə,siːdʒə/ *noun* in the United States, a committee of the American Institute of Certified Public Accountants that was responsible between 1939 and 1959 for issuing accounting principles, some of which are still part of the Generally Accepted Accounting Principles

commodity /kə'mɒdɪti/ *noun* something sold in very large quantities, especially a raw material such as a metal or a food such as wheat

commodity exchange /kə'mɒdɪti ɪks ,tʃeɪndʒ/ *noun* a place where commodities are bought and sold

commodity futures /kə,mɒdɪti 'fjuːtʃəz/ *plural noun* commodities traded for delivery at a later date ○ *Silver rose 5% on the commodity futures market yesterday.*

commodity market /kə'mɒdɪti ,mɑːkɪt/ *noun* a place where people buy and sell commodities

commodity trader /kə'mɒdɪti ,treɪdə/ *noun* a person whose business is buying and selling commodities

common cost /,kɒmən 'kɒst/ *noun* a cost which is apportioned to two or more cost centres

Common Market /'kɒmən 'mɑːkɪt/ *noun* □ **the European Common Market** formerly the name for the European Community, an organization which links several European countries for the purposes of trade

common ownership /,kɒmən 'əʊnəʃɪp/ *noun* a situation where a business is owned by the employees who work in it

common pricing /,kɒmən 'praɪsɪŋ/ *noun* the illegal fixing of prices by several businesses so that they all charge the same price

common stock /,kɒmən 'stɒk/ *noun US* ordinary shares in a company, giving shareholders a right to vote at meetings and to receive dividends

Compagnie Nationale des Commissaires aux Comptes *noun* in France, an organisation that regulates external audit. Abbreviation **CNCC**

Companies Registration Office /,kʌmp(ə)niz ,redʒɪ'streɪʃ(ə)n ,ɒfɪs/ *noun* an office of the Registrar of Companies, the official organisation where the records of companies must be deposited, so that they can be inspected by the public. Abbreviation **CRO**. Also called **Companies House**

company /'kʌmp(ə)ni/ *noun* a business organisation, a group of people organised to buy, sell or provide a service, usually for profit

company auditor /,kʌmp(ə)ni 'ɔːdɪtə/ *noun* the individual or firm of accountants a company appoints to audit its annual accounts

company car /,kʌmp(ə)ni 'kɑː/ *noun* a car which belongs to a company and is lent to an employee to use for business or other purposes

company director /,kʌmp(ə)ni daɪ 'rektə/ *noun* a person appointed by the shareholders to help run a company

company flat /,kʌmp(ə)ni 'flæt/ *noun* a flat owned by a company and used by members of staff from time to time (NOTE: The US term is **company apartment**.)

company law /,kʌmp(ə)ni 'lɔː/ *noun* laws which refer to the way companies work

company pension scheme /,kʌmp(ə)ni 'penʃən skiːm/ *noun* same as **occupational pension scheme** ○ *She decided to join the company's pension scheme.*

company promoter /,kʌmp(ə)ni prə 'məʊtə/ *noun* a person who organises the setting up of a new company

company registrar /,kʌmp(ə)ni 'redʒɪstrɑː/ *noun* the person who keeps the share register of a company

company secretary /,kʌmp(ə)ni 'sekrɪt(ə)ri/ *noun* a person who is responsible for a company's legal and financial affairs

comparability /ˌkɒmp(ə)rə'bɪlɪti/ *noun* a feature in the financial statements of two or more companies that enables an analyst to make a faithful comparison between them

comparable /'kɒmp(ə)rəb(ə)l/ *adjective* possible to compare ○ *The two sets of figures are not comparable.*

comparative balance sheet /kəm ˌpærətɪv 'bæləns ʃiːt/ *noun* one of two or more financial statements prepared on different dates that lend themselves to a comparative analysis of the financial condition of an organisation

compare with /kəm'peə wɪð/ *verb* to examine two things to see where they are the same and where they differ ○ *How do the sales this year compare with last year's?* ○ *Compared with the previous month, last month was terrific.*

compensate /'kɒmpənseɪt/ *verb* to give someone money to make up for a loss or injury ○ *In this case we will compensate a manager for loss of commission.* ○ *The company will compensate the employee for the burns suffered in the accident.* (NOTE: You compensate someone **for** something.)

compensating balance /ˌkɒmpənseɪtɪŋ 'bæləns/ *noun* the amount of money which a customer has to keep in a bank account in order to get free services from the bank

compensating errors /ˌkɒmpənseɪtɪŋ 'erəz/ *plural noun* two or more errors which are set against each other so that the accounts still balance

compensation /ˌkɒmpən'seɪʃ(ə)n/ *noun* **1.** □ **compensation for damage** payment for damage done □ **compensation for loss of office** payment to a director who is asked to leave a company before their contract ends □ **compensation for loss of earnings** payment to someone who has stopped earning money or who is not able to earn money **2.** *US* a salary

'…compensation can also be via the magistrates courts for relatively minor injuries' [*Personnel Management*]

compensation deal /ˌkɒmpən'seɪʃ(ə)n diːl/ *noun* a deal where an exporter is paid (at least in part) in goods from the country to which he or she is exporting

compensation fund /ˌkɒmpən'seɪʃ(ə)n fʌnd/ *noun* a fund operated by the Stock Exchange to compensate investors for losses suffered when members of the Stock Exchange default

compensation package /ˌkɒmpən 'seɪʃ(ə)n ˌpækɪdʒ/ *noun* the salary, pension and other benefits offered with a job

'…golden parachutes are liberal compensation packages given to executives leaving a company' [*Publishers Weekly*]

compete /kəm'piːt/ *verb* □ **to compete with someone** *or* **with a company** to try to do better than another person or another company ○ *We have to compete with cheap imports from the Far East.* ○ *They were competing unsuccessfully with local companies on their home territory.* □ **the two companies are competing for a market share** *or* **for a contract** each company is trying to win a larger part of the market, trying to win the contract

competition /ˌkɒmpə'tɪʃ(ə)n/ *noun* a situation where companies or individuals are trying to do better than others, e.g. trying to win a larger share of the market, or to produce a better or cheaper product or to control the use of resources

'…profit margins in the industries most exposed to foreign competition are worse than usual' [*Sunday Times*]

'…competition is steadily increasing and could affect profit margins as the company tries to retain its market share' [*Citizen (Ottawa)*]

competitive /kəm'petɪtɪv/ *adjective* involving competition

'…the company blamed fiercely competitive market conditions in Europe for a £14m operating loss last year' [*Financial Times*]

competitive devaluation /kəm,petɪtɪv ,diːvælju'eɪʃ(ə)n/ *noun* a devaluation of a currency to make a country's goods more competitive on the international markets

competitive pricing /kəm,petɪtɪv 'praɪsɪŋ/ *noun* the practice of putting low prices on goods so as to compete with other products

competitive products /kəm,petɪtɪv 'prɒdʌkts/ *plural noun* products made to compete with existing products

competitor /kəm'petɪtə/ *noun* a person or company that is competing with another ○ *Two German firms are our main competitors.*

'…sterling labour costs continue to rise between 3% and 5% a year faster than in most of our competitor countries' [*Sunday Times*]

complete /kəm'pliːt/ *verb* to sign a contract for the sale of a property and to exchange it with the other party, so making it legal

completed contract method /kəm ,pliːtɪd 'kɒntrækt ,meθəd/ *noun* a way of accounting for a particular contractual obligation, e.g., a long-term construction project, whereby the profit is not recorded until the final completion of the project, even if there has been some revenue while the project was still in progress

completion /kəm'pli:ʃ(ə)n/ *noun* the act of finishing something

completion date /kəm'pli:ʃ(ə)n deit/ *noun* a date when something will be finished

compliance /kəm'plaɪəns/ *noun* agreement to do what is ordered

compliance costs /kəm'plaɪəns kɒsts/ *noun* expenses incurred as a result of meeting legal requirements, e.g., for safety requirements or to comply with company law

compliance department /kəm'plaɪəns dɪˌpɑːtmənt/ *noun* a department in a stockbroking firm which makes sure that the Stock Exchange rules are followed and that confidentiality is maintained in cases where the same firm represents rival clients

compliance officer /kəm'plaɪəns ˌɒfɪsə/ *noun* an employee of a financial organisation whose job is to make sure that the organisation complies with the regulations governing its business

composition /ˌkɒmpə'zɪʃ(ə)n/ *noun* an agreement between a debtor and creditors, where the debtor settles a debt by repaying only part of it

compound /kəm'paʊnd/ *verb* **1.** to agree with creditors to settle a debt by paying part of what is owed **2.** to add to ○ *The interest is compounded daily.*

compound discount /ˌkɒmpaʊnd 'dɪskaʊnt/ *noun* the difference between the nominal amount of a particular sum in the future and its present discounted value. So, if £150 in a year's time is worth £142 now, the compound discount is £8.

compound interest /ˌkɒmpaʊnd 'ɪntrəst/ *noun* interest which is added to the capital and then earns interest itself

compound journal entry /ˌkɒmpaʊnd ˌdʒɜːn(ə)l 'entri/ *noun* an entry in a journal that comprises more than individual equally matched debit and credit items

comprehensive income /ˌkɒmprɪhensɪv 'ɪnkʌm/ *noun* a company's total income for a given accounting period, taking into account all gains and losses, not only those included in a normal income statement. In the United States, comprehensive income must be declared whereas in the United Kingdom it appears in the statement of total recognised gains and losses.

comprehensive insurance /ˌkɒmprɪhensɪv ɪn'ʃʊərəns/, **comprehensive policy** /ˌkɒmprɪhensɪv 'pɒlɪsi/ *noun* an insurance policy which covers you against all risks which are likely to happen

comprehensive tax allocation /ˌkɒmprɪhensɪv 'tæks ˌæləkeɪʃ(ə)n/ *noun* the setting aside of money to cover deferred tax

compromise /'kɒmprəmaɪz/ *noun* an agreement between two sides, where each side gives way a little ○ *Management offered £5 an hour, the union asked for £9, and a compromise of £7.50 was reached.* ■ *verb* to reach an agreement by giving way a little ○ *She asked £15 for it, I offered £7 and we compromised on £10.*

comptroller /kən'trəʊlə/ *noun* a financial controller

Comptroller and Auditor General /kənˌtrəʊlə ən ˌɔːdɪtə 'dʒen(ə)rəl/ *noun* in the United Kingdom, the head of the National Audit Office who reports back to Parliament on the audit of government departments

compulsory annuity /kəmˌpʌlsəri ə'njuːɪti/ *noun* in the United Kingdom, the legal requirement that at least 75% of the funds built-up in a personal pension plan have to be used to purchase an annuity by the age of 75

compulsory liquidation /kəmˌpʌlsəri ˌlɪkwɪ'deɪʃ(ə)n/ *noun* liquidation which is ordered by a court

compulsory winding up /kəmˌpʌlsəri ˌwaɪndɪŋ 'ʌp/ *noun* liquidation which is ordered by a court

computable /kəm'pjuːtəb(ə)l/ *adjective* possible to calculate

computation /ˌkɒmpjʊ'teɪʃ(ə)n/ *noun* a calculation

computational error /ˌkɒmpjʊteɪʃ(ə)nəl 'erə/ *noun* a mistake made in calculating

compute /kəm'pjuːt/ *verb* to calculate, to do calculations

computer /kəm'pjuːtə/ *noun* an electronic machine which calculates or stores information and processes it automatically

computer department /kəm'pjuːtə dɪˌpɑːtmənt/ *noun* a department in a company which manages the company's computers

computer file /kəm'pjuːtə faɪl/ *noun* a section of information on a computer, e.g. the payroll, list of addresses or list of customer accounts

computerise /kəm'pjuːtəraɪz/, **computerize** *verb* to change something from a manual system to one using computers ○ *We have computerised all our records.* ○ *Stock control is now completely computerised.*

computerised /kəmˈpjuːtəraɪzd/, **computerized** *adjective* carried out by computers ○ *a computerised invoicing* or *filing system*

computer listing /kəmˌpjuːtə ˈlɪstɪŋ/ *noun* a printout of a list of items taken from data stored in a computer

computer manager /kəmˈpjuːtə ˌmænɪdʒə/ *noun* a person in charge of a computer department

computer network /kəmˌpjuːtə ˈnetwɜːk/ *noun* a computer system where several PCs are linked so that they all draw on the same database

computer operator /kəmˈpjuːtər ˌɒpəreɪtə/ *noun* a person who operates a computer

computer program /kəmˈpjuːtə ˌprəʊɡræm/ *noun* instructions to a computer telling it to do a particular piece of work ○ *to buy a graphics program* ○ *The accounts department is running a new payroll program.*

computer programmer /kəmˌpjuːtə ˈprəʊɡræmə/ *noun* a person who writes computer programs

computer programming /kəmˌpjuːtə ˈprəʊɡræmɪŋ/ *noun* the work of writing programs for computers

computer-readable /kəmˌpjuːtə ˈriːdəb(ə)l/ *adjective* able to be read and understood by a computer ○ *computer-readable codes*

computer services /kəmˌpjuːtə ˈsɜːvɪsɪz/ *plural noun* work using a computer, done by a computer bureau

computer system /kəmˈpjuːtə ˌsɪstəm/ *noun* a set of programs, commands, etc., which run a computer

computing /kəmˈpjuːtɪŋ/ *noun* the operating of computers

computing speed /kəmˈpjuːtɪŋ spiːd/ *noun* the speed at which a computer calculates

concealment of assets /kənˌsiːlmənt əv ˈæsets/ *noun* the act of hiding assets so that creditors do not know they exist

concept /ˈkɒnsept/ *noun* an idea □ **concept of capital maintenance** idea that profit is only recorded if the capital of the company, measured in terms of its net assets, increases during an accounting period (assets can be measured at historical cost or in units of constant purchasing power) □ **concept of maintenance of operating capacity** concept of capital maintenance measured in terms of the changes in the current values of fixed assets, stock and working capital (profit can only be taken if the total value of these assets, called the 'net operating assets', including adjustments for changes in prices affecting these assets, increases during an accounting period)

conceptual framework /kənˌseptʃuəl ˈfreɪmwɜːk/ *noun* a set of theoretical principles that underlies the practice and regulation of financial accounting. In the United States, this is expressed in the Statements of Financial Accounting Concepts issued by the Financial Accounting Standards Board. In the United Kingdom, it is expressed in the Statement of Principles issued by the Accounting Standards Board.

concern /kənˈsɜːn/ *noun* a business or company

concession /kənˈseʃ(ə)n/ *noun* **1.** the right to use someone else's property for business purposes **2.** the right to be the only seller of a product in a place ○ *She runs a jewellery concession in a department store.* **3.** an allowance, e.g. a reduction of tax or price

concessionaire /kənˌseʃəˈneə/ *noun* a person or business that has the right to be the only seller of a product in a place

concessionary fare /kənˌseʃ(ə)nəri ˈfeə/ *noun* a reduced fare for some types of passenger such as pensioners, students or employees of a transport company

conciliation /kənˌsɪliˈeɪʃ(ə)n/ *noun* the practice of bringing together the parties in a dispute with an independent third party, so that the dispute can be settled through a series of negotiations

condition /kənˈdɪʃ(ə)n/ *noun* **1.** something which has to be carried out as part of a contract or which has to be agreed before a contract becomes valid **2.** a general state or the general way of life in a place ○ *item sold in good condition* ○ *The union has complained of the bad working conditions in the factory.* ○ *What was the condition of the car when it was sold?* ○ *Adverse trading conditions affected our profits.*

conditional /kənˈdɪʃ(ə)n(ə)l/ *adjective* provided that specific conditions are taken into account

conditionality /kənˌdɪʃ(ə)ˈnælɪti/ *noun* the fact of having conditions attached

conditional sale /kənˌdɪʃ(ə)nəl ˈseɪl/ *noun* a sale which is subject to conditions, such as a hire- purchase agreement

conditions of employment /kənˌdɪʃ(ə)nz əv ɪmˈplɔɪmənt/ *plural noun* the terms of a contract of employment

conditions of sale /kən‚dɪʃ(ə)nz əv ‚seɪl/ *plural noun* agreed ways in which a sale takes place, e.g. discounts or credit terms

Confederation of Asian and Pacific Accountants /kən‚fedə‚reɪʃ(ə)n əv ‚eɪʒ(ə)n ən pə‚sɪfɪk ə'kaʊntənts/ *noun* full form of **CAPA**

conference proceedings /'kɒnf(ə)rəns prə‚siːdɪŋz/ *plural noun* a written report of what has taken place at a conference

confidential report /‚kɒnfɪdenʃəl rɪ'pɔːt/ *noun* a secret document which must not be shown to other people

confirm /kən'fɜːm/ *verb* to say again that something agreed before is correct ○ *to confirm a hotel reservation* or *a ticket* or *an agreement* or *a booking*

confirmation /‚kɒnfə'meɪʃ(ə)n/ *noun* the act of making certain

conflict of interest /‚kɒnflɪkt əv 'ɪntrəst/ *noun* a situation where a person or firm may profit personally from decisions taken in an official capacity

conglomerate /kən'glɒmərət/ *noun* a group of subsidiary companies linked together and forming a group, each making very different types of products

connected persons /kə‚nektɪd 'pɜːs(ə)ns/ *noun* for purposes of disclosure under the UK Companies Act, certain people who are related to or connected with members of the board of directors, including his or her spouse and children

Conseil National de la Comptabilité *noun* in France, a committee appointed by the government that is responsible for drawing up the Plan Comptable Général (General Accounting Plan)

consensus ad idem /kən‚sensəs æd 'aɪdem/ *Latin phrase meaning* 'agreement to this same thing': real agreement to a contract by both parties

conservative /kən'sɜːvətɪv/ *adjective* careful, not overestimating ○ *His forecast of expenditure was very conservative* or *She made a conservative forecast of expenditure.*

'…we are calculating our next budget income at an oil price of $15 per barrel. We know it is a conservative projection, but we do not want to come in for a shock should prices dive at any time during the year' [*Lloyd's List*]

conservatively /kən'sɜːvətɪvli/ *adverb* not overestimating ○ *The total sales are conservatively estimated at £2.3m.*

consider /kən'sɪdə/ *verb* to think seriously about something

consideration /kən‚sɪdə'reɪʃ(ə)n/ *noun* **1.** serious thought ○ *We are giving consideration to moving the head office to Scotland.* **2.** something valuable exchanged as part of a contract

consignation /‚kɒnsaɪ'neɪʃ(ə)n/ *noun* the act of consigning

consignee /‚kɒnsaɪ'niː/ *noun* a person who receives goods from someone for their own use or to sell for the sender

consignment /kən'saɪnmənt/ *noun* **1.** the sending of goods to someone who will sell them for you **2.** a group of goods sent for sale ○ *A consignment of goods has arrived.* ○ *We are expecting a consignment of cars from Japan.*

'…some of the most prominent stores are gradually moving away from the traditional consignment system, under which manufacturers agree to repurchase any unsold goods, and in return dictate prices and sales strategies and even dispatch staff to sell the products' [*Nikkei Weekly*]

consignment accounts /kən‚saɪnmənt ə'kaʊnts/ *plural noun* accounts kept by both consignee and consignor, showing quantities, dates of shipment, and payments for stocks held

consignment note /kən'saɪnmənt nəʊt/ *noun* a note saying that goods have been sent

consignor /kən'saɪnə/ *noun* a person who consigns goods to someone

consistency /kən'sɪstənsi/ *noun* one of the basic accounting concepts, that items in the accounts should be treated in the same way from year to year

consolidate /kən'sɒlɪdeɪt/ *verb* **1.** to include the accounts of several subsidiary companies as well as the holding company in a single set of accounts **2.** to group goods together for shipping

consolidated accounts /kən‚sɒlɪdeɪtɪd ə'kaʊnts/ *plural noun* accounts where the financial position of several different companies, i.e. a holding company and its subsidiaries, are recorded together

consolidated balance sheet /kən‚sɒlɪdeɪtɪd 'bæləns ʃiːt/ *noun* a balance sheets of subsidiary companies grouped together into the balance sheet of the parent company

consolidated cash flow statement /kən‚sɒlɪdeɪtɪd kæʃ fləʊ 'steɪtmənt/ *noun* a cash flow statement for a group of enterprises and its parent company as a whole

consolidated fund /kən‚sɒlɪdeɪtɪd 'fʌnd/ *noun* money in the Exchequer which comes from tax revenues and is used to pay for government expenditure

consolidated income statement /kən ˌsɒlɪdeɪtɪd ˈɪnkʌm ˌsteɪtmənt/ *noun* an income statement for a group of enterprises and its parent company as a whole

consolidated profit and loss account /kənˌsɒlɪdeɪtɪd ˌprɒfɪt ən ˈlɒs əˌkaʊnt/ *noun* profit and loss accounts of the holding company and its subsidiary companies, grouped together into a single profit and loss account (NOTE: The US term is **profit and loss statement** or **income statement**.)

consolidated shipment /kən ˌsɒlɪdeɪtɪd ˈʃɪpmənt/ *noun* goods from different companies grouped together into a single shipment

consolidation /kənˌsɒlɪˈdeɪʃ(ə)n/ *noun* **1.** the grouping together of goods for shipping **2.** the act of taking profits from speculative investments and investing them safely in blue-chip companies

consolidation adjustments /kənˌsɒlɪ ˈdeɪʃ(ə)n əˌdʒʌstmənts/ *noun* necessary changes and deletions made to financial records when consolidating the accounts of a group of enterprises

consolidation difference /kənˌsɒlɪ ˈdeɪʃ(ə)n ˌdɪf(ə)rəns/ *noun* the difference between the price paid for a subsidiary and the value of the assets and liabilities obtained in the purchase

consols /ˈkɒnsɒlz/ *plural noun* government bonds which pay interest but do not have a maturity date

consortium /kənˈsɔːtiəm/ *noun* a group of companies which work together ○ *A consortium of Canadian companies* or *A Canadian consortium has tendered for the job.* (NOTE: The plural is **consortia**.)

'…the consortium was one of only four bidders for the £2 billion contract to run the lines, seen as potentially the most difficult contract because of the need for huge investment' [*Times*]

constant /ˈkɒnstənt/ *adjective* unchanging ○ *The calculations are in constant dollars.*

constant purchasing power /ˌkɒnstənt ˈpɜːtʃɪsɪŋ ˌpaʊə/ *noun* same as **current purchasing power**

consult /kənˈsʌlt/ *verb* to ask an expert for advice ○ *We consulted our accountant about our tax.*

consultancy /kənˈsʌltənsi/ *noun* the act of giving specialist advice ○ *a consultancy firm* ○ *She offers a consultancy service.*

Consultative Committee of Accountancy Bodies /kənˌsʌltətɪv kə ˌmɪti əv əˈkaʊntənsi ˌbɒdiz/ *noun* an organisation established in 1974 that represents and encourages coordination between the six professional accountancy bodes in the United Kingdom and Ireland

consulting /kənˈsʌltɪŋ/ *adjective* giving specialist advice ○ *a consulting engineer*

consulting actuary /kənˌsʌltɪŋ ˈæktjuəri/ *noun* an independent actuary who advises large pension funds

consumable goods /kənˌsjuːməb(ə)l ˈɡʊdz/, **consumables** /kənˈsjuːməb(ə)lz/ *plural noun* goods which are bought by members of the public and not by companies. Also called **consumer goods**

consumer /kənˈsjuːmə/ *noun* a person or company that buys and uses goods and services ○ *Gas consumers are protesting at the increase in prices.* ○ *The factory is a heavy consumer of water.*

'…forecasting consumer response is one problem which will never be finally solved' [*Marketing Week*]

'…consumer tastes in the UK are becoming much more varied' [*Marketing*]

'…the marketing director's brief will be to develop the holiday villages as a consumer brand, aimed at the upper end of the tourist market' [*Marketing Week*]

consumer council /kənˌsjuːmə ˈkaʊns(ə)l/ *noun* a group representing the interests of consumers

consumer credit /kənˌsjuːmə ˈkredɪt/ *noun* the credit given by shops, banks and other financial institutions to consumers so that they can buy goods (NOTE: Lenders have to be licensed under the Consumer Credit Act, 1974. The US term is **installment credit**.)

Consumer Credit Act, 1974 /kən ˌsjuːmə ˈkredɪt ækt/ *noun* an Act of Parliament which licenses lenders, and requires them to state clearly the full terms of loans which they make, including the APR

consumer goods /kənˌsjuːmə ˈɡʊdz/ *plural noun* same as **consumable goods**

consumer panel /kənˈsjuːmə ˌpæn(ə)l/ *noun* a group of consumers who report on products they have used so that the manufacturers can improve them or use what the panel says about them in advertising

Consumer Price Index /kənˌsjuːmə ˈpraɪs ˌɪndeks/ *noun* an American index showing how prices of consumer goods have risen over a period of time, used as a way of measuring inflation and the cost of living.

Abbreviation **CPI** (NOTE: The UK term is **retail prices index**.)

'…analysis of the consumer price index for the first half of the year shows that the rate of inflation went down by about 12.9 per cent' [*Business Times (Lagos)*]

consumer protection /kən,sjuːmə prə'tekʃən/ *noun* the activity of protecting consumers against unfair or illegal traders

consumer research /kən,sjuːmə rɪ'sɜːtʃ/ *noun* research into why consumers buy goods and what goods they may want to buy

consumer spending /kən,sjuːmə 'spendɪŋ/ *noun* spending by private households on goods and services

'…companies selling in the UK market are worried about reduced consumer spending as a consequence of higher interest rates and inflation' [*Business*]

consumption tax /kən'sʌmpʃ(ə)n tæks/ *noun* a tax used to encourage people to buy less of a particular good or service by increasing its price. This type of tax is often levied in times of national hardship.

Contact Committee /,kɒntækt kə'mɪti/ *noun* an advisory body, established by the European Union, that oversees the application of European accounting directives and makes recommendations to the European Commission about changes to those directives

contango /kən'tæŋgəʊ/ *noun* **1.** the payment of interest by a stockbroker for permission to carry payment for shares from one account to the next (NOTE: Contango is no longer applied on the London Stock Exchange because of the rolling account system, but it is still applied on some other exchanges.) **2.** a cash price which is lower than the forward price

contango day /kən'tæŋgəʊ deɪ/ *noun* formerly, the day when the rate of contango payments was fixed

contested takeover /kən,testɪd 'teɪkəʊvə/ *noun* a takeover bid where the board of the target company does not recommend it to the shareholders and tries to fight it. Also called **hostile bid**

contingency /kən'tɪndʒənsi/ *noun* a possible state of emergency when decisions will have to be taken quickly

contingency fund /kən'tɪndʒənsi fʌnd/ *noun* money set aside in case it is needed urgently

contingent expenses /kən,tɪndʒənt ɪk'spensɪz/ *plural noun* expenses which will be incurred only if something happens

contingent gain /kən,tɪndʒənt 'geɪn/ *noun* a gain or loss which is incurred only if something happens

contingent liability /kən,tɪndʒənt laɪə'bɪlɪti/ *noun* a liability which may or may not occur, but for which provision is made in a company's accounts, as opposed to 'provisions', where money is set aside for an anticipated expenditure

contingent loss /kən,tɪndʒənt 'lɒs/ *noun* a possible loss that is conditional on the occurrence of a certain event in the future

contingent policy /kən,tɪndʒənt 'pɒlɪsi/ *noun* an insurance policy which pays out only if something happens, such as if a person named in the policy dies before the person due to benefit

continuous /kən'tɪnjʊəs/ *adjective* with no end or with no breaks ○ *a continuous production line*

continuous disclosure /kən,tɪnjʊəs dɪs'kləʊʒə/ *noun* in Canada, the practice of ensuring that complete, timely, accurate, and balanced information about a public company is made available to shareholders

continuously contemporary accounting /kən,tɪnjʊəsli kən,temp(ə)rəri ə'kaʊntɪŋ/ *noun* an accounting system that measures assets and liabilities at their current cash price. Profit and loss can therefore be viewed in terms of changes in the value as all items are measured in the same way. Abbreviation **CoCoA**

contra /'kɒntrə/ *noun* an accounting term used when debits are matched with related credits in an account or set of accounts

contra account /'kɒntrə ə,kaʊnt/ *noun* an account which offsets another account, e.g. where a company's supplier is not only a creditor in that company's books but also a debtor because it has purchased goods on credit

contract *noun* /'kɒntrækt/ **1.** a legal agreement between two parties ○ *to draw up a contract* ○ *to draft a contract* ○ *to sign a contract* ○ **the contract is binding on both parties** both parties signing the contract must do what is agreed □ **under contract** bound by the terms of a contract ○ *The firm is under contract to deliver the goods by November.* □ **to void a contract** to make a contract invalid **2.** □ **by private contract** by private legal agreement **3.** an agreement for the supply of a service or goods ○ *to enter into a contract to supply spare parts* ○ *to sign a contract for £10,000 worth of spare parts* **4.** (*Stock Exchange*) a deal to buy or sell shares, or an agreement to purchase options or futures ■

verb /kən'trækt/ to agree to do some work on the basis of a legally binding contract ○ *to contract to supply spare parts* or *to contract for the supply of spare parts*

contract costing /ˌkɒntrækt 'kɒstɪŋ/ *noun* a method of costing large projects, where the contracted work will run over several accounting periods

contracting party /kənˌtræktɪŋ 'pɑːti/ *noun* a person or company that signs a contract

contract note /'kɒntrækt nəʊt/ *noun* a note showing that shares have been bought or sold but not yet paid for, also including the commission

contract of employment /ˌkɒntrækt əv ɪm'plɔɪmənt/ *noun* a contract between an employer and an employee stating all the conditions of work. Also called **employment contract**

contract of service /ˌkɒntrækt əv 'sɜːvɪs/ *noun* a legal agreement between an employer and an employee whereby the employee will work for the employer and be directed by them, in return for payment

contractor /kən'træktə/ *noun* a person or company that does work according to a written agreement

contractual /kən'træktʃʊəl/ *adjective* according to a contract ○ *contractual conditions* □ **to fulfil your contractual obligations** to do what you have agreed to do in a contract

contractual liability /kənˌtræktʃʊəl ˌlaɪə'bɪlɪti/ *noun* a legal responsibility for something as stated in a contract

contractually /kən'træktjʊəli/ *adverb* according to a contract ○ *The company is contractually bound to pay our expenses.*

contractual obligation /kənˌtræktʃʊəl ˌɒblɪ'geɪʃ(ə)n/ *noun* something that a person is legally forced to do through having signed a contract to do □ **to fulfil your contractual obligations** to do what you have agreed to do in a contract

contract work /'kɒntrækt wɜːk/ *noun* work done according to a written agreement

contra entry /'kɒntrə ˌentri/ *noun* an entry made in the opposite side of an account to make an earlier entry worthless, i.e. a debit against a credit

contribute /kən'trɪbjuːt/ *verb* to give money or add to money ○ *We agreed to contribute 10% of the profits.* ○ *They had contributed to the pension fund for 10 years.*

contribution /ˌkɒntrɪ'bjuːʃ(ə)n/ *noun* **1.** money paid to add to a sum **2.** the difference

between sales value and the variable costs of a unit sold. This goes to cover fixed costs and provide the profit.

contribution income statement /ˌkɒntrɪbjuːʃ(ə)n 'ɪnkʌm ˌsteɪtmənt/ *noun* a way of presenting an income statement in which fixed costs are shown as a deduction from the total contribution. This format is often used as part of management accounting.

contribution margin /ˌkɒntrɪ'bjuːʃ(ə)n ˌmɑːdʒɪn/ *noun* a way of showing how much individual products or services contribute to net profit

contribution of capital /kɒntrɪ ˌbjuːʃ(ə)n əv 'kæpɪt(ə)l/ *noun* money paid to a company as additional capital

contributor of capital /kənˌtrɪbjʊtər əv 'kæpɪt(ə)l/ *noun* a person who contributes capital

contributory /kən'trɪbjʊt(ə)ri/ *adjective* causing or helping to cause ○ *Falling exchange rates have been a contributory factor in the company's loss of profits.*

contributory pension scheme /kən ˌtrɪbjʊt(ə)ri 'penʃən skiːm/ *noun* a scheme where the employee pays a proportion of his or her salary into the pension fund

control account /kənˌtrəʊl ə'kaʊnt/ *noun* an account used to record the total amounts entered in a number of different ledger accounts. It also acts as a means of checking the accuracy of the ledger accounts.

controllable variance /kənˌtrəʊləb(ə)l 'veəriəns/ *noun* a difference between actual and budgeted amounts that is considered as being within the control of the budget centre manager

controlled /kən'trəʊld/ *adjective* ruled or kept in check

controlled company /kənˌtrəʊld 'kʌmp(ə)ni/ *noun* company where more than 50% (or in the USA, 25%) of the shares belong to one owner

controlled economy /kənˌtrəʊld ɪ 'kɒnəmi/ *noun* an economy where most business activity is directed by orders from the government

controller /kən'trəʊlə/ *noun* **1.** a person who controls something, especially the finances of a company **2.** *US* the chief accountant in a company

control period /kənˌtrəʊl 'pɪəriəd/ *noun* the fraction of the financial year, e.g., a month, for which separate totals are given in a budget

conversion /kən'vɜːʃ(ə)n/ *noun* **1.** a change **2.** the action of changing convertible loan stock into ordinary shares

conversion costs /kən'vɜːʃ(ə)n kɒsts/ *plural noun* cost of changing raw materials into finished or semi-finished products, including wages, other direct production costs and the production overhead

conversion of funds /kən‚vɜːʃ(ə)n əv 'fʌndz/ *noun* the act of using money which does not belong to you for a purpose for which it is not supposed to be used

conversion period /kən'vɜːʃ(ə)n ‚pɪəriəd/ *noun* a time during which convertible loan stock may be changed into ordinary shares

conversion price /kən'vɜːʃ(ə)n praɪs/, **conversion rate** /kən'vɜːʃ(ə)n reɪt/ *noun* **1.** a price at which preference shares are converted into ordinary shares **2.** a rate at which a currency is changed into a foreign currency

conversion value /kən'vɜːʃ(ə)n ‚væljuː/ *noun* a value of convertible stock, including the extra value of the ordinary shares into which they may be converted

convert /kən'vɜːt/ *verb* **1.** to change money of one country for money of another ○ *We converted our pounds into Swiss francs.* **2.** □ **to convert funds to your own use** to use someone else's money for yourself

convertibility /kən‚vɜːtə'bɪləti/ *noun* the ability of a currency to be exchanged for another easily

convertible currency /kən‚vɜːtəb(ə)l 'kʌrənsi/ *noun* a currency which can easily be exchanged for another

convertible debenture /kən‚vɜːtəb(ə)l dɪ'bentʃə/ *noun* a debenture or loan stock which can be exchanged for ordinary shares at a later date

convertible loan stock /kən‚vɜːtəb(ə)l 'ləʊn stɒk/ *noun* money lent to a company which can be converted into shares at a later date

convertibles /kən'vɜːtəb(ə)lz/ *plural noun* corporate bonds or preference shares which can be converted into ordinary shares at a set price on set dates

conveyance /kən'veɪəns/ *noun* a legal document which transfers a property from the seller to the buyer

conveyancer /kən'veɪənsə/ *noun* a person who draws up a conveyance

conveyancing /kən'veɪənsɪŋ/ *noun* the work of legally transferring a property from a seller to a buyer

cooling-off period /‚kuːlɪŋ 'ɒf ‚pɪəriəd/ *noun* **1.** (*during an industrial dispute*) a period when negotiations have to be carried on and no action can be taken by either side **2.** a period during which someone who is about to enter into an agreement may reflect on all aspects of the arrangement and change his or her mind if necessary ○ *New York has a three day cooling-off period for telephone sales.*

cooperative /kəʊ'ɒp(ə)rətɪv/ *adjective* willing to work together ○ *The workforce has not been cooperative over the management's productivity plan.*

cooperative society /kəʊ'ɒp(ə)rətɪv sə‚saɪəti/ *noun* an organisation where customers and employees are partners and share the profits

cooperative store /kəʊ'ɒp(ə)rətɪv stɔː/ *noun* a store owned by those who shop there as well as by its workers

coproperty /kəʊ'prɒpəti/ *noun* ownership of property by two or more people together

coproprietor /‚kəʊprə'praɪətə/ *noun* a person who owns a property with another person or several other people

copying machine /'kɒpiɪŋ mə‚ʃiːn/ *noun* a machine which makes copies of documents

copyright /'kɒpiraɪt/ *noun* an author's legal right to publish his or her own work and not to have it copied, lasting seventy years after the author's death

Copyright Act /'kɒpi‚raɪt ækt/ *noun* an Act of Parliament making copyright legal, and controlling the copying of copyright material

copyright deposit /‚kɒpiraɪt dɪ'pɒzɪt/ *noun* the act of depositing a copy of a published work in a copyright library, which is part of the formal copyrighting of copyright material

copyright holder /‚kɒpiraɪt 'həʊldə/ *noun* a person who owns a copyright and who can expect to receive royalties from it

copyright law /'kɒpiraɪt lɔː/ *noun* laws concerning the protection of copyright

copyright notice /‚kɒpiraɪt 'nəʊtɪs/ *noun* a note in a book showing who owns the copyright and the date of ownership

corporate /'kɔːp(ə)rət/ *adjective* referring to corporations or companies, or to a particular company as a whole

'…the prime rate is the rate at which banks lend to their top corporate borrowers' [*Wall Street Journal*]

'…if corporate forecasts are met, sales will exceed \$50 million next year' [*Citizen (Ottawa)*]

corporate bond /ˈkɔːp(ə)rət bɒnd/ *noun* a loan stock officially issued by a company to raise capital, usually against the security of some of its assets (NOTE: The company promises to pay an amount of interest on a set date every year until the redemption date, when it repays the loan.)

corporate finance /ˌkɔːp(ə)rət ˈfaɪnæns/ *noun* the financial affairs of companies

corporate governance /ˌkɔːp(ə)rət ˈgʌv(ə)nəns/ *noun* a theory of the way companies should be run

corporate loan /ˌkɔːp(ə)rət ˈləʊn/ *noun* a loan issued by a corporation

corporate name /ˌkɔːp(ə)rət ˈneɪm/ *noun* the name of a large corporation

corporate plan /ˌkɔːp(ə)rət ˈplæn/ *noun* a plan for the future work of a whole company

corporate planning /ˌkɔːp(ə)rət ˈplænɪŋ/ *noun* **1.** the process of planning the future work of a whole company **2.** planning the future financial state of a group of companies

corporate profits /ˌkɔːp(ə)rət ˈprɒfɪts/ *plural noun* the profits of a corporation

'…corporate profits for the first quarter showed a 4 per cent drop from last year' [*Financial Times*]

corporate raider /ˌkɔːp(ə)rət ˈreɪdə/ *noun* a person or company which buys a stake in another company before making a hostile takeover bid

corporation /ˌkɔːpəˈreɪʃ(ə)n/ *noun* **1.** a large company **2.** *US* a company which is incorporated in the United States **3.** a municipal authority

corporation income tax /ˌkɔːpəreɪʃ(ə)n ˈɪnkʌm tæks/ *noun* a tax on profits made by incorporated companies

corporation loan /ˌkɔːpəˈreɪʃ(ə)n ləʊn/ *noun* a loan issued by a local authority

corporation tax /ˌkɔːpəˈreɪʃ(ə)n tæks/ *noun* a tax on profits and capital gains made by companies, calculated before dividends are paid. Abbreviation **CT**

correcting entry /kəˌrektɪŋ ˈentri/ *noun* an entry made in accounts to make something right which was previously wrong

correction /kəˈrekʃən/ *noun* an act of making something correct ○ *She made some corrections to the text of the speech.*

'…there were fears in October that shares were overvalued and bears were ready to enter the market. This only proved to be a small correction' [*Investors Chronicle*]

COSA *abbr* cost of sales adjustment

cost /kɒst/ *noun* the amount of money which has to be paid for something ○ *What is the cost of a first class ticket to New York?* ○ *Computer costs are falling each year.* ○ *We cannot afford the cost of two cars.*

cost accountant /ˈkɒst əˌkaʊntənt/ *noun* an accountant who gives managers information about their business costs

cost accounting /ˈkɒst əˌkaʊntɪŋ/ *noun* the process of preparing special accounts of manufacturing and sales costs

cost allocation /kɒst ˌæləˈkeɪʃ(ə)n/ *noun* a way in which overhead expenses are related to various cost centres

cost analysis /ˈkɒst əˌnæləsɪs/ *noun* the process of calculating in advance what a new product will cost

cost apportionment /kɒst əˈpɔːʃ(ə)nmənt/ *noun* the sharing out of common overhead costs among various cost centres

cost-benefit analysis /kɒst ˈbenɪfɪt əˌnæləsɪs/ *noun* the process of comparing the costs and benefits of various possible ways of using available resources. Also called **benefit-cost analysis**

cost centre /ˈkɒst ˌsentə/ *noun* **1.** a person or group whose costs can be itemised and to which costs can be allocated in accounts **2.** a unit, a process, or an individual that provides a service needed by another part of an organisation and whose cost is therefore accepted as an overhead of the business

cost (at cost) concept /ˌkɒst ət ˈkɒst ˌkɒnsept/ *noun* the practice of valuing assets with reference to their acquisition cost

cost-cutting /ˈkɒst ˌkʌtɪŋ/ *adjective* intended to reduce costs ○ *We have taken out the second telephone line as a cost-cutting exercise.* ■ *noun* the process of reducing costs ○ *As a result of cost-cutting, we have had to make three secretaries redundant.*

cost-effective /ˌkɒstɪ ˈfektɪv/ *adjective* giving good value when compared with the original cost ○ *We find advertising in the Sunday newspapers very cost-effective.*

cost-effectiveness /ˌkɒst ɪˈfektɪvnəs/, **cost efficiency** *noun* the quality of being cost-effective ○ *Can we calculate the cost-effectiveness of air freight against shipping by sea?*

cost factor /ˈkɒst ˌfæktə/ *noun* the problem of cost

costing /ˈkɒstɪŋ/ *noun* a calculation of the manufacturing costs, and so the selling price, of a product ○ *The costings give us a retail price of $2.95.* ○ *We cannot do the costing* *until we have details of all the production expenditure.*

costly /'kɒstlɪ/ *adjective* costing a lot of money, or costing too much money ○ *Defending the court case was a costly process.* ○ *The mistakes were time-consuming and costly.*

cost management /kɒst 'mænɪdʒmənt/ *noun* the application of management accounting concepts, methods of data collection, analysis, and presentation, in order to provide the information required to enable costs to be planned, monitored, and controlled

cost of borrowing /kɒst əv 'bɒrəʊɪŋ/ *noun* an interest rate paid on borrowed money

cost of capital /ˌkɒst əv 'kæpɪt(ə)l/ *noun* interest paid on the capital used in operating a business

cost of goods sold /ˌkɒst əv ˌgʊdz 'səʊld/ *noun* same as **cost of sales**

cost of living /ˌkɒst əv 'lɪvɪŋ/ *noun* money which has to be paid for basic items such as food, heating or rent ○ *to allow for the cost of living in the salary adjustments*

cost-of-living allowance /ˌkɒst əv 'lɪvɪŋ əˌlaʊəns/ *noun* an addition to normal salary to cover increases in the cost of living (NOTE: The US term is **COLA**.)

cost-of-living bonus /ˌkɒst əv 'lɪvɪŋ ˌbəʊnəs/ *noun* money paid to meet an increase in the cost of living

cost-of-living increase /ˌkɒst əv 'lɪvɪŋ ˌɪnkriːs/ *noun* an increase in salary to allow it to keep up with the increased cost of living

cost-of-living index /ˌkɒst əv 'lɪvɪŋ ˌɪndeks/ *noun* a way of measuring the cost of living which is shown as a percentage increase on the figure for the previous year. It is similar to the consumer price index, but includes other items such as the interest on mortgages.

cost of sales /ˌkɒst əv 'seɪlz/ *noun* all the costs of a product sold, including manufacturing costs and the staff costs of the production department, before general overheads are calculated. Also called **cost of goods sold**

cost of sales adjustment /ˌkɒst əv 'seɪlz əˌdʒʌstmənt/ *noun* an adjustment made in current cost accounting to a company's historical cost profit figure to take into account the effect of inflation on the value of materials used in production during the accounting period. If prices are rising, the

COSA will reduce historical cost profit. Abbreviation **COSA**

cost plus /ˌkɒst 'plʌs/ *noun* a system of calculating a price, by taking the cost of production of goods or services and adding a percentage to cover the supplier's overheads and margin ○ *We are charging for the work on a cost plus basis.*

cost price /'kɒst praɪs/ *noun* a selling price which is the same as the price, either the manufacturing price or the wholesale price, which the seller paid for the item

costs /kɒsts/ *plural noun* the expenses involved in a court case ○ *The judge awarded costs to the defendant.* ○ *Costs of the case will be borne by the prosecution.*

cost-volume-profit analysis /ˌkɒst ˌvɒljuːm 'prɒfɪt əˌnæləsɪs/ *noun* an analysis of the relationship between gross profit and costs of production at different selling prices and output volumes. Also called **CVP analysis**

council tax /'kaʊnsəl tæks/ *noun* a tax paid by individuals or companies to a local authority, Introduced in April 1993 as a replacement for the much maligned community charge, or 'poll tax', council tax depends on the value of the residential or commercial property occupied

count /kaʊnt/ *verb* **1.** to add figures together to make a total ○ *She counted up the sales for the six months to December.* **2.** to include something ○ *Did you count my trip to New York as part of my sales expenses?*

counter- /kaʊntə/ *prefix* against

counterbid /'kaʊntəbɪd/ *noun* a higher bid in reply to a previous bid ○ *When I bid £20 she put in a counterbid of £25.*

counter-claim /'kaʊntə kleɪm/ *noun* a claim for damages made in reply to a previous claim ○ *Jones claimed £25,000 in damages against Smith, and Smith entered a counter-claim of £50,000 for loss of office.*

counterfeit /'kaʊntəfɪt/ *adjective* referring to false or imitation money ○ *Shops in the area have been asked to look out for counterfeit £20 notes.* ■ *verb* to make imitation money

counterfoil /'kaʊntəfɔɪl/ *noun* a slip of paper kept after writing a cheque, an invoice or a receipt, as a record of the deal which has taken place

countermand /ˌkaʊntə'mɑːnd/ *verb* to say that an order must not be carried out ○ *to countermand an order* □ **to countermand an order** to say that an order must not be carried out

counter-offer /ˈkaʊntər ˌɒfə/ *noun* a higher or lower offer made in reply to another offer ○ *Smith Ltd made an offer of £1m for the property, and Blacks replied with a counter-offer of £1.4m.*

'…the company set about paring costs and improving the design of its product. It came up with a price cut of 14%, but its counter-offer – for an order that was to have provided 8% of its workload next year – was too late and too expensive' [*Wall Street Journal*]

counterparty /ˈkaʊntəpɑːti/ *noun* the other party in a deal

counterpurchase /ˈkaʊntəpɜːtʃɪs/ *noun* an international trading deal, where a company agrees to use money received on a sale to purchase goods in the country where the sale was made

countersign /ˈkaʊntəsaɪn/ *verb* to sign a document which has already been signed by someone else ○ *All our cheques have to be countersigned by the finance director.* ○ *The sales director countersigns all my orders.*

countertrade /ˈkaʊntətreɪd/ *noun* a trade which does not involve payment of money, but something such as a barter or a buy-back deal instead

countervailing duty /ˈkaʊntəveɪlɪŋ ˌdjuːti/ *noun* a duty imposed by a country on imported goods, where the price of the goods includes a subsidy from the government in the country of origin. Also called **anti-dumping duty**

counting house /ˈkaʊntɪŋ haʊs/ *noun* a department dealing with cash (*dated*)

country risk /ˈkʌntri rɪsk/ *noun* the risk associated with undertaking transactions with, or holding assets in, a particular country. Sources of risk might be political, economic, or regulatory instability affecting overseas taxation, repatriation of profits, nationalisation, currency instability, etc.

coupon /ˈkuːpɒn/ *noun* 1. a piece of paper used in place of money 2. a slip of paper attached to a government bond certificate which can be cashed to provide the annual interest

coupon rate /ˈkuːpɒn reɪt/ *noun* percentage fixed interest rate on a government bond or a debenture

coupon security /ˈkuːpɒn sɪˌkjʊərɪti/ *noun* a government security which carries a coupon and pays interest, as opposed to one which pays no interest but is sold at a discount to its face value

covenant /ˈkʌvənənt/ *noun* a legal contract ■ *verb* to agree to pay annually a specified sum of money to a person or organisation by contract. When payments are made under covenant to a charity, the charity can reclaim the tax paid by the donee. ○ *to covenant to pay £10 per annum*

cover /ˈkʌvə/ *noun* an amount of money large enough to guarantee that something can be paid for ○ *Do you have sufficient cover for this loan?* ■ *verb* 1. to provide protection by insurance against something ○ *The insurance covers fire, theft and loss of work.* □ **to cover a risk** to be protected by insurance against a risk 2. to have, earn or provide enough money to pay for something ○ *We do not make enough sales to cover the expense of running the shop.* ○ *Breakeven point is reached when sales cover all costs.* 3. to earn enough money to pay for costs, expenses, etc. ○ *We do not make enough sales to cover the expense of running the shop.* ○ *Breakeven point is reached when sales cover all costs.* 4. to ask for security against a loan which you are making

'…three export credit agencies have agreed to provide cover for large projects in Nigeria' [*Business Times (Lagos)*]

coverage /ˈkʌv(ə)rɪdʒ/ *noun* US protection guaranteed by insurance ○ *Do you have coverage against fire damage?*

'…from a PR point of view it is easier to get press coverage when you are selling an industry and not a brand' [*PR Week*]

covered bear /ˌkʌvəd ˈbeə/ *noun* a bear who holds the stock which he or she is selling

cover note /ˈkʌvə nəʊt/ *noun* a letter from an insurance company giving details of an insurance policy and confirming that the policy exists

cover price /ˈkʌvə praɪs/ *noun* the price of a newspaper or magazine which is printed on the cover and paid by the final purchaser

CP *abbr* commercial paper

CPA *abbr* certified public accountant

CPI *abbr* Consumer Price Index

creative accountancy /kriˌeɪtɪv əˈkaʊntɪŋ/, **creative accounting** *noun* an adaptation of a company's figures to present a better picture than is correct, usually intended to make a company more attractive to a potential buyer, or done for some other reason which may not be strictly legal

credit /ˈkredɪt/ *noun* 1. a period of time allowed before a customer has to pay a debt incurred for goods or services ○ *to give someone six months' credit* ○ *to sell on good credit terms* 2. an amount entered in accounts to show a decrease in assets or expenses or an increase in liabilities, revenue or capital. In accounts, credits are entered in the right-hand column. ○ *to enter £100 to someone's credit* ○ *to pay in £100 to the credit of Mr Smith*

Compare **debit** ∎ *verb* to put money into someone's account, or to note money received in an account ○ *to credit an account with £100* or *to credit £100 to an account*

credit account /ˈkredɪt əˌkaʊnt/ *noun* an account which a customer has with a shop which allows him or her to buy goods and pay for them later

credit balance /ˈkredɪt ˌbæləns/ *noun* a balance in an account showing that more money has been received than is owed ○ *The account has a credit balance of £100.*

credit bank /ˈkredɪt bæŋk/ *noun* a bank which lends money

credit card /ˈkredɪt kɑːd/ *noun* a plastic card which allows you to borrow money and to buy goods without paying for them immediately. You must pay the balance to the credit card company at a later date.

credit card holder /ˈkredɪt kɑːd ˌhəʊldə/ *noun* **1.** a person who has a credit card **2.** a plastic wallet for keeping credit cards

credit card sale /ˈkredɪt kɑːd ˌseɪl/ *noun* the act of selling where the buyer uses a credit card to pay

credit column /ˈkredɪt ˌkɒləm/ *noun* the right-hand column in accounts showing money received

credit control /ˈkredɪt kənˌtrəʊl/ *noun* a check that customers pay on time and do not owe more than their credit limit

credit controller /ˈkredɪt kənˌtrəʊlə/ *noun* a member of staff whose job is to try to get payment of overdue invoices

credit entry /ˈkredɪt ˌentri/ *noun* an entry on the credit side of an account

credit facilities /ˈkredɪt fəˌsɪlɪtiz/ *plural noun* an arrangement with a bank or supplier to have credit so as to buy goods

credit freeze /ˈkredɪt friːz/ *noun* a period when lending by banks is restricted by the government

credit limit /ˈkredɪt ˌlɪmɪt/ *noun* the largest amount of money which a customer can borrow

credit line /ˈkredɪt laɪn/ *noun* an overdraft, the amount by which a person can draw money from an account with no funds, with the agreement of the bank

credit note /ˈkredɪt nəʊt/ *noun* a note showing that money is owed to a customer ○ *The company sent the wrong order and so had to issue a credit note.* Abbreviation **C/N**

creditor /ˈkredɪtə/ *noun* a person or company that is owed money, i.e. a company's creditors are its liabilities

creditor days /ˈkredɪtə deɪs/ *noun* the number of days on average that a company requires to pay its creditors. ◊ **debtor days**

creditors /ˈkredɪtəz/ *noun* a list of all liabilities in a set of accounts, including overdrafts, amounts owing to other companies in the group, trade creditors, payments received on account for goods not yet supplied, etc.

creditors' meeting /ˈkredɪtəz ˌmiːtɪŋ/ *noun* a meeting of all the people to whom an insolvent company owes money, to decide how to obtain the money owed

credit rating /ˈkredɪt ˌreɪtɪŋ/ *noun* an amount which a credit agency feels a customer will be able to repay

credit reference /ˌkredɪt ˈref(ə)rəns/ *noun* a credit rating or other indication of the creditworthiness of a company or individual

credit report /ˌkredɪt rɪˈpɔːt/ *noun* information about an individual or entity relevant to a decision to grant credit

credit risk /ˈkredɪt rɪsk/ *noun* a risk that a borrower may not be able to repay a loan

credit side /ˈkredɪt saɪd/ *noun* the right-hand column of accounts showing money received

credit squeeze /ˈkredɪt skwiːz/ *noun* a period when lending by the banks is restricted by the government

credit union /ˈkredɪt ˌjuːnjən/ *noun* a group of people who pay in regular deposits or subscriptions which earn interest and are used to make loans to other members of the group

creditworthiness /ˈkredɪtˌwɜːðinəs/ *noun* the ability of a customer to pay for goods bought on credit

creditworthy /ˈkredɪtwɜːði/ *adjective* having enough money to be able to buy goods on credit ○ *We will do some checks on her to see if she is creditworthy.*

crisis /ˈkraɪsɪs/ *noun* a serious economic situation where decisions have to be taken rapidly ○ *a banking crisis* ○ *The government stepped in to try to resolve the international crisis.* ○ *Withdrawals from the bank have reached crisis level.*

crisis management /ˈkraɪsɪs ˌmænɪdʒmənt/ *noun* **1.** management of a business or a country's economy during a period of crisis **2.** actions taken by an organisation to protect itself when unexpected events or situations occur that could threaten its success or continued operation (NOTE: Crisis situations may result from external factors such as the development of a new product by a competitor or changes in legislation, or from internal factors such as a product failure or faulty decision-making, and often involve the need to make quick decisions on the basis of uncertain or incomplete information.)

critical-path method /ˌkrɪtɪk(ə)l ˈpɑːθ ˌmeθəd/ *noun* a technique used in project management to identify the activities within a project that are critical to its success, usually by showing on a diagram or flow chart the order in which activities must be carried out so that the project can be completed in the shortest time and at the least cost

CRO *abbr* Companies Registration Office

cross-border /ˌkrɒs ˈbɔːdə/ *adjective* from one country to another, covering several countries

cross-border services /krɒs ˌbɔːdə ˈsɜːvɪsɪz/ *plural noun* accountancy services provided by an accountancy firm in one country for a client in another country

crossed cheque /ˌkrɒst ˈtʃek/ *noun* a cheque with two lines across it showing that it can only be deposited at a bank and not exchanged for cash

cross holding /ˈkrɒs ˌhəʊldɪŋ/ *noun* a situation where two companies own shares in each other in order to stop either from being taken over ○ *The two companies have protected themselves from takeover by a system of cross holdings.*

cross out /ˌkrɒs ˈaʊt/ *verb* to put a line through something which has been written ○ *She crossed out £250 and put in £500.*

cross rate /ˈkrɒs reɪt/ *noun* an exchange rate between two currencies expressed in a third currency

cross-selling /ˌkrɒs ˈselɪŋ/ *noun* the act of selling two products which go with each other, by placing them side by side in a store

crown jewels /ˌkraʊn ˈdʒuːəlz/ *plural noun* the most valuable assets of a company, the reason why other companies may want to make takeover bids

crude petroleum /ˌkruːd pəˈtrəʊliəm/ *noun* raw petroleum which has not been processed

crystallise /ˈkrɪstəlaɪz/, **crystallize** *verb* to become chargeable on an asset ○ *a deferred gain is crystallised when you realise the gain by selling the asset*

CT *abbr* corporation tax

cum /kʌm/ *preposition* with

cum all /ˌkʌm ˈɔːl/ *adverb* including all entitlements

cum coupon /kʌm ˈkuːpɒn/ *adverb* with a coupon attached or before interest due on a security is paid

cum rights /ˌkʌm ˈraɪts/ *adverb* sold with the right to purchase new shares in a rights issue

cumulative /ˈkjuːmjʊlətɪv/ *adjective* added to regularly over a period of time

cumulative interest /ˌkjuːmjʊlətɪv ˈɪntrəst/ *noun* the interest which is added to the capital each year

cumulative preference share /ˌkjuːmjʊlətɪv ˈpref(ə)rəns ʃeə/, **cumulative preferred stock** /ˌkjuːmjʊlətɪv prɪ ˌfɜːd ˈstɒk/ *noun* a preference share which will have the dividend paid at a later date even if the company is not able to pay a dividend in the current year

cumulative weighted average cost /ˌkjuːmjʊlətɪv ˌweɪtɪd ˈæv(ə)rɪdʒ kɒst/, **cumulative weighted average price** /ˌkjuːmjʊlətɪv ˌweɪtɪd ˈæv(ə)rɪdʒ praɪs/ *noun* the average price per unit of stock delivered in a period calculated each time a new delivery is received (as opposed 'periodic weighted average')

currency /ˈkʌrənsɪ/ *noun* **1.** money in coins and notes which is used in a particular country **2.** a foreign currency, the currency of another country (NOTE: **Currency** has no plural when it refers to the money of one country: *He was arrested trying to take currency out of the country.*)

'…today's wide daily variations in exchange rates show the instability of a system based on a single currency, namely the dollar' [*Economist*]

'…the level of currency in circulation increased to N4.9 billion in the month of August' [*Business Times (Lagos)*]

currency backing /ˈkʌrənsi ˌbækɪŋ/ *noun* gold or government securities which maintain the strength of a currency

currency band /ˈkʌrənsi bænd/ *noun* the exchange rate levels between which a currency is allowed to move without full devaluation

currency basket /ˈkʌrənsi ˌbɑːskɪt/ *noun* a group of currencies, each of which is weighted, calculated together as a single unit against which another currency can be measured

currency clause /ˈkʌrənsi clɔːz/ *noun* a clause in a contract which avoids problems of payment caused by changes in exchange rates, by fixing the exchange rate for the various transactions covered by the contract

currency futures /'kʌrənsi ˌfjuːtʃəz/ plural noun purchases of foreign currency for delivery at a future date

currency hedging /'kʌrənsi ˌhedʒɪŋ/ noun a method of reducing exchange rate risk by diversifying currency holdings and adjusting them according to changes in exchange rates

currency mismatching /'kʌrənsi ˌmɪsmætʃɪŋ/ noun the activity of borrowing money in the currency of a country where interest rates are low and depositing it in the currency of a country with higher interest rates. The potential profit from the interest rate margin may be offset by changes in the exchange rates which increase the value of the loan in the company's balance sheet.

currency movements /'kʌrənsi ˌmuːvmənts/ plural noun changes in exchange rates between countries

currency note /'kʌrənsi nəʊt/ noun a bank note

currency reserves /'kʌrənsi rɪˌzɜːvz/ noun foreign money held by a government to support its own currency and to pay its debts

currency swap /'kʌrənsi swɒp/ noun **1.** an agreement to use a certain currency for payments under a contract in exchange for another currency (the two companies involved can each buy one of the currencies at a more favourable rate than the other) **2.** the buying or selling of a fixed amount of a foreign currency on the spot market, and the selling or buying of the same amount of the same currency on the forward market

current account /'kʌrənt əˌkaʊnt/ noun **1.** an account in an bank from which the customer can withdraw money when he or she wants. Current accounts do not always pay interest. ○ *to pay money into a current account* Also called **cheque account** (NOTE: The US term is **checking account**.) **2.** an account of the balance of payments of a country relating to the sale or purchase of raw materials, goods and invisibles

'…a surplus in the current account is of such vital importance to economists and currency traders because the more Japanese goods that are exported, the more dollars overseas customers have to pay for these products. That pushes up the value of the yen' [*Nikkei Weekly*]

'…customers' current deposit and current accounts also rose to $655.31 million at the end of December' [*Hongkong Standard*]

current assets /ˌkʌrənt 'æsets/ plural noun the assets used by a company in its ordinary work, e.g. materials, finished goods, cash and monies due, and which are held for a short time only

current cost /ˌkʌrənt 'kɒst/ noun the amount it would cost to replace an asset at current prices

current cost accounting /ˌkʌrənt 'kɒst əˌkaʊntɪŋ/ noun a method of accounting which notes the cost of replacing assets at current prices, rather than valuing assets at their original cost. Abbreviation **CCA**

current liabilities /ˌkʌrənt laɪəˈbɪlɪtiz/ plural noun the debts which a company has to pay within the next accounting period. In a company's annual accounts, these would be debts which must be paid within the year and are usually payments for goods or services received.

current purchasing power /ˌkʌrənt 'pɜːtʃɪsɪŋ ˌpaʊə/ noun a method of accounting which takes inflation into account by using constant monetary units (actual amounts multiplied by a general price index). Also called **constant purchasing power**

current rate of exchange /ˌkʌrənt reɪt əv ɪks'tʃeɪndʒ/ noun today's rate of exchange

current ratio /ˌkʌrənt 'reɪʃiəʊ/ noun a ratio of current assets to current liabilities showing if a company may not be able to meet its immediate debts

current year /ˌkʌrənt 'jɪə/ noun the year in which an accounting period falls ○ *Under self-assessment, income is taxed on a current year basis – i.e. it is taxed in the year in which it is received.*

current yield /ˌkʌrənt 'jiːld/ noun a dividend calculated as a percentage of the current price of a share on the stock market

curve /kɜːv/ noun a line which is not straight, e.g. a line on a graph ○ *The graph shows an upward curve.*

cushion /'kʊʃ(ə)n/ noun money which allows a company to pay interest on its borrowings or to survive a loss ○ *We have sums on deposit which are a useful cushion when cash flow is tight.*

custodian /kʌ'stəʊdiən/ noun a bank whose principal function is to maintain and grow the assets contained in a trust

custom /'kʌstəm/ noun the use of a shop by regular shoppers

customer /'kʌstəmə/ noun a person or company that buys goods ○ *The shop was full of customers.* ○ *Can you serve this customer first please?* ○ *She's a regular customer of ours.* (NOTE: The customer may not be the consumer or end user of the product.)

'…unless advertising and promotion is done in the context of an overall customer orientation, it cannot seriously be thought of as marketing' [*Quarterly Review of Marketing*]

customer service department /ˌkʌstəmə ˈsɜːvɪs dɪˌpɑːtmənt/ *noun* a department which deals with customers and their complaints and orders

customise /ˈkʌstəmaɪz/, **customize** *verb* to change something to fit the special needs of a customer ○ *We use customised computer terminals.*

customs barrier /ˈkʌstəmz ˌbæriə/ *noun* customs duty intended to make trade more difficult

customs broker /ˈkʌstəmz ˌbrəʊkə/ *noun* a person or company that takes goods through customs for a shipping company

customs clearance /ˈkʌstəmz ˌklɪərəns/ *noun* **1.** the act of passing goods through customs so that they can enter or leave the country **2.** a document given by customs to a shipper to show that customs duty has been paid and the goods can be shipped ○ *to wait for customs clearance*

customs declaration /ˈkʌstəmz deklə ˌreɪʃ(ə)n/ *noun* a statement showing goods being imported on which duty will have to be paid ○ *to fill in a customs declaration form*

customs duty /ˈkʌstəmz ˌdjuːti/ *noun* a tax on goods imported into a country

customs entry point /ˌkʌstəmz ˈentri pɔɪnt/ *noun* a place at a border between two countries where goods are declared to customs

customs examination /ˈkʌstəmz ɪg ˌzæmɪneɪʃ(ə)n/ *noun* an inspection of goods or baggage by customs officials

customs formalities /ˈkʌstəmz fɔː ˌmælɪtiz/ *plural noun* a declaration of goods by the shipper and examination of them by customs

customs officer /ˈkʌstəmz ˌɒfɪsə/ *noun* a person working for the Customs and Excise Department

customs official /ˈkʌstəmz əˌfɪʃ(ə)l/ *noun* a person working for the Customs and Excise Department

customs seal /ˈkʌstəmz siːl/ *noun* a seal attached by a customs officer to a box, to

show that the contents have not passed through customs

customs tariff /ˈkʌstəmz ˌtærɪf/ *noun* a list of taxes to be paid on imported goods

customs union /ˈkʌstəmz ˌjuːnjən/ *noun* an agreement between several countries that goods can travel between them, without paying duty, while goods from other countries have to pay special duties

cut /kʌt/ *noun* **1.** the sudden lowering of a price, salary or the number of jobs ○ *price cuts* or *cuts in prices* □ **he took a cut in salary**, **he took a salary cut** he accepted a lower salary **2.** a share in a payment ○ *She introduces new customers and gets a cut of the sales rep's commission.* ■ *verb* **1.** to lower something suddenly ○ *We are cutting prices on all our models.* ○ *We have taken out the second telephone line in order to try to cut costs.* **2.** to reduce the number of something

'…state-owned banks cut their prime rates a percentage point to 11%' [*Wall Street Journal*]

'…the US bank announced a cut in its prime from 10½ per cent to 10 per cent' [*Financial Times*]

'Opec has on average cut production by one third since 1979' [*Economist*]

cutback /ˈkʌtbæk/ *noun* a reduction ○ *cutbacks in government spending*

cut down (on) /ˌkʌt ˈdaʊn ɒn/ *verb* to reduce suddenly the amount of something used ○ *The government is cutting down on welfare expenditure.* ○ *The office is trying to cut down on electricity consumption.* ○ *We have installed networked computers to cut down on paperwork.*

cut-off /ˈkʌt ɒf/ *noun* a date and procedure for isolating the flow of cash and goods, stocktaking and the related documentation, to ensure that all aspects of a transaction are dealt with in the same financial period

CVP analysis *noun* same as **cost-volume-profit analysis**

cycle /ˈsaɪk(ə)l/ *noun* a set of events which happen in a regularly repeated sequence

cyclical factors /ˌsɪklɪk(ə)l ˈfæktəz/ *plural noun* the way in which a trade cycle affects businesses

D

D/A *abbr* deposit account

Daimyo bond /ˈdaɪmjəʊ bɒnd/ *noun* a Japanese bearer bond which can be cleared through European clearing houses

damages /ˈdæmɪdʒɪz/ *plural noun* money claimed as compensation for harm done ○ *to claim £1000 in damages* ○ *to be liable for damages* ○ *to pay £25,000 in damages*

D & B *abbr* Dun and Bradstreet

danger money /ˈdeɪndʒə ˌmʌni/ *noun* extra money paid to employees in dangerous jobs ○ *The workforce has stopped work and asked for danger money.* ○ *He decided to go to work on an oil rig because of the danger money offered as an incentive.*

data bank /ˈdeɪtə bæŋk/ *noun* a store of information in a computer

data capture /ˈdeɪtə ˌkæptʃə/, **data entry** /ˌdeɪtə ˈentri/ *noun* the act of putting information onto a computer by keyboarding or by scanning

data processing /ˌdeɪtə ˈprəʊsesɪŋ/ *noun* the act of selecting and examining data in a computer to produce information in a special form

Datastream /ˈdeɪtəstriːm/ *noun* a data system available online, giving information about securities, prices, stock exchange transactions, etc.

dated /ˈdeɪtɪd/ *adjective* with a date written on it ○ *Thank you for your letter dated June 15th.*

date of bill /ˌdeɪt əv ˈbɪl/ *noun* a date when a bill will mature

date of record /ˌdeɪt əv ˈrekɔːd/ *noun* the date when a shareholder must be registered to qualify for a dividend

date stamp /ˈdeɪt stæmp/ *noun* a stamp with rubber figures which can be moved, used for marking the date on documents

dawn raid /ˈdɔːn ˈreɪd/ *noun* a sudden planned purchase of a large number of a company's shares at the beginning of a day's trading (NOTE: Up to 15% of a company's shares may be bought in this way, and the purchaser must wait for seven days before purchasing any more shares. Sometimes a dawn raid is the first step towards a takeover of the target company.)

day book /ˈdeɪ bʊk/ *noun* a book with an account of sales and purchases made each day

day order /ˈdeɪ ˌɔːdə/ *noun* an order to a stockbroker to buy or sell on a specific day

day shift /ˈdeɪ ʃɪft/ *noun* a shift worked during the daylight hours

day trader /ˈdeɪ ˌtreɪdə/ *noun* a person who buys shares and sells them within the same day

DCF *abbr* discounted cash flow

DD *abbr* direct debit

dead account /ˌded əˈkaʊnt/ *noun* an account which is no longer used

dead loss /ˌded ˈlɒs/ *noun* a total loss ○ *The car was written off as a dead loss.*

dead money /ˌded ˈmʌni/ *noun* money which is not invested to make a profit

dead season /ˈded ˌsiːz(ə)n/ *noun* the time of year when there are few tourists about

deal /diːl/ *noun* a business agreement, affair or contract ○ *The sales director set up a deal with a Russian bank.* ○ *The deal will be signed tomorrow.* ○ *They did a deal with an American airline.* ■ *verb* to buy and sell □ **to deal in leather** *or* **options** to buy and sell leather or options

dealer /ˈdiːlə/ *noun* **1.** a person who buys and sells ○ *a used-car dealer* **2.** a person or firm that buys or sells on their own account, not on behalf of clients

dealing /ˈdiːlɪŋ/ *noun* **1.** the business of buying and selling on the Stock Exchange, commodity markets or currency markets □ **dealing for** *or* **within the account** buying shares and selling the same shares during an account, which means that the dealer has only to pay the difference between the price of the shares bought and the price obtained for them when they are sold **2.** the business of buying and selling goods

dear /dɪə/ *adjective* expensive, costing a lot of money ○ *Property is very dear in this area.*

dear money /ˈdɪə ˌmʌni/ *noun* money which has to be borrowed at a high interest rate, and so restricts expenditure by companies. Also called **tight money**

death /deθ/ *noun* the act of dying

death benefit /ˈdeθ ˌbenɪfɪt/ *noun* insurance benefit paid to the family of someone who dies in an accident at work

death in service /ˌdeθ ɪn ˈsɜːvɪs/ *noun* an insurance benefit or pension paid when someone dies while employed by a company

debenture /dɪˈbentʃə/ *noun* agreement to repay a debt with fixed interest using the company's assets as security ○ *The bank holds a debenture on the company.*

debenture bond /dɪˈbentʃə bɒnd/ *noun* US **1.** a certificate showing that a debenture has been issued **2.** an unsecured loan

debenture capital /dɪˈbentʃə ˌkæpɪt(ə)l/ *noun* a capital borrowed by a company, using its fixed assets as security

debenture holder /dɪˈbentʃə ˌhəʊldə/ *noun* a person who holds a debenture for money lent

debenture stock /dɪˈbentʃə stɒk/ *noun* a capital borrowed by a company, using its fixed assets as security

debit /ˈdebɪt/ *noun* an amount entered in accounts which shows an increase in assets or expenses or a decrease in liabilities, revenue or capital. In accounts, debits are entered in the left-hand column. Compare **credit**

debitable /ˈdebɪtəb(ə)l/ *adjective* able to be debited

debit balance /ˈdebɪt ˌbæləns/ *noun* a balance in an account showing that more money is owed than has been received ○ *Because of large payments to suppliers, the account has a debit balance of £1,000.*

debit card /ˈdebɪt kɑːd/ *noun* a plastic card, similar to a credit card, but which debits the holder's account immediately through an EPOS system

debit column /ˈdebɪt ˌkɒləm/ *noun* the left-hand column in accounts showing the money paid or owed to others

debit entry /ˈdebɪt ˌentri/ *noun* an entry on the debit side of an account

debit note /ˈdebɪt nəʊt/ *noun* a note showing that a customer owes money ○ *We undercharged Mr Smith and had to send him a debit note for the extra amount.*

debits and credits /ˌdebɪts ən ˈkredɪts/ *plural noun* money which a company owes

and money it receives, or figures which are entered in the accounts to record increases or decreases in assets, expenses, liabilities, revenue or capital

debit side /ˈdebɪt saɪd/ *noun* a left-hand column of accounts showing money owed or paid to others

debt /det/ *noun* money owed for goods or services ○ *The company stopped trading with debts of over £1 million.* □ **he is in debt to the tune of £250,000** he owes £250,000

debt collecting /ˈdet kəˌlektɪŋ/ *noun* collecting money which is owed

debt collection /ˈdet kəˌlekʃən/ *noun* the act of collecting money which is owed

debt collection agency /ˈdet kəˌlekʃən ˌeɪdʒənsi/ *noun* a company which collects debts for other companies for a commission

debt collector /ˈdet kəˌlektə/ *noun* a person who collects debts

debt counselling /ˈdet ˌkaʊnsəlɪŋ/ *noun* the work of advising people who are in debt of the best ways to arrange their finances so as to pay off their debts

debt factoring /ˈdet ˌfæktərɪŋ/ *noun* the business of buying debts at a discount. A factor collects a company's debts when due, and pays the creditor in advance part of the sum to be collected, so 'buying' the debt.

debtor /ˈdetə/ *noun* a person who owes money

debtor days /ˈdetə deɪs/ *noun* the number of days on average that it takes a company to receive payment for what it sells. ◊ **creditor days**

debtors /ˈdetəz/ *noun* all money owed to a company as shown in the accounts

debtors control account /ˌdetəz kən ˈtrəʊl əˌkaʊnt/ *noun* an account used to summarise the balances on the individual sales ledger accounts

debtor side /ˈdetə saɪd/ *noun* the debit side of an account

debtors ledger /ˌdetəz ˈledʒə/ *noun* sales ledger

debtors turnover ratio /ˌdetəz ˈtɜːnəʊvə ˌreɪʃiəʊ/ *noun* the average time which debtors take to pay

debt ratio /ˈdet ˌreɪʃiəʊ/ *noun* the debts of a company shown as a percentage of its equity plus loan capital

debt rescheduling /ˈdet riːˌʃedjuːlɪŋ/ *noun* FINANCE, BANKING, AND ACCOUNTING, GENERAL MANAGEMENT the process of reorganising the way in which debts are repaid. Debt rescheduling may be necessary if a company is unable to pay its debts and may involve postponing debt payments, postponing payment of interest, or negotiating a new loan.

decile /'desaɪl/ *noun* one of a series of nine figures below which one tenth or several tenths of the total fall

decimalisation /ˌdesɪm(ə)laɪ'zeɪʃ(ə)n/, **decimalization** *noun* the process of changing to a decimal system

decimalise /'desɪm(ə)laɪz/, **decimalize** *verb* to change something to a decimal system

decimal point /ˌdesɪm(ə)l 'pɔɪnt/ *noun* a dot which indicates the division between the whole unit and its smaller parts, e.g. 4.75

decimal system /'desɪm(ə)l ˌsɪstəm/ *noun* a system of mathematics based on the number 10

decision support system /dɪˌsɪʒ(ə)n sə'pɔːt ˌsɪstəm/ *noun* a computer-based system which presents auditor judgements in a structured way and can be used to create audit programmes or document the assessment of business risk

decision tree /dɪ'sɪʒ(ə)n triː/ *noun* a model for decision-making, showing the possible outcomes of different decisions ○ *This computer programme incorporates a decision tree.*

declaration /ˌdeklə'reɪʃ(ə)n/ *noun* an official statement

declaration date /ˌdeklə'reɪʃ(ə)n deɪt/ *noun US* the date on which a board of directors declares the dividend to be paid

declaration of bankruptcy /ˌdekləreɪʃ(ə)n əv 'bæŋkrʌptsi/ *noun* an official statement that someone is bankrupt

declaration of solvency /ˌdeklə ˌreɪʃ(ə)n əv 'sɒlv(ə)nsi/ *noun* a document, lodged with the Registrar of Companies, that lists the assets and liabilities of a company seeking voluntary liquidation to show that the company is capable of repaying its debts within 12 months

declare /dɪ'kleə/ *verb* to make an official statement of something, or announce something to the public ○ *to declare someone bankrupt* ○ *The company declared an interim dividend of 10p per share.*

declared /dɪ'kleəd/ *adjective* having been made public or officially stated

declared value /dɪˌkleəd 'vælju:/ *noun* the value of goods entered on a customs declaration

decline /dɪ'klaɪn/ *verb* to fall slowly or decrease ○ *Shares declined in a weak market.* ○ *New job applications have declined over the*

last year. ○ *The economy declined during the last government.* ○ *The purchasing power of the pound declined over the decade.*

'Saudi oil production has declined by three quarters to around 2.5m barrels a day' [*Economist*]

'...this gives an average monthly decline of 2.15 per cent during the period' [*Business Times (Lagos)*]

'...share prices disclosed a weak tendency right from the onset of business and declined further, showing losses over a broad front' [*The Hindu*]

declining balance method /dɪˌklaɪnɪŋ 'bæləns ˌmeθəd/ *noun US* same as **reducing balance method**

decrease /dɪ'kriːs/ *verb* to fall or to become less ○ *Imports are decreasing.* ○ *The value of the pound has decreased by 5%.*

deduct /dɪ'dʌkt/ *verb* to take money away from a total ○ *to deduct £3 from the price* ○ *to deduct a sum for expenses* ○ *After deducting costs the gross margin is only 23%.* ○ *Expenses are still to be deducted.*

deductible /dɪ'dʌktɪb(ə)l/ *adjective* possible to deduct

deduction /dɪ'dʌkʃən/ *noun* the removing of money from a total, or the amount of money removed from a total ○ *Net salary is salary after deduction of tax and social security.* ○ *The deduction from her wages represented the cost of repairing the damage she had caused to the machinery.* □ **deductions from salary** *or* **salary deductions** *or* **deductions at source** money which a company removes from salaries to give to the government as tax, national insurance contributions, etc.

deed /diːd/ *noun* a legal document or written agreement

deed of arrangement /ˌdiːd əv ə'reɪndʒmənt/ *noun* agreement made between a debtor and creditors whereby the creditors accept an agreed sum in settlement of their claim rather than make the debtor bankrupt

deed of assignment /ˌdiːd əv ə'saɪnmənt/ *noun* a document which legally transfers a property from a debtor to a creditor

deed of covenant /ˌdiːd əv 'kʌvənənt/ *noun* a legal document in which a person or organisation promises to pay a third party a sum of money on an annual basis. In certain countries this arrangement may have tax advantages. For example, in the United Kingdom, it is often used for making regular payments to a charity.

deed of partnership /ˌdiːd əv 'pɑːtnəʃɪp/ *noun* agreement which sets up a partnership

deed of transfer /ˌdiːd əv ˈtrænsfɜː/ *noun* a document which transfers the ownership of shares

deep discount /ˌdiːp ˈdɪskaʊnt/ *noun* a very large discount

'…when it needed to make its financial results look good, it shipped a lot of inventory. It did this by offering deep discounts to distributors' [*Forbes*]

deep discounted bonds /diːp ˌdɪskaʊntɪd ˈbɒndz/ *plural noun* Eurobonds which are issued at a very large discount but which do not produce any interest

deep pocket /ˌdiːp ˈpɒkɪt/ *noun* company which provides finance for another

defalcation /ˌdiːfælˈkeɪʃ(ə)n/ *noun* an illegal use of money by someone who is not the owner but who has been trusted to look after it

default /dɪˈfɔːlt/ *noun* a failure to carry out the terms of a contract, especially failure to pay back a debt ■ *verb* to fail to carry out the terms of a contract, especially to fail to pay back a debt ○ *There was a major financial crisis when the bank defaulted.*

defaulter /dɪˈfɔːltə/ *noun* a person who defaults

default notice /dɪˌfɔːlt ˈnəʊtɪs/ *noun* a formal document issued by a lender to a borrower who is in default (NOTE: The US term is **notice of default**.)

defence counsel /dɪˈfens ˌkaʊnsəl/ *noun* a lawyer who represents the defendant in a lawsuit

defer /dɪˈfɜː/ *verb* to put back to a later date, to postpone ○ *We will have to defer payment until January.* ○ *The decision has been deferred until the next meeting.* (NOTE: **deferring – deferred**)

deferment /dɪˈfɜːmənt/ *noun* the act of leaving until a later date ○ *deferment of payment* ○ *deferment of a decision*

deferred /dɪˈfɜːd/ *adjective* put back to a later date

deferred consideration /dɪˌfɜːd kənˌsɪdəˈreɪʃ(ə)n/ *noun* instalment payments for the acquisition of new subsidiaries usually made in the form of cash and shares, where the balance due after the initial deposit depends on the performance of the business acquired

deferred creditor /dɪˌfɜːd ˈkredɪtə/ *noun* a person who is owed money by a bankrupt but who is paid only after all other creditors

deferred expenditure /dɪˌfɜːd ɪkˈspendɪtʃə/ *noun* expenditure incurred now but reflected in the accounts of future years

deferred payment /dɪˌfɜːd ˈpeɪmənt/ *noun* **1.** money paid later than the agreed date **2.** payment for goods by instalments over a long period

deferred payments /dɪˌfɜːd ˈpeɪməntz/ *noun* money paid later than the agreed date ○ *The company agreed to defer payments for three months.*

deferred revenue /dɪˌfɜːd ˈrevənjuː/ *noun* revenue carried forward to future accounting periods

deferred tax /dɪˌfɜːd ˈtæks/ *noun* a tax which may become payable at some later date

deficiency /dɪˈfɪʃ(ə)nsi/ *noun* a lack of something, or the amount by which something, e.g. a sum of money, is less than it should be ○ *There is a £10 deficiency in the petty cash.*

deficit /ˈdefɪsɪt/ *noun* the amount by which spending is higher than income

deficit financing /ˈdefɪsɪt ˌfaɪnænsɪŋ/ *noun* a type of financial planning by a government in which it borrows money to cover the difference between its tax income and its expenditure

deflation /diːˈfleɪʃ(ə)n/ *noun* a general reduction in economic activity as a result of a reduced supply of money and credit, leading to lower prices ○ *The oil crisis resulted in worldwide deflation.* Opposite **inflation**

'…the reluctance of people to spend is one of the main reasons behind 26 consecutive months of price deflation, a key economic ill that has led to price wars, depressed the profit margins of state enterprises and hit incomes among the rural population' [*Financial Times*]

deflationary /diːˈfleɪʃ(ə)n(ə)ri/ *adjective* causing deflation ○ *The government has introduced some deflationary measures in the budget.*

'…the strong dollar's deflationary impact on European economies as national governments push up interest rates' [*Duns Business Month*]

deflator /diːˈfleɪtə/ *noun* the amount by which a country's GNP is reduced to take inflation into account

degearing /diːˈɡɪərɪŋ/ *noun* a reduction in gearing, reducing a company's loan capital in relation to the value of its ordinary shares

degressive tax /rɪˌɡresɪv ˈtæk/ *noun* a tax whose payments depend on an individual's salary. Those on smaller salaries pay a lower percentage their income than those with larger salaries.

del credere /ˌdel ˈkreɪdəri/ *noun* an amount added to a charge to cover the possibility of not being paid

del credere agent /del ˈkreɪdəri ˌeɪdʒənt/ *noun* an agent who receives a high commission because he or she guarantees payment by customers

delinquency /dɪˈlɪŋkwənsi/ *noun US* the fact of being overdue in payment of an account, an interest payment, etc.

delinquent /dɪˈlɪŋkwənt/ *adjective US* referring to an account or payment of tax which is overdue

deliver /dɪˈlɪvə/ *verb* to transport goods to a customer □ **goods delivered free** *or* **free delivered goods** goods transported to the customer's address at a price which includes transport costs □ **goods delivered on board** goods transported free to the ship or plane but not to the customer's warehouse

delivered price /dɪˈlɪvəd praɪs/ *noun* a price which includes packing and transport

delivery /dɪˈlɪv(ə)ri/ *noun* **1.** a consignment of goods being delivered ○ *We take in three deliveries a day.* ○ *There were four items missing in the last delivery.* **2.** the transport of a commodity to a purchaser **3.** the transfer of a bill of exchange or other negotiable instrument to the bank which is due to make payment

delivery month /dɪˈlɪv(ə)ri mʌnθ/ *noun* a month in a futures contract when actual delivery will take place

delivery note /dɪˈlɪv(ə)ri nəʊt/ *noun* a list of goods being delivered, given to the customer with the goods

delivery of goods /dɪˌlɪv(ə)ri əv ˈɡʊdz/ *noun* the transport of goods to a customer's address

delivery order /dɪˈlɪv(ə)ri ˌɔːdə/ *noun* the instructions given by the customer to the person holding her goods, to tell her where and when to deliver them

delivery time /dɪˈlɪv(ə)ri taɪm/ *noun* the number of days before something will be delivered

delivery van /dɪˈlɪv(ə)ri væn/ *noun* a van for delivering goods to customers

demand /dɪˈmɑːnd/ *noun* **1.** an act of asking for payment **2.** an act of asking for something and insisting on getting it ○ *the union's list of demands* ○ *The management refused to give in to union demands for a meeting.* ■ *verb* **1.** the need that customers have for a product or their eagerness to buy it ○ *There was an active demand for oil shares on the stock market.* ○ *The factory had to cut production when demand slackened.* ○ *The office cleaning company cannot keep up with the demand for its services.* □ **this book is in**

great demand *or* **there is a great demand for this book** many people want to buy it □ **to meet** *or* **fill a demand** to supply what is needed ○ *The factory had to increase production to meet the extra demand.* **2.** to ask for something and expect to get it ○ *She demanded a refund.* ○ *The suppliers are demanding immediate payment of their outstanding invoices.* ○ *The shop stewards demanded an urgent meeting with the managing director.*

'…spot prices are now relatively stable in the run-up to the winter's peak demand' [*Economist*]

'…the demand for the company's products remained strong throughout the first six months of the year with production and sales showing significant increases' [*Business Times (Lagos)*]

'…growth in demand is still coming from the private rather than the public sector' [*Lloyd's List*]

demand bill /dɪˈmɑːnd bɪl/ *noun* a bill of exchange which must be paid when payment is asked for

demand price /dɪˈmɑːnd praɪs/ *noun* the price at which a quantity of goods will be bought

demerge /diːˈmɜːdʒ/ *verb* to separate a company into several separate parts

demerger /diːˈmɜːdʒə/ *noun* the separation of a company into several separate parts, especially used of companies which have grown by acquisition

demise /dɪˈmaɪz/ *noun* **1.** a death ○ *On his demise the estate passed to his daughter.* **2.** the act of granting a property on a lease

demonetisation /diːˌmʌnɪtaɪˈzeɪʃ(ə)n/, **demonetization** *noun* the act of stopping a coin or note being used as money

demonetise /diːˈmʌnɪtaɪz/, **demonetize** *verb* to stop a coin or note being used as money

demurrage /dɪˈmʌrɪdʒ/ *noun* money paid to a customer when a shipment is delayed at a port or by customs

demutualisation /diːˌmjuːtjuəlaɪˈzeɪʃ(ə)n/, **demutualization** *noun* the process by which a mutual society, such as a building society, becomes a publicly owned corporation

demutualise /diːˈmjuːtjuəlaɪz/, **demutualize** /diːˈmjuːtʃuəˌlaɪz/ *verb* to stop having mutual status, by becoming a Plc and selling shares to the general public on the stock market

denomination /dɪˌnɒmɪˈneɪʃ(ə)n/ *noun* a unit of money on a coin, banknote or stamp ○ *We collect coins of all denominations for charity.* ○ *Small denomination notes are not often counterfeited.*

departmental /ˌdiːpɑːt'ment(ə)l/ *adjective* referring to a department

departmental accounts /ˌdiːpɑːtment(ə)l ə'kaʊnts/ *plural noun* accounts which analyse the sales of different departments or products of a company

Department of Trade and Industry /dɪˌpɑːtmənt əv ˌtreɪd ənd 'ɪndəstri/ *noun* a British government department which deals with areas such as commerce, international trade and the stock exchange. Abbreviation **DTI**

deposit /dɪ'pɒzɪt/ *noun* **1.** money placed in a bank for safe keeping or to earn interest **2.** money given in advance so that the thing which you want to buy will not be sold to someone else ○ *to pay a deposit on a watch* ○ *to leave £10 as deposit* ■ *verb* **1.** to put documents somewhere for safe keeping ○ *to deposit shares with a bank* ○ *We have deposited the deeds of the house with the bank.* ○ *He deposited his will with his solicitor.* **2.** to put money into a bank account ○ *to deposit £100 in a current account*

deposit account /dɪ'pɒzɪt əˌkaʊnt/ *noun* a bank account which pays interest but on which notice has to be given to withdraw money. Abbreviation **D/A**

depositary /dɪ'pɒzɪtəri/ *noun US* a person or corporation which can place money or documents for safekeeping with a depository. ◊ **American Depositary Receipt** (NOTE: Do not confuse with **depository**.)

depositor /dɪ'pɒzɪtə/ *noun* a person who deposits money in a bank, building society, etc.

depository /dɪ'pɒzɪt(ə)ri/ *noun* a person or company with whom money or documents can be deposited (NOTE: Do not confuse with **depositary**.)

deposit slip /dɪ'pɒzɪt slɪp/ *noun* a piece of paper stamped by the cashier to prove that you have paid money into your account

deposit-taking institution /dɪˌpɒzɪt ˌteɪkɪŋ ˌɪnstɪ'tjuːʃ(ə)n/, **depository institution** /dɪˌpɒzɪt(ə)ri ˌɪnstɪ'tjuːʃ(ə)n/ *noun* an institution which is licensed to receive money on deposit from private individuals and to pay interest on it, e.g. a building society, bank or friendly society

depreciable /dɪ'priːʃiəb(ə)l/ *adjective* possible to depreciate

depreciable asset /dɪˌpriːʃiəb(ə)l 'æset/ *noun* an asset which will be used over more than one accounting period, but which has a limited life and so can be depreciated

depreciate /dɪ'priːʃieɪt/ *verb* **1.** to reduce the value of assets in accounts ○ *We depreciate our company cars over three years.* **2.** to lose value ○ *a share which has depreciated by 10% over the year* ○ *The pound has depreciated by 5% against the dollar.*

'...this involved reinvesting funds on items which could be depreciated against income for three years' [*Australian Financial Review*]

'...buildings are depreciated at two per cent per annum on the estimated cost of construction' [*Hongkong Standard*]

'...the euro's downward drift sparked alarmed reactions from the European Central Bank which has seen the new currency depreciate by almost 15% since its launch' [*Times*]

depreciation /dɪˌpriːʃi'eɪʃ(ə)n/ *noun* **1.** a reduction in value of an asset **2.** a loss of value ○ *a share which has shown a depreciation of 10% over the year* ○ *the depreciation of the pound against the dollar*

depreciation rate /dɪˌpriːʃi'eɪʃ(ə)n reɪt/ *noun* the rate at which an asset is depreciated each year in the company accounts

depress /dɪ'pres/ *verb* to reduce something ○ *Reducing the money supply has the effect of depressing demand for consumer goods.*

depressed market /dɪˌprest 'mɑːkɪt/ *noun* a market where there are more goods than customers

deregulate /diː'regjʊleɪt/ *verb* to remove government controls from an industry ○ *The US government deregulated the banking sector in the 1980s.*

deregulation /diːˌregjʊ'leɪʃ(ə)n/ *noun* the reduction of government control over an industry ○ *the deregulation of the airlines*

'...after the slump in receipts last year that followed liner shipping deregulation in the US, carriers are probably still losing money on their transatlantic services. But with a possible contraction in capacity and healthy trade growth, this year has begun in a much more promising fashion than last' [*Lloyd's List*]

derivative instruments /dɪˌrɪvətɪv 'ɪnstrʊmənts/, **derivatives** /dɪ'rɪvətɪvz/ *plural noun* any forms of traded security such as option contracts, which are derived from ordinary bonds and shares, exchange rates or stock market indices

designated account /ˌdezɪgneɪtɪd ə'kaʊnt/ *noun* an account opened and held in one person's name, but which also features another person's name for extra identification purposes

devaluation /ˌdiːvæljuː'eɪʃ(ə)n/ *noun* a reduction in the value of a currency against other currencies ○ *the devaluation of the rand*

devalue /diːˈvæljuː/ *verb* to reduce the value of a currency against other currencies ○ *The pound has been devalued by 7%.*

development costs /dɪˈveləpmənt kɒsts/ *plural noun* costs of developing new or improved products

devise /dɪˈvaɪz/ *noun* the act of giving freehold land to someone in a will ■ *verb* to give freehold property to someone in a will

devisee /dɪvaɪˈziː/ *noun* a person who receives freehold property in a will

differential /ˌdɪfəˈrenʃəl/ *adjective* showing a difference

differential tariffs /ˌdɪfərenʃəl ˈtærɪfs/ *plural noun* different tariffs for different classes of goods as, e.g., when imports from some countries are taxed more heavily than similar imports from other countries

digit /ˈdɪdʒɪt/ *noun* a single number ○ *a seven-digit phone number*

digital analysis /ˌdɪdʒɪt(ə)l əˈnæləsɪs/ *noun* auditing techniques that investigate the digits in accounting numbers to reveal fraud and error

digital computer /ˌdɪdʒɪt(ə)l kəmˈpjuːtə/ *noun* a computer which calculates on the basis of numbers

dilution of shareholding /daɪˌluːʃ(ə)n əv ˈʃeəhəʊldɪŋ/ *noun* a situation where the ordinary share capital of a company has been increased, but without an increase in the assets so that each share is worth less than before (NOTE: The US term is **stockholding**.)

dime /daɪm/ *noun US* ten cent coin (*informal*)

diminish /dɪˈmɪnɪʃ/ *verb* to become smaller ○ *Our share of the market has diminished over the last few years.*

direct cost /daɪˌrekt ˈkɒst/ *noun* a cost which can be directly related to the making of a product, i.e. its production cost

direct cost variance /daɪˌrekt kɒst ˈveəriəns/ *noun* the difference between the planned direct costs for a product and the actual direct costs

direct debit /daɪˌrekt ˈdebɪt/ *noun* a system where a customer allows a company to charge costs to his or her bank account automatically and where the amount charged can be increased or decreased with the agreement of the customer ○ *I pay my electricity bill by direct debit.* Abbreviation **DD**

direct expenses /daɪˌrekt ɪkˈspensɪz/ *plural noun* expenses excluding materials, labour or purchase of stock for resale which are incurred in making a product

directional testing /daɪˌrekʃən(ə)l ˈtestɪŋ/ *noun* an auditing technique by which work is reduced by testing debits only for overstatement and credits only for understatement

directive /daɪˈrektɪv/ *noun* an order or command to someone to do something, especially an order from the Council of Ministers or Commission of the European Union referring to a particular problem ○ *The Commission issued a directive on food prices.*

direct labour costs /daɪˌrekt ˈleɪbə ˌkɒsts/ *noun* the cost of the employees employed which can be allocated to a product, not including materials or overheads

direct mail /daɪˌrekt ˈmeɪl/ *noun* the practice of selling a product by sending publicity material to possible buyers through the post ○ *These calculators are only sold by direct mail.* ○ *The company runs a successful direct-mail operation.*

'…all of those who had used direct marketing techniques had used direct mail, 79% had used some kind of telephone technique and 63% had tried off-the-page selling' [*Precision marketing*]

direct-mail advertising /daɪˌrekt meɪl ˈædvətaɪzɪŋ/ *noun* advertising by sending leaflets to people through the post

direct materials cost /daɪˌrekt mə ˈtɪəriəls kɒst/ *noun* the cost of the materials which are used in making a product and for which costs can be directly related to that product

directorate /daɪˈrekt(ə)rət/ *noun* a group of directors

director's fees /daɪˈrektəz fiːz/ *plural noun* money paid to a director for attendance at board meetings

directorship /daɪˈrektəʃɪp/ *noun* the post of director ○ *She was offered a directorship with Smith Ltd.*

'…what benefits does the executive derive from his directorship? In the first place compensation has increased sharply in recent years' [*Duns Business Month*]

directors' report /daɪˌrektəz rɪˈpɔːt/ *noun* the annual report from the board of directors to the shareholders

direct product profitability /daɪˌrekt ˌprɒdʌkt ˌprɒfɪtəˈbɪlɪti/ *noun* used primarily within the retail sector, DPP involves the attribution of costs other than the purchase price (e.g., distribution, warehousing, retailing) to each product line. Thus a net profit, as opposed to a gross profit, can be identified for each product.

direct selling /daɪˌrekt ˈselɪŋ/ *noun* the work of selling a product direct to the customer without going through a shop

direct share ownership /daɪˌrekt ˈʃeə ˌəʊnəʃɪp/ *noun* the ownership of shares by private individuals, buying or selling through brokers, and not via holdings in unit trusts

direct tax /daɪˌrekt ˈtæks/ *noun* a tax paid directly to the government, e.g. income tax

direct taxation /daɪˌrekt tækˈseɪʃ(ə)n/ *noun* a tax which is paid direct to the government, e.g. income tax ○ *The government raises more money by direct taxation than by indirect.*

dirty float /ˈdɜːti fləʊt/ *noun* a process of floating a currency, where the government intervenes to regulate the exchange rate

disallow /ˌdɪsəˈlaʊ/ *verb* not to accept a claim for insurance ○ *She claimed £2,000 for fire damage, but the claim was disallowed.*

disallowable /ˌdɪsəˈlaʊəb(ə)l/ *adjective* not able to be allowed for tax relief ○ *The use of a car for private travel is a disallowable expense.* Opposite **allowable**

disburse /dɪsˈbɜːs/ *verb* to pay money

disbursement /dɪsˈbɜːsmənt/ *noun* the payment of money

discharge *noun* /ˈdɪstʃɑːdʒ/ **1.** a payment of debt □ **in full discharge of a debt** as full payment of a debt **2.** □ **in discharge of her duties as director** while carrying out her duties as director ■ *verb* /dɪsˈtʃɑːdʒ/ **1.** □ **to discharge a bankrupt** to release someone from bankruptcy because they have has paid their debts **2.** □ **to discharge a debt, to discharge your liabilities** to pay a debt or your liabilities in full **3.** to dismiss an employee ○ *to discharge an employee for negligence*

discharged bankrupt /dɪsˌtʃɑːdʒd ˈbæŋkrʌpt/ *noun* a person who has been released from being bankrupt because his or her debts have been paid

disclaimer /dɪsˈkleɪmə/ *noun* a legal refusal to accept responsibility

disclose /dɪsˈkləʊz/ *verb* to tell something that was previously unknown to other people or secret ○ *The bank has no right to disclose details of my account to the tax office.*

disclosure /dɪsˈkləʊʒə/ *noun* the act of telling something that was previously unknown to other people or secret ○ *The disclosure of the takeover bid raised the price of the shares.*

disclosure of shareholding /dɪsˌkləʊʒər əv ˈʃeəhəʊldɪŋ/ *noun* the act of making public the fact that someone owns shares in a company

discount *noun* /ˈdɪskaʊnt/ **1.** the percentage by which the seller reduces the full price for the buyer ○ *to give a discount on bulk purchases* □ **to sell goods at a discount** *or* at **a discount price** to sell goods below the normal price □ **10% discount for cash** *or* **10% cash discount** you pay 10% less if you pay in cash **2.** the amount by which something is sold for less than its value ■ *verb* /dɪsˈkaʊnt/ **1.** to reduce prices to increase sales **2.** □ **to discount bank bills, to re-discount bank bills** to buy bills, issued by banks, at less than their face value (the Central Bank buys the bills and in this way is able to provide the banks with cash) **3.** to react to something which may happen in the future, such as a possible takeover bid or currency devaluation

'…pressure on the Federal Reserve Board to ease monetary policy and possibly cut its discount rate mounted yesterday' [*Financial Times*]

'…banks refrained from quoting forward US/Hong-kong dollar exchange rates as premiums of 100 points replaced the previous day's discounts of up to 50 points' [*South China Morning Post*]

discountable /ˈdɪskaʊntəb(ə)l/ *adjective* possible to discount ○ *These bills are not discountable.*

discount broker /ˈdɪskaʊnt ˌbrəʊkə/ *noun* a broker who charges a lower commission than other brokers

discounted cash flow /ˌdɪskaʊntɪd ˈkæʃ fləʊ/ *noun* the calculation of the forecast return on capital investment by discounting future cash flows from the investment, usually at a rate equivalent to the company's minimum required rate of return. Abbreviation **DCF**

discounted value /ˌdɪskaʊntɪd ˈvæljuː/ *noun* the difference between the face value of a share and its lower market price

discounter /ˈdɪskaʊntə/ *noun* a person or company that discounts bills or invoices, or sells goods at a discount

'…invoice discounting is an instant finance raiser. Cash is advanced by a factor or discounter against the value of invoices sent out by the client company. Debt collection is still in the hands of the client company, which also continues to run its own bought ledger' [*Times*]

'…a 100,000 square-foot warehouse generates ten times the volume of a discount retailer; it can turn its inventory over 18 times a year, more than triple a big discounter's turnover' [*Duns Business Month*]

discount house /ˈdɪskaʊnt haʊs/ *noun* **1.** a financial company which specialises in discounting bills **2.** a shop which specialises in selling cheap goods bought at a high discount

discount price /ˈdɪskaʊnt praɪs/ *noun* the full price less a discount

discount rate /ˈdɪskaʊnt reɪt/ *noun* the rate charged by a central bank on any loans it makes to other banks

discount store /'dɪskaʊnt stɔː/ *noun* a shop which specialises in cheap goods bought at a high discount

discrepancy /dɪ'skrepənsi/ *noun* a situation where figures are not correct

discretion /dɪ'skreʃ(ə)n/ *noun* the ability to decide what should be done

discretionary /dɪ'skreʃ(ə)n(ə)ri/ *adjective* possible if someone wants

discretionary account /dɪ‚skreʃ(ə)n(ə)ri ə'kaʊnt/ *noun* a client's account with a stockbroker, where the broker invests and sells at his or her own discretion without the client needing to give him specific instructions

discretionary client /dɪ‚skreʃ(ə)n(ə)ri 'klaɪənt/ *noun* a client whose funds are managed on a discretionary basis

discretionary funds /dɪ‚skreʃ(ə)n(ə)ri 'fʌndz/ *plural noun* funds managed on a discretionary basis

discretionary trust /dɪ‚skreʃ(ə)n(ə)ri 'trʌst/ *noun* a trust where the trustees decide how to invest the income and when and how much income should be paid to the beneficiaries

diseconomies of scale /dɪsɪ‚kɒnəmiz əv 'skeɪl/ *plural noun* a situation where increased production leads to a higher production cost per unit or average production cost

disequilibrium /‚dɪsiːkwɪ'lɪbriəm/ *noun* an imbalance in the economy when supply does not equal demand

dishonoured cheque /dɪs‚ɒnəd 'tʃek/ *noun* a cheque which the bank will not pay because there is not enough money in the account to pay it

disinvest /‚dɪsɪn'vest/ *verb* to reduce investment by not replacing capital assets when they wear out

disinvestment /‚dɪsɪn'vestmənt/ *noun* a reduction in capital assets by not replacing them when they wear out

disk drive /'dɪsk draɪv/ *noun* a part of a computer which makes a disk spin round in order to read it or store information on it

dispatch /dɪ'spætʃ/ *verb* to send goods to customers ○ *The goods were dispatched last Friday.*

dispatch note /dɪ'spætʃ nəʊt/ *noun* a note saying that goods have been sent

dispensation /‚dɪspen'seɪʃ(ə)n/ *noun* arrangement between an employer and the Inland Revenue by which business expenses paid to an employee are not declared for tax

disposable personal income /dɪ‚spəʊzəb(ə)l ‚pɜːs(ə)nəl 'ɪnkʌm/ *noun* the income left after tax and national insurance have been deducted. Also called **take-home pay**

disposal /dɪ'spəʊz(ə)l/ *noun* a sale ○ *a disposal of securities* ○ *The company has started a systematic disposal of its property portfolio.* □ **lease** or **business for disposal** a lease or business for sale

disqualification /dɪs‚kwɒlɪfɪ'keɪʃ(ə)n/ *noun* **1.** the act of making someone disqualified to do something **2.** a court order which forbids a person from being a director of a company. A variety of offences, even those termed as 'administrative', can result in some being disqualified for up to five years.

'Even 'administrative offences' can result in disqualification. A person may be disqualified for up to five years following persistent breach of company legislation in terms of failing to file returns, accounts and other documents with the Registrar' [*Accountancy*]

disqualify /dɪs'kwɒlɪfaɪ/ *verb* to make a person unqualified to do something, such as to be a director of a company

dissolution /‚dɪsə'luːʃ(ə)n/ *noun* the ending of a partnership

dissolve /dɪ'zɒlv/ *verb* to bring to an end ○ *to dissolve a partnership*

distrain /dɪ'streɪn/ *verb* to seize goods to pay for debts

distress /dɪ'stres/ *noun* the act of taking someone's goods to pay for debts

distress merchandise /dɪ'stres ‚mɜːtʃəndaɪs/ *noun US* goods sold cheaply to pay a company's debts

distress sale /dɪ'stres seɪl/ *noun* a sale of goods at low prices to pay a company's debts

distributable /dɪs'trɪbjʊtəb(ə)l/ *adjective* possible to distribute

distributable profits /dɪs‚trɪbjʊtəb(ə)l 'prɒfɪts/ *plural noun* profits which can be distributed to shareholders as dividends if the directors decide to do so

distribute /dɪ'strɪbjuːt/ *verb* **1.** to share out dividends ○ *Profits were distributed among the shareholders.* **2.** to send out goods from a manufacturer's warehouse to retail shops ○ *Smith Ltd distributes for several smaller companies.* ○ *All orders are distributed from our warehouse near Oxford.*

distributed profits /dɪ‚strɪbjʊtɪd 'prɒfɪts/ *plural noun* profits passed to shareholders in the form of dividends

distribution /‚dɪstrɪ'bjuːʃ(ə)n/ *noun* the act of sending goods from the manufacturer to the wholesaler and then to retailers ○ *Stock is held in a distribution centre which deals with all order processing.* ○ *Distribution* *costs have risen sharply over the last 18 months.* ○ *She has several years' experience as distribution manager.*

'British distribution companies are poised to capture a major share of the European market' [*Management News*]

distribution cost /ˌdɪstrɪˈbjuːʃ(ə)n kɒst/, **distribution expense** /ˌdɪstrɪˌbjuːʃ(ə)n ɪkˈspens/, **distribution overhead** /ˌdɪstrɪˌbjuːʃ(ə)n ˈəʊvəhed/ *noun* expenditure involved in warehousing, packing and sending stocks for sale

distribution network /ˌdɪstrɪˈbjuːʃ(ə)n ˌnetwɜːk/ *noun* a series of points or small warehouses from which goods are sent all over a country

distribution of income /ˌdɪstrɪbjuːʃ(ə)n əv ˈɪnkʌm/ *noun* payment of dividends to shareholders

distribution slip /ˌdɪstrɪˈbjuːʃ(ə)n slɪp/ *noun* a paper attached to a document or to a magazine, showing all the people in an office who should read it

distributor /dɪˈstrɪbjʊtə/ *noun* a company which sells goods for another company which makes them

distributorship /dɪˈstrɪbjʊtəʃɪp/ *noun* the position of being a distributor for a company

District Bank /ˌdɪstrɪkt ˈbæŋk/ *noun* one of the 12 US banks that make up the Federal Reserve System. Each District Bank is responsible for all banking activity in its area.

diversification /daɪˌvɜːsɪfɪˈkeɪʃ(ə)n/ *noun* the process of adding another quite different type of business to a firm's existing trade

diversify /daɪˈvɜːsɪfaɪ/ *verb* **1.** to add new types of business to existing ones ○ *The company is planning to diversify into new products.* **2.** to invest in different types of shares or savings so as to spread the risk of loss

divestiture /daɪˈvestɪtʃə/ *noun* a sale of an asset

dividend /ˈdɪvɪdend/ *noun* a percentage of profits paid to shareholders □ **to raise** *or* **increase the dividend** to pay out a higher dividend than in the previous year □ **to omit** *or* **pass the dividend** to pay no dividend

dividend cover /ˈdɪvɪdend ˌkʌvə/ *noun* the ratio of profits to dividends paid to shareholders

dividend forecast /ˈdɪvɪdend ˌfɔːkɑːst/ *noun* a forecast of the amount of an expected dividend

dividend mandate /ˌdɪvɪdend mæn ˈdeɪt/ *noun* an authorisation by a shareholder

to the company, to pay his or her dividends directly into a bank account

dividend per share /ˌdɪvɪdend pə ˈʃeə/ *noun* an amount of money paid as dividend for each share held

dividend warrant /ˌdɪvɪdend ˈwɒrənt/ *noun* a cheque which makes payment of a dividend (NOTE: The US term is **dividend check**.)

dividend yield /ˈdɪvɪdend jiːld/ *noun* a dividend expressed as a percentage of the current market price of a share

dividend yield basis /ˌdɪvɪdend jiːld ˈbeɪsɪs/ *noun* a method of valuing shares in a company, calculated as the dividend per share divided by the expected dividend yield

divisional headquarters /dɪˌvɪʒ(ə)nəl ˌhedˈkwɔːtəz/ *plural noun* the main office of a division of a company

divisor /dɪˈvaɪzə/ *noun* an operand used to divide a dividend in a division operation

document /ˈdɒkjʊmənt/ *noun* a paper, especially an official paper, with written information on it ○ *He left a file of documents in the taxi.* ○ *She asked to see the documents relating to the case.*

documentary /ˌdɒkjʊˈment(ə)ri/ *adjective* in the form of documents ○ *documentary evidence*

documentary credit /ˌdɒkjʊment(ə)ri ˈkredɪt/ *noun* a credit document used in export trade, when a bank issues a letter of credit against shipping documents

documentary proof /ˌdɒkjʊment(ə)ri ˈpruːf/ *noun* a proof in the form of a document

documentation /ˌdɒkjʊmenˈteɪʃ(ə)n/ *noun* all the documents referring to something ○ *Please send me the complete documentation concerning the sale.*

dole queue /ˈdəʊl kjuː/ *noun* a line of people waiting to collect their unemployment money (NOTE: The US term is **dole line**.)

dollar /ˈdɒlə/ *noun* a unit of currency used in the US and other countries such as Australia, Bahamas, Barbados, Bermuda, Brunei, Canada, Fiji, Hong Kong, Jamaica, New Zealand, Singapore and Zimbabwe ○ *The US dollar rose 2%.* ○ *They sent a cheque for fifty Canadian dollars.* ○ *It costs six Australian dollars.*

dollar area /ˈdɒlər ˌeəriə/ *noun* an area of the world where the US dollar is the main trading currency

dollar balances /ˈdɒlə ˌbælənsɪz/ *noun* a country's trade balances expressed in US dollars

dollar crisis /'dɒlə ˌkraɪsɪs/ *noun* a fall in the exchange rate for the US dollar

dollar gap /ˌdɒlə 'gæp/ *noun* a situation where the supply of US dollars is not enough to satisfy the demand for them from overseas buyers

dollar millionaire /ˌdɒlə ˌmɪljə'neə/ *noun* a person who has more than one million dollars

dollar stocks /'dɒlə stɒkz/ *plural noun* shares in US companies

domestic production /də,mestɪk prə'dʌkʃən/ *noun* the production of goods for use in the home country

domicile /'dɒmɪsaɪl/ *noun* the country where someone lives or where a company's office is registered ■ *verb* □ **she is domiciled in Denmark** she lives in Denmark officially

donation /dəʊ'neɪʃ(ə)n/ *noun* a gift, especially to a charity

donee /ˌdəʊ'niː/ *noun* a person who receives a gift from a donor

donor /'dəʊnə/ *noun* a person who gives, especially someone who gives money

dormant /'dɔːmənt/ *adjective* no longer active or no longer operating

dormant account /ˌdɔːmənt ə'kaʊnt/ *noun* **1.** a bank account which is no longer used **2.** a past customer who is no longer buying ○ *Let's re-establish contact with some of our dormant accounts.* ○ *All the old reports on dormant accounts have been filed away.*

dormant company /ˌdɔːmənt 'kʌmp(ə)ni/ *noun* company which has not made any transactions during an accounting period

double-entry bookkeeping /ˌdʌb(ə)l ˌentri 'bʊkkiːpɪŋ/ *noun* the most commonly used system of bookkeeping, based on the principle that every financial transaction involves the simultaneous receiving and giving of value, and is therefore recorded twice

double taxation /ˌdʌb(ə)l tæk'seɪʃ(ə)n/ *noun* the act of taxing the same income twice

double taxation agreement /ˌdʌb(ə)l tæk'seɪʃ(ə)n ə,griːmənt/, **double taxation treaty** /ˌdʌb(ə)l tæk'seɪʃ(ə)n ,triːti/ *noun* an agreement between two countries that a person living in one country shall not be taxed in both countries on the income earned in the other country

double taxation relief /ˌdʌb(ə)l tæk 'seɪʃ(ə)n rɪ,liːf/ *noun* a reduction of tax payable in one country by the amount of tax on income, profits or capital gains already paid in another country

doubtful debt /ˌdaʊtf(ə)l 'det/ *noun* a debt which may never be paid

doubtful loan /ˌdaʊtf(ə)l 'ləʊn/ *noun* a loan which may never be repaid

down /daʊn/ *adverb, preposition* in a lower position or to a lower position ○ *The inflation rate is gradually coming down.* ○ *Shares are slightly down on the day.* ○ *The price of petrol has gone down.*

downgrade /'daʊngreɪd/ *verb* **1.** to reduce the importance of someone or of a job ○ *The post was downgraded in the company reorganisation.* **2.** to reduce the forecast for a share

down payment /ˌdaʊn 'peɪmənt/ *noun* a part of a total payment made in advance ○ *We made a down payment of $100.*

downside factor /'daʊnsaɪd ˌfæktə/, **downside potential** /ˌdaʊnsaɪd pə 'tenʃ(ə)l/ *noun* the possibility of making a loss in an investment

downside risk /'daʊnsaɪd rɪsk/ *noun* a risk that an investment will fall in value. Opposite **upside potential**

down time /'daʊn taɪm/ *noun* the time when a machine is not working or not available because it is broken or being mended

downturn /'daʊntɜːn/ *noun* the movement towards lower prices, sales or profits ○ *a downturn in the market price* ○ *The last quarter saw a downturn in the economy.*

draft /drɑːft/ *noun* **1.** an order for money to be paid by a bank ○ *We asked for payment by banker's draft.* **2.** a first rough plan or document which has not been finished ○ *The finance depart* ○ *A draft of the contract* or *The draft contract is waiting for the MD's comments.* ○ *He drew up the draft agreement on the back of an envelope.* ■ *verb* to make a first rough plan of a document ○ *to draft a letter* ○ *to draft a contract* ○ *The contract is still being drafted* or *is still in the drafting stage.*

drafting /'drɑːftɪŋ/ *noun* an act of preparing the draft of a document ○ *The drafting of the contract took six weeks.*

drain /dreɪn/ *noun* a gradual loss of money flowing away ○ *The costs of the London office are a continual drain on our resources.* ■ *verb* to remove something gradually ○ *The expansion plan has drained all our profits.* ○ *The company's capital resources have drained away.*

draw /drɔː/ *verb* **1.** to take money away ○ *to draw money out of an account* **2.** to write a cheque ○ *She paid the invoice with a cheque* *drawn on an Egyptian bank.* (NOTE: **drawing – drew – has drawn**)

drawback /'drɔːbæk/ *noun* **1.** something which is not convenient or which is likely to cause problems ○ *One of the main drawbacks of the scheme is that it will take six years to complete.* **2.** a rebate on customs duty for imported goods when these are then used in producing exports

drawdown /'drɔːdaʊn/ *noun* the act of drawing money which is available under a credit agreement

drawee /drɔː'iː/ *noun* the person or bank asked to make a payment by a drawer

drawer /'drɔːə/ *noun* the person who writes a cheque or a bill asking a drawee to pay money to a payee

drawing account /'drɔːɪŋ ə,kaʊnt/ *noun* a current account, or any account from which the customer may take money when he or she wants

drawings /'drɔːɪŋz/ *plural noun* money or trading stock taken by a partner from a partnership, or by a sole trader from his or her business

drawings account /,drɔːɪŋs ə'kaʊnt/ *noun* an account showing amounts drawn by partners in a partnership

draw up /,drɔː 'ʌp/ *verb* to write a legal document ○ *to draw up a contract or an agreement* ○ *to draw up a company's articles of association*

drop /drɒp/ *noun* a fall ○ *a drop in sales* ○ *Sales show a drop of 10%.* ○ *The drop in prices resulted in no significant increase in sales.* ■ *verb* to fall ○ *Sales have dropped by 10% or have dropped 10%.* ○ *The pound dropped three points against the dollar.*

'…while unemployment dropped by 1.6 per cent in the rural areas, it rose by 1.9 per cent in urban areas during the period under review' [*Business Times (Lagos)*]

'…corporate profits for the first quarter showed a 4 per cent drop from last year's final three months' [*Financial Times*]

'…since last summer American interest rates have dropped by between three and four percentage points' [*Sunday Times*]

droplock bond /'drɒplɒk bɒnd/ *noun* a floating rate bond which will convert to a fixed rate of interest if interest rates fall to some level

dry goods /,draɪ 'ɡʊdz/ *plural noun* cloth, clothes and household goods

DTI *abbr* Department of Trade and Industry

dual /'djuːəl/ *adjective* referring to two things at the same time

dual currency bond /,djuːəl 'kʌrənsi bɒnd/ *noun* a bond which is paid for in one currency but which is repayable in another on redemption

dual listing /,djuːəl 'lɪstɪŋ/ *noun* the listing of a share on two stock exchanges

dual pricing /,djuːəl 'praɪsɪŋ/ *noun* the fact of giving different prices to the same product depending on the market in which it is sold

dual resident /,djuːəl 'rezɪd(ə)nt/ *noun* a person who is legally resident in two countries

dud /dʌd/ *noun, adjective* referring to a coin or banknote which is false or not good, or something which does not do what it is supposed to do (*informal*) ○ *The £50 note was a dud.*

dud cheque /,dʌd 'tʃek/ *noun* a cheque which cannot be cashed because the person writing it has not enough money in the account to pay it

due /djuː/ *adjective* owed ○ *a sum due from a debtor* □ **to fall** *or* **become due** to be ready for payment

'…many expect the US economic indicators for April, due out this Thursday, to show faster economic growth' [*Australian Financial Review*]

due diligence /,djuː 'dɪlɪdʒəns/ *noun* the examination of a company's accounts prior to a potential takeover by another organisation. This assessment is often undertaken by an independent third party.

dues /djuːz/ *plural noun* orders taken but not supplied until new stock arrives

dumping /'dʌmpɪŋ/ *noun* the act of getting rid of excess goods cheaply in an overseas market ○ *The government has passed anti-dumping legislation.* ○ *Dumping of goods on the European market is banned.*

Dun and Bradstreet /,dʌn ən 'brædstriːt/ *noun* an international organisation that sources credit information from companies and their creditors which it then makes available to subscribers. Abbreviation **D&B**

duplicate /'djuːplɪkət/ *noun* a copy ○ *He sent me the duplicate of the contract.*

duplicating machine /'djuːplɪkeɪtɪŋ mə,ʃiːn/ *noun* a machine which makes copies of documents

duplication /,djuːplɪ'keɪʃ(ə)n/ *noun* the act of doing something that is already being done in the same way by somebody else, copying

Dutch auction /,dʌtʃ 'ɔːkʃən/ *noun* an auction in which the auctioneer offers an item for sale at a high price and then gradually reduces the price until someone makes a bid

duty /'djuːti/ *noun* a tax which has to be paid ○ *Traders are asking the government to take the duty off alcohol* or *to put a duty on cigarettes.*

'Canadian and European negotiators agreed to a deal under which Canada could lower its import duties on $150 million worth of European goods' [*Globe and Mail (Toronto)*]

'…the Department of Customs and Excise collected a total of N79m under the new advance duty payment scheme' [*Business Times (Lagos)*]

duty-free /ˌdjuːti 'friː/ *adjective, adverb* sold with no duty to be paid ○ *She bought duty-free perfume at the airport.* ○ *He bought the watch duty-free.*

duty-free shop /ˌdjuːti 'friː ʃɒp/ *noun* a shop at an airport or on a ship where goods can be bought without paying duty

duty-paid goods /ˌdjuːti 'peɪd gʊdz/ *plural noun* goods where the duty has been paid

E

e- /iː/ *prefix* referring to electronics or the Internet

EAA *abbr* European Accounting Association

e. & o.e. *abbr* errors and omissions excepted

early withdrawal /ˌɜːli wɪð'drɔːəl/ *noun* the act of withdrawing money from a deposit account before the due date ○ *Early withdrawal usually incurs a penalty.*

earmark /'ɪəmɑːk/ *verb* /'ɪəˌmɑːk/ to reserve for a special purpose ○ *to earmark funds for a project* ○ *The grant is earmarked for computer systems development.*

earn /ɜːn/ *verb* **1.** to be paid money for working ○ *to earn £100 a week* ○ *Our agent in Paris certainly does not earn his commission.* ○ *Her new job is more of a transfer than a promotion, since she doesn't earn any more.* ○ *How much do you earn in your new job?* **2.** to produce interest or dividends ○ *a building society account which earns interest at 10%* ○ *What level of dividend do these shares earn?*

earned income /ɜːnd 'ɪnkʌm/ *noun* income from wages, salaries, pensions, fees, rental income, etc., as opposed to 'unearned' income from investments

earnest /'ɜːnɪst/ *noun* money paid as an initial payment by a buyer to a seller, to show commitment to the contract of sale

earning capacity /'ɜːnɪŋ kəˌpæsɪti/ *noun* the amount of money someone should be able to earn

earning potential /'ɜːnɪŋ pəˌtenʃəl/ *noun* **1.** the amount of money a person should be able to earn in his or her professional capacity **2.** the amount of dividend which a share is capable of earning

earning power /'ɜːnɪŋ ˌpaʊə/ *noun* the amount of money someone should be able to earn ○ *She is such a fine designer that her earning power is very large.*

earnings /'ɜːnɪŋz/ *plural noun* **1.** salary, wages, dividends or interest received ○ *High earnings in top management reflect the heavy responsibilities involved.* ○ *The calculation is based on average earnings over three years.* **2.** the profit made by a company

'…the US now accounts for more than half of our world-wide sales. It has made a huge contribution to our earnings turnaround' [*Duns Business Month*]

'…last fiscal year the chain reported a 116% jump in earnings, to $6.4 million or $1.10 a share' [*Barrons*]

earnings before interest, taxes, depreciation and amortisation /ˌɜːnɪŋz bɪˌfɔː ˌɪntrəst ˌtæksɪz dɪˌpriːʃieɪʃ(ə)n ənd əˌmɔːtaɪˈzeɪʃ(ə)n/ *plural noun* the earnings generated by a business's fundamental operating performance, frequently used in accounting ratios for comparison with other companies. Interest on borrowings, tax payable on those profits, depreciation, and amortisation are excluded on the basis that they can distort the underlying performance. Abbreviation **EBIT, EBITDA**

earnings before interest and tax /ˌɜːnɪŋz bɪˌfɔː 'ɪntrəst ən tæks/ *noun* the amount earned by a business before deductions are made for tax and interest payments

earnings cap /'ɜːnɪŋz kæp/ *noun* the upper limit on the amount of salary that can be taken into account when calculating pensions

earnings performance /'ɜːnɪŋz pəˌfɔːməns/ *noun* a way in which shares earn dividends

earnings per share /ˌɜːnɪŋz pə 'ʃeə/ *plural noun* the money earned in dividends per share, shown as a percentage of the market price of one share. Abbreviation **EPS**

earnings-related contributions /ˌɜːnɪŋz rɪˌleɪtɪd ˌkɒntrɪ'bjuːʃ(ə)nz/ *plural noun* contributions to social security which rise as the employee's earnings rise

earnings-related pension /ˌɜːnɪŋz rɪ ˌleɪtɪd 'penʃən/ *noun* a pension which is linked to the size of a person's salary

earnings yield /'ɜːnɪŋz jiːld/ *noun* the money earned in dividends per share as a percentage of the current market price of the share

ease /iːz/ *verb* to fall a little ○ *The share index eased slightly today.*

easy market /ˌiːzi 'mɑːkɪt/ *noun* a market where few people are buying, so prices are lower than they were before ○ *The Stock Exchange was easy yesterday.*

easy money /'iːzi 'mʌni/ *noun* **1.** money which can be earned with no difficulty **2.** a loan available on easy repayment terms

easy money policy /'iːzi 'mʌni/ *noun* a government policy of expanding the economy by making money more easily available, e.g. through lower interest rates and easy access to credit

easy terms /ˌiːzi 'tɜːmz/ *plural noun* financial terms which are not difficult to accept ○ *The shop is let on very easy terms.*

EBITDA, EBIT *abbr* earnings before interest, taxes, depreciation and amortization

EBRD *abbr* European Bank for Reconstruction and Development

e-business /'iː ˌbɪznəs/ *noun* a general term that refers to any type of business activity on the Internet, including marketing, branding and research ○ *E-business is a rising part of the economy.*

'...the enormous potential of e-business is that it can automate the link between suppliers and customers' [*Investors Chronicle*]

ECB *abbr* European Central Bank

ECGD *abbr* Export Credit Guarantee Department

e-commerce /'iː ˌkɒmɜːs/ *noun* a general term that is usually used to refer to the process of buying and selling goods over the Internet

'...the problem is that if e-commerce takes just a 3 per cent slice of the market that would be enough to reduce margins to ribbons' [*Investors Chronicle*]

'...the new economy requires new company structures. He believes that other blue-chip organizations are going to find that new set-ups would be needed to attract and retain the best talent for e-commerce' [*Times*]

econometrics /ɪˌkɒnə'metrɪks/ *plural noun* the study of the statistics of economics, using computers to analyse these statistics and make forecasts using mathematical models

economic /ˌiːkə'nɒmɪk/ *adjective* **1.** providing enough money to make a profit ○ *The flat is let at an economic rent.* ○ *It is hardly economic for the company to run its own warehouse.* **2.** referring to the financial state of a country ○ *economic planning* ○ *economic trends* ○ *Economic planners are expecting a consumer-led boom.* ○ *The government's economic policy is in ruins after the devaluation.* ○ *The economic situation is getting worse.* ○ *The country's economic system needs more regulation.*

'...each of the major issues on the agenda at this week's meeting is important to the government's success in overall economic management' [*Australian Financial Review*]

economical /ˌiːkə'nɒmɪk(ə)l/ *adjective* saving money or materials or being less expensive ○ *This car is very economical.* □ **an economical use of resources** the fact of using resources as carefully as possible

Economic and Monetary Union /ˌiːkənɒmɪk ən ˌmʌnɪt(ə)ri 'juːnjən/ *noun* abbreviation **EMU.** same as **European Monetary Union**

economic crisis /ˌiːkənɒmɪk 'kraɪsɪs/, **economic depression** /ˌiːkəˌnɒmɪk dɪ 'preʃ(ə)n/ *noun* a situation where a country is in financial collapse ○ *The government has introduced import controls to solve the current economic crisis.*

economic cycle /ˌiːkənɒmɪk 'saɪk(ə)l/ *noun* a period during which trade expands, then slows down and then expands again

economic development /ˌiːkənɒmɪk dɪ'veləpmənt/ *noun* the expansion of the commercial and financial situation ○ *The government has offered tax incentives to speed up the economic development of the region.* ○ *Economic development has been rel-*

atively slow in the north, compared with the rest of the country.

economic forecaster /ˌiːkənɒmɪk ˈfɔːkɑːstə/ *noun* a person who says how he or she thinks a country's economy will perform in the future

economic growth /ˌiːkənɒmɪk ˈɡrəʊθ/ *noun* the rate at which a country's national income grows

economic model /ˌiːkənɒmɪk ˈmɒd(ə)l/ *noun* a computerised plan of a country's economic system, used for forecasting economic trends

economic order quantity /ˌiːkənɒmɪk ˈɔːdə ˌkwɒntɪti/ *noun* the quantity of stocks which a company should hold, calculated on the basis of the costs of warehousing, of lower unit costs because of higher quantities purchased, the rate at which stocks are used and the time it takes for suppliers to deliver new orders. Abbreviation **EOQ**

economic planning /ˌiːkənɒmɪk ˈplænɪŋ/ *noun* the process of planning the future financial state of the country for the government

economics /ˌiːkəˈnɒmɪks/ *noun* the study of the production, distribution, selling and use of goods and services ■ *plural noun* the study of financial structures to show how a product or service is costed and what returns it produces ○ *I do not understand the economics of the coal industry.* (NOTE: [all senses] takes a singular verb)

'…believers in free-market economics often find it hard to sort out their views on the issue' [*Economist*]

economic sanctions /ˌiːkənɒmɪk ˈsæŋkʃ(ə)ns/ *plural noun* restrictions on trade with a country in order to influence its political situation or in order to make its government change its policy ○ *to impose economic sanctions on a country*

economic stagnation /ˌiːkənɒmɪk stæɡˈneɪʃ(ə)n/ *noun* a lack of expansion in the economy

economic value added /ˌiːkənɒmɪk ˌvæljuː ˈædɪd/ *noun* a way of judging financial performance by measuring the amount by which the earnings of a project, an operation, or a company exceed or fall short of the total amount of capital that was originally invested by its owners. Abbreviation **EVA**

economies of scale /ɪˌkɒnəmiz əv ˈskeɪl/ *plural noun* a situation in which a product is made more profitable by manufacturing it in larger quantities so that each unit costs less to make. Compare **diseconomies of scale**

economies of scope /ɪˌkɒnəmiz əv ˈskəʊp/ *plural noun* reductions in unit average costs caused by the simultaneous production of a number of related products, permitting benefits such as the sharing of joint costs over a larger volume than would otherwise be possible

economist /ɪˈkɒnəmɪst/ *noun* a person who specialises in the study of economics ○ *Government economists are forecasting a growth rate of 3% next year.* ○ *An agricultural economist studies the economics of the agriculture industry.*

economy /ɪˈkɒnəmi/ *noun* **1.** an action which is intended to stop money or materials from being wasted, or the quality of being careful not to waste money or materials ○ **to introduce economies** *or* **economy measures into the system** to start using methods to save money or materials **2.** the financial state of a country, or the way in which a country makes and uses its money ○ *The country's economy is in ruins.*

'…the European economies are being held back by rigid labor markets and wage structures, huge expenditures on social welfare programs and restrictions on the free movement of goods' [*Duns Business Month*]

economy class /ɪˈkɒnəmi klɑːs/ *noun* a lower-quality, less expensive way of travelling ○ *I travel economy class because it is cheaper.* ○ *I always travels first class because economy class is too uncomfortable.*

economy drive /ɪˈkɒnəmi draɪv/ *noun* a vigorous effort to save money or materials

economy size /ɪˈkɒnəmi saɪz/ *noun* a large size or large packet which is cheaper than usual

ECP /ˌiː siː ˈpiː/ *abbr* Eurocommercial Paper

ecu /ˈekjuː/, **ECU** *abbr* European Currency Unit

ED *abbr* exposure draft

EDI /ˌiː diː ˈaɪ/ *abbr* electronic data interchange

editorial board /ˌedɪˌtɔːriəl ˈbɔːd/ *noun* a group of editors on a newspaper or other publication

effect /ɪˈfekt/ *noun* **1.** a result ○ *The effect of the pay increase was to raise productivity levels.* **2.** an operation ○ **terms of a contract which take effect** *or* **come into effect from January 1st** terms which start to operate on January 1st **3.** meaning ○ **a clause to the effect that** a clause which means that ■ *verb* to carry out

effective /ɪˈfektɪv/ *adjective* **1.** actual, as opposed to theoretical **2.** ○ **a clause effective**

as from January 1st a clause which starts to be applied on January 1st **3.** producing results ○ *Advertising in the Sunday papers is the most effective way of selling.* ○ *She is an effective marketing manager.* ◊ **cost-effective**

effective annual rate /ɪˌfektɪv ˈænjuəl/ *noun* the average interest rate paid on a deposit for a period of a year. It is the total interest received over 12 months expressed as a percentage of the principal at the beginning of the period.

effective date /ɪˈfektɪv deɪt/ *noun* the date on which a rule or contract starts to be applied, or on which a transaction takes place

effective demand /ɪˌfektɪv dɪˈmɑːnd/ *noun* the actual demand for a product which can be paid for

effective exchange rate /ɪˌfektɪv ɪks ˈtʃeɪndʒ ˌreɪt/ *noun* a rate of exchange for a currency calculated against a basket of currencies

effectiveness /ɪˈfektɪvnəs/ *noun* the quality of working successfully or producing results ○ *I doubt the effectiveness of television advertising.* ○ *Her effectiveness as a manager was due to her quick grasp of detail.* ◊ **cost-effectiveness**

effective price /ɪˌfektɪv ˈpraɪs/ *noun* a share price which has been adjusted to allow for a rights issue

effective rate /ɪˌfektɪv ˈreɪt/ *noun* a real interest rate on a loan or deposit, i.e., the APR

effective tax rate /ɪˌfektɪv ˈtæks ˌreɪt/ *noun* the average tax rate applicable to a given transaction, whether it is income from work undertaken, the sale of an asset, or a gift, taking into account personal allowances and scales of tax. It is the amount of money generated by the transaction divided by the additional tax payable because of it.

effective yield /ɪˌfektɪv ˈjiːld/ *noun* an actual yield shown as a percentage of the price paid after adjustments have been made

efficiency /ɪˈfɪʃ(ə)nsi/ *noun* the ability to work well or to produce the right result or the right work quickly ○ *a business efficiency exhibition* ○ *The bus system is run with a high degree of efficiency.* ○ *We called in an efficiency expert to report on ways of increasing profitability.*

'…increased control means improved efficiency in purchasing, shipping, sales and delivery' [*Duns Business Month*]

efficient /ɪˈfɪʃ(ə)nt/ *adjective* able to work well or to produce the right result quickly ○ *the efficient working of a system* ○ *An effi-*

cient assistant is invaluable. ○ *An efficient new machine would save time.*

efficiently /ɪˈfɪʃ(ə)ntli/ *adverb* in an efficient way ○ *She organised the sales conference very efficiently.*

efficient markets hypothesis /ɪˌfɪʃ(ə)nt ˈmɑːkɪts/ *noun* the theory that stock markets respond with varying degrees of efficiency to information about the companies listed. Abbreviation **EMH**

EFT /ˌiː ef ˈtiː/ *abbr* electronic funds transfer

EFTPOS /ˌiː ef ˌtiː piː əʊ ˈes/ *abbr* electronic funds transfer at a point of sale

EIB *abbr* European Investment Bank

EIS /ˌiː aɪ ˈes/ *abbr* Enterprise Investment Scheme

elastic /ɪˈlæstɪk/ *adjective* able to expand or contract easily because of small changes in price

elasticity /ˌɪlæˈstɪsɪti/ *noun* the ability to change easily in response to a change in circumstances

eldercare /ˈeldəkeə/ *noun* assurance services sold to elderly people and their families

-elect /ɪlekt/ *suffix* referring to a person who has been elected but has not yet started the term of office

electronic banking /ˌelektrɒnɪk ˈbæŋkɪŋ/ *noun* the use of computers to carry out banking transactions such as withdrawals through cash dispensers or transfer of funds at point of sale

electronic data interchange /ˌelektrɒnɪk ˈdeɪtə ˌɪntətʃeɪndʒ/ *noun* a standard format used when business documents such as invoices and purchase orders are exchanged over electronic networks such as the Internet. Abbreviation **EDI**

electronic funds transfer /ˌelektrɒnɪk ˌfʌndz ˌtrænsfɜː ət ˌpɔɪnt əv ˈseɪl/ *noun* the system used by banking organisations for the movement of funds between accounts and for the provision of services to the customer. Abbreviation **EFT**

electronic funds transfer at point of sale /ˌelektrɒnɪk ˌfʌndz ˌtrænsfɜː ət ˌpɔɪnt əv ˈseɪl/ *noun* the payment for goods or services by a bank customer using a card that is swiped through an electronic reader on the till, thereby transferring the cash from the customer's account to the retailer's or service provider's account. Abbreviation **EFTPOS**

Electronic Lodgement Service /ˌelektrɒnɪk ˈlɒdʒmənt ˌsɜːvɪs/ *noun* British system for filing your tax return electronically. Abbreviation **ELS**

electronic point of sale /ˌelɪktrɒnɪk pɔɪnt əv ˈseɪl/ *noun* a system where sales are charged automatically to a customer's credit card and stock is controlled by the shop's computer. Abbreviation **EPOS**

Electronic Version of the Tax Return /ˌelektrɒnɪk ˌvɜːʒ(ə)n əv ðə tæks rɪˈtɜːn/ *noun* a method of making an individual's tax return using email. Abbreviation **EVR**

eligibility /ˌelɪdʒɪˈbɪlɪti/ *noun* the fact of being eligible ○ *The chairman questioned her eligibility to stand for re-election.*

eliminate /ɪˈlɪmɪneɪt/ *verb* to remove ○ *to eliminate defects in the system* ○ *Using a computer should eliminate all possibility of error.* ○ *We have decided to eliminate this series of old products from our range.* ○ *Most of the candidates were eliminated after the first batch of tests.*

ELS *abbr* Electronic Lodgement Service

emailing /ˈiːmeɪlɪŋ/ *noun* the process of sending something by email

embargo /ɪmˈbɑːɡəʊ/ *noun* **1.** a government order which stops a type of trade □ **to lay** *or* **put an embargo on trade with a country** to say that trade with a country must not take place ○ *The government has put an embargo on the export of computer equipment.* **2.** a period of time during which specific information in a press release must not be published (NOTE: The plural is **embargoes**.) ■ *verb* **1.** to stop trade, or not to allow something to be traded ○ *The government has embargoed trade with the Eastern countries.* **2.** not to allow publication of information for a period of time ○ *The news of the merger has been embargoed until next Wednesday.*

'…the Commerce Department is planning to loosen export controls for products that have been embargoed but are readily available elsewhere in the West' [*Duns Business Month*]

embezzle /ɪmˈbez(ə)l/ *verb* to use illegally money which is not yours, or which you are looking after for someone ○ *He was sent to prison for six months for embezzling his clients' money.*

embezzlement /ɪmˈbez(ə)lmənt/ *noun* the act of embezzling ○ *He was sent to prison for six months for embezzlement.*

embezzler /ɪmˈbez(ə)lə/ *noun* a person who embezzles

EMH *abbr* efficient markets hypothesis

emoluments /ɪˈmɒljʊmənts/ *plural noun* pay, salary or fees, or the earnings of directors who are not employees (NOTE: US English uses the singular **emolument**.)

employ /ɪmˈplɔɪ/ *verb* to give someone regular paid work

'70 per cent of Australia's labour force was employed in service activity' [*Australian Financial Review*]

employed /ɪmˈplɔɪd/ *adjective* **1.** in regular paid work **2.** referring to money used profitably ■ *plural noun* people who are working ○ *the employers and the employed*

employee /ɪmˈplɔɪiː/ *noun* a person employed by another ○ *Employees of the firm are eligible to join a profit-sharing scheme.* ○ *Relations between management and employees are good.* ○ *The company has decided to take on new employees.*

'…companies introducing robotics think it important to involve individual employees in planning their introduction' [*Economist*]

employee contribution /ɪmˌplɔɪiː ˌkɒntrɪˈbjuːʃ(ə)n/ *noun* a contribution paid by an employee towards his or her pension

employee share ownership plan /ɪm ˈplɔɪiː ˌʃeə ˈəʊnəʃɪp plæn/, **employee share ownership programme** /ɪmˌplɔɪiː ˈʃeə ˌəʊnəʃɪp ˌprəʊɡræm/, **employee share scheme** /ɪmˌplɔɪiː ˈʃeə skiːm/ *noun* a plan which allows employees to obtain shares in the company for which they work, though tax may be payable if the shares are sold to employees at a price which is lower than the current market price. Abbreviation **ESOP**

employer /ɪmˈplɔɪə/ *noun* a person or company that has regular employees and pays them

employer's contribution /ɪmˌplɔɪəz ˌkɒntrɪˈbjuːʃ(ə)n/ *noun* money paid by an employer towards an employee's pension

employers' liability insurance /ɪm ˌplɔɪəz ˌlaɪəˈbɪlɪti ɪnˌʃʊərəns/ *noun* insurance to cover accidents which may happen at work, and for which the company may be responsible

employment /ɪmˈplɔɪmənt/ *noun* regular paid work

'…the blue-collar unions are the people who stand to lose most in terms of employment growth' [*Sydney Morning Herald*]

employment agency /ɪmˈplɔɪmənt ˌeɪdʒənsi/ *noun* an office which finds jobs for staff

employment income /ɪmˌplɔɪmənt ˈɪnkʌm/ *noun* money received from an employer, e.g. salary, fees, commission, bonus, fringe benefits

employment office /ɪmˈplɔɪmənt ˌɒfɪs/ *noun* an office which finds jobs for people

EMS /ˌiː em ˈes/ *abbr* European Monetary System

EMU *abbr* **1.** Economic and Monetary Union **2.** European Monetary Union

encash /ɪnˈkæʃ/ *verb* to cash a cheque, to exchange a cheque for cash

encashable /ɪnˈkæʃəb(ə)l/ *adjective* possible to cash

encashment /ɪnˈkæʃmənt/ *noun* an act of exchanging for cash

encumbrance /ɪnˈkʌmbrəns/ *noun* a liability which is attached usually to a property or land, e.g. a mortgage or charge

endorse /ɪnˈdɔːs/ *verb* to say that a product is good □ **to endorse a bill** *or* **a cheque** to sign a bill or cheque on the back to show that you accept it

endorsee /ˌendɔːˈsiː/ *noun* a person whose name is written on a bill or cheque as having the right to cash it

endorsement /ɪnˈdɔːsmənt/ *noun* **1.** the act of endorsing **2.** a signature on a document which endorses it **3.** a note on an insurance policy which adds conditions to the policy

endorser /ɪnˈdɔːsə/ *noun* a person who endorses a bill or cheque which is then paid to him or her

endowment /ɪnˈdaʊmənt/ *noun* the act of giving money to provide a regular income

endowment assurance /ɪnˈdaʊmənt ɪnˌʃʊərəns/, **endowment insurance** *noun* an insurance policy where a sum of money is paid to the insured person on a specific date or to his heirs if he dies before that date

endowment mortgage /ɪnˈdaʊmənt ˌmɔːɡɪdʒ/ *noun* a mortgage backed by an endowment policy

endowment policy /ɪnˈdaʊmənt ˌpɒlɪsi/ *noun* same as **endowment assurance**

end product /ˌend ˈprɒdʌkt/ *noun* a manufactured product resulting from a production process

energy costs /ˈenədʒi kɒsts/ *plural noun* costs of gas, electricity, etc., as shown in accounts

energy shares /ˈenədʒi ʃeəz/ *plural noun* shares in companies which provide energy

enforce /ɪnˈfɔːs/ *verb* to make sure something is done or that a rule is obeyed ○ *to enforce the terms of a contract*

enforcement /ɪnˈfɔːsmənt/ *noun* the act of making sure that something is obeyed ○ *enforcement of the terms of a contract*

engagement /ɪnˈɡeɪdʒmənt/ *noun* an agreement to do something

engagement letter /ɪnˌɡeɪdʒmənt ˈletə/ *noun* a letter, usually required by professional standards, sent by an accountant to a client setting out the work the accountant is to do

and further administrative matters, such as any limit on the accountant's liability

entail /ɪnˈteɪl/ *noun* a legal condition which passes ownership of a property only to some specific persons ■ *verb* to involve ○ *Itemising the sales figures will entail about ten days' work.*

entering /ˈentərɪŋ/ *noun* the act of writing items in a record

enterprise /ˈentəpraɪz/ *noun* **1.** a system of carrying on a business **2.** a business

Enterprise Investment Scheme /ˌentəpraɪz ɪnˈvestmənt skiːm/ *noun* a scheme which provides income and CGT relief for people prepared to risk investing in a single unquoted or AIM-listed trading company. Abbreviation **EIS**

enterprise zone /ˈentəpraɪz zəʊn/ *noun* an area of the country where businesses are encouraged to develop by offering special conditions such as easy planning permission for buildings or a reduction in the business rate

entertain /ˌentəˈteɪn/ *verb* to offer such things as meals, hotel accommodation and theatre tickets for the comfort and enjoyment of business visitors

entertainment /ˌentəˈteɪnmənt/ *noun* the practice of offering meals or other recreation to business visitors

entertainment allowance /ˌentə ˈteɪnmənt əˌlaʊəns/ *noun* money which managers are allowed by their company to spend on meals with visitors

entertainment expenses /ˌentə ˈteɪnmənt ɪkˌspensɪz/ *plural noun* money spent on giving meals to business visitors

entitle /ɪnˈtaɪt(ə)l/ *verb* to give the right to someone to have something ○ *After one year's service the employee is entitled to four weeks' holiday*

entitlement /ɪnˈtaɪt(ə)lmənt/ *noun* a person's right to something

entity /ˈentɪti/ *noun* a single separate body or organisation

entrepreneur /ˌɒntrəprəˈnɜː/ *noun* a person who directs a company and takes commercial risks

entrepreneurial /ˌɒntrəprəˈnɜːriəl/ *adjective* taking commercial risks ○ *an entrepreneurial decision*

entry /ˈentri/ *noun* **1.** an item of written information put in an accounts ledger (NOTE: The plural is **entries**.) **2.** an act of going in or the place where you can go in ○ *to pass a customs entry point* ○ *entry of goods under bond*

entry price /'entri praɪs/ *noun* a price at which an accounting entity buys, i.e., the current replacement cost

EOQ *abbr* economic order quantity

epos /'iːpɒs/, **EPOS**, **EPoS** *abbr* electronic point of sale

EPS *abbr* earnings per share

equal /'iːkwəl/ *adjective* exactly the same ○ *Male and female employees have equal pay.* ■ *verb* to be the same as ○ *Production this month has equalled our best month ever.* (NOTE: UK English is **equalling – equalled**, but the US spelling is **equaling – equaled**.)

equalise /'iːkwəlaɪz/, **equalize** *verb* to make equal ○ *to equalise dividends*

equally /'iːkwəli/ *adverb* so that each has or pays the same, or to the same degree ○ *Costs will be shared equally between the two parties.* ○ *They were both equally responsible for the disastrous launch.*

equate /ɪ'kweɪt/ *verb* to reduce to a standard value

equation /ɪ'kweɪʒ(ə)n/ *noun* a set of mathematical rules applied to solve a problem ○ *The basic accounting equation is that assets equal liabilities plus equity.*

equilibrium /ˌiːkwɪ'lɪbriəm/ *noun* the state of balance in the economy where supply equals demand or a country's balance of payments is neither in deficit nor in excess

equities /'ekwɪtiz/ *plural noun* ordinary shares

'...in the past three years commercial property has seriously underperformed equities and dropped out of favour as a result' [*Investors Chronicle*]

equity accounting /'ekwɪti əˌkaʊntɪŋ/ *noun* a method of accounting which puts part of the profits of a subsidiary into the parent company's books

equity capital /'ekwɪti ˌkæpɪt(ə)l/ *noun* the nominal value of the shares owned by the ordinary shareholders of a company (NOTE: Preference shares are not equity capital. If the company were wound up, none of the equity capital would be distributed to preference shareholders.)

equity dividend cover /ˌekwɪti 'dɪvɪdend ˌkʌvə/ *noun* an accounting ratio, calculated by dividing the distributable profits during a given period by the actual dividend paid in that period, that indicates the likelihood of the dividend being maintained in future years. ◊ **capital reserves**

equity finance /'ekwɪti ˌfaɪnæns/ *noun* finance for a company in the form of ordinary shares paid for by shareholders

equity gearing /'ekwɪti ˌɡɪərɪŋ/ *noun* the ratio between a company's borrowings at interest and its ordinary share capital

equity kicker /'ekwɪti ˌkɪkə/ *noun US* an incentive given to people to lend a company money, in the form of a warrant to share in future earnings (NOTE: The UK term is **equity sweetener**.)

equity share capital /ˌekwɪti ʃeə 'kæpɪt(ə)l/ *noun* a company's issued share capital less capital which carries preferential rights. Equity share capital normally comprises ordinary shares.

equity sweetener /'ekwɪti ˌswiːt(ə)nə/ *noun* an incentive to encourage people to lend a company money, in the form of a warrant giving the right to buy shares at a later date and at an agreed price

equivalence /ɪ'kwɪvələns/ *noun* the condition of having the same value or of being the same

equivalent /ɪ'kwɪvələnt/ *noun* a person who is the equal of someone else

equivalent unit /ɪˌkwɪvələnt 'juːnɪt/ *noun* a unit of unfinished production calculated for valuation purposes when work started during the period is not finished at the end of the period, or when work started during the previous period is finished during the current period

error /'erə/ *noun* a mistake ○ *He made an error in calculating the total.* ○ *Someone must have made a keyboarding error.*

errors and omissions excepted /ˌerəz ənd əʊˌmɪʃ(ə)nz ɪk'septɪd/ *phrase* words written on an invoice to show that the company has no responsibility for mistakes in the invoice. Abbreviation **e. & o.e.**

ESC /ɪ'skeɪp/ *noun* a charter for employees, drawn up by the EU in 1989, by which employees have the right to a fair wage, and to equal treatment for men and women, a safe work environment, training, freedom of association and collective bargaining, provision for disabled workers, freedom of movement from country to country, guaranteed standards of living both for the working population and for retired people. Full form **European Social Charter**. Also called **Social Charter**

escalate /'eskəleɪt/ *verb* to increase steadily

escalation clause /ˌeskə'leɪʃ(ə)n klɔːz/ *noun* same as **escalator clause**

escalator clause /'eskəleɪtə klɔːz/ *noun* a clause in a contract allowing for regular price increases because of increased costs, or regular wage increases because of the increased cost of living

escape clause /ɪ'skeɪp klɔːz/ *noun* a clause in a contract which allows one of the parties to avoid carrying out the terms of the contract under conditions

escrow /'eskrəʊ/ *noun US* an agreement between two parties that something should be held by a third party until conditions are fulfilled

escrow account /'eskrəʊ ə,kaʊnt/ *noun US* an account where money is held in escrow until a contract is signed or until goods are delivered

ESOP *abbr* employee share ownership plan

establishment /ɪ'stæblɪʃmənt/ *noun* **1.** a commercial business ○ *He runs an important printing establishment.* **2.** the number of people working in a company

establishment charges /ɪ'stæblɪʃmənt ,tʃɑːdʒɪz/ *plural noun* the cost of people and property in a company's accounts

estate /ɪ'steɪt/ *noun* property left by a dead person

estate agency /ɪ'steɪt ,eɪdʒənsi/ *noun* an office which arranges for the sale of properties

estate duty /ɪ'steɪt ,djuːti/ *noun* a tax paid on the property left by a dead person (NOTE: now called **inheritance tax**)

estimate *noun* /'estɪmət/ **1.** a calculation of the probable cost, size or time of something ○ *Can you give me an estimate of how much time was spent on the job?* **2.** a calculation by a contractor or seller of a service of how much something is likely to cost, given to a client in advance of an order ○ *You should ask for an estimate before committing yourselves.* ○ *Before we can give the grant we must have an estimate of the total costs involved.* ○ *Unfortunately the final bill was quite different from the estimate.* ■ *verb* /'estɪmeɪt/ to calculate the probable cost, size or time of something ○ *to estimate that it will cost £1m* or *to estimate costs at £1m* ○ *We estimate current sales at only 60% of last year.*

estimated /'estɪmeɪtɪd/ *adjective* calculated approximately ○ *estimated sales* ○ *Costs were slightly more than the estimated figure.*

estimation /,estɪ'meɪʃ(ə)n/ *noun* an approximate calculation

estimator /'estɪmeɪtə/ *noun* a person whose job is to calculate estimates for carrying out work

EU *abbr* European Union ○ *EU ministers met today in Brussels.* ○ *The USA is increasing its trade with the EU.*

euro /'jʊərəʊ/ *noun* a unit of currency adopted as legal tender in several European countries from January 1st, 1999 ○ *Many articles are priced in euros.* ○ *What's the exchange rate for the euro?* (NOTE: The plural is **euro** or **euros**.)

'...cross-border mergers in the European Union have shot up since the introduction of the euro' [*Investors Chronicle*]

Euro- /jʊərəʊ/ *prefix* referring to Europe or the European Union

euro account /'jʊərəʊ ə,kaʊnt/ *noun* a bank account in euros (NOTE: written Ä before numbers: **Ä250:** say: 'two hundred and fifty euros')

Eurobond /'jʊərəʊbɒnd/ *noun* a long-term bearer bond issued by an international corporation or government outside its country of origin and sold to purchasers who pay in a Eurocurrency, sold on the Eurobond market

Eurocheque /'jʊərəʊtʃek/ *noun* a cheque which can be cashed in any European bank. The Eurocheque system is based in Brussels.

Eurocommercial paper /,jʊərəʊkəmɜːʃ(ə)l 'peɪpə/ *noun* a form of short-term borrowing in Eurocurrencies. Abbreviation **ECP**

eurocredit /'jʊərəʊ,kredɪt/ *noun* a large bank loan in a Eurocurrency, usually provided by a group of banks to a large commercial undertaking

Eurocurrency /'jʊərəʊkʌrənsi/ *noun* any currency used for trade within Europe but outside its country of origin, the Eurodollar being the most important ○ *a Eurocurrency loan* ○ *the Eurocurrency market*

eurodeposit /'jʊərəʊdɪ,pɒzɪt/ *noun* a deposit of Eurodollars in a bank outside the US

Eurodollar /'jʊərəʊdɒlə/ *noun* a US dollar deposited in a bank outside the US, used mainly for trade within Europe ○ *a Eurodollar loan* ○ *the Eurodollar markets*

euroequity /'jʊərəʊ,ekwɪti/ *noun* a share in an international company traded on European stock markets outside its country of origin

Euroland /'jʊərəʊlænd/ *noun* same as **Eurozone**

euronote /'jʊərəʊ,nəʊt/ *noun* a short-term Eurocurrency bearer note

euro-option /'jʊərəʊ ,ɒpʃ(ə)n/ *noun* an option to buy European bonds at a later date

Europe /'jʊərəp/ *noun* **1.** the continent of Europe, the part of the world to the west of

Asia, from Russia to Ireland ○ *Most of the countries of Western Europe are members of the EU.* ○ *Poland is in eastern Europe, and Greece, Spain and Portugal are in southern Europe.* **2.** the European Union, including the UK ○ *Canadian exports to Europe have risen by 25%.*

European /ˌjʊərəˈpiːən/ *adjective* referring to Europe ○ *They do business with several European countries.*

European Accounting Association /ˌjʊərəpiːən əˈkaʊntɪŋ əˌsəʊsieɪʃ(ə)n/ *noun* an organisation for teachers and researchers in accountancy, founded in 1977 and based in Brussels, that EAA aims to be a forum for European research in the subject. Abbreviation **EAA**

European Bank for Reconstruction and Development /ˌjʊərəpiːən bæŋk fə riːkənˌstrʌktʃ(ə)n ən dɪˈveləpmənt/ *noun* a bank, based in London, which channels aid from the EU to Eastern European countries. Abbreviation **EBRD**

European Central Bank /ˌjʊərəpiːən ˌsentrəl ˈbæŋk/ *noun* central bank for most of the countries in the European Union, those which have accepted European Monetary Union and have the euro as their common currency. Abbreviation **ECB**

'...the ECB begins with some $300 billion of foreign exchange reserves, far more than any other central bank' [*Investors Chronicle*]

'...any change in the European bank's statutes must be agreed and ratified by all EU member nations' [*The Times*]

European Currency Unit /ˌjʊərəpiːən ˈkʌrənsi ˌjuːnɪt/ *noun* a monetary unit used within the EU. Abbreviation **ECU**

European Investment Bank /ˌjʊərəpiːən ɪnˈvestmənt bæŋk/ *noun* a financial institution whose main task is to further regional development within the EU by financing capital projects, modernising or converting undertakings, and developing new activities. Abbreviation **EIB**

European Monetary System /ˌjʊərəpiːən ˈmʌnɪt(ə)ri ˌsɪstəm/ *noun* the first stage of economic and monetary union of the EU, which came into force in March 1979, giving stable, but adjustable, exchange rates. Abbreviation **EMS**

European Monetary Union /ˌjʊərəpiːən ˈmʌnɪt(ə)ri ˌjuːnjən/ *noun* the process by which some of the member states of the EU joined together to adopt the euro as their common currency on 1st January 1999. Abbreviation **EMU**

European Social Charter /ˌjʊərəpiːən ˌsəʊʃ(ə)l ˈtʃɑːtə/ *noun* full form of **ESC**

European Union /ˌjʊərəpiːən ˈjuːnjən/ *noun* a group of European countries linked together by the Treaty of Rome. The European Community was set up in 1957 and changed its name to the European Union when it adopted the single market. It has now grown to include twenty-five member states. These are: Austria, Belgium, Cyprus, the Czech Republic, Denmark, Estonia, Finland, France, Germany, Greece, Hungary, Ireland, Italy, Latvia, Lithuania, Luxembourg, Malta, the Netherlands, Poland, Portugal, Slovakia, Slovenia, Spain, Sweden and the United Kingdom. The member states of the EU are linked together by the Treaty of Rome in such a way that trade is more free, that money can be moved from one country to another freely, that people can move from one country to another more freely and that people can work more freely in other countries of the group (the four fundamental freedoms).

euroyen /ˈjʊərəʊˌjen/ *noun* a Japanese yen deposited in a European bank and used for trade within Europe

Eurozone /ˈjʊərəʊzəʊn/ *noun* the European countries which use the euro as a common currency, seen as a group. Also called **Euroland**

'...the European Central Bank left the door open yesterday for a cut in Eurozone interest rates' [*Financial Times*]

'...a sustained recovery in the euro will require either a sharp slowdown in US growth or a rise in inflation and interest rates in the Eurozone beyond that already discounted' [*Investors Chronicle*]

EVA *abbr* economic value added

evade /ɪˈveɪd/ *verb* to try to avoid something

evaluate /ɪˈvæljueɪt/ *verb* to calculate a value for something ○ *to evaluate costs* ○ *We will evaluate jobs on the basis of their contribution to the organisation as a whole.* ○ *We need to evaluate the experience and qualifications of all the candidates.*

evaluation /ɪˌvæljuˈeɪʃ(ə)n/ *noun* the calculation of value

evasion /ɪˈveɪʒ(ə)n/ *noun* the act of avoiding something

EVR *abbr* Electronic Version of the Tax Return

ex /eks/ *prefix* out of or from ■ without

exact /ɪɡˈzækt/ *adjective* strictly correct, not varying in any way from, e.g. not any more or less than, what is stated ○ *The exact time is 10.27.* ○ *The salesgirl asked me if I had the exact sum, since the shop had no change.*

exact interest /ɪɡˌzækt ˈɪntrəst/ *noun* an annual interest calculated on the basis of 365 days, as opposed to ordinary interest which is calculated on 360 days

exactly /ɪgˈzæktli/ *adverb* not varying in any way from, e.g. not any more or less than, what is stated ○ *The total cost was exactly £6,500.*

ex-all /ˌeks ˈɔːl/ *adjective* referring to a share price where the share is sold without the dividend, rights issue, or any other current issue. Abbreviation **xa**

examination /ɪgˌzæmɪˈneɪʃ(ə)n/ *noun* an act of looking at something very carefully to see if it is acceptable

examine /ɪgˈzæmɪn/ *verb* to look at someone or something very carefully ○ *Customs officials asked to examine the inside of the car.* ○ *The police are examining the papers from the managing director's safe.*

examiner /ɪgˈzæmɪnə/ *noun* a person who examines something to see if it is correct

ex ante /ˌeks ˈænti/ *adverb* before the event. An ex ante budget, or standard, is set before a period of activity commences, and is based on the best information available at that time on expected levels of cost, performance, etc. Compare **ex post**

exceed /ɪkˈsiːd/ *verb* to be more than ○ *a discount not exceeding 15%* ○ *Last year costs exceeded 20% of income for the first time.*

except /ɪkˈsept/ *preposition, conjunction* not including ○ *VAT is levied on all goods and services except books, newspapers and children's clothes.* ○ *Sales are rising in all markets except the Far East.*

excepted /ɪkˈseptɪd/ *adverb* not including

exceptional /ɪkˈsepʃ(ə)l/ *adjective* different or not usual

exceptional items /ɪkˌsepʃ(ə)l ˈaɪtəmz/ *plural noun* **1.** items which arise from normal trading but which are unusual because of their size or nature; such items are shown separately in a note to the company's accounts but not on the face of the P & L account unless they are profits or losses on the sale or termination of an operation, or costs of a fundamental reorganisation or restructuring which have a material effect on the nature and focus of the reporting entity's operations, or profits or losses on the disposal of fixed assets **2.** items in a balance sheet which do not appear there each year and which are included in the accounts before the pre-tax profit is calculated, as opposed to extraordinary items which are calculated after the pre-tax profit

excess /ˈekses/; /ɪkˈses/ *noun, adjective* an amount which is more than what is allowed ○ *an excess of expenditure over revenue* ○ *Excess costs have caused us considerable problems.*

'…most airlines give business class the same baggage allowance as first class, which can save large sums in excess baggage' [*Business Traveller*]

'…control of materials provides manufacturers with an opportunity to reduce the amount of money tied up in excess materials' [*Duns Business Month*]

excess capacity /ˌekses kəˈpæsɪti/ *noun* spare capacity which is not being used

excessive /ɪkˈsesɪv/ *adjective* too large ○ *Excessive production costs made the product uneconomic.*

excess profit /ˌekses ˈprɒfɪt/ *noun* a profit which is higher than what is thought to be normal

excess profits tax /ˌekses ˈprɒfɪts tæks/ *noun* a tax on profits which are higher than what is thought to be normal

excess reserves /ɪkˌses rɪˈzɜːvz/ *plural noun* US reserves held by a financial institution that are higher than those required by the regulatory authorities. As such reserves may indicate that demand for loans is low, banks often sell their excess reserves to other institutions.

exchange /ɪksˈtʃeɪndʒ/ *noun* **1.** the act of giving one thing for another **2.** a market for shares, commodities, futures, etc. ■ *verb* **1.** □ **to exchange something (for something else)** to give one thing in place of something else ○ *He exchanged his motorcycle for a car.* ○ *Goods can be exchanged only on production of the sales slip.* **2.** to change money of one country for money of another ○ *to exchange euros for pounds*

'…under the barter agreements, Nigeria will export crude oil in exchange for trucks, food, planes and chemicals' [*Wall Street Journal*]

exchangeable /ɪksˈtʃeɪndʒəb(ə)l/ *adjective* possible to exchange

exchange control /ɪksˈtʃeɪndʒ kənˌtrəʊl/ *noun* the control by a government of the way in which its currency may be exchanged for foreign currencies

exchange controls /ɪksˈtʃeɪndʒ kənˌtrəʊlz/ *plural noun* government restrictions on changing the local currency into foreign currency ○ *The government had to impose exchange controls to stop the rush to buy dollars.* ○ *They say the government is going to lift exchange controls.*

exchange cross rates /ɪksˌtʃeɪndʒ ˈkrɒs reɪts/ *plural noun* rates of exchange for two currencies, shown against each other, but in terms of a third currency, often the US dollar. Also called **cross rates**

exchange dealer /ɪks'tʃeɪndʒ ˌdiːlə/ noun a person who buys and sells foreign currency

exchange dealings /ɪks'tʃeɪndʒ ˌdiːlɪŋz/ plural noun the buying and selling of foreign currency

exchange gain /ɪks'tʃeɪndʒ ɡeɪn/, **exchange loss** /ɪks'tʃeɪndʒ lɒs/ noun a gain or loss made from changes in the exchange rate which take place during the period of the transaction

exchange of contracts /ɪks ˌtʃeɪndʒ əv 'kɒntrækts/ noun the point in the sale of property when the buyer and the seller both sign the contract of sale, which then becomes binding

exchange premium /ɪks'tʃeɪndʒ ˌpriːmiəm/ noun an extra cost above the usual rate for buying a foreign currency

exchanger /ɪks'tʃeɪndʒə/ noun a person who buys and sells foreign currency

exchange rate mechanism /ɪks 'tʃeɪndʒ reɪt ˌmekənɪz(ə)m/ noun a former method of stabilising exchange rates within the European Monetary System, where currencies could only move up or down within a narrow band (usually 2.25% either way, but for some currencies this is widened to 6%) without involving a realignment of all the currencies in the system

exchange transaction /ɪks'tʃeɪndʒ trænˌzækʃən/ noun a purchase or sale of foreign currency

Exchequer /ɪks'tʃekə/ ◇ **the Exchequer** 1. the fund of all money received by the government of the UK from taxes and other revenues 2. the British government's account with the Bank of England 3. the British government department dealing with public revenue

excise duty /'eksaɪz ˌdjuːti/ noun a tax on goods such as alcohol and petrol which are produced in the country

exciseman /'eksaɪzmæn/ noun a person who works in the Excise Department

excise tax /'ɪksaɪz tæks/ noun US a tax levied for a particular purpose

exclude /ɪk'skluːd/ verb to keep out, or not to include ○ The interest charges have been excluded from the document. ○ Damage by fire is excluded from the policy.

exclusion /ɪk'skluːʒ(ə)n/ noun the act of not including something

exclusion clause /ɪk'skluːʒ(ə)n klɔːz/ noun a clause in an insurance policy or war-

ranty which says which items or events are not covered

exclusive agreement /ɪkˌskluːsɪv ə 'griːmənt/ noun an agreement where a person is made sole agent for a product in a market

exclusive of tax /ɪkˌskluːsɪv əv 'tæks/ adjective not including tax ○ All payments are exclusive of tax.

exclusivity /ˌeksklu'sɪvɪti/ noun the exclusive right to market a product

ex coupon /eks 'kuːpɒn/ adverb without the interest coupons or after interest has been paid

execute /'eksɪkjuːt/ verb to carry out an order ○ Failure to execute orders may lead to dismissal. ○ There were many practical difficulties in executing the managing director's instructions.

execution /ˌeksɪ'kjuːʃ(ə)n/ noun the carrying out of a commercial order or contract

executive /ɪɡ'zekjʊtɪv/ adjective putting decisions into action

executive committee /ɪɡˌzekjʊtɪv kə 'mɪti/ noun a committee which runs a society or a club

executive director /ɪɡˌzekjʊtɪv daɪ 'rektə/ noun 1. a director who works full-time in the company, as opposed to a 'non-executive director' 2. a senior employee of an organisation who is usually in charge of one or other of its main functions, e.g. sales or human relations, and is usually, but not always, a member of the board of directors

executive power /ɪɡˌzekjʊtɪv 'paʊə/ noun a right to act as director or to put decisions into action

executive share option scheme /ɪɡ ˌzekjʊtɪv 'ʃeər ɒpʃən ˌskiːm/ noun a special scheme for senior managers, by which they can buy shares in the company they work for at a fixed price at a later date

executor /ɪɡ'zekjʊtə/ noun a person or firm that sees that the terms of a will are carried out ○ She was named executor of her brother's will.

executrix /ɪɡ'zekjʊtrɪks/ noun a female executor

exemplary damages /ɪɡˌzempləri 'dæmɪdʒɪz/ plural noun heavy damages which punish the defendant for the loss or harm caused to the claimant, awarded to show that the court feels the defendant has behaved badly towards the claimant

exempt /ɪɡ'zempt/ adjective not forced to do something, especially not forced to obey a particular law or rule, or not forced to pay something ○ *Anyone over 65 is exempt from charges* ○ *He was exempt from military service in his country.* □ **exempt from tax** not required to pay tax ○ *As a non-profit-making organisation we are exempt from tax.*

'Companies with sales under $500,000 a year will be exempt from the minimum-wage requirements' [*Nation's Business*]

exempt assets /ɪɡˌzempt 'æsets/ *plural noun* assets such as cars which are not subject to capital gains tax when sold

exempt gift /ɪɡˌzempt 'ɡɪft/ *noun* a gift that is not subject to US gift tax

exempt investment fund /ɪɡˌzempt ɪn 'vestmənt fʌnd/ *noun* in the United Kingdom, a collective investment, usually a unit trust, for investors who have certain tax privileges, e.g., charities or contributors to pension plans

exemption /ɪɡ'zempʃ(ə)n/ *noun* the act of exempting something from a contract or from a tax □ **exemption from tax**, **tax exemption** the fact of being free from having to pay tax ○ *As a non-profit-making organisation you can claim tax exemption.*

exempt supplies /ɪɡˌzempt sə'plaɪz/ *plural noun* products or services on which the supplier does not have to charge VAT, e.g., the purchase of, or rent on, property and financial services

exercise /'eksəsaɪz/ *noun* **1.** a use of something **2.** a financial year ○ *during the current exercise* ■ *verb* to use ○ *The chairwoman exercised her veto to block the motion.*

exercise date /'eksəsaɪz deɪt/ *noun* a date when an option can be put into effect

exercise price /'eksəsaɪz praɪs/ *noun* a price at which an option will be put into effect

ex gratia /ˌeks 'ɡreɪʃə/ *adjective* as an act of favour, without obligation

exit charge /'eɡzɪt tʃɑːdʒ/, **exit fee** /'eɡzɪt fiː/ *noun* a charge sometimes made by a trust when selling units in a unit trust or when selling out of a PEP

exit price /'eksɪt praɪs/ *noun* the price at which an investor sells an investment or at which a firm sells up and leaves a market

ex officio /ˌeks ə'fɪʃiəʊ/ *adjective, adverb* because of an office held ○ *The treasurer is ex officio a member* or *an ex officio member of the finance committee.*

expand /ɪk'spænd/ *verb* to get bigger, or make something bigger ○ *an expanding economy* ○ *The company is expanding fast.* ○ *We have had to expand our sales force.*

expansion /ɪk'spænʃən/ *noun* an increase in size ○ *The expansion of the domestic market.* ○ *The company had difficulty in financing its current expansion programme.*

'…inflation-adjusted GNP moved up at a 1.3% annual rate, its worst performance since the economic expansion began' [*Fortune*]

'…the businesses we back range from start-up ventures to established businesses in need of further capital for expansion' [*Times*]

'…the group is undergoing a period of rapid expansion and this has created an exciting opportunity for a qualified accountant' [*Financial Times*]

ex parte /ˌeks 'pɑːti/ *Latin phrase meaning* 'on behalf of'

expected value /ɪkˌspektɪd 'væljuː/ *noun* the future value of a course of action, weighted according to the probability that the course of action will actually occur. If the possible course of action produces income of £10,000 and has a 10% chance of occurring, its expected value is 10% of £10,000 or £1,000.

expenditure /ɪk'spendɪtʃə/ *noun* the amount of money spent

expense /ɪk'spens/ *noun* money spent ○ *It is not worth the expense.* ○ *The expense is too much for my bank balance.* ○ *The likely profits do not justify the expense of setting up the project.* ○ *It was well worth the expense to get really high-quality equipment.*

expense account /ɪk'spens əˌkaʊnt/ *noun* an allowance of money which a business pays for an employee to spend on travelling and entertaining clients in connection with that business ○ *I'll put this lunch on my expense account.*

expenses /ɪk'spensɪz/ *plural noun* money paid to cover the costs incurred by someone when doing something ○ *The salary offered is £10,000 plus expenses.* ○ *She has a high salary and all her travel expenses are paid by the company.*

expert system /'ekspɜːt ˌsɪstəm/ *noun* software that applies the knowledge, advice and rules defined by experts in a particular field to a user's data to help solve a problem

expiration /ˌekspə'reɪʃ(ə)n/ *noun* the act of coming to an end ○ *the expiration of an insurance policy* ○ *to repay before the expiration of the stated period*

expire /ɪk'spaɪə/ *verb* to come to an end ○ *The lease expires in 2010.*

expiry /ɪk'spaɪəri/ *noun* the act of coming to an end ○ *the expiry of an insurance policy*

exponent /ɪk'spəʊnənt/ *noun* a number indicating how many times a base number is to be multiplied to produce a power. It is printed in small characters after the base number.

export /ɪk'spɔːt/ *verb* to send goods to foreign countries for sale ○ *50% of our production is exported.* ○ *The company imports raw materials and exports the finished products.*

exportation /ˌekspɔː'teɪʃ(ə)n/ *noun* the act of sending goods to foreign countries for sale

Export Credit Guarantee Department /ˌekspɔːt ˌkredɪt gæærən'tiː dɪ ˌpɑːtmənt/ *noun* a British government department which insures sellers of exports sold on credit against the possibility of non-payment by the purchasers. Abbreviation **ECGD**

export department /'ekspɔːt dɪ ˌpɑːtmənt/ *noun* the section of a company which deals in sales to foreign countries

export duty /'ekspɔːt ˌdjuːti/ *noun* a tax paid on goods sent out of a country for sale

exporter /ɪk'spɔːtə/ *noun* a person, company or country that sells goods in foreign countries ○ *a major furniture exporter* ○ *Canada is an important exporter of oil* or *an important oil exporter.*

export house /'ekspɔːt haʊs/ *noun* a company which specialises in the export of goods manufactured by other companies

exporting /ek'spɔːtɪŋ/ *adjective* sending goods out of a country

export licence /'ekspɔːt ˌlaɪs(ə)ns/ *noun* a government permit allowing something to be exported ○ *The government has refused an export licence for computer parts.*

export manager /'ekspɔːt ˌmænɪdʒə/ *noun* the person in charge of an export department in a company ○ *The export manager planned to set up a sales force in Southern Europe.* ○ *Sales managers from all export markets report to our export manager.*

exports /'ekspɔːts/ *plural noun* goods sent to a foreign country to be sold ○ *Exports to Africa have increased by 25%.* (NOTE: Usually used in the plural, but the singular form is used before a noun.)

ex post /ˌeks 'pəʊst/ *adverb* after the event. An ex post budget, or standard, is set after the end of a period of activity, when it can represent the optimum achievable level of performance in the conditions which were experienced. Thus the budget can be flexed, and standards can reflect factors such as unanticipated changes in technology and in price levels. Compare **ex ante**

exposure /ɪk'spəʊʒə/ *noun* **1.** publicity given to an organisation or product ○ *Our*

company has achieved more exposure since we decided to advertise nationally. **2.** the amount of risk which a lender or investor runs ○ *He is trying to limit his exposure in the property market.*

'…it attributed the poor result to the bank's high exposure to residential mortgages, which showed a significant slowdown in the past few months' [*South China Morning Post*]

exposure draft /ɪk'spəʊʒə drɑːft/ *noun* a document produced by a body before a new authoritative pronouncement is published. It invites accountants and other interested parties to comment on matters raised by the draft. Abbreviation **ED**

express delivery /ɪkˌspres dɪ'lɪv(ə)ri/ *noun* a very fast delivery

expressly /ɪk'spresli/ *adverb* clearly in words ○ *The contract expressly forbids sales to the United States.*

extend /ɪk'stend/ *verb* **1.** to offer something ○ *to extend credit to a customer* **2.** to make something longer ○ *Her contract of employment was extended for two years.* ○ *We have extended the deadline for making the appointment by two weeks.*

extended credit /ɪkˌstendɪd 'kredɪt/ *noun* **1.** credit allowing the borrower a very long time to pay ○ *We sell to Australia on extended credit.* **2.** *US* an extra long credit used by commercial banks borrowing from the Federal Reserve

extension /ɪk'stenʃən/ *noun* **1.** a longer time allowed for something than was originally agreed **2.** (*in an office*) an individual telephone linked to the main switchboard ○ *The sales manager is on extension 53.* ○ *Can you get me extension 21?* ○ *Extension 21 is engaged.*

'…the White House refusal to ask for an extension of the auto import quotas' [*Duns Business Month*]

extensive /ɪk'stensɪv/ *adjective* very large or covering a wide area ○ *an extensive network of sales outlets* ○ *an extensive recruitment drive*

external /ɪk'stɜːn(ə)l/ *adjective* **1.** outside a country. Opposite **internal 2.** outside a company

external account /ɪkˌstɜːn(ə)l ə'kaʊnt/ *noun* an account in a British bank belonging to someone who is living in another country

external audit /ɪkˌstɜːn(ə)l 'ɔːdɪt/ *noun* **1.** an audit carried out by an independent auditor who is not employed by the company **2.** an evaluation of the effectiveness of a company's public relations carried out by an outside agency

external auditing /ɪkˌstɜːn(ə)l ˈɔːdɪtɪŋ/ noun an action of auditing a set of accounts by an external auditor

external auditor /ɪkˌstɜːn(ə)l ˈɔːdɪtə/ noun an independent person who audits the company's accounts

external debt /ɪkˌstɜːn(ə)l ˈdet/ noun money which a company has borrowed from outside sources such as a bank, as opposed to money raised from shareholders

external funds /ɪkˌstɜːn(ə)l ˈfʌndz/ plural noun same as **external debt**

external growth /ɪkˌstɜːn(ə)l ˈɡrəʊθ/ noun growth by buying other companies, rather than by expanding existing sales or products. Opposite **internal growth**

external liabilities /ɪkˌstɜːn(ə)l ˌlaɪəˈbɪlɪtiz/ plural noun money owed to lenders and other creditors outside a company

external trade /ɪkˌstɜːn(ə)l ˈtreɪd/ noun trade with foreign countries. Opposite **internal trade**

extract /ˈekstrækt/ noun a printed document which is part of a larger document ○ He sent me an extract of the accounts.

extraordinary /ɪkˈstrɔːd(ə)n(ə)ri/ adjective different from normal

extraordinary items /ɪkˈstrɔːd(ə)n(ə)ri ˌaɪtəmz/ plural noun formerly, large items of income or expenditure which did not arise from usual trading and which did not occur every year. They were shown separately in the P&L account, after taxation.

extraordinary resolution /ɪkˌstrɔːd(ə)n(ə)ri ˌrezəˈluːʃ(ə)n/ noun a resolution which needs 75% of the votes before it can be carried

F

face value /ˌfeɪs ˈvæljuː/ noun the value written on a coin, banknote or share certificate

'…travellers cheques cost 1% of their face value – some banks charge more for small amounts' [Sunday Times]

facility /fəˈsɪlɪti/ noun the total amount of credit which a lender will allow a borrower

facility fee /fəˈsɪlɪti fiː/ noun a charge made to a borrower by a bank for arranging credit facilities

facility-sustaining activities /fəˌsɪlɪti səˌsteɪnɪŋ ækˈtɪvɪtiz/ noun activities undertaken to support the organisation as a whole, which cannot be logically linked to individual units of output. Accounting is a facility-sustaining activity.

factor /ˈfæktə/ noun **1.** something which is important, or which is taken into account when making a decision ○ The drop in sales is an important factor in the company's lower profits. ○ Motivation was an important factor in drawing up the new pay scheme. **2.** a number used in multiplication to produce another number □ **by a factor of ten** ten times **3.** a person or company which is responsible for collecting debts for companies, by buying debts at a discount on their face value **4.** a person who sells for a business or another person and earns a commission ■ verb to buy debts from a company at a discount

'…factors 'buy' invoices from a company, which then gets an immediate cash advance representing most of their value. The balance is paid when the debt is met. The client company is charged a fee as well as interest on the cash advanced' [Times]

factorial /fækˈtɔːriəl/ noun the product of all the numbers below a number ○ example: 4 factorial = 1x2x3x4 = 24 (NOTE: **4 factorial** is written **4!**)

factoring /ˈfæktərɪŋ/ noun the business of buying debts from a firm at a discount and then getting the debtors to pay

factoring charges /ˈfæktərɪŋ ˌtʃɑːdʒɪz/ plural noun the cost of selling debts to a factor for a commission

factors of production /ˌfæktəz əv prəˈdʌkʃən/ plural noun land, labour and capital, i.e. the three things needed to produce a product

factory gate price /ˌfækt(ə)rɪ 'geɪt praɪs/ *noun* the actual cost of manufacturing goods before any mark-up is added to give profit (NOTE: The factory gate price includes direct costs such as labour, raw materials and energy, and indirect costs such as interest on loans, plant maintenance or rent.)

factory overhead /ˌfækt(ə)ri 'əʊvəhed/ *noun* a production overhead, indirect costs of production which are absorbed into the cost of goods produced

FAE *abbr* Final Admitting Exam

fail /feɪl/ *verb* to be unsuccessful ○ *The prototype failed its first test.*

failure /'feɪljə/ *noun* an act of breaking down or stopping ○ *the failure of the negotiations*

fair /feə/ *adjective* reasonable, with equal treatment

fair copy /ˌfeə 'kɒpi/ *noun* a document which is written or typed with no changes or mistakes

fair dealing /ˌfeə 'diːlɪŋ/ *noun* the legal buying and selling of shares

fair price /ˌfeə 'praɪs/ *noun* a good price for both buyer and seller

fair trade /feə 'treɪd/ *noun* an international business system where countries agree not to charge import duties on some items imported from their trading partners

fair value /ˌfeə 'væljuː/ *noun* **1.** a price paid by a buyer who knows the value of what he or she is buying, to a seller who also knows the value of what is being sold, i.e., neither is cheating the other **2.** a method of valuing the assets and liabilities of a business based on the amount for which they could be sold to independent parties at the time of valuation

fair wear and tear /ˌfeə weər ən 'teə/ *noun* acceptable damage caused by normal use ○ *The insurance policy covers most damage but not fair wear and tear to the machine.*

fall /fɔːl/ *noun* a sudden reduction or loss of value ○ *a fall in the exchange rate* ○ *a fall in the price of gold* ○ *a fall on the Stock Exchange* ○ *Profits showed a 10% fall.* ■ *verb* **1.** to be reduced suddenly to a lower price or value ○ *Shares fell on the market today.* ○ *Gold shares fell 10% or fell 45 cents on the Stock Exchange.* ○ *The price of gold fell for the second day running.* ○ *The pound fell against the euro.* **2.** to happen or to take place ○ *The public holiday falls on a Tuesday.*

'…market analysts described the falls in the second half of last week as a technical correction to the market' [*Australian Financial Review*]

'…for the first time since mortgage rates began falling in March a financial institution has raised charges on homeowner loans' [*Globe and Mail (Toronto)*]

'…interest rates were still falling as late as June, and underlying inflation remains below the government's target of 2.5 per cent' [*Financial Times*]

fall away /ˌfɔːl ə'weɪ/ *verb* to become less ○ *Hotel bookings have fallen away since the tourist season ended.*

fall back /ˌfɔːl 'bæk/ *verb* to become lower or cheaper after rising in price ○ *Shares fell back in light trading.*

fall behind /ˌfɔːl bɪ'haɪnd/ *verb* to be late in doing something ○ *They fell behind with their mortgage repayments.*

falling /'fɔːlɪŋ/ *adjective* becoming smaller or dropping in price

'…falling profitability means falling share prices' [*Investors Chronicle*]

fall off /ˌfɔːl 'ɒf/ *verb* to become lower, cheaper or less ○ *Sales have fallen off since the tourist season ended.*

false /fɔːls/ *adjective* not true or not correct ○ *to make a false claim for a product* ○ *to make a false entry in the balance sheet*

false accounting /ˌfɔːls ə'kaʊntɪŋ/ *noun* a criminal offence of changing, destroying or hiding accounting records for a dishonest purpose, such as to gain money

false market /ˌfɔːls 'mɑːkɪt/ *noun* a market in shares caused by persons or companies conspiring to buy or sell and so influence the share price to their advantage

false weight /ˌfɔːls 'weɪt/ *noun* a weight as measured on a shop scales which is wrong and so cheats customers

falsification /ˌfɔːlsɪfɪ'keɪʃ(ə)n/ *noun* the act of making false entries in accounts

falsify /'fɔːlsɪfaɪ/ *verb* to change something to make it wrong ○ *They were accused of falsifying the accounts.*

family company /'fæm(ə)li ˌkʌmp(ə)ni/ *noun* a company where most of the shares are owned by members of a family

f. & f. *abbr* fixtures and fittings

FASB *abbr* Financial Accounting Standards Board

favourable /'feɪv(ə)rəb(ə)l/ *adjective* giving an advantage (NOTE: The US spelling is **favorable**.)

favourable trade balance /ˌfeɪv(ə)rəb(ə)l 'treɪd ˌbæləns/ *noun* a situation where a country exports more than it imports ○ *The country has had an adverse balance of trade for the second month running.*

favourable variance /ˌfeɪv(ə)rəb(ə)l ˈveərɪəns/ *noun* variance which shows that the actual result is better than expected

fax /fæks/ *noun* a system for sending the exact copy of a document via telephone lines ○ *Can you confirm the booking by fax?* ■ *verb* to send a message by fax ○ *The details of the offer were faxed to the brokers this morning.* ○ *I've faxed the documents to our New York office.*

FCA *abbr* Fellow of the Institute of Chartered Accountants in England and Wales

FCCA *abbr* Fellow of the Association of Chartered Certified Accountants

federal /ˈfed(ə)rəl/ *adjective* **1.** referring to a system of government where a group of states are linked together in a federation **2.** referring to the central government of the United States ○ *Most federal offices are in Washington.*

'…federal examiners will determine which of the privately-insured savings and loans qualify for federal insurance' [*Wall Street Journal*]

'…since 1978 America has freed many of its industries from federal rules that set prices and controlled the entry of new companies' [*Economist*]

Federal Funds /ˌfed(ə)rəl ˈfʌndz/ *plural noun* deposits by commercial banks with the Federal Reserve Banks, which can be used for short-term loans to other banks

Federal Reserve /ˌfed(ə)rəl rɪˈzɜːv/, **Federal Reserve System** /ˌfed(ə)rəl rɪˈzɜːv ˌsɪstəm/ *noun* the system of federal government control of the US banks, where the Federal Reserve Board regulates money supply, prints money, fixes the discount rate and issues government bonds

federation /ˌfedəˈreɪʃ(ə)n/ *noun* a group of societies, companies or organisations which have a central organisation which represents them and looks after their common interests ○ *a federation of trades unions* ○ *the employers' federation*

Fed Funds /ˈfed fʌndz/ *plural noun US* same as **Federal Funds** (*informal*)

fed funds rate /ˈfed fʌndz ˌreɪt/ *noun* the rate charged by banks for lending money deposited with the Federal Reserve to other banks ○ *most federal offices are in Washington*

fee /fiː/ *noun* money paid for work carried out by a professional person such as an accountant, a doctor or a lawyer ○ *We charge a small fee for our services.* ○ *The consultant's fee was much higher than we expected.*

fee work /ˈfiː wɜːk/ *noun* FINANCE, BANKING, AND ACCOUNTING, GENERAL MANAGEMENT any work on a project carried out by in-

dependent workers or contractors, rather than by the organisation's employees

fellow /ˈfeləʊ/ *noun* a title given to senior members of a professional association. Junior members are usually called 'associates'.

fiat money /ˈfiːæt ˌmʌni/ *noun* coins or notes which are not worth much as paper or metal, but are said by the government to have a value and are recognised as legal tender

fictitious assets /fɪkˌtɪʃəs ˈæsets/ *plural noun* assets which do not really exist, but are entered as assets to balance the accounts

fiddle /ˈfɪd(ə)l/ (*informal*) *noun* an act of cheating ○ *It's all a fiddle.* ■ *verb* to cheat ○ *He tried to fiddle his tax returns.* ○ *The salesman was caught fiddling his expense account.*

fiduciary /fɪˈdjuːʃəri/ *noun, adjective* a person in a position of trust ○ *Directors have fiduciary duty to act in the best interests of the company.*

fiduciary deposits /fɪˌdjuːʃəri dɪ ˈpɒzɪtz/ *plural noun* bank deposits which are managed for the depositor by the bank

FIFO /ˈfaɪfəʊ/ *abbr* first in first out

fifty-fifty /ˌfɪfti ˈfɪfti/ *adjective, adverb* half

figure /ˈfɪɡə/ *noun* **1.** a number, or a cost written in numbers ○ *The figure in the accounts for heating is very high.* **2.** □ *his income runs into six figures or he has a six-figure income* his income is more than £100,000

figures /ˈfɪɡəz/ *plural noun* **1.** written numbers **2.** the results for a company ○ *the figures for last year or last year's figures*

file /faɪl/ *noun* **1.** documents kept for reference **2.** a section of data on a computer, e.g. payroll, address list, customer accounts ○ *How can we protect our computer files?* ■ *verb* **1.** to make an official request **2.** to register something officially ○ *to file an application for a patent* ○ *to file a return to the tax office*

file copy /ˈfaɪl ˌkɒpi/ *noun* a copy of a document which is kept for reference in an office

filing date /ˈfaɪlɪŋ deɪt/ *noun* the date by which income tax returned must be filed with the Inland Revenue

filing system /ˈfaɪlɪŋ ˌsɪstəm/ *noun* a way of putting documents in order for easy reference

final /ˈfaɪn(ə)l/ *adjective* last, coming at the end of a period ○ *to pay the final instalment* ○ *to make the final payment* ○ *to put the final details on a document*

final accounts /ˌfaɪn(ə)l əˈkaʊntz/ *noun* the accounts produced at the end of an accounting period, including the balance sheet and profit and loss account

Final Admitting Exam /ˌfaɪn(ə)l əd ˈmɪtɪŋ ɪgˈzæm/ *noun* a final examination set by the ICAEW to admit student accountants as Chartered Accountants. Abbreviation **FAE**

final closing date /ˌfaɪn(ə)l ˈkləʊzɪŋ deɪt/ *noun* the last date for acceptance of a takeover bid, when the bidder has to announce how many shareholders have accepted his or her offer ○ *to pay the final instalment* ○ *to make the final payment* ○ *to put the final details on a document*

final demand /ˌfaɪn(ə)l dɪˈmɑːnd/ *noun* the last reminder from a supplier, after which they will sue for payment

final discharge /ˌfaɪn(ə)l dɪsˈtʃɑːdʒ/ *noun* the last payment of what is left of a debt

final dividend /ˌfaɪn(ə)l ˈdɪvɪdend/ *noun* a dividend paid at the end of a year's trading, which has to be approved by the shareholders at an AGM

finalise /ˈfaɪnəlaɪz/, **finalize** *verb* to agree final details ○ *We hope to finalise the agreement tomorrow.* ○ *After six weeks of negotiations the loan was finalised yesterday.*

final settlement /ˌfaɪn(ə)l ˈset(ə)lmənt/ *noun* the last payment which settles a debt

finance /ˈfaɪnæns/ *noun* **1.** money used by a company, provided by the shareholders or by loans ○ *Where will they get the necessary finance for the project?* **2.** money (used by a club, local authority, etc.) ○ *She is the secretary of the local authority finance committee.* ■ *verb* to provide money to pay for something ○ *They plan to finance the operation with short-term loans.*

'…an official said that the company began to experience a sharp increase in demand for longer-term mortgages at a time when the flow of money used to finance these loans diminished' [*Globe and Mail*]

Finance Act /ˈfaɪnæns ækt/ *noun* an annual Act of Parliament which gives the government the power to obtain money from taxes as proposed in the Budget

Finance Bill /ˈfaɪnæns bɪl/ *noun* **1.** a bill which lists the proposals in a chancellor's budget and which is debated before being voted into law as the Finance Act **2.** *US* a short-term bill of exchange which provides credit for a corporation so that it can continue trading

finance controller /ˌfaɪnæns kən ˈtrəʊlə/ *noun* an accountant whose main task is to manage the company's monetary resources

finance lease /ˈfaɪnæns liːs/ *noun* a lease which requires the lessee company to show the asset acquired under the lease in its balance sheet and to depreciate it in the usual way

finance leasing /ˌfaɪnæns ˈliːsɪŋ/ *noun* leasing a property under a finance lease

finance market /ˈfaɪnæns ˌmɑːkɪt/ *noun* a place where large sums of money can be lent or borrowed

finances /ˈfaɪnænsɪz/ *plural noun* money or cash which is available ○ *the bad state of the company's finances*

financial /faɪˈnænʃəl/ *adjective* concerning money

Financial Accountant /faɪˌnænʃ(ə)l əˈkaʊntənt/ *noun* a qualified accountant, a member of the Institute of Financial Accountants, who advises on accounting matters or who works as the financial director of a company

Financial Accounting Standards Board /faɪˌnænʃ(ə)l əˈkaʊntɪŋ/ *noun* the body which regulates accounting standards in the USA. Abbreviation **FASB**

financial adviser /faɪˌnænʃəl ədˈvaɪzə/ *noun* a person or company which gives advice on financial problems for a fee

financial aid /faɪˌnænʃəl ˈeɪd/ *noun* monetary assistance given to an individual, organisation, or nation. International financial aid, that is from one country to another, is often used to fund educational, health-related, or other humanitarian activities.

financial assistance /faɪˌnænʃəl əˈsɪstəns/ *noun* help in the form of money

financial calendar /faɪˌnænʃəl ˈkælɪndə/ *noun* a list of significant events and dates in a company's financial reporting year

financial correspondent /faɪˌnænʃəl ˌkɒrɪsˈpɒndənt/ *noun* a journalist who writes articles on money matters for a newspaper

financial futures /faɪˌnænʃəl ˈfjuːtʃəz/, **financial futures contract** /faɪˌnænʃəl ˈfjuːtʃəz ˌkɒntrækt/ *noun* a contract for the purchase of gilt-edged securities for delivery at a date in the future

financial futures market /faɪˌnænʃəl ˈfjuːtʃəz ˌmɑːkɪt/ *noun* the market in gilt-edged securities for delivery at a date in the future

financial institution /faɪˌnænʃəl ˌɪnstɪ ˈtjuːʃ(ə)n/ *noun* a bank, investment trust or insurance company whose work involves lending or investing large sums of money

financial instrument /faɪˌnænʃəl ˈɪnstrʊmənt/ *noun* **1.** a document showing that money has been lent or borrowed, invested or passed from one account to another, e.g. a bill of exchange, share certificate, certificate of deposit, an IOU **2.** any form of investment in the stock market or in other financial markets, e.g. shares, government stocks, certificates of deposit or bills of exchange

financial intermediary /faɪˌnænʃəl ˌɪntəˈmiːdiəri/ *noun* an institution which takes deposits or loans from individuals and lends money to clients

financial leverage /faɪˌnænʃəl ˈliːvərɪdʒ/ *noun* ▶ **gearing**

financially /fɪˈnænʃəli/ *adverb* regarding money □ **a company which is financially sound** a company which is profitable and has strong assets

financial management /faɪˌnænʃəl ˈmænɪdʒmənt/ *noun* management of the acquisition and use of long- and short-term capital by a business

financial position /faɪˌnænʃəl pəˈzɪʃ(ə)n/ *noun* the state of a person's or company's bank balance in terms of assets and debts ○ *She must think of her financial position.*

financial report /faɪˌnænʃəl rɪˈpɔːt/ *noun* a document which gives the financial position of a company or of a club, etc.

Financial Reporting Review Panel /faɪˌnænʃ(ə)l rɪˌpɔːtɪŋ rɪˈvjuː ˌpæn(ə)l/ *noun* a UK body that receives and investigates complaints about the annual accounts of companies in respect of apparent departures from the accounting requirements of the Companies Act, including the requirement to give a true and fair view. Abbreviation **FRRP**

Financial Reporting Standards *plural noun* a series of accounting standards issued by the Accounting Standards Board outlining common accounting practice. Abbreviation **FRSs**

financial resources /faɪˌnænʃəl rɪˈzɔːsɪz/ *plural noun* the supply of money for something ○ *a company with strong financial resources*

financial review /faɪˌnænʃəl rɪˈvjuː/ *noun* an examination of an organisation's finances

financial risk /faɪˌnænʃəl ˈrɪsk/ *noun* the possibility of losing money ○ *The company is taking a considerable financial risk in manufacturing 25 million units without doing any market research.* ○ *There is always some financial risk in selling on credit.*

financials /faɪˈnænʃəlz/ *plural noun* same as **financial futures**

Financial Services Act /faɪˌnænʃəl ˈsɜːvɪsɪz ækt/ *noun* an Act of the British Parliament which regulates the offering of financial services to the general public and to private investors

Financial Services Authority /faɪˌnænʃ(ə)l ˈsɜːvɪsɪz ɔːˌθɒrəti/ *noun* an independent non-governmental body formed in 1997 as a result of reforms in the regulation of financial services in the United Kingdom. The Securities and Investments Board (SIB) became responsible for the supervision of banking and investment services and changed its name to become the Financial Services Authority. The FSA's four statutory objectives were specified by the Financial Services and Markets Act 2000: maintaining market confidence; increasing public knowledge of the finance system; ensuring appropriate protection for consumers; and reducing financial crime. Abbreviation **FSA**

financial statement /faɪˌnænʃəl ˈsteɪtmənt/ *noun* a document which shows the financial situation of a company ○ *The accounts department has prepared a financial statement for the shareholders.*

financial supermarket /faɪˌnænʃəl ˈsuːpəmɑːkɪt/ *noun* a company which offers a range of financial services, e.g. a bank offering loans, mortgages, pensions and insurance as well as the usual personal banking services

financial year /faɪˌnænʃəl ˈjɪə/ *noun* the twelve-month period for which a company produces accounts. A financial year is not necessarily the same as a calendar year.

financier /faɪˈnænsiə/ *noun* a person who lends large amounts of money to companies or who buys shares in companies as an investment

financing /ˈfaɪnænsɪŋ/ *noun* the act of providing money for a project ○ *The financing of the project was done by two international banks.*

finder's fee /ˈfaɪndəz fiː/ *noun* a fee paid to a person who finds a client for another, e.g., someone who introduces a client to a stockbroking firm

fine /faɪn/ *noun* money paid because of something wrong which has been done ○ *She was asked to pay a $25,000 fine.* ○ *We had to pay a £50 parking fine.*

fine-tuning /faɪn ˈtjuːnɪŋ/ *noun* the act of making of small adjustments in areas such as interest rates, tax bands or the money supply, to improve a nation's economy

fire insurance /ˈfaɪər ɪnˌʃʊərəns/ *noun* insurance against damage by fire

fire sale /ˈfaɪə seɪl/ *noun* a sale of fire-damaged goods

firm /fɜːm/ *noun* a company, business or partnership ○ *a manufacturing firm* ○ *an important publishing firm* ○ *She is a partner in a law firm.* ■ *adjective* **1.** unchangeable ○ *to make a firm offer for something* ○ *to place a firm order for two aircraft* **2.** not dropping in price and possibly going to rise ○ *Sterling was firmer on the foreign exchange markets.* ○ *Shares remained firm.* ■ *verb* to remain at a price and seem likely to rise ○ *The shares firmed at £1.50.*

'…some profit-taking was noted, but underlying sentiment remained firm' [*Financial Times*]

firmness /ˈfɜːmnəs/ *noun* the fact of being steady at a particular price, or likely to rise ○ *the firmness of the pound on foreign exchanges*

'Toronto failed to mirror New York's firmness as a drop in gold shares on a falling bullion price left the market closing on a mixed note' [*Financial Times*]

firm price /ˌfɜːm ˈpraɪs/ *noun* a price which will not change ○ *They are quoting a firm price of $1.23 a unit.*

firm sale /ˌfɜːm ˈseɪl/ *noun* a sale which does not allow the purchaser to return the goods

firm up /ˌfɜːm ˈʌp/ *verb* to agree on the final details of something ○ *We expect to firm up the deal at the next trade fair.*

first /fɜːst/ *noun* a person or thing that is there at the beginning or earlier than others ○ *Our company was one of the first to sell into the European market.*

first-class /ˌfɜːst ˈklɑːs/ *adjective* top-quality or most expensive ○ *She is a first-class accountant.*

first in first out /ˌfɜːst ɪn ˌfɜːst ˈaʊt/ *phrase* an accounting policy where it is assumed that stocks in hand were purchased last, and that stocks sold during the period were purchased first. Abbreviation **FIFO**. Compare **last in first out**

first option /ˌfɜːst ˈɒpʃən/ *noun* allowing someone to be the first to have the possibility of deciding something

first quarter /ˌfɜːst ˈkwɔːtə/ *noun* the period of three months from January to the end of March ○ *The first quarter's rent is payable in advance.*

first year allowance /ˌfɜːst jɪə ə ˈlaʊəns/ *noun* an allowance which can be claimed on capital expenditure by a business or self-employed person during the year in which the purchase was made. After the first

year, the written down allowance (WDA) applies. Abbreviation **FYA**

fiscal /ˈfɪskəl/ *adjective* referring to tax or to government revenues

fiscal drag /ˌfɪskəl ˈdræg/ *noun* **1.** the effect of inflation on a government's tax revenues. As inflation increases so do prices and wages, and tax revenues rise proportionally. Even if inflation is low, increased earnings will give the government increased revenues anyway. **2.** the negative effect of higher personal taxation on an individual's work performance

fiscal measures /ˌfɪskəl ˈmeʒəz/ *plural noun* tax changes made by a government to improve the working of the economy

fiscal year /ˌfɪskəl ˈjɪə/ *noun* a twelve-month period on which taxes are calculated. In the UK this is April 6th to April 5th.

'…last fiscal year the chain reported a 116% jump in earnings' [*Barron's*]

fittings /ˈfɪtɪŋz/ *plural noun* items in a property which are sold with it but are not permanently fixed, e.g. carpets or shelves. ◊ **fixtures**

five dollar bill /ˌfaɪv ˌdɒlə ˈbɪl/ *noun* a banknote for five dollars

fixed /fɪkst/ *adjective* unable to be changed or removed

'…you must offer shippers and importers fixed rates over a reasonable period of time' [*Lloyd's List*]

fixed assets /fɪkst ˈæsets/ *plural noun* property or machinery which a company owns and uses, but which the company does not buy or sell as part of its regular trade, including the company's investments in shares of other companies

fixed budget /ˌfɪkst ˈbʌdʒɪt/ *noun* a budget which refers to a specific level of business, i.e., a sales turnover which produces a specific level of profit

fixed capital /fɪkst ˈkæpɪt(ə)l/ *noun* capital in the form of buildings and machinery

fixed charge /ˌfɪkst ˈtʃɑːdʒ/ *noun* a charge over a particular asset *or* property

fixed costs /fɪkst ˈkɒsts/ *plural noun* business costs which do not change with the quantity of the product made

fixed deduction /ˌfɪkst dɪˈdʌkʃən/ *noun* a deduction agreed by the Inland Revenue and a group of employees, such as a trade union, which covers general expenditure on clothes or tools used in the course of employment

fixed deposit /ˌfɪkst dɪˈpɒzɪt/ *noun* a deposit which pays a stated interest over a set period

fixed exchange rate /ˌfɪkst ɪks'tʃeɪndʒ ˌreɪt/ *noun* a rate of exchange of one currency against another which cannot fluctuate, and can only be changed by devaluation or revaluation

fixed expenses /ˌfɪkst ɪk'spensɪz/ *plural noun* expenses which do not vary with different levels of production, e.g. rent, secretaries' salaries and insurance

fixed income /ˌfɪkst 'ɪnkʌm/ *noun* income which does not change from year to year, as from an annuity

fixed-interest /ˌfɪkst 'ɪntrəst/ *adjective* having an interest rate which does not vary

fixed-interest investments /ˌfɪkst ˌɪntrəst ɪn'vestmənts/ *plural noun* investments producing an interest which does not change

fixed-interest securities /fɪkst ˌɪntrəst sɪ'kjʊərɪtiz/ *plural noun* securities such as government bonds which produce an interest which does not change

fixed-price /ˌfɪkst 'praɪs/ *adjective* having a price which cannot be changed

fixed-price agreement /ˌfɪkst 'praɪs ə ˌgriːmənt/ *noun* an agreement where a company provides a service or a product at a price which stays the same for the whole period of the agreement

fixed rate /ˌfɪkst 'reɪt/ *noun* a rate, e.g. an exchange rate, which does not change

fixed rate loan /ˌfɪkst reɪt 'ləʊn/ *noun* a loan on which the rate of interest stays the same for the duration of the loan

fixed scale of charges /ˌfɪkst skeɪl əv 'tʃɑːdʒɪz/ *noun* a rate of charging which does not change

fixed yield /ˌfɪkst 'jiːld/ *noun* a percentage return which does not change

fixer /'fɪksə/ *noun* a person who has a reputation for arranging business deals, often illegally

fixing /'fɪksɪŋ/ *noun* **1.** arranging ○ *the fixing of charges* ○ *the fixing of a mortgage rate* **2.** a regular meeting to set a price

fixtures /'fɪkstʃəz/ *plural noun* items in a property which are permanently attached to it, e.g. sinks and lavatories

fixtures and fittings /ˌfɪkstʃəz ən 'fɪtɪŋz/ *plural noun* objects in a property which are sold with the property, both those which cannot be removed and those which can. Abbreviation **f. & f.**

flat /flæt/ *adjective* **1.** referring to market prices which do not fall or rise, because of low demand ○ *The market was flat today.* **2.**

not changing in response to different conditions

'...the government revised its earlier reports for July and August. Originally reported as flat in July and declining by 0.2% in August, industrial production is now seen to have risen by 0.2% and 0.1% respectively in those months' [*Sunday Times*]

flat rate /ˌflæt 'reɪt/ *noun* a charge which always stays the same ○ *a flat-rate increase of 10%* ○ *We pay a flat rate for electricity each quarter.* ○ *He is paid a flat rate of £2 per thousand.*

flat tax /ˌflæt 'tæks/ *noun* a tax levied at one fixed rate whatever an individual's income

flat yield /ˌflæt 'jiːld/ *noun* an interest rate as a percentage of the price paid for fixed- interest stock

flexibility /ˌfleksɪ'bɪlɪti/ *noun* the ability to be easily changed ○ *There is no flexibility in the company's pricing policy.*

'...they calculate interest on their 'flexible' mortgage on an annual basis rather than daily. Charging annual interest makes a nonsense of the whole idea of flexibility which is supposed to help you pay off your mortgage more quickly' [*Financial Times*]

flexible /'fleksɪb(ə)l/ *adjective* possible to alter or change ○ *We try to be flexible where the advertising budget is concerned.* ○ *The company has adopted a flexible pricing policy.*

flexible budget /ˌfleksɪb(ə)l 'bʌdʒɪt/ *noun* a budget which changes in response to changes in sales turnover or output

flight of capital /ˌflaɪt əv 'kæpɪt(ə)l/ *noun* a rapid movement of capital out of one country because of lack of confidence in that country's economic future

flight to quality /ˌflaɪt tə 'kwɒlɪti/ *noun* a tendency of investors to buy safe blue-chip securities when the economic outlook is uncertain

float /fləʊt/ *noun* **1.** cash taken from a central supply and used for running expenses ○ *The sales reps have a float of £100 each.* **2.** the process of starting a new company by selling shares in it on the Stock Exchange ○ *The float of the new company was a complete failure.* **3.** the process of allowing a currency to settle at its own exchange rate, without any government intervention **4.** the period between the presentation of a cheque as payment and the actual payment to the payee or the financial advantage provided by this period to the drawer of a cheque ■ *verb* to let a currency find its own exchange rate on the international markets and not be fixed ○ *The government has let sterling float.* ○ *The government has decided to float the pound.*

floating /ˈfləʊtɪŋ/ *adjective* not fixed ○ *floating exchange rates* ○ *the floating pound*
'...in a world of floating exchange rates the dollar is strong because of capital inflows rather than weak because of the nation's trade deficit' [*Duns Business Month*]

floating charge /ˈfləʊtɪŋ tʃɑːdʒ/ *noun* a charge linked to any of the company's assets in a category, but not to any specific item

floating rate /ˈfləʊtɪŋ reɪt/ *noun* 1. same as **variable rate** 2. an exchange rate for a currency which can vary according to market demand, and is not fixed by the government

floating-rate notes /ˌfləʊtɪŋ reɪt ˈnəʊts/ *plural noun* eurocurrency loans arranged by a bank which are not at a fixed rate of interest. Abbreviation **FRNs**

floor /flɔː/ *noun* a bottom level of something, e.g. the lowest exchange rate which a government will accept for its currency or the lower limit imposed on an interest rate ○ *The government will impose a floor on wages to protect the poor.*

floor broker /ˈflɔː ˌbrəʊkə/ *noun* a stockbroker who is a member of a brokerage house

floor price /ˈflɔː praɪs/ *noun* a lowest price, a price which cannot go any lower

floor space /ˈflɔː speɪs/ *noun* an area of floor in an office or warehouse ○ *We have 3,500 square metres of floor space to let.*

floor trader /ˈflɔː ˌtreɪdə/ *noun* an independent trader on a Stock Exchange, who buys and sells on his or her own account

flop /flɒp/ *noun* a failure, or something which has not been successful ○ *The new model was a flop.*

floppy disk /ˌflɒpi ˈdɪsk/, **floppy** /ˈflɒpi/ *noun* a flat circular flexible disk onto which data can be stored in a magnetic form. A floppy disk cannot store as much data as a hard disk, but is easily removed, and is protected by a plastic sleeve.

flow chart /ˈfləʊ tʃɑːt/ *noun* a diagram showing the arrangement of various work processes in a series

fluctuate /ˈflʌktʃueɪt/ *verb* to move up and down ○ *Prices fluctuated between £1.10 and £1.25.* ○ *The pound fluctuated all day on the foreign exchange markets*

fluctuating /ˈflʌktʃueɪtɪŋ/ *adjective* moving up and down ○ *fluctuating dollar prices*

fluctuation /ˌflʌktʃuˈeɪʃ(ə)n/ *noun* an up and down movement ○ *the fluctuations of the yen* ○ *the fluctuations of the exchange rate*

folio /ˈfəʊliəʊ/ *noun* a page with a number, especially two facing pages in an account book which have the same number ■ *verb* to put a number on a page

force /fɔːs/ *noun* 1. strength 2. a group of people ■ *verb* to make someone do something ○ *Competition has forced the company to lower its prices.* ○ *After the takeover several of the managers were forced to take early retirement.*

forced sale /ˌfɔːst ˈseɪl/ *noun* a sale which takes place because a court orders it or because it is the only way to avoid a financial crisis

force majeure /ˌfɔːs mæˈʒɜː/ *noun* something which happens which is out of the control of the parties who have signed a contract, e.g. a strike, war or storm

forecast /ˈfɔːkɑːst/ *noun* a description or calculation of what will probably happen in the future ○ *The chairman did not believe the sales director's forecast of higher turnover.*

forecast dividend /ˌfɔːkɑːst ˈdɪvɪdend/ *noun* a dividend which a company expects to pay at the end of the current year. Also called **prospective dividend**

forecaster /ˈfɔːkɑːstə/ *noun* a person who says what he or she thinks will happen in the future

forecasting /ˈfɔːkɑːstɪŋ/ *noun* the process of calculating what will probably happen in the future ○ *Manpower planning will depend on forecasting the future levels of production.*

foreclose /fɔːˈkləʊz/ *verb* to sell a property because the owner cannot repay money which he or she has borrowed, using the property as security ○ *to foreclose on a mortgaged property*

foreclosure /fɔːˈkləʊʒə/ *noun* an act of foreclosing

foreign /ˈfɒrɪn/ *adjective* not belonging to your own country ○ *Foreign cars have flooded our market.* ○ *We are increasing our trade with foreign countries.*
'...a sharp setback in foreign trade accounted for most of the winter slowdown' [*Fortune*]

foreign banks /ˌfɒrɪn ˈbæŋks/ *plural noun* banks from other countries which have branches in a country

foreign branch /ˌfɒrɪn ˈbrɑːntʃ/ *noun* a branch of a company in another country. The accounts of foreign branches may cause problems because of varying exchange rates.

foreign company /ˌfɒrɪn ˈkʌmp(ə)ni/ *noun* company which is not resident in the UK

foreign currency /ˌfɒrɪn ˈkʌrənsi/ *noun* money of another country

foreign currency account /ˌfɒrɪn ˈkʌrənsi əˌkaʊnt/ *noun* a bank account in the currency of another country, e.g. a dollar account in a British bank

foreign currency reserves /ˌfɒrɪn ˈkʌrənsi rɪˌzɜːvz/ *plural noun* a country's reserves held in currencies of other countries. Also called **foreign exchange reserves, international reserves**

'...the treasury says it needs the cash to rebuild its foreign reserves which have fallen from $19 billion when the government took office to $7 billion in August' [*Economist*]

foreign earnings /ˌfɒrɪn ˈɜːnɪŋz/ *plural noun* earning received from employment outside the UK

foreign entity /ˌfɒrɪn ˈentɪti/ *noun* a person or incorporated company outside the UK

foreign exchange /ˌfɒrən ɪksˈtʃeɪndʒ/ *noun* **1.** the business of exchanging the money of one country for that of another **2.** foreign currencies

'...the dollar recovered a little lost ground on the foreign exchanges yesterday' [*Financial Times*]

foreign exchange broker /ˌfɒrɪn ɪks ˈtʃeɪndʒ ˌbrəʊkə/, **foreign exchange dealer** *noun* a person who deals on the foreign exchange market

foreign exchange dealing /ˌfɒrɪn ɪks ˈtʃeɪndʒ ˌdiːlɪŋ/ *noun* the business of buying and selling foreign currencies

foreign exchange market /ˌfɒrɪn ɪks ˈtʃeɪndʒ ˌmɑːkɪt/ *noun* **1.** a market where people buy and sell foreign currencies ○ *She trades on the foreign exchange market.* **2.** dealings in foreign currencies ○ *Foreign exchange markets were very active after the dollar devalued.*

foreign exchange reserves /ˌfɒrɪn ɪks ˈtʃeɪndʒ rɪˌzɜːvz/ *plural noun* foreign money held by a government to support its own currency and pay its debts

foreign exchange transfer /ˌfɒrɪn ɪks ˈtʃeɪndʒ ˌtrænsfɜː/ *noun* the sending of money from one country to another

foreign income /ˌfɒrɪn ˈɪnkʌm/ *noun* income which comes from outside the UK

foreign investments /ˌfɒrɪn ɪn ˈvestmənts/ *plural noun* money invested in other countries

foreign money order /ˌfɒrɪn ˈmʌni ˌɔːdə/ *noun* a money order in a foreign currency which is payable to someone living in a foreign country

foreign rights /ˌfɒrɪn ˈraɪts/ *plural noun* a legal entitlement to sell something in a foreign country, e.g. the right to translate a book into a foreign language

foreign trade /ˈfɒrɪn treɪd/ *noun* a trade with other countries

forensic /fəˈrensɪk/ *adjective* referring to the courts or to the law in general

forensic accounting /fəˌrensɪk əˈkaʊntɪŋ/ *noun* the scrutinisation of an entity's past financial activities in orde to discover whether illegal practices have been used at any time

forensic partner /fəˌrensɪk ˈpɑːtnə/ *noun* a partner in an accountancy firm who deals with litigation

foreseeable loss /fɔːˌsiːəb(ə)l ˈlɒs/ *noun* loss which is expected to occur during a long-term contract

forfaiting /ˈfɔːfɪtɪŋ/ *noun* the action of providing finance for exporters, where an agent or forfaiter accepts a bill of exchange from an overseas customer; he or she buys the bill at a discount, and collects the payments from the customer in due course

forfeit clause /ˈfɔːfɪt klɔːz/ *noun* a clause in a contract which says that goods or a deposit will be taken away if the contract is not obeyed

forfeiture /ˈfɔːfɪtʃə/ *noun* the act of forfeiting a property

form /fɔːm/ *noun* **1.** □ **form of words** words correctly laid out for a legal document □ **receipt in due form** a correctly written receipt **2.** an official printed paper with blank spaces which have to be filled in with information ○ *a pad of order forms* ○ *You have to fill in form A20.* ○ *Each passenger was given a customs declaration form.* ○ *The reps carry pads of order forms.*

formal /ˈfɔːm(ə)l/ *adjective* clearly and legally written ○ *to make a formal application* ○ *to send a formal order* ○ *Is this a formal job offer?* ○ *The factory is prepared for the formal inspection by the government inspector.*

formal documents /ˌfɔːm(ə)l ˈdɒkjʊmənts/ *plural noun* documents giving full details of a takeover bid

formality /fɔːˈmælɪti/ *noun* something which has to be done to obey the law

formation /fɔːˈmeɪʃ(ə)n/, **forming** /ˈfɔːmɪŋ/ *noun* the act of organising ○ *the formation of a new company*

form letter /ˈfɔːm ˌletə/ *noun* a letter which can be sent without any change to several correspondents, e.g. a letter chasing payment

fortune /ˈfɔːtʃən/ *noun* a large amount of money ○ *He made a fortune from investing in oil shares.* ○ *She left her fortune to her three children.*

forward /ˈfɔːwəd/ *adjective* in advance or to be paid at a later date

forward contract /ˈfɔːwəd ˌkɒntrækt/ *noun* a one-off agreement to buy foreign currency or shares or commodities for delivery at a later date at a specific price

forward cover /ˈfɔːwəd ˌkʌvə/ *noun* an arrangement to cover the risks on a forward contract

forward delivery /ˌfɔːwəd dɪˈlɪv(ə)ri/ *noun* a delivery at some date in the future which has been agreed between the buyer and seller

forwarding address /ˈfɔːwədɪŋ əˌdres/ *noun* the address to which a person's mail can be sent on

forwarding agent /ˈfɔːwədɪŋ ˌeɪdʒənt/ *noun* a person or company which arranges shipping and customs documents

forward margin /ˌfɔːwəd ˈmɑːdʒɪn/ *noun* the difference between the current price and the forward price

forward market /ˌfɔːwəd ˈmɑːkɪt/ *noun* a market for purchasing foreign currency, oil or commodities for delivery at a later date

forward sales /ˈfɔːwəd seɪlz/ *plural noun* the sales of shares, commodities or foreign exchange for delivery at a later date

forwards spreading /ˌfɔːwədz ˈspredɪŋ/ *noun* the act of spreading lump sum income over several years in the future

forward trading /ˈfɔːwəd ˌtreɪdɪŋ/ *noun* the activity of buying or selling commodities forward

foul bill of lading /ˌfaʊl bɪl əv ˈleɪdɪŋ/ *noun* a bill of lading which says that the goods were in bad condition when received by the shipper

founder /ˈfaʊndə/ *noun* a person who starts a company

fourth quarter /ˌfɔːθ ˈkwɔːtə/ *noun* a period of three months from 1st October to the end of the year

fraction /ˈfrækʃən/ *noun* a very small amount ○ *Only a fraction of the new share issue was subscribed.*

fractional /ˈfrækʃənəl/ *adjective* very small

fractional certificate /ˈfrækʃənəl səˌtɪfɪkət/ *noun* a certificate for part of a share

franc /fræŋk/ *noun* **1.** a former unit of currency in France and Belgium ○ *French francs* or *Belgian francs* **2.** a unit of currency in Switzerland and several other currencies ○ *It costs twenty-five Swiss francs.*

franchise /ˈfræntʃaɪz/ *noun* a licence to trade using a brand name and paying a royalty for it ○ *He's bought a printing franchise* or *a pizza franchise.* ■ *verb* to sell licences for people to trade using a brand name and paying a royalty ○ *His sandwich bar was so successful that he decided to franchise it.*

'…many new types of franchised businesses will join the ranks of the giant chains of fast-food restaurants, hotels and motels and rental car agencies' [*Franchising Opportunities*]

franchisee /ˌfræntʃaɪˈziː/ *noun* a person who runs a franchise

franchiser /ˈfræntʃaɪzə/ *noun* a person who licenses a franchise

franchising /ˈfræntʃaɪzɪŋ/ *noun* the act of selling a licence to trade as a franchise ○ *She runs her sandwich chain as a franchising operation.*

franco /ˈfræŋkəʊ/ *adverb* free

franked /fræŋkd/ *adjective* on which tax has already been paid

fraud /frɔːd/ *noun* an act of making money by making people believe something which is not true ○ *He got possession of the property by fraud.* ○ *She was accused of frauds relating to foreign currency.*

fraudulent /ˈfrɔːdjʊlənt/ *adjective* not honest, or aiming to cheat people ○ *a fraudulent transaction*

fraudulently /ˈfrɔːdjʊləntli/ *adverb* not honestly ○ *goods imported fraudulently*

fraudulent misrepresentation /ˌfrɔːdjʊlənt mɪsˌreprɪzenˈteɪʃ(ə)n/ *noun* the act of making a false statement with the intention of tricking a customer

fraudulent trading /ˌfrɔːdjʊlənt ˈtreɪdɪŋ/ *noun* the process of carrying on the business of a company, knowing that the company is insolvent

free /friː/ *adjective, adverb* **1.** not costing any money ○ *I have been given a free ticket to the exhibition.* ○ *The price includes free delivery.* ○ *All goods in the store are delivered free.* ○ *A catalogue will be sent free on request.* **2.** with no restrictions □ **free of tax** with no tax having to be paid ○ *Interest is paid free of tax.* □ **free of duty** with no duty to be paid ○ *to import wine free of duty* ■ *verb* to make something available or easy ○ *The government's decision has freed millions of pounds for investment.*

'American business as a whole is increasingly free from heavy dependence on manufacturing' [*Sunday Times*]

free competition /ˌfriː kɒmpəˈtɪʃ(ə)n/ *noun* the fact of being free to compete without government interference

free currency /ˌfriː ˈkʌrənsi/ *noun* a currency which is allowed by the government to be bought and sold without restriction

free enterprise /ˌfriː ˈentəpraɪz/ *noun* a system of business free from government interference

freeholder /ˈfriːhəʊldə/ *noun* a person who owns a freehold property

freehold property /ˈfriːhəʊld ˌprɒpəti/ *noun* property which the owner holds for ever and on which no rent is paid

free issue /ˌfriː ˈɪʃuː/ *noun* same as **scrip issue**

free market /friː ˈmɑːkɪt/ *noun* a market in which there is no government control of supply and demand, and the rights of individuals and organisations to physical and intellectual property are upheld

free market economy /friː ˌmɑːkɪt ɪ ˈkɒnəmi/ *noun* a system where the government does not interfere in business activity in any way

free on board /ˌfriː ɒn ˈbɔːd/ *adjective* **1.** including in the price all the seller's costs until the goods are on the ship for transportation. Abbreviation **f.o.b. 2.** including in the price all the seller's costs until the goods are delivered to a place

free reserves /ˌfriː rɪ ˈzɜːvz/ *plural noun* the part of a bank's reserves which are above the statutory level and so can be used for various purposes as the bank wishes

free-standing additional voluntary contribution /friː ˌstændɪŋ əˌdɪʃ(ə)nəl ˌvɒlənt(ə)ri ˌkɒntrɪˈbjuːʃ(ə)n/ *noun* a payment made by an individual into an independent pension fund to supplement an occupational pension scheme. The anticipated benefits from the two schemes together must be less than the maximum permitted under the rules laid down by the Inland Revenue. Abbreviation **FSAVC**

free trade /friː ˈtreɪd/ *noun* a system where goods can go from one country to another without any restrictions

'…can free trade be reconciled with a strong dollar resulting from floating exchange rates?' [*Duns Business Month*]

free trade area /friː ˈtreɪd ˌeəriə/ *noun* a group of countries practising free trade

free trader /ˌfriː ˈtreɪdə/ *noun* a person who is in favour of free trade

'…free traders hold that the strong dollar is the primary cause of the nation's trade problems' [*Duns Business Month*]

free trade zone /friː ˈtreɪd ˌzəʊn/ *noun* an area where there are no customs duties

free trial /ˌfriː ˈtraɪəl/ *noun* an opportunity to test a machine or product with no payment involved

freeze /friːz/ *noun* □ **a freeze on wages and prices** period when wages and prices are not allowed to be increased ■ *verb* to keep something such as money or costs at their present level and not allow them to rise ○ *to freeze wages and prices* ○ *to freeze credits* ○ *to freeze company dividends* ○ *We have frozen expenditure at last year's level.* (NOTE: **freezing – froze – frozen**)

freight /freɪt/ *noun* the cost of transporting goods by air, sea or land ○ *At an auction, the buyer pays the freight.*

freightage /ˈfreɪtɪdʒ/ *noun* the cost of transporting goods

freight costs /ˈfreɪt kɒsts/ *plural noun* money paid to transport goods

freight forward /ˌfreɪt ˈfɔːwəd/ *noun* a deal where the customer pays for transporting the goods

friendly society /ˈfrendli səˌsaɪəti/ *noun* a group of people who pay regular subscriptions which are used to help members of the group when they are ill or in financial difficulties

fringe benefit /frɪndʒ ˈbenɪfɪt/ *noun* an extra item given by a company to employees in addition to a salary, e.g. company cars or private health insurance ○ *The fringe benefits make up for the poor pay.* ○ *Use of the company recreation facilities is one of the fringe benefits of the job.*

FRN *abbr* floating rate note

front /frʌnt/ *noun* □ **money up front** payment in advance ○ *They are asking for £10,000 up front before they will consider the deal.* ○ *He had to put money up front before he could clinch the deal.*

front-end /ˌfrʌnt ˈend/ *adjective* referring to the start of an investment or insurance

front-end loaded /ˈfrʌnt end ˌləʊdɪd/ *adjective* referring to an insurance or investment scheme where most of the management charges are incurred in the first year of the investment or insurance, and are not spread out over the whole period. Compare **back-end loaded**

frozen /ˈfrəʊz(ə)n/ *adjective* not allowed to be changed or used ○ *Wages have been frozen at last year's rates.*

frozen account /ˈfrəʊz(ə)n əˌkaʊnt/ *noun* a bank account where the money cannot be moved or used because of a court order

frozen assets /ˌfrəʊz(ə)n ˈæsets/ *plural noun* a company's assets which by law cannot be sold because someone has a claim against them

frozen credits /ˌfrəʊz(ə)n 'kredɪtz/ *plural noun* credits in an account which cannot be moved

FRRP *abbr* Financial Reporting Review Panel

FRSs *abbr* Financial Reporting Standards

frustrate /frʌ'streɪt/ *verb* to prevent something, especially the terms of a contract, being fulfilled

FSA *abbr* Financial Services Authority

FSAVC *abbr* free-standing additional voluntary contribution

FT 500 Share Index *noun* an index based on the market prices of 500 leading companies in the manufacturing, retailing and service sectors

FT Actuaries Share Indices /ˌef tiː ˌæktjʊəriz 'ʃeə ˌɪndɪsiz/ *plural noun* several indices based on prices on the London Stock Exchange, which are calculated by and published in the Financial Times in conjunction with the Institute of Actuaries and the Faculty of Actuaries

FT Industrial Group Share Index *noun* an index based on the market prices of more than 470 leading industrial companies

FT Ordinary Share Index *noun* an index based on the market prices of thirty blue-chip companies This index is the oldest of the FT indices, and is now considered too narrow to have much relevance

FTSE 100 /ˌfʊtsi wʌn 'hʌndrəd/ *noun* an index based on the prices of one hundred leading companies (this is the main London index)

'…the benchmark FTSE 100 index ended the session up 94.3 points' [*Times*]

FT-Stock Exchange 100 Share Index *noun* the main London index based on the prices of one hundred leading companies. Also called **FT-SE 100**

full /fʊl/ *adjective* **1.** with as much inside it as possible ○ *The train was full of commuters.* ○ *Is the container full yet?* ○ *We sent a lorry full of spare parts to our warehouse.* ○ *When the disk is full, don't forget to make a backup copy.* **2.** complete, including everything

'…a tax-free lump sum can be taken partly in lieu of a full pension' [*Investors Chronicle*]

full cover /ˌfʊl 'kʌvə/ *noun* insurance cover against all risks

full employment /ˌfʊl ɪm'plɔɪmənt/ *noun* a situation where all the people who can work have jobs

full price /'fʊl praɪs/ *noun* a price with no discount ○ *She bought a full-price ticket.*

full production costs /ˌfʊl prə'dʌkʃən ˌkɒsts/ *plural noun* all the costs of manufacturing a product, including both fixed and variable costs

full rate /ˌfʊl 'reɪt/ *noun* the full charge, with no reductions

full repairing lease /ˌfʊl rɪ'peərɪŋ ˌliːs/ *noun* a lease where the tenant has to pay for all repairs to the property

full-scale /'fʊl skeɪl/ *adjective* complete or very thorough ○ *The MD ordered a full-scale review of credit terms.* ○ *The HR department will start a full-scale review of the present pay structure.*

'…the administration launched a full-scale investigation into maintenance procedures' [*Fortune*]

full-service banking /fʊl ˌsɜːvɪs 'bæŋkɪŋ/ *noun* banking that offers a whole range of services including mortgages, loans, pensions, etc.

full-time /'fʊl taɪm/ *adjective, adverb* working the usual working time, i.e. about eight hours a day, five days a week ○ *She's in full-time work* or *She works full-time* or *She's in full-time employment.* ○ *He is one of our full-time staff.*

full-time employment /ˌfʊl taɪm ɪm 'plɔɪmənt/ *noun* work for all of a working day ○ *to be in full-time employment*

fully /'fʊli/ *adverb* completely

'…issued and fully paid capital is $100 million' [*Hongkong Standard*]

fully diluted earnings per share /ˌfʊli daɪˌluːtɪd ˌɜːnɪŋz pə 'ʃeə/, **fully diluted EPS** /ˌfʊli ˌdaɪluːtɪd ˌiː piː 'es/ *plural noun* earnings per share calculated over the whole number of shares assuming that convertible shares have been converted to ordinary shares

fully paid-up capital /ˌfʊli peɪd ʌp 'kæpɪt(ə)l/ *noun* all money paid for the issued capital shares

function /'fʌŋkʃən/ *verb* to work ○ *The advertising campaign is functioning smoothly.* ○ *The new management structure does not seem to be functioning very well.*

functional /'fʌŋkʃən(ə)l/ *adjective* referring to a job

functional budget /ˌfʌŋkʃən(ə)l 'bʌdʒɪt/ *noun* a budget relating to a specific function such as marketing or personnel

functional diagram /ˌfʌŋkʃ(ə)nəl 'daɪəɡræm/ *noun* a drawing of the internal workings and processes of a machine or piece of software

functional specification /ˌfʌŋkʃ(ə)nəl ˌspesɪfɪˈkeɪʃ(ə)n/ *noun* a specification which defines the results which a program is expected to produce

functional unit /ˌfʌŋkʃən(ə)l ˈjuːnɪt/ *noun* hardware or software that works as it should

fund /fʌnd/ *noun* **1.** money set aside for a special purpose **2.** money invested in an investment trust as part of a unit trust, or given to a financial adviser to invest on behalf of a client. ◊ **funds** ■ *verb* to provide money for a purpose ○ *The company does not have enough resources to fund its expansion programme.*

'…the S&L funded all borrowers' development costs, including accrued interest' [*Barrons*]

fund accounting /ˈfʌnd əˌkaʊntɪŋ/ *noun* the preparation of financial statements for an entity which is a fund

fundamental /ˌfʌndəˈment(ə)l/ *adjective* basic or most important

fundamental assumptions /ˌfʌndəment(ə)l əˈsʌmpʃ(ə)ns/ *plural noun* the basic assumptions on which the preparation of accounts depends: that the company is a going concern, that the principles on which the accounts are prepared do not change from year to year, that revenues and costs are accrued (i.e., they are written into the accounts when they occur, not when they are received or paid)

fundamental issues /ˌfʌndəment(ə)l ˈɪʃuːz/ *plural noun* matters relating to a company's profits or assets

fundamental research /ˌfʌndəment(ə)l rɪˈsɜːtʃ/, **fundamental analysis** /ˌfʌndəment(ə)l əˈnæləsɪs/ *noun* an examination of the basic factors which affect a market

fundamentals /ˌfʌndəˈment(ə)lz/ *plural noun* the basic realities of a stock market or of a company, e.g. its assets, profitability and dividends

funded /ˈfʌndɪd/ *adjective* backed by long-term loans ○ *long-term funded capital*

funded scheme /ˌfʌndɪd ˈskiːm/ *noun* a pension scheme where money is invested in securities to create a fund from which the pension is later paid

funding /ˈfʌndɪŋ/ *noun* **1.** money for spending ○ *The bank is providing the funding for the new product launch.* **2.** the act of changing a short-term debt into a long-term loan ○ *The capital expenditure programme requires long-term funding.*

fund management /ˈfʌnd ˌmænɪdʒmənt/ *noun* the business of dealing with the investment of sums of money on behalf of clients

funds /fʌndz/ *plural noun* **1.** money which is available for spending ○ *The company has no funds to pay for the research programme.* □ **to convert funds to your own use** to use someone else's money for yourself □ **budgeted funds flow statement** plan of anticipated incoming funds and the use to which they will be put □ **funds flow method of budgeting** preparing a budget of funds flow, as opposed to a budget of expenditure □ **funds flow statement** statement which shows the amount of funds (cash and working capital) which have come into a business during the last financial period, the sources of these funds, and the use made of the funds (see FRS1, formerly SSAP10) **2.** government stocks and securities □ **the Funds** government stocks and securities

'…small innovative companies have been hampered for lack of funds' [*Sunday Times*]

'…the company was set up with funds totalling NorKr 145m' [*Lloyd's List*]

fungibility /ˌfʌndʒəˈbɪlɪti/ *noun* the ability to be exchanged for something similar

fungible /ˈfʌndʒəb(ə)l/ *adjective* referring to a security which can be exchanged for another of the same type

funny money /ˈfʌni ˌmʌni/ *noun* an unusual type of financial instrument created by a company

furnished lettings /ˌfɜːnɪʃt ˈletɪŋs/ *plural noun* a furnished property to let

furniture depository /ˈfɜːnɪtʃə dɪˌpɒzɪt(ə)ri/ *noun* a warehouse where you can store household furniture

future /ˈfjuːtʃə/ *adjective* referring to time to come or to something which has not yet happened

future delivery /ˌfjuːtʃə dɪˈlɪv(ə)ri/ *noun* delivery at a later date

futures /ˈfjuːtʃəz/ *plural noun* shares, currency or commodities that are bought or sold for now for delivery at a later date ○ *Gold rose 5% on the commodity futures market yesterday.*

'…cocoa futures plummeted in November to their lowest levels in seven years' [*Business in Africa*]

futures contract /ˈfjuːtʃəz ˌkɒntrækt/ *noun* a contract for the purchase of commodities for delivery at a date in the future

futures exchange /ˈfjuːtʃəz ɪks ˌtʃeɪndʒ/ *noun* a commodity market which only deals in futures

future value /ˌfjuːtʃə ˈvæljuː/ *noun* the value to which a sum of money will increase if invested for a certain period of time at some rate of interest. Abbreviation **FV**

FV *abbr* full value

FYA *abbr* first year allowance

G

GAAP *abbr* Generally Accepted Accounting Principles

gain /geɪn/ *noun* **1.** an increase, or the act of becoming larger **2.** an increase in profit, price or value ○ *Oil shares showed gains on the Stock Exchange.* ○ *Property shares put on gains of 10%-15%.* ■ *verb* **1.** to get or to obtain ○ *She gained some useful experience working in a bank.* □ **to gain control of a business** to buy more than 50% of the shares so that you can direct the business **2.** to rise in value ○ *The dollar gained six points on the foreign exchange markets.*

galloping inflation /ˌɡæləpɪŋ ɪnˈfleɪʃ(ə)n/ *noun* very rapid inflation which is almost impossible to reduce

gap analysis /ˈɡæp əˌnæləsɪs/ *noun* analysis of a market to try to find a particular area that is not at present being satisfied ○ *Gap analysis showed that there was a whole area of the market we were not exploiting.* ○ *The computer performed a gap analysis and came up with suggestions for a medium-priced machine suitable for the small business market.*

gap financing /ˈɡæp ˌfaɪnænsɪŋ/ *noun* arranging extra loans such as a bridging loan to cover a purchase not covered by an existing loan

garnishee /ˌɡɑːnɪˈʃiː/ *noun* a person who owes money to a creditor and is ordered by a court to pay that money to a creditor of the creditor, and not to the creditor himself

garnishee order /ˌɡɑːnɪˈʃiː ˌɔːdə/ *noun* a court order, making a garnishee pay money not to the debtor, but to a third party

GAS *abbr* Government Accountancy Service

gazumping /ɡəˈzʌmpɪŋ/ *noun* the practice of offering a higher price for a house than

another buyer has already agreed with the seller

gear /ɡɪə/ *verb* to link something to something else

gearing /ˈɡɪərɪŋ/ *noun* **1.** a ratio of capital borrowed by a company at a fixed rate of interest to the company's total capital. Also called **leverage 2.** the act of borrowing money at fixed interest which is then used to produce more money than the interest paid

general audit /ˌdʒen(ə)rəl ˈɔːdɪt/ *noun* a process of examining all the books and accounts of a company

general average /ˌdʒen(ə)rəl ˈæv(ə)rɪdʒ/ *noun* a process by which the cost of lost goods is shared by all parties to an insurance, such as in cases where some goods have been lost in an attempt to save the rest of the cargo

General Commissioners /ˌdʒen(ə)rəl kəˈmɪʃ(ə)nəz/ *noun* a body of unpaid individuals appointed by the Lord Chancellor in England, Wales, and Northern Ireland, and the Secretary of State for Scotland in Scotland, to hear appeals on tax matters

general damages /ˌdʒen(ə)rəl ˈdæmɪdʒɪz/ *plural noun* damages awarded by court to compensate for a loss which cannot be calculated such as an injury

general expenses /ˌdʒen(ə)rəl ɪkˈspensɪz/ *plural noun* all kinds of minor expenses, the money spent on the day-to-day costs of running a business

general fund /ˈdʒen(ə)rəl fʌnd/ *noun* a unit trust with investments in a variety of stocks

general insurance /ˌdʒen(ə)rəl ɪnˈʃʊərəns/ *noun* insurance covering all kinds of risk, e.g. theft, loss or damage, but excluding life insurance

general ledger /ˌdʒen(ə)rəl 'ledʒə/ *noun* a book which records a company's income and expenditure in general

general lien /ˌdʒen(ə)rəl 'liːən/ *noun* **1.** a right to hold goods or property until a debt has been paid **2.** a lien against the personal possessions of a borrower, but not against his or her house or land. ◊ **banker's lien**

Generally Accepted Accounting Principles /ˌdʒen(ə)rəli əkˌseptɪd ə 'kaʊntɪŋ ˌprɪnsɪp(ə)lz/ *plural noun US* a summary of best practice in respect of the form and content of financial statements and auditor's reports, and of accounting policies and disclosures adopted for the preparation of financial information. GAAP does not have any statutory or regulatory authority in the United Kingdom, unlike in a number of other countries where the term is in use, such as the United States, Canada. Abbreviation **GAAP**

general manager /ˌdʒen(ə)rəl 'mænɪdʒə/ *noun* a manager in charge of the administration of a company

general meeting /ˌdʒen(ə)rəl 'miːtɪŋ/ *noun* a meeting of all the shareholders of a company or of all the members of a society

general office /'dʒen(ə)rəl ˌɒfɪs/ *noun* the main administrative office of a company

general partner /ˌdʒen(ə)rəl 'pɑːtnə/ *noun* a partner in a partnership whose responsibility for its debts is not limited

general partnership /ˌdʒen(ə)rəl 'pɑːtnəʃɪp/ *noun* a partnership where the liability of each partner is not limited

general undertaking /ˌdʒen(ə)rəl ˌʌndə'teɪkɪŋ/ *noun* an undertaking signed by the directors of a company applying for a Stock Exchange listing, promising to work within the regulations of the Stock Exchange

gensaki /dʒen'sɑːki/ *noun* a Japanese bond market, dealing in bonds issued with agreements to repurchase at less than twelve months' notice

get back /ˌget 'bæk/ *verb* to receive something which you had before ○ *I got my money back after I had complained to the manager.* ○ *He got his initial investment back in two months.*

get out /ˌget 'aʊt/ *verb* **1.** to produce something ○ *The accounts department got out the draft accounts in time for the meeting.* **2.** to sell an investment (*informal*) ○ *He didn't like what he read in the company's annual report, so he got out before the company collapsed.*

get out of /ˌget 'aʊt əv/ *verb* to stop trading in a product or an area ○ *The company is*

getting out of computers. ○ *We got out of the South American market.*

get round /ˌget 'raʊnd/ *verb* to avoid ○ *We tried to get round the embargo by shipping from Canada.*

gift /gɪft/ *noun* a thing which is given to someone

gift aid /'gɪft eɪd/ *noun* payment above some limit made to a registered charity, meaning that the charity is able to reclaim the basic rate tax which you have paid on the gift

gift coupon /'gɪft ˌkuːpɒn/, **gift token** /'gɪft ˌtəʊkən/, **gift voucher** /'gɪft ˌvaʊtʃə/ *noun* a card that can be used to buy specified goods up to the value printed on it, often issued by chain stores. The person receiving the voucher is able to redeem it in any store in the chain. ○ *We gave her a gift token for her birthday.*

gift inter vivos /ˌgɪft ɪntə 'viːvəʊs/ *noun* a gift given to another living person. Abbreviation **GIV**

gilt-edged /'gɪlt edʒd/ *adjective* referring to an investment which is very safe

gilt-edged securities /ˌgɪlt edʒd sɪ 'kjʊərɪtiz/ *plural noun* investments in British government stock

gilts /gɪlts/ *plural noun* same as **government bonds**

giro /'dʒaɪrəʊ/ *noun* same as **bank giro**

GIV *abbr* gift inter vivos

GM *abbr* gross margin

GNP *abbr* gross national product

go back on /ˌgəʊ 'bæk ɒn/ *verb* not to carry out something which you have promised to do it ○ *Two months later they went back on the agreement.*

go-go fund /'gəʊ gəʊ ˌfʌnd/ *noun* a fund which aims to give very high returns because it is invested in speculative stocks

going /'gəʊɪŋ/ *adjective* current

going concern /ˌgəʊɪŋ kən'sɜːn/ *noun* a company that is actively trading and making a profit

going concern value /ˌgəʊɪŋ kən'sɜːn ˌvæljuː/ *noun* the value of a corporation as it continues trading as opposed to its breakup value

go into /ˌgəʊ 'ɪntuː/ *verb* to examine something carefully ○ *The bank wants to go into the details of the inter-company loans.*

go into business /ˌgəʊ ɪntə 'bɪznɪs/ *verb* to start in business ○ *He went into business as a car dealer.* ○ *She went into business in partnership with her son.*

gold bullion /ˌgəʊld 'bʊliən/ *noun* bars of gold

gold card /ˈgəʊld kɑːd/ *noun* a credit card issued to important customers, i.e., those with a high income, which gives certain privileges such as a higher spending limit than ordinary credit cards

golden handshake /ˌgəʊld(ə)n ˈhændʃeɪk/ *noun* a large, usually tax-free, sum of money given to a director who retires from a company before the end of his or her service contract ○ *The retiring director received a golden handshake of £250,000.*

golden share /ˌgəʊld(ə)n ˈʃeə/ *noun* a share in a privatised company which is retained by the government and carries special privileges such as the right to veto foreign takeover bids

gold fixing /ˈgəʊld ˌfɪksɪŋ/ *noun* a system where the world price for gold is set twice a day in US dollars on the London Gold Exchange and in Paris and Zurich

goldmine /ˈgəʊldmaɪn/ *noun* a mine which produces gold

gold point /ˈgəʊld pɔɪnt/ *noun* an amount by which a currency which is linked to gold can vary in price

gold reserves /ˈgəʊld rɪˌzɜːvz/ *plural noun* the country's store of gold kept to pay international debts

goods /gʊdz/ *plural noun* items which can be moved and are for sale □ **goods received** goods which have been sent by a seller and received by a purchaser during an accounting period □ **goods received note** internal note within a company which shows the date when goods were received, by whom and in what quantities

'…profit margins are lower in the industries most exposed to foreign competition – machinery, transportation equipment and electrical goods' [*Sunday Times*]

'…the minister wants people buying goods ranging from washing machines to houses to demand facts on energy costs' [*Times*]

goods and chattels /ˌgʊdz ən ˈtʃæt(ə)lz/ *plural noun* moveable personal possessions

Goods and Services Tax /ˌgʊdz ən ˈsɜːvɪsɪz tæks/ *noun* a Canadian tax on the sale of goods or the provision of services, similar to VAT. Abbreviation **GST**

goodwill /gʊdˈwɪl/ *noun* good feeling towards someone ○ *To show goodwill, the management increased the terms of the offer.*

go private /ˌgəʊ ˈpraɪvət/ *verb* to become a private company again, by concentrating all its shares in the hands of one or a few shareholders and removing its stock exchange listing

go public /ˌgəʊ ˈpʌblɪk/ *verb* to become a public company by placing some of its shares for sale on the stock market so that anyone can buy them

govern /ˈgʌv(ə)n/ *verb* to rule a country ○ *The country is governed by a group of military leaders.*

governance /ˈgʌv(ə)nəns/ *noun* the philosophy of ruling, whether a country or a company

'…the chairman has committed the cardinal sin in corporate governance – he acted against the wishes and interests of the shareholders' [*Investors Chronicle*]

'…in two significant decisions, the Securities and Exchange Board of India today allowed trading of shares through the Internet and set a deadline for companies to conform to norms for good corporate governance' [*The Hindu*]

government /ˈgʌv(ə)nmənt/ *adjective* coming from the government, referring to the government ○ *a government ban on the import of arms* ○ *Government intervention or Intervention by the government helped to solve the dispute.* ○ *Government employees can belong to one of two unions.*

Government Accountancy Service /ˌgʌv(ə)nmənt əˈkaʊntənsi ˌsɜːvɪs/ *noun* part of HM Treasury, a service whose remit it is to ensure that best accounting practice is observed and conducted across the whole of the Civil Service. Abbreviation **GAS**

governmental /ˌgʌv(ə)nˈment(ə)l/ *adjective* referring to a government

government-backed /ˌgʌv(ə)nmənt ˈbækt/ *adjective* backed by the government

government bonds /ˌgʌv(ə)nmənt ˈbɒndz/ *plural noun* bonds or other securities issued by the government on a regular basis as a method of borrowing money for government expenditure

government contractor /ˌgʌv(ə)nmənt kənˈtræktə/ *noun* a company which supplies the government with goods by contract

government-controlled /ˌgʌv(ə)nmənt kənˈtrəʊld/ *adjective* under the direct control of the government ○ *Advertisements cannot be placed in the government-controlled newspapers.*

government economic indicators /ˌgʌv(ə)nmənt iːkəˌnɒmɪk ˈɪndɪkeɪtəz/ *plural noun* statistics which show how the country's economy is going to perform in the short or long term

government grant /ˌgʌv(ə)nmənt ˈgrɑːnt/ *noun* a grant of money or assets given by a central government, a local government or a government agency ○ *The labora-*

tory has a government grant to cover the cost of the development programme ○ the government has allocated grants towards the costs of the scheme.

government loan /ˌgʌv(ə)nmənt ˈləʊn/ *noun* money lent by the government

government-regulated /ˈgʌv(ə)nmənt ˌregjʊleɪtɪd/ *adjective* regulated by the government

government securities /ˌgʌv(ə)nmənt sɪˈkjʊərɪtiz/ *plural noun* same as **government bonds**

government-sponsored /ˈgʌv(ə)nmənt ˌspɒnsəd/ *adjective* encouraged by the government and backed by government money ○ She is working in a government-sponsored scheme to help small businesses.

government stock /ˌgʌv(ə)nmənt ˈstɒk/ *noun* same as **government bonds**

government support /ˌgʌv(ə)nmənt sə ˈpɔːt/ *noun* a financial help given by the government ○ The aircraft industry relies on government support.

governor /ˈgʌv(ə)nə/ *noun* **1.** a person in charge of an important institution **2.** *US* one of the members of the Federal Reserve Board

grace /greɪs/ *noun* a favour shown by granting a delay ○ to give a creditor a period of grace or two weeks' grace

gradual /ˈgrædʒuəl/ *adjective* slow and steady ○ The company saw a gradual return to profits. ○ Her CV describes her gradual rise to the position of company chairman.

gradually /ˈgrædʒuəli/ *adverb* slowly and steadily ○ The company has gradually become more profitable. ○ She gradually learnt the details of the import-export business.

graduate /ˈgrædʒuət/ *noun* a person who has obtained a degree

graduated /ˈgrædʒueɪtɪd/ *adjective* changing in small regular stages

graduated income tax /ˌgrædʒueɪtɪd ˈɪnkʌm tæks/ *noun* a tax which rises in steps, each level of income being taxed at a higher percentage

graduated pension scheme /ˌgrædʒueɪtɪd ˈpenʃən skiːm/ *noun* a pension scheme where the benefit is calculated as a percentage of the salary of each person in the scheme

graduated taxation /ˌgrædʒueɪtɪd tæk ˈseɪʃ(ə)n/ *noun* a tax system where the percentage of tax paid rises as the income rises

grand /grænd/ *noun* one thousand pounds or dollars (*informal*) ○ They offered him fifty grand for the information. ○ She's earning fifty grand plus car and expenses.

grand total /ˌgrænd ˈtəʊt(ə)l/ *noun* the final total made by adding several subtotals

grant /grɑːnt/ *verb* to agree to give someone something ○ to grant someone a loan or a subsidy ○ to grant someone three weeks' leave of absence ○ The local authority granted the company an interest-free loan to start up the new factory.

'…the budget grants a tax exemption for $500,000 in capital gains' [*Toronto Star*]

grantor /grɑːnˈtɔː/ *noun* a person who grants a property to another

graph /grɑːf/ *noun* a diagram which shows the relationship between two sets of quantities or values, each of which is represented on an axis ○ A graph was used to show salary increases in relation to increases in output. ○ According to the graph, as average salaries have risen so has absenteeism. ○ We need to set out the results of the questionnaire in a graph.

gratis /ˈgrætɪs/ *adverb* free or not costing anything ○ We got into the exhibition gratis.

gratuity /grəˈtjuːɪti/ *noun* a tip, money given to someone who has helped you ○ The staff are instructed not to accept gratuities.

greenback /ˈgriːnbæk/ *noun* US a dollar bill (*informal*)

'…gold's drop this year is of the same magnitude as the greenback's 8.5% rise' [*Business Week*]

green card /ˈgriːn kɑːd/ *noun* **1.** a special British insurance certificate to prove that a car is insured for travel abroad **2.** an identity card and work permit for a person going to live in the USA

green currency /ˌgriːn ˈkʌrənsiː/ *noun* formerly, a currency used in the EU for calculating agricultural payments. Each country had an exchange rate fixed by the Commission, so there were 'green pounds', 'green francs', 'green marks', etc.

green form /ˈgriːn fɔːm/ *noun* a form for giving free or subsidised legal advice to clients who are eligible for Legal Aid

greenmail /ˈgriːnmeɪl/ *noun* the practice of making a profit by buying a large number of shares in a company, threatening to take the company over, and then selling the shares back to the company at a higher price

'…he proposes that there should be a limit on greenmail, perhaps permitting payment of a 20% premium on a maximum of 8% of the stock' [*Duns Business Month*]

Green Paper /ˈgriːn ˈpeɪpə/ *noun* a report from the British government on proposals for a new law to be discussed in Parliament. Compare **White Paper**

green pound /ˈgriːn ˈpaʊnd/ *noun* a value for the British pound used in calculating agricultural prices and subsidies in the EU

green report /ˌgriːn rɪˈpɔːt/ *noun* a part of a company's annual report dealing with ecological matters

grey market /ˈgreɪ ˌmɑːkɪt/ *noun* an unofficial market run by dealers, where new issues of shares are bought and sold before they officially become available for trading on the Stock Exchange even before the share allocations are known

gross /grəʊs/ *noun* twelve dozen (144) ○ *He ordered four gross of pens.* (NOTE: no plural) ■ *adjective* total, with no deductions ■ *adverb* with no deductions ○ *My salary is paid gross.*

> '…gross wool receipts for the selling season to end June appear likely to top $2 billion' [*Australian Financial Review*]

gross domestic product /grəʊs dəˌmestɪk ˈprɒdʌkt/ *noun* the annual value of goods sold and services paid for inside a country. Abbreviation **GDP**

gross earnings /ˌgrəʊs ˈɜːnɪŋz/ *plural noun* total earnings before tax and other deductions

gross income /grəʊs ˈɪnkʌm/ *noun* a salary before tax is deducted

gross interest /ˌgrəʊs ˈɪntrəst/ *noun* the interest earned on a deposit or security before the deduction of tax. ◊ **net interest**

gross margin /grəʊs ˈmɑːdʒɪn/ *noun* the percentage difference between the received price and the unit manufacturing cost or purchase price of goods for resale. Abbreviation **GM**

gross national product /grəʊs ˌnæʃ(ə)nəl ˈprɒdʌkt/ *noun* the annual value of goods and services in a country including income from other countries. Abbreviation **GNP**

gross profit /grəʊs ˈprɒfɪt/ *noun* a profit calculated as sales income less the cost of the goods sold, i.e. without deducting any other expenses

gross receipts /ˌgrəʊs rɪˈsiːts/ *plural noun* the total amount of money received before expenses are deducted

gross salary /ˌgrəʊs ˈsæləri/ *noun* a salary before tax is deducted

gross sales /ˌgrəʊs ˈseɪlz/ *plural noun* money received from sales before deductions for goods returned, special discounts, etc. ○ *Gross sales are impressive since many buyers seem to be ordering more than they will eventually need.*

gross turnover /ˌgrəʊs ˈtɜːnəʊvə/ *noun* the total turnover including VAT and discounts

gross weight /ˌgrəʊs ˈweɪt/ *noun* the weight of both the container and its contents

gross yield /ˌgrəʊs ˈjiːld/ *noun* a profit from investments before tax is deducted

ground landlord /ˈgraʊnd ˌlændlɔːd/ *noun* a person or company that owns the freehold of a property which is then let and sublet ○ *Our ground landlord is an insurance company.*

ground rent /ˈgraʊnd rent/ *noun* a rent paid by the main tenant to the ground landlord

group /gruːp/ *noun* **1.** several things or people together ○ *A group of managers has sent a memo to the chairman complaining about noise in the office.* ○ *The respondents were interviewed in groups of three or four, and then singly.* **2.** several companies linked together in the same organisation ○ *the group chairman* or *the chairman of the group* ○ *group turnover* or *turnover for the group* ○ *the Granada Group*

group accounts /ˌgruːp əˈkaʊntz/ *noun* accounts for a holding company and its subsidiaries

group balance sheet /ˌgruːp ˈbæləns ˌʃiːt/ *noun* a consolidated balance sheet, the balance sheets of subsidiary companies grouped together into the balance sheet of the parent company

group results /ˌgruːp rɪˈzʌlts/ *plural noun* the results of a group of companies taken together

growth /grəʊθ/ *noun* the fact of becoming larger or increasing

> '…a general price freeze succeeded in slowing the growth in consumer prices' [*Financial Times*]

> '…growth in demand is still coming from the private rather than the public sector' [*Lloyd's List*]

> '…population growth in the south-west is again reflected by the level of rental values' [*Lloyd's List*]

growth index /ˈgrəʊθ ˌɪndeks/ *noun* an index showing how something has grown

growth prospects /ˈgrəʊθ ˌprɒspekts/ *plural noun* potential for growth in a share

growth rate /ˈgrəʊθ reɪt/ *noun* the speed at which something grows

GST *abbr* Goods and Services Tax

> '…because the GST is applied only to fees for brokerage and appraisal services, the new tax does not appreciably increase the price of a resale home' [*Toronto Globe & Mail*]

guarantee /ˌgærənˈtiː/ *noun* **1.** a legal document in which the producer agrees to compensate the buyer if the product is faulty or becomes faulty before a specific date after purchase ○ *a certificate of guarantee* or *a guarantee certificate* ○ *The guarantee lasts for two years.* ○ *It is sold with a twelve-month guarantee.* **2.** a promise that someone will pay another person's debts □ **company limited by guarantee** company where each member stated in the memorandum of association how much money he will contribute to the company if it becomes insolvent (as opposed to a company limited by shares) **3.**

something given as a security ○ *to leave share certificates as a guarantee* ■ *verb* to give a promise that something will happen

guaranteed wage /ˌɡærəntiːd ˈweɪdʒ/ *noun* a wage which a company promises will not fall below a specific figure

guarantor /ˌɡærənˈtɔː/ *noun* a person who promises to pay someone's debts ○ *She stood guarantor for her brother.*

H

half /hɑːf/ *noun* one of two equal parts into which something is divided ○ *The first half of the agreement is acceptable.* ■ *adjective* divided into two parts

'...economists believe the economy is picking up this quarter and will do better in the second half of the year' [*Sunday Times*]

half a per cent /ˌhɑːf ə pə ˈsent/ *noun* 0.5%

half-commission man /ˌhɑːf kə ˈmɪʃ(ə)n ˌmæn/ *noun* a dealer who introduces new clients to a stockbroker, and takes half the broker's commission as a fee

half-dollar /ˌhɑːf ˈdɒlə/ *noun US* fifty cents

half-price sale /ˌhɑːf praɪs ˈseɪl/ *noun* a sale of items at half the usual price

half-year /ˌhɑːf ˈjɪə/ *noun* six months of an accounting period

half-yearly /ˌhɑːf ˈjɪəli/ *adjective* happening every six months, or referring to a period of six months ○ *half-yearly accounts* ○ *half-yearly payment* ○ *half-yearly statement* ○ *a half-yearly meeting* ■ *adverb* every six months ○ *We pay the account half-yearly.*

handling charge /ˈhændlɪŋ tʃɑːdʒ/ *noun* money to be paid for packing, invoicing and dealing with goods which are being shipped

hard bargain /ˌhɑːd ˈbɑːɡɪn/ *noun* a bargain with difficult terms

hard cash /ˌhɑːd ˈkæʃ/ *noun* money in notes and coins, as opposed to cheques or credit cards

hard currency /hɑːd ˈkʌrənsi/ *noun* the currency of a country which has a strong economy, and which can be changed into other currencies easily ○ *to pay for imports in hard currency* ○ *to sell raw materials to earn hard currency* Also called **scarce currency**. Opposite **soft currency**

hard disk /ˌhɑːd ˈdɪsk/ *noun* a computer disk which has a sealed case and can store large quantities of information

'...hard disks help computers function more speedily and allow them to store more information' [*Australian Financial Review*]

hardening /ˈhɑːd(ə)nɪŋ/ *adjective* (*of a market*) slowly moving upwards

hard landing /ˌhɑːd ˈlændɪŋ/ *noun* a change in economic strategy to counteract inflation which has serious results for the population such as high unemployment, rising interest rates, etc.

hard market /ˌhɑːd ˈmɑːkɪt/ *noun* a market which is strong and not likely to fall

hardware /ˈhɑːdweə/ *noun* machines used in data processing, including the computers and printers, but not the programs

haulage contractor /ˈhɔːlɪdʒ kən ˌtræktə/ *noun* a company which transports goods by contract

head /hed/ *adjective* most important or main ○ *Ask the head waiter for a table.*

head and shoulders /ˌhed ən ˈʃəʊldəz/ *noun* a term used by chartists showing a share price which rises to a peak, then falls slightly, then rises to a much higher peak, then falls sharply and rises to a lower peak before falling again, looking similar to a person's head and shoulders when shown on a graph

head buyer /ˌhed ˈbaɪə/ *noun* the most important buyer in a store

heading /ˈhedɪŋ/ *noun* the words at the top of a piece of text ○ *Items are listed under several headings.* ○ *Look at the figure under the heading 'Costs 2001–02'.*

headlease /ˈhedliːs/ *noun* a lease from the freehold owner to a tenant

headline inflation rate /ˌhedlaɪn ɪn ˈfleɪʃ(ə)n ˌreɪt/ *noun* a British inflation figure which includes items such as mortgage interest and local taxes, which are not included in the inflation figures for other countries

head office /ˌhed ˈɒfɪs/ *noun* an office building where the board of directors works and meets

headquarters /hedˈkwɔːtəz/ *plural noun* the main office, where the board of directors meets and works ○ *The company's headquarters are in New York.*

heads of agreement /ˌhedz əv ə ˈɡriːmənt/ *plural noun* **1.** a draft agreement with not all the details complete **2.** the most important parts of a commercial agreement

health insurance /ˈhelθ ɪnˌʃʊərəns/ *noun* insurance which pays the cost of treatment for illness, especially when travelling abroad

healthy /ˈhelθi/ *adjective* □ **a healthy balance sheet** balance sheet which shows a good profit

heavily /ˈhevɪli/ *adverb* □ **the issue was heavily stagged** large numbers of stags applied for the issue of new shares

'…the steel company had spent heavily on new equipment' [*Fortune*]

heavy industry /ˌhevi ˈɪndəstri/ *noun* an industry which deals in heavy raw materials such as coal or makes large products such as ships or engines

hedge /hedʒ/ *noun* a protection against a possible loss, which involves taking an action which is the opposite of an action taken earlier ■ *verb* to protect against the risk of a loss □ **to hedge your bets** to make investments in several areas so as to be protected against loss in one of them □ **to hedge against inflation** to buy investments which will rise in value faster than the increase in the rate of inflation

'…during the 1970s commercial property was regarded by investors as an alternative to equities, with many of the same inflation-hedge qualities' [*Investors Chronicle*]

'…the move saved it from having to pay its creditors an estimated \$270 million owed in connection with hedge contracts which began working against the company when the price of gold rose unexpectedly during September' [*Business in Africa*]

hedge fund /ˈhedʒ fʌnd/ *noun* a partnership open to a small number of rich investors, which invests in equities, currency futures and derivatives and may produce high returns but carries a very high risk

'…much of what was described as near hysteria was the hedge funds trying to liquidate bonds to repay bank debts after losing multi-million dollar bets on speculations that the yen would fall against the dollar' [*Times*]

'…hedge funds generally have in common an ability to sell short (that is, sell stocks you do not own), and to increase growth prospects – and risk – by borrowing to enhance the fund's assets' [*Money Observer*]

'…the stock is a hedge fund – limited by the Securities and Exchange Commission to only wealthy individuals and qualified institutions' [*Smart Money*]

hedging /ˈhedʒɪŋ/ *noun* the act of buying investments at a fixed price for delivery later, so as to protect against possible loss

hereafter /hɪərˈɑːftə/ *adverb* from this time on

hereby /hɪəˈbaɪ/ *adverb* in this way, by this letter ○ *We hereby revoke the agreement of January 1st 1982.*

hereditament /herɪˈdɪtəmənt/ *noun* a property, including land and buildings

hidden asset /ˌhɪd(ə)n ˈæset/ *noun* an asset which is valued much less in the company's accounts than its true market value

hidden tax /ˈhɪd(ə)n tæks/ *noun* a tax that is not immediately apparent. For example, while a consumer may be aware of a tax on retail purchases, a tax imposed at the wholesale level, which consequently increases the cost of items to the retailer, will not be apparent.

high /haɪ/ *adjective* large, not low ○ *High overhead costs increase the unit price.* ○ *High prices put customers off.* ○ *They are budgeting for a high level of expenditure.* ○ *High interest rates are crippling small businesses.* □ **higher rate of tax** top rate of income tax (currently in the UK, 40% on taxable income above œ28,000) ■ *noun* a point where prices or sales are very large ○ *Prices have dropped by 10% since the high of January 2nd.*

'American interest rates remain exceptionally high in relation to likely inflation rates' [*Sunday Times*]

'…faster economic growth would tend to push US interest rates, and therefore the dollar, higher' [*Australian Financial Review*]

'…in a leveraged buyout the acquirer raises money by selling high-yielding debentures to private investors' [*Fortune*]

higher-rate tax /ˌhaɪə reɪt 'tæks/ *noun* in the United Kingdom, the highest of the three bands of income tax. Most countries have bands of income tax with different rates applicable to income within each band.

highest bidder /ˌhaɪəst 'bɪdə/ *noun* a person who offers the most money at an auction ○ *The property was sold to the highest bidder.*

high finance /ˌhaɪ 'faɪnæns/ *noun* the lending, investing and borrowing of very large sums of money organised by financiers

high gearing /ˌhaɪ 'ɡɪərɪŋ/ *noun* a situation where a company has a high level of borrowing compared to its share price

high-grade bond /ˌhaɪ ɡreɪd 'bɒnd/ *noun* a bond which has the highest rating

high-income /ˌhaɪ 'ɪnkʌm/ *adjective* giving a large income ○ *high-income shares* ○ *a high-income portfolio*

highly-geared company /ˌhaɪli ɡɪəd 'kʌmp(ə)ni/ *noun* company which has a high proportion of its funds from fixed-interest borrowings

highly-paid /ˌhaɪli 'peɪd/ *adjective* earning a large salary

highly-placed /ˌhaɪli 'pleɪst/ *adjective* occupying an important post ○ *The delegation met a highly-placed official in the Trade Ministry.*

highly-priced /ˌhaɪli 'praɪst/ *adjective* with a large price

high yield /ˌhaɪ 'jiːld/ *noun* a dividend yield which is higher than is usual for the type of company

hike /haɪk/ *US noun* an increase ■ *verb* to increase

hire /'haɪə/ *noun* an arrangement whereby customers pay money to be able to use a car, boat or piece of equipment owned by someone else for a time

hire car /'haɪə kɑː/ *noun* a car which has been rented ○ *He was driving a hire car when the accident happened.*

hire purchase /ˌhaɪə 'pɜːtʃɪs/ *noun* a system of buying something by paying a sum regularly each month ○ *to buy a refrigerator on hire purchase* (NOTE: The US term is **installment credit**, **installment plan** or **installment sale**.)

hire purchase agreement /ˌhaɪə 'pɜːtʃɪs əˌɡriːmənt/ *noun* a contract to pay for something by instalments

hire-purchase company /ˌhaɪə 'pɜːtʃɪs ˌkʌmp(ə)ni/ *noun* a company which provides money for hire purchase

historic /hɪ'stɒrɪk/, **historical** /hɪ'stɒrɪk(ə)l/ *adjective* dating back over a period of time

'…the Federal Reserve Board has eased interest rates in the past year, but they are still at historically high levels' [*Sunday Times*]

'…the historic p/e for the FTSE all-share index is 28.3 and the dividend yield is barely 2 per cent. Both indicators suggest that the stock markets are very highly priced' [*Times*]

historical cost accounting /hɪˌstɒrɪk(ə)l 'kɒst əˌkaʊntɪŋ/ *noun* the preparation of accounts on the basis of historical cost, with assets valued at their original cost of purchase. Compare **replacement cost accounting**

historical cost concept /hɪˌstɒrɪk(ə)l kɒst 'kɒnsept/, **historical cost convention** /hɪˌstɒrɪk(ə)l kɒst kən'venʃən/ *noun* a basis for treatment of assets in financial statements where they are recorded at their historical cost, without adjustment for inflation or other price variations (NOTE: Use 'historical cost convention' not 'historic cost convention'.)

historical cost depreciation /hɪˌstɒrɪk(ə)l 'kɒst dɪˌpriːʃieɪʃ(ə)n/ *noun* depreciation based on the original cost of the asset

historical figures /hɪˌstɒrɪk(ə)l 'fɪɡəz/ *plural noun* figures which were current in the past

historical pricing /hɪˌstɒrɪk(ə)l 'praɪsɪŋ/ *noun* a method of setting prices for a good or service that is based on prices previously set. Sometimes revised prices may take into account the effects of inflation.

historical summary /hɪˌstɒrɪk(ə)l 'sʌməri/ *noun* in the United Kingdom, an optional synopsis of a company's results over a period of time, often five or ten years, featured in the annual accounts

historical trading range /hɪˌstɒrɪk(ə)l 'treɪdɪŋ reɪndʒ/ *noun* the difference between the highest and lowest price for a share or bond over a period of time

hive off /ˌhaɪv 'ɒf/ *verb* to split off part of a large company to form a smaller subsidiary ○ *The new managing director hived off the retail sections of the company.*

HM Treasury /ˌeɪtʃ ˌem 'treʒəri/ *noun* the UK government department responsible for managing the country's public revenues. The department is run on a day-to-day basis by the Chancellor of the Exchequer.

hoard /hɔːd/ *verb* to buy and store goods in case of need

hoarder /ˈhɔːdə/ *noun* a person who buys and stores goods in case of need

hold /həʊld/ *noun* **1.** the bottom part of a ship or aircraft, in which cargo is carried **2.** the action of keeping something ■ *verb* **1.** to own or to keep something ○ *She holds 10% of the company's shares.* **2.** to make something happen ○ *The receiver will hold an auction of the company's assets.* **3.** not to sell ○ *You should hold these shares – they look likely to rise.*

'…as of last night, the bank's shareholders no longer hold any rights to the bank's shares' [*South China Morning Post*]

hold back /ˌhəʊld ˈbæk/ *verb* to wait, not to do something at the present time

hold down /ˌhəʊld ˈdaʊn/ *verb* to keep at a low level ○ *We are cutting margins to hold our prices down.*

'…real wages have been held down; they have risen at an annual rate of only 1% in the last two years' [*Sunday Times*]

holder /ˈhəʊldə/ *noun* **1.** a person who owns or keeps something ○ *holders of government bonds* or *bondholders* ○ *holder of stock* or *of shares in a company* ○ *holder of an insurance policy* or *policy holder* **2.** a thing which keeps something, which protects something

hold harmless letter /həʊld ˌhɑːmləs ˈletə/ *noun* a letter issued by parties to a business deal to reporting accountants stating that the accountants will not be held responsible for any losses suffered on the deal

holding /ˈhəʊldɪŋ/ *noun* a group of shares owned ○ *She has sold all her holdings in the Far East.* ○ *The company has holdings in German manufacturing companies.*

holding company /ˈhəʊldɪŋ ˌkʌmp(ə)ni/ *noun* **1.** a company which owns more than 50% of the shares in another company. ◊ **subsidiary company 2.** a company which exists only or mainly to own shares in subsidiary companies. ◊ **subsidiary** (NOTE: [all senses] The US term is **proprietary company**.)

holding cost /ˈhəʊldɪŋ kɒst/ *noun* the cost of keeping items of stock including warehousing and handling costs, insurance, losses through deterioration, wastage, theft, etc. and the cost of capital used to acquire the stock measured in terms of the interest lost on the money which was spent on purchasing the stock in the first place or the interest paid on the loans which were needed to finance the purchase of the stock

hold on /ˌhəʊld ˈɒn/ *verb* to wait, not to change

hold out for /ˌhəʊld ˈaʊt fɔː/ *verb* to wait and ask for something

hold to /ˈhəʊld tuː/ *verb* not to allow something or someone to change

hold up /ˌhəʊld ˈʌp/ *verb* **1.** to stay at a high level ○ *Share prices have held up well.* ○ *Sales held up during the tourist season.* **2.** to delay something ○ *The shipment has been held up at customs.* ○ *Payment will be held up until the contract has been signed.* ○ *The strike will hold up dispatch for some weeks.* ○ *The employees are holding up production as a form of protest against poor conditions.*

holiday entitlement /ˈhɒlɪdeɪ ɪnˌtaɪt(ə)lmənt/ *noun* the number of days of paid holiday which an employee has the right to take ○ *She has not used up all her holiday entitlement.*

hologram /ˈhɒləɡræm/ *noun* a three-dimensional picture which is used on credit cards as a means of preventing forgery

home banking /ˌhəʊm ˈbæŋkɪŋ/ *noun* a system of banking using a personal computer in your own home to carry out various financial transactions such as paying invoices or checking your bank account

home loan /ˈhəʊm ləʊn/ *noun* a loan by a bank or building society to help someone buy a house

home trade /ˈhəʊm treɪd/ *noun* trade in the country where a company is based

honorarium /ˌɒnəˈreəriəm/ *noun* money paid to a professional person such as an accountant or a lawyer when a specific fee has not been requested (NOTE: The plural is **honoraria**.)

honorary /ˈɒnərəri/ *adjective* not paid a salary for the work done for an organisation ○ *He is honorary president of the translators' association.*

honorary secretary /ˌɒnərəri ˈsekrət(ə)ri/ *noun* a person who keeps the minutes and official documents of a committee or club, but is not paid a salary

honorary treasurer /ˌɒnərəri ˈtreʒərə/ *noun* a treasurer who does not receive any fee

honour /ˈɒnə/ *verb* to pay something because it is owed and is correct ○ *to honour a bill* (NOTE: The US spelling is **honor**.)

horizontal integration /ˌhɒrɪzɒnt(ə)l ˌɪntɪˈɡreɪʃ(ə)n/ *noun* the process of joining similar companies or taking over a company in the same line of business as yourself

hot money /ˌhɒt ˈmʌni/ *noun* **1.** money which is moved from country to country to get the best returns **2.** money that has been obtained by dishonest means. ◊ **money laundering**

hour /aʊə/ *noun* **1.** a period of time lasting sixty minutes **2.** sixty minutes of work ○ *She earns £14 an hour.* ○ *We pay £16 an hour.*

house /haʊs/ *noun* a company ○ *the largest London finance house* ○ *a broking house* ○ *a publishing house*

house agent /'haʊz ˌeɪdʒənt/ *noun* an estate agent who deals in buying or selling houses or flats

household goods /ˌhaʊshəʊld 'ɡʊdz/ *plural noun* items which are used in the home

human capital accounting /ˌhjuːmən 'kæpɪt(ə)l əˌkaʊntɪŋ/ *noun* an attempt to place a financial value on the knowledge and skills possessed by the employees of an organisation. Also called **human asset accounting, human resource accounting**

human resource accounting /ˌhjuːmən rɪˈzɔːs əˌkaʊntɪŋ/ *noun* same as **human capital accounting**

hybrid /'haɪbrɪd/ *noun* a combination of financial instruments, e.g., a bond with warrants attached, or a range of cash and derivative instruments designed to mirror the performance of a financial market

hyper- /haɪpə/ *prefix* very large

hyperinflation /ˌhaɪpərɪnˈfleɪʃ(ə)n/ *noun* inflation which is at such a high percentage rate that it is almost impossible to reduce

I

IASB *abbr* International Accounting Standards Board

IASC *abbr* International Accounting Standards Committee

ICAEW *abbr* Institute of Chartered Accountants in England and Wales

ICAI *abbr* Institute of Chartered Accountants in Ireland

ICANZ *abbr* Institute of Chartered Accountants of New Zealand

ICAS *abbr* Institute of Chartered Accountants in Scotland

ICSID *abbr* International Centre for Settlement of Investment Disputes

ideal /aɪ'dɪəl/ *adjective* perfect, very good for something ○ *This is the ideal site for a new hypermarket.*

idle /'aɪd(ə)l/ *adjective* not working ○ *2,000 employees were made idle by the recession.*

idle capital /ˌaɪd(ə)l 'kæpɪt(ə)l/ *noun* capital which is not being used productively

idle time /'aɪd(ə)l taɪm/ *noun* the time for which employees are paid although they are unable to work because of factors beyond their control ○ *Idle time in January was attributed to the temporary closing down of one of the company's factories.* ○ *Workers were laid off to avoid excessive idle time.*

IFA[1] *abbr* independent financial adviser

IFA[2] *abbr* Institute of Financial Accountants

illegal /ɪ'liːɡ(ə)l/ *adjective* not legal or against the law

illegality /ˌɪliːˈɡælɪti/ *noun* the fact of being illegal

illegally /ɪ'liːɡəli/ *adverb* against the law ○ *He was accused of illegally laundering money.*

illicit /ɪ'lɪsɪt/ *adjective* not legal or not permitted ○ *the illicit sale of alcohol* ○ *trade in illicit alcohol*

illiquid /ɪ'lɪkwɪd/ *adjective* **1.** referring to an asset which is not easy to change into cash **2.** used to describe a person or business that lacks cash or assets such as securities that can readily be converted into cash

IMA *abbr* Investment Management Association

IMF *abbr* International Monetary Fund

immovable /ɪ'muːvəb(ə)l/ *adjective* impossible to move

immovable property /ɪˌmuːvəb(ə)l ˈprɒpəti/ *noun* houses and other buildings on land

impact /ˈɪmpækt/ *noun* a shock or strong effect ○ *the impact of new technology on the cotton trade* ○ *The new design has made little impact on the buying public.*

'…the strong dollar's deflationary impact on European economies as governments push up interest rates to support their sinking currencies' [*Duns Business Month*]

impairment /ɪmˈpeəmənt/ *noun* a condition in which a sense or function is harmed so that it does not work properly ○ *His hearing impairment does not affect his work.*

impersonal account /ɪmˌpɜːs(ə)n(ə)l əˈkaʊnt/ *noun* any account other than a personal account, being classified as either a real account, in which property is recorded, or a nominal account, in which income, expenses, and capital are recorded. ◊ **account**

implement /ˈɪmplɪˌment/ *verb* to put into action ○ *to implement an agreement* ○ *to implement a decision*

implementation /ˌɪmplɪmenˈteɪʃ(ə)n/ *noun* the process of putting something into action ○ *the implementation of new rules*

import /ɪmˈpɔːt/ *verb* to bring goods from abroad into a country for sale ○ *The company imports television sets from Japan.* ○ *This car was imported from France.*

'European manufacturers rely heavily on imported raw materials which are mostly priced in dollars' [*Duns Business Month*]

importation /ˌɪmpɔːˈteɪʃ(ə)n/ *noun* the act of importing ○ *The importation of arms is forbidden.* ○ *The importation of livestock is subject to very strict controls.*

import ban /ˈɪmpɔːt bæn/ *noun* an order forbidding imports ○ *The government has imposed an import ban on arms.*

import duty /ˈɪmpɔːt ˌdjuːti/ *noun* a tax on goods imported into a country

importer /ɪmˈpɔːtə/ *noun* a person or company that imports goods ○ *a cigar importer* ○ *The company is a big importer of foreign cars.*

import-export /ˌɪmpɔːt ˈekspɔːt/ *adjective, noun* referring to business which deals with both bringing foreign goods into a country and sending locally made goods abroad ○ *Rotterdam is an important centre for the import-export trade.* ○ *She works in import-export.*

importing /ɪmˈpɔːtɪŋ/ *adjective* bringing goods into a country ○ *oil-importing countries* ○ *an importing company*

import levy /ˈɪmpɔːt ˌlevi/ *noun* a tax on imports, especially in the EU a tax on imports of farm produce from outside the EU

import quota /ˈɪmpɔːt ˌkwəʊtə/ *noun* a fixed quantity of a particular type of goods which the government allows to be imported ○ *The government has imposed a quota on the importation of cars.* ○ *The quota on imported cars has been lifted.*

import restrictions /ˈɪmpɔːt rɪˌstrɪkʃ(ə)nz/ *plural noun* actions taken by a government to reduce the level of imports by imposing quotas, duties, etc.

imports /ˈɪmpɔːts/ *plural noun* goods brought into a country from abroad for sale ○ *Imports from Poland have risen to $1m a year.* (NOTE: Usually used in the plural, but the singular is used before a noun.)

import surcharge /ˈɪmpɔːt ˌsɜːtʃɑːdʒ/ *noun* the extra duty charged on imported goods, to try to stop them from being imported and to encourage local manufacture

impose /ɪmˈpəʊz/ *verb* to give orders for something regarded as unpleasant or unwanted such as a tax or a ban ○ *to impose a tax on bicycles* ○ *They tried to impose a ban on smoking.* ○ *The government imposed a special duty on oil.*

imposition /ˌɪmpəˈzɪʃ(ə)n/ *noun* the act of imposing something

impound /ɪmˈpaʊnd/ *verb* to take something away and keep it until a tax is paid ○ *customs impounded the whole cargo*

impounding /ɪmˈpaʊndɪŋ/ *noun* an act of taking something and keeping it until a tax is paid

imprest account /ˈɪmprest əˌkaʊnt/ *noun* a UK term for a record of the transactions of a type of petty cash system. An employee is given an advance of money, an imprest, for incidental expenses and when most of it has been spent, he or she presents receipts for the expenses to the accounts department and is then reimbursed with cash to the total value of the receipts.

imprest system /ˈɪmprest ˌsɪstəm/ *noun* a system of controlling petty cash, where cash is paid out against a written receipt and the receipt is used to get more cash to bring the float to the original level

improve /ɪmˈpruːv/ *verb* to make something better, or to become better ○ *We are trying to improve our image with a series of TV commercials.* ○ *They hope to improve the company's market share.* ○ *We hope the cash flow position will improve or we will have difficulty in paying our bills.*

'…we also invest in companies whose growth and profitability could be improved by a management buyout' [*Times*]

improved offer /ɪmˌpruːvd ˈɒfə/ *noun* an offer which is larger or has better terms than the previous offer

impulse buyer /ˈɪmpʌls ˌbaɪə/ *noun* a person who buys something on impulse, not because he or she intended to buy it

impulse buying /ˈɪmpʌls ˌbaɪɪŋ/ *noun* the practice of buying items which you have just seen, not because you had planned to buy them

imputation system /ˌɪmpjuːˈteɪʃ(ə)n ˌsɪstəm/ *noun* a system of taxation of dividends, where the company pays advance corporation tax on the dividends it pays to its shareholders, and the shareholders pay no tax on the dividends received, assuming that they pay tax at the standard rate. The ACT is shown as a tax credit which is imputed to the shareholder.

inactive /ɪnˈæktɪv/ *adjective* not active or not busy

inactive account /ɪnˌæktɪv əˈkaʊnt/ *noun* a bank account which is not used over a period of time

inactive market /ɪnˌæktɪv ˈmɑːkɪt/ *noun* a stock market with few buyers or sellers

incentive /ɪnˈsentɪv/ *noun* something which encourages a customer to buy, or employees to work better

'…some further profit-taking was seen yesterday as investors continued to lack fresh incentives to renew buying activity' [*Financial Times*]

'…a well-designed plan can help companies retain talented employees and offer enticing performance incentives – all at an affordable cost' [*Fortune*]

'…the right incentives can work when used strategically' [*Management Today*]

'…an additional incentive is that the Japanese are prepared to give rewards where they are due' [*Management Today*]

incentive bonus /ɪnˈsentɪv ˌbəʊnəs/, **incentive payment** /ɪnˈsentɪv ˌpeɪmənt/ *noun* an extra payment offered to employees to make them work better

incentive scheme /ɪnˈsentɪv skiːm/ *noun* a plan to encourage better work by paying higher commission or bonuses ○ *Incentive schemes are boosting production.*

inchoate /ɪnˈkəʊət/ *adjective* referring to an instrument which is incomplete

incidence of tax /ˌɪnsɪd(ə)ns əv ˈtæks/ *noun* used to indicate where the final burden of a tax lies. For example, although a retailer pays any sales tax to the tax collecting authority, the tax itself is ultimately paid by the customer.

incidental /ˌɪnsɪˈdent(ə)l/ *adjective* not important, but connected with something else

incidental expenses /ˌɪnsɪdent(ə)l ɪkˈspensɪz/ *plural noun* small amounts of money spent at various times in addition to larger amounts

include /ɪnˈkluːd/ *verb* to count something along with other things ○ *The charge includes VAT.* ○ *The total is £140 not including insurance and freight.* ○ *The account covers services up to and including the month of June.*

inclusive /ɪnˈkluːsɪv/ *adjective* counting something in with other things ○ *inclusive of tax* ○ *not inclusive of VAT*

income /ˈɪnkʌm/ *noun* **1.** money which a person receives as salary or dividends □ **lower income bracket**, **upper income bracket** the groups of people who earn low or high salaries considered for tax purposes **2.** money which an organisation receives as gifts or from investments ○ *The hospital has a large income from gifts.*

'…there is no risk-free way of taking regular income from your money much higher than the rate of inflation' [*Guardian*]

income distribution /ˈɪnkʌm dɪstrɪˌbjuːʃ(ə)n/ *noun* the UK term for the payment to investors of the income generated by a collective investment, less management charges, tax, and expenses. It is distributed in proportion to the number of units or shares held by each investor. US term **income dividend**

income gearing /ˈɪnkʌm ˌɡɪərɪŋ/ *noun* the ratio of the interest a company pays on its borrowing shown as a percentage of its pre-tax profits before the interest is paid

income shares /ˈɪnkʌm ʃeəz/ *plural noun* shares in an investment trust which receive income from the investments, but do not benefit from the rise in capital value of the investments

income smoothing /ˌɪnkʌm ˈsmuːðɪŋ/ *noun* a UK term for a form of creative accounting that involves the manipulation of a company's financial statements to show steady annual profits rather than large fluctuations

income statement /ˈɪnkʌm ˌsteɪtmənt/ *noun* US a statement of company expenditure and sales which shows whether the company has made a profit or loss (NOTE: The UK term is **profit and loss account**.)

income tax /ˈɪnkʌm tæks/ *noun* **1.** the tax on a person's income, both earned and unearned **2.** the tax on the profits of a corporation

income tax form /ˈɪnkʌm tæks ˌfɔːm/ *noun* a form to be completed which declares all income to the tax office

income units /ˈɪnkʌm ˌjuːnɪts/ *plural noun* units in a unit trust, from which the investor receives dividends in the form of income

incomplete records /ˌɪnkəmpliːt ˈrekɔːdz/ *noun* an accounting system which is not double-entry bookkeeping. Various degrees of incompleteness can occur, e.g., **single-entry bookkeeping**, in which usually only a cash book is maintained.

inconvertible /ˌɪnkənˈvɜːtəb(ə)l/ *adjective* referring to currency which cannot be easily converted into other currencies

incorporate /ɪnˈkɔːpəreɪt/ *verb* **1.** to bring something in to form part of a main group ○ *Income from the 1998 acquisition is incorporated into the accounts.* **2.** to form a registered company ○ *a company incorporated in the USA* ○ *an incorporated company* ○ *J. Doe Incorporated*

incorporation /ɪnˌkɔːpəˈreɪʃ(ə)n/ *noun* an act of incorporating a company

increase *noun* /ˈɪnkriːs/ **1.** an act of becoming larger ○ *There have been several increases in tax or tax increases in the last few years.* ○ *There is an automatic 5% increase in price or price increase on January 1st.* ○ *Profits showed a 10% increase or an increase of 10% on last year.* **2.** a higher salary ○ *increase in pay or pay increase* ○ *The government hopes to hold salary increases to 3%.* □ **she had two increases last year** her salary went up twice ■ *verb* /ɪnˈkriːs/ **1.** to grow bigger or higher ○ *Profits have increased faster than the increase in the rate of inflation.* ○ *Exports to Africa have increased by more than 25%.* ○ *The price of oil has increased twice in the past week.* □ **to increase in size** *or* **value** to become larger or more valuable **2.** to make something bigger or higher □ **the company increased her salary to £20,000** the company gave her a rise in salary to £20,000

'…turnover has the potential to be increased to over 1 million dollars with energetic management and very little capital' [*Australian Financial Review*]

'…competition is steadily increasing and could affect profit margins as the company tries to retain its market share' [*Citizen (Ottawa)*]

increment /ˈɪŋkrɪmənt/ *noun* a regular automatic increase in salary ○ *an annual increment* □ **salary which rises in annual increments of £1000** each year the salary is increased by £1000

incremental /ˌɪŋkrɪˈment(ə)l/ *adjective* rising automatically in stages

incremental budgeting /ˌɪŋkrɪment(ə)l ˈbʌdʒɪtɪŋ/ *noun* a method of setting budgets in which the prior period budget is used as a base for the current budget, which is set by adjusting the prior period budget to take account of any anticipated changes

incremental cost /ˌɪŋkrɪment(ə)l ˈkɒst/ *noun* the cost of making extra units above the number already planned. This may then include further fixed costs.

incremental increase /ˌɪŋkrɪment(ə)l ˈɪnkriːs/ *noun* an increase in salary according to an agreed annual increment

incremental scale /ˌɪŋkrɪment(ə)l ˈskeɪl/ *noun* a salary scale with regular annual salary increases

incur /ɪnˈkɜː/ *verb* to make yourself liable to something

'…the company blames fiercely competitive market conditions in Europe for a £14m operating loss last year, incurred despite a record turnover' [*Financial Times*]

indebted /ɪnˈdetɪd/ *adjective* owing money to someone ○ *to be indebted to a property company*

indemnification /ɪndemnɪfɪˈkeɪʃən/ *noun* payment for damage

indemnify /ɪnˈdemnɪfaɪ/ *verb* to pay for damage ○ *to indemnify someone for a loss*

indemnity /ɪnˈdemnɪti/ *noun* **1.** a guarantee of payment after a loss ○ *She had to pay an indemnity of £100.* **2.** compensation paid after a loss

indent /ˈɪndent/ *noun* an order placed by an importer for goods from overseas ○ *They put in an indent for a new stock of soap.*

indenture /ɪnˈdentʃə/ *noun US* a formal agreement showing the terms of a bond issue

independent /ˌɪndɪˈpendənt/ *adjective* not under the control or authority of anyone else

independent company /ˌɪndɪpendənt ˈkʌmp(ə)ni/ *noun* a company which is not controlled by another company

independent financial adviser /ˌɪndɪpendənt faɪˌnænʃ(ə)l ədˈvaɪzə/ *noun* a person who gives impartial advice on financial matters, who is not connected with any financial institution. Abbreviation **IFA**

independent trader /ˌɪndɪpendənt ˈtreɪdə/, **independent shop** /ˌɪndɪpendənt ˈʃɒp/ *noun* a shop which is owned by an individual proprietor, not by a chain

index /ˈɪndeks/ *noun* **1.** a list of items classified into groups or put in alphabetical order **2.** a regular statistical report which shows rises and falls in prices, values or levels **3.** a figure based on the current market price of shares on a stock exchange ■ *verb* to link a payment to an index ○ *salaries indexed to the cost of living*

'...the index of industrial production sank 0.2 per cent for the latest month after rising 0.3 per cent in March' [*Financial Times*]

'...an analysis of the consumer price index for the first half of the year shows that the rate of inflation went down by 12.9 per cent' [*Business Times (Lagos)*]

indexation /ˌɪndek'seɪʃ(ə)n/ *noun* the linking of something to an index

index card /'ɪndeks kɑːd/ *noun* a card used to make a card index

indexed portfolio /ˌɪndekst pɔːt 'fəʊliəʊ/ *noun* a portfolio of shares in all the companies which form the basis of a stock exchange index

index fund /'ɪndeks fʌnd/ *noun* an investment fund consisting of shares in all the companies which are used to calculate a Stock Exchange index (NOTE: The plural is **indexes** or **indices**.)

index letter /'ɪndeks ˌletə/ *noun* a letter of an item in an index

index-linked /ˌɪndeks 'lɪŋkt/ *adjective* rising automatically by the percentage increase in the cost of living ○ *index-linked government bonds* ○ *Inflation did not affect her as she has an index-linked pension.*

'...two-year index-linked savings certificates now pay 3 per cent a year tax free, in addition to index-linking' [*Financial Times*]

index number /'ɪndeks ˌnʌmbə/ *noun* **1.** a number of something in an index **2.** a number showing the percentage rise of something over a period

index tracker /'ɪndeks ˌtrækə/ *noun* an investor or fund manager who tracks an index

index-tracking /'ɪndeks ˌtrækɪŋ/ *adjective* following an index

indicate /'ɪndɪkeɪt/ *verb* to show something ○ *The latest figures indicate a fall in the inflation rate.* ○ *Our sales for last year indicate a move from the home market to exports.*

indicator /'ɪndɪkeɪtə/ *noun* something which indicates

'...it reduces this month's growth in the key M3 indicator from about 19% to 12%' [*Sunday Times*]

'...we may expect the US leading economic indicators for April to show faster economic growth' [*Australian Financial Review*]

'...other indicators, such as high real interest rates, suggest that monetary conditions are extremely tight' [*Economist*]

indirect /ˌɪndaɪ'rekt/ *adjective* not direct

indirect expenses /ˌɪndaɪrekt ɪk 'spensɪz/ *noun* costs which are not directly

attached to the making of a product, e.g. cleaning, rent, administration

indirect labour costs /ˌɪndaɪrekt 'leɪbə ˌkɒsts/ *plural noun* the cost of paying employees not directly involved in making a product such as cleaners or canteen staff. Such costs cannot be allocated to a cost centre.

indirect material cost /ˌɪndaɪˌrekt mə 'tɪəriəl kɒst/, **indirect materials cost** /ˌɪndaɪˌrekt mə'tɪəriəls kɒst/ *noun* the cost of materials which cannot be allocated to the production of a particular product

indirect tax /ˌɪndaɪrekt 'tæks/ *noun* a tax such as VAT paid to someone who then pays it to the government

indirect taxation /ˌɪndaɪrekt tæk 'seɪʃ(ə)n/ *noun* taxes which are not paid direct to the government, e.g. sales tax ○ *The government raises more money by indirect taxation than by direct.*

individual /ˌɪndɪ'vɪdʒuəl/ *noun* one single person ○ *a savings plan tailored to the requirements of the private individual*

Individual Savings Account /ˌɪndɪvɪdʒuəl 'seɪvɪŋz əˌkaʊnt/ *noun* a British scheme by which individuals can invest for their retirement by putting a limited amount of money each year in a tax-free account. Abbreviation **ISA**

Individual Voluntary Agreement *abbr* IVA

Individual Voluntary Arrangement /ˌɪndɪvɪdʒuəl ˌvɒlənt(ə)ri ə'reɪndʒmənt/ *noun* a legally binding arrangement between a debtor and creditors by which the debtor offers the creditors the best deal he or she can afford by realising his assets, and so the expense of bankruptcy proceedings is avoided. Abbreviation **IVA**

inducement /ɪn'djuːsmənt/ *noun* something which helps to persuade someone to do something ○ *They offered her a company car as an inducement to stay.*

industrial arbitration tribunal /ɪn ˌdʌstriəl ɑːbɪ'treɪʃ(ə)n traɪˌbjuːn(ə)l/ *noun* a court which decides in industrial disputes

industrial tribunal /ɪnˌdʌstriəl traɪ 'bjuːn(ə)l/ *noun* a court which can decide in disputes about employment

'ACAS has a legal obligation to try and solve industrial grievances before they reach industrial tribunals' [*Personnel Today*]

ineligible /ɪn'elɪdʒɪb(ə)l/ *adjective* not eligible

inflation /ɪn'fleɪʃ(ə)n/ *noun* a greater increase in the supply of money or credit than in the production of goods and services, resulting in higher prices and a fall in the purchasing power of money ○ *to take measures to reduce inflation* ○ *High interest rates tend to increase inflation.* □ **we have 3% inflation** *or* **inflation is running at 3%** prices are 3% higher than at the same time last year

inflation accounting /ɪnˈfleɪʃ(ə)n əˌkaʊntɪŋ/ *noun* an accounting system, where inflation is taken into account when calculating the value of assets and the preparation of accounts

inflationary /ɪnˈfleɪʃ(ə)n(ə)ri/ *adjective* tending to increase inflation ○ *inflationary trends in the economy*

'...inflationary expectations fell somewhat this month, but remained a long way above the actual inflation rate, according to figures released yesterday. The annual rate of inflation measured by the consumer price index has been below 2 per cent for over 18 months' [*Australian Financial Review*]

inflation-proof /ɪnˈfleɪʃ(ə)n pruːf/ *adjective* referring to a pension, etc. which is index-linked, so that its value is preserved in times of inflation

inflow /ˈɪnfləʊ/ *noun* the act of coming in or being brought in

'...the dollar is strong because of capital inflows rather than weak because of the trade deficit' [*Duns Business Month*]

influx /ˈɪnflʌks/ *noun* an inflow, especially one where people or things come in in large quantities ○ *an influx of foreign currency into the country* ○ *an influx of cheap labour into the cities*

'...the retail sector will also benefit from the expected influx of tourists' [*Australian Financial Review*]

information retrieval /ˌɪnfəmeɪʃ(ə)n rɪˈtriːv(ə)l/ *noun* the finding of stored data in a computer

inherit /ɪnˈherɪt/ *verb* to get something from a person who has died ○ *When her father died she inherited the shop.* ○ *He inherited £10,000 from his grandfather.*

inheritance /ɪnˈherɪt(ə)ns/ *noun* property which is received from a dead person

inheritance tax /ɪnˈherɪt(ə)ns tæks/ *noun* tax payable on wealth or property worth above a certain amount and inherited after the death of someone. The current threshold is £250,000, and the estate is liable for 40% tax on the excess amount. Abbreviation **IHT** (NOTE: The US term is **death duty**.)

in-house /ˌɪn ˈhaʊs/ *adverb, adjective* done by someone employed by a company on their premises, not by an outside contractor ○ *the in-house staff* ○ *We do all our data processing in-house.*

initial /ɪˈnɪʃ(ə)l/ *adjective* first or starting ○ *The initial response to the TV advertising has been very good.*

'...the founding group has subscribed NKr 14.5m of the initial NKr 30m share capital' [*Financial Times*]

'...career prospects are excellent for someone with potential, and initial salary is negotiable around $45,000 per annum' [*Australian Financial Review*]

initial capital /ɪˌnɪʃ(ə)l ˈkæpɪt(ə)l/ *noun* capital which is used to start a business

initials /ɪˈnɪʃ(ə)lz/ *plural noun* a first letters of the words in a name ○ *What do the initials IMF stand for?* ○ *The chairman wrote his initials by each alteration in the contract he was signing.*

initial sales /ɪˌnɪʃ(ə)l ˈseɪlz/ *plural noun* the first sales of a new product

initial yield /ɪˌnɪʃ(ə)l ˈjiːld/ *noun* the estimated yield of an investment fund at the time when it is launched

initiate /ɪˈnɪʃieɪt/ *verb* to start ○ *to initiate discussions*

initiative /ɪˈnɪʃətɪv/ *noun* the decision to start something

injection /ɪnˈdʒekʃən/ *noun* □ **a capital injection of £100,000** *or* **an injection of £100,000 capital** putting £100,000 into an existing business

injunction /ɪnˈdʒʌŋkʃən/ *noun* a court order telling someone not to do something ○ *He got an injunction preventing the company from selling his car.* ○ *The company applied for an injunction to stop their rival from marketing a similar product.*

inland /ˈɪnlənd/ *adjective* inside a country

inland freight charges /ˌɪnlənd ˈfreɪt ˌtʃɑːdʒɪz/ *plural noun* charges for carrying goods from one part of the country to another

inland postage /ˌɪnlənd ˈpəʊstɪdʒ/ *noun* postage for a letter to another part of the same country

Inland Revenue /ˌɪnlənd ˈrevənjuː/ *noun* a British government department dealing with taxes such as income tax, corporation tax, capital gains tax, inheritance tax, etc., but not duties, such as VAT, which are collected by the Customs and Excise ○ *He received a letter from the Inland Revenue.* (NOTE: The US term is **Internal Revenue Service** or **IRS**.)

Inland Revenue Commissioner /ɪn ˌlænd ˌrevənjuː kəˈmɪʃ(ə)nə/ *noun* a person appointed officially to supervise the collection of taxes, including income tax, capital gains tax and corporation tax, but not Value Added Tax. Abbreviation **IRC**

inputs /'ɪnpʊts/ *plural noun* goods or services bought by a company and which may be liable to VAT

input tax /'ɪnpʊt tæks/ *noun* VAT which is paid by a company on goods or services bought

inquiry office /ɪn'kwaɪəri ˌɒfɪs/ *noun* an office which members of the public can go to to have their questions answered

inside /ɪn'saɪd/ *adjective, adverb* in, especially in a company's office or building ○ *We do all our design work inside.*

insider /ɪn'saɪdə/ *noun* a person who works in an organisation and therefore knows its secrets

insider buying /ɪnˌsaɪdə 'baɪɪŋ/, **insider dealing** /ɪnˌsaɪdə 'diːlɪŋ/ *noun* the illegal buying or selling of shares by staff of a company or other persons who have secret information about the company's plans

insider trading /ɪnˌsaɪdə 'treɪdɪŋ/ *noun* same as **insider buying**

inside worker /'ɪnsaɪd ˌwɜːkə/ *noun* an employee who works in an office or factory

insolvency /ɪn'sɒlvənsi/ *noun* the fact of not being able to pay debts. Opposite **solvency**

'…hundreds of thrifts found themselves on the brink of insolvency after a deregulation programme prompted them to enter dangerous financial waters' [*Times*]

insolvency practitioner /ɪn'sɒlvənsi prækˌtɪʃ(ə)nə/ *noun* a person who advises insolvent companies

insolvent /ɪn'sɒlvənt/ *adjective* not able to pay debts ○ *The company was declared insolvent.* (NOTE: see note at **insolvency**)

inspect /ɪn'spekt/ *verb* to examine in detail ○ *to inspect a machine* or *an installation* ○ *The gas board is sending an engineer to inspect the central heating system.* ○ *Officials from the DTI have come to inspect the accounts.*

inspection /ɪn'spekʃən/ *noun* the close examination of something ○ *to make an inspection* or *to carry out an inspection of a machine* or *an installation* ○ *the inspection of a product for defects*

inspection stamp /ɪn'spekʃən stæmp/ *noun* a stamp placed on something to show it has been inspected

inspector /ɪn'spektə/ *noun* an official who inspects ○ *The inspectors will soon be round to make sure the building is safe.*

inspectorate /ɪn'spekt(ə)rət/ *noun* all inspectors

inspector of taxes /ɪnˌspektər əv 'tæksɪz/ *noun* in the United Kingdom, an official who reports to the Board of Inland Revenue and is responsible for issuing tax returns and assessments, agreeing tax liabilities, and conducting appeals on matters of tax

inspector of weights and measures /ɪnˌspektər əv ˌweɪts ən 'meʒəz/ *noun* a government official who inspects weighing machines and goods sold in shops to see if the quantities and weights are correct

instability /ˌɪnstə'bɪlɪti/ *noun* the state of being unstable or moving up and down □ **a period of instability in the money markets** a period when currencies fluctuate rapidly

instalment /ɪn'stɔːlmənt/ *noun* a part of a payment which is paid regularly until the total amount is paid ○ *The first instalment is payable on signature of the agreement.* (NOTE: The US spelling is **installment**.) □ **to pay £25 down and monthly instalments of £20** to pay a first payment of £25 and the rest in payments of £20 each month

institute /'ɪnstɪtjuːt/ *noun* a society or organisation which represents a particular profession or activity ○ *the Institute of Chartered Accountants* ○ *the Chartered Institute of Personnel and Development*

Institute of Chartered Accountants in England and Wales /ˌɪnstɪtjuːt əv ˌtʃɑːtəd əˌkaʊntənts ɪn ˌɪŋglənd ən 'weɪlz/ *noun* the largest professional accountancy body in Europe, providing qualification by examinations, ensuring high standards of education and training, and supervising professional conduct. Abbreviation **ICAEW**

Institute of Chartered Accountants in Ireland /ˌɪnstɪtjuːt əv ˌtʃɑːtəd əˌkaʊntənts ɪn 'aɪələnd/ *noun* the oldest and largest professional body for accountants in Ireland, founded in 1888 with the aims of in promoting best practice in chartered accountancy and maintaining high standards of professionalism among its members. Abbreviation **ICAI**

Institute of Chartered Accountants in Scotland /ˌɪnstɪtjuːt əv ˌtʃɑːtəd əˌkaʊntənts ɪn 'skɒtlənd/ *noun* the world's oldest professional body for accountants, based in Edinburgh. Abbreviation **ICAS**

Institute of Chartered Accountants of New Zealand /ˌɪnstɪtjuːt əv ˌtʃɑːtəd əˌkaʊntənts əv njuː 'ziːlənd/ *noun* the only professional accounting body in New Zealand, representing over 26,000 members in that country and abroad. Abbreviation **ICANZ**

Institute of Financial Accountants /ˌɪnstɪˌtjuːt əv faɪˌnænʃ(ə)l ə'kaʊntənts/

noun a professional body, established in 1916, which aims to set technical and ethical standards in UK financial accountancy. Abbreviation **IFA**

institution /ˌɪnstɪˈtjuːʃ(ə)n/ *noun* an organisation or society set up for a particular purpose. ◊ **financial institution**

institutional /ˌɪnstɪˈtjuːʃ(ə)n(ə)l/ *adjective* referring to an institution, especially a financial institution

> '…during the 1970s commercial property was regarded by big institutional investors as an alternative to equities' [*Investors Chronicle*]

instruction /ɪnˈstrʌkʃən/ *noun* an order which tells what should be done or how something is to be used ○ *She gave instructions to his stockbroker to sell the shares immediately.*

instrument /ˈɪnstrʊmənt/ *noun* **1.** a tool or piece of equipment ○ *The technician brought instruments to measure the output of electricity.* **2.** a legal document

insurable /ɪnˈʃʊərəb(ə)l/ *adjective* possible to insure

insurable interest /ɪnˌʃʊərəb(ə)l ˈɪntrəst/ *adjective* the value of the thing insured which is attributed to the person who is taking out the insurance

insurance /ɪnˈʃʊərəns/ *noun* an agreement that in return for regular payments called 'premiums', a company will pay compensation for loss, damage, injury or death ○ *to take out insurance* ○ *Repairs will be paid for by the insurance.*

insurance agent /ɪnˈʃʊərəns ˌeɪdʒənt/, **insurance broker** /ɪnˈʃʊərəns ˌbrəʊkə/ *noun* a person who arranges insurance for clients

insurance claim /ɪnˈʃʊərəns kleɪm/ *noun* a request to an insurance company to pay compensation for damage or loss

insurance company /ɪnˈʃʊərəns ˌkʌmp(ə)ni/ *noun* a company whose business is insurance

insurance contract /ɪnˈʃʊərəns ˌkɒntrækt/ *noun* an agreement by an insurance company to insure

insurance cover /ɪnˈʃʊərəns ˌkʌvə/ *noun* protection guaranteed by an insurance policy ○ *Do you have cover against theft?*

insurance policy /ɪnˈʃʊərəns ˌpɒlɪsi/ *noun* a document which shows the conditions of an insurance contract

insurance premium /ɪnˈʃʊərəns ˌpriːmiəm/ *noun* an annual payment made by a person or a company to an insurance company

insurance premium tax /ɪnˈʃʊərəns ˈpriːmiəm tæks/ *noun* a tax on household, motor vehicle, travel, and other general insurance

insurance rates /ɪnˈʃʊərəns reɪts/ *plural noun* the amount of premium which has to be paid per £1000 of insurance

insure /ɪnˈʃʊə/ *verb* to have a contract with a company whereby, if regular small payments are made, the company will pay compensation for loss, damage, injury or death ○ *to insure a house against fire* ○ *to insure someone's life* ○ *to insure baggage against loss* ○ *to insure against loss of earnings* ○ *She was insured for £100,000.*

insurer /ɪnˈʃʊərə/ *noun* a company which insures (NOTE: For life insurance, UK English prefers to use **assurer**.)

intangible /ɪnˈtændʒɪb(ə)l/ *adjective* not possible to touch

intangible assets /ɪnˌtændʒɪb(ə)l ˈæsets/, **intangibles** /ɪnˈtændʒɪb(ə)lz/ *plural noun* assets which have a value, but which cannot be seen, e.g. goodwill, or a patent or a trademark

intangible fixed assets /ɪnˌtændʒɪb(ə)l fɪkst ˈæsets/ *plural noun* assets which have a value, but which cannot be seen, e.g. goodwill, copyrights, patents or trademarks

integrate /ˈɪntɪɡreɪt/ *verb* to link things together to form one whole group

integrated accounts /ˌɪntɪˌɡreɪtɪd əˈkaʊnts/ *noun* accounting records that show both financial and cost accounts

integration /ˌɪntɪˈɡreɪʃ(ə)n/ *noun* the act of bringing several businesses together under a central control

intent /ɪnˈtent/ *noun* something that someone plans to do

inter- /ɪntə/ *prefix* between

inter-bank /ˌɪntə ˈbæŋk/ *adjective* between banks

inter-bank loan /ˌɪntə bæŋk ˈləʊn/ *noun* a loan from one bank to another

inter-company /ɪnˌtɜː ˈkʌmp(ə)ni/ *adjective* between companies

inter-company dealings /ɪnˌtɜː ˌkʌmp(ə)ni ˈdiːlɪŋz/, **inter-company transactions** /ɪnˌtɜː ˌkʌmp(ə)ni trænˈzækʃ(ə)ns/ *plural noun* dealings or transactions between two companies in the same group

interest /ˈɪntrəst/ *noun* **1.** special attention ○ *The buyers showed a lot of interest in our new product range.* **2.** payment made by a borrower for the use of money, calculated as a percentage of the capital borrowed □ **high interest, low interest** interest at a high or low percentage **3.** money paid as income on investments or loans ○ *to receive interest at 5%* ○ *the loan pays 5% interest* ○ *deposit which yields* or *gives* or *produces* or *bears 5% interest* ○ *account which earns interest at 10%* or *which earns 10% interest* ○ *The bank pays 10% interest on deposits.* **4.** a part of the ownership of something, e.g. if you invest money in a company you acquire a financial share or interest in it

interest-bearing deposits /ˌɪntrəst ˌbeərɪŋ dɪˈpɒzɪts/ *plural noun* deposits which produce interest

interest charges /ˈɪntrəst ˌtʃɑːdʒɪz/ *plural noun* money paid as interest on a loan

interest cover /ˈɪntrəst ˌkʌvə/ *noun* the ability to pay interest payments on a loan

interested party /ˌɪntrestɪd ˈpɑːti/ *noun* a person or company with a financial interest in a company

interest-free credit /ˌɪntrəst friː ˈkredɪt/ *noun* a credit or loan where no interest is paid by the borrower ○ *The company gives its staff interest-free loans.*

interest rate margin /ˈɪntrəst reɪt ˌmɑːdʒɪn/ *noun* the difference between the interest a bank pays on deposits and the interest it charges on loans

interest rate swap /ˈɪntrəst reɪt ˌswɒp/ *noun* an agreement between two companies to exchange borrowings. A company with fixed-interest borrowings might swap them for variable interest borrowings of another company. Also called **plain vanilla swap**

interest sensitive /ˌɪntrəst ˈsensɪtɪv/ *noun* used to describe assets, generally purchased with credit, that are in demand when interest rates fall but considered less attractive when interest rates rise

interest yield /ˈɪntrəst jiːld/ *noun* a yield on a fixed-interest investment

interim /ˈɪntərɪm/ *adjective* made, measured or happening in the middle of a period, such as the financial year, and before the final result for the period is available ■ *noun* a statement of interim profits or dividends

'…the company plans to keep its annual dividend unchanged at 7.5 per share, which includes a 3.75 interim payout' [*Financial Times*]

interim dividend /ˌɪntərɪm ˈdɪvɪˌdend/ *noun* a dividend paid at the end of a half-year

interim financial statement /ˌɪntərɪm faɪˌnænʃəl ˈsteɪtmənt/ *noun* a financial statement that covers a period other than a full financial year. Although UK companies are not legally obliged to publish interim fi-

nancial statements, those listed on the London Stock Exchange are obliged to publish a half-yearly report of their activities and a profit and loss account which may either be sent to shareholders or published in a national newspaper. In the United States, the practice is to issue quarterly financial statement.

interim payment /ˌɪntərɪm ˈpeɪmənt/ *noun* a payment of part of a dividend

interim receiver /ˌɪntərɪm rɪˈsiːvə/ *noun* a receiver appointed to deal with a person's affairs until a bankruptcy order is made

intermediary /ˌɪntəˈmiːdiəri/ *noun* a person who is the link between people or organisations who do not agree or who are negotiating ○ *He refused to act as an intermediary between the two directors.*

intermediate debt /ˌɪntəˈmiːdiət det/ *noun* debts which have to be repaid between four and ten years' time

internal /ɪnˈtɜːn(ə)l/ *adjective* **1.** inside a company **2.** inside a country or a region

internal audit /ɪnˌtɜːn(ə)l ˈɔːdɪt/ *noun* an audit carried out by a department inside the company

internal auditor /ɪnˌtɜːn(ə)l ˈɔːdɪtə/ *noun* a member of staff who audits a company's accounts

internal control /ɪnˌtɜːn(ə)l kənˈtrəʊl/ *noun* a system set up by the management of a company to monitor and control the company's activities

internal growth /ɪnˌtɜːn(ə)l ˈɡrəʊθ/ *noun* the development of a company by growing its existing business with its own finances, as opposed to acquiring other businesses. Also called **organic growth**. Opposite **external growth**

internal rate of return /ɪnˌtɜːn(ə)l reɪt əv rɪˈtɜːn/ *noun* an average annual yield of an investment, where the interest earned over a period of time is the same as the original cost of the investment. Abbreviation **IRR**

Internal Revenue Service /ɪnˌtɜːn(ə)l ˈrevənjuː ˌsɜːvɪs/ *noun US* in the United States, the branch of the federal government charged with collecting the majority of federal taxes. Abbreviation **IRS**

internal telephone /ɪnˌtɜːn(ə)l ˈtelɪfəʊn/ *noun* a telephone which is linked to other telephones in an office

internal trade /ɪnˌtɜːn(ə)l ˈtreɪd/ *noun* trade between various parts of a country. Opposite **external trade**

international /ˌɪntəˈnæʃ(ə)nəl/ *adjective* working between countries

International Accounting Standards Board /ˌɪntənæʃ(ə)nəl əˌkaʊntɪŋ 'stændədz ˌbɔːd/ *noun* an independent and privately funded accounting standards setting organisation, based in London. The Board, whose members come from nine countries and a range of backgrounds, is committed to developing a single set of high quality, understandable, and enforceable global standards that require transparent and comparable information in general purpose financial statements. It also works with national. Abbreviation **IASB**

International Accounting Standards Committee /ˌɪntənæʃ(ə)nəl əˌkaʊntɪŋ 'stændədz kəˌmɪti/ *noun* an organisation based in London that works towards achieving global agreement on accounting standards. Abbreviation **IASC**

International Centre for Settlement of Investment Disputes /ˌɪntə ˌnæʃ(ə)nəl ˌsentə fə ˌset(ə)lmənt əv ɪn 'vestmənt/ *noun* one of the five institutions that comprises the World Bank Group. It was established in 1966 to undertake the role previously undertaken in a personal capacity by the President of the World Bank in assisting in mediation or conciliation of investment disputes between governments and private foreign investors. The overriding consideration in its establishment was that a specialist institution could help to promote increased flows of international investment. Although ICSID has close links to the World Bank, it is an autonomous organisation. Abbreviation **ICSID**

International Monetary Fund /ˌɪntənæʃ(ə)nəl 'mʌnɪt(ə)ri ˌfʌnd/ *noun* a type of bank which is part of the United Nations and helps member states in financial difficulties, gives financial advice to members and encourages world trade. Abbreviation **IMF**

international money markets /ˌɪntənæʃ(ə)nəl 'mʌni ˌmɑːkɪts/ *plural noun* markets such as the Euromarket, the international market for lending or borrowing in eurocurrencies

international trade /ˌɪntənæʃ(ə)nəl 'treɪd/ *noun* trade between different countries

Internet banking /ˌɪntənet 'bæŋkɪŋ/ *noun* the operation of a bank account over the internet

intervene /ˌɪntə'viːn/ *verb* to try to make a change in a situation in which you have not been involved before

intervention /ˌɪntə'venʃən/ *noun* the act of becoming involved in a situation in order to change it ○ *the central bank's intervention in the banking crisis* ○ *the government's intervention in the labour dispute*

intervention mechanism /ˌɪntə 'venʃən ˌmekənɪz(ə)m/ *noun* a method used by central banks in maintaining exchange rate parities, e.g. buying or selling foreign currency

inter vivos /ˌɪntə 'viːvəʊs/ *phrase* a Latin phrase, 'between living people'

inter vivos trust /ˌɪntə 'viːvəʊs trʌst/ *noun* a trust set up by one person for another living person

intestacy /ɪn'testəsi/ *noun* the state of having died without having made a will

intrinsic value /ɪnˌtrɪnsɪk 'væljuː/ *noun* the material value of something ○ *These objects have sentimental value, but no intrinsic value at all.* ○ *The intrinsic value of jewellery makes it a good investment.*

introductory offer /ˌɪntrədʌkt(ə)ri 'ɒfə/ *noun* a special price offered on a new product to attract customers

invalid /ɪn'vælɪd/ *adjective* not valid or not legal ○ *This permit is invalid.* ○ *The claim has been declared invalid.*

invalidate /ɪn'vælɪdeɪt/ *verb* to make something invalid ○ *Because the company has been taken over, the contract has been invalidated.*

invalidation /ɪnˌvælɪ'deɪʃən/ *noun* the act of making invalid

invalidity /ˌɪnvə'lɪdɪti/ *noun* the fact of being invalid ○ *the invalidity of the contract*

inventory /'ɪnvənt(ə)ri/ *noun* **1.** *especially US* all the stock or goods in a warehouse or shop ○ *to carry a high inventory* ○ *to aim to reduce inventory* (NOTE: The UK term is **stock.**) **2.** a list of the contents of a building such as a house for sale or an office for rent ○ *to draw up an inventory of fixtures and fittings* ■ *verb* to make a list of stock or contents

    '…a warehouse needs to tie up less capital in inventory and with its huge volume spreads out costs over bigger sales' [*Duns Business Month*]

inventory control /'ɪnvənt(ə)ri kən ˌtrəʊl/ *noun especially US* a system of checking that there is not too much stock in a warehouse, but just enough to meet requirements

inventory financing /'ɪnvənt(ə)ri ˌfaɪnænsɪŋ/ *noun especially US* the use of money from working capital to purchase stock for resale

inventory turnover /ˌɪnvənt(ə)ri ˈtɜːnəʊvə/ *noun especially US* the total value of stock sold during a year, divided by the value of the goods remaining in stock

invest /ɪnˈvest/ *verb* **1.** to put money into shares, bonds, a building society, etc., hoping that it will produce interest and increase in value ○ *He invested all his money in unit trusts.* ○ *She was advised to invest in real estate* or *in government bonds.* **2.** to spend money on something which you believe will be useful ○ *to invest money in new machinery* ○ *to invest capital in a new factory*

'…we have substantial venture capital to invest in good projects' [*Times*]

investment /ɪnˈvestmənt/ *noun* **1.** the placing of money so that it will produce interest and increase in value ○ *They called for more government investment in new industries.* ○ *She was advised to make investments in oil companies.* **2.** a share, bond or piece of property bought in the hope that it will produce more money than was used to buy it

'…investment trusts, like unit trusts, consist of portfolios of shares and therefore provide a spread of investments' [*Investors Chronicle*]

'…investment companies took the view that prices had reached rock bottom and could only go up' [*Lloyd's List*]

investment analyst /ɪnˌvestmənt ˈænəlɪst/ *noun* a person working for a stockbroking firm, who analyses the performance of companies in a sector of the market, or the performance of a market sector as a whole, or economic trends in general

investment bank /ɪnˈvestmənt bæŋk/ *noun US* a bank which deals with the underwriting of new issues, and advises corporations on their financial affairs (NOTE: The UK term is **issuing house**.)

investment company /ɪnˈvestmənt ˈkʌmp(ə)ni/ *noun* company whose shares can be bought on the Stock Exchange, and whose business is to make money by buying and selling stocks and shares

investment grant /ɪnˈvestmənt grɑːnt/ *noun* a government grant to a company to help it to invest in new machinery

investment income /ɪnˈvestmənt ˌɪnkʌm/ *noun* income from investments, e.g. interest and dividends. Compare **earned income**

Investment Management Association /ɪnˌvestmənt ˈmænɪdʒmənt əˌsəʊsieɪʃ(ə)n/ *noun* the trade body for the UK investment industry, formed in February 2002 following the merger of the Association of Unit Trusts and Investment Funds (AU-

TIF) and the Fund Manager's Association. Abbreviation **IMA**

investment property /ɪnˌvestmənt ˈprɒpəti/ *noun* property which is held for letting

investment revaluation reserve /ɪn ˌvestmənt riːˌvæljʊˌeɪʃən rɪˈzɜːv/ *noun* the capital reserve where changes in the value of a business's investment properties are disclosed when they are revalued

investment trust /ɪnˈvestmənt trʌst/ *noun* a company whose shares can be bought on the Stock Exchange and whose business is to make money by buying and selling stocks and shares

investor /ɪnˈvestə/ *noun* a person who invests money

investor protection /ɪnˈvestə prəˌtekʃ(ə)n/ *noun* legislation to protect small investors from unscrupulous investment brokers and advisers

Investors in Industry /ɪnˌvestəz ɪn ˈɪndəstri/ *plural noun* a finance group partly owned by the big British High Street banks, providing finance especially to smaller companies. Abbreviation **3i**

invisible assets /ɪnˌvɪzɪb(ə)l ˈæsets/ *plural noun* assets which have a value but which cannot be seen, e.g. goodwill or patents

invisible earnings /ɪnˌvɪzɪb(ə)l ˈɜːnɪŋz/ *plural noun* foreign currency earned by a country by providing services, receiving interests or dividends, but not by selling goods

invisible exports /ɪnˌvɪzəb(ə)l ˈekspɔːts/ *plural noun* services such as banking, insurance or tourism which do not involve selling a product and which are provided to foreign customers and paid for in foreign currency. Opposite **visible exports**

invisible imports /ɪnˌvɪzɪb(ə)l ˈɪmpɔːtz/ *noun* services such as banking, insurance or tourism which do not involve selling a product and which are provided by foreign companies and paid for in local currency. Opposite **visible imports**

invisibles /ɪnˈvɪzɪb(ə)lz/ *plural noun* invisible imports and exports

invisible trade /ɪnˌvɪzəb(ə)l ˈtreɪd/ *noun* trade involving invisible imports and exports. Opposite **visible trade**

invitation /ˌɪnvɪˈteɪʃ(ə)n/ *noun* an act of asking someone to do something ○ *to issue an invitation to someone to join the board* ○ *They advertised the invitation to tender for a contract.* ○ *Invitation to subscribe a new issue.*

invoice /'ɪnvɔɪs/ *noun* a note asking for payment for goods or services supplied ○ *your invoice dated November 10th* ○ *to make out an invoice for £250* ○ *to settle* or *to pay an invoice* ○ *They sent in their invoice six weeks late.* ■ *verb* to send an invoice to someone ○ *to invoice a customer*

invoice clerk /'ɪnvɔɪs klɑːk/ *noun* an office employee who deals with invoices

invoice discounting /'ɪnvɔɪs ˌdɪskaʊntɪŋ/ *noun* a method of obtaining early payment of invoices by selling them at a discount to a company which will receive payment of the invoices when they are paid. The debtor is not informed of this arrangement, as opposed to factoring, where the debtor is informed.

invoice price /'ɪnvɔɪs praɪs/ *noun* the price as given on an invoice, including any discount and VAT

invoice register /ˌɪnvɔɪs 'redʒɪstə/ *noun* a list of purchase invoices recording the date of receipt of the invoice, the supplier, the invoice value, and the person to whom the invoice has been passed to ensure that all invoices are processed by the accounting system

invoicing /'ɪnvɔɪsɪŋ/ *noun* the work of sending invoices ○ *All our invoicing is done by computer.*

invoicing department /'ɪnvɔɪsɪŋ dɪ ˌpɑːtmənt/ *noun* the department in a company which deals with preparing and sending invoices

involuntary bankruptcy /ɪn ˌvɒlənt(ə)ri 'bæŋkrʌptsi/ *noun US* an application by creditors to have a person or corporation made bankrupt (NOTE: The UK term is **compulsory winding up**.)

inward /'ɪnwəd/ *adjective* towards the home country

inward bill /ˌɪnwəd 'bɪl/ *noun* a bill of lading for goods arriving in a country

inward mission /ˌɪnwəd 'mɪʃ(ə)n/ *noun* a visit to your home country by a group of foreign businesspeople

IOU /ˌaɪ əʊ 'juː/ *noun* 'I owe you', a signed document promising that you will pay back money borrowed ○ *to pay a pile of IOUs* ○ *I have a pile of IOUs which need paying.*

IRC *abbr* Inland Revenue Commissioner

irrecoverable /ˌɪrɪ'kʌv(ə)rəb(ə)l/ *adjective* not possible to get back

irrecoverable debt /ɪrɪˌkʌv(ə)rəb(ə)l 'det/ *noun* a debt which will never be paid

irredeemable /ɪrɪ'diːməb(ə)l/ *adjective* not possible to redeem

irredeemable bond /ɪrɪˌdiːməb(ə)l 'bɒnd/ *noun* a government bond which has no date of maturity and which therefore provides interest but can never be redeemed at full value

irrevocable /ɪ'revəkəb(ə)l/ *adjective* unchangeable

irrevocable letter of credit /ɪ ˌrevəkəb(ə)l ˌletər əv 'kredɪt/ *noun* a letter of credit which cannot be cancelled or changed, except if agreed between the two parties involved

IRS *abbr US* Internal Revenue Service

ISA /'aɪsə/ *abbr* Individual Savings Account

issue /'ɪʃuː/ *verb* to put out or to give out ○ *to issue a letter of credit* ○ *to issue shares in a new company* ○ *to issue a writ against someone* ○ *The government issued a report on London's traffic.*

'…the company said that its recent issue of 10.5 per cent convertible preference shares at A$8.50 a share has been oversubscribed' [*Financial Times*]

issued capital /ˌɪʃuːd 'kæpɪt(ə)l/ *noun* an amount of capital which is given out as shares to shareholders

issue price /'ɪʃuː praɪs/ *noun* a price of shares when they are offered for sale for the first time

issuer /'ɪʃuə/ *noun* a financial institution that issues credit and debit cards and maintains the systems for billing and payment

issuing /'ɪʃuɪŋ/ *adjective* organising an issue of shares

item /'aɪtəm/ *noun* **1.** something for sale □ **we are holding orders for out-of-stock items** we are holding orders for goods which are not in stock ○ *Please find enclosed an order for the following items from your catalogue.* **2.** a piece of information ○ *items on a balance sheet* **3.** a point on a list

itemise /'aɪtəmaɪz/, **itemize** *verb* to make a detailed list of things ○ *Itemising the sales figures will take about two days.*

JK

J curve /'dʒeɪ 'kɜːv/ *noun* a line on a graph shaped like a letter 'J', with an initial short fall, followed by a longer rise, used to describe the effect of a falling exchange rate on a country's balance of trade

job /dʒɒb/ *noun* **1.** an order being worked on ○ *We are working on six jobs at the moment.* ○ *The shipyard has a big job starting in August.* **2.** regular paid work ○ *She is looking for a job in the computer industry.* ○ *He lost his job when the factory closed.* ○ *Thousands of jobs will be lost if the factories close down.* □ **to give up your job** to resign or retire from your work □ **to retire from your job** to leave work and take a pension □ **to give up your job** to resign from your work □ **to retire from your job** to leave work and take a pension

'…he insisted that the tax advantages he directed toward small businesses will help create jobs' [*Toronto Star*]

job card /'dʒɒb kɑːd/ *noun* a record card relating to a job and giving details of the time taken to do a piece of work and the materials used. This is used to allocate direct labour and materials costs.

job centre /'dʒɒb ˌsentə/ *noun* a government office which lists jobs which are vacant ○ *There was a long queue of unemployed people waiting at the job centre.*

job costing /'dʒɒb ˌkɒstɪŋ/ *noun* the process of calculating the cost of a single job or batch of work. Also called **specific order costing**

job evaluation /'dʒɒb ɪvælju̩eɪʃ(ə)n/ *noun* the process of examining different jobs within an organisation to see what skills and qualifications are needed to carry them out

joint /dʒɔɪnt/ *adjective* **1.** carried out or produced together with others ○ *a joint undertaking* **2.** one of two or more people who work together or who are linked ○ *They are joint beneficiaries of the will.* ○ *She and her brother are joint managing directors.* ○ *The two countries are joint signatories of the treaty.*

joint account /'dʒɔɪnt əˌkaʊnt/ *noun* a bank or building society account shared by two people ○ *Many married couples have joint accounts so that they can pay for household expenses.*

joint and several liability /ˌdʒɔɪnt ən ˌsev(ə)rəl laɪəˈbɪlɪti/ *noun* a situation where someone who has a claim against a group of people can sue them separately or together as a group

joint cost /ˌdʒɔɪnt kɒst/ *noun* the cost of which can be allocated to more than one product, project or service

joint-life annuity /'dʒɔɪnt laɪf əˌnjuəti/ *noun* an annuity that continues until both parties have died. They are attractive to married couples as they ensure that the survivor has an income for the rest of his or her life.

jointly /'dʒɔɪntli/ *adverb* together with one or more other people ○ *to own a property jointly* ○ *to manage a company jointly* ○ *They are jointly liable for damages.*

joint management /ˌdʒɔɪnt ˈmænɪdʒmənt/ *noun* management done by two or more people

joint ownership /ˌdʒɔɪnt ˈəʊnəʃɪp/ *noun* the owning of a property by several owners

joint-stock bank /ˌdʒɔɪnt ˈstɒk ˌbæŋk/ *noun* a bank which is a public company quoted on the Stock Exchange

joint-stock company /'dʒɔɪnt stɒk ˌkʌmp(ə)ni/ *noun* formerly, a public company whose shares were owned by very many people. Now called a Public Limited Company or Plc.

joint venture /dʒɔɪnt ˈventʃə/ *noun* a situation where two or more companies join together for one specific large business project

journal /'dʒɜːn(ə)l/ *noun* a book with the account of sales and purchases made each day

judgement /'dʒʌdʒmənt/, **judgment** *noun* a legal decision or official decision of a court □ **to pronounce judgement**, **to give your judgement on something** to give an official or legal decision about something □ **to pronounce judgement**, **to give your judgement on something** to give an official or legal decision about something

judgment creditor /ˌdʒʌdʒmənt ˈkredɪtə/ *noun* a person who has been given a court order making a debtor pay him a debt

junior /ˈdʒuːniə/ *adjective* **1.** younger or lower in rank **2.** less important than something else

junior capital /ˌdʒuːniə ˈkæpɪt(ə)l/ *adjective* capital in the form of shareholders' equity, which is repaid only after secured loans called 'senior capital' have been paid if the firm goes into liquidation

junior mortgage /ˌdʒuːniə ˈmɔːɡɪdʒ/ *noun* a second mortgage

junior partner /ˌdʒuːniə ˈpɑːtnə/ *noun* a person who has a small part of the shares in a partnership

junior security /ˌdʒuːniə sɪˈkjʊərɪti/ *noun* a security which is repaid after other securities

K *abbreviation* one thousand □ '**salary: £20K+**' salary more than £20,000 per annum

keep /kiːp/ *verb* **1.** to do what is necessary for something **2.** to hold items for sale or for information **3.** to hold things at some level ○ *to keep spending to a minimum* ○ *We must keep our mailing list up to date.* ○ *The price of oil has kept the pound at a high level.* ○ *Lack of demand for the product has kept prices down.* (NOTE: **keeping – kept**)

keep back /ˌkiːp ˈbæk/ *verb* to hold on to something which you could give to someone ○ *to keep back information* or *to keep something back from someone* ○ *to keep £10 back from someone's salary*

Keogh plan /ˈkiːəʊ ˌplæn/ *noun US* a private pension system allowing self-employed businesspeople and professionals to set up pension and retirement plans for themselves

key money /ˈkiː ˌmʌni/ *noun* a premium paid when taking over the keys of a flat or office which you are renting

key-person insurance /ˈkiː pɜːs(ə)n ɪn ˌʃʊərəns/ *noun* an insurance policy taken out to cover the costs of replacing an employee who is particularly important to an organisation if he or she dies or is ill for a long time

key rate /ˈkiː reɪt/ *noun* an interest rate which gives the basic rate on which other rates are calculated, e.g. the former bank base rate in the UK, or the Federal Reserve's discount rate in the USA

kickback /ˈkɪkbæk/ *noun* an illegal commission paid to someone, especially a government official, who helps in a business deal

kicker /ˈkɪkə/ *noun* a special inducement to buy a bond, e.g. making it convertible to shares at a preferential rate (*informal*)

kite /kaɪt/ *verb* **1.** *US* to write cheques on one account which may not be able to honour them and deposit them in another, withdrawing money from the second account before the cheques are cleared **2.** to use stolen credit cards or cheque books

kite flier /ˈkaɪt ˌflaɪə/ *noun* a person who tries to impress people by putting forward a proposal

kite-flying /ˈkaɪt ˌflaɪɪŋ/ *noun* the practice of trying to impress people by putting forward grand plans

kitty /ˈkɪti/ *noun* money which has been collected by a group of people to be used later, such as for an office party ○ *We each put £5 into the kitty.*

know-how /ˈnəʊ haʊ/ *noun* knowledge or skill in a particular field ○ *to acquire computer know-how* ○ *If we cannot recruit staff with the right know-how, we will have to initiate an ambitious training programme.*

know-how fund /ˈnəʊ haʊ ˌfʌnd/ *noun* a fund created by the UK government to provide technical training and advice to countries of Eastern Europe

L

labour /ˈleɪbə/ *noun* **1.** heavy work (NOTE: The US spelling is **labor**.) □ **labour is charged at £5 an hour** each hour of work costs £5 **2.** workers, the workforce ○ *We will need to employ more labour if production is to be increased.* ○ *The costs of labour are rising in line with inflation.* (NOTE: The US spelling is **labor**.)

'…the possibility that British goods will price themselves back into world markets is doubtful as long as sterling labour costs continue to rise faster than in competitor countries' [*Sunday Times*]

labour costs /ˈleɪbə kɒsts/ *noun* the cost of the employees employed to make a product, not including materials or overheads

labour force /ˈleɪbə fɔːs/ *noun* all the employees in a company or in an area ○ *The management has made an increased offer to the labour force.* ○ *We are opening a new factory in the Far East because of the cheap local labour force.*

'70 per cent of Australia's labour force is employed in service activity' [*Australian Financial Review*]

labour market /ˈleɪbə ˌmɑːkɪt/ *noun* the number of people who are available for work ○ *25,000 school-leavers have just come on to the labour market.*

'European economies are being held back by rigid labor markets and wage structures' [*Duns Business Month*]

labour relations /ˈleɪbə rɪˌleɪʃ(ə)nz/ *plural noun* relations between management and employees ○ *The company has a history of bad labour relations.*

labour turnover /ˈleɪbə ˌtɜːnəʊvə/ *noun* the movement of employees with some leaving their jobs and others joining. Also called **turnover of labour**

lading /ˈleɪdɪŋ/ *noun* the work of putting goods on a ship

Laffer curve /ˈlæfə kɜːv/ *noun* a chart showing that cuts in tax rates increase output in the economy. Alternatively, increases in tax rates initially produce more revenue and then less as the economy slows down.

lag /læg/ *verb* to be behind or to be slower than something

lagging indicator /ˈlægɪŋ ˌɪndɪkeɪtə/ *noun* an indicator which shows a change in economic trends later than other indicators, e.g. the gross national product. Opposite **leading indicator**

land agent /ˈlænd ˌeɪdʒənt/ *noun* a person who runs a farm or a large area of land for the owner

landed costs /ˌlændɪd ˈkɒsts/ *plural noun* the costs of goods which have been delivered to a port, unloaded and passed through customs

landing charges /ˈlændɪŋ ˌtʃɑːdʒɪz/ *plural noun* payments for putting goods on land and paying customs duties

landing order /ˈlændɪŋ ˌɔːdə/ *noun* a permit which allows goods to be unloaded into a bonded warehouse without paying customs duty

landlord /ˈlændlɔːd/ *noun* a person or company which owns a property which is let

land register /ˈlænd ˌredʒɪstə/ *noun* a list of pieces of land, showing who owns each and what buildings are on it

land registration /ˈlænd redʒɪˌstreɪʃ(ə)n/ *noun* a system of registering land and its owners

land tax /ˈlænd tæks/ *noun* a tax on the amount of land owned

lapse /læps/ *verb* to stop being valid, or to stop being active ○ *The guarantee has lapsed.*

lapsed option /ˌlæpst ˈɒpʃən/ *noun* an option which has not been taken up, and now has expired

last /lɑːst/ *adjective, adverb* coming at the end of a series ○ *Out of a queue of twenty people, I was served last.* ○ *This is our last board meeting before we move to our new offices.* ○ *We finished the last items in the order just two days before the promised delivery date.*

last in first out /ˌlɑːst ɪn ˌfɜːst ˈaʊt/ *noun* **1.** a redundancy policy using the principle that the people who have been most recently appointed are the first to be made redundant **2.** an accounting method where stock is valued at the price of the earliest purchases. Abbreviation **LIFO**. Compare **first in first out**

last quarter /ˌlɑːst ˈkwɔːtə/ *noun* a period of three months at the end of the financial year

last will and testament /ˌlɑːst ˌwɪl ən ˈtestəmənt/ *noun* a will, a document by which a person says what he or she wants to happen to their property when they die

launder /ˈlɔːndə/ *verb* to pass illegal profits, money from selling drugs, money which has not been taxed, etc., into the banking system ○ *to launder money through an offshore bank*

'…it has since emerged that the bank was being used to launder drug money and some of its executives have been given lengthy jail sentences' [*Times*]

LAUTRO *abbr* Life Assurance and Unit Trust Regulatory Organization

law /lɔː/ *noun* **1.** □ **inside** *or* **within the law** obeying the laws of a country □ **against** *or* **outside the law** not according to the laws of a country ○ *The company is possibly operating outside the law.* □ **to break the law** to do something which is not allowed by law ○ *He is breaking the law by trading without a licence.* ○ *You will be breaking the law if you try to take that computer out of the country without an export licence.* **2.** a rule governing some aspect of human activity made and enforced by the state

lawful /ˈlɔːf(ə)l/ *adjective* acting within the law

law of supply and demand /ˌlɔːr əv sə ˌplaɪ ən dɪˈmɑːnd/ *noun* a general rule that the amount of a product which is available is related to the needs of potential customers

laws /lɔːz/ *noun* rules by which a country is governed and the activities of people and organisations controlled

lay out /ˌleɪ ˈaʊt/ *verb* to spend money ○ *We had to lay out half our cash budget on equipping the new factory.*

layout /ˈleɪaʊt/ *noun* the arrangement of the inside space of a building or its contents ○ *They have altered the layout of the offices.*

LBO *abbr* leveraged buyout

L/C *abbr* letter of credit

LCM *abbr* lower of cost or market

LDT *abbr* licensed deposit-taker

lead /liːd/ *adjective* most important, in the front

lead bank /ˌliːd ˈbæŋk/ *noun* the main bank in a loan syndicate

leader /ˈliːdə/ *noun* a product which sells best

leading indicator /ˌliːdɪŋ ˈɪndɪkeɪtə/ *noun* an indicator such as manufacturing order books which shows a change in economic trends earlier than other indicators. Opposite **lagging indicator**

lead manager /ˌliːd ˈmænɪdʒə/ *noun* a person who organises a syndicate of underwriters for a new issue of securities

leads and lags /ˌliːdz ən ˈlægz/ *plural noun* in businesses that deal in foreign currencies, the practice of speeding up the receipt of payments (leads) if a currency is going to weaken, and slowing down the payment of costs (lags) if a currency is thought to be about to strengthen, in order to maximise gains and reduce losses

lead time /ˈliːd taɪm/ *noun* the time between deciding to place an order and receiving the product ○ *The lead time on this item is more than six weeks.*

lead underwriter /ˌliːd ˈʌndəraɪtə/ *noun* an underwriting firm which organises the underwriting of a share issue (NOTE: The US term is **managing underwriter**.)

learning curve /ˈlɜːnɪŋ kɜːv/ *noun* **1.** a process of learning something that starts slowly and then becomes faster **2.** a line on a graph which shows the relationship between experience in doing something and competence at carrying it out **3.** a diagram or graph that represents the way in which people gain knowledge or experience over time (NOTE: A steep learning curve represents a situation where people learn a great deal in a short time; a shallow curve represents a slower learning process. The curve eventually levels out, representing the time when the knowledge gained is being consolidated.) **4.** the decrease in the effort required to produce each single item when the total number of items produced is doubled (NOTE: The concept of the learning curve has its origin in productivity research in the aircraft industry of the 1930s, when it was discovered that the time and effort needed to assemble an aircraft decreased by 20% each time the total number produced doubled.)

lease /liːs/ *noun* a written contract for letting or renting a building, a piece of land or a piece of equipment for a period against payment of a fee ○ *to rent office space on a twenty-year lease* □ **the lease expires next year** *or* **the lease runs out next year** the lease comes to an end next year ■ *verb* **1.** to let or rent offices, land or machinery for a period ○ *to lease offices to small firms* ○ *to lease* *equipment* **2.** to use an office, land or machinery for a time and pay a fee ○ *to lease an office from an insurance company* ○ *All our company cars are leased.*

lease back /ˌliːs ˈbæk/ *verb* to sell a property or machinery to a company and then take it back on a lease ○ *They sold the office building to raise cash, and then leased it back on a twenty-five year lease.*

leasehold /ˈliːshəʊld/ *noun, adjective* possessing property on a lease, for a fixed time ○ *to buy a property leasehold* ○ *We are currently occupying a leasehold property.* ○ *The company has some valuable leaseholds.*

leaseholder /ˈliːshəʊldə/ *noun* a person who holds a property on a lease

leasing /ˈliːsɪŋ/ *noun* the use of a lease or of equipment under a lease ○ *an equipment-leasing company* ○ *to run a copier under a leasing arrangement* ○ *The company has branched out into car leasing.* ◊ **lessee**

leasing agreement /ˌliːsɪŋ əˈɡriːmənt/ *noun* a contract between an owner and a lessee, by which the lessee has the exclusive use of a piece of equipment for a period of time, against payment of a fee

ledger /ˈledʒə/ *noun* a book in which accounts are written

legacy /ˈleɡəsi/ *noun* a piece of property given by someone to someone else in a will

legal /ˈliːɡ(ə)l/ *adjective* **1.** according to the law or allowed by the law ○ *The company's action in sacking the accountant was completely legal.* **2.** referring to the law

legal charge /ˌliːɡ(ə)l ˈtʃɑːdʒ/ *noun* a legal document held by the Land Registry showing who has a claim on a property

legal claim /ˈliːɡ(ə)l kleɪm/ *noun* a statement that someone owns something legally ○ *He has no legal claim to the property.*

legal costs /ˈliːɡ(ə)l kɒsts/, **legal charges** /ˈliːɡ(ə)l ˌtʃɑːdʒɪz/, **legal expenses** /ˈliːɡ(ə)l ɪkˌspensɪz/ *plural noun* money spent on fees to lawyers ○ *The clerk could not afford the legal expenses involved in suing her boss.*

legal currency /ˌliːɡ(ə)l ˈkʌrənsi/ *noun* money which is legally used in a country

legal tender /ˌliːɡ(ə)l ˈtendə/ *noun* coins or notes which can be legally used to pay a debt

legatee /ˌleɡəˈtiː/ *noun* a person who receives property from someone who has died

legislation /ˌledʒɪˈsleɪʃ(ə)n/ *noun* laws

lend /lend/ *verb* to allow someone to use something for a period ○ *to lend something to someone* or *to lend someone something* ○ *to lend money against security* ○ *He lent the company money* or *He lent money to the company.* ○ *The bank lent her £50,000 to start her business.* (NOTE: **lending – lent**)

lender /ˈlendə/ *noun* a person who lends money

lender of the last resort /ˌlendə əv ðə ˌlɑːst rɪˈzɔːt/ *noun* a central bank which lends money to commercial banks

lending /ˈlendɪŋ/ *noun* an act of letting someone use money for a time

lending limit /ˈlendɪŋ ˌlɪmɪt/ *noun* a restriction on the amount of money a bank can lend

lending margin /ˈlendɪŋ ˌmɑːdʒɪn/ *noun* an agreed spread for lending, based on the LIBOR

less /les/ *adjective* smaller than, of a smaller size or of a smaller value ○ *We do not grant credit for sums of less than £100.* ○ *He sold it for less than he had paid for it.* ■ *preposition* minus, with a sum removed ○ *purchase price less 15% discount* ○ *interest less service charges* ■ *adverb* not as much

lessee /leˈsiː/ *noun* a person who has a lease or who pays money for a property he or she leases

lessor /leˈsɔː/ *noun* a person who grants a lease on a property

let /let/ *verb* to allow the use of a house, an office or a farm to someone for the payment of rent

letter /ˈletə/ *noun* a piece of writing sent from one person or company to another to ask for or to give information

letter of acknowledgement /ˌletər əv əkˈnɒlɪdʒmənt/ *noun* a letter which says that something has been received

letter of application /ˌletər əv æplɪˈkeɪʃ(ə)n/ *noun* a letter in which someone applies for a job

letter of appointment /ˌletər əv əˈpɔɪntmənt/ *noun* a letter in which someone is appointed to a job

letter of credit /ˌletər əv ˈkredɪt/ *noun* a document issued by a bank on behalf of a customer authorising payment to a supplier when the conditions specified in the document are met. Abbreviation **L/C**

letter of indemnity /ˌletər əv ɪnˈdemnɪti/ *noun* a letter promising payment as compensation for a loss

letter of intent /ˌletər əv ɪnˈtent/ *noun* a letter which states what a company intends to do if something happens

letter of licence /ˌletə əv ˈlaɪs(ə)ns/ *noun* a letter from a creditor to a debtor who is having problems repaying money owed, giving the debtor a certain period of time to raise the money and an undertaking not to bring legal proceedings to recover the debt during that period

letter of reference /ˌletər əv 'ref(ə)rəns/ *noun* a letter in which an employer recommends someone for a new job

letters patent /ˌletəz 'peɪtənt/ *plural noun* the official term for a patent

letting agency /ˈletɪŋ ˌeɪdʒənsi/ *noun* an agency which deals in property to let

level /ˈlev(ə)l/ *verb* □ **to level off** *or* **to level out** to stop rising or falling ○ *Profits have levelled off over the last few years.* ○ *Prices are levelling out.*

leverage /ˈliːvərɪdʒ/ *noun* **1.** a ratio of capital borrowed by a company at a fixed rate of interest to the company's total capital **2.** the act of borrowing money at fixed interest which is then used to produce more money than the interest paid

leveraged /ˈliːvərɪdʒ/ *adjective* using borrowings for finance

leveraged buyout /ˌliːvərɪdʒd 'baɪaʊt/, **leveraged takeover** /ˌliːvərɪdʒd 'teɪkəʊvə/ *noun* an act of buying all the shares in a company by borrowing money against the security of the shares to be bought. Abbreviation **LBO**

> '…the offer came after management had offered to take the company private through a leveraged buyout for $825 million' [*Fortune*]

levy /ˈlevi/ *noun* money which is demanded and collected by the government

> '…royalties have been levied at a rate of 12.5% of full production' [*Lloyd's List*]

liabilities /ˌlaɪə'bɪlɪtiz/ *plural noun* the debts of a business, including dividends owed to shareholders ○ *The balance sheet shows the company's assets and liabilities.* □ **to discharge your liabilities in full** to pay everything which you owe

liability /ˌlaɪə'bɪlɪti/ *noun* **1.** a legal responsibility for damage, loss or harm ○ *The two partners took out insurance to cover employers' liability.* **2.** responsibility for a payment such as the repayment of a loan

LIBOR *abbr* London Interbank Offered Rate

licence /ˈlaɪs(ə)ns/ *noun* an official document which allows someone to do something (NOTE: The US spelling is **license**.)

license /ˈlaɪs(ə)ns/ *noun* US spelling of **licence**

licensed deposit-taker /ˌlaɪs(ə)nst dɪ 'pɒzɪt ˌteɪkə/, **licensed institution** /ˌlaɪs(ə)nst ˌɪnstɪ'tjuːʃ(ə)n/ *noun* a deposit-

taking institution which is licensed to receive money on deposit from private individuals and to pay interest on it, e.g. a building society, bank or friendly society. Abbreviation **LDT**

licensee /ˌlaɪs(ə)n'siː/ *noun* a person who has a licence, especially a licence to sell alcohol or to manufacture something

licensing /ˈlaɪs(ə)nsɪŋ/ *adjective* referring to licences ○ *a licensing agreement* ○ *licensing laws*

lien /ˈliːən/ *noun* the legal right to hold someone's goods and keep them until a debt has been paid

life /laɪf/ *noun* the period of time for which something or someone exists

life assurance /ˈlaɪf əˌʃʊərəns/ *noun* insurance which pays a sum of money when someone dies, or at an agreed date if they are still alive

Life Assurance and Unit Trust Regulatory Organization /laɪf əˌʃɔːrəns ən ˌjuːnɪt trʌst ˌregjʊlət(ə)ri ˌɔːgənaɪ 'zeɪʃ(ə)n/ *noun* an organisation set up to regulate the operations of life assurance companies and unit trusts, now replaced by the FSA. Abbreviation **LAUTRO**

life assurance company /laɪf ə 'ʃɔːrəns ˌkʌmp(ə)ni/ *noun* a company providing life assurance, but usually also providing other services such as investment advice

life-cycle costing /laɪf ˌsaɪk(ə)l 'kɒstɪŋ/ *noun* the maintenance of physical asset cost records over the life of an entire asset, so that decisions concerning the acquisition, use, or disposal of the assets can be made in a way that achieves the optimum asset usage at the lowest possible cost to the entity. The term may be applied to the profiling of cost over a product's life, including the pre-production stage (**terotechnology**), and to both company and industry life cycles.

life expectancy /ˈlaɪf ɪkˌspekt ənsi/ *noun* the number of years a person is likely to live

life insurance /ˈlaɪf ɪnˌʃʊərəns/ *noun* same as **life assurance**

life interest /ˌlaɪf 'ɪntrəst/ *noun* a situation where someone benefits from a property as long as he or she is alive

LIFO /ˈlaɪfəʊ/ *abbr* last in first out

limit /ˈlɪmɪt/ *noun* the point at which something ends or the point where you can go no further

> '…the biggest surprise of 1999 was the rebound in the price of oil. In the early months of the year commentators were talking about a fall to $5 a barrel but for the first time in two decades, the oil exporting countries got their act together, limited production

and succeeded in pushing prices up' [*Financial Times*]

limitation /ˌlɪmɪˈteɪʃ(ə)n/ *noun* the act of allowing only a specific quantity of something ○ *The contract imposes limitations on the number of cars which can be imported.*

limited /ˈlɪmɪtɪd/ *adjective* restricted

limited company /ˌlɪmɪtɪd ˈkʌmp(ə)ni/ *noun* a company where each shareholder is responsible for the company's debts only to the amount that he or she has invested in the company. Limited companies must be formed by at least 2 directors. Abbreviation **Ltd**. Also called **limited liability company**

limited liability /ˌlɪmɪtɪd laɪəˈbɪlɪti/ *noun* a situation where someone's liability for debt is limited by law

limited liability company /ˌlɪmɪtɪd laɪə ˈbɪlɪti ˌkʌmp(ə)ni/ *noun* same as **limited company**

limited partner /ˌlɪmɪtɪd ˈpɑːtnə/ *noun* a partner who is responsible for the debts of the firm only up to the amount of money which he or she has provided to the business

limited partnership /ˌlɪmɪtɪd ˈpɑːtnəʃɪp/ *noun* a registered business where the liability of the partners is limited to the amount of capital they have each provided to the business and where the partners may not take part in the running of the business

limiting /ˈlɪmɪtɪŋ/ *adjective* not allowing something to go beyond a point, restricting ○ *a limiting clause in a contract* ○ *The short holiday season is a limiting factor on the hotel trade.*

limiting factor /ˌlɪmɪtɪŋ ˈfæktə/ *noun* a factor which limits a company's ability to achieve its goals, e.g. sales demand being too low for the company to make enough profit ○ *The short holiday season is a limiting factor on the hotel trade.*

line /laɪn/ *noun* a row of letters or figures on a page

'…cash paid for overstocked lines, factory seconds, slow sellers, etc.' [*Australian Financial Review*]

line item budget /laɪn ˌaɪtəm ˈbʌdʒɪt/ *noun* a well-established budget layout that shows the costs of a cost object analysed by their nature in a line-by-line format

link /lɪŋk/ *verb* to join or to attach to something else ○ *to link pensions to inflation* ○ *to link bonus payments to productivity* ○ *His salary is linked to the cost of living.* ◊ **index-linked**

liquid /ˈlɪkwɪd/ *adjective* easily converted to cash, or containing a large amount of cash

liquid assets /ˌlɪkwɪd ˈæsets/ *plural noun* cash, or investments which can be quickly converted into cash

liquidation /ˌlɪkwɪˈdeɪʃ(ə)n/ *noun* **1.** the sale of assets for cash □ **liquidation of a debt** payment of a debt **2.** the winding up or closing of a company and selling of its assets □ **the company went into liquidation** the company was closed and its assets sold

liquidator /ˈlɪkwɪdeɪtə/ *noun* a person named to supervise the closing of a company which is in liquidation

liquidity /lɪˈkwɪdɪti/ *noun* cash, or the fact of having cash or assets which can be changed into cash

liquidity ratio /lɪˈkwɪdɪti ˌreɪʃiəʊ/ *noun* an accounting ratio used to measure an organisation's liquidity. It is calculated by taking the business's current assets, minus its stocks, divided by its current liabilities. Also called **acid test ratio, quick ratio**

list /lɪst/ *noun* several items written one after the other ○ *They have an attractive list of products* or *product list.* ○ *I can't find that item on our stock list.* ○ *Please add this item to the list.* ○ *She crossed the item off her list.*

listed company /ˌlɪstɪd ˈkʌmp(ə)ni/ *noun* a company whose shares can be bought or sold on the Stock Exchange

listed securities /ˌlɪstɪd sɪˈkjʊərɪtiz/ *plural noun* shares which can be bought or sold on the Stock Exchange, shares which appear on the official Stock Exchange list

Listing Agreement /ˈlɪstɪŋ əˌgriːmənt/ *noun* a document which a company signs when being listed on the Stock Exchange, in which it promises to abide by stock exchange regulations

listing requirements /ˈlɪstɪŋ rɪ ˌkwaɪəmənts/ *plural noun* the conditions which must be met by a corporation before its stock can be listed on the New York Stock Exchange

list price /ˈlɪst praɪs/ *noun* the price for something as given in a catalogue

litigation /ˌlɪtɪˈgeɪʃ(ə)n/ *noun* the bringing of a lawsuit against someone

Lloyd's broker /ˌlɔɪdz ˈbrəʊkə/ *noun* an agent who represents a client who wants insurance and who arranges this insurance for him through a Lloyd's underwriting syndicate

Lloyd's Register /ˌlɔɪdz ˈredʒɪstə/ *noun* a classified list showing details of all the ships in the world and estimates of their condition

Lloyd's underwriter /ˌlɔɪdz ˈʌndəraɪtə/ *noun* a member of an insurance group at Lloyd's who accepts to underwrite insurances

loan /ləʊn/ *noun* money which has been lent

'…over the last few weeks, companies raising new loans from international banks have been forced to pay more, and an unusually high number of attempts to syndicate loans among banks has failed' [*Financial Times*]

loan capital /ˈləʊn ˌkæpɪt(ə)l/ *noun* a part of a company's capital which is a loan to be repaid at a later date

loan stock /ˈləʊn stɒk/ *noun* stock issued by a company at a fixed rate of interest, as a means of raising a loan

local /ˈləʊk(ə)l/ *adjective* **1.** located in or providing a service for a restricted area **2.** referring to a particular area, especially one near where a factory or an office is based

'…each cheque can be made out for the local equivalent of £100 rounded up to a convenient figure' [*Sunday Times*]

'…the business agent for Local 414 of the Store Union said his committee will recommend that the membership ratify the agreement' [*Toronto Star*]

'EC regulations insist that customers can buy cars anywhere in the EC at the local pre-tax price' [*Financial Times*]

local authority /ˌləʊk(ə)l ɔːˈθɒrɪti/ *noun* an elected section of government which runs a small area of the country

local currency /ˌləʊk(ə)l ˈkʌrənsi/ *noun* the currency of a particular country where a transaction is being carried out ○ *Because of the weakness of the local currency, all payments are in dollars.*

local government /ˌləʊk(ə)l ˈgʌv(ə)nmənt/ *noun* elected authorities and administrative organisations which deal with the affairs of small areas of a country

local labour /ˌləʊk(ə)l ˈleɪbə/ *noun* workers who are recruited near a factory, and are not brought there from a distance

lock into /ˌlɒk ˈɪntə/, **lock in** /ˌlɒk ˈɪn/ *verb* to be fixed to an interest rate or exchange rate ○ *By buying francs forward the company is in effect locking itself into a pound-franc exchange rate of 10.06.*

London Interbank Offered Rate /ˌlʌndən ˌɪntəbæŋk ˈɒfəd reɪt/ *noun* the rate at which banks offer to lend eurodollars to other banks. Abbreviation **LIBOR**

long /lɒŋ/ *adjective* for a large period of time

long bond /ˈlɒŋ bɒnd/, **long coupon bond** /lɒŋ ˈkuːpɒn bɒnd/ *adjective* a bond which will mature in more than ten years' time

long credit /ˌlɒŋ ˈkredɪt/ *noun* credit terms which allow the borrower a long time to pay

long-dated bill /ˌlɒŋ ˌdeɪtɪd ˈbɪl/ *noun* a bill which is payable in more than three months' time

long-dated stocks /ˌlɒŋ ˌdeɪtɪd ˈstɒks/ *plural noun* same as **longs**

long lease /ˌlɒŋ ˈliːs/ *noun* a lease which runs for fifty years or more ○ *to take an office building on a long lease*

long position /ˌlɒŋ pəˈzɪʃ(ə)n/ *noun* a situation where an investor sells long, i.e. sells forward shares which he or she owns. Compare **short position**

long-range /ˌlɒŋ ˈreɪndʒ/ *adjective* for a long period of time in the future

longs /lɒŋz/ *plural noun* government stocks which will mature in over fifteen years' time. Also called **long-dated stocks**

long-term borrowings /ˌlɒŋ tɜːm ˈbɒrəʊɪŋz/ *plural noun* borrowings which do not have to be repaid for some years

loose change /ˌluːs ˈtʃeɪndʒ/ *noun* money in coins

lose /luːz/ *verb* **1.** not to have something any more **2.** to have less money ○ *He lost £25,000 in his father's computer company.*

loss /lɒs/ *noun* **1.** the state or process of not having something any more **2.** the state of having less money than before or of not making a profit □ **the car was written off as a dead loss** *or* **a total loss** the car was so badly damaged that the insurers said it had no value □ **to cut your losses** to stop doing something which is losing money

'…against losses of FFr 7.7m two years ago, the company made a net profit of FFr 300,000 last year' [*Financial Times*]

loss adjuster /ˈlɒs əˌdʒʌstə/ *noun* a person who calculates how much insurance should be paid on a claim

loss-leader /ˈlɒs ˌliːdə/ *noun* an article which is sold at a loss to attract customers ○ *We use these cheap films as a loss-leader.*

loss relief /ˈlɒs rɪˌliːf/ *noun* an amount of tax not to be paid on one year's profit to offset a loss in the previous year

lot /lɒt/ *noun* **1.** a group of items sold together at an auction ○ *to bid for lot 23* ○ *At the end of the auction half the lots were unsold.* **2.** a group of shares which are sold ○ *to sell a lot of shares* ○ *to sell shares in small lots*

lottery /ˈlɒtəri/ *noun* a game where numbered tickets are sold and prizes given for some of the numbers

low /ləʊ/ *adjective* not high or not much ○ *Low overhead costs keep the unit cost low.* ○ *We try to keep our wages bill low.* ○ *The company offered him a mortgage at a low rate of interest.* ○ *The pound is at a very low rate of exchange against the dollar.*

'…after opening at 79.1 the index touched a peak of 79.2 and then drifted to a low of 78.8' [*Financial Times*]

'…the pound which had been as low as $1.02 earlier this year, rose to $1.30' [*Fortune*]

lower /ˈləʊə/ *adjective* smaller or less high ○ *a lower rate of interest* ○ *Sales were lower in December than in November.*

lower of cost or market /ˌləʊə əv kɒst ɔː ˈmɑːkɪt/ *noun* a method used by manufacturing and supply firms when accounting for their homogeneous stocks that involves valuing them either at their original cost or the current market price, whichever is lower. Abbreviation **LCM**

low gearing /ˌləʊ ˈɡɪərɪŋ/ *noun* the fact of not having much borrowing in proportion to your capital

low yield /ˌləʊ ˈjiːld/ *noun* a yield on the share price which is low for the sector, suggesting that investors anticipate that the company will grow fast, and have pushed up the share price in expectation of growth

loyalty bonus /ˈlɔɪəlti ˌbəʊnəs/ *noun* a special privilege given to shareholders who keep their shares for a long period of time, used especially to attract investors to privatisation issues

Ltd *abbr* limited company

lump sum /ˌlʌmp ˈsʌm/ *noun* money paid in one single amount, not in several small sums ○ *When he retired he was given a lump-sum bonus.* ○ *She sold her house and invested the money as a lump sum.*

luncheon voucher /ˈlʌnʃtən ˌvaʊtʃə/ *noun* a ticket given by an employer to an employee in addition to their wages, which can be exchanged for food in a restaurant

luxury tax /ˈlʌkʃəri tæks/ *noun* a tax on goods or services that are considered non-essential

M

machine hour rate /məˌʃiːn ˈaʊə ˌreɪt/
noun a method of calculating production
overhead absorption rate, where the number
of hours the machines are expected to work is
divided into the budgeted production overhead to give a rate per hour

macro- /mækrəʊ/ *prefix* very large, covering a wide area

macroeconomics /ˌmækrəʊiːkə
ˈnɒmɪks/ *plural noun* a study of the economics of a whole area, a whole industry, a whole
group of the population or a whole country,
in order to help in economic planning. Compare **microeconomics** (NOTE: takes a singular verb)

magnetic card /mægˌnetɪk ˈkɑːd/ *noun*
plastic card with a strip of magnetic recording material on its surface, allowing data to
be stored and used

mail-order selling /ˈmeɪl ɔːdə ˌselɪŋ/
noun a method of selling in which orders are
taken and products are delivered by mail

mainstream corporation tax
/ˌmeɪnstriːm ˌkɔːpəˈreɪʃ(ə)n tæks/ *noun*
the total tax paid by a company on its profits
less any advance corporation tax, which a
company has already paid when distributing
profits to its shareholders in the form of dividends. Abbreviation **MCT**

maintain /meɪnˈteɪn/ *verb* **1.** to keep
something going or working ○ We try to
maintain good relations with our customers.
○ Her trip aims to maintain contact with her
important overseas markets. **2.** to keep something working at the same level ○ to maintain
an interest rate at 5% ○ The company has
maintained the same volume of business in
spite of the recession.

maintenance /ˈmeɪntənəns/ *noun* **1.** the
process of keeping things going or working ○
Maintenance of contacts is important for a
sales rep. ○ It is essential to ensure the maintenance of supplies to the factory. **2.** the process of keeping a machine in good working order ○ We offer a full maintenance service.

'…responsibilities include the maintenance of large
computerized databases' [*Times*]

'…the federal administration launched a full-scale
investigation into the airline's maintenance procedures' [*Fortune*]

major /ˈmeɪdʒə/ *adjective* important ○
There is a major risk of fire.

'…if the share price sinks much further the company
is going to look tempting to any major takeover merchant' [*Australian Financial Review*]

'…monetary officials have reasoned that coordinat-
ed greenback sales would be able to drive the dollar
down against other major currencies' [*Duns Business Month*]

'…a client base which includes many major commercial organizations and nationalized industries'
[*Times*]

majority /məˈdʒɒrɪti/ *noun* more than half
of a group

majority shareholder /məˌdʒɒrəti
ˈʃeəhəʊldə/ *noun* a person who owns more
than half the shares in a company

majority shareholding /məˌdʒɒrəti
ˈʃeəhəʊldɪŋ/ *noun* a group of shares which
are more than half the total

majority vote /məˈdʒɒrɪti vəʊt/, **majority decision** /məˈdʒɒrɪti dɪˌsɪʒ(ə)n/ *noun* a
decision which represents the wishes of the
largest group as shown by a vote

make /meɪk/ *verb* **1.** to produce or to manufacture ○ The employees spent ten weeks
making the table. ○ The factory makes three
hundred cars a day. **2.** to earn money ○ He
makes £50,000 a year or £25 an hour. **3.** to
increase in value ○ The shares made $2.92 in
today's trading. **4.** □ **to make a profit** to have
more money after a deal □ **to make a loss** to
have less money after a deal □ **to make a
killing** to make a very large profit

make over /ˌmeɪk ˈəʊvə/ *verb* to transfer
property legally ○ to make over the house to
your children

maker /ˈmeɪkə/ *noun* a person or company
which makes something ○ a major car maker
○ a furniture maker

make up /ˌmeɪk ˈʌp/ *verb* to compensate
for something □ **to make up a loss** *or* **differ-**

ence to pay extra so that the loss or difference is covered

maladministration /ˌmælədˌmɪnɪ'streɪʃ(ə)n/ *noun* incompetent administration

manage /'mænɪdʒ/ *verb* to direct or to be in charge of something ○ *to manage a branch office* ○ *A competent and motivated person is required to manage an important department in the company.*

'…the research director will manage and direct a team of graduate business analysts reporting on consumer behaviour throughout the UK' [*Times*]

managed fund /ˌmænɪdʒd 'fʌnd/ *noun* a unit trust fund which is invested in specialist funds within the group and can be switched from one specialised investment area to another

managed rate /ˌmænɪdʒd 'reɪt/ *noun* a rate of interest charged by a financial institution for borrowing that is not prescribed as a margin over base rate but is set from time to time by the institution

managed unit trust /ˌmænɪdʒd 'juːnɪt trʌst/ *noun* same as **managed fund**

management /'mænɪdʒmənt/ *noun* **1.** the process of directing or running a business ○ *a management graduate* or *a graduate in management* ○ *She studied management at university.* ○ *Good management* or *efficient management is essential in a large organisation.* ○ *Bad management* or *inefficient management can ruin a business.* **2.** a group of managers or directors ○ *The management has decided to give everyone a pay increase.* (NOTE: Where **management** refers to a group of people it is sometimes followed by a plural verb.)

'…the management says that the rate of loss-making has come down and it expects further improvement in the next few years' [*Financial Times*]

management accountant /'mænɪdʒmənt əˌkaʊntənt/ *noun* an accountant who prepares financial information for managers so that they can take decisions

management accounting /'mænɪdʒmənt əˌkaʊntɪŋ/ *noun* the preparation and use of financial information to support management decisions

management accounts /'mænɪdʒmənt əˌkaʊnts/ *plural noun* financial information prepared for a manager so that decisions can be made, including monthly or quarterly financial statements, often in great detail, with analysis of actual performance against the budget

management by objectives /ˌmænɪdʒmənt baɪ əb'dʒektɪvz/ *noun* a way of managing a business by planning

work for the managers to do and testing if it is completed correctly and on time

management consultant /'mænɪdʒmənt kənˌsʌltənt/ *noun* a person who gives advice on how to manage a business

management course /'mænɪdʒmənt kɔːs/ *noun* a training course for managers

management team /'mænɪdʒmənt tiːm/ *noun* all the managers who work in a particular company

manager /'mænɪdʒə/ *noun* **1.** the head of a department in a company ○ *She's a department manager in an engineering company.* ○ *Go and see the human resources manager if you have a problem.* ○ *The production manager has been with the company for only two weeks.* ○ *Our sales manager started as a rep in London.* **2.** the person in charge of a branch or shop ○ *Mr Smith is the manager of our local Lloyds Bank.* ○ *The manager of our Lagos branch is in London for a series of meetings.*

'…the No. 1 managerial productivity problem in America is managers who are out of touch with their people and out of touch with their customers' [*Fortune*]

managing director /ˌmænədʒɪŋ daɪ'rektə/ *noun* the director who is in charge of a whole company. Abbreviation **MD**

mandate /'mændeɪt/ *noun* an order which allows something to take place

mandatory /'mændət(ə)ri/ *adjective* obligatory ○ *Wearing a suit is mandatory for all managerial staff.*

'…the wage talks are focusing on employment issues such as sharing of work among employees and extension of employment beyond the mandatory retirement age of 60 years' [*Nikkei Weekly*]

mandatory bid /ˌmændət(ə)ri 'bɪd/ *noun* an offer to purchase the shares of a company which has to be made when a shareholder acquires 30% of that company's shares

manipulate /mə'nɪpjʊleɪt/ *verb* □ **to manipulate the accounts** to make false accounts so that the company seems profitable

manpower forecasting /'mænpaʊə ˌfɔːkɑːstɪŋ/ *noun* the process of calculating how many employees will be needed in the future, and how many will actually be available

manpower planning /'mænpaʊə ˌplænɪŋ/ *noun* the process of planning to obtain the right number of employees in each job

manufacturing /ˌmænjʊ'fæktʃərɪŋ/ *noun* the production of machine-made products for sale ○ *We must try to reduce the man-*

ufacturing overheads. ○ *Manufacturing processes are continually being updated.*

manufacturing profit /ˌmænjʊ
ˈfæktʃərɪŋ ˌprɒfɪt/ *noun* the difference between the cost of buying a product from another supplier and the cost to the company of manufacturing it itself

margin /ˈmɑːdʒɪn/ *noun* **1.** the difference between the money received when selling a product and the money paid for it **2.** extra space or time allowed **3.** the difference between interest paid to depositors and interest charged to borrowers by a bank, building society, etc. **4.** a deposit paid when purchasing a futures contract

    '…profit margins in the industries most exposed to foreign competition – machinery, transportation equipment and electrical goods – are significantly worse than usual' [*Australian Financial Review*]

marginal /ˈmɑːdʒɪn(ə)l/ *adjective* hardly worth the money paid

marginal cost /ˌmɑːdʒɪn(ə)l ˈkɒst/ *noun* the cost of making a single extra unit above the number already planned

marginal costing /ˌmɑːdʒɪn(ə)l ˈkɒstɪŋ/ *noun* the costing of a product on the basis of its variable costs only, excluding fixed costs

marginal land /ˌmɑːdʒɪn(ə)l ˈlænd/ *noun* land which is almost not worth farming

marginal pricing /ˌmɑːdʒɪn(ə)l ˈpraɪsɪŋ/ *noun* **1.** the practice of basing the selling price of a product on its variable costs of production plus a margin, but excluding fixed costs **2.** the practice of making the selling price the same as the cost of a single extra unit above the number already planned

marginal purchase /ˌmɑːdʒɪn(ə)l ˈpɜːtʃɪs/ *noun* something which a buyer feels is only just worth buying

marginal rate of tax /ˌmɑːdʒɪn(ə)l reɪt əv ˈtæks/, **marginal rate of taxation** /ˌmɑːdʒɪn(ə)l reɪt əv tæksˈeɪʃ(ə)n/ *noun* the percentage of tax which a taxpayer pays at the top rate, which he or she therefore pays on every further pound or dollar he earns

    '…pensioner groups claim that pensioners have the highest marginal rates of tax. Income earned by pensioners above $30 a week is taxed at 62.5 per cent, more than the highest marginal rate' [*Australian Financial Review*]

marginal revenue /ˌmɑːdʒɪn(ə)l ˈrevenjuː/ *noun* the income from selling a single extra unit above the number already sold

marginal tax rate /ˌmɑːdʒɪn(ə)l ˈtæks reɪt/ *noun* same as **marginal rate of tax**

margin call /ˈmɑːdʒɪn kɔːl/ *noun* a request for a purchaser of a futures contract or an option to pay more margin, since the fall

in the price of the securities or commodity has removed the value of the original margin deposited

margin of safety /ˌmɑːdʒɪn əv ˈseɪfti/ *noun* the units produced or sales of such units which are above the breakeven point

marine underwriter /məˌriːn ˈʌndəraɪtə/ *noun* a person or company that insures ships and their cargoes

maritime lawyer /ˌmærɪtaɪm ˈlɔːjə/ *noun* a lawyer who specialises in legal matters concerning ships and cargoes

mark down /ˌmɑːk ˈdaʊn/ *verb* to make the price of something lower

mark-down /ˈmɑːk daʊn/ *noun* **1.** a reduction of the price of something to less than its usual price **2.** the percentage amount by which a price has been lowered ○ *There has been a 30% mark-down on all goods in the sale.*

market /ˈmɑːkɪt/ *noun* **1.** an area where a product might be sold or the group of people who might buy a product ○ *There is no market for this product.* ○ *Our share of the Far eastern market has gone down.* **2.** the possible sales of a specific product or demand for a specific product ○ *There's no market for word processors* ○ *The market for home computers has fallen sharply.* ○ *We have 20% of the British car market.* **3.** a place where money or commodities are traded **4.** □ **sell at the market** an instruction to stockbroker to sell shares at the best price possible **5.** □ **to put something on the market** to start to offer something for sale ○ *They put their house on the market.* ○ *I hear the company has been put on the market.* □ **the company has priced itself out of the market** the company has raised its prices so high that its products do not sell

    '…market analysts described the falls in the second half of last week as a technical correction to a market which had been pushed by demand to over the 900 index level' [*Australian Financial Review*]

marketability /ˌmɑːkɪtəˈbɪlɪti/ *noun* the fact of being able to be sold easily ○ *the marketability of shares in electronic companies*

marketable /ˈmɑːkɪtəb(ə)l/ *adjective* easily sold

market analysis /ˌmɑːkɪt əˈnæləsɪs/ *noun* the detailed examination and report of a market

market capitalisation /ˌmɑːkɪt ˌkæpɪtəlaɪˈzeɪʃ(ə)n/ *noun* the total market value of a company, calculated by multiplying the price of its shares on the Stock Exchange by the number of shares outstanding ○ *company with a £1m capitalisation*

market economist /ˌmɑːkɪt ɪ'kɒnəmɪst/ *noun* a person who specialises in the study of financial structures and the return on investments in the stock market

market forces /ˌmɑːkɪt 'fɔːsɪz/ *plural noun* the influences on the sales of a product which bring about a change in prices

marketing /'mɑːkɪtɪŋ/ *noun* the business of presenting and promoting goods or services in such a way as to make customers want to buy them

'…reporting to the marketing director, the successful applicant will be responsible for the development of a training programme for the new sales force' [*Times*]

marketing agreement /'mɑːkɪtɪŋ ə ˌgriːmənt/ *noun* a contract by which one company will market another company's products

marketing cost /'mɑːkɪtɪŋ kɒst/ *noun* the cost of selling a product, including advertising, packaging, etc.

marketing department /'mɑːkɪtɪŋ dɪ ˌpɑːtmənt/ *noun* the section of a company dealing with marketing and sales

marketing manager /'mɑːkɪtɪŋ ˌmænɪdʒə/ *noun* a person in charge of a marketing department ○ *The marketing manager has decided to start a new advertising campaign.*

market leader /ˌmɑːkɪt 'liːdə/ *noun* **1.** a product which sells most in a market **2.** the company with the largest market share ○ *We are the market leader in home computers.*

'…market leaders may benefit from scale economies or other cost advantages; they may enjoy a reputation for quality simply by being at the top, or they may actually produce a superior product that gives them both a large market share and high profits' [*Accountancy*]

marketmaker /'mɑːkɪtmeɪkə/ *noun* a person who buys or sells shares on the stock market and offers to do so. A marketmaker operates a book, listing the securities he or she is willing to buy or sell, and makes his or her money by charging a commission on each transaction.

market opportunities /ˌmɑːkɪt ɒpə 'tjuːnɪtiz/ *noun* the possibility of finding new sales in a market

market optimism /ˌmɑːkɪt 'ɒptɪ ˌmɪzəm/ *noun* a feeling that the stock market will rise

market price /'mɑːkɪt praɪs/ *noun* **1.** the price at which a product can be sold **2.** the price at which a share stands in a stock market

market rate /ˌmɑːkɪt 'reɪt/ *noun* the usual price in the market ○ *We pay the market rate*

for secretaries or *We pay secretaries the market rate.*

'…after the prime rate cut yesterday, there was a further fall in short-term market rates' [*Financial Times*]

market research /ˌmɑːkɪt rɪ'sɜːtʃ/ *noun* the process of examining the possible sales of a product and the possible customers for it before it is put on the market

market trends /ˌmɑːkɪt 'trendz/ *plural noun* gradual changes taking place in a market

market value /ˌmɑːkɪt 'væljuː/ *noun* the value of an asset, a share, a product or a company if sold today

mark up /ˌmɑːk 'ʌp/ *verb* to increase the price of something

mark-up /'mɑːk ʌp/ *noun* **1.** an increase in price ○ *We put into effect a 10% mark-up of all prices in June.* ○ *Since I was last in the store they have put at least a 5% mark-up on the whole range of items.* **2.** the difference between the cost of a product or service and its selling price □ **we work to a 3.5 times mark-up** *or* **to a 350% mark-up** we take the unit cost and multiply by 3.5 to give the selling price

mass production /mæs prə'dʌkʃən/ *noun* the manufacture of large quantities of identical products

mass unemployment /ˌmæs ˌʌnɪm 'plɔɪmənt/ *noun* unemployment affecting large numbers of people

matching /'mætʃɪŋ/ *noun* the relating of costs to sales in order to calculate profits during an accounting period

material /mə'tɪəriəl/ *noun* a substance which can be used to make a finished product

material facts /məˌtɪəriəl 'fækts/ *noun* **1.** in an insurance contract, information that the insured has to reveal at the time that the policy is taken out, e.g., that a house is located on the edge of a crumbling cliff. Failure to reveal material facts can result in the contract being declared void. **2.** information that has to be disclosed in a prospectus. ◊ **listing requirements**

materiality /məˌtɪəri'ælɪti/ *noun* the state of being material

material news /məˌtɪəriəl 'njuːz/ *noun* price sensitive developments in a company, e.g., proposed acquisitions, mergers, profit warnings, and the resignation of directors, that most stock exchanges require a company to announce immediately to the exchange (NOTE: The US term is **material information**.)

materials requisition /məˌtɪəriəlz ˌrekwɪˈzɪʃ(ə)n/ *noun* an official note from a production department, asking for materials to be moved from the store to the workshop

materials transfer note /məˌtɪəriəls ˈtrænsfɜː nəʊt/ *noun* an official note made out when materials are moved from one workplace to another

maturity date /məˈtʃʊərɪti deɪt/ *noun* a date when a government stock, an assurance policy or a debenture will become due for payment. Also called **date of maturity**

MAXI ISA /ˈmæksi ˌaɪsə/ *noun* an ISA for somebody who uses only one firm to handle all ISA funds. ◊ **MINI ISA**

maximisation /ˌmæksɪmaɪˈzeɪʃ(ə)n/, **maximization** *noun* the process of making something as large as possible ○ *profit maximisation* or *maximisation of profit*

maximise /ˈmæksɪmaɪz/, **maximize** *verb* to make something as large as possible ○ *Our aim is to maximise profits.* ○ *The cooperation of the workforce will be needed if we are to maximise production.* ○ *She is paid on results, and so has to work flat out to maximise her earnings.*

maximum /ˈmæksɪməm/ *noun* the largest possible number, price or quantity ○ *It is the maximum the insurance company will pay.* (NOTE: The plural is **maxima** or **maximums**.) ○ *up to a maximum of £10* no more than £10 ■ *adjective* largest possible ○ *40% is the maximum income tax rate* or *the maximum rate of tax.* ○ *The maximum load for the truck is one ton.* ○ *Maximum production levels were reached last week.*

MCT *abbr* mainstream corporation tax

MD *abbr* managing director ○ *She was appointed MD of a property company.*

mean /miːn/ *adjective* average ○ *The mean annual increase in sales is 3.20%.*

means /miːnz/ *noun* a way of doing something ○ *Do we have any means of copying all these documents quickly?* ○ *Bank transfer is the easiest means of payment.* (NOTE: The plural is **means.**) ■ *plural noun* money or resources ○ *The company has the means to launch the new product.* ○ *Such a level of investment is beyond the means of a small private company.*

means test /ˈmiːnz test/ *noun* an inquiry into how much money someone earns to see if they are eligible for state benefits ■ *verb* to find out how much money someone has in savings and assets ○ *All applicants will be means-tested.*

measure /ˈmeʒə/ *noun* **1.** a way of calculating size or quantity **2.** a type of action ■ *verb* □ **to measure a company's performance** to judge how well a company is doing

measurement /ˈmeʒəmənt/ *noun* a way of judging something ○ *growth measurement* ○ *performance measurement* or *measurement of performance*

measurement of profitability /ˌmeʒəmənt əv ˌprɒfɪtəˈbɪlɪti/ *noun* a way of calculating how profitable something is

median /ˈmiːdiən/ *noun* the middle number in a list of numbers

medical insurance /ˈmedɪk(ə)l ɪn ˌʃʊərəns/ *noun* insurance which pays the cost of medical treatment, especially when someone is travelling abroad

medium /ˈmiːdiəm/ *adjective* middle or average ○ *The company is of medium size.*

medium of exchange /ˌmiːdiəm əv ɪks ˈtʃeɪndʒ/ *noun* anything that is used to pay for goods. Nowadays, this usually takes the form of money (banknotes and coins), but in ancient societies, it included anything from cattle to shells.

mediums /ˈmiːdiəmz/ *plural noun* government stocks which mature in seven to fifteen years' time

medium-sized company /ˌmiːdiəm saɪzd ˈkʌmp(ə)ni/ *noun* a company which has a turnover of less than £5.75m and does not employ more than 250 staff ○ *a medium-sized engineering company*

medium-term /ˌmiːdiəm ˈtɜːm/ *adjective* referring to a point between short term and long term

medium-term bond /ˌmiːdiəm tɜːm ˈbɒnd/ *noun* a bond which matures within five to fifteen years

member /ˈmembə/ *noun* **1.** a person who belongs to a group, society or organisation ○ *Committee members voted on the proposal.* ○ *They were elected members of the board.* ○ *Every employer is a member of the employers' federation.* **2.** a shareholder in a company **3.** an organisation which belongs to a larger organisation ○ *the member companies of a trade association* ○ *The member states of the EU.* ○ *The members of the United Nations.*

'…this is the first opportunity for party members and trade union members to express their views on the tax package' [*Australian Financial Review*]

member bank /ˌmembə ˈbæŋk/ *noun* a bank which is part of the Federal Reserve system

member firm /ˌmembə ˈfɜːm/ *noun* a stockbroking firm which is a member of a stock exchange

membership /'membəʃɪp/ *noun* **1.** the fact of belonging to a group, society or organisation ○ *membership qualifications* ○ *conditions of membership* ○ *membership card* ○ *to pay your membership or your membership fees* ○ *membership of the EU* **2.** all the members of a group ○ *The membership was asked to vote for the new president.*

'…the bargaining committee will recommend that its membership ratify the agreement at a meeting called for June' [*Toronto Star*]

members' voluntary winding up /ˌmembəz ˌvɒlənt(ə)ri ˌwaɪndɪŋ 'ʌp/ *noun* the winding up of a company by the shareholders themselves

mercantile /'mɜːkəntaɪl/ *adjective* commercial

mercantile marine /ˌmɜːkəntaɪl mə'riːn/ *noun* all the commercial ships of a country

merchant /'mɜːtʃənt/ *noun* **1.** a businessperson who buys and sells, especially one who buys imported goods in bulk for retail sale ○ *a coal merchant* ○ *a wine merchant* **2.** a company, shop or other business which accepts a credit card for purchases

merchant bank /'mɜːtʃənt bæŋk/ *noun* **1.** a bank which arranges loans to companies, deals in international finance, buys and sells shares and launches new companies on the Stock Exchange, but does not provide banking services to the general public **2.** *US* a bank which operates a credit card system, accepting payment on credit cards from retailers or 'merchants'

merchant banker /ˌmɜːtʃənt 'bæŋkə/ *noun* a person who has a high position in a merchant bank

merchant number /'mɜːtʃənt ˌnʌmbə/ *noun* a number of the merchant, printed at the top of the report slip when depositing credit card payments

merge /mɜːdʒ/ *verb* to join together ○ *The two companies have merged.* ○ *The firm merged with its main competitor.*

merger /'mɜːdʒə/ *noun* the joining together of two or more companies ○ *As a result of the merger, the company is now the largest in the field.*

merger accounting /'mɜːdʒə əˌkaʊntɪŋ/ *noun* a way of presenting the accounts of a newly acquired company within the group accounts, so as to show it in the best possible light

merit increase /'merɪt ˌɪnkriːs/ *noun* an increase in pay given to an employee because his or her work is good

merit rating /'merɪt ˌreɪtɪŋ/ *noun* the process of judging how well an employee works, so that payment can be according to merit

mezzanine finance /ˌmetsəniːn 'faɪnæns/ *noun* finance provided to a company after it has received start-up finance

micro- /maɪkrəʊ/ *prefix* very small

microeconomics /'maɪkrəʊ iːkə ˌnɒmɪks/ *plural noun* the study of the economics of people or single companies. Compare **macroeconomics** (NOTE: takes a singular verb)

microfiche /'maɪkrəʊfiːʃ/ *noun* an index sheet, made of several microfilm photographs ○ *We hold our records on microfiche.*

microfilm /'maɪkrəʊfɪlm/ *noun* a roll of film on which a document is photographed in very small scale ○ *We hold our records on microfilm.*

mid- /mɪd/ *prefix* middle

middle management /ˌmɪd(ə)l 'mænɪdʒmənt/ *noun* department managers in a company, who carry out the policy set by the directors and organise the work of a group of employees

middle price /'mɪd(ə)l praɪs/ *noun* a price between the buying and selling price, usually shown in indices

mid-month /ˌmɪd 'mʌnθ/ *adjective* happening in the middle of the month ○ *mid-month accounts*

mid-week /ˌmɪd 'wiːk/ *adjective* happening in the middle of a week ○ *the mid-week lull in sales*

millionaire /ˌmɪljə'neə/ *noun* a person who has more than one million pounds or dollars

MINI ISA /'mɪni ˌaɪsə/ *noun* an ISA for somebody who uses up to three firms for handling the components of the ISA. ◊ **MAXI ISA**

minimisation /ˌmɪnɪmaɪ'zeɪʃ(ə)n/ *noun* making as small as possible

minimum /'mɪnɪməm/ *noun* the smallest possible quantity, price or number ○ *to keep expenses to a minimum* ○ *to reduce the risk of a loss to a minimum* (NOTE: The plural is **minima** or **minimums.**) ■ *adjective* smallest possible

minimum lending rate /ˌmɪnɪməm 'lendɪŋ reɪt/ *noun* the lowest rate of interest formerly charged by the Bank of England to discount houses, now replaced by the base rate

minimum reserves /ˌmɪnɪməm rɪ 'zɜːvz/ *plural noun* the smallest amount of reserves which a commercial bank must hold with a central bank

minimum wage /ˌmɪnɪməm ˈweɪdʒ/ noun the lowest hourly wage which a company can legally pay its employees

mining concession /ˈmaɪnɪŋ kənˌseʃ(ə)n/ noun the right to dig a mine on a piece of land

minor /ˈmaɪnə/ adjective less important ○ Items of minor expenditure are not listed separately. ○ The minor shareholders voted against the proposal.

minority /maɪˈnɒrɪti/ noun a number or quantity which is less than half of the total ○ A minority of board members opposed the chairman.

minority shareholder /maɪˌnɒrəti ˌʃeəˈhəʊldə/ noun a person who owns a group of shares but less than half of the shares in a company

minority shareholding /maɪˌnɒrəti ˈʃeəhəʊldɪŋ/ noun a group of shares which are less than half the total ○ He acquired a minority shareholding in the company.

minus /ˈmaɪnəs/ preposition, adverb less, without ○ Net salary is gross salary minus tax and National Insurance deductions. ○ Gross profit is sales minus production costs.

minus factor /ˈmaɪnəs ˌfæktə/ noun an unfavourable factor ○ To have lost sales in the best quarter of the year is a minus factor for the sales team.

misappropriate /ˌmɪsəˈprəʊprieɪt/ verb to use illegally money which is not yours, but with which you have been trusted

misappropriation /ˌmɪsəprəʊpriˈeɪʃ(ə)n/ noun the illegal use of money by someone who is not the owner but who has been trusted to look after it

miscalculate /mɪsˈkælkjʊleɪt/ verb to calculate wrongly, or to make a mistake in calculating something ○ The salesman miscalculated the discount, so we hardly broke even on the deal.

miscalculation /ˌmɪsˌkælkjʊˈleɪʃ(ə)n/ noun a mistake in calculating

miscount noun /ˈmɪskaʊnt/ a mistake in counting ■ verb /mɪsˈkaʊnt/ to count wrongly, or to make a mistake in counting something ○ The shopkeeper miscounted, so we got twenty-five bars of chocolate instead of two dozen.

mismanage /mɪsˈmænɪdʒ/ verb to manage something badly ○ The company had been badly mismanaged under the previous MD.

mismanagement /mɪsˈmænɪdʒmənt/ noun bad management ○ The company failed because of the chairman's mismanagement.

misrepresent /ˌmɪsreprɪˈzent/ verb to report facts or what someone says wrongly ○ Our spokesman was totally misrepresented in the Sunday papers.

misrepresentation /ˌmɪsˌreprɪzenˈteɪʃ(ə)n/ noun the act of making a wrong statement in order to persuade someone to enter into a contract such as one for buying a product or service

misuse /mɪsˈjuːs/ noun a wrong use ○ the misuse of funds or of assets

mixed /mɪkst/ adjective **1.** made up of different sorts or of different types of things together **2.** neither good nor bad

'…prices closed on a mixed note after a moderately active trading session' [Financial Times]

mixed economy /ˌmɪkst ɪˈkɒnəmi/ noun a system which contains both nationalised industries and private enterprise

mode /məʊd/ noun a way of doing something

modified accounts /ˌmɒdɪfaɪd əˈkaʊntz/ plural noun ♦ abbreviated accounts

monetarism /ˈmʌnɪtəˌrɪz(ə)m/ noun a theory that the amount of money in the economy affects the level of prices, so that inflation can be controlled by regulating money supply

monetarist /ˈmʌnɪtərɪst/ noun a person who believes in monetarism and acts accordingly ■ adjective according to monetarism ○ monetarist theories

monetary /ˈmʌnɪt(ə)ri/ adjective referring to money or currency

'…the decision by the government to tighten monetary policy will push the annual inflation rate above the year's previous high' [Financial Times]

'…it is not surprising that the Fed started to ease monetary policy some months ago' [Sunday Times]

'…a draft report on changes in the international monetary system' [Wall Street Journal]

monetary assets /ˌmʌnɪt(ə)ri ˈæsets/ noun assets, principally accounts receivable, cash, and bank balances, that are realisable at the amount stated in the accounts. Other assets, e.g., facilities and machinery, inventories, and marketable securities will not necessarily realise the sum stated in a business's balance sheet.

monetary items /ˌmʌnɪt(ə)ri ˈaɪtəms/ plural noun monetary assets such as cash or debtors, and monetary liabilities such as an overdraft or creditors, whose values stay the same in spite of inflation

monetary standard /ˌmʌnɪt(ə)ri ˈstændəd/ *noun* the fixing of a fixed exchange rate for a currency

monetary targets /ˌmʌnɪt(ə)ri ˈtɑːɡɪtz/ *plural noun* figures which are given as targets by the government when setting out its budget for the forthcoming year, e.g. the money supply or the PSBR

monetary unit /ˈmʌnɪt(ə)ri ˌjuːnɪt/ *noun* a main item of currency of a country

money /ˈmʌni/ *noun* coins and notes used for buying and selling □ **money up front** payment in advance ○ *They are asking for £10,000 up front before they will consider the deal.* ○ *He had to put money up front before he could clinch the deal.*

money at call /ˌmʌni ət ˈkɔːl/, **money on call** /ˌmʌni ɒn ˈkɔːl/ *noun* same as **call money**

money at call and short notice /ˌmʌni ət kɔːl ən ʃɔːt ˈnəʊtɪs/ *noun* in the United Kingdom, balances in an account that are either available upon demand (call) or within 14 days (short notice)

money broker /ˈmʌni ˌbrəʊkə/ *noun* a dealer operating in the interbank and foreign exchange markets

money laundering /ˈmʌni ˌlɔːndərɪŋ/ *noun* the act of passing illegal money into the banking system

moneylender /ˈmʌniˌlendə/ *noun* a person who lends money at interest

money lying idle /ˌmʌni ˌlaɪɪŋ ˈaɪd(ə)l/ *noun* money which is not being used to produce interest, which is not invested in business

money-making /ˈmʌni ˌmeɪkɪŋ/ *adjective* able to turn over a profit ○ *a money-making plan*

money market fund /ˈmʌni ˌmɑːkɪt fʌnd/ *noun* an investment fund, which only invests in money market instruments

money market instruments /ˈmʌni ˌmɑːkɪt ˌɪnstrʊmənts/ *plural noun* short-term investments which can be easily turned into cash and are traded on the money markets, e.g. cds

money order /ˈmʌni ˌɔːdə/ *noun* a document which can be bought as a way of sending money through the post

money rates /ˈmʌni reɪts/ *plural noun* rates of interest for borrowers or lenders

money-spinner /ˈmʌni ˌspɪnə/ *noun* an item which sells very well or which is very profitable ○ *The home-delivery service has proved to be a real money-spinner.*

money supply /ˈmʌni səˌplaɪ/ *noun* the amount of money which exists in a country

monies /ˈmʌniz/ *plural noun* sums of money ○ *monies owing to the company* ○ *to collect monies due*

monitor /ˈmɒnɪtə/ *verb* to check or to examine how something is working ○ *She is monitoring the progress of sales.* ○ *How do you monitor the performance of the sales reps?* ○ *How do you monitor the performance of a unit trust?*

monopoly /məˈnɒpəli/ *noun* a situation where one person or company is the only supplier of a particular product or service ○ *to be in a monopoly situation* ○ *The company has the monopoly of imports of Brazilian wine.* ○ *The factory has the absolute monopoly of jobs in the town.* (NOTE: The more usual US term is **trust**.)

Monte Carlo method /ˌmɒnti ˈkɑːləʊ ˌmeθəd/ *noun* a statistical analysis technique for calculating an unknown quantity which has an exact value by using an extended series of random trials (NOTE: The name refers to the fact that a roulette wheel in a casino, as in Monte Carlo, continually generates random numbers.)

month /mʌnθ/ *noun* one of twelve periods which make a year ○ *bills due at the end of the current month* ○ *The company pays him £100 a month.* ○ *She earns £2,000 a month.*

month end /ˌmʌnθ ˈend/ *noun* the end of a calendar month, when accounts have to be drawn up ○ *The accounts department are working on the month-end accounts.*

monthly /ˈmʌnθli/ *adjective* happening every month or which is received every month ○ *We get a monthly statement from the bank.* ○ *She makes monthly payments to the credit card company.* ○ *He is paying for his car by monthly instalments.* ○ *My monthly salary cheque is late* □ **monthly statement** a statement sent to a customer at the end of each month, itemising transactions which have taken place in his or her account ■ *adverb* every month ○ *She asked if she could pay monthly by direct debit.* ○ *The account is credited monthly.*

moonlight /ˈmuːnlaɪt/ *verb* to do a second job for cash, often in the evening, as well as a regular job (*informal*)

moonlighting /ˈmuːnlaɪtɪŋ/ *noun* the practice of doing a second job ○ *He makes thousands a year from moonlighting.*

moral hazard /ˌmɒrəl ˈhæzəd/ *noun* a risk that somebody will behave immorally because insurance, the law, or some other agency protects them against loss that the immoral behaviour might otherwise cause

moratorium /ˌmɒrəˈtɔːriəm/ *noun* a temporary stop to repayments of interest on loans or capital owed ○ *The banks called for a moratorium on payments.* (NOTE: The plural is **moratoria** or **moratoriums**.)

mortgage /ˈmɔːɡɪdʒ/ *noun* agreement where someone lends money to another person so that he or she can buy a property, the property being the security ○ *to take out a mortgage on a house*

'…mortgage payments account for just 20 per cent of the average first-time buyer's gross earnings against an average of 24 per cent during the past 15 years' [*Times*]

'…mortgage money is becoming tighter. Applications for mortgages are running at a high level and some building societies are introducing quotas' [*Times*]

'…for the first time since mortgage rates began falling a financial institution has raised charges on homeowner loans' [*Globe and Mail (Toronto)*]

mortgage bond /ˈmɔːɡɪdʒ bɒnd/ *noun* a certificate showing that a mortgage exists and that property is security for it

mortgage debenture /ˈmɔːɡɪdʒ dɪˌbentʃə/ *noun* a debenture where the lender can be repaid by selling the company's property

mortgagee /mɔːɡəˈdʒiː/ *noun* a person or company which lends money for someone to buy a property

mortgage famine /ˈmɔːɡɪdʒ ˌfæmɪn/ *noun* a situation where there is not enough money available to offer mortgages to house buyers

mortgager /ˈmɔːɡɪdʒə/, **mortgagor** *noun* a person who borrows money to buy a property

movable /ˈmuːvəb(ə)l/, **moveable** *adjective* possible to move ○ *All the moveable property has been seized by the bailiffs.*

movable property /ˌmuːvəb(ə)l ˈprɒpəti/ *noun* chattels and other objects which can be moved, as opposed to land

moveables /ˈmuːvəb(ə)lz/ *plural noun* moveable property

mover /ˈmuːvə/ *noun* a person who proposes a motion

moving average /ˌmuːvɪŋ ˈæv(ə)rɪdʒ/ *noun* an average of share prices on a stock market, where the calculation is made over a period which moves forward regularly

multi- /mʌlti/ *prefix* referring to many things

multicurrency /ˌmʌltiˈkʌrənsi/ *adjective* in several currencies

multifunctional card /ˌmʌltifʌnkʃən(ə)l ˈkɑːd/ *noun* a plastic card that may be used for two or more purposes, e.g., as a cash card, a cheque card, and a debit card

multilateral /ˌmʌltiˈlæt(ə)rəl/ *adjective* between several organisations or countries ○ *a multilateral agreement*

multilateral netting /ˌmʌltilæt(ə)rəl ˈnetɪŋ/ *noun* a method of putting together sums from various sources into one currency, used by groups of banks trading in several currencies at the same time

multimillion /ˌmʌltiˈmɪljən/ *adjective* referring to several million pounds or dollars ○ *They signed a multimillion pound deal.*

multimillionaire /ˌmʌltimɪljəˈneə/ *noun* a person who owns property or investments worth several million pounds or dollars

multiple /ˈmʌltɪp(ə)l/ *adjective* many

multiple exchange rate /ˌmʌltɪp(ə)l ɪksˈtʃeɪndʒ reɪt/ *noun* a two-tier rate of exchange used in certain countries where the more advantageous rate may be for tourists or for businesses proposing to build a factory

multiple ownership /ˌmʌltɪp(ə)l ˈəʊnəʃɪp/ *noun* a situation where something is owned by several parties jointly

multiplication sign /ˌmʌltɪplɪˈkeɪʃ(ə)n saɪn/ *noun* a sign (x) used to show that a number is being multiplied by another

multiplier /ˈmʌltɪplaɪə/ *noun* a number which multiplies another, or a factor which tends to multiply something, as the effect of new expenditure on total income and reserves

multiply /ˈmʌltɪplaɪ/ *verb* **1.** to calculate the sum of various numbers added together a particular number of times ○ *If you multiply twelve by three you get thirty-six.* ○ *Square measurements are calculated by multiplying length by width.* **2.** to grow or to increase ○ *Profits multiplied in the boom years.*

municipal bond /mjuːˌnɪsɪp(ə)l ˈbɒnd/ *noun* US a bond issued by a town or district (NOTE: The UK term is **local authority bond**.)

mutual /ˈmjuːtʃuəl/ *adjective* belonging to two or more people

N

naked /'neɪkɪd/ *adjective* without any hedge or without any reserves to protect a position

name /neɪm/ *noun* a person who provides security for insurance arranged by a Lloyd's of London syndicate

named /neɪmd/ *adjective* □ **the person named in the policy** the person whose name is given on an insurance policy as the person insured

NAO *abbr* National Audit Office

narration /nə'reɪʃ(ə)n/, **narrative** /'nærətɪv/ *noun* a series of notes and explanations relating to transactions in the accounts

national /'næʃ(ə)nəl/ *adjective* referring to the whole of a particular country

National Audit Office /,næʃ(ə)nəl ,ɔːdɪt 'ɒfɪs/ *noun* a body which investigates the use of public money by central government departments. It acts on behalf of the Parliamentary Public Accounts Committee. Abbreviation **NAO**

national bank /'næʃ(ə)nəl bæŋk/ *noun* **US** a bank which is chartered by the federal government and is part of the Federal Reserve system as opposed to a 'state bank'

national income /,næʃ(ə)nəl 'ɪnkʌm/ *noun* the value of income from the sales of goods and services in a country

national income accounts /,næʃ(ə)nəl 'ɪnkʌm/ *plural noun* economic statistics that show the state of a nation's economy over a given period of time, usually a year. ◊ **gross domestic product, gross national product**

National Insurance /,næʃ(ɔ)nəl ɪn'ʃʊərəns/ *noun* state insurance in the United Kingdom, organised by the government, which pays for medical care, hospitals, unemployment benefits, etc. Abbreviation **NI**

National Insurance contributions /,næʃ(ə)nəl ɪn'ʃʊərəns ,kɒntrɪbjuːʃ(ə)nz/ *noun* payments made by both employers and employees to the government. The contribu-

tions, together with other government receipts, are used to finance state pensions and other benefits such as unemployment benefit. Abbreviation **NIC**

National Insurance number /,næʃ(ə)nəl ɪn'ʃʊərəns ,nʌmbə/ *noun* a number given to each British citizen, which is the number by which he or she is known to the social security services

National Savings & Investments /,næʃ(ə)nəl ,seɪvɪŋz ənd ɪn'vestmənts/ *noun* a part of the Exchequer, a savings scheme for small investors including savings certificates and premium bonds. Abbreviation **NS&I**

National Savings Bank /,næʃ(ə)nəl 'seɪvɪŋz ,bæŋk/ *noun* in the United Kingdom, a savings scheme established in 1861 as the Post Office Savings Bank and now operated by National Savings. Abbreviation **NSB**

National Savings Certificate /,næʃ(ə)nəl 'seɪvɪŋz sə,tɪfɪkət/ *noun* in the United Kingdom, either a fixed-interest or an index-linked certificate issued for two or five year terms by National Savings with returns that are free of income tax. Abbreviation **NSC**

National Savings Stock Register /,næʃ(ə)nəl ,seɪvɪŋz 'stɒk ,redʒɪstə/ *noun* an organisation, run by the Department for National Savings, which gives private individuals the opportunity to buy British government stocks by post without going through a stockbroker

NBV *abbr* net book value

negative carry /,negətɪv 'kæri/ *noun* a deal where the cost of finance is more than the return on the capital used

negative cash flow /,negətɪv 'kæʃ fləʊ/ *noun* a situation where more money is going out of a company than is coming in

negative equity /,negətɪv 'ekwiti/ *noun* a situation where a house bought with a mortgage becomes less valuable than the money borrowed to buy it because of falling house prices

negative goodwill /ˌnegətɪv gʊdˈwɪl/ *noun* negative goodwill arises when the aggregate fair values of the identifiable assets and liabilities of the entity exceed the acquisition cost

negative yield curve /ˌnegətɪv ˈjiːld kɜːv/ *noun* a situation where the yield on a long-term investment is less than that on a short-term investment

negotiable instrument /nɪˌɡəʊʃiəb(ə)l ˈɪnstrʊmənt/ *noun* a document which can be exchanged for cash, e.g. a bill of exchange or a cheque

negotiable order of withdrawal /nɪˌɡəʊʃiəb(ə)l ˌɔːdə əv wɪðˈdrɔːəl/ *adjective* a cheque written on a NOW account

negotiable paper /nɪˌɡəʊʃiəb(ə)l ˈpeɪpə/ *noun* a document which can be transferred from one owner to another for cash

negotiate /nɪˈɡəʊʃieɪt/ *verb* □ **to negotiate terms and conditions** *or* **a contract** to discuss and agree the terms of a contract □ **he negotiated a £250,000 loan with the bank** he came to an agreement with the bank for a loan of £250,000 ■ *noun* to transfer financial instruments, e.g. bearer securities, bills of exchange, cheques, and promissory notes, to another person in return for a consideration

'…many of the large travel agency chains are able to negotiate even greater discounts' [*Duns Business Month*]

negotiation /nɪˌɡəʊʃiˈeɪʃ(ə)n/ *noun* the discussion of terms and conditions in order to reach an agreement □ **to enter into** *or* **to start negotiations** to start discussing a problem

'…after three days of tough negotiations, the company reached agreement with its 1,200 unionized workers' [*Toronto Star*]

nest egg /ˈnest eɡ/ *noun* money which someone has saved over a period of time, usually kept in an interest-bearing account and intended for use after retirement

net /net/ *adjective* referring to a price, weight, pay, etc., after all deductions have been made ■ *verb* to make a true profit ○ *to net a profit of £10,000* (NOTE: **netting – netted**)

'…out of its earnings a company will pay a dividend. When shareholders receive this it will be net, that is it will have had tax deducted at 30 per cent' [*Investors Chronicle*]

net asset value per share /net ˌæset ˌvæljuː pə ˈʃeə/ *noun* the value of a company calculated by dividing the shareholders' funds by the number of shares issued

net book value /net bʊk ˈvæljuː/ *noun* the historical cost of an asset less any accumulated depreciation or other provision for diminution in value, e.g., reduction to net realisable value, or asset value which has been revalued downwards to reflect market conditions. Abbreviation **NBV**. Also called **written-down value**

net borrowings /ˌnet ˈbɒrəʊɪŋz/ *plural noun* a company's borrowings, less any cash the company is holding in its bank accounts

net cash flow /net ˈkæʃ fləʊ/ *noun* the difference between the money coming in and the money going out

net current assets /net ˌkʌrənt ˈæsets/ *plural noun* the current assets of a company, i.e. cash and stocks, less any liabilities. Also called **net working capital**

net current liabilities /net ˌkʌrənt ˌlaɪə ˈbɪlɪtiz/ *plural noun* current liabilities of a company less its current assets

net dividend per share /net ˌdɪvɪdend pə ˈʃeə/ *noun* the dividend per share after deduction of personal income tax

net income /net ˈɪnkʌm/ *noun* a person's or organisation's income which is left after taking away tax and other deductions

net interest /ˌnet ˈɪntrəst/ *noun* gross interest less tax

net liquid funds /ˌnet ˌlɪkwɪd ˈfʌndz/ *noun* an organisation's cash plus its marketable investments less its short-term borrowings, such as overdrafts and loans

net loss /ˌnet ˈlɒs/ *noun* an actual loss, after deducting overheads

net margin /ˌnet ˈmɑːdʒɪn/ *noun* the percentage difference between received price and all costs, including overheads

net present value /ˌnet ˌprezənt ˈvæljuː/ *noun* the value of future cash inflows less future cash outflows discounted at a certain discount rate, usually the company's cost of capital. Abbreviation **NPV**

net price /ˌnet ˈpraɪs/ *noun* the price of goods or services which cannot be reduced by a discount

net profit /net ˈprɒfɪt/ *noun* the amount by which income from sales is larger than all expenditure. Also called **profit after tax**

net profit ratio /net ˌprɒfɪt ˈreɪʃiəʊ/ *noun* the ratio of an organisation's net profit to its total net sales. Comparing the net profit ratios of companies in the same sector shows which are the most efficient.

net realisable value /net ˌrɪəlaɪzəb(ə)l ˈvæljuː/ *noun* the price at which goods in stock could be sold, less any costs incurred in making the sale. Abbreviation **NRV**

net receipts /ˌnet rɪˈsiːts/ *plural noun* receipts after deducting commission, tax, discounts, etc.

net relevant earnings /net ˌreləv(ə)nt ˈɜːnɪŋz/ *plural noun* earnings which qualify for calculating pension contributions and against which relief against tax can be claimed. Such earnings can be income from employment which is not pensionable, profits of a self-employed sole trader, etc.

net residual value /net rɪˌzɪdjuəl ˈvæljuː/ *noun* the anticipated proceeds of an asset at the end of its useful life, less the costs of selling it, e.g., transport and commission. It is used when calculating the annual charge for the straight-line method of depreciation. Abbreviation **NRV**

net return /ˌnet rɪˈtɜːn/ *noun* a return on an investment after tax has been paid

net salary /ˌnet ˈsæləri/ *noun* the salary which is left after deducting tax and National Insurance contributions

net sales /ˌnet ˈseɪlz/ *plural noun* the total amount of sales less damaged or returned items and discounts to retailers

net turnover /net ˈtɜːnˌəʊvə/ *noun* turnover before VAT and after trade discounts have been deducted

net working capital /net ˌwɜːkɪŋ ˈkæpɪt(ə)l/ *noun* same as **net current assets**

net worth /net ˈwɜːθ/ *noun* the value of all the property of a person or company after taking away what the person or company owes ○ *The upmarket product is targeted at individuals of high net worth.*

net yield /net ˈjiːld/ *noun* the profit from investments after deduction of tax

new issues department /njuː ˈɪʃuːz dɪˌpɑːtmənt/ *noun* the section of a bank which deals with issues of new shares

NI *abbr* National Insurance

NIC /ˌen aɪ ˈsiː/ *abbr* National Insurance contributions

NIF *abbr* note issuance facility

night safe /ˈnaɪt seɪf/ *noun* a safe in the outside wall of a bank, where money and documents can be deposited at night, using a special door

nil /nɪl/ *noun* zero or nothing ○ *The advertising budget has been cut to nil.*

nil paid shares /ˌnɪl peɪd ˈʃeəz/ *plural noun* new shares which have not yet been paid for

nil return /ˌnɪl rɪˈtɜːn/ *noun* a report showing no sales, income, tax, etc.

no-claims bonus /nəʊ ˈkleɪmz ˌbəʊnəs/ *noun* **1.** a reduction of premiums on an insurance policy because no claims have been made **2.** a lower premium paid because no claims have been made against the insurance policy

nominal /ˈnɒmɪn(ə)l/ *adjective* (*of a payment*) very small ○ *They are paying a nominal rent.* ○ *The employment agency makes a nominal charge for its services.*

nominal account /ˌnɒmɪn(ə)l əˈkaʊnt/ *noun* an account for recording transactions relating to a particular type of expense or receipt

nominal interest rate /ˌnɒmɪn(ə)l ˈɪntrəst reɪt/ *noun* an interest rate expressed as a percentage of the face value of a bond, not on its market value

nominal ledger /ˌnɒmɪn(ə)l ˈledʒə/ *noun* a book which records a company's transactions in the various accounts

nominal share capital /ˌnɒmɪn(ə)l ˈʃeə ˌkæpɪt(ə)l/ *noun* the total of the face value of all the shares which a company is authorised to issue according to its memorandum of association

nominal value /ˌnɒmɪn(ə)l ˈvæljuː/ *noun* same as **face value**

nominee /ˌnɒmɪˈniː/ *noun* a person who is nominated, especially someone who is appointed to deal with financial matters on your behalf

nominee account /ˌnɒmɪˈniː əˌkaʊnt/ *noun* an account held on behalf of someone

non- /nɒn/ *prefix* not

non-acceptance /ˌnɒn əkˈseptəns/ *noun* a situation in which the person who is to pay a bill of exchange does not accept it

non-cash item /ˌnɒn ˌkæʃ ˈaɪtəm/ *noun* an item in an income statement that is not cash, such as depreciation expenses, and gains or losses from investments

noncash items /ˌnɒn kæʃ ˈaɪtəmz/ *plural noun* cheques, drafts and similar items which are not in the form of cash

non-cumulative preference share /ˌnɒn ˌkjuːmjʊlətɪv ˈpref(ə)rəns ˌʃeə/ *noun* a preference share where, if the dividend is not paid in the current year, it is lost

non-historic /ˌnɒn hɪˈstɒrɪk/ *adjective* not calculated on a historical cost basis

non-monetary /ˌnɒn ˈmʌnɪt(ə)ri/ *adjective* items or assets which are not money, and can be valued at a higher value than their original purchase price

non-negotiable instrument /ˌnɒn nɪ
ˌɡəʊʃəb(ə)l 'ɪnstrʊmənt/ *noun* a document
which cannot be exchanged for cash, e.g. a
crossed cheque

non-performing loan /ˌnɒn pɜːˌfɔːmɪŋ
'ləʊn/ *noun US* a loan where the borrower is
not likely to pay any interest nor to repay the
principal, as in the case of loans to Third
World countries by western banks

non-profit-making   organisation
/'nɒn'prɒfɪt'meɪkɪŋ ɔːɡənaɪ'zeɪʃən/, **non-
profit organisation** /ˌnɒn 'prɒfɪt ɔːɡənaɪ
ˌzeɪʃ(ə)n/ *noun* an organisation which is not
allowed by law to make a profit ○ *Non-profit-
making organisations are exempted from tax.*
(NOTE: Non-profit organisations include
charities, professional associations, trade
unions, and religious, arts, community, research, and campaigning bodies. The US
term is **non-profit corporation**.)

non-recurring items /ˌnɒn rɪˌkɜːrɪŋ
'aɪtəmz/ *plural noun* special items in a set of
accounts which appear only once

non-refundable /ˌnɒn rɪ'fʌndəb(ə)l/ *adjective* not possible to refund ○ *You will be
asked to make a non-refundable deposit.*

non-resident /ˌnɒn 'rezɪd(ə)nt/ *noun,
adjective* a person who is not considered a
resident of a country for tax purposes ○ *He
has a non-resident bank account.*

non-tariff barriers *noun* barriers to international trade other than tariffs. They include
over-complicated documentation; verification of goods for health and safety reasons
and blocked deposits payable by importers to
obtain foreign currency. Abbreviation **NTBs**

non-taxable /ˌnɒn 'tæksəb(ə)l/ *adjective*
not subject to tax ○ *non-taxable income* ○
Lottery prizes are non-taxable.

non-trade   creditor /ˌnɒn 'treɪd
ˌkredɪtə/ *noun* a creditor who is not owed
money in the normal trade of a business, e.g.
a debenture holder or the Inland Revenue

non-voting shares /ˌnɒn 'vəʊtɪŋ ʃeəz/
plural noun shares which do not allow the
shareholder to vote at meetings. ◊ **A shares**

normal /'nɔːm(ə)l/ *adjective* usual or
which happens regularly ○ *Normal deliveries are made on Tuesdays and Fridays.* ○
*Now that supply difficulties have been re-
solved we hope to resume normal service as
soon as possible.*

normalise /'nɔːməlaɪz/, **normalize** *verb*
1. to store and represent numbers in a pre-
agreed form, usually to provide maximum
precision **2.** to convert data into a form which
can be read by a particular computer system

normal loss /ˌnɔːm(ə)l 'lɒs/ *noun* loss
which is usual in the type of business being
carried on, e.g. loss of small quantities of materials during the manufacturing process

notary public /ˌnəʊtəri 'pʌblɪk/ *noun* a
lawyer who has the authority to witness documents and spoken statements, making them
official (NOTE: The plural is **notaries public**.)

note /nəʊt/ *noun* **1.** a short document or
piece of writing, or a short piece of information ○ *to send someone a note* ○ *I left a note
on her desk.* **2.** paper showing that money has
been borrowed

note issuance facility /nəʊt 'ɪʃʊəns fə
ˌsɪlɪti/ *noun* a credit facility where a company obtains a loan underwritten by banks and
can issue a series of short-term eurocurrency
notes to replace others which have expired.
Abbreviation **NIF**

note of hand /ˌnəʊt əv 'hænd/ *noun* a
document stating that someone promises to
pay an amount of money on an agreed date

notice of coding /ˌnəʊtɪs əv 'kəʊdɪŋ/
noun a notice which informs someone of the
code number given to indicate the amount of
tax allowances a person has

notional /'nəʊʃ(ə)n(ə)l/ *adjective* probable but not known exactly or not quantifiable

notional income /ˌnəʊʃ(ə)n(ə)l 'ɪnkʌm/
noun an invisible benefit which is not money
or goods and services

notional rent /ˌnəʊʃ(ə)n(ə)l 'rent/ *noun* a
sum put into accounts as rent where the company owns the building it is occupying and so
does not pay an actual rent

not negotiable /ˌnɒt nɪ'ɡəʊʃiəb(ə)l/
noun wording appearing on a cheque or bill
of exchange that it is deprived of its inherent
quality of negotiability. When such a document is transferred from one person to another, the recipient obtains no better title to it
than the signatory. ◊ **negotiable instrument**

novation /nəʊ'veɪʃ(ə)n/ *noun* an agreement to change a contract by substituting a
third party for one of the two original parties

NOW account /'naʊ əˌkaʊnt/ *noun US* an
interest-bearing account with a bank or savings and loan association, on which cheques
called 'negotiable orders of withdrawal' can
be drawn. Full form **negotiable order of
withdrawal account**

NPV *abbr* net present value

NRV *abbr* **1.** net realisable value **2.** net residual value

NS&I *abbr* National Savings & Investments

NSB *abbr* National Savings Bank

NSC *abbr* National Savings Certificate

NTBs *abbr* non-tariff barriers

number /'nʌmbə/ *noun* **1.** a quantity of things or people ○ *The number of persons on the payroll has increased over the last year.* ○ *The number of days lost through strikes has fallen.* **2.** a printed or written figure that identifies a particular thing ○ *Please write your account number on the back of the cheque.* ○ *If you have a complaint to make, always quote the batch number.* ○ *She noted the cheque number in the ledger.* ■ *verb* to put a figure on a document ○ *to number an order* ○ *I refer to your invoice numbered 1234.*

numbered account /,nʌmbəd ə'kaʊnt/ *noun* a bank account, usually in Switzerland, which is referred to only by a number, the name of the person holding it being kept secret

numeral /'njuːm(ə)rəl/ *noun* a character or symbol which represents a number

numeric /njuː'merɪk/, **numerical** /njuː'merɪk(ə)l/ *adjective* referring to numbers

numerical order /njuː,merɪk(ə)l 'ɔːdə/ *noun* an arrangement by numbers ○ *Put these invoices in numerical order.*

numeric data /njuː,merɪk 'deɪtə/ *noun* data in the form of figures

numeric keypad /njuː,merɪk 'kiːpæd/ *noun* the part of a computer keyboard which is a programmable set of numbered keys

O

O & M *abbr* organisation and methods

OAP *abbr* old age pensioner

objective /əb'dʒektɪv/ *noun* something which you hope to achieve ○ *The company has achieved its objectives.* ○ *We set the sales forces specific objectives.* ○ *Our recruitment objectives are to have well-qualified and well-placed staff.*

objectivity /,ɒbdʒek'tɪvɪti/ *noun* a lack of any opinion or bias

obligation /,ɒblɪ'geɪʃ(ə)n/ *noun* **1.** a duty to do something ○ *There is no obligation to help out in another department* ○ *There is no obligation to buy.* □ **to fulfil your contractual obligations** to do what is stated in a contract **2.** a debt □ **to meet your obligations** to pay your debts

obsolescence /,ɒbsə'les(ə)ns/ *noun* the process of a product going out of date because of progress in design or technology, and therefore becoming less useful or valuable

obsolete /'ɒbsəliːt/ *adjective* no longer used ○ *Computer technology changes so fast that hardware soon becomes obsolete.*

occupational /,ɒkjʊ'peɪʃ(ə)nəl/ *adjective* referring to a job

occupational pension /,ɒkjʊpeɪʃ(ə)nəl 'penʃə/ *noun* a pension which is paid by the company by which an employee has been employed

occupational pension scheme /,ɒkjʊpeɪʃ(ə)nəl 'penʃən skiːm/ *noun* a pension scheme where the employee gets a pension from a fund set up by the company he or she has worked for, which is related to the salary he or she was earning. Also called **company pension scheme**

occupier /'ɒkjʊpaɪə/ *noun* a person who lives in a property

O/D *abbr* overdraft

odd lot /,ɒd 'lɒt/ *noun* **1.** a group of miscellaneous items for sale at an auction **2.** a group of miscellaneous items, such as a small block of shares

Oeic *abbr* open-ended investment company

off /ɒf/ *adverb* **1.** not working or not in operation ○ *to take three days off* ○ *The agreement is off.* ○ *They called the strike off.* ○ *We give the staff four days off at Christmas.* ○ *It's my day off tomorrow.* **2.** taken away from

a price ○ *We give 5% off for quick settlement.*
3. lower than a previous price ○ *The shares closed 2% off.* ■ *preposition* **1.** subtracted from ○ *to take £25 off the price* ○ *We give 10% off our usual prices.* **2.** not included □ **items off balance sheet** *or* **off balance sheet assets** financial items which do not appear in a company's balance sheet as assets, such as equipment acquired under an operating lease

'...its stock closed Monday at $21.875 a share in NYSE composite trading, off 56% from its high last July' [*Wall Street Journal*]

off-balance-sheet financing /ˌɒf ˌbæləns ʃiːt ˈfaɪnænsɪŋ/ *noun* financing by leasing equipment instead of buying it, so that it does not appear in the balance sheet as an asset

offer /ˈɒfə/ *noun* **1.** a statement that you are willing to give or do something, especially to pay a specific amount of money to buy something ○ *to make an offer for a company* ○ *We made an offer of £10 a share.* ○ *We made a written offer for the house.* ○ *£1,000 is the best offer I can make.* ○ *We accepted an offer of £1,000 for the car.* □ **or near offer** *US,* **or best offer** or an offer of a price which is slightly less than the price asked ○ *The car is for sale at £2,000 or near offer.* **2.** a statement that you are willing to sell something **3.** a statement that you are willing to employ someone □ **she received six offers of jobs** *or* **six job offers** six companies told her she could have a job with them **4.** a statement that a company is prepared to buy another company's shares and take the company over ■ *verb* **1.** to say that you are willing to pay a specific amount of money for something ○ *to offer someone £100,000 for their house* ○ *She offered £10 a share.* **2.** to say that you are willing to sell something ○ *We offered the house for sale.* ○ *They are offering special prices on winter holidays in the USA.*

offer document /ˈɒfə ˌdɒkjʊmənt/ *noun* a formal document where a company offers to buy shares at some price as part of a take-over bid

offer for sale /ˌɒfə fə ˈseɪl/ *noun* a situation where a company advertises new shares for sale to the public as a way of launching itself on the Stock Exchange (NOTE: The other ways of launching a company are a 'tender' or a 'placing.')

offering /ˈɒf(ə)rɪŋ/ *noun* an action of stating that you are prepared to sell something at some price

'...shares of newly public companies posted their worst performance of the year last month as a spate of initial public offerings disappointed followers' [*Wall Street Journal*]

'...if the partnership supports a sale, a public offering of shares would be set for as early as the fourth quarter' [*Wall Street Journal*]

offering circular /ˈɒf(ə)rɪŋ ˌsɜːkjʊlə/ *noun* a document which gives information about a company whose shares are being sold to the public for the first time

offeror /ˈɒfərə/ *noun* a person who makes an offer

offer period /ˈɒfə ˌpɪəriəd/ *noun* a time during which a takeover bid for a company is open

offer price /ˈɒfə praɪs/ *noun* the price at which investors buy new shares or units in a unit trust. The opposite, i.e. the selling price, is called the 'bid price', the difference between the two is the 'spread'.

office hours /ˌɒfɪs ˈaʊəz/ *plural noun* the time when an office is open ○ *Do not make private phone calls during office hours.*

Office of Fair Trading /ˌɒfɪs əv feə ˈtreɪdɪŋ/ *noun* a government department which protects consumers against unfair or illegal business. Abbreviation **OFT**

Office of Management and Budget /ˌɒfɪs əv ˌmænɪdʒmənt ən ˈbʌdʒɪt/ *noun* *US* a government department which prepares the US federal budget. Abbreviation **OMB**

Office of Thrift Supervision /ˌɒfɪs əv ˈθrɪft suːpəˌvɪʒ(ə)n/ *noun* a US government department which regulates the Savings and Loan Associations

officer /ˈɒfɪsə/ *noun* a person who has an official position, especially an unpaid one in a club or other association ○ *The election of officers takes place next week.*

official /əˈfɪʃ(ə)l/ *adjective* from a government department or organisation ○ *She went to France on official business.* ○ *He left official documents in his car.* ○ *She received an official letter of explanation.*

official books of account /əˌfɪʃ(ə)l bʊks əv əˈkaʊnt/ *noun* the official financial records of an institution

Official List /əˌfɪʃ(ə)l ˈlɪst/ *noun* a daily publication by the London Stock Exchange of the highest and lowest prices recorded for each share during the trading session

official receiver /əˌfɪʃ(ə)l rɪˈsiːvə/ *noun* a government official who is appointed to run a company which is in financial difficulties, to pay off its debts as far as possible and to close it down ○ *The company is in the hands of the official receiver.*

official return /əˌfɪʃ(ə)l rɪˈtɜːn/ *noun* an official report

off-line /ˌɒf ˈlaɪn/ *adverb* not connected to a network or central computer

offload /ɒfˈləʊd/ *verb* to pass something which you do not want to someone else

offset /ɒfˈset/ *verb* to balance one thing against another so that they cancel each other out ○ *to offset losses against tax* ○ *Foreign exchange losses more than offset profits in the domestic market.* (NOTE: **offsetting – offset**)

offshore /ˈɒfʃɔː/ *adjective, adverb* **1.** on an island or in the sea near to land ○ *an offshore oil field* ○ *an offshore oil platform* **2.** on an island which is a tax haven **3.** based outside a country, especially in a tax haven

offshore banking /ˌɒfʃɔː ˈbæŋkɪŋ/ *noun* banking in a tax haven

offshore finance subsidiary /ˌɒfʃɔː ˈfaɪnæns səbˌsɪdiəri/ *noun* a company created in another country to handle financial transactions, giving the owning company certain tax and legal advantages in its home country (NOTE: The US term is **offshore financial subsidiary.**)

offshore financial centre /ˌɒfʃɔː faɪˈnænʃəl/ *noun* a country or other political unit that has banking laws intended to attract business from industrialised nations

offshore fund /ˌɒf ʃɔː ˈfʌnd/ *noun* a fund which is based outside the UK, and usually in a country which has less strict taxation than in the UK, such as the Bahamas

off-the-job training /ˌɒf ðə dʒɒb ˈtreɪnɪŋ/ *noun* training given to employees away from their place of work, such as at a college or school

off-the-shelf company /ˌɒf ðə ˌʃelf ˈkʌmp(ə)ni/ *noun* a company which has already been registered by an accountant or lawyer, and which is ready for sale to someone who wants to set up a new company quickly

OFT *abbr* Office of Fair Trading

oil-exporting country /ˈɔɪl ɪkˌspɔːtɪŋ ˌkʌntri/ *noun* a country which produces oil and sells it to others

old age pension /ˌəʊld eɪdʒ ˈpenʃən/ *noun* a state pension given to people over some age (currently to a man who is 65 or to a woman who is 60)

old age pensioner /ˌəʊld eɪdʒ ˈpenʃ(ə)nə/ *noun* a person who receives the retirement pension. Abbreviation **OAP**

OMB *abbr* Office of Management and Budget

ombudsman /ˈɒmbʊdzmən/ *noun* a management employee who is given the freedom to move around the workplace to locate and remedy unfair practices (NOTE: plural is **ombudsmen**)

'…radical changes to the disciplinary system, including appointing an ombudsman to review cases where complainants are not satisfied with the outcome, are proposed in a consultative paper the Institute of Chartered Accountants issued last month' [*Accountancy*]

omission /əʊˈmɪʃ(ə)n/ *noun* a thing which has been omitted, or the act of omitting something

omit /əʊˈmɪt/ *verb* to leave something out, not to put something in ○ *Her assistant omitted the date when typing the contract.*

oncosts /ˈɒnkɒsts/ *plural noun* money spent in producing a product, which does not rise with the quantity of the product made. Also called **fixed costs**

on demand /ˌɒn dɪˈmɑːnd/ *adjective* used to describe an account from which withdrawals may be made without giving a period of notice

one-man business /ˌwʌn mæn ˈbɪznɪs/, **one-man firm** /ˌwʌn mæn ˈfɜːm/, **one-man company** /ˌwʌn mæn ˈkʌmp(ə)ni/ *noun* a business run by one person alone with no staff or partners

one-off /ˌwʌn ˈɒf/ *adjective* done or made only once ○ *one-off item* ○ *one-off deal* ○ *one-off payment*

one-sided /ˌwʌn ˈsaɪdɪd/ *adjective* favouring one side and not the other in a negotiation

one-year money /ˌwʌn jɪə ˈmʌni/ *noun* money placed for one year

online /ɒnˈlaɪn/, /ˈɒnlaɪn/ *adjective, adverb* linked via a computer directly to another computer, a computer network or, especially, the Internet; on the Internet ○ *The sales office is online to the warehouse.* ○ *We get our data online from the stock control department.*

'…there may be a silver lining for 'clicks-and-mortar' stores that have both an online and a high street presence. Many of these are accepting returns of goods purchased online at their traditional stores. This is a service that may make them more popular as consumers become more experienced online shoppers' [*Financial Times*]

'…a survey found that even among experienced users – those who shop online at least once a month – about 10% abandoned a planned purchase because of annoying online delays and procedures' [*Financial Times*]

'…some online brokers failed to foresee the huge increase in private dealing and had problems coping with the rising volume. It has been the year when private investors were able to trade online quickly, cheaply, and on the whole, with little bother' [*Financial Times*]

on-the-job training /ˌɒn ðə dʒɒb ˈtreɪnɪŋ/ *noun* training given to employees at their place of work

open /ˈəʊpən/ *adjective* **1.** at work, not closed ○ *The store is open on Sunday mornings.* ○ *Our offices are open from 9 to 6.* ○ *They are open for business every day of the week.* **2.** ready to accept something ■ *verb* **1.** to start a new business ○ *She has opened a shop in the High Street.* ○ *We have opened a branch in London.* **2.** to start work, to be at work ○ *The office opens at 9 a.m.* ○ *We open for business on Sundays.* **3.** to begin something **4.** to set something up or make something available ○ *to open a bank account* ○ *to open a line of credit* ○ *to open a loan* **5.** □ **shares opened lower** share prices were lower at the beginning of the day's trading

'…after opening at 79.1 the index touched a peak of 79.2 and then drifted to a low of 78.8' [*Financial Times*]

open account /ˌəʊpən əˈkaʊnt/ *noun* an account where the supplier offers the purchaser credit without security

open cheque /ˌəʊpən ˈtʃek/ *noun* same as **uncrossed cheque**

open credit /ˌəʊpən ˈkredɪt/ *noun* credit given to good customers without security

open-ended /ˌəʊpən ˈendɪd/ *adjective* with no fixed limit or with some items not specified ○ *They signed an open-ended agreement.* ○ *The candidate was offered an open-ended contract with a good career plan.* (NOTE: The US term is **open-end**.)

open-ended credit /ˌəʊpən ˌendɪd ˈkredɪt/ *noun* same as **revolving credit**

open-ended fund /ˌəʊpən ˈendɪd fʌnd/ *noun* a fund such as a unit trust where investors buy units, the money being invested in a range of securities. This is as opposed to a closed fund, such as an investment trust, where the investor buys shares in the trust company, and receives dividends.

Open-ended investment company /ˌəʊpən ˌendɪd ɪnˈvestmənt ˌkʌmp(ə)ni/ *noun* a new form of unit trust, in which the investor purchases shares at a single price, as opposed to the offer/bid pricing system used by ordinary unit trusts. Abbreviation **Oeic**

open-ended management company /ˌəʊpən ˌendɪd ˈmænɪdʒmənt ˌkʌmp(ə)ni/ *noun* a company that sells unit trusts (NOTE: The US term is **open-end management company**.)

opening /ˈəʊp(ə)nɪŋ/ *noun* the act of starting a new business ○ *the opening of a new branch* ○ *the opening of a new market* or *of a new distribution network*

opening balance /ˌəʊp(ə)nɪŋ ˈbæləns/ *noun* a balance at the beginning of an accounting period

opening balance sheet /ˌəʊp(ə)nɪŋ ˈbæləns ʃiːt/ *noun* an account showing an organisation's opening balances

opening bid /ˈəʊp(ə)nɪŋ bɪd/ *noun* the first bid at an auction

opening entry /ˈəʊp(ə)nɪŋ ˌentri/ *noun* the first entry in an account

opening price /ˈəʊp(ə)nɪŋ praɪs/ *noun* a price at the start of a day's trading

opening stock /ˈəʊp(ə)nɪŋ stɒk/ *noun* on a balance sheet, the closing stock at the end of one accounting period that is transferred forward and becomes the opening stock in the one that follows (NOTE: The US term is **beginning inventory**.)

open market /ˌəʊpən ˈmɑːkɪt/ *noun* a market where anyone can buy or sell

open-market value /ˌəʊpən ˈmɑːkɪt ˌvæljuː/ *noun* the price that an asset or security would realise if it was offered on a market open to all

operate /ˈɒpəreɪt/ *verb* to be in force ○ *The new terms of service will operate from January 1st.* ○ *The rules operate on inland postal services only.*

'…the company gets valuable restaurant locations which will be converted to the family-style restaurant chain that it operates and franchises throughout most parts of the US' [*Fortune*]

operating /ˈɒpəreɪtɪŋ/ *noun* the general running of a business or of a machine

'…the company blamed over-capacity and competitive market conditions in Europe for a £14m operating loss last year' [*Financial Times*]

operating budget /ˈɒpəreɪtɪŋ ˌbʌdʒɪt/ *noun* a forecast of income and expenditure over a period of time

operating costing /ˌɒpəreɪtɪŋ ˈkɒstɪŋ/ *noun* costing which is based on the costs of services provided

operating cycle /ˌɒpəreɪtɪŋ ˈsaɪk(ə)l/ *noun* the time it takes for purchases of materials for production to generate revenue from sales

operating lease /ˈɒpəreɪtɪŋ liːs/ *noun* a lease which does not require the lessee company to show the asset acquired under the lease in its balance sheet but the annual rental charge for such assets must be disclosed in a note to the accounts

operating leverage /ˌɒpəreɪtɪŋ ˈliːvərɪdʒ/ *noun* the ratio of a business's fixed costs to its total costs. As the fixed costs have to be paid regardless of output, the higher the ratio, the higher the risk of losses in an economic downturn.

operating manual /ˈɒpəreɪtɪŋ ˌmænjʊəl/ *noun* a book which shows how to work a machine

operating profit /ˈɒpəreɪtɪŋ ˌprɒfɪt/ *noun* the difference between a company's revenues and any related costs and expenses, not including income or expenses from any sources other than its normal methods of providing a good or a service

operating statement /ˈɒpəreɪtɪŋ ˌsteɪtmənt/ *noun* a financial statement which shows a company's expenditure and income and consequently its final profit or loss ○ *The operating statement shows unexpected electricity costs.* ○ *Let's look at the operating statement to find last month's expenditure.*

operating system /ˈɒpəreɪtɪŋ ˌsɪstəm/ *noun* the main program which operates a computer

operation /ˌɒpəˈreɪʃ(ə)n/ *noun* **1.** an activity or a piece of work, or the task of running something ○ *the company's operations in West Africa* ○ *He heads up the operations in Northern Europe.* **2.** □ **in operation** working or being used ○ *The system will be in operation by June.* ○ *The new system came into operation on January 1st.*

'…a leading manufacturer of business, industrial and commercial products requires a branch manager to head up its mid-western Canada operations based in Winnipeg' [*Globe and Mail (Toronto)*]

operational /ˌɒpəˈreɪʃ(ə)nəl/ *adjective* referring to the day-to-day activities of a business or to the way in which something is run

operational budget /ˌɒpəreɪʃ(ə)nəl ˈbʌdʒɪt/ *noun* a forecast of expenditure on running a business

operational costs /ˌɒpəreɪʃ(ə)nəl ˈkɒsts/ *plural noun* the costs of running a business

operational gearing /ˌɒpəreɪʃ(ə)nəl ˈɡɪərɪŋ/ *noun* a situation where a company has high fixed costs which are funded by borrowings

operational planning /ˌɒpəreɪʃ(ə)nəl ˈplænɪŋ/ *noun* the planning of how a business is to be run

operational research /ˌɒpəreɪʃ(ə)nəl rɪˈsɜːtʃ/ *noun* a study of a company's way of working to see if it can be made more efficient and profitable

operations review /ˌɒpəreɪʃ(ə)nz rɪˈvjuː/ *noun* an act of examining the way in which a company or department works to see

how it can be made more efficient and profitable

operation time /ˌɒpəˈreɪʃ(ə)n taɪm/ *noun* a period of time that an operation requires for its operation cycle

operator /ˈɒpəreɪtə/ *noun* **1.** a person who works a machine ○ *a keyboard operator* ○ *a computer operator* **2.** a person who runs a business

'…a number of block bookings by American tour operators have been cancelled' [*Economist*]

opportunity cost /ˌɒpəˈtjuːnɪti kɒst/ *noun* **1.** the cost of a business initiative in terms of profits that could have been gained through an alternative plan ○ *It's a good investment plan and we will not be deterred by the opportunity cost.* **2.** the value of another method of investment which could have been used, instead of the one adopted

oppose /əˈpəʊz/ *verb* to try to stop something happening; to vote against something ○ *A minority of board members opposed the motion.* ○ *We are all opposed to the takeover.*

optimal /ˈɒptɪm(ə)l/ *adjective* best

optimise /ˈɒptɪmaɪz/ *noun* to allocate such things as resources or capital as efficiently as possible

optimum /ˈɒptɪməm/ *adjective* best ○ *The market offers optimum conditions for sales.*

option /ˈɒpʃən/ *noun* the opportunity to buy or sell something within a fixed period of time at a fixed price □ **to take up an option** *or* **to exercise an option** to accept the option which has been offered and to put it into action ○ *They exercised their option or they took up their option to acquire sole marketing rights to the product.*

optional /ˈɒpʃ(ə)nəl/ *adjective* able to be done or not done, taken or not taken, as a person chooses ○ *The insurance cover is optional.* ○ *Attendance at staff meetings is optional, although the management encourages employees to attend.*

option contract /ˈɒpʃən ˌkɒntrækt/ *noun* a right to buy or sell shares at a fixed price

option dealing /ˈɒpʃən ˌdiːlɪŋ/ *noun* the activity of buying and selling share options

option trading /ˈɒpʃ(ə)n ˌtreɪdɪŋ/ *noun* the business of buying and selling share options

order /ˈɔːdə/ *noun* **1.** the way in which records such as filing cards or invoices are arranged ○ *in alphabetical or numerical order* **2.** an official request for goods to be supplied ○ *to give someone an order* or *to place an order with someone for twenty filing cabinets* ○ *The management ordered the workforce to* *leave the factory.* □ **to fill an order, to fulfil an order** to supply items which have been ordered ○ *We are so understaffed we cannot fulfil any more orders before Christmas.* □ **items available to order only** items which will be manufactured only if someone orders them □ **on order** ordered but not delivered ○ *This item is out of stock, but is on order.* **3.** a document which allows money to be paid to someone ○ *She sent us an order on the Chartered Bank.* **4.** (*Stock Exchange*) an instruction to a broker to buy or sell **5.** □ **pay to Mr Smith or order** pay money to Mr Smith or as he orders □ **pay to the order of Mr Smith** pay money directly to Mr Smith or to his account ■ *verb* to ask for goods to be supplied ○ *They ordered a new Rolls Royce for the managing director.*

order book /'ɔːdə bʊk/ *noun* a book which records orders received

order fulfilment /'ɔːdə fʊl,fɪlmənt/ *noun* the process of supplying items which have been ordered

order processing /'ɔːdə ,prəʊsesɪŋ/ *noun* the work of dealing with orders

ordinarily resident /,ɔːd(ə)n(ə)rɪli 'rezɪd(ə)nt/ *adjective* normally living in a country ○ *Mr Schmidt is ordinarily resident in Canada*

ordinary activities /,ɔːd(ə)n(ə)ri æk'tɪvɪtiz/ *noun* the usual trading of a company, that is, what the company usually does

ordinary interest /,ɔːd(ə)n(ə)ri 'ɪntrəst/ *noun* annual interest calculated on the basis of 360 days, as opposed to 'exact interest' which is calculated on 365 days

ordinary resolution /,ɔːd(ə)n(ə)ri ,rezə'luːʃ(ə)n/ *noun* a resolution put before an AGM, usually referring to some general procedural matter, and which requires a simple majority of votes to be accepted

ordinary share capital /,ɔːd(ə)n(ə)ri 'ʃeə ,kæpɪt(ə)l/ *noun* the capital of a company in the form of money paid for ordinary shares

ordinary shareholder /,ɔːd(ə)n(ə)ri 'ʃeəhəʊldə/ *noun* a person who owns ordinary shares in a company

ordinary shares /'ɔːd(ə)n(ə)ri ʃeəz/ *plural noun* normal shares in a company, which have no special benefits or restrictions (NOTE: The US term is **common stock.**)

organic growth /ɔː,gænɪk 'grəʊθ/ *noun* same as **internal growth**

organisation /,ɔːgənaɪ'zeɪʃ(ə)n/, **organization** *noun* **1.** a way of arranging something so that it works efficiently ○ *the organ-*

isation of the head office into departments ○ *The chairman handles the organisation of the AGM.* ○ *The organisation of the group is too centralised to be efficient.* **2.** a group or institution which is arranged for efficient work

'...working with a client base which includes many major commercial organizations and nationalized industries' [*Times*]

organisational /,ɔːgənaɪ'zeɪʃ(ə)n)l/, **organizational** *adjective* referring to the way in which something is organised ○ *The paper gives a diagram of the company's organisational structure.*

organisation and methods /,ɔːgənaɪzeɪʃ(ə)n ən 'meθədz/ *noun* a process of examining how an office works, and suggesting how it can be made more efficient. Abbreviation **O & M**

organise /'ɔːgənaɪz/, **organize** *verb* **1.** to set up a system for doing something ○ *The company is organised into six profit centres.* ○ *The group is organised by sales areas.* **2.** to arrange something so that it works

'...we organize a rate with importers who have large orders and guarantee them space at a fixed rate so that they can plan their costs' [*Lloyd's List*]

other capital /,ʌðə 'kæpɪt(ə)l/ *noun* capital that is not listed in specific categories

other long-term capital /,ʌθə ,lɒŋ tɜːm 'kæpɪt(ə)l/ *noun* long-term capital that is not listed in specific categories

other long-term liabilities /,ʌθə ,lɒŋ tɜːm ,laɪə'bɪlɪtiz/ *noun* obligations with terms greater than one year on which there is no charge for interest in the next year

other short-term capital /,ʌθə ,ʃɔːt tɜːm 'kæpɪt(ə)l/ *noun* short-term capital that is not listed in specific categories

out /aʊt/ *adverb* □ **we are £20,000 out in our calculations** we have £20,000 too much or too little

outgoings /'aʊtgəʊɪŋz/ *plural noun* money which is paid out

outlay /'aʊtleɪ/ *noun* money spent, expenditure

outlook /'aʊtlʊk/ *noun* a view of what is going to happen in the future ○ *The economic outlook is not good.* ○ *The stock market outlook is worrying.*

'American demand has transformed the profit outlook for many European manufacturers' [*Duns Business Month*]

out-of-date cheque /,aʊt əv deɪt 'tʃek/ *noun* a cheque which has not been cleared because its date is too old, normally more than six months

out of pocket /,aʊt əv 'pɒkɪt/ *adjective, adverb* having paid out money personally ○ *The deal has left me out of pocket.*

out-of-pocket expenses /ˌaʊt əv ˌpɒkɪt ɪkˈspensɪz/ *plural noun* an amount of money paid back to an employee who has spent his or her personal money on company business

output /ˈaʊtpʊt/ *noun* **1.** the amount which a company, person or machine produces ○ *Output has increased by 10%.* ○ *25% of our output is exported.* **2.** information which is produced by a computer

'...crude oil output plunged during the last month and is likely to remain near its present level for the near future' [*Wall Street Journal*]

output per hour /ˌaʊtpʊt pər ˈaʊə/ *noun* the amount of something produced in one hour

output tax /ˈaʊtpʊt tæks/ *noun* VAT charged by a company on goods or services sold, and which the company pays to the government

outright /ˌaʊtˈraɪt/ *adverb, adjective* completely

outside /ˈaʊtsaɪd/ *adjective, adverb* not in a company's office or building

outsource /ˈaʊtˌsɔːs/ *verb* to use a source outside a company or business to do the work that is needed

outsourcing /ˈaʊtsɔːsɪŋ/ *noun* the practice of obtaining services from specialist bureaux or other companies, rather than employing full-time members of staff to provide them

'...organizations in the public and private sectors are increasingly buying in specialist services – or outsourcing – allowing them to cut costs and concentrate on their core business activities' [*Financial Times*]

outstanding /aʊtˈstændɪŋ/ *adjective* not yet paid or completed

outstanding cheque /aʊtˌstændɪŋ ˈtʃek/ *noun* a cheque which has been written and therefore has been entered in the company's ledgers, but which has not been presented for payment and so has not been debited from the company's bank account

outvote /aʊtˈvəʊt/ *verb* to defeat someone in a vote

overabsorbed overhead /ˌaʊvərəbzɔːbd ˈaʊvəhed/ *noun* an absorbed overhead which ends up by being higher than the actual overhead incurred

overabsorption /ˌaʊvərəbˈzɔːpʃ(ə)n/ *noun* a situation where the actual overhead incurred is less than the absorbed overhead

overall /ˌaʊvərˈɔːl/ *adjective* covering or including everything □ **the company reported an overall fall in profits** the company reported a general fall in profits

overall balance of payments /ˌaʊvərɔːl ˌbæləns əv ˈpeɪmənts/ *noun* the total of current and long-term balance of payments

overall capitalisation rate /ˌaʊvərɔːl ˌkæpɪt(ə)laɪˈzeɪʃ(ə)n ˌreɪt/ *noun* net operating income, other than debt service, divided by value

overall return /ˌaʊvərɔːl rɪˈtɜːn/ *noun* the aggregate of all the dividends received over an investment's life together with its capital gain or loss at the date of its realisation, calculated either before or after tax. It is one of the ways an investor can look at the performance of an investment.

overborrowed /ˌaʊvəˈbɒrəʊd/ *adjective* referring to a company which has very high borrowings compared to its assets, and has difficulty in meeting its interest payments

overcapitalised /ˌaʊvəˈkæpɪtəlaɪzd/, **overcapitalized** *adjective* referring to a company with more capital than it needs

overcharge *noun* /ˈaʊvətʃɑːdʒ/ a charge which is higher than it should be ○ *to pay back an overcharge* ■ *verb* /ˌaʊvəˈtʃɑːdʒ/ to ask someone for too much money ○ *They overcharged us for our meals.* ○ *We asked for a refund because we'd been overcharged.*

overdraft /ˈaʊvədrɑːft/ *noun* **1.** an amount of money which a company or person can withdraw from a bank account, with the bank's permission, despite the fact that the account is empty ○ *The bank has allowed me an overdraft of £5,000.* Abbreviation **O/D** (NOTE: The US term is **overdraft protection.**) □ **we have exceeded our overdraft facilities** we have taken out more than the overdraft allowed by the bank **2.** *US* a negative amount of money in an account, i.e. a situation where a cheque is more than the money in the account on which it is drawn

overdraw /ˌaʊvəˈdrɔː/ *verb* to take out more money from a bank account than there is in it

overdue /ˌaʊvəˈdjuː/ *adjective* having not been paid on time

overdue account /ˌaʊvədjuː əˈkaʊnt/ *noun* an account whose holder owes money that should have been paid earlier

overestimate /ˌaʊvərˈestɪmeɪt/ *verb* to think something is larger or worse than it really is ○ *She overestimated the amount of time needed to fit out the factory.* ○ *They overestimated the costs of moving the offices to central London.*

overgeared /ˌaʊvəˈɡɪərd/ *adjective* referring to a company which has high borrowings in comparison to its assets

overhang /ˈəʊvəhæŋ/ *noun* a large quantity of shares or of a commodity or of unsold stock available for sale, which has the effect of depressing the market price

overhead absorption rate /ˌəʊvəhed əbˈzɔːpʃən reɪt/ *noun* a rate at which production costs are increased to absorb higher overhead costs

overhead budget /ˌəʊvəhed ˈbʌdʒɪt/ *noun* a plan of probable overhead costs

overhead costs /ˌəʊvəhed ˈkɒsts/, **overhead expenses** /ˌəʊvəhed ɪkˈspensɪz/ *plural noun* same as **overheads**

overhead cost variance /ˌəʊvəhed kɒst ˈveəriəns/ *noun* the difference between the overhead cost absorbed and the actual overhead costs incurred, both fixed and variable

overhead expenditure variance /ˌəʊvəhed ɪkˈspendɪtʃə ˌveəriəns/ *noun* the difference between the budgeted overhead costs and the actual expenditure

overheads /ˈəʊvəhedz/ *plural noun* the indirect costs of the day-to-day running of a business, i.e. not money spent of producing goods, but money spent on such things as renting or maintaining buildings and machinery ○ *The sales revenue covers the manufacturing costs but not the overheads.* (NOTE: The usual US term is **overhead**.)

overlap profit /ˌəʊvəlæp ˈprɒfɪt/ *noun* a profit which occurs in two accounting periods, i.e. when two accounting periods overlap, and on which overlap relief can be claimed

overpaid /ˌəʊvəˈpeɪd/ *adjective* paid too much ○ *Our staff are overpaid and underworked.*

overpay /ˌəʊvəˈpeɪ/ *verb* to pay too much to someone or for something ○ *We overpaid the invoice by $245.*

overpayment /ˌəʊvəˈpeɪmənt/ *noun* an act of paying too much

overrider /ˈəʊvəraɪdə/, **overriding commission** /ˈəʊvəraɪdɪŋ kəˌmɪʃ(ə)n/ *noun* a special extra commission which is above all other commissions

overseas /ˌəʊvəˈsiːz/ *noun* foreign countries ○ *The profits from overseas are far higher than those of the home division.*

overseas division /ˌəʊvəsiːz dɪˈvɪʒ(ə)n/ *noun* the section of a company dealing with trade with other countries

overseas funds /ˌəʊvəˈsiːz fʌndz/ *plural noun* investment funds based in other countries

overseas markets /ˌəʊvəsiːz ˈmɑːkɪts/ *plural noun* markets in foreign countries

overseas taxation /ˌəʊvəsiːz tækˈseɪʃ(ə)n/ *noun* ♦ **double taxation, double taxation agreement**

overseas trade /ˌəʊvəsiːz ˈtreɪd/ *noun* same as **foreign trade**

overspend /ˌəʊvəˈspend/ *verb* to spend too much □ **to overspend your budget** to spend more money than is allowed in your budget

overspending /ˌəʊvəˈspendɪŋ/ *noun* the act of spending more than is allowed ○ *The board decided to limit the overspending by the production departments.*

overstate /ˌəʊvəˈsteɪt/ *verb* to make something seem more than it really is ○ *the company accounts overstate the real profit*

overstatement /ˌəʊvəˈsteɪtmənt/ *noun* making something seem more than it really is

overstock /ˌəʊvəˈstɒk/ *verb* to have a bigger stock of something than is needed

'Cash paid for your stock: any quantity, any products, overstocked lines, factory seconds' [*Australian Financial Review*]

overstocks /ˈəʊvəstɒks/ *plural noun US* more stock than is needed to supply orders ○ *We will have to sell off the overstocks to make room in the warehouse.*

over-the-counter market /ˌəʊvə ðə ˈkaʊntə ˌmɑːkɪt/ *noun* a secondary market in shares which are not listed on the main Stock Exchange

over-the-counter sales /ˌəʊvə ðə ˈkaʊntə ˌseɪlz/ *plural noun* the legal selling of shares which are not listed in the official Stock Exchange list, usually carried out by telephone

overtime /ˈəʊvətaɪm/ *noun* hours worked in addition to your usual working hours ○ *to work six hours' overtime* ○ *The overtime rate is one and a half times normal pay.*

overtime pay /ˈəʊvətaɪm peɪ/ *noun* pay for extra time worked

overtrading /ˌəʊvəˈtreɪdɪŋ/ *noun* a situation where a company increases sales and production too much and too quickly, so that it runs short of cash

overvalue /ˌəʊvəˈvæljuː/ *verb* to give a higher value to something or someone than is right □ **these shares are overvalued at £1.25** the shares are worth less than the £1.25 for which they are selling

'…the fact that sterling has been overvalued for the past three years shows that currencies can remain above their fair value for very long periods' [*Investors Chronicle*]

owe /əʊ/ *verb* to have to pay money ○ *He owes the bank £250,000.* □ **they still owe the company for the stock they purchased last year** they have still not paid for the stock

owing /ˈəʊɪŋ/ *adjective* owed ○ *money owing to the directors* ○ *How much is still owing to the company by its debtors?*

own /əʊn/ *verb* to have or to possess ○ *She owns 50% of the shares.*

owner-occupier /ˌəʊnər ˈɒkjʊpaɪə/ *noun* a person who owns the property in which he or she lives

owners' equity /ˌəʊnəz ˈekwɪti/ *noun* a value of the shares in a company owned by the owners of the company

ownership /ˈəʊnəʃɪp/ *noun* the fact of owning something

P

package /ˈpækɪdʒ/ *noun* goods packed and wrapped for sending by mail ○ *The Post Office does not accept bulky packages.* ○ *The goods are to be sent in airtight packages.*

package deal /ˌpækɪdʒ ˈdiːl/ *noun* an agreement which deals with several different items at the same time ○ *They agreed a package deal which involves the construction of the factory, training of staff and purchase of the product.*

paid /peɪd/ *adjective* **1.** for which money has been given ○ *The invoice is marked 'paid'.* **2.** referring to an amount which has been settled ○ *The order was sent carriage paid.*

paid assistant /ˌpeɪd əˈsɪst(ə)nt/ *noun* an assistant who receives a salary

paid-up shares /ˌpeɪd ʌp ˈʃeəz/ *noun* shares which have been completely paid for by the shareholders

panic buying /ˈpænɪk ˌbaɪɪŋ/ *noun* a rush to buy something at any price because stocks may run out

paper /ˈpeɪpə/ *noun* **1.** a document which can represent money, e.g. a bill of exchange or a promissory note **2.** shares in the form of share certificates

paper loss /ˌpeɪpə ˈlɒs/ *noun* a loss made when an asset has fallen in value but has not been sold

paper millionaire /ˌpeɪpə ˌmɪljəˈneə/ *noun* a person who owns shares which, if sold, would be worth one million pounds or dollars

paper money /ˌpeɪpə ˈmʌni/ *noun* payments in paper form, e.g., cheques

paper offer /ˌpeɪpə ˈɒfə/ *noun* a takeover bid, where the purchasing company offers its shares in exchange for shares in the company being taken over as opposed to a cash offer

paper profit /ˌpeɪpə ˈprɒfɪt/ *noun* a profit on an asset which has increased in price but has not been sold ○ *He is showing a paper profit of £25,000 on his investment.* Also called **paper gain, unrealised profit**

paperwork /ˈpeɪpəwɜːk/ *noun* an office work, especially writing memos and filling in forms ○ *Exporting to Russia involves a large amount of paperwork.*

par /pɑː/ *adjective* equal, at the same price

parameter /pəˈræmɪtə/ *noun* a fixed limit ○ *The budget parameters are fixed by the finance director.* ○ *Spending by each department has to fall within agreed parameters.*

parcel of shares /ˌpɑːs(ə)l əv ˈʃeəz/ *noun* a fixed number of shares which are sold as a group ○ *The shares are on offer in parcels of 50.*

parent company /ˈpeərənt ˌkʌmp(ə)ni/ *noun* a company which owns more than 50% of the shares of another company

Pareto's Law /pəˈriːtəʊz lɔː/, **Pareto Effect** /pəˈriːtəʊ ɪˌfekt/ *noun* the theory that incomes are distributed in the same way in all countries, whatever tax regime is in force, and that a small percentage of a total is responsible for a large proportion of value or resources. Also called **eighty/twenty law**

pari passu /ˌpæri ˈpæsuː/ *adverb* a Latin phrase meaning 'equally' ○ *The new shares will rank pari passu with the existing ones.*

parity /ˈpærɪti/ *noun* **1.** the state of being equal □ **the pound fell to parity with the dollar** the pound fell to a point where one pound equalled one dollar **2.** a situation when the price of a commodity, foreign currency, or security is the same in different markets

'…the draft report on changes in the international monetary system casts doubt about any return to fixed exchange-rate parities' [*Wall Street Journal*]

part exchange /ˌpɑːt ɪksˈtʃeɪndʒ/ *noun* the act of giving an old product as part of the payment for a new one ○ *to take a car in part exchange*

partial /ˈpɑːʃ(ə)l/ *adjective* not complete

participate /pɑːˈtɪsɪpeɪt/ *verb* to take part in an activity or enterprise ○ *The staff are encouraged to participate actively in the company's decision-making processes.*

participating preference shares /pɑːˌtɪsɪpeɪtɪŋ ˈpref(ə)rəns ʃeəz/, **participating preferred stock** /pɑːˌtɪsɪpeɪtɪŋ prɪˌfɜːd ˈstɒk/ *plural noun* preference shares which get an extra bonus dividend if company profits reach a high level

participative budgeting /pɑːˌtɪsɪpətɪv ˈbʌdʒɪtɪŋ/ *noun* a budgeting system in which all budget holders are given the opportunity to participate in setting their own budgets. Also called **bottom-up budgeting**

partly /ˈpɑːtli/ *adverb* not completely

partly-paid capital /ˌpɑːt(ə)li peɪd ˈkæpɪt(ə)l/ *noun* a capital which represents partly-paid shares

partly-paid up shares /ˌpɑːt(ə)li peɪd ʌp ˈʃeəz/, **partly-paid shares** /ˌpɑːt(ə)li peɪd ˈʃeəz/ *plural noun* shares where the shareholders have not paid the full face value

partner /ˈpɑːtnə/ *noun* a person who works in a business and has an equal share in it with other partners ○ *I became a partner in a firm of solicitors.*

partnership /ˈpɑːtnəʃɪp/ *noun* an unregistered business where two or more people (but not more than twenty) share the risks and profits according to a partnership agreement ○ *to go into partnership with someone* ○ *to join with someone to form a partnership*

partnership accounts /ˌpɑːtnəʃɪp əˈkaʊnts/ *noun* the capital and current accounts of each partner in a partnership, or the accounts recording the partnership's business activities

partnership agreement /ˈpɑːtnəʃɪp əˈgriːmənt/ *noun* a document setting up a partnership, giving the details of the business and the amount each partner is contributing to it. Also called **articles of partnership**

part-owner /ˌpɑːt ˈəʊnə/ *noun* a person who owns something jointly with one or more other people ○ *I am part-owner of the restaurant.*

part-ownership /ˌpɑːt ˈəʊnəʃɪp/ *noun* a situation where two or more persons own the same property

part payment /ˌpɑːt ˈpeɪmənt/ *noun* the paying of part of a whole payment ○ *I gave him £250 as part payment for the car.*

part-time /ˌpɑːt ˈtaɪm/ *adjective, adverb* not working for the whole working week ○ *a part-time employee* ○ *It is a part-time job that* ○ *We are looking for part-time staff to work our computers.* ○ *She only works part-time as she has small children to look after.*

party /ˈpɑːti/ *noun* a person or organisation involved in a legal dispute or legal agreement ○ *How many parties are there to the contract?* ○ *The company is not a party to the agreement.*

par value /pɑː ˈvæljuː/ *noun* same as **face value**

passbook /ˈpɑːsbʊk/ *noun* same as **bank book**

'…instead of customers having transactions recorded in their passbooks, they will present plastic cards and have the transactions printed out on a receipt' [*Australian Financial Review*]

patent /ˈpeɪtənt, ˈpætənt/ *noun* an official document showing that a person has the exclusive right to make and sell an invention ○ *to take out a patent for a new type of light bulb* ○ *to apply for a patent for a new invention* □ **'patent applied for'**, **'patent pending'** words on a product showing that the inventor has applied for a patent for it

patent agent /ˈpeɪtənt ˌeɪdʒənt/ *noun* a person who advises on patents and applies for patents on behalf of clients

patent office /ˈpeɪtənt ˌɒfɪs/ *noun* a government office which grants patents and supervises them

patent rights /ˈpeɪtənt raɪts/ *plural noun* the rights which an inventor holds because of a patent

pawnbroker /ˈpɔːnbrəʊkə/ *noun* a person who lends money against the security of valuable objects

pawnshop /ˈpɔːnʃɒp/ *noun* a pawnbroker's shop

pawn ticket /ˈpɔːn ˌtɪkɪt/ *noun* a receipt given by the pawnbroker for an object left in pawn

pay /peɪ/ *noun* a salary or wages, money given to someone for regular work ■ *verb* **1.** to give money to buy an item or a service ○ *to pay £1,000 for a car* ○ *How much did you pay to have the office cleaned?* (NOTE: **paying – paid**) □ **'pay cash'** words written on a crossed cheque to show that it can be paid in cash if necessary **2.** to produce or distribute money (NOTE: **paying – paid**) **3.** to give an employee money for work done ○ *The workforce has not been paid for three weeks.* ○ *We pay good wages for skilled workers.* ○ *How much do they pay you per hour?* (NOTE: **paying – paid**) □ **to be paid at piecework rates** to get money for each piece of work finished **4.** to give money which is owed or which has to be paid ○ *He was late paying the bill.* ○ *We phoned to ask when they were going to pay the invoice.* ○ *You will have to pay duty on these imports.* ○ *She pays tax at the highest rate.* (NOTE: **paying – paid**) □ **please pay the sum of £10** please give £10 in cash or by cheque

'…recession encourages communication not because it makes redundancies easier, but because it makes low or zero pay increases easier to accept' [*Economist*]

'…the yield figure means that if you buy the shares at their current price you will be getting 5% before tax on your money if the company pays the same dividend as in its last financial year' [*Investors Chronicle*]

payable /ˈpeɪəb(ə)l/ *adjective* due to be paid

payable to order /ˌpeɪəb(ə)l tə ˈɔːdə/ *adjective* words written on a bill of exchange or cheque to indicate that it may be transferred

pay back /ˌpeɪ ˈbæk/ *verb* to give money back to someone ○ *Banks are warning students not to take out loans which they cannot pay back.* ○ *I lent him £50 and he promised to pay me back in a month.* ○ *She has never paid me back the money she borrowed.* ■ *noun* the time required for the cash inflows from a capital investment project to equal the cash outflows

payback /ˈpeɪbæk/ *noun* the act of paying back money which has been borrowed

payback clause /ˈpeɪbæk klɔːz/ *noun* a clause in a contract which states the terms for repaying a loan

payback period /ˈpeɪbæk ˌpɪəriəd/ *noun* **1.** a period of time over which a loan is to be repaid or an investment is to pay for itself **2.** the length of time it will take to earn back the money invested in a project

pay day /ˈpeɪ deɪ/ *noun* a day on which wages are paid to employees, usually Friday for employees paid once a week and during the last week of the month for employees who are paid once a month

pay desk /ˈpeɪ desk/ *noun* a place in a store where you pay for goods bought

paydown /ˈpeɪdaʊn/ *noun* a repayment of part of a sum which has been borrowed

payee /peɪˈiː/ *noun* a person who receives money from someone, or the person whose name is on a cheque

payer /ˈpeɪə/ *noun* a person who gives money to someone

pay hike /ˈpeɪ haɪk/ *noun* an increase in salary

paying /ˈpeɪɪŋ/ *adjective* **1.** making a profit ○ *It is a paying business.* **2.** producing money, source of money ■ *noun* the act of giving money

paying agent /ˈpeɪɪŋ ˌeɪdʒənt/ *noun* a bank which pays dividend or interest to a bondholder

paying-in book /ˌpeɪɪŋ ˈɪn bʊk/ *noun* a book of forms for paying money into a bank account or a building society account

paying-in slip /ˌpeɪɪŋ ˈɪn slɪp/ *noun* a printed form which is filled in when money is being deposited in a bank

paymaster /ˈpeɪmɑːstə/ *noun* the person responsible for paying an organisation's employees

payment /ˈpeɪmənt/ *noun* **1.** the act of giving money in exchange for goods or a service ○ *We always ask for payment in cash* or *cash payment and not payment by cheque.* ○ *The payment of interest* or *the interest payment should be made on the 22nd of each month.* **2.** money paid

payment terms /ˈpeɪmənt tɜːmz/ *plural noun* the conditions laid down by a business regarding when it should be paid for goods or services that it supplies, e.g. cash with order, payment on delivery or payment within a particular number of days of the invoice date

pay negotiations /ˈpeɪ nɪɡəʊʃ ˌeɪʃ(ə)nz/, **pay talks** /ˈpeɪ tɔːks/ *plural noun* discussions between management and employees about pay increases

pay off /ˌpeɪ ˈɒf/ *verb* **1.** to finish paying money which is owed for something ○ *He won the lottery and paid off his mortgage.* ○ *She is trying to pay off the loan by monthly instalments.* **2.** to terminate somebody's employment and pay all wages that are due ○

When the company was taken over the factory was closed and all the employees were paid off.

payoff /ˈpeɪɒf/ *noun* money paid to finish paying something which is owed, such as money paid to an employee when his or her employment is terminated

'...the finance director of the group is to receive a payoff of about £300,000 after deciding to leave the company and pursue other business opportunities' [*Times*]

pay out /ˌpeɪ ˈaʊt/ *verb* to give money ○ *The company pays out thousands of pounds in legal fees.* ○ *We have paid out half our profits in dividends.*

payout /ˈpeɪaʊt/ *noun* money paid to help a company or person in difficulties, a subsidy ○ *The company only exists on payouts from the government.*

'...after a period of recession followed by a rapid boost in incomes, many tax payers embarked upon some tax planning to minimize their payouts' [*Australian Financial Review*]

pay packet /ˈpeɪ ˌpækɪt/ *noun* an envelope containing the pay slip and the cash pay

pay rise /ˈpeɪ raɪz/ *noun* an increase in pay

payroll /ˈpeɪrəʊl/ *noun* the list of people employed and paid by a company ○ *The company has 250 on the payroll.*

payroll giving scheme /ˌpeɪrəʊl ˈgɪvɪŋ ˌskiːm/ *noun* a scheme by which an employee pays money to a charity directly out of his or her salary. The money is deducted by the employer and paid to the charity; the employee gets tax relief on such donations.

payroll ledger /ˈpeɪrəʊl ˌledʒə/ *noun* a list of staff and their salaries

payroll tax /ˈpeɪrəʊl tæks/ *noun* a tax on the people employed by a company

pay scale /ˈpeɪ skeɪl/ *noun* a hierarchy of wage levels, typically varying according to job title, salary or length of service. Also called **salary scale, wage scale**

pay threshold /ˈpeɪ ˌθreʃhəʊld/ *noun* a point at which pay increases because of a threshold agreement

pay up /ˌpeɪ ˈʌp/ *verb* to give money which is owed ○ *The company only paid up when we sent them a letter from our solicitor.* ○ *She finally paid up six months late.*

PBIT *abbr* profit before interest and tax

P/C *abbr* petty cash

P/E *abbr* price/earnings

pecuniary /pɪˈkjuːniəri/ *adjective* referring to money

peg /peg/ *verb* to maintain or fix something at a specific level

penalise /ˈpiːnəlaɪz/, **penalize** *verb* to punish or fine someone ○ *to penalise a supplier for late deliveries* ○ *They were penalised for bad time-keeping.*

penalty /ˈpen(ə)lti/ *noun* **1.** a punishment, often a fine, which is imposed if something is not done or is done incorrectly or illegally **2.** an arbitrary pre-arranged sum that becomes payable if one party breaks a term of a contract or an undertaking. The most common penalty is a high rate of interest on an unauthorised overdraft.

pension /ˈpenʃən/ *noun* money paid regularly to someone who no longer works

pensionable /ˈpenʃənəb(ə)l/ *adjective* able to receive a pension

pensionable earnings /ˌpenʃənəb(ə)l ˈɜːnɪŋz/ *plural noun* earnings being received at the moment of retirement, on which the pension is calculated

pension contributions /ˈpenʃən kɒntrɪˌbjuːʃ(ə)nz/ *plural noun* money paid by a company or employee into a pension fund

pension entitlement /ˈpenʃən ɪnˌtaɪt(ə)lmənt/ *noun* the amount of pension which someone has the right to receive when he or she retires

pensioner /ˈpenʃənə/ *noun* a person who receives a pension

pension fund /ˈpenʃən fʌnd/ *noun* a large sum of money made up of contributions from employees and their employer which provides pensions for retired employees

pension funds /ˈpenʃ(ə)n fʌndz/ *plural noun* investments managed by pension companies to produce pensions for investors

pension income /ˌpenʃən ˈɪnkʌm/ *noun* income which you receive from a pension scheme

pension plan /ˈpenʃən plæn/, **pension scheme** /ˈpenʃən skiːm/ *noun* a plan worked out by an insurance company which arranges for employees to pay part of their salary over many years and receive a regular payment when they retire

PEP *abbr* Personal Equity Plan

per /pɜː, pə/ *preposition* **1.** □ **as per** according to **2.** for each □ **we pay £10 per hour** we pay £10 for each hour worked □ **the earnings per share** the dividend received for each share □ **the average sales per representative** the average sales achieved by one representative

'...a 100,000 square-foot warehouse generates $600 in sales per square foot of space' [*Duns Business Month*]

PER *abbr* price/earnings ratio

per annum /pər ˈænəm/ adverb in a year ○ What is their turnover per annum? ○ What is his total income per annum? ○ She earns over £100,000 per annum.

per capita /pə ˈkæpɪtə/ adjective, adverb for each person

per capita income /pə ˌkæpɪtə ˈɪnkʌm/ noun **1.** the average income of one person. Also called **income per capita, income per head 2.** the average income of each member of a particular group of people, e.g., the citizens of a country

per cent /pə ˈsent/ adjective, adverb out of each hundred, or for each hundred

'…this would represent an 18 per cent growth rate – a slight slackening of the 25 per cent turnover rise in the first half' [Financial Times]

'…buildings are depreciated at two per cent per annum on the estimated cost of construction' [Hongkong Standard]

percentage /pəˈsentɪdʒ/ noun an amount shown as part of one hundred

'…state-owned banks cut their prime rates a percentage point to 11%' [Wall Street Journal]

'…a good percentage of the excess stock was taken up during the last quarter' [Australian Financial Review]

'…the Federal Reserve Board, signalling its concern about the weakening American economy, cut the discount rate by one-half percentage point to 6.5%' [Wall Street Journal]

percentage discount /pəˌsentɪdʒ dɪs ˈkaʊnt/ noun a discount calculated at an amount per hundred

percentage increase /pəˌsentɪdʒ ˈɪnkriːs/ noun an increase calculated on the basis of a rate for one hundred

percentage point /pəˈsentɪdʒ pɔɪnt/ noun 1 per cent

percentile /pəˈsentaɪl/ noun one of a series of ninety-nine figures below which a percentage of the total falls

per day /pə ˈdeɪ/, **per diem** /pə ˈdiːem/ adverb for each day

perform /pəˈfɔːm/ verb to do well or badly

performance /pəˈfɔːməns/ noun **1.** the way in which someone or something acts ○ Last year saw a dip in the company's performance. □ **performance of staff against objectives** how staff have worked, measured against the objectives set **2.** the way in which a share increases in value

'…inflation-adjusted GNP edged up at a 1.3% annual rate, its worst performance since the economic expansion began' [Fortune]

performance rating /pəˈfɔːməns ˌreɪtɪŋ/ noun a judgement of how well a share or a company has performed

performance review /pəˈfɔːməns rɪ ˌvjuː/ noun a yearly interview between a manager and each employee to discuss how the employee has worked during the year

per head /pə ˈhed/ adverb for each person ○ Allow £15 per head for expenses. ○ Representatives cost on average £50,000 per head per annum.

period bill /ˈpɪərɪəd bɪl/ noun a bill of exchange payable on a certain date rather than on demand. Also known as **term bill**

period cost /ˈpɪərɪəd kɒst/ noun a fixed cost, such as rent or insurance, which is related to a period of time

periodic /ˌpɪəriˈɒdɪk/, **periodical** /ˌpɪəri ˈɒdɪk(ə)l/ adjective happening from time to time ○ a periodic review of the company's performance

periodicity concept /ˌpɪəriəˈdɪsɪti ˌkɒnsept/ noun a legal requirement that states entities must produce required financial documentation at agreed times

periodic stock check /ˌpɪəriˈɒdɪk stɒk tʃek/ noun the counting of stock at some point in time, usually at the end of an accounting period

periodic weighted average cost /ˌpɪəriˌɒdɪk ˌweɪtɪd ˈæv(ə)rɪdʒ kɒst/, **periodic weighted average price** /ˌpɪəriˌɒdɪk ˌweɪtɪd ˈæv(ə)rɪdʒ praɪs/ noun the average price per unit of stock delivered in a period calculated at the end of the period, as opposed to 'cumulative weighted average'

period of account /ˌpɪərɪəd əv əˈkaʊnt/ noun the period usually covered by a firm's accounts

period of qualification /ˌpɪərɪəd əv ˌkwɒlɪfɪˈkeɪʃ(ə)n/ noun the time which has to pass before someone qualifies for something

perk /pɜːk/ noun an extra item given by a company to employees in addition to their salaries, e.g. company cars or private health insurance (informal) ○ She earns a good salary and in addition has all sorts of perks.

permit /pəˈmɪt/ verb to allow someone to do something ○ This document permits you to export twenty-five computer systems. ○ The ticket permits three people to go into the exhibition. ○ Will we be permitted to use her name in the advertising copy? ○ Smoking is not permitted in the design studio. (NOTE: **permitting – permitted**)

perpetual inventory system /pɜː ˌpetjʊəl ˈɪnventəri ˌsɪstəm/ noun a stock control system by which the stock is continually counted as it moves into and out of the warehouse, so avoiding having to close the warehouse for annual stock checks. Abbreviation **PIS**

perpetuity /ˌpɜːpɪˈjuːɪti/ *noun* same as **annuity**

per pro /pə ˈprəʊ/ *abbr* per procurationem ○ *The secretary signed per pro the manager.*

perquisite /ˈpɜːkwɪzɪt/ *noun* same as **perk**

person /ˈpɜːs(ə)n/ *noun* a man or a woman ○ *an insurance policy which covers a named person*

personal /ˈpɜːs(ə)n(ə)l/ *adjective* referring to one person □ **apart from the family shares, she has a personal shareholding in the company** apart from shares belonging to her family as a group, she has shares which she owns herself

personal allowance /ˌpɜːs(ə)n(ə)l əˈlaʊəns/ *noun* a part of a person's income which is not taxed

personal assets /ˌpɜːs(ə)n(ə)l ˈæsets/ *plural noun* moveable assets which belong to a person

Personal Equity Plan /ˌpɜːs(ə)nəl ˈekwɪti plæn/ *noun* an account held under a UK-government-backed scheme to encourage share-ownership and investment in industry, allowing individual taxpayers to invest some amount of money in shares each year, and not pay tax on either the income or the capital gains, provided that the shares are held for an agreed period of time. PEPs were replaced by ISAs in April 1999, but existing schemes will continue. Abbreviation **PEP**

personal financial planning /ˌpɜːs(ə)n(ə)l faɪˌnænʃəl ˈplænɪŋ/ *noun* short- and long-term financial planning by an individual, either independently or with the assistance of a professional adviser. It will include the use of tax efficient schemes such as Individual Savings Accounts, ensuring adequate provisions are being made for retirement, and examining short- and long-term borrowing requirements such as overdrafts and mortgages.

Personal Identification Number /ˌpɜːs(ə)n(ə)l aɪˌdentɪfɪˈkeɪʃ(ə)n ˌnʌmbə/ *noun* a unique number allocated to the holder of a cash card or credit card, by which he or she can enter an automatic banking system, as e.g., to withdraw cash from a cash machine or to pay in a store. Abbreviation **PIN**

personal income /ˌpɜːs(ə)n(ə)l ˈɪnkʌm/ *noun* the income received by an individual person before tax is paid

Personal Investment Authority /ˌpɜːs(ə)nəl ɪnˌvestmənt ɔːˈθɒrəti/ *noun* a self-regulatory organisation responsible for supervising the activities of financial intermediaries selling financial products to individuals. Abbreviation **PIA**

personal loan /ˌpɜːs(ə)nəl ˈləʊn/ *noun* a loan to a person for household or other personal use, not for business use

personal pension plan /ˌpɜːs(ə)n(ə)l ˈpenʃən plæn/ *noun* a pension plan which applies to one employee only, usually a self-employed person, not to a group. Abbreviation **PPP**

personal property /ˌpɜːs(ə)n(ə)l ˈprɒpəti/ *noun* things which belong to a person ○ *The fire caused considerable damage to personal property.*

personal representative /ˌpɜːs(ə)n(ə)l ˌreprɪˈzentətɪv/ *noun* a person who is the executor of a will or the administrator of the estate of a deceased person

PERT /pɜːt/ *abbr* programme evaluation and review technique

petition /pəˈtɪʃ(ə)n/ *noun* an official request

petroleum revenues /pəˈtrəʊliəm ˌrevənjuːz/ *plural noun* income from selling oil

petroleum revenue tax /pəˌtrəʊliəm ˈrevənjuː ˌtæks/ *noun* a British tax on revenues from companies extracting oil from the North Sea. Abbreviation **PRT**

petty cash /ˌpeti ˈkæʃ/ *noun* a small amount of money kept in an office to pay small debts. Abbreviation **P/C**

petty cash voucher /ˌpeti ˈkæʃ ˌvaʊtʃə/ *noun* a piece of paper on which cash expenditure is noted so that an employee can be reimbursed for what he or she has spent on company business

petty expenses /ˌpeti ɪkˈspensɪz/ *plural noun* small sums of money spent

phase /feɪz/ *noun* a period or part of something which takes place ○ *the first phase of the expansion programme*

phase in /ˌfeɪz ˈɪn/ *verb* to bring something in gradually ○ *The new invoicing system will be phased in over the next two months.*

'…the budget grants a tax exemption for $500,000 in capital gains, phased in over the next six years' [*Toronto Star*]

phase out /ˌfeɪz ˈaʊt/ *verb* to remove something gradually ○ *Smith Ltd will be phased out as a supplier of spare parts.*

phoenix company /ˈfiːnɪks ˌkʌmp(ə)ni/ *noun* a company formed by the directors of a company which has gone into receivership, which trades in the same way as the first company, and in most respects (except its name) seems to be exactly the same as the first company

'...the prosecution follows recent calls for a reform of insolvency legislation to prevent directors from leaving behind a trail of debt while continuing to trade in phoenix companies – businesses which fold only to rise again, often under a slightly different name in the hands of the same directors and management' [*Financial Times*]

physical asset /ˌfɪzɪk(ə)l 'æset/ *noun* an asset that is a physically existing thing, as opposed to cash or securities

physical inventory /ˌfɪzɪk(ə)l 'ɪnvənt(ə)ri/ *noun* an act of counting actual items of stock

physical market /ˌfɪzɪk(ə)l 'mɑːkɪt/ *noun* a commodity market where purchasers actually buy the commodities, as opposed to the futures market, where they buy and sell the right to purchase commodities at a future date

physical price /ˌfɪzɪk(ə)l 'praɪs/ *noun* a current cash price for a commodity for immediate delivery

physicals /'fɪzɪk(ə)lz/ *plural noun* actual commodities which are sold on the current market, as opposed to futures

physical stock /ˌfɪzɪk(ə)l 'stɒk/ *noun* the actual items of stock held in a warehouse

PIA /ˌpiː aɪ 'eɪ/ *abbr* Personal Investment Authority

piece rate /'piːs reɪt/ *noun* a rate of pay calculated as an amount for each product produced or for each piece of work done and not as an amount for each hour worked ○ *to earn piece rates*

piecework /'piːswɜːk/ *noun* work for which employees are paid in accordance with the number of products produced or pieces of work done and not at an hourly rate

pie chart /'paɪ tʃɑːt/ *noun* a diagram where information is shown as a circle cut up into sections of different sizes

pilferage /'pɪlfərɪdʒ/, **pilfering** /'pɪlfərɪŋ/ *noun* the stealing of small amounts of money or small items from an office or shop

PIN /pɪn/ *abbr* Personal Identification Number

PIS *abbr* perpetual inventory system

placement /'pleɪsmənt/ *noun* **1.** the act of finding work for someone ○ *The bureau specialises in the placement of former executives.* **2.** US the act of finding buyers for an issue of new shares (NOTE: The UK term is **placing**.)

placing /'pleɪsɪŋ/ *noun* the act of finding a single buyer or a group of institutional buyers for a large number of shares in a new company or a company that is going public

plain vanilla swap /ˌpleɪn vəˌnɪlə 'swɒp/ *noun* an interest rate swap, where a company with fixed interest borrowings may swap them for variable interest borrowings of another company

plan /plæn/ *noun* **1.** an organised way of doing something ○ *an investment plan* ○ *a pension plan* ○ *a savings plan* **2.** a way of saving or investing money ■ *verb* to organise carefully how something should be done in the future

'...the benefits package is attractive and the compensation plan includes base, incentive and car allowance totalling $50,000+' [*Globe and Mail (Toronto)*]

plan comptable *noun* in France, a uniformly structured and detailed bookkeeping system that companies are required to comply with

planned economy /ˌplænd ɪ'kɒnəmi/ *noun* a system where the government plans all business activity, regulates supply, sets production targets and itemises work to be done. Also called **command economy, central planning**

planned obsolescence /ˌplænd ˌɒbsə'les(ə)ns/ *adjective* built-in obsolescence ○ *Planned obsolescence was condemned by the consumer organisation as a cynical marketing ploy.*

planning /'plænɪŋ/ *noun* the process of organising how something should be done in the future ○ *Setting up a new incentive scheme with insufficient planning could be a disaster.* ○ *The long-term planning or short-term planning of the project has been completed.*

'...buildings are closely regulated by planning restrictions' [*Investors Chronicle*]

plant and machinery /ˌplɑːnt ən məˈʃiːnəri/ *noun* equipment used to help someone trade such as trucks, tools, office furniture, computers, ladders, etc.

plastic money /ˌplæstɪk 'mʌni/ *noun* credit cards and charge cards

pledge /pledʒ/ *noun* an object given to a pawnbroker as security for money borrowed

plus /plʌs/ *preposition* added to ○ *Her salary plus commission comes to more than £45,000.* ○ *Production costs plus overheads are higher than revenue.* ■ *adverb* more than □ **houses valued at £100,000 plus** houses valued at over £100,000

pocket /'pɒkɪt/ *noun* □ **to be £25 in pocket** to have made a profit of £25 □ **to be £25 out of pocket** to have lost £25

point /pɔɪnt/ *noun* **1.** a place or position **2.** a unit for calculations □ **government stocks rose by one point** they rose by £1

policy /ˈpɒlɪsi/ *noun* a course of action or set of principles determining the general way of doing something ○ *a company's trading policy* ○ *The country's economic policy seems to lack any direction.* ○ *We have a policy of only hiring qualified staff.* ○ *Our policy is to submit all contracts to the legal department.*

policy cost /ˈpɒlɪsi kɒst/ *noun* a fixed cost, such as advertising cost, which is governed by the management's policy on the amount of advertising to be done

portable /ˈpɔːtəb(ə)l/ *adjective* possible to carry ○ *a portable computer*

portable pension plan /ˌpɔːtəb(ə)l ˈpenʃən plæn/ *noun* a pension plan which an employee can carry from one company to another as he changes jobs

portfolio investments /pɔːtˌfəʊliəʊ ɪnˈvestmənts/ *plural noun* investments in shares and government stocks, as opposed to investments in property, etc.

portfolio management /pɔːtˈfəʊliəʊ ˌmænɪdʒmənt/ *noun* the buying and selling shares to make profits for a single investor

portfolio theory /pɔːtˈfəʊliəʊ ˌθɪəri/ *noun* a basis for managing a portfolio of investments, i.e. a mix of safe stocks and more risky ones

position /pəˈzɪʃ(ə)n/ *noun* **1.** a situation or state of affairs **2.** a point of view **3.** a job or paid work in a company ○ *to apply for a position as manager* ○ *We have several positions vacant.* ○ *All the vacant positions have been filled.* ○ *She retired from her position in the accounts department.* **4.** the state of a person's current financial holding in a stock

position audit /pəˌzɪʃ(ə)n ˈɔːdɪt/ *noun* part of the planning process which examines the current state of an entity in respect of the following: resources of tangible and intangible assets and finance; products, brands, and markets; operating systems such as production and distribution; internal organisation; current results; and returns to stockholders

positive carry /ˌpɒzɪtɪv ˈkæri/ *noun* a deal where the cost of the finance is less than the return

positive cash flow /ˌpɒzɪtɪv ˈkæʃ fləʊ/ *noun* a situation where more money is coming into a company than is going out

positive goodwill /ˌpɒzɪtɪv gʊdˈwɪl/ *noun* positive goodwill arises when the ac-

quisition cost exceeds the aggregate fair values of the identifiable assets and liabilities

positive yield curve /ˌpɒzɪtɪv ˈjiːld ˌkɜːv/ *noun* a situation where the yield on a short-term investment is less than that on a long-term investment

possess /pəˈzes/ *verb* to own something ○ *The company possesses property in the centre of the town.* ○ *He lost all he possessed in the collapse of his company.* Compare **repossess**

possession /pəˈzeʃ(ə)n/ *noun* the fact of owning or having something

possessions /pəˈzeʃ(ə)nz/ *plural noun* property, things owned ○ *They lost all their possessions in the fire.* Compare **repossession**

post-acquisition /pəʊst ˌækwɪˈzɪʃ(ə)n/ *adjective* taking place after a company has been acquired

post-acquisition profit /pəʊst ˌækwɪˈzɪʃ(ə)n ˈprɒfɪt/ *noun* a profit of a subsidiary company in the period after it has been acquired, which is treated as revenue and transferred to the consolidated reserves of the holding company

post a credit /ˌpəʊst eɪ ˈkredɪt/ *verb* to enter a credit item in a ledger

post-balance sheet event /pəʊst ˌbæləns ʃiːt ɪˈvent/ *noun* something which happens after the date when the balance sheet is drawn up, and before the time when the balance sheet is officially approved by the directors, which affects a company's financial position

postdate /ˌpəʊstˈdeɪt/ *verb* to put a later date on a document ○ *He sent us a postdated cheque.* ○ *Her cheque was postdated to June.*

post-purchase costs /ˌpəʊst ˈpɜːtʃɪs ˌkɒsts/ *noun* costs incurred after a capital expenditure decision has been implemented and facilities acquired. These costs may include training, maintenance, and the cost of upgrades.

pound /paʊnd/ *noun* **1.** a measure of weight (= 0.45 kilos) ○ *to sell oranges by the pound* ○ *a pound of oranges* ○ *Oranges cost 50p a pound.* (NOTE: Usually written **lb** after a figure: **25lb**. Note also that the pound is now no longer officially used in the UK) **2.** a unit of currency used in the UK and many other countries including Cyprus, Egypt, Lebanon, Malta, Sudan, Syria and, before the euro, Ireland

poundage /ˈpaʊndɪdʒ/ *noun* a rate charged per pound in weight

pound sterling /paʊnd ˈstɜːlɪŋ/ *noun* the official term for the British currency

power /ˈpaʊə/ *noun* **1.** strength or ability **2.** a force or legal right **3.** a mathematical term describing the number of times a number is to be multiplied by itself ○ *5 to the power 2 is equal to 25* (NOTE: written as small figures in superscript: 10^5: say: 'ten to the power five')

power of attorney /ˌpaʊər əv əˈtɜːni/ *noun* a legal document which gives someone the right to act on someone's behalf in legal matters

PPI *abbr* producers' price index

PPP /ˌpiː piː ˈpiː/ *abbr* personal pension plan

practice /ˈpræktɪs/ *noun* a way of doing things, a custom or habit ○ *Her practice was to arrive at work at 7.30 and start counting the cash.*

> '…the EC demanded international arbitration over the pricing practices of the provincial boards' [*Globe and Mail (Toronto)*]

pre-acquisition /ˌpriː ˌækwɪˈzɪʃən/ *adjective* before the acquisition of a company

pre-acquisition profits /ˌpriː ˌækwɪzɪʃən ˈprɒfɪts/ *plural noun* profits of a company in the part of its accounting period before it was acquired by another company. Under acquisition accounting methods, the holding company deducts these profits from the combined reserves of the group.

pre-acquisition write-down /ˌpriː ˌækwɪzɪʃən ˈraɪt ˌdaʊn/ *noun* a reduction in the fair value of a new subsidiary in the balance sheet of a holding company against the potential future costs or the possible revaluation of the subsidiary's assets after acquisition

prebilling /priːˈbɪlɪŋ/ *noun* the practice of submitting a bill for a product or service before it has actually been delivered

preceding year /prɪˌsiːdɪŋ ˈjɪə/ *noun* the year before the accounting year in question □ **taxed on a preceding year basis** tax on income or capital gains arising in the previous year is payable in the current year

pre-empt /priː ˈempt/ *verb* to stop something happening or stop someone doing something by taking action quickly before anyone else can ○ *They staged a management buyout to pre-empt a takeover bid.*

pre-emption right /priːˈempʃən raɪt/ *noun* the right of an existing shareholder to be first to buy a new stock issue

pre-emptive /priː ˈemptɪv/ *adjective* done before anyone else takes action in order to stop something happening

preference dividend /ˌpref(ə)rəns ˈdɪvɪdend/ *noun* a dividend paid on preference shares

preference shares /ˈpref(ə)rəns ʃeəz/ *plural noun* shares, often with no voting rights, which receive their dividend before all other shares and are repaid first at face value if the company goes into liquidation (NOTE: The US term is **preferred stock**.)

preferential /ˌprefəˈrenʃəl/ *adjective* showing that something is preferred more than another

preferential creditor /ˌprefəˌrenʃ(ə)l ˈkredɪtə/, **preferred creditor** /prɪˌfɜːd ˈkredɪtə/ *noun* a creditor who must be paid first if a company is in liquidation

preferential debt /ˌprefəˈrenʃəl det/ *noun* a debt which is paid before all others

preferential payment /ˌprefərenʃəl ˈpeɪmənt/ *noun* a payment to a preferential creditor

preferential shares /ˌprefəˈrenʃəl ʃeəz/ *plural noun* shares which are part of a new issue and are set aside for the employees of the company

preferred creditor /prɪˌfɜːd ˈkredɪtə/ *noun* a creditor who must be paid first if a company is in liquidation

preferred shares /prɪˌfɜːd ˈʃeəz/, **preferred stock** /prɪˌfɜːd ˈstɒk/ *plural noun* same as **preference shares**

pre-financing /priːˈfaɪnænsɪŋ/ *noun* financing in advance

preliminary /prɪˈlɪmɪn(ə)ri/ *adjective* early, happening before anything else

> '…preliminary indications of the level of business investment and activity during the March quarter will be available this week' [*Australian Financial Review*]

preliminary announcement /prɪ ˌlɪmɪn(ə)ri əˈnaʊnsmənt/ *noun* an announcement of a company's full-year results, given out to the press before the detailed annual report is released

premium /ˈpriːmiəm/ *noun* **1.** a regular payment made to an insurance company for the protection provided by an insurance policy **2.** an amount to be paid to a landlord or a tenant for the right to take over a lease ○ *flat to let with a premium of £10,000* ○ *annual rent: £8,500, premium: £25,000* **3.** an extra sum of money in addition to a usual charge, wage, price or other amount **4.** a gift, discount or other incentive to encourage someone to buy

> '…greenmail, the practice of buying back stock at a premium from an acquirer who threatens a takeover' [*Duns Business Month*]

'…responsibilities include the production of premium quality business reports' [*Times*]

premium bond /ˈpriːmiəm bɒnd/ *noun* a government bond, part of the National Savings scheme, which pays no interest, but gives the owner the chance to win a weekly or monthly prize

premium bonds /ˈpriːmiəm bɒndz/ *plural noun* British government bonds, part of the national savings scheme, which pay no interest, but give the owner the chance to win a monthly prize

premium income /ˌpriːmiəm ˈɪnkʌm/ *noun* income which an insurance company derives from premiums paid by insured persons

premium offer /ˈpriːmiəm ˌɒfə/ *noun* a free gift offered to attract more customers

premium on redemption /ˌpriːmiəm ɒn rɪˈdempʃən/ *noun* an extra amount above the nominal value of a share or debenture paid to the holder by a company buying back its share or loan stock

prepaid /priːˈpeɪd/ *adjective* paid in advance

prepaid expenses /priːˌpeɪd ɪkˈspensɪz/ *plural noun* expenditure on items such as rent, which is made in one accounting period but covers part of the next period also

prepaid interest /priːˌpeɪd ˈɪntrəst/ *noun* interest paid in advance of its due date

prepay /priːˈpeɪ/ *verb* to pay something in advance (NOTE: **prepaying – prepaid**)

prepayment /priːˈpeɪmənt/ *noun* **1.** a payment in advance, or the act of paying in advance **2.** *US* the repayment of the principal of a loan before it is due

prepayment penalty /priːˈpeɪmənt ˌpen(ə)lti/ *noun US* a charge levied on someone who repays a loan such as a mortgage before it is due

present /ˈprez(ə)nt/; /prɪˈzent/ *verb* to bring or send and show a document

presentation /ˌprez(ə)nˈteɪʃ(ə)n/ *noun* the showing of a document

present value /ˌprez(ə)nt ˈvæljuː/ *noun* **1.** the value something has now ○ *In 1984 the pound was worth five times its present value.* **2.** the value now of a specified sum of money to be received in the future, if invested at current interest rates. Abbreviation **PV 3.** a price which a share must reach in the future to be the equivalent of today's price, taking inflation into account

preservation of capital /ˌprezəveɪʃ(ə)n əv ˈkæpɪt(ə)l/ *noun* an approach to financial management that protects

a person's or company's capital by arranging additional forms of finance

pressing /ˈpresɪŋ/ *adjective* urgent

pre-tax /ˈpriːtæks/, **pretax** *adjective* before tax has been deducted or paid

'…the company's goals are a growth in sales of up to 40 per cent, a rise in pre-tax earnings of nearly 35 per cent and a rise in after-tax earnings of more than 25 per cent' [*Citizen (Ottawa)*]

'EC regulations which came into effect in July insist that customers can buy cars anywhere in the EC at the local pre-tax price' [*Financial Times*]

pretax profit /ˌpriːtæks ˈprɒfɪt/ *noun* the amount of profit a company makes before taxes are deducted ○ *The dividend paid is equivalent to one quarter of the pretax profit.* Also called **profit before tax, profit on ordinary activities before tax**

pretax profit margin /ˌpriːtæks ˈprɒfɪt ˌmɑːdʒɪn/ *noun* the pretax profit shown as a percentage of turnover in a profit and loss account

previous /ˈpriːviəs/ *adjective* happening earlier or which existed before ○ *List all previous positions with the salaries earned.*

previous balance /ˌpriːviəs ˈbæləns/ *noun* a balance in an account at the end of the accounting period before the current one

price /praɪs/ *noun* money which has to be paid to buy something □ **cars in the £18–19,000 price range** cars of different makes, selling for between £18,000 and £19,000 ■ *verb* to give a price to a product ○ *We have two used cars for sale, both priced at £5,000.*

'…the average price per kilogram for this season has been 300c' [*Australian Financial Review*]

'European manufacturers rely heavily on imported raw materials which are mostly priced in dollars' [*Duns Business Month*]

'…after years of relying on low wages for their competitive edge, Spanish companies are finding that rising costs and the strength of the peseta are pricing them out of the market' [*Wall Street Journal*]

'…that British goods will price themselves back into world markets is doubtful as long as sterling labour costs continue to rise' [*Sunday Times*]

price ceiling /ˈpraɪs ˌsiːlɪŋ/ *noun* the highest price which can be reached

price change /ˈpraɪs tʃeɪndʒ/ *noun* an amount by which the price of a share moves during a day's trading

price control /ˈpraɪs kənˌtrəʊl/ *noun* a legal measures to stop prices rising too fast

price controls /ˈpraɪs kənˌtrəʊlz/ *plural noun* legal measures to prevent prices rising too fast

price cutting /ˈpraɪs ˌkʌtɪŋ/ *noun* a sudden lowering of prices

'…in today's circumstances, price-cutting is inevitable in an attempt to build up market share' [*Marketing Week*]

price-cutting war /'praɪs ˌkʌtɪŋ wɔː/ *noun* same as **price war**

price differential /'praɪs dɪfəˌrenʃəl/ *noun* the difference in price between products in a range

price/earnings ratio /ˌpraɪs 'ɜːnɪŋz ˌreɪʃiəʊ/ *noun* a ratio between the current market price of a share and the earnings per share (the current dividend it produces), calculated by dividing the market price by the earnings per share ○ *these shares sell at a P/E ratio of 7* Also called **P/E ratio**. Abbreviation **PER** (NOTE: The US term is **price/earnings multiple**.)

price fixing /'praɪs ˌfɪksɪŋ/ *noun* an illegal agreement between companies to charge the same price for competing products

price-insensitive /ˌpraɪs ɪn'sensətɪv/ *adjective* used to describe a good or service for which sales remain constant no matter what its price because it is essential to buyers

price label /'praɪs ˌleɪb(ə)l/ *noun* a label which shows a price

price list /'praɪs lɪst/ *noun* a sheet giving prices of goods for sale

price range /'praɪs reɪndʒ/ *noun* a series of prices for similar products from different suppliers

price tag /'praɪs tæg/ *noun* a label attached to an item being sold that shows its price

price war /'praɪs wɔː/ *noun* a competition between companies to get a larger market share by cutting prices. Also called **price-cutting war**

pricing /'praɪsɪŋ/ *noun* the act of giving a price to a product

pricing model /'praɪsɪŋ ˌmɒd(ə)l/ *noun* a computerised system for calculating a price, based on costs, anticipated margins, etc.

pricing policy /'praɪsɪŋ ˌpɒlisi/ *noun* a company's policy in giving prices to its products ○ *Our pricing policy aims at producing a 35% gross margin.*

primary /'praɪməri/ *adjective* basic

'...farmers are convinced that primary industry no longer has the capacity to meet new capital taxes or charges on farm inputs' [*Australian Financial Review*]

primary commodities /ˌpraɪməri kə 'mɒdɪtiz/ *plural noun* farm produce grown in large quantities, e.g. corn, rice or cotton

primary industry /ˌpraɪməri 'ɪndəstri/ *noun* an industry dealing with basic raw materials such as coal, wood or farm produce

primary market /ˌpraɪməri 'mɑːkɪt/ *noun* a market where new securities or bonds are issued. Also called **new issue market**

prime /praɪm/ *adjective* **1.** most important **2.** basic

prime bills /ˌpraɪm 'bɪlz/ *plural noun* bills of exchange which do not involve any risk

prime cost /ˌpraɪm 'kɒst/ *noun* the cost involved in producing a product, excluding overheads

prime rate /'praɪm reɪt/, **prime** /praɪm/ *noun US* the best rate of interest at which an American bank lends to its customers

'...the base lending rate, or prime rate, is the rate at which banks lend to their top corporate borrowers' [*Wall Street Journal*]

prime sites /ˌpraɪm 'saɪts/ *plural noun* the most valuable commercial sites, i.e. in main shopping streets, as opposed to secondary sites

prime time /'praɪm taɪm/ *noun* the most expensive advertising time for TV commercials ○ *We are putting out a series of prime-time commercials.*

priming /'praɪmɪŋ/ *noun* ♦ **pump priming**

principal /'prɪnsɪp(ə)l/ *noun* **1.** a person or company that is represented by an agent ○ *The agent has come to London to see his principals.* **2.** a person acting for him or herself, such as a marketmaker buying securities on his or her own account **3.** money invested or borrowed on which interest is paid ○ *to repay principal and interest* ○ *We try to repay part of principal each month.* (NOTE: Do not confuse with **principle**.) ■ *adjective* most important ○ *The principal shareholders asked for a meeting.* ○ *The country's principal products are paper and wood.* ○ *The company's principal asset is its design staff.*

'...the company was set up with funds totalling NorKr 145m with the principal aim of making capital gains on the secondhand market' [*Lloyd's List*]

principle /'prɪnsɪp(ə)l/ *noun* a basic point or general rule

prior /'praɪə/ *adjective* earlier

prior charge percentage *noun* same as **priority percentage**

priority /praɪ'ɒrɪti/ *noun* □ **to have priority over** *or* **to take priority over something** to be more important than something ○ *Reducing overheads takes priority over increasing turnover.* ○ *Debenture holders have priority over ordinary shareholders.*

priority percentage /praɪˌɒrɪti pə 'sentɪdʒ/ *noun* the proportion of a business's net profit that is paid in interest to preference shareholders and holders of debt capital. Also called **prior charge percentage**

prior year adjustments /ˌpraɪə jɪə ə 'dʒʌs(t)mənts/ *plural noun* adjustments made to accounts for previous years, because of changes in accounting policies or because of errors

private /ˈpraɪvət/ *adjective* belonging to a single person or to individual people, not to a company or the state □ **a letter marked 'private and confidential'** a letter which must not be opened by anyone other than the person it is addressed to □ **to sell (a house) by private treaty** to sell (a house) to another person not by auction

'…in the private sector the total number of new house starts was 3 per cent higher than in the corresponding period last year, while public sector starts were 23 per cent lower' [*Financial Times*]

'…management had offered to take the company private through a leveraged buyout for $825 million' [*Fortune*]

private bank /ˌpraɪvət ˈbæŋk/ *noun* **1.** a bank that is owned by a single person or a limited number of private shareholders **2.** a bank that provides banking facilities to high net worth individuals. ◊ **private banking**

private banking /ˌpraɪvət ˈbæŋkɪŋ/ *noun* a service offered by certain financial institutions to high net worth individuals. In addition to standard banking services, it will typically include portfolio management and advisory services on taxation, including estate planning.

private company /ˌpraɪvət ˈkʌmp(ə)ni/ *noun* a registered company whose shares are not offered for sale to the public

private debt /ˌpraɪvət ˈdet/ *noun* money owed by individuals and organisations other than governments

private enterprise /ˌpraɪvət ˈentəpraɪz/ *noun* businesses which are owned privately, not nationalised ○ *The project is completely funded by private enterprise.*

private income /ˌpraɪvət ˈɪnkʌm/ *noun* income from dividends, interest or rent which is not part of a salary

private investor /ˌpraɪvət ɪnˈvestə/ *noun* an ordinary person with money to invest

private limited company /ˌpraɪvət ˌlɪmɪtɪd ˈkʌmp(ə)ni/ *noun* **1.** a company with a small number of shareholders, whose shares are not traded on the Stock Exchange (NOTE: shortened to **Ltd**) **2.** a subsidiary company whose shares are not listed on the Stock Exchange, while those of its parent company are ▶ abbreviation **Pty Ltd**

privately held company /ˌpraɪvətli held ˈkʌmp(ə)ni/ *noun US* company controlled by a few shareholders or its directors. Also called **closed corporation**

private ownership /ˌpraɪvət ˈəʊnəʃɪp/ *noun* a situation where a company is owned by private shareholders

private placing /ˌpraɪvət ˈpleɪsɪŋ/, **private placement** /ˌpraɪvət ˈpleɪsmənt/ *noun* the act of placing a new issue of shares with a group of selected financial institutions

private practice /ˌpraɪvət ˈpræktɪs/ *noun* accounting services offered to clients, as opposed to accounting work carried out as an employee of a company

private property /ˌpraɪvət ˈprɒpəti/ *noun* property which belongs to a private person, not to the public

private sector /ˈpraɪvət ˌsektə/ *noun* all companies which are owned by private shareholders, not by the state ○ *The expansion is completely funded by the private sector.* ○ *Salaries in the private sector have increased faster than in the public sector.*

'…in the private sector the total number of new house starts was 3 per cent higher than in the corresponding period last year, while public sector starts were 23 per cent lower' [*Financial Times*]

private treaty /ˌpraɪvət ˈtriːti/ *noun* agreement between individual persons

pro /prəʊ/ *preposition* for

probability /ˌprɒbəˈbɪlɪti/ *noun* the likelihood that something will happen, expressed mathematically

probable /ˈprɒbəb(ə)l/ *adjective* likely to happen ○ *They are trying to prevent the probable collapse of the company.* ○ *It is probable that the company will collapse if a rescue package is not organised before the end of the month.*

probate /ˈprəʊbeɪt/ *noun* legal acceptance that a document, especially a will, is valid □ **the executor was granted probate *or* obtained a grant of probate** the executor was told officially that the will was valid

procedure /prəˈsiːdʒə/ *noun* a way in which something is done ○ *The inquiry found that the company had not followed the approved procedures.*

'…this was a serious breach of disciplinary procedure and the dismissal was unfair' [*Personnel Management*]

proceed /prəˈsiːd/ *verb* to go on, to continue ○ *The negotiations are proceeding slowly.*

proceeds /ˈprəʊsiːdz/ *plural noun* money received from selling something

process /ˈprəʊses/ *verb* to deal with something in the usual routine way ○ *It usually takes at least two weeks to process an insurance claim.* ○ *Orders are processed in our warehouse.*

process costing /prəʊˌses ˈkɒstɪŋ/ noun a method of costing something which is manufactured from a series of continuous processes, where the total costs of those processes are divided by the number of units produced

processing /ˈprəʊsesɪŋ/ noun the act of sorting information ○ the processing of information or of statistics by a computer

producers' price index /prəˌdjuːsə ˈpraɪs ˌɪndeks/ noun US a measure of the annual increase in the prices of goods and services charged by producers which is used to indicate the rate of inflation in the US economy. Abbreviation **PPI**

product /ˈprɒdʌkt/ noun **1.** something which is made or manufactured **2.** a manufactured item for sale

product advertising /ˈprɒdʌkt ˌædvətaɪzɪŋ/ noun the advertising of a particular named product, not the company which makes it

product analysis /ˌprɒdʌkt əˈnæləsɪs/ noun an examination of each separate product in a company's range to find out why it sells, who buys it, etc.

product design /ˈprɒdʌkt dɪˌzaɪn/ noun the design of consumer products

product development /ˌprɒdʌkt dɪˈveləpmənt/ noun the process of improving an existing product line to meet the needs of the market

product engineer /ˌprɒdʌkt ˌendʒɪˈnɪə/ noun an engineer in charge of the equipment for making a product

production /prəˈdʌkʃən/ noun **1.** the act of showing something **2.** the work of making or manufacturing of goods for sale ○ We are hoping to speed up production by installing new machinery. ○ Higher production is rewarded with higher pay.

production cost /prəˈdʌkʃən kɒst/ noun the cost of making a product

production department /prəˈdʌkʃən dɪˌpɑːtmənt/ noun the section of a company which deals with the making of the company's products

production line /prəˈdʌkʃən laɪn/ noun a system of making a product, where each item such as a car moves slowly through the factory with new sections added to it as it goes along ○ He works on the production line. ○ She is a production-line employee.

production manager /prəˈdʌkʃən ˌmænɪdʒə/ noun the person in charge of the production department

production overhead /prəˌdʌkʃən ˈəʊvəhed/ noun a factory overhead, the indirect costs of production which are absorbed into the cost of goods produced

production target /prəˈdʌkʃən ˌtɑːgɪt/ noun the amount of units a factory is expected to produce

production unit /prəˈdʌkʃən ˌjuːnɪt/ noun a separate small group of employees producing a product

productive /prəˈdʌktɪv/ adjective producing something, especially something useful

productive capital /prəˌdʌktɪv ˈkæpɪt(ə)l/ noun capital which is invested to give interest

productivity /ˌprɒdʌkˈtɪvɪti/ noun the rate of output per employee or per machine in a factory ○ Bonus payments are linked to productivity. ○ The company is aiming to increase productivity. ○ Productivity has fallen or risen since the company was taken over.

'…though there has been productivity growth, the absolute productivity gap between many British firms and their foreign rivals remains' [*Sunday Times*]

productivity agreement /ˌprɒdʌkˈtɪvɪti əˌgriːmənt/ noun an agreement to pay a productivity bonus

productivity bonus /ˌprɒdʌkˈtɪvɪti ˌbəʊnəs/ noun an extra payment made to employees because of increased production per employee

productivity drive /ˌprɒdʌkˈtɪvɪti draɪv/ noun an extra effort to increase productivity

product management /ˌprɒdʌkt ˈmænɪdʒmənt/ noun the process of directing the making and selling of a product as an independent item

product mix /ˈprɒdʌkt mɪks/ noun a range of different products which a company has for sale

profession /prəˈfeʃ(ə)n/ noun **1.** an occupation for which official qualifications are needed and which is often made a lifelong career ○ The managing director is an accountant by profession. ○ HR management is now more widely recognised as a profession. **2.** a group of specialised workers ○ the accounting profession ○ the legal profession □ **the accounting profession** all qualified accountants □ **the banking profession** all qualified bankers

'…one of the key advantages of an accountancy qualification is its worldwide marketability. Other professions are not so lucky: lawyers, for example, are much more limited in where they can work' [*Accountancy*]

professional /prəˈfeʃ(ə)n(ə)l/ *adjective* referring to one of the professions ○ *The accountant sent in his bill for professional services.* ○ *We had to ask our lawyer for professional advice on the contract.* ○ *The professional institute awards diplomas.* □ **professional man**, **professional woman** a man or woman who works in one of the professions such as a lawyer, doctor or accountant

professional fees /prəˌfeʃ(ə)n(ə)l ˈfiːz/ *plural noun* fees paid to lawyers, accountants, architects, etc.

profit /ˈprɒfɪt/ *noun* money gained from a sale which is more than the money spent on making the item sold or on providing the service offered □ **to take your profit** to sell shares at a higher price than was paid for them, and so realise the profit, rather than to keep them as an investment □ **to make a profit** to have more money as a result of a deal

> '...because capital gains are not taxed and money taken out in profits and dividends is taxed, owners of businesses will be using accountants and tax experts to find loopholes in the law' [*Toronto Star*]

> '...the bank transferred $5 million to general reserve compared with $10 million the previous year which made the consolidated profit and loss account look healthier' [*Hongkong Standard*]

profitability /ˌprɒfɪtəˈbɪlɪti/ *noun* **1.** the ability to make a profit ○ *We doubt the profitability of the project.* **2.** the amount of profit made as a percentage of costs

profitable /ˈprɒfɪtəb(ə)l/ *adjective* making a profit ○ *She runs a very profitable employment agency.*

profitably /ˈprɒfɪtəbli/ *adverb* making a profit ○ *The aim of every company must be to trade profitably.*

profit after tax /ˌprɒfɪt ɑːftə ˈtæks/ *noun* same as **net profit**

profit and loss account /ˌprɒfɪt ən ˈlɒs əˌkaʊnt/ *noun* the accounts for a company showing expenditure and income over a period of time, usually one calendar year, balanced to show a final profit or loss. Also called **P&L account** (NOTE: The US term is **profit and loss statement** or **income statement**.)

profit before interest and tax /ˌprɒfɪt bɪˌfɔː ˈɪntrəst ən tæks/ *noun* operating profit shown before deducting interest on borrowings and tax due to the Inland Revenue. Abbreviation **PBIT**

profit centre /ˈprɒfɪt ˌsentə/ *noun* a person, unit or department within an organisation which is considered separately for the purposes of calculating a profit ○ *We count*

the kitchen equipment division as a single profit centre.

profit distribution /ˌprɒfɪt ˌdɪstrɪˈbjuːʃ(ə)n/ *noun* the allocation of profits to different recipients such as shareholders and owners, or for different purposes such as research or investment

profiteer /ˌprɒfɪˈtɪə/ *noun* a person who makes too much profit, especially when goods are rationed or in short supply

profiteering /ˌprɒfɪˈtɪərɪŋ/ *noun* the practice of making too much profit

profit from ordinary activities /ˌprɒfɪt frəm ˌɔːd(ə)n(ə)ri ækˈtɪvɪtiz/ *noun* profits earned in the normal course of business, as opposed to profits from extraordinary sources such as windfall payments

profit-making /ˈprɒfɪt ˌmeɪkɪŋ/ *adjective* making a profit ○ *The whole project was expected to be profit-making by 2001 but it still hasn't broken even.* ○ *It is hoped to make it into a profit-making concern.*

profit margin /ˈprɒfɪt ˌmɑːdʒɪn/ *noun* the percentage difference between sales income and the cost of sales

profit on ordinary activities before tax /ˌprɒfɪt ɒn ˌɔːd(ə)n(ə)ri ækˌtɪvɪtiz bɪ ˌfɔː ˈtæks/ *noun* same as **pretax profit**

profit-related /ˈprɒfɪt rɪˌleɪtɪd/ *adjective* linked to profit

profit-related bonus /ˌprɒfɪt rɪˌleɪtɪd ˈbəʊnəs/ *noun* a bonus paid which is related to the amount of profit a company makes

profit-related pay /ˌprɒfɪt rɪˌleɪtɪd ˈpeɪ/ *noun* pay including bonuses which is linked to profit

profit retained for the year /ˌprɒfɪt rɪ ˈteɪnɪd fə ðə ˈjɪə/ *noun* non-distributed profit retained as a distributable reserve

profit-sharing /ˈprɒfɪt ˌʃeərɪŋ/ *noun* **1.** an arrangement where employees get a share of the profits of the company they work for ○ *The company runs a profit-sharing scheme.* **2.** the practice of dividing profits among employees

profit squeeze /ˈprɒfɪt skwiːz/ *noun* a strict control of the amount of profits which companies can pay out as dividend

profit-taking /ˈprɒfɪt ˌteɪkɪŋ/ *noun* the act of selling investments to realise the profit, rather than keeping them ○ *Share prices fell under continued profit-taking.*

> '...some profit-taking was seen yesterday as investors continued to lack fresh incentives to renew buying activity' [*Financial Times*]

pro forma /prəʊ ˈfɔːmə/ *verb* to issue a pro forma invoice ○ *Can you pro forma this order?*

pro-forma financial statement /prəʊ ˌfɔːmə faɪˌnænʃəl ˈsteɪtmənt/ *noun* a projection showing a business's financial statements after the completion of a planned transaction

programmable /ˈprəʊɡræməb(ə)l/ *adjective* possible to programme

programme evaluation and review technique /ˌprəʊɡræm ɪvæljuˌeɪʃ(ə)n ən rɪˈvjuː tekˌniːk/ *noun* a way of planning and controlling a large project, concentrating on scheduling and completion on time. Abbreviation **PERT**

programming engineer /ˈprəʊɡræmɪŋ ˌendʒɪnɪə/ *noun* an engineer in charge of programming a computer system

progress *noun* /ˈprəʊɡres/ the movement of work towards completion ○ *to report on the progress of the work* or *of the negotiations* ■ *verb* /prəʊˈɡres/ to move forward, to go ahead ○ *The contract is progressing through various departments.*

progressive /prəˈɡresɪv/ *adjective* moving forward in stages

progressive taxation /prəˌɡresɪv tæk ˈseɪʃ(ə)n/ *noun* a taxation system where tax levels increase as the income is higher. Also called **graduated taxation**. Compare **regressive taxation**

prohibitive /prəʊˈhɪbɪtɪv/ *adjective* with a price so high that you cannot afford to pay it ○ *The cost of redesigning the product is prohibitive.*

project /ˈprɒdʒekt/ *noun* **1.** a plan ○ *She has drawn up a project for developing new markets in Europe.* **2.** a particular job of work which follows a plan ○ *We are just completing an engineering project in North Africa.* ○ *The company will start work on the project next month.*

projected /prəˈdʒektɪd/ *adjective* planned or expected

project finance /ˌprɒdʒekt ˈfaɪnæns/ *noun* money raised for a specific undertaking, usually a construction or development project

projection /prəˈdʒekʃən/ *noun* a forecast of something which will happen in the future ○ *Projection of profits for the next three years.* ○ *The sales manager was asked to draw up sales projections for the next three years.*

promise /ˈprɒmɪs/ *noun* an act of saying that you will do something ■ *verb* to say that you will do something ○ *They promised to pay the last instalment next week.* ○ *The per-*

sonnel manager promised he would look into the grievances of the office staff.

promissory note /ˈprɒmɪsəri ˌnəʊt/ *noun* a document stating that someone promises to pay an amount of money on a specific date

promote /prəˈməʊt/ *verb* **1.** to give someone a more important job or to move someone to a higher grade ○ *He was promoted from salesman to sales manager.* **2.** to advertise a product

promotion /prəˈməʊʃ(ə)n/ *noun* the fact of being moved up to a more important job ○ *I ruined my chances of promotion when I argued with the managing director.* ○ *The job offers good promotion chances* or *promotion prospects.*

    '…finding the right promotion to appeal to children is no easy task' [*Marketing*]

    '…you have to study the profiles and people involved very carefully and tailor the promotion to fill those needs' [*Marketing Week*]

promotional /prəˈməʊʃ(ə)n(ə)l/ *adjective* used in an advertising campaign ○ *The admen are using balloons as promotional material.*

    '…the simplest way to boost sales at the expense of regional newspapers is by a heavyweight promotional campaign' [*Marketing Week*]

prompt /prɒmpt/ *adjective* rapid or done immediately ○ *We got very prompt service at the complaints desk.* ○ *Thank you for your prompt reply to my letter.*

    '…they keep shipping costs low and can take advantage of quantity discounts and other allowances for prompt payment' [*Duns Business Month*]

proof /pruːf/ *noun* evidence which shows that something is true

-proof /pruːf/ *suffix* preventing something getting in or getting out or harming something ○ *a dustproof cover* ○ *an inflation-proof pension* ○ *a soundproof studio*

property /ˈprɒpəti/ *noun* **1.** land and buildings ○ *Property taxes are higher in the inner city.* ○ *They are assessing damage to property* or *property damage after the storm.* ○ *The commercial property market is booming.* **2.** a building ○ *We have several properties for sale in the centre of the town.*

property bond /ˈprɒpəti bɒnd/ *noun* an investment in a fund invested in properties or in property companies

property company /ˈprɒpəti ˌkʌmp(ə)ni/ *noun* a company which buys buildings to lease them

proportion /prəˈpɔːʃ(ə)n/ *noun* a part of a total ○ *A proportion of the pre-tax profit is set aside for contingencies.* ○ *Only a small proportion of our sales comes from retail shops.*

proportional /prə'pɔːʃ(ə)n(ə)l/ *adjective* directly related ○ *The increase in profit is proportional to the reduction in overheads.*

proportionately /prə'pɔːʃ(ə)nətli/ *adverb* in a way that is directly related

proprietary /prə'praɪət(ə)ri/ *noun, adjective* a product, e.g. a medicine which is made and owned by a company

proprietary company /prə,praɪət(ə)ri 'kʌmp(ə)ni/ *noun US* a company formed to invest in stock of other companies so as to control them. Abbreviation **pty** (NOTE: The UK term is **holding company**.)

proprietary drug /prə,praɪət(ə)ri 'drʌg/ *noun* a drug which is made by a particular company and marketed under a brand name

proprietor /prə'praɪətə/ *noun* the owner of a business, especially in the hospitality industry ○ *She is the proprietor of a hotel* or *a hotel proprietor.* ○ *The restaurant has a new proprietor.*

proprietors' interest /prə,praɪətəz 'ɪntrəst/ *noun* the amount which the owners of a business have invested in the business

pro rata /prəʊ 'rɑːtə/ *adjective, adverb* at a rate which varies according to the size or importance of something ○ *When part of the shipment was destroyed we received a pro rata payment.* ○ *The full-time pay is £500 a week and the part-timers are paid pro rata.*

prospect /'prɒspekt/ *noun* a chance or possibility that something will happen in the future □ **her job prospects are good** she is very likely to find a job

prospective /prə'spektɪv/ *adjective* possibly happening in the future

prospective dividend /prə,spektɪv 'dɪvɪdend/ *noun* a dividend which a company expects to pay at the end of the current year

prospective P/E ratio /prə,spektɪv ,piː 'iː ,reɪʃiəʊ/ *noun* a P/E ratio expected in the future on the basis of forecast dividends

prospects /'prɒspekts/ *plural noun* the possibilities for the future

prospectus /prə'spektəs/ *noun* a document which gives information to attract buyers or customers ○ *The restaurant has people handing out prospectuses in the street.*

'…when the prospectus emerges, existing shareholders and any prospective new investors can find out more by calling the free share information line; they will be sent a leaflet. Non-shareholders who register in this way will receive a prospectus when it is published; existing shareholders will be sent one automatically' [*Financial Times*]

prosperity /prɒ'sperɪti/ *noun* the state of being rich

prosperous /'prɒsp(ə)rəs/ *adjective* rich ○ *a prosperous shopkeeper* ○ *a prosperous town*

protectionism /prə'tekʃənɪz(ə)m/ *noun* the practice of protecting producers in the home country against foreign competitors by banning or taxing imports or by imposing import quotas

protective tariff /prə,tektɪv 'tærɪf/ *noun* a tariff which tries to ban imports to stop them competing with local products

pro tem /,prəʊ 'tem/ *adverb* temporarily, for a time

protest /'prəʊtest/ *noun* an official document which proves that a bill of exchange has not been paid

provide /prə'vaɪd/ *verb* **1.** to give or supply something **2.** to put money aside in accounts to cover expenditure or loss in the future ○ *£25,000 is provided against bad debts.*

provident /'prɒvɪd(ə)nt/ *adjective* providing benefits in case of illness, old age or other cases of need ○ *a provident fund* ○ *a provident society*

provider of capital /prə,vaɪdə əv 'kæpɪt(ə)l/ *noun* a person or company which provides capital to a business, usually by being a shareholder

provision /prə'vɪʒ(ə)n/ *noun* **1.** an amount of money put aside in accounts for anticipated expenditure where the timing or amount of expenditure is uncertain, often for doubtful debts ○ *The bank has made a £2m provision for bad debts* or *a $5bn provision against Third World loans.* **2.** □ **there is no provision for** *or* **no provision has been made for car parking in the plans for the office block** the plans do not include space for cars to park

'…landlords can create short lets of dwellings which will be free from the normal security of tenure provisions' [*Times*]

provisional /prə'vɪʒ(ə)n(ə)l/ *adjective* temporary, not final or permanent ○ *She was given a provisional posting to see* ○ *The sales department has been asked to make a provisional forecast of sales.* ○ *The provisional budget has been drawn up for each department.* ○ *They faxed their provisional acceptance of the contract.*

provisionally /prə'vɪʒ(ə)nəli/ *adverb* not finally ○ *The contract has been accepted provisionally.*

provisions /prə'vɪʒ(ə)nz/ *noun* money put aside in accounts for anticipated expenditure where the timing or amount of expenditure is uncertain. If the expenditure is not certain to occur at all, then the money set aside is called a 'contingent liability'.

proxy /'prɒksi/ *noun* **1.** a document which gives someone the power to act on behalf of someone else ○ *to sign by proxy* **2.** a person who acts on behalf of someone else ○ *She asked the chairman to act as proxy for her.*

proxy form /'prɒksi fɔːm/, **proxy card** /'prɒksi kɑːd/ *noun* a form which a shareholders receive with their invitations to attend an AGM, and which they fill in if they want to appoint a proxy to vote for them on a resolution

proxy statement /'prɒksi ˌsteɪtmənt/ *noun* a document, filed with the SEC, outlining executive pay packages, option grants and other perks, and also giving details of dealings by executives in shares of the company

proxy vote /'prɒksi vəʊt/ *noun* a vote made by proxy ○ *The proxy votes were all in favour of the board's recommendation.*

PRT *abbr* petroleum revenue tax

prudence /'pruːdəns/ *noun* the use of care and judgement

prudent /'pruːdənt/ *adjective* careful, not taking any risks

prudential ratio /pruˌdenʃ(ə)l 'reɪʃiəʊ/ *noun* a ratio of capital to assets which a bank feels it is prudent to have, according to EU regulations

PSBR *abbr* Public Sector Borrowing Requirement

Pty *abbr* proprietary company

Pty Ltd *abbr* private limited company

public /'pʌblɪk/ *adjective* **1.** referring to all the people in general **2.** referring to the government or the state

Public Accounts Committee /ˌpʌblɪk əˈkaʊnts kəˌmɪti/ *noun* a committee of the House of Commons which examines the spending of each department and ministry

public debt /ˌpʌblɪk 'det/ *noun* the money that a government or a set of governments owes

public deposits /ˌpʌblɪk dɪ'pɒzɪts/ *noun* in the United Kingdom, the government's credit monies held at the Bank of England

public expenditure /ˌpʌblɪk ɪk'spendɪtʃə/ *noun* money spent by the local or central government

public finance /ˌpʌblɪk 'faɪnæns/ *noun* the raising of money by governments by taxes or borrowing, and the spending of it

public funds /ˌpʌblɪk 'fʌndz/ *plural noun* government money available for expenditure

public holiday /ˌpʌblɪk 'hɒlɪdeɪ/ *noun* a day when all employees are entitled to take a holiday

publicity budget /pʌ'blɪsɪti ˌbʌdʒɪt/ *noun* money allowed for expenditure on publicity

public limited company /ˌpʌblɪk ˌlɪmɪtɪd 'kʌmp(ə)ni/ *noun* a company whose shares can be bought on the Stock Exchange. Abbreviation **Plc, PLC, plc**. Also called **public company**

publicly held company /ˌpʌblɪkli held 'kʌmp(ə)ni/ *noun US* company controlled by a few shareholders or its directors, but which is quoted on the Stock Exchange and where the public hold a few shares

public ownership /ˌpʌblɪk 'əʊnəʃɪp/ *noun* a situation where the government owns a business, i.e. where an industry is nationalised

public placing /ˌpʌblɪk 'pleɪsɪŋ/, **public placement** /ˌpʌblɪk 'pleɪsmənt/ *noun* an act of offering a new issue of shares to investing institutions, though not to private investors in general

public sector /'pʌblɪk ˌsektə/ *noun* nationalised industries and services ○ *a report on wage rises in the public sector* or *on public-sector wage settlements* Also called **government sector**

Public Sector Borrowing Requirement /ˌpʌblɪk ˌsektə 'bɒrəʊɪŋ rɪ ˌkwaɪəmənt/ *noun* the amount of money which a government has to borrow to pay for its own spending. Abbreviation **PBSR**

public spending /ˌpʌblɪk 'spendɪŋ/ *noun* spending by the government or by local authorities

Public Trustee /ˌpʌblɪk ˌtrʌ'stiː/ *noun* an official who is appointed as a trustee of an individual's property

published accounts /ˌpʌblɪʃɪd ə 'kaʊnts/ *noun* the accounts of a company which have been prepared and audited and then must be published by sending to the shareholders and other interested parties

pump priming /'pʌmp ˌpraɪmɪŋ/ *noun* government investment in new projects which it hopes will benefit the economy

purchase /'pɜːtʃɪs/ *noun* a product or service which has been bought

purchase book /'pɜːtʃɪs bʊk/ *noun* a book in which purchases are recorded

purchase daybook, purchases daybook *noun* a book which records the purchases made each day

purchase invoice /ˌpɜːtʃɪs ˈɪnvɔɪs/ *noun* an invoice received by a purchaser from a seller

purchase ledger /ˈpɜːtʃɪs ˌledʒə/ *noun* a book in which expenditure is noted

purchase order /ˈpɜːtʃɪs ˌɔːdə/ *noun* an official order made out by a purchasing department for goods which a company wants to buy ○ *We cannot supply you without a purchase order number.*

purchase price /ˈpɜːtʃɪs praɪs/ *noun* a price paid for something

purchaser /ˈpɜːtʃɪsə/ *noun* a person or company that purchases ○ *The company has found a purchaser for its warehouse.*

purchase requisition /ˌpɜːtʃɪs ˌrekwɪˈzɪʃ(ə)n/ *noun* an instruction from a department within an organisation to its purchasing department to buy goods or services, stating the kind and quantity required, and forming the basis of a purchase order

purchase tax /ˈpɜːtʃɪs tæks/ *noun* a tax paid on things which are bought

purchasing /ˈpɜːtʃɪsɪŋ/ *noun, adjective* buying

purchasing department /ˈpɜːtʃɪsɪŋ dɪ ˌpɑːtmənt/ *noun* the section of a company which deals with the buying of stock, raw materials, equipment, etc.

purchasing manager /ˈpɜːtʃɪsɪŋ ˌmænɪdʒə/ *noun* the head of a purchasing department

purchasing officer /ˈpɜːtʃɪsɪŋ ˌɒfɪsə/ *noun* a person in a company or organisation who is responsible for buying stock, raw materials, equipment, etc.

purchasing power /ˈpɜːtʃɪsɪŋ ˌpaʊə/ *noun* the quantity of goods which can be bought by a particular group of people or with a particular sum of money ○ *the purchasing power of the school market* ○ *The purchasing power of the pound has fallen over the last five years.*

pure endowment /ˌpjʊə ɪnˈdaʊmənt/ *noun* a gift whose use is fully prescribed by the donor

put down /ˌpʊt ˈdaʊn/ *verb* **1.** to make a deposit ○ *to put down money on a house* **2.** to write an item in a ledger or an account book ○ *to put down a figure for expenses*

put up /ˌpʊt ˈʌp/ *verb* **1.** □ **who put up the money for the shop?** who provided the investment money for the shop to start? □ **to put something up for sale** to advertise that something is for sale ○ *When he retired he decided to put his town flat up for sale.* **2.** to increase something, to make something higher ○ *The shop has put up all its prices by 5%.*

PV *abbr* present value

pyramid selling /ˈpɪrəmɪd ˌselɪŋ/ *noun* an illegal way of selling goods or investments to the public, where each selling agent pays for the franchise to sell the product or service, and sells that right on to other agents together with stock, so that in the end the person who makes most money is the original franchiser, and sub-agents or investors may lose all their investments

'…much of the population had committed their life savings to get-rich-quick pyramid investment schemes – where newcomers pay the original investors until the money runs out – which inevitably collapsed' [*Times*]

Q

qualification /ˌkwɒlɪfɪˈkeɪʃ(ə)n/ *noun* a document or some other formal proof of the fact that someone has successfully completed a specialised course of study or has acquired a skill ○ *You must have the right qualifications for the job.* ○ *Job-hunting is difficult if you have no qualifications.*

'...personnel management is not an activity that can ever have just one set of qualifications as a requirement for entry into it' [*Personnel Management*]

qualified /ˈkwɒlɪfaɪd/ *adjective* **1.** having passed special examinations in a subject ○ *She is a qualified accountant.* ○ *We have appointed a qualified designer to supervise the decorating of the new reception area.* **2.** with some reservations or conditions ○ *qualified acceptance of a contract* ○ *The plan received qualified approval from the board.*

'...applicants will be professionally qualified and ideally have a degree in Commerce and postgraduate management qualifications' [*Australian Financial Review*]

qualified acceptance of a bill /ˌkwɒlɪfaɪd əkˈseptəns əv eɪ bɪl/ *noun* acceptance of a bill which takes place only if conditions are met

qualified accounts /ˌkwɒlɪfaɪd əˈkaʊnts/ *plural noun* accounts which have been noted by the auditors because they contain something with which the auditors do not agree

qualified domestic trust /ˌkwɒlɪfaɪd dəˈmestɪk trʌst/ *noun* a trust for the non-citizen spouse of a US citizen, affording tax advantages at the time of the citizen's death

qualified valuer /ˌkwɒlɪfaɪd ˈvæljʊə/ *noun* a person conducting a valuation who holds a recognised and relevant professional qualification and has recent post-qualification experience, and sufficient knowledge of the state of the market, with reference to the location and category of the tangible fixed asset being valued

qualifying distribution /ˌkwɒlɪfaɪɪŋ ˌdɪstrɪˈbjuːʃ(ə)n/ *noun* a payment of a dividend to a shareholder, on which advance corporation tax is paid

qualifying period /ˈkwɒlɪfaɪɪŋ ˌpɪəriəd/ *noun* a time which has to pass before something or someone qualifies for something, e.g. a grant or subsidy ○ *There is a six-month qualifying period before you can get a grant from the local authority.*

qualifying shares /ˌkwɒlɪfaɪɪŋ ˈʃeəz/ *plural noun* the number of shares which you need to earn to get a bonus issue or to be a director of the company, etc.

quality control /ˈkwɒlɪti kənˌtrəʊl/ *noun* the process of making sure that the quality of a product is good

quango /ˈkwæŋgəʊ/ *noun* an official body, set up by a government to investigate or deal with a special problem (NOTE: plural is **quangos**)

quantifiable /ˈkwɒntɪfaɪəb(ə)l/ *adjective* possible to quantify ○ *The effect of the change in the discount structure is not quantifiable.*

quantity discount /ˌkwɒntɪti ˈdɪskaʊnt/ *noun* a discount given to people who buy large quantities

quantum meruit /ˌkwæntʊm ˈmeruɪt/ *phrase* a Latin phrase meaning 'as much as has been earned'

quarter /ˈkwɔːtə/ *noun* **1.** one of four equal parts (25%) ○ *She paid only a quarter of the list price.* **2.** a period of three months ○ *The instalments are payable at the end of each quarter.*

'...corporate profits for the first quarter showed a 4 per cent drop from last year's final three months' [*Financial Times*]

'...economists believe the economy is picking up this quarter and will do better still in the second half of the year' [*Sunday Times*]

quarter day /ˈkwɔːtə deɪ/ *noun* a day at the end of a quarter, when rents, fees etc. should be paid

quarterly /ˈkwɔːtəli/ *adjective, adverb* happening once every three months ○ *There is a quarterly charge for electricity.* ○ *The bank sends us a quarterly statement.* ○ *We* *agreed to pay the rent quarterly* or *on a quarterly basis.*

quarterly report /ˌk(w)ɔːtəlɪ rɪˈpɔːt/ *noun* the results of a corporation, produced each quarter

quartile /ˈkwɔːtaɪl/ *noun* one of a series of three figures below which 25%, 50% or 75% of the total falls

quasi- /kweɪzaɪ/ *prefix* almost or which seems like ○ *a quasi-official body*

quasi-loan /ˌkweɪzaɪ ˈləʊn/ *noun* an agreement between two parties where one agrees to pay the other's debts, provided that the second party agrees to reimburse the first at some later date

quasi-public corporation /ˌkweɪzaɪ ˌpʌblɪk ˌkɔːpəˈreɪʃ(ə)n/ *noun US* a US institution which is privately owned, but which serves a public function, such as the Federal National Mortgage Association

queue /kjuː/ *noun* **1.** a line of people waiting one behind the other ○ *to form a queue* or *to join a queue* ○ *Queues formed at the doors of the bank when the news spread about its possible collapse.* **2.** a series of documents such as orders or application forms which are dealt with in order ■ *verb* to form a line one after the other for something ○ *When food was rationed, people had to queue for bread.* ○ *We queued for hours to get tickets.* ○ *A list of companies queueing to be launched on the Stock Exchange.* ○ *The candidates queued outside the interviewing room.*

queuing time /ˈkjuːɪŋ taɪm/ *noun* a period of time messages have to wait before they can be processed or transmitted

quick ratio /ˌkwɪk ˈreɪʃiəʊ/ *noun* same as **liquidity ratio**

quid /kwɪd/ *noun* one pound Sterling (*slang*) □ **to be quids in** to make a profit, to be in luck ○ *He was quids in after the sale.*

quid pro quo /ˌkwɪd prəʊ ˈkwəʊ/ *noun* money paid or an action carried out in return for something ○ *She agreed to repay the loan early, and as a quid pro quo the bank released the collateral.*

quorum /ˈkwɔːrəm/ *noun* a minimum number of people who have to be present at a meeting to make it valid

quota /ˈkwəʊtə/ *noun* a limited amount of something which is allowed to be produced, imported, etc.

'Canada agreed to a new duty-free quota of 600,000 tonnes a year' [*Globe and Mail (Toronto)*]

quota system /ˈkwəʊtə ˌsɪstəm/ *noun* **1.** a system where imports or supplies are regulated by fixed maximum amounts **2.** an arrangement for distribution which allows each distributor only a specific number of items

quotation /kwəʊˈteɪʃ(ə)n/ *noun* an estimate of how much something will cost ○ *They sent in their quotation for the job.* ○ *Our quotation was much lower than all the others.* ○ *We accepted the lowest quotation.*

quote /kwəʊt/ *verb* **1.** to repeat words or a reference number used by someone else ○ *He quoted figures from the annual report.* ○ *In reply please quote this number.* ○ *When making a complaint please quote the batch number printed on the box.* ○ *She replied, quoting the number of the account.* **2.** to estimate what a cost or price is likely to be ○ *to quote a price for supplying stationery* ○ *Their prices are always quoted in dollars.* ○ *He quoted me a price of £1,026.* ○ *Can you quote for supplying 20,000 envelopes?* ■ *noun* an estimate of how much something will cost (*informal*) ○ *to give someone a quote for supplying computers* ○ *We have asked for quotes for refitting the shop.* ○ *Her quote was the lowest of three.* ○ *We accepted the lowest quote.*

'…banks operating on the foreign exchange market refrained from quoting forward US/Hongkong dollar exchange rates' [*South China Morning Post*]

quoted company /ˌkwəʊtɪd ˈkʌmp(ə)ni/ *noun* a company whose shares can be bought or sold on the Stock Exchange

quoted investments /ˌkwəʊtɪd ɪn ˈvestmənts/ *noun* investments which are listed on a Stock Exchange

quote-driven system /ˈkwəʊt ˌdrɪv(ə)n ˌsɪstəm/ *noun* a system of working a stock market, where marketmakers quote a price for a stock, as opposed to an order-driven system

quoted shares /ˌkwəʊtɪd ˈʃeəz/ *plural noun* shares which can be bought or sold on the Stock Exchange

R

racket /'rækɪt/ *noun* an illegal deal which makes a lot of money ○ *She runs a cut-price ticket racket.*

rack rent /'ræk rent/ *noun* a very high rent

raise /reɪz/ *noun US* an increase in salary ○ *He asked the boss for a raise.* ○ *She is pleased – she has had her raise.* ○ *She got her raise last month.* (NOTE: The UK term is **rise.**) ■ *verb* **1.** to increase or to make higher ○ *The government has raised the tax levels.* ○ *Air fares will be raised on June 1st.* ○ *The company raised its dividend by 10%.* ○ *When the company raised its prices, it lost half of its share of the market.* ○ *The organisation will raise wages if inflation gets worse.* ○ *This increase in production will raise the standard of living in the area.* **2.** to obtain money or to organise a loan ○ *The company is trying to raise the capital to fund its expansion programme.* ○ *The government raises more money by indirect taxation than by direct.* ○ *Where will he raise the money from to start up his business?*

'…the company said yesterday that its recent share issue has been oversubscribed, raising A$225.5m' [*Financial Times*]

'…investment trusts can raise capital, but this has to be done as a company does, by a rights issue of equity' [*Investors Chronicle*]

'…over the past few weeks, companies raising new loans from international banks have been forced to pay more' [*Financial Times*]

rally /'ræli/ *noun* a rise in price when the trend has been downwards ○ *Shares staged a rally on the Stock Exchange.* ○ *After a brief rally shares fell back to a new low.* ■ *verb* to rise in price, when the trend has been downwards ○ *Shares rallied on the news of the latest government figures.*

'…when Japan rallied, it had no difficulty in surpassing its previous all-time high, and this really stretched the price-earnings ratios into the stratosphere' [*Money Observer*]

'…bad news for the US economy ultimately may have been the cause of a late rally in stock prices yesterday' [*Wall Street Journal*]

R&D *abbr* research and development

random /'rændəm/ *adjective* done without making any special selection

random check /ˌrændəm 'tʃek/ *noun* a check on items taken from a group without any special selection

random sample /ˌrændəm 'sɑːmpəl/ *noun* a sample taken without any selection

range /reɪndʒ/ *noun* **1.** a series of items ○ *Their range of products* or *product range is too narrow.* ○ *We offer a wide range of sizes* or *range of styles.* ○ *There are a whole range of alternatives for the new salary scheme.* **2.** a scale of items from a low point to a high one □ **range of prices** the difference between the highest and lowest price for a share or bond over a period of time

rank /ræŋk/ *noun* a position in a company or an organisation, especially one which shows how important someone is relative to others ○ *All managers are of equal rank.* ○ *Promotion means moving up from a lower rank.* ■ *verb* **1.** to classify in order of importance ○ *Candidates are ranked in order of their test results.* ○ *Deferred ordinary shares do not rank for dividend.* **2.** to be in a position ○ *The non-voting shares rank equally with the voting shares.* ○ *Deferred ordinary shares do not rank for dividend.*

rate /reɪt/ *noun* **1.** the money charged for time worked or work completed **2.** an amount of money paid, e.g. as interest or dividend, shown as a percentage **3.** the value of one currency against another ○ *What is today's rate* or *the current rate for the dollar?* **4.** an amount, number or speed compared with something else ○ *the rate of increase in redundancies* ○ *The rate of absenteeism* or *The absenteeism rate always increases in fine weather.*

'…state-owned banks cut their prime rate a percentage point to 11%' [*Wall Street Journal*]

'…the unions had argued that public sector pay rates had slipped behind rates applying in private sector employment' [*Australian Financial Review*]

'…royalties have been levied at a rate of 12.5% of full production' [*Lloyd's List*]

'...the minister is not happy that banks are paying low interest on current accounts of less than 10 per cent, but are charging rates of between 60 and 71 per cent on loans' [*Business in Africa*]

rateable value /ˌreɪtəb(ə)l 'væljuː/ *noun* a value of a property as a basis for calculating local taxes

rate of return /ˌreɪt əv rɪ'tɜːn/ *noun* the amount of interest or dividend which comes from an investment, shown as a percentage of the money invested

rate of sales /ˌreɪt əv 'seɪlz/ *noun* the speed at which units are sold

rates *plural noun* local UK taxes formerly levied on property in the UK and now replaced by the council tax

rating /'reɪtɪŋ/ *noun* **1.** the act of giving something a value, or the value given **2.** the valuing of property for local taxes

rating agency /'reɪtɪŋ ˌeɪdʒənsi/ *noun* an organisation which gives a rating to companies or other organisations issuing bonds

rating officer /'reɪtɪŋ ˌɒfɪsə/ *noun* an official in a local authority who decides the rateable value of a commercial property

ratio /'reɪʃiəʊ/ *noun* a proportion or quantity of something compared to something else ○ *the ratio of successes to failures* ○ *Our product outsells theirs by a ratio of two to one.* ○ *With less manual work available, the ratio of employees to managers is decreasing.*

ratio analysis /'reɪʃiəʊ əˌnæləsɪs/ *noun* a method of analysing the performance of a company by showing the figures in its accounts as ratios and comparing them with those of other companies

raw data /ˌrɔː 'deɪtə/ *noun* data as it is put into a computer, without being analysed

raw materials /ˌrɔː mə'tɪəriəlz/ *plural noun* basic materials which have to be treated or processed in some way before they can be used, e.g. wood, iron ore or crude petroleum

R/D *abbr* refer to drawer

RDPR *abbr* refer to drawer please represent

re- /riː/ *prefix* again

readjust /ˌriːə'dʒʌst/ *verb* to adjust something again or in a new way, or to change in response to new conditions ○ *to readjust prices to take account of the rise in the costs of raw materials* ○ *to readjust salary scales* ○ *Share prices readjusted quickly to the news of the devaluation.*

readjustment /ˌriːə'dʒʌstmənt/ *noun* an act of readjusting ○ *a readjustment in pricing* ○ *After the devaluation there was a period of readjustment in the exchange rates.*

ready cash /ˌredi 'kæʃ/ *noun* money which is immediately available for payment

ready money /ˌredi 'mʌni/ *noun* cash or money which is immediately available

real /rɪəl/ *adjective* genuine and not an imitation ○ *His case is made of real leather* or *he has a real leather case.* ○ *That car is a real bargain at £300.*

'...real wages have been held down dramatically: they have risen as an annual rate of only 1% in the last two years' [*Sunday Times*]

'...sterling M3 rose by 13.5% in the year to August – seven percentage points faster than the rate of inflation and the biggest increase in real terms for years' [*Economist*]

'Japan's gross national product for the April-June quarter dropped 0.4% in real terms from the previous quarter' [*Nikkei Weekly*]

'...the Federal Reserve Board has eased interest rates in the past year, but they are still at historically high levels in real terms' [*Sunday Times*]

real asset /ˌrɪəl 'æset/ *noun* a non-movable asset such as land or a building

real estate /'rɪəl ɪˌsteɪt/ *noun* property in the form of land or buildings

'...on top of the cost of real estate, the investment in inventory and equipment to open a typical warehouse comes to around $5 million' [*Duns Business Month*]

real estate agent /'rɪəl ɪˌsteɪt ˌeɪdʒənt/ *noun US* a person who sells property for customers

real estate investment trust /rɪəl ɪ ˌsteɪt ɪn'vestmənt trʌst/ *noun* a public trust company which invests only in property. Abbreviation **REIT**

real exchange rate /ˌrɪəl ɪks'tʃeɪndʒ ˌreɪt/ *noun* an exchange rate that has been adjusted for inflation

real interest rate /ˌrɪəl 'ɪntrəst ˌreɪt/ *noun* an interest rate after taking inflation into account

real investment /ˌrɪəl ɪn'vestmənt/ *noun* the purchase of assets such as land, property, and plant and machinery as opposed to the acquisition of securities

realisation /ˌrɪəlaɪ'zeɪʃ(ə)n/, **realization** *noun* the act of making real □ **the realisation of a project** putting a project into action ○ *The plan moved a stage nearer realisation when the contracts were signed.*

realisation concept /ˌrɪəlaɪ'zeɪʃ(ə)n ˌkɒnsept/ *noun* the principle that increases in value should only be recognised when the assets in question are realised by being sold to an independent purchaser

realise /'rɪəlaɪz/, **realize** *verb* **1.** to make something become real □ **to realise a project or a plan** to put a project or a plan into action **2.** to sell for money ○ *The company was run-*

ning out of cash, so the board decided to realise some property or assets. ○ *The sale realised £100,000.* □ **realised gain** *or* **loss** a gain or loss made when assets are sold

realised profit /ˌrɪəlaɪzd ˈprɒfɪt/ *noun* an actual profit made when something is sold, as opposed to paper profit

real rate of return /rɪəl ˌreɪt əv rɪˈtɜːn/ *noun* an actual rate of return, calculated after taking inflation into account

real return after tax /rɪəl rɪˌtɜːn ˌɑːftə ˈtæks/ *noun* the return calculated after deducting tax and inflation

real time /ˈrɪəl taɪm/ *noun* the time when a computer is working on the processing of data while the event to which the data refers is actually taking place ○ *The website allows you to check share prices in real time* or *gives real time information on share prices.*

real-time system /ˈrɪəl taɪm ˌsɪstəm/ *noun* a computer system where data is inputted directly into the computer which automatically processes it to produce information which can be used immediately

realty /ˈrɪəlti/ *noun* property or real estate

real value /ˌrɪəl ˈvæljuː/ *noun* a value of an investment which is kept the same, e.g. by index-linking

reasonable /ˈriːz(ə)nəb(ə)l/ *adjective* **1.** sensible, or not annoyed ○ *The manager of the shop was very reasonable when I tried to explain that I had left my credit cards at home.* **2.** moderate or not expensive ○ *The union has decided to put in a reasonable wage claim.*

reassess /ˌriːəˈses/ *verb* to assess again ○ *The manager was asked to reassess the department staff, after the assessments were badly done by the supervisors.*

reassessment /ˌriːəˈsesmənt/ *noun* a new assessment

rebate /ˈriːbeɪt/ *noun* **1.** a reduction in the amount of money to be paid ○ *We are offering a 10% rebate on selected goods* **2.** money returned to someone because they have paid too much ○ *She got a tax rebate at the end of the year.*

recapitalisation /riːˌkæpɪt(ə)laɪˈzeɪʃ(ə)n/, **recapitalization** *noun* a change in the capital structure of a company as when new shares are issued, especially when undertaken to avoid the company going into liquidation

receipt /rɪˈsiːt/ *noun* **1.** a piece of paper showing that money has been paid or that something has been received ○ *He kept the customs receipt to show that he had paid duty*

on the goods. ○ *She lost her taxi receipt.* ○ *Keep the receipt for items purchased in case you need to change them later.* **2.** the act of receiving something ○ *Goods will be supplied within thirty days of receipt of order.* ○ *Invoices are payable within thirty days of receipt.* ○ *On receipt of the notification, the company lodged an appeal.* ■ *verb* to stamp or to sign a document to show that it has been received, or to stamp an invoice to show that it has been paid ○ *Receipted invoices are filed in the ring binder.*

receipts /rɪˈsiːts/ *plural noun* money taken in sales ○ *to itemise receipts and expenditure* ○ *Receipts are down against the same period of last year.*

'…the public sector borrowing requirement is kept low by treating the receipts from selling public assets as a reduction in borrowing' [*Economist*]

'…gross wool receipts for the selling season to end June appear likely to top $2 billion' [*Australian Financial Review*]

receipts and payments account /rɪˌsiːts ən ˈpeɪmənts əˌkaʊnt/ *noun* a report of cash transactions during a period. It is used in place of an income and expenditure account when it is not considered appropriate to distinguish between capital and revenue transactions or to include accruals.

receivable /rɪˈsiːvəb(ə)l/ *adjective* able to be received

receivables /rɪˈsiːvəb(ə)lz/ *plural noun* money which is owed to a company

receive /rɪˈsiːv/ *verb* to get something which is given or delivered to you ○ *We received the payment ten days ago.* ○ *The employees have not received any salary for six months.* ○ *The goods were received in good condition.*

receiver /rɪˈsiːvə/ *noun* a person who receives something ○ *He signed as receiver of the shipment.*

Receiver of Revenue /rɪˌsiːvə əv ˈrevənjuː/ *noun* an informal term for the South African Revenue Service as a whole

receiving /rɪˈsiːvɪŋ/ *noun* an act of getting something which has been delivered

receiving clerk /rɪˈsiːvɪŋ klɑːk/ *noun* an official who works in a receiving office

receiving department /rɪˈsiːvɪŋ dɪˌpɑːtmənt/ *noun* a section of a company which deals with incoming goods or payments

receiving office /rɪˈsiːvɪŋ ˌɒfɪs/ *noun* an office where goods or payments are received

receiving order /rɪˈsiːvɪŋ ˌɔːdə/ *noun* an order from a court appointing an official receiver to a company

recession /rɪˈseʃ(ə)n/ *noun* a period where there is a decline in trade or in the economy ○ *The recession has reduced profits in many companies.* ○ *Several firms have closed factories because of the recession.*

reciprocal /rɪˈsɪprək(ə)l/ *adjective* done by one person, company or country to another one, which does the same thing in return ○ *We signed a reciprocal agreement* or *a reciprocal contract with a Russian company.*

reciprocal holdings /rɪˌsɪprək(ə)l ˈhəʊldɪŋz/ *plural noun* a situation where two companies own shares in each other to prevent takeover bids

reciprocal trade /rɪˌsɪprək(ə)l ˈtreɪd/ *noun* trade between two countries

reciprocate /rɪˈsɪprəkeɪt/ *verb* to do the same thing for someone as that person has done for you ○ *They offered us an exclusive agency for their cars and we reciprocated with an offer of the agency for our buses.*

'...in 1934 Congress authorized President Roosevelt to seek lower tariffs with any country willing to reciprocate' [*Duns Business Month*]

reckon /ˈrekən/ *verb* to calculate something ○ *to reckon the costs at £25,000* ○ *We reckon the loss to be over £1m.* ○ *They reckon the insurance costs to be too high.*

recognise /ˈrekəgnaɪz/, **recognize** *verb* □ **statement of total recognised gains and losses** financial statement showing changes in shareholders' equity during an accounting period (see FRS 3)

recognised professional body /ˌrekəgnaɪzd prəˌeʃ(ə)nəl ˈbɒdi/ *noun* a professional body which is in charge of the regulation of the conduct of its members and is recognised by the FSA. Abbreviation **RPB**

recognized qualification /ˌrekəgnaɪzd ˌkwɒlɪfɪˈkeɪʃ(ə)n/ *noun* a qualification which is well-known to employers and professional bodies

reconcile /ˈrekənsaɪl/ *verb* to make two financial accounts or statements agree ○ *She is trying to reconcile one account with another* or *to reconcile the two accounts.*

reconciliation /ˌrekənsɪliˈeɪʃ(ə)n/, **reconcilement** /ˈrekənsaɪlmənt/ *noun* the act of making two accounts or statements agree

reconciliation statement /ˌrekənsɪli ˈeɪʃ(ə)n ˌsteɪtmənt/ *noun* a statement which explains how two accounts can be made to agree

reconstruction /ˌriːkənˈstrʌkʃən/ *noun* **1.** the process of building again ○ *The economic reconstruction of an area after a disaster.* **2.** new way of organizing

record /ˈrekɔːd/ *noun* **1.** a report of something which has happened ○ *The chairman signed the minutes as a true record of the last meeting.* ○ *She has a very poor timekeeping record.* □ **for the record** or **to keep the record straight** in order that everyone knows what the real facts of the matter are ○ *For the record, I should like to say that these sales figures have not yet been checked by the sales department.* **2.** a description of what has happened in the past ○ *the salesperson's record of service* or *service record* ○ *the company's record in industrial relations* ○ *He has a very poor timekeeping record.* **3.** a success which is better than anything before ○ *Last year was a record year for the company.* ○ *Our top sales rep has set a new record for sales per call.*

record book /ˈrekɔːd bʊk/ *noun* a book in which minutes of meetings are kept

record date /ˈrekɔːd deɪt/ *noun* same as **date of record**

recorded delivery /rɪˌkɔːdɪd dɪˈlɪv(ə)ri/ *noun* a mail service where the letters are signed for by the person receiving them ○ *We sent the documents (by) recorded delivery.*

recording /rɪˈkɔːdɪŋ/ *noun* the act of making a note of something ○ *the recording of an order* or *of a complaint*

records /ˈrekɔːdz/ *plural noun* documents which give information ○ *The names of customers are kept in the company's records.* ○ *We find from our records that our invoice number 1234 has not been paid.*

recoup /rɪˈkuːp/ *verb* □ **to recoup your losses** to get back money which you thought you had lost

recourse /rɪˈkɔːs/ *noun* a right of a lender to compel a borrower to repay money borrowed

recover /rɪˈkʌvə/ *verb* **1.** to get back something which has been lost ○ *to recover damages from the driver of the car* ○ *to start a court action to recover property* ○ *He never recovered his money.* ○ *The initial investment was never recovered.* **2.** to get better, to rise ○ *The market has not recovered from the rise in oil prices.* ○ *The stock market fell in the morning, but recovered during the afternoon.*

recoverable /rɪˈkʌv(ə)rəb(ə)l/ *adjective* possible to get back

recoverable amount /rɪˌkʌv(ə)rəb(ə)l ə ˈmaʊnt/ *noun* the value of an asset, either the price it would fetch if sold, or its value to the company when used, whichever is the larger figure

recovery /rɪˈkʌv(ə)ri/ *noun* **1.** the act of getting back something which has been lost

○ *to start an action for recovery of property* ○ *We are aiming for the complete recovery of the money invested.* **2.** a movement upwards of shares or of the economy ○ *signs of recovery after a slump* ○ *The economy staged a recovery.*

rectification /ˌrektɪfɪ'keɪʃ(ə)n/ *noun* correction

rectify /'rektɪfaɪ/ *verb* to correct something, to make something right ○ *to rectify an entry* (NOTE: **rectifies – rectifying – rectified**)

recurrent /rɪ'kʌrənt/ *adjective* happening again and again ○ *a recurrent item of expenditure* ○ *There is a recurrent problem in supplying this part.*

recurring payments /rɪˌkɜːrɪŋ 'peɪmənts/ *plural noun* payments, such as mortgage interest or payments on a hire purchase agreement, which are made each month

recycle /riː'saɪk(ə)l/ *verb* to take waste material and process it so that it can be used again

red /red/ *noun* the colour of debit or overdrawn balances in some bank statements □ **in the red** showing a debit or loss ○ *My bank account is in the red.* ○ *The company went into the red in 1998.* ○ *The company is out of the red for the first time since 1990.*

Red Book /'red bʊk/ *noun* a document published on Budget Day, with the text of the Chancellor of the Exchequer's financial statement and budget

redeem /rɪ'diːm/ *verb* to pay off a loan or a debt ○ *to redeem a mortgage* ○ *to redeem a debt*

redeemable /rɪ'diːməb(ə)l/ *adjective* referring to a bond which can be sold for cash

redeemable government stock /rɪ ˌdiːməb(ə)l ˌgʌv(ə)nmənt 'stɒk/ *noun* stock which can be redeemed for cash at some time in the future. In the UK, only the War Loan is irredeemable.

redeemable preference share /rɪ ˌdiːməb(ə)l 'pref(ə)rəns ʃeə/ *noun* a preference share which must be bought back by the company at an agreed date and for an agreed price

redeemable security /rɪˌdiːməb(ə)l sɪ 'kjʊərɪti/ *noun* a security which can be redeemed at its face value at a specific date in the future

redemption /rɪ'dempʃən/ *noun* the repayment of a loan

redemption date /rɪ'dempʃən deɪt/ *noun* a date on which a loan or debt is due to be repaid

redemption value /rɪ'dempʃən ˌvæljuː/ *noun* a value of a security when redeemed

redemption yield /rɪ'dempʃən jiːld/ *noun* a yield on a security including interest and its redemption value

redistribute /ˌriːdɪ'strɪbjuːt/ *verb* to move items, work or money to different areas or people ○ *The government aims to redistribute wealth by taxing the rich and giving grants to the poor.* ○ *The orders have been redistributed among the company's factories.*

redistribution of wealth /ˌriːdɪstrɪbjuːʃən əv 'welθ/ *noun* the process of sharing wealth among the whole population

reduce /rɪ'djuːs/ *verb* to make something smaller or lower ○ *We must reduce expenditure if we want to stay in business.* ○ *They have reduced prices in all departments.* ○ *We were expecting the government to reduce taxes not to increase them.* ○ *We have made some staff redundant to reduce overmanning.* ○ *The company reduced output because of a fall in demand.* ○ *The government's policy is to reduce inflation to 5%.*

reduced /rɪ'djuːst/ *adjective* lower ○ *Reduced prices have increased unit sales.* ○ *Prices have fallen due to a reduced demand for the goods.*

reducing balance method /rɪˌdjuːsɪŋ 'bæləns ˌmeθəd/ *noun* a method of depreciating assets, where the asset is depreciated at a constant percentage of it cost each year. Also called **declining balance method**

reduction /rɪ'dʌkʃən/ *noun* an act of making something smaller or less ○ *Reduction in demand has led to the cancellation of several new projects.* ○ *The company was forced to make reductions in its advertising budget.* ○ *Price reductions have had no effect on our sales.* ○ *Working only part-time will mean a significant reduction in take-home pay.*

redundancy /rɪ'dʌndənsi/ *noun* the dismissal of a person whose job no longer needs to be done

redundancy payment /rɪ'dʌndənsi ˌpeɪmənt/ *noun* a payment made to an employee to compensate for losing his or her job

redundancy rebate /rɪ'dʌndənsi ˌriːbeɪt/ *noun* a payment made to a company to compensate for redundancy payments made

redundant /rɪ'dʌndənt/ *adjective* more than is needed, useless ○ *a redundant clause* *in a contract* ○ *The new legislation has made clause 6 redundant.* ○ *Retraining can help employees whose old skills have become redundant.*

redundant staff /rɪˌdʌndənt 'stɑːf/ *noun* staff who have lost their jobs because they are not needed any more

re-export /ˌriːek'spɔːt/ *verb* to export something which has been imported

re-exportation /ˌriːekspɔː'teɪʃ(ə)n/ *noun* the exporting of goods which have been imported

refer /rɪ'fɜː/ *verb* □ **'refer to drawer'** words written on a cheque which a bank refuses to pay and returns it to the person who wrote it. Abbreviation **R** *or* **D**

reference /'ref(ə)rəns/ *noun* **1.** the process of mentioning or dealing with something ○ *with reference to your letter of May 25th* **2.** a series of numbers or letters which make it possible to find a document which has been filed ○ *our reference: PC/MS 1234* ○ *Thank you for your letter (reference 1234).* ○ *Please quote this reference in all correspondence.* **3.** a written report on someone's character or ability ○ *to write someone a reference* or *to give someone a reference* ○ *to ask applicants to supply references* □ **to ask a company for trade references** *or* **for bank references** to ask for reports from traders or a bank on the company's financial status and reputation

referral /rɪ'fɜːrəl/ *noun* an action of referring or recommending someone to someone

refer to drawer please represent /rɪ ˌfɜː tə ˌdrɔːə pliːz ˌriːprɪ'zent/ *noun* in the United Kingdom, written on a cheque by the paying banker to indicate that there are currently insufficient funds to meet the payment, but that the bank believes sufficient funds will be available shortly. Abbreviation **RDPR**

refinance /ˌriː'faɪnæns/ *verb* to replace one source of finance with another

refund *noun* /'riːfʌnd/ money paid back ○ *The shoes don't fit – I'm going to ask for a refund.* ○ *She got a refund after complaining to the manager.* ■ *verb* /rɪ'fʌnd/ to pay back money ○ *to refund the cost of postage* ○ *All money will be refunded if the goods are not satisfactory.*

refundable /rɪ'fʌndəb(ə)l/ *adjective* possible to pay back ○ *We ask for a refundable deposit of £20.* ○ *The entrance fee is refundable if you purchase £5 worth of goods.*

register /'redʒɪstə/ *noun* an official list ○ *to enter something in a register* ○ *to keep a register up to date* ○ *people on the register of electors* ■ *verb* **1.** to write something in an official list ○ *to register a fall in the numbers*

of unemployed teenagers ○ *To register a company you must pay a fee to Companies House.* ○ *When a property is sold, the sale is registered at the Land Registry.* **2.** to send a letter by registered post ○ *I registered the letter, because it contained some money.*

registered /'redʒɪstəd/ *adjective* having been noted on an official list ○ *a registered share transaction*

registered cheque /ˌredʒɪstəd 'tʃek/ *noun* a cheque written on a bank account on behalf of a client who does not have a bank account

registered company /ˌredʒɪstəd 'kʌmp(ə)ni/ *noun* company which has been officially set up and registered with the Registrar of Companies

registered letter /ˌredʒɪstəd 'letə/, **registered parcel** /ˌredʒɪstəd 'pɑːs(ə)l/ *noun* a letter or parcel which is noted by the post office before it is sent, so that the sender can claim compensation if it is lost

registered office /ˌredʒɪstəd 'ɒfɪs/ *noun* the office address of a company which is officially registered with the Companies' Registrar

registered security /ˌredʒɪstəd sɪ 'kjʊərɪti/ *noun* a security such as a share in a quoted company which is registered with Companies House and whose holder is listed in the company's share register

register of companies /ˌredʒɪstə əv 'kʌmp(ə)niz/ *noun* in the United Kingdom, the list of companies maintained at Companies House. ◊ **company, corporation**

register of directors /ˌredʒɪstə əv daɪ 'rektəz/ *noun* an official list of the directors of a company which has to be sent to the Registrar of Companies

registrant /'redʒɪstrənt/ *noun US* company applying to register with the Securities and Exchange Commission

registrar /ˌredʒɪ'strɑː/ *noun* a person who keeps official records

Registrar of Companies /ˌredʒɪstrɑː əv 'kʌmp(ə)nɪz/ *noun* a government official whose duty is to ensure that companies are properly registered, and that, when registered, they file accounts and other information correctly

registration /ˌredʒɪ'streɪʃ(ə)n/ *noun* the act of having something noted on an official list ○ *the registration of a trademark* or *of a share transaction*

registration fee /ˌredʒɪ'streɪʃ(ə)n fiː/ *noun* **1.** money paid to have something registered **2.** money paid to attend a conference

registration number /ˌredʒɪˈstreɪʃ(ə)n ˌnʌmbə/ *noun* an official number, e.g. the number of a car

registration statement /ˌredʒɪ ˈstreɪʃ(ə)n ˌsteɪtmənt/ *noun* a document which gives information about a company when it is registered and listed on a stock exchange (NOTE: The UK term is **listing particulars**.)

regression analysis /rɪˈgreʃ(ə)n ə ˌnæləsɪs/, **regression model** /rɪˈgreʃ(ə)n ˌmɒd(ə)l/ *noun* a method of discovering the ratio of one dependent variable and one or more independent variables, so as to give a value to the dependent variable

regressive taxation /rɪˌgresɪv tæk ˈseɪʃ(ə)n/ *noun* a system of taxation in which tax gets progressively less as income rises. Compare **progressive taxation**

regular /ˈreɡjʊlə/ *adjective* occurring at the same time each day, each week, each month or each year ○ *His regular train is the 12.45.* ○ *The regular flight to Athens leaves at 06.00.*

regular income /ˌreɡjʊlər ˈɪnkʌm/ *noun* an income which comes in every week or month ○ *She works freelance so she does not have a regular income.*

regulate /ˈreɡjʊleɪt/ *verb* **1.** to adjust something so that it works well or is correct **2.** to change or maintain something by law

regulated consumer credit agreement /ˌreɡjʊleɪtɪd kənˌsjuːmə ˈkredɪt ə ˌgriːmənt/ *noun* a credit agreement according to the Consumer Credit Act

regulation /ˌreɡjʊˈleɪʃ(ə)n/ *noun* **1.** a law or rule ○ *the new government regulations on housing standards* ○ *Fire regulations or Safety regulations were not observed at the restaurant.* ○ *Regulations concerning imports and exports are set out in this leaflet.* **2.** the use of laws or rules stipulated by a government or regulatory body, such as the Financial Services Authority, to provide orderly procedures and to protect consumers and investors ○ *government regulation of trading practices*

'EC regulations which came into effect in July insist that customers can buy cars anywhere in the EC at the local pre-tax price' [*Financial Times*]

'...a unit trust is established under the regulations of the Department of Trade, with a trustee, a management company and a stock of units' [*Investors Chronicle*]

'...fear of audit regulation, as much as financial pressures, is a major factor behind the increasing number of small accountancy firms deciding to sell their practices or merge with another firm' [*Accountancy*]

regulations /ˌreɡjʊˈleɪʃ(ə)nz/ *noun* laws or rules ○ *the new government regulations on housing standards* ○ *Fire regulations or Safety regulations were not observed at the restaurant.* ○ *Regulations concerning imports and exports are set out in this leaflet.*

Regulation S-X /ˌreɡjʊleɪʃ(ə)n es ˈeks/ *noun* the rule of the US Securities and Exchange Commission which regulates annual reports from companies

regulator /ˈreɡjʊleɪtə/ *noun* a person whose job it is to see that regulations are followed

'...the regulators have sought to protect investors and other market participants from the impact of a firm collapsing' [*Banking Technology*]

regulatory /ˈreɡjʊlət(ə)ri/ *adjective* applying regulations

regulatory body /ˌreɡjʊlət(ə)ri ˈbɒdi/ *noun* FINANCE, BANKING, AND ACCOUNTING, GENERAL MANAGEMENT an independent organisation, usually established by a government, that makes rules and sets standards for an industry and oversees the activities of companies within it

regulatory powers /ˈreɡjʊlət(ə)ri ˌpaʊəz/ *noun* powers to enforce government regulations

reimburse /ˌriːɪmˈbɜːs/ *verb* □ **to reimburse someone their expenses** to pay someone back for money which they have spent ○ *You will be reimbursed for your expenses* or *Your expenses will be reimbursed.*

reimbursement /ˌriːɪmˈbɜːsmənt/ *noun* the act of paying back money ○ *reimbursement of expenses*

reinvest /ˌriːɪnˈvest/ *verb* to invest money again ○ *She sold her shares and reinvested the money in government stocks.*

reinvestment /ˌriːɪnˈvestmənt/ *noun* **1.** the act of investing money again in the same securities **2.** the act of investing a company's earnings in its own business by using them to create new products for sale

'...many large US corporations offer shareholders the option of reinvesting their cash dividend payments in additional company stock at a discount to the market price. But to some big securities firms these discount reinvestment programs are an opportunity to turn a quick profit' [*Wall Street Journal*]

REIT *abbr US* real estate investment trust

reject *noun* /ˈriːdʒekt/, *adjective* something which has been thrown out because it is not of the usual standard ○ *sale of rejects* or *of reject items* ○ *to sell off reject stock* ■ *verb* /rɪˈdʒekt/ to refuse to accept something, or to say that something is not satisfactory ○ *The board rejected the draft budget.*

related /rɪˈleɪtɪd/ *adjective* connected or linked ○ *related items on the agenda*

related company /rɪˌleɪtɪd ˈkʌmp(ə)ni/ *noun* a company in which another company makes a long-term capital investment in order to gain control or influence

related party /rɪˌleɪtɪd ˈpɑːti/ *noun* any person or company which controls or participates in the policy decisions of an accounting entity

relative error /ˌrelətɪv ˈerə/ *noun* the difference between an estimate and its correct value

release /rɪˈliːs/ *noun* the act of setting someone free or of making something or someone no longer subject to an obligation or restriction ○ *release from a contract* ○ *the release of goods from customs* ○ *She was offered early release so that she could take up her new job.*

'…pressure to ease monetary policy mounted yesterday with the release of a set of pessimistic economic statistics' [*Financial Times*]

'…the national accounts for the March quarter released by the Australian Bureau of Statistics showed a real increase in GDP' [*Australian Financial Review*]

relevant /ˈreləv(ə)nt/ *adjective* having to do with what is being discussed or the current situation ○ *Which is the relevant government department?* ○ *Can you give me the relevant papers?* ○ *The new assistant does not have any relevant experience.*

relevant benefits /ˌreləv(ə)nt ˈbenɪfɪts/ *plural noun* benefits such as pension, endowment insurance, etc. provided by a pension scheme

relief /rɪˈliːf/ *noun* help

relief shift /rɪˈliːf ʃɪft/ *noun* a shift which comes to take the place of another shift, usually the shift between the day shift and the night shift

relocation /ˌriːləʊˈkeɪʃ(ə)n/ *noun* the act of moving to a different place ○ *We will pay all the staff relocation costs.*

relocation package /ˌriːləʊˈkeɪʃ(ə)n ˌpækɪdʒ/ *noun* payments made by an employer to an employee when the employee is asked to move to a new area in order to work. Payments up to a minimum level are exempt from tax.

remainder /rɪˈmeɪndə/ *noun* things left behind ○ *The remainder of the stock will be sold off at half price.*

reminder /rɪˈmaɪndə/ *noun* a letter to remind a customer that he or she has not paid an invoice ○ *to send someone a reminder*

remission of taxes /rɪˌmɪʃ(ə)n əv ˈtæksɪz/ *noun* a refund of taxes which have been overpaid

remit /rɪˈmɪt/ *verb* to send money ○ *to remit by cheque* (NOTE: **remitting – remitted**)

remittance /rɪˈmɪt(ə)ns/ *noun* money which is sent to pay back a debt or to pay an invoice ○ *Please send remittances to the treasurer.* ○ *The family lives on a weekly remittance from their father in the USA.*

remittance advice /rɪˈmɪt(ə)ns əd ˌvaɪs/, **remittance slip** /rɪˈmɪt(ə)ns slɪp/ *noun* an advice note sent with payment, showing why it is being made, i.e. quoting the invoice number or a reference number

remitting bank /rɪˈmɪtɪŋ bæŋk/ *verb* a bank into which a person has deposited a cheque, and which has the duty to collect the money from the account of the writer of the cheque

remunerate /rɪˈmjuːnəreɪt/ *verb* to pay someone for doing something ○ *The company refused to remunerate them for their services.*

remuneration /rɪˌmjuːnəˈreɪʃ(ə)n/ *noun* payment for services ○ *The job is interesting but the remuneration is low.* ○ *She receives a small remuneration of £400 a month.* ○ *No one will work hard for such poor remuneration.*

renegotiate /ˌriːnɪˈɡəʊʃieɪt/ *verb* to negotiate something again ○ *The company was forced to renegotiate the terms of the loan.*

renew /rɪˈnjuː/ *verb* to continue something for a further period of time ○ *We have asked the bank to renew the bill of exchange.* ○ *The tenant wants to renew his lease.* ○ *Her contract was renewed for a further three years.*

renewal /rɪˈnjuːəl/ *noun* the act of renewing ○ *renewal of a lease* or *of a subscription* or *of a bill* ○ *renewal of a contract* ○ *Her contract is up for renewal* ○ *When is the renewal date of the bill?*

renewal notice /rɪˈnjuːəl ˌnəʊtɪs/ *noun* a note sent by an insurance company asking the insured person to renew the insurance

renewal premium /rɪˈnjuːəl ˌpriːmiəm/ *noun* a premium to be paid to renew an insurance

rent /rent/ *noun* money paid to use an office, house or factory for a period of time ■ *verb* **1.** to pay money to hire an office, house, factory or piece of equipment for a period of time ○ *to rent an office* or *a car* ○ *He rents an office in the centre of town.* ○ *They were driving a rented car when they were stopped by the police.* **2.** □ **rent a room** scheme by which a taxpayer can let a room in his or her house and be exempt from tax on the rental income below a certain level

rental /'rent(ə)l/ *noun* money paid to use an office, house, factory, car, piece of equipment, etc., for a period of time ○ *The car rental bill comes to over £1000 a quarter.*

'…top quality office furniture: short or long-term rental 50% cheaper than any other rental company' [*Australian Financial Review*]

'…until the vast acres of empty office space start to fill up with rent-paying tenants, rentals will continue to fall and so will values. Despite the very sluggish economic recovery under way, it is still difficult to see where the new tenants will come from' [*Australian Financial Review*]

rental value /'rent(ə)l ˌvæljuː/ *noun* a full value of the rent for a property if it were charged at the current market rate, i.e. calculated between rent reviews

rent control /'rent kənˌtrəʊl/ *noun* government regulation of rents

rent review /'rent rɪˌvjuː/ *noun* an increase in rents which is carried out during the term of a lease. Most leases allow for rents to be reviewed every three or five years.

rent tribunal /'rent traɪˌbjuːn(ə)l/ *noun* a court which can decide if a rent is too high or low

renunciation /rɪˌnʌnsi'eɪʃ(ə)n/ *noun* an act of giving up ownership of shares

reorder /riː'ɔːdə/ *noun* a further order for something which has been ordered before ○ *The product has only been on the market ten days and we are already getting reorders.* ■ *verb* to place a new order for something ○ *We must reorder these items because stock is getting low.*

reorder level /riː'ɔːdə ˌlev(ə)l/ *noun* a minimum amount of an item which a company holds in stock, such that, when stock falls to this amount, the item must be reordered

reorder quantity /riː'ɔːdə ˌkwɒntəti/ *noun* a quantity of a product which is reordered, especially the economic order quantity (EOQ)

reorganisation /riːˌɔːgənaɪ'zeɪʃ(ə)n/, **reorganization** *noun* the process of organising a company in a different way, as in the USA when a bankrupt company applies to be treated under Chapter 11 to be protected from its creditors while it is being reorganised

repay /rɪ'peɪ/ *verb* to pay something back, or to pay back money to someone ○ *to repay money owed* ○ *The company had to cut back on expenditure in order to repay its debts.*

repayable /rɪ'peɪəb(ə)l/ *adjective* possible to pay back ○ *loan which is repayable over ten years*

repayment /rɪ'peɪmənt/ *noun* the act of paying money back or money which is paid back ○ *The loan is due for repayment next year.*

repayment mortgage /rɪ'peɪmənt ˌmɔːgɪdʒ/ *noun* a mortgage where the borrower pays back both interest and capital over the period of the mortgage. This is opposed to an endowment mortgage, where only the interest is repaid, and an insurance is taken out to repay the capital at the end of the term of the mortgage.

replacement cost accounting /rɪˌpleɪsmənt kɒst ə'kaʊntɪŋ/ *noun* a method of accounting in which assets are valued at the amount it would cost to replace them, rather than at the original cost. Also called **current cost accounting**. Compare **historical cost accounting**

replacement cost depreciation /rɪˌpleɪsmənt kɒst dɪˌpriːʃi'eɪʃ(ə)n/ *noun* depreciation based on the actual cost of replacing the asset in the current year

replacement price /rɪ'pleɪsmənt praɪs/ *noun* a price at which the replacement for an asset would have to be bought

replacement value /rɪ'pleɪsmənt ˌvæljuː/ *noun* the value of something for insurance purposes if it were to be replaced ○ *The computer is insured at its replacement value.*

report /rɪ'pɔːt/ *noun* a statement describing what has happened or describing a state of affairs ○ *to make a report* or *to present a report* or *to send in a report on market opportunities in the Far East* ○ *The accountants are drafting a report on salary scales.* ○ *The sales manager reads all the reports from the sales team.* ○ *The chairman has received a report from the insurance company.* ■ *verb* **1.** to make a statement describing something ○ *The salesforce reported an increased demand for the product.* ○ *He reported the damage to the insurance company.* ○ *We asked the bank to report on his financial status.* **2.** to publish the results of a company for a period and declare the dividend

'…a draft report on changes in the international monetary system' [*Wall Street Journal*]

'…responsibilities include the production of premium quality business reports' [*Times*]

'…the research director will manage a team of business analysts monitoring and reporting on the latest development in retail distribution' [*Times*]

'…the successful candidate will report to the area director for profit responsibility for sales of leading brands' [*Times*]

report form /rɪ'pɔːt fɔːm/ *noun* a balance sheet laid out in vertical form. It is the opposite of 'account' or 'horizontal' form. Also called **vertical form**

reporting entity /rɪˌpɔːtɪŋ 'entɪti/ *noun* any organisation, such as a limited company, which reports its accounts to its shareholders

repossess /ˌriːpəˈzes/ *verb* to take back an item which someone is buying under a hire-purchase agreement, or a property which someone is buying under a mortgage, because the purchaser cannot continue the payments

repossession /ˌriːpəˈzeʃ(ə)n/ *noun* an act of repossessing ○ *Repossessions are increasing as people find it difficult to meet mortgage repayments.*

reprice /riːˈpraɪs/ *verb* to change the price on an item, usually to increase it

repudiation /rɪˌpjuːdiˈeɪʃ(ə)n/ *noun* a refusal to accept something such as a debt

repurchase /riːˈpɜːtʃɪs/ *verb* to buy something again, especially something which you have recently bought and then sold

require /rɪˈkwaɪə/ *verb* to ask for or to demand something ○ *to require a full explanation of expenditure* ○ *The law requires you to submit all income to the tax authorities.*

required rate of return /rɪˌkwaɪəd reɪt əv rɪˈtɜːn/ *noun* the minimum return for a proposed project investment to be acceptable. ◊ **discounted cash flow**

resale /ˈriːseɪl/ *noun* the selling of goods which have been bought ○ *to purchase something for resale* ○ *The contract forbids resale of the goods to the USA.*

resale price maintenance /ˌriːseɪl ˈpraɪs ˌmeɪntənəns/ *noun* a system in which the price for an item is fixed by the manufacturer and the retailer is not allowed to sell it at a lower price. Abbreviation **RPM**

reschedule /riːˈʃedjuːl/ *verb* **1.** to arrange a new timetable for something ○ *She missed her plane, and all the meetings had to be rescheduled.* **2.** to arrange new credit terms for the repayment of a loan ○ *Third World countries which are unable to keep up the interest payments on their loans from western banks have asked for their loans to be rescheduled.*

rescind /rɪˈsɪnd/ *verb* to annul or to cancel something ○ *to rescind a contract* or *an agreement*

research and development expenditure /rɪˌsɜːtʃ ən dɪˈveləpmənt ɪkˌspendɪtʃə/ *noun* money spent on R & D

resell /riːˈsel/ *verb* to sell something which has just been bought ○ *The car was sold in*

June and the buyer resold it to an dealer two months later. (NOTE: **reselling – resold**)

reseller /riːˈselə/ *noun* somebody in the marketing chain who buys to sell to somebody else, e.g. wholesalers, distributors, and retailers

reserve currency /rɪˈzɜːv ˌkʌrənsi/ *noun* a strong currency used in international finance, held by other countries to support their own weaker currencies

reserve for fluctuations /rɪˌzɜːv fə ˌflʌktʃuˈeɪʃ(ə)nz/ *noun* money set aside to allow for changes in the values of currencies

reserve fund /rɪˈzɜːv fʌnd/ *noun* profits in a business which have not been paid out as dividend but have been ploughed back into the business

reserve price /rɪˈzɜːv praɪs/ *noun* the lowest price which a seller will accept, e.g. at an auction or when selling securities through a broker ○ *The painting was withdrawn when it failed to reach its reserve price.*

reserves /rɪˈzɜːvz/ *plural noun* **1.** supplies kept in case of need ○ *Our reserves of fuel fell during the winter.* ○ *The country's reserves of gas* or *gas reserves are very large.* **2.** money from profits not paid as dividend, but kept back by a company in case it is needed for a special purpose

residence /ˈrezɪd(ə)ns/ *noun* **1.** a house or flat where someone lives ○ *He has a country residence where he spends his weekends.* **2.** the fact of living or operating officially in a country

residence permit /ˈrezɪd(ə)ns ˌpɜːmɪt/ *noun* an official document allowing a foreigner to live in a country ○ *He has applied for a residence permit.* ○ *She was granted a residence permit for one year* or *a one-year residence permit.*

resident /ˈrezɪd(ə)nt/ *noun, adjective* a person or company considered to be living or operating in a country for official or tax purposes ○ *The company is resident in France.*

residential property /ˌrezɪdenʃ(ə)l ˈprɒpəti/ *noun* houses or flats owned or occupied by individual residents

residual /rɪˈzɪdjuəl/ *adjective* remaining after everything else has gone

residual income /rɪˌzɪdjuəl ˈɪnkʌm/ *noun* pretax profits less an imputed interest charge for invested capital. It is used to assess divisional performance.

residual value /rɪˌzɪdjuəl ˈvæljuː/ *noun* a value of an asset after it has been depreciated in the company's accounts

residue /ˈrezɪdjuː/ noun money left over ○ *After paying various bequests the residue of his estate was split between his children.*

resolution /ˌrezəˈluːʃ(ə)n/ noun a decision to be reached at a meeting

resolve /rɪˈzɒlv/ verb to decide to do something ○ *The meeting resolved that a dividend should not be paid.*

responsibility accounting /rɪˌspɒnsɪ ˈbɪlɪti əˌkaʊntɪŋ/ noun the keeping of financial records with an emphasis on who is responsible for each item

restated balance sheet /ˌriːsteɪtd ˈbæləns ʃiːt/ noun a balance sheet reframed to serve a particular purpose, such as highlighting depreciation on assets

restrict /rɪˈstrɪkt/ verb to limit something or to impose controls on something ○ *to restrict credit* ○ *to restrict the flow of trade* or *to restrict imports* ○ *We are restricted to twenty staff by the size of our offices.*

restrictive /rɪˈstrɪktɪv/ adjective not allowing something to go beyond a point, limiting

restrictive covenant /rɪˌstrɪktɪv ˈkʌvənənt/ noun a clause in a contract which prevents someone from doing something

restructure /riːˈstrʌktʃə/ verb to reorganise the financial basis of a company

restructuring /riːˈstrʌktʃərɪŋ/ noun the process of reorganising the financial basis of a company

result /rɪˈzʌlt/ noun **1.** a profit or loss account for a company at the end of a trading period ○ *The company's results for last year were an improvement on those of the previous year.* **2.** something which happens because of something else ○ *What was the result of the price investigation?* ○ *The company doubled its sales force with the result that the sales rose by 26%.*

'...the company has received the backing of a number of oil companies who are willing to pay for the results of the survey' [*Lloyd's List*]

'...some profit-taking was noted, but underlying sentiment remained firm in a steady stream of strong corporate results' [*Financial Times*]

retail /ˈriːteɪl/ noun the sale of small quantities of goods to the general public □ **the goods in stock have a retail value of £1m** the value of the goods if sold to the public is £1m, before discounts and other factors are taken into account ■ adverb □ **he buys wholesale and sells retail** he buys goods in bulk at a wholesale discount and sells in small quantities to the public ■ verb to sell

for a price □ **these items retail at or for £2.50** the retail price of these items is £2.50

retail banking /ˈriːteɪl ˌbæŋkɪŋ/ noun services provided by commercial banks to individuals as opposed to business customers, e.g. current accounts, deposit and savings accounts, as well as credit cards, mortgages, and investments (NOTE: In the United Kingdom, although this service was traditionally provided by high street banks, separate organisations are now providing Internet and telephone banking services.)

retail dealer /ˈriːteɪl ˌdiːlə/ noun a person who sells to the general public

retail deposit /ˈriːteɪl dɪˌpɒzɪt/ noun a deposit placed by an individual with a bank

retailer /ˈriːteɪlə/ noun a person who runs a retail business, selling goods direct to the public

retailing /ˈriːteɪlɪŋ/ noun the selling of full-price goods to the public ○ *From car retailing the company branched out into car leasing.*

retail investor /ˈriːteɪl ɪnˌvestə/ noun a private investor, as opposed to institutional investors

retail price /ˈriːteɪl ˌpraɪs/ noun the price at which the retailer sells to the final customer

retain /rɪˈteɪn/ verb to keep something or someone ○ *measures to retain experienced staff* ○ *Out of the profits, the company has retained £50,000 as provision against bad debts.*

retained earnings /rɪˌteɪnd ˈɜːnɪŋz/ plural noun an amount of profit after tax which a company does not pay out as dividend to the shareholders, but which is kept to be used for the further development of the business. Also called **retentions**

retained income /rɪˌteɪnd ˈɪnkʌm/, **retained profit** /rɪˌteɪnd ˈprɒfɪt/ noun same as **retained earnings**

retainer /rɪˈteɪnə/ noun money paid in advance to someone so that they will work for you, and not for someone else ○ *We pay them a retainer of £1,000.*

retiral /rɪˈtaɪərəl/ noun US same as **retirement**

retire /rɪˈtaɪə/ verb **1.** to stop work and take a pension ○ *She retired with a £15,000 pension.* ○ *The founder of the company retired at the age of 85.* ○ *The shop is owned by a retired policeman.* **2.** to make an employee stop work and take a pension ○ *They decided to retire all staff over 50.*

retirement /rɪˈtaɪəmənt/ *noun* the act of retiring from work ○ *I am looking forward to my retirement.* ○ *Older staff are planning what they will do in retirement.*

retirement age /rɪˈtaɪəmənt eɪdʒ/ *noun* the age at which people retire. In the UK this is usually 65 for men and 60 (but soon to become 65) for women.

retirement annuity /rɪˈtaɪəmənt ə ˌnjuːɪti/ *noun* an annuity bought when someone retires, using part of the sum put into a personal pension plan

retirement benefits /rɪˈtaɪəmənt ˈbenɪfɪts/ *plural noun* benefits which are payable by a pension scheme to a person on retirement

retirement pension /rɪˈtaɪəmənt ˌpenʃən/ *noun* a state pension given to a man who is over 65 or and woman who is over 60

retroactive /ˌretrəʊˈæktɪv/ *adjective* which takes effect from a time in the past ○ *They got a pay rise retroactive to last January.*

'The salary increases, retroactive from April of the current year, reflect the marginal rise in private sector salaries' [*Nikkei Weekly*]

retroactively /ˌretrəʊˈæktɪvli/ *adverb* going back to a time in the past

return /rɪˈtɜːn/ *noun* **1.** a profit or income from money invested ○ *We are buying technology shares because they bring in a quick return.* ○ *What is the gross return on this line?* **2.** an official statement or form that has to be sent in to the authorities ■ *verb* to make a statement ○ *to return income of £15,000 to the tax authorities*

'…with interest rates running well above inflation, investors want something that offers a return for their money' [*Business Week*]

'Section 363 of the Companies Act 1985 requires companies to deliver an annual return to the Companies Registration Office. Failure to do so before the end of the period of 28 days after the company's return date could lead to directors and other officers in default being fined up to £2000' [*Accountancy*]

return date /rɪˈtɜːn deɪt/ *noun* a date by which a company's annual return has to be made to the Registrar of Companies

return on assets /rɪˌtɜːn ɒn ˈæsets/, **return on capital employed** /rɪˌtɜːn ɒn ˈekwɪti/, **return on equity** *noun* a profit shown as a percentage of the capital or money invested in a business. Abbreviation **ROA, ROCE, ROE**

return on investment /rɪˌtɜːn ɒn ɪn ˈvestmənt/ *noun* a ratio of the profit made in a financial year as a percentage of an investment. Abbreviation **ROI**

return on net assets /rɪˌtɜːn ɒn net ˈæsets/ *noun* a ratio of the profit made in a financial year as a percentage of the assets of a company

returns /rɪˈtɜːnz/ *plural noun* profits or income from investment ○ *The company is looking for quick returns on its investment.*

revaluation /riːˌvæljuˈeɪʃən/ *noun* an act of revaluing ○ *The balance sheet takes into account the revaluation of the company's properties.*

revaluation method /riːˌvæljuˈeɪʃən ˌmeθəd/ *noun* a method of calculating the depreciation of assets, by which the asset is depreciated by the difference in its value at the end of the year over its value at the beginning of the year

revaluation reserve /riːˌvæljuˈeɪʃən rɪ ˌzɜːv/ *noun* money set aside to account for the fact that the value of assets may vary as a result of accounting in different currencies

revalue /riːˈvæljuː/ *verb* to value something again, usually setting a higher value on it than before ○ *The company's properties have been revalued.* ○ *The dollar has been revalued against all world currencies.*

revenue /ˈrevənjuː/ *noun* **1.** money received ○ *revenue from advertising* or *advertising revenue* ○ *Oil revenues have risen with the rise in the dollar.* **2.** money received by a government in tax

revenue account /ˈrevənjuː əˌkaʊnt/ *noun* an accounting system which records the revenue and expenditure incurred by a company during its usual business

revenue accounts /ˈrevənjuː əˌkaʊnts/ *plural noun* accounts of a business which record money received as sales, commission, etc.

revenue expenditure /ˌrevənjuː ɪk ˈspendɪtʃə/ *noun* expenditure on purchasing stock but not capital items, which is then sold during the current accounting period

revenue ledger /ˌrevənjuː ˈledʒə/ *noun* a record of all the income received by an organisation

revenue officer /ˈrevənjuː ˌɒfɪsə/ *noun* a person working in the government tax offices

revenue reserves /ˈrevənjuː rɪˌzɜːvs/ *plural noun* retained earnings which are shown in the company's balance sheet as part of the shareholders' funds. Also called **company reserves**

revenue sharing /ˌrevənjuː ˈʃeərɪŋ/ *noun* the distribution of income within limited partnerships

reverse /rɪ'vɜːs/ *adjective* opposite or in the opposite direction ■ *verb* to change a decision to the opposite ○ *The committee reversed its decision on import quotas.*

'…the trade balance sank $17 billion, reversing last fall's brief improvement' [*Fortune*]

reverse leverage /rɪˌvɜːs 'liːvərɪdʒ/ *noun* the borrowing of money at a rate of interest higher than the expected rate of return on investing the money borrowed

reverse takeover /rɪˌvɜːs 'teɪkəʊvə/ *noun* a takeover where the company which has been taken over ends up owning the company which has taken it over. The acquiring company's shareholders give up their shares in exchange for shares in the target company.

reverse yield gap /rɪˌvɜːs 'jiːld ˌgæp/ *noun* the amount by which bond yield exceeds equity yield, or interest rates on loans exceed rental values as a percentage of the costs of properties

reversing entry /rɪ'vɜːsɪŋ ˌentri/ *noun* an entry in a set of accounts which reverses an entry in the preceding accounts

reversion /rɪ'vɜːʃ(ə)n/ *noun* a return of property to an original owner

reversionary /rɪ'vɜːʃ(ə)n(ə)ri/ *adjective* referring to property which passes to another owner on the death of the present one

reversionary annuity /rɪˌvɜːʃ(ə)n(ə)ri ə'njuːɪti/ *noun* an annuity paid to someone on the death of another person

reversionary bonus /rɪˌvɜːʃ(ə)n(ə)ri 'bəʊnəs/ *noun* an annual bonus on a life assurance policy, declared by the insurer

review /rɪ'vjuː/ *noun* a general examination ○ *to conduct a review of distributors* ■ *verb* to examine something generally

revise /rɪ'vaɪz/ *verb* to change something which has been calculated or planned ○ *Sales forecasts are revised annually.* ○ *The chairman is revising his speech to the AGM.*

revolving credit /rɪˌvɒlvɪŋ 'kredɪt/ *noun* a system where someone can borrow money at any time up to an agreed amount, and continue to borrow while still paying off the original loan. Also called **open-ended credit**

revolving loan /rɪˌvɒlvɪŋ 'ləʊn/ *noun* a loan facility whereby the borrower can choose the number and timing of withdrawals against their bank loan and any money repaid may be reborrowed at a future date. Such loans are available both to businesses and personal customers.

rider /'raɪdə/ *noun* an additional clause ○ *to add a rider to a contract*

right /raɪt/ *noun* a legal entitlement to something ○ *There is no automatic right of renewal to this contract.* ○ *She has a right to the property.* ○ *He has no right to the patent.* ○ *The staff have a right to know how the company is doing.*

right of way /ˌraɪt əv 'weɪ/ *noun* a legal title to go across someone's property

rights issue /'raɪts ˌɪʃuː/ *noun* an arrangement which gives shareholders the right to buy more shares at a lower price (NOTE: The US term is **rights offering**.)

ring fence /'rɪŋ fens/ *verb* 1. to separate valuable assets or profitable businesses from others in a group which are unprofitable and may make the whole group collapse 2. to identify money from certain sources and only use it in certain areas ○ *The grant has been ring-fenced for use in local authority education projects only.*

rise /raɪz/ *noun* 1. an increase ○ *A rise in the price of raw materials.* ○ *Oil price rises brought about a recession in world trade.* ○ *There has been a rise in sales of 10% or Sales show a rise of 10%.* ○ *Salaries are increasing to keep up with the rises in the cost of living.* ○ *The recent rise in interest rates has made mortgages dearer.* ○ *There needs to be an increase in salaries to keep up with the rise in the cost of living.* 2. an increase in pay ○ *She asked her boss for a rise.* ○ *He had a 6% rise in January.* (NOTE: The US term is **raise**.) ■ *verb* to move upwards or to become higher ○ *Prices or Salaries are rising faster than inflation.* ○ *Interest rates have risen to 15%.* ○ *Salaries are rising faster than inflation.* (NOTE: **rising – rose – risen**)

'…the index of industrial production sank 0.2 per cent for the latest month after rising 0.3 per cent in March' [*Financial Times*]

'…the stock rose to over $20 a share, higher than the $18 bid' [*Fortune*]

'…customers' deposit and current accounts also rose to $655.31 million at the end of December' [*Hong-kong Standard*]

'…the government reported that production in the nation's factories and mines rose 0.2% in September' [*Sunday Times*]

risk /rɪsk/ *noun* possible harm or a chance of danger

'…remember, risk isn't volatility. Risk is the chance that a company's earnings power will erode – either because of a change in the industry or a change in the business that will make the company significantly less profitable in the long term' [*Fortune*]

risk-adjusted return on capital /ˌrɪsk əˌdʒʌstɪd rɪˌtɜːn ɒn 'kæpɪt(ə)l/ *adjective* calculated in a way that takes into account the risks associated with income

risk arbitrage /ˌrɪsk ˈɑːbɪtrɑːʒ/ *noun* the business of buying shares in companies which are likely to be taken over and so rise in price

risk arbitrageur /rɪsk ˌɑːbɪtrɑːˈʒɜː/ *noun* a person whose business is risk arbitrage

risk asset ratio /ˌrɪsk ˌæset ˈreɪʃiəʊ/ *noun* a proportion of a bank's capital which is in risk assets

risk capital /ˈrɪsk ˌkæpɪt(ə)l/ *noun* same as **venture capital**

risk-free /ˌrɪsk ˈfriː/, **riskless** /ˈrɪskləs/ *adjective* with no risk involved ○ *a risk-free investment*

'…there is no risk-free way of taking regular income from your money higher than the rate of inflation and still preserving its value' [*Guardian*]

'…many small investors have also preferred to put their spare cash with risk-free investments such as building societies rather than take chances on the stock market. The returns on a host of risk-free investments have been well into double figures' [*Money Observer*]

risk management /ˈrɪsk ˌmænɪdʒmənt/ *noun* the work of managing a company's exposure to risk from its credit terms or exposure to interest rate or exchange rate fluctuations

risk premium /ˈrɪsk ˌpriːmiəm/ *noun* an extra payment, e.g. increased dividend or higher than usual profits, for taking risks

risk-weighted assets /ˌrɪsk ˌweɪtɪd ˈæsets/ *plural noun* assets which include off-balance sheet items for insurance purposes

risky /ˈrɪski/ *adjective* dangerous or which may cause harm ○ *We lost all our money in some risky ventures in South America.*

'…while the bank has scaled back some of its more risky trading operations, it has retained its status as a top-rate advisory house' [*Times*]

ROA *abbr* return on assets

ROCE *abbr* return on capital employed

ROE *abbr* return on equity

ROI *abbr* return on investment

rolled-up coupons /ˌrəʊld ʌp ˈkuːpɒnz/ *plural noun* interest coupons on securities, which are not paid out, but added to the capital value of the security

rolling account /ˈrəʊlɪŋ əˌkaʊnt/ *noun* US a system where there are no fixed account days, but stock exchange transactions are paid at a fixed period after each transaction has taken place, as opposed to the British system, where an account day is fixed each month

rolling budget /ˌrəʊlɪŋ ˈbʌdʒɪt/ *noun* a budget which moves forward on a regular basis, such as a budget covering a twelve-month period which moves forward each month or quarter

rolling settlement /ˌrəʊlɪŋ ˈset(ə)lmənt/ *noun* US same as **rolling account**

roll over /ˌrəʊl ˈəʊvə/ *verb* □ **to roll over a credit** to make credit available over a continuing period □ **to roll over a debt** to allow a debt to stand after the repayment date

'…at the IMF in Washington, officials are worried that Japanese and US banks might decline to roll over the principal of loans made in the 1980s to Southeast Asian and other developing countries' [*Far Eastern Economic Review*]

rollover /ˈrəʊləʊvə/ *noun* an extension of credit or of the period of a loan, though not necessarily on the same terms as previously

rollover relief /ˌrəʊləʊvə rɪˈliːf/ *noun* tax relief, where profit on the sale of an asset is not taxed if the money realised is used to acquire another asset. The profit on the eventual sale of this second asset will be taxed unless the proceeds of the second sale are also invested in new assets.

roll up /ˌrəʊl ˈʌp/ *verb* to extend a loan, by adding the interest due to be paid to the capital

Romalpa clause /rəʊˈmɒlpə ˌklɔːz/ *noun* a clause in a contract, whereby the seller provides that title to the goods does not pass to the buyer until the buyer has paid for them

Roman numerals /ˌrəʊmən ˈnjuːmərəlz/ *plural noun* figures written I, II, III, IV, etc.

root /ruːt/ *noun* a fractional power of a number

rough /rʌf/ *adjective* approximate, not very accurate

rough calculation /ˌrʌf ˌkælkjʊˈleɪʃ(ə)n/ *noun* a way of working out a mathematical problem approximately, or the approximate result arrived at ○ *I made some rough calculations on the back of an envelope.*

rough estimate /ˌrʌf ˈestɪmət/ *noun* a very approximate calculation

rough out /ˌrʌf ˈaʊt/ *verb* to make a draft or a general design of something, which may be changed later ○ *The finance director roughed out a plan of investment.*

round down /ˌraʊnd ˈdaʊn/ *verb* to decrease a fractional figure to the nearest full figure

round figures /ˌraʊnd ˈfɪɡəz/ *noun* figures that have been adjusted up or down to the nearest 10, 100, 1,000, and so on

round off /ˌraʊnd ˈɒf/ *verb* to reduce the digits in a decimal number by removing the final zeros

round up /ˌraʊnd ˈʌp/ *verb* to increase a fractional figure to the nearest full figure ○ *to round up the figures to the nearest pound*

'…each cheque can be made out for the local equivalent of œ100 rounded up to a convenient figure' [*Sunday Times*]

royalty /ˈrɔɪəlti/ *noun* money paid to an inventor, writer or the owner of land for the right to use their property, usually a specific percentage of sales, or a specific amount per sale ○ *The country will benefit from rising oil royalties.* ○ *He is still receiving substantial royalties from his invention.*

RPB *abbr* recognised professional body

RPM *abbr* resale price maintenance

rubber check /ˌrʌbə ˈtʃek/ *noun US* a cheque which cannot be cashed because the person writing it does not have enough money in the account to pay it (NOTE: The UK term is **bouncing cheque**.)

rule /ruːl/ *noun* a statement that directs how people should behave ○ *It is a company rule that smoking is not allowed in the offices.* ○ *The rules of the organisation are explained during the induction sessions.* ■ *verb* **1.** to give an official decision ○ *The commission of inquiry ruled that the company was in breach of contract.* ○ *The judge ruled that the documents had to be deposited with the court.* **2.** to be in force or to be current ○ *Prices which are ruling at the moment.* ○ *The current ruling agreement is being redrafted.*

rulebook /ˈruːlbʊk/ *noun* a set of rules by which the members of a self-regulatory organisation must operate

rule of 72 /ˌruːl əv ˌsev(ə)nti ˈtuː/ *noun* a calculation that an investment will double in value at compound interest after a period shown as 72 divided by the interest percentage, so interest at 10% compound will double the capital invested in 7.2 years

rule of 78 /ˌruːl əv ˌsev(ə)nti ˈeɪt/ *noun* a method used to calculate the rebate on a loan with front-loaded interest that has been repaid early. It takes into account the fact that as the loan is repaid, the share of each monthly payment related to interest decreases, while the share related to repayment increases.

run /rʌn/ *noun* **1.** a period of time during which a machine is working **2.** a rush to buy something ○ *The Post Office reported a run on the new stamps.* □ **a run on the bank** a rush by customers to take deposits out of a bank which they think may close down ■ *verb* **1.** to be in force ○ *The lease runs for twenty years.* ○ *The lease has only six months to run.* **2.** to amount to ○ *The costs ran into thousands of pounds.* **3.** to work on a machine ○ *Do not run the photocopier for more than four hours at a time.* ○ *The computer was running invoices all night.*

'…applications for mortgages are running at a high level' [*Times*]

'…with interest rates running well above inflation, investors want something that offers a return for their money' [*Business Week*]

run into /ˌrʌn ˈɪntʊ/ *verb* to amount to ○ *Costs have run into thousands of pounds.* □ **he has an income running into five figures** he earns more than £10,000

running account credit /ˌrʌnɪŋ ə ˌkaʊnt ˈkredɪt/ *noun* an overdraft facility, credit card, or similar system that allows customers to borrow up to a specific limit and re-borrow sums previously repaid by either writing a cheque or using their card

running total /ˌrʌnɪŋ ˈtəʊt(ə)l/ *noun* the total carried from one column of figures to the next

running yield /ˈrʌnɪŋ jiːld/ *noun* a yield on fixed interest securities, where the interest is shown as a percentage of the price paid

run up /ˌrʌn ˈʌp/ *verb* to make debts or costs go up quickly ○ *He quickly ran up a bill for £250.*

S

safe deposit /ˌseɪf dɪˌpɒzɪt/ *noun* a bank safe where you can leave jewellery or documents

safe deposit box /ˌseɪf dɪˈpɒzɪt ˌbɒks/ *noun* a small box which you can rent to keep jewellery or documents in a bank's safe

safe investment /ˌseɪf ɪnˈvestmənt/ *noun* something, e.g. a share, which is not likely to fall in value

safe keeping /ˌseɪf ˈkiːpɪŋ/ *noun* the fact of being looked after carefully ○ *We put the documents into the bank for safe keeping.*

safety /ˈseɪfti/ *noun* the fact of being free from danger or risk □ **to take safety precautions** *or* **safety measures** to act to make sure something is safe

salaried /ˈsælərid/ *adjective* earning a salary ○ *The company has 250 salaried staff.*

salaried partner /ˌsælərid ˈpɑːtnə/ *noun* a partner, often a junior one, who receives a regular salary in accordance with the partnership agreement

salary /ˈsæləri/ *noun* a regular payment for work done, made to an employee usually as a cheque at the end of each month ○ *The company froze all salaries for a six-month period.* ○ *If I get promoted, my salary will go up.* ○ *The salary may be low, but the fringe benefits attached to the job are good.* ○ *She got a salary increase in June.*

salary cheque /ˈsæləri tʃek/ *noun* a monthly cheque by which an employee is paid

salary cut /ˈsæləri kʌt/ *noun* a sudden reduction in salary

salary deductions /ˈsæləri dɪˌdʌkʃənz/ *plural noun* money which a company removes from salaries to pay to the government as tax, National Insurance contributions, etc.

salary scale /ˈsæləri skeɪl/ *noun* same as **pay scale** ○ *He was appointed at the top end of the salary scale.*

sale /seɪl/ *noun* **1.** an act of giving an item or doing a service in exchange for money, or for the promise that money will be paid □ **to offer something for sale** *or* **to put something up for sale** to announce that something is ready to be sold ○ *They put the factory up for sale.* ○ *His shop is for sale.* ○ *These items are not for sale to the general public.* **2.** an act of selling goods at specially low prices ○ *The shop is having a sale to clear old stock.* ○ *The sale price is 50% of the usual price.*

'…the latest car sales for April show a 1.8 per cent dip from last year's total' [*Investors Chronicle*]

sale and lease-back /ˌseɪl ən ˈliːs bæk/ *noun* **1.** a situation where a company sells a property to raise cash and then leases it back from the purchaser **2.** the sale of an asset, usually a building, to somebody else who then leases it back to the original owner

sales /seɪlz/ *plural noun* money received for selling something ○ *Sales have risen over the first quarter.*

sales analysis /ˈseɪlz əˌnæləsɪs/ *noun* an examination of the reports of sales to see why items have or have not sold well

sales book /ˈseɪlz bʊk/ *noun* a record of sales

sales budget /ˈseɪlz ˌbʌdʒɪt/ *noun* a plan of probable sales

sales chart /ˈseɪlz tʃɑːt/ *noun* a diagram showing how sales vary from month to month

sales curve /ˈseɪlz kɜːv/ *noun* a graph showing how sales increase or decrease

sales department /ˈseɪlz dɪˌpɑːtmənt/ *noun* the section of a company which deals with selling the company's products or services

sales figures /ˈseɪlz ˌfɪgəz/ *plural noun* total sales

sales force /ˈseɪlz fɔːs/ *noun* a group of sales staff

sales forecast /ˈseɪlz ˌfɔːkɑːst/ *noun* an estimate of future sales

sales invoice /ˈseɪlz ˌɪnvɔɪs/ *noun* an invoice relating to a sale

sales journal /ˈseɪlz ˌdʒɜːn(ə)l/ *noun* the book in which non-cash sales are recorded with details of customer, invoice, amount and date. These details are later posted to each customer's account in the sales ledger.

sales ledger /ˈseɪlz ˌledʒə/ *noun* a book in which sales to each customer are entered

sales ledger clerk /ˈseɪlz ledʒə ˌklɑːk/ *noun* an office employee who deals with the sales ledger

sales manager /ˈseɪlz ˌmænɪdʒə/ *noun* a person in charge of a sales department

sales mix /ˈseɪlz mɪks/ *noun* the sales and profitability of a wide range of products sold by a single company

sales mix profit variance /ˌseɪls mɪks ˈprɒfɪt ˌveəriəns/ *noun* the differing profitability of different products within a product range

sales price variance /ˌseɪlz praɪs ˈveəriəns/ *noun* the difference between expected revenue from actual sales and actual revenue

sales return /ˈseɪlz rɪˌtɜːn/ *noun* a report of sales made each day or week or quarter

sales revenue /ˈseɪlz ˌrevənjuː/ *noun* US the income from sales of goods or services (NOTE: The UK term is **turnover**.)

sales slip /ˈseɪlz slɪp/ *noun* a paper showing that an article was bought at a specific shop ○ *Goods can be exchanged only on production of a sales slip.*

sales target /ˈseɪlz ˌtɑːgɪt/ *noun* the amount of sales a sales representative is expected to achieve

sales tax /ˈseɪlz tæks/ *noun* a tax which is paid on each item sold and is collected when the purchase is made. Also called **turnover tax**

sales value /ˈseɪlz ˌvæljuː/ *noun* the amount of money which would be received if something is sold

sales volume /ˈseɪlz ˌvɒljuːm/ *noun* the number of units sold (NOTE: The UK term is **turnover**.)

sales volume profit variance /ˌseɪlz ˌvɒljuːm ˈprɒfɪt ˌveəriəns/ *noun* the difference between the profit on the number of units actually sold and the forecast figure

salvage /ˈsælvɪdʒ/ *noun* **1.** the work of saving a ship or a cargo from being destroyed **2.** goods saved from a wrecked ship, from a fire or from some other accident ○ *a sale of flood salvage items* (NOTE: no plural) ■ *verb* **1.** to save goods or a ship from being destroyed ○ *We are selling off a warehouse full of salvaged goods.* **2.** to save something from loss ○ *The company is trying to salvage its reputation after the managing director was*

sent to prison for fraud. ○ *The receiver managed to salvage something from the collapse of the company.*

salvage money /ˈsælvɪdʒ ˌmʌni/ *noun* payment made by the owner of a ship or a cargo to the person who has saved it

salvage vessel /ˈsælvɪdʒ ˌves(ə)l/ *noun* a ship which specialises in saving other ships and their cargoes

S&L *abbr* savings and loan

SAS *abbr* Statement of Auditing Standards

save /seɪv/ *verb* to keep, not to spend (money) ○ *He is trying to save money by walking to work.* ○ *She is saving to buy a house.*

save-as-you-earn /ˌseɪv əz juː ˈɜːn/ *noun* a scheme where employees can save money regularly by having it deducted automatically from their wages and invested in National Savings. Abbreviation **SAYE**

saver /ˈseɪvə/ *noun* a person who saves money

savings /ˈseɪvɪŋz/ *plural noun* money saved (i.e. money which is not spent) ○ *She put all her savings into a deposit account.*

savings account /ˈseɪvɪŋz əˌkaʊnt/ *noun* an account where you put money in regularly and which pays interest, often at a higher rate than a deposit account

savings and loan /ˈseɪvɪŋz ən ˈləʊn/, **savings and loan association** /ˈseɪvɪŋz ən ˈləʊn əˌsəʊsieɪʃ(ə)n/ *noun* US a financial association which accepts and pays interest on deposits from investors and lends money to people who are buying property. The loans are in the form of mortgages on the security of the property being bought. S&Ls are regulated by the Office of Thrift Supervision and are protected by the Savings Association Insurance Fund. Abbreviation **S&L**. Also called **thrift** (NOTE: The UK term is **building society**.)

savings bank /ˈseɪvɪŋz bæŋk/ *noun* a bank where you can deposit money and receive interest on it

savings certificate /ˈseɪvɪŋz səˌtɪfɪkət/ *noun* a document showing that you have invested money in a government savings scheme (NOTE: The US term is **savings bond**.)

savings income /ˌseɪvɪŋz ˈɪnkʌm/ *noun* income in the form of interest on deposits with banks and building societies, government bonds, etc., but not income from dividends or rental income from property

savings-related share option scheme /ˌseɪvɪŋz rɪˌleɪtɪd ˈʃeə ˌɒpʃən ˌskiːm/ *noun* a scheme which allows employees of a company to buy shares with money which they have contributed to a savings scheme

SAYE *abbr* save-as-you-earn

SBA *abbr* Small Business Administration

scale /skeɪl/ *noun* a system which is graded into various levels □ **scale of charges** *or* **scale of prices** a list showing various prices □ **scale of salaries** a list of salaries showing different levels of pay in different jobs in the same company

scarcity value /'skeəsɪti ˌvæljuː/ *noun* the value something has because it is rare and there is a large demand for it

schedule /'ʃedjuːl/ *noun* **1.** a timetable, a plan of how time should be spent, drawn up in advance ○ *The managing director has a busy schedule of appointments.* ○ *Her assistant tried to fit us into her schedule.* **2.** a list, especially a list forming an additional document attached to a contract ○ *the schedule of territories to which a contract applies* ○ *Please find enclosed our schedule of charges.* ○ *See the attached schedule* or *as per the attached schedule.* **3.** a list of interest rates

Schedule A /ˌʃedjuːl 'eɪ/ *noun* a schedule under which tax is charged on income from land or buildings

Schedule B /ˌʃedjuːl 'biː/ *noun* a schedule under which tax was formerly charged on income from woodlands

Schedule C /ˌʃedjuːl 'siː/ *noun* a schedule under which tax is charged on profits from government stock

Schedule D /ˌʃedjuːl 'diː/ *noun* a schedule under which tax is charged on income from trades or professions, interest and other earnings not derived from being employed

Schedule E /ˌʃedjuːl 'iː/ *noun* a schedule under which tax is charged on income from salaries, wages or pensions

Schedule F /ˌʃedjuːl 'ef/ *noun* a schedule under which tax is charged on income from dividends

scheme /skiːm/ *noun* a plan, arrangement or way of working ○ *Under the bonus scheme all employees get 10% of their annual pay as a Christmas bonus.* ○ *She has joined the company pension scheme.* ○ *We operate a profit-sharing scheme for managers.* ○ *The new payment scheme is based on reward for individual effort.*

scheme of arrangement /ˌskiːm əv ə 'reɪndʒmənt/ *noun* a scheme drawn up by an individual or company to offer ways of paying debts, so as to avoid bankruptcy pro-

ceedings. Also called **voluntary arrangement**

scorched earth policy /ˌskɔːtʃt 'ɜːθ ˌpɒlɪsi/ *noun* a way of combating a takeover bid, where the target company sells valuable assets or purchases unattractive assets

scrap /skræp/ *noun* material left over after an industrial process, and which still has some value, as opposed to waste, which has no value ○ *to sell a ship for scrap*

scrap value /'skræp ˌvæljuː/ *noun* the value of an asset if sold for scrap ○ *Its scrap value is £2,500.*

scrip /skrɪp/ *noun* a security, e.g. a share, bond, or the certificate issued to show that someone has been allotted a share or bond

> '…under the rule, brokers who fail to deliver stock within four days of a transaction are to be fined 1% of the transaction value for each day of missing scrip' [*Far Eastern Economic Review*]

scrip dividend /'skrɪp ˌdɪvɪdend/ *noun* a dividend which takes the form of new shares in the company, as opposed to cash

scrip issue /'skrɪp ˌɪʃuː/ *noun* an issue of shares whereby a company transfers money from reserves to share capital and issues free extra shares to the shareholders. The value of the company remains the same, and the total market value of shareholders' shares remains the same, the market price being adjusted to account for the new prices. Also called **free issue, capitalisation issue**

SDRs *abbr* special drawing rights

seal /siːl/ *noun* **1.** a special symbol, often one stamped on a piece of wax, which is used to show that a document is officially approved by the organisation that uses the symbol **2.** a piece of paper, metal or wax attached to close something, so that it can be opened only if the paper, metal or wax is removed or broken ■ *verb* **1.** to close something tightly ○ *The computer disks were sent in a sealed container.* **2.** to attach a seal, to stamp something with a seal ○ *Customs sealed the shipment.*

sealed envelope /ˌsiːld 'envələʊp/ *noun* an envelope where the flap has been stuck down to close it ○ *to send the information in a sealed envelope*

seasonal adjustment /ˌsiːz(ə)n(ə)l ə 'dʒʌstmənt/ *noun* an adjustment made to accounts to allow for any short-term seasonal factors, such as Christmas sales, that may distort the figures

seasonal business /ˌsiːz(ə)n(ə)l 'bɪznɪs/ *noun* trade that varies depending on the time of the year, e.g. trade in goods such as suntan products or Christmas trees

SEC *abbr* Securities and Exchange Commission

second /'sekənd/ *noun, adjective* the thing which comes after the first ■ *verb* /sɪ'kɒnd/ **1.** /'sekənd/; /sɪ'kɒnd/ □ **to second a motion** to be the first person to support a proposal put forward by someone else ○ *Mrs Smith seconded the motion* or *The motion was seconded by Mrs Smith.* **2.** to lend a member of staff to another company, organisation or department for a fixed period of time ○ *He was seconded to the Department of Trade for two years.*

secondary /'sekənd(ə)ri/ *adjective* second in importance

secondary industry /'sekənd(ə)ri ˌɪndəstri/ *noun* an industry which uses basic raw materials to produce manufactured goods

seconder /'sekəndə/ *noun* a person who seconds a proposal ○ *There was no seconder for the motion so it was not put to the vote.*

second half /ˌsekənd 'hɑːf/ *noun* a period of six months from 1st July to 31st December ○ *The figures for the second half are up on those for the first part of the year.*

second half-year /ˌsekənd 'hɑːf jɪə/ *noun* the six-month period from July to the end of December

secondment /sɪ'kɒndmənt/ *noun* the fact or period of being seconded to another job for a period ○ *She is on three years' secondment to an Australian college.*

second mortgage /ˌsekənd 'mɔːgɪdʒ/ *noun* a further mortgage on a property which is already mortgaged

second quarter /ˌsekənd 'kwɔːtə/ *noun* a period of three months from April to the end of June

secret /'siːkrət/ *adjective* being deliberately kept hidden from people, or which is not known about by many people ○ *The MD kept the contract secret from the rest of the board.* ○ *The management signed a secret deal with a foreign supplier.* ■ *noun* something which is kept hidden or which is not known about by many people ○ *to keep a secret*

secretary /'sekrət(ə)ri/ *noun* an official of a company or society whose job is to keep records and write letters

secret reserves /ˌsiːkrət rɪ'zɜːvz/ *plural noun* reserves which are illegally kept hidden in a company's balance sheet, as opposed to 'hidden reserves' which are simply not easy to identify

section /'sekʃən/ *noun* one of the parts of an Act of Parliament

secure /sɪ'kjʊə/ *adjective* safe, which cannot change

secured /sɪ'kjʊəd/ *adjective* used to describe a type of borrowing such as a mortgage where the lender has a legal right to take over an asset or assets of the borrower, if the borrower does not repay the loan

secured creditor /sɪˌkjʊəd 'kredɪtə/ *noun* a person who is owed money by someone, and can legally claim the same amount of the borrower's property if the borrower fails to pay back the money owed

secured loan /sɪ'kjʊəd ləʊn/ *noun* a loan which is guaranteed by the borrower giving assets as security

securities /sɪ'kjʊərɪtiz/ *plural noun* investments in stocks and shares

securities account /sɪˌkjʊərɪtiz ə 'kaʊnt/ *noun* an account that shows the value of financial assets held by a person or organisation

Securities and Exchange Commission /sɪˌkjʊərɪtiz ən ɪks'tʃeɪndʒ kə 'mɪʃ(ə)n/ *noun* the official body which regulates the securities markets in the USA. Abbreviation **SEC**

Securities and Futures Authority /sɪ ˌkjʊərətiz ən 'fjuːtʃəz ɔːˌθɒrəti/ *noun* in the UK, a self-regulatory organisation which supervises the trading in shares and futures, now part of the FSA. Abbreviation **SFA**

Securities and Investments Board /sɪˌkjʊərɪtiz ən ɪn'vestmənts bɔːd/ *noun* the former regulatory body which regulated the securities markets in the UK It has been superseded by the FSA. Abbreviation **SIB**

securitisation /sɪˌkjʊərɪtaɪ'zeɪʃ(ə)n/, **securitization** *noun* the process of making a loan or mortgage into a tradeable security by issuing a bill of exchange or other negotiable paper in place of it

security /sɪ'kjʊərɪti/ *noun* **1.** a guarantee that someone will repay money borrowed ○ *to give something as security for a debt* ○ *to use a house as security for a loan* ○ *The bank lent him £20,000 without security.* □ **to stand security for someone** to guarantee that if the person does not repay a loan, you will repay it for him **2.** a stock or share

security deposit /sɪˌkjʊərɪti dɪ'pɒzɪt/ *noun* an amount of money paid before a transaction occurs to compensate the seller in the event that the transaction is not concluded and this is the buyer's fault

seed money /'siːd ˌmʌni/ *noun* venture capital invested when a new project is starting up and therefore more risky than secondary finance

segmental reporting /seg,ment(ə)l rɪ'pɔːtɪŋ/ *noun* the act of showing in company reports the results of a company or sections of it, separated according to the type of business or geographical area

self /self/ *pronoun* your own person

self- /self/ *prefix* referring to yourself

self-assessment /self ə'sesmənt/ *noun* the process of calculating how much tax you should pay and reporting it to the Inland Revenue on time ○ *Self-assessment forms should be returned to the tax office by 31st January.*

self-employed /,self ɪm'plɔɪd/ *adjective* working for yourself or not on the payroll of a company ○ *a self-employed engineer* ○ *He worked for a bank for ten years but is now self-employed.*

self-employed contributions /,self ɪm,plɔɪd ,kɒntrɪ'bjuːʃ(ə)nz/ *plural noun* National Insurance contributions made by self-employed people

self-financing /,self faɪ'nænsɪŋ/ *noun* the financing of development costs, the purchase of capital assets, etc. by a company from its own resources

self-regulation /self ,regjʊ'leɪʃ(ə)n/ *noun* the regulation of an industry by itself, through a committee which issues a rulebook and makes sure that members of the industry follow the rules (NOTE: For example, the Stock Exchange is regulated by the Stock Exchange Council.)

self-regulatory /self ,regjʊ'leɪt(ə)ri/ *adjective* referring to an organisation which regulates itself

sell /sel/ *noun* an act of selling ■ *verb* **1.** to give goods in exchange for money ○ *to sell something on credit* ○ *The shop sells washing machines and refrigerators.* ○ *They tried to sell their house for £100,000.* ○ *Their products are easy to sell.* **2.** to be sold ○ *These items sell well in the pre-Christmas period.* ○ *Those packs sell for £25 a dozen.* (NOTE: **selling – sold**)

seller /'selə/ *noun* a person who sells ○ *There were few sellers in the market, so prices remained high.*

seller's market /,selə 'mɑːkɪt/ *noun* a market where the seller can ask high prices because there is a large demand for the product. Opposite **buyer's market**

selling costs /'selɪŋ kɒsts/, **selling overhead** /,selɪŋ 'əʊvəhed/ *plural noun* the amount of money to be paid for the advertis-

ing, reps' commissions and other expenses involved in selling something

selling price /'selɪŋ praɪs/ *noun* the price at which someone is willing to sell something

selling price variance /'selɪŋ praɪs ,veəriəns/ *noun* the difference between the actual selling price and the budgeted selling price

semi- /semi/ *prefix* half or part

semiannual /,semi'ænjuəl/ *adjective* referring to interest paid every six months

semi-fixed cost /,semi fɪkst 'kɒst/ *noun* same as **semi-variable cost**

semi-variable cost /,semi ,veəriəb(ə)l 'kɒst/ *noun* money paid to produce a product which increases, though less than proportionally, with the quantity of the product made ○ *Stepping up production will mean an increase in semi-variable costs.* Also called **semi-fixed cost**

senior /'siːniə/ *adjective* **1.** referring to an employee who is more important **2.** referring to an employee who is older or who has been employed longer than another **3.** referring to a sum which is repayable before others

senior capital /,siːniə 'kæpɪt(ə)l/ *noun* capital in the form of secured loans to a company. It is repaid before junior capital, such as shareholders' equity, in the event of liquidation.

seniority /,siːni'ɒrɪti/ *noun* the fact of being more important ○ *in order of seniority* □ **the managers were listed in order of seniority** the manager who had been an employee the longest was put at the top of the list

senior manager /,siːniə 'mænɪdʒə/, **senior executive** /,siːniər ɪg'zekjʊtɪv/ *noun* a manager or director who has a higher rank than others

sensitivity analysis /,sensə'tɪvəti ə,næləsɪs/ *noun* the analysis of the effect of a small change in a calculation on the final result

separable /'sep(ə)rəb(ə)l/ *adjective* possible to separate

separable net assets /,sep(ə)rəb(ə)l net 'æsets/ *plural noun* assets which can be separated from the rest of the assets of a business and sold off

separate /'sep(ə)rət/ *adjective* not connected with something

sequester /sɪ'kwestə/, **sequestrate** /'siːkwɪstreɪt, sɪ'kwestreɪt/ *verb* to take and keep a bank account or property because a court has ordered it ○ *The union's funds have been sequestrated.*

sequestration /ˌsiːkweˈstreɪʃ(ə)n/ *noun* the act of taking and keeping property on the order of a court, especially of seizing property from someone who is in contempt of court

sequestrator /ˈsiːkwɪstreɪtə, sɪˈkwestreɪtə/ *noun* a person who takes and keeps property on the order of a court

series /ˈsɪəriːz/ *noun* a group of items following one after the other ○ *A series of successful takeovers made the company one of the largest in the trade.* (NOTE: plural is **series**)

Serious Fraud Office /ˌsɪəriəs ˈfrɔːd ˌɒfɪs/ *noun* a British government department in charge of investigating major fraud in companies. Abbreviation **SFO**

SERPS /sɜːps/ *abbr* State Earnings-Related Pension Scheme

service /ˈsɜːvɪs/ *noun* **1.** the fact of working for an employer, or the period of time during which an employee has worked for an employer ○ *retiring after twenty years service to the company* ○ *The amount of your pension depends partly on the number of your years of service.* **2.** the work of dealing with customers ○ *The service in that restaurant is extremely slow* **3.** payment for help given to the customer ○ *to add on 10% for service*

service bureau /ˈsɜːvɪs ˌbjʊərəʊ/ *noun* an office which specialises in helping other offices

service charge /ˈsɜːvɪs tʃɑːdʒ/ *noun* **1.** a charge added to the bill in a restaurant to pay for service **2.** an amount paid by tenants in a block of flats or offices for general maintenance, insurance and cleaning **3.** *US* a charge which a bank makes for carrying out work for a customer (NOTE: The UK term is **bank charge**.)

service contract /ˈsɜːvɪs ˌkɒntrækt/ *noun* a contract between a company and a director showing all conditions of work ○ *She worked unofficially with no service contract.*

service industry /ˈsɜːvɪs ˌɪndəstri/ *noun* an industry which does not produce raw materials or manufacture products but offers a service such as banking, retailing or accountancy

services /ˈsɜːvɪsɪz/ *plural noun* **1.** benefits which are sold to customers or clients, e.g. transport or education ○ *We give advice to companies on the marketing of services.* ○ *We must improve the exports of both goods and services.* **2.** business of providing help in some form when it is needed, e.g. insurance, banking, etc., as opposed to making or selling goods

set /set/ *adjective* fixed or which cannot be changed ○ *There is a set fee for all our consultants.* ■ *verb* to fix or to arrange something ○ *We have to set a price for the new computer.* ○ *The price of the calculator has been set low, so as to achieve maximum unit sales.* (NOTE: **setting – set**)

set against /ˌset əˈgenst/ *verb* to balance one group of figures against another group to try to make them cancel each other out ○ *to set the costs against the sales revenue* ○ *Can you set the expenses against tax?*

set off /ˌset ˈɒf/ *verb* to use a debt owed by one party to reduce a debt owed to them

set-off /ˈset ɒf/ *noun* an agreement between two parties to balance one debt against another or a loss against a gain

settle /ˈset(ə)l/ *verb* to place a property in trust

settlement /ˈset(ə)lmənt/ *noun* **1.** the payment of an account □ **we offer an extra 5% discount for rapid settlement** we take a further 5% off the price if the customer pays quickly **2.** an agreement after an argument or negotiations ○ *a wage settlement*

'…he emphasised that prompt settlement of all forms of industrial disputes would guarantee industrial peace in the country and ensure increased productivity' [*Business Times (Lagos)*]

settlement date /ˈset(ə)lmənt deɪt/ *noun* a date when a payment has to be made

settlement day /ˈset(ə)lmənt deɪ/ *noun* **1.** the day on which shares which have been bought must be paid for. On the London Stock Exchange the account period is three business days from the day of trade. **2.** in the USA, the day on which securities bought actually become the property of the purchaser

settle on /ˈset(ə)l ɒn/ *verb* to leave property to someone when you die ○ *He settled his property on his children.*

set up /ˌset ˈʌp/ *verb* to begin something, or to organise something new ○ *to set up an inquiry* or *a working party*

'…the concern announced that it had acquired a third large tanker since being set up' [*Lloyd's List*]

seven-day money /ˌsev(ə)n deɪ ˈmʌni/ *noun* an investment in financial instruments which mature in seven days' time

several /ˈsev(ə)rəl/ *adjective* more than a few, some ○ *Several managers are retiring this year.* ○ *Several of our products sell well in Japan.*

severally /ˈsev(ə)rəli/ *adverb* separately, not jointly

severance pay /ˈsev(ə)rəns peɪ/ *noun* money paid as compensation to an employee whose job is no longer needed

SFA *abbr* Securities and Futures Authority

SFAS *abbr* Statement of Financial Accounting Standards

SFO *abbr* Serious Fraud Office

shadow director /ˌʃædəʊ daɪˈrektə/ *noun* a person who is not a director of a company, but who tells the directors of the company how to act

share /ʃeə/ *noun* **1.** a part of something that has been divided up among several people or groups **2.** one of many equal parts into which a company's capital is divided ○ *He bought a block of shares in Marks and Spencer.* ○ *Shares fell on the London market.* ○ *The company offered 1.8m shares on the market.*

'…falling profitability means falling share prices' [*Investors Chronicle*]

'…the share of blue-collar occupations declined from 48 per cent to 43 per cent' [*Sydney Morning Herald*]

share account /ˈʃeə əˌkaʊnt/ *noun* an account at a building society where the account holder is a member of the society. Building societies usually offer another type of account, a deposit account, where the account holder is not a member. A share account is generally paid a better rate of interest, but in the event of the society going into liquidation, deposit account holders are given preference.

share at par /ˌʃeə ət ˈpɑː/ *noun* a share whose value on the stock market is the same as its face value

share capital /ˈʃeə ˌkæpɪt(ə)l/ *noun* the value of the assets of a company held as shares

share certificate /ˈʃeə səˌtɪfɪkət/ *noun* a document proving that you own shares

share disposals /ˈʃeə dɪˌspəʊz(ə)lz/ *plural noun* selling of shares

shareholder /ˈʃeəhəʊldə/ *noun* a person who owns shares in a company ○ *to call a shareholders' meeting* (NOTE: The US term is **stockholder**.)

'…as of last night the bank's shareholders no longer hold any rights to the bank's shares' [*South China Morning Post*]

'…the company said that its recent issue of 10.5% convertible preference shares at A$8.50 has been oversubscribed, boosting shareholders' funds to A$700 million plus' [*Financial Times*]

shareholders' equity /ˌʃeəhəʊldəz ˈekwɪti/ *noun* **1.** the value of a company which is the property of its ordinary shareholders (the company's assets less its liabilities) **2.** a company's capital which is invested by shareholders, who thus become owners of the company

shareholders' funds /ˌʃeəhəʊldəz ˈfʌndz/ *noun* the capital and reserves of a company

shareholder value /ˌʃeəhəʊldə ˈvæljuː/ *noun* the total return to the shareholders in terms of both dividends and share price growth, calculated as the present value of future free cash flows of the business discounted at the weighted average cost of the capital of the business less the market value of its debt

shareholder value analysis /ˌʃeəhəʊldə ˌvæljuː əˈnæləsɪs/ *noun* a calculation of the value of a company made by looking at the returns it gives to its shareholders. It assumes that the objective of a company director is to maximise the wealth of the company's shareholders, and is based on the premise that discounted cash flow principles can be applied to the business as a whole. Abbreviation **SVA**

shareholding /ˈʃeəhəʊldɪŋ/ *noun* a group of shares in a company owned by one owner

share option /ˈʃeər ˌɒpʃən/ *noun* a right to buy or sell shares at an agreed price at a time in the future

share premium /ˈʃeə ˌpriːmiəm/ *noun* an amount to be paid above the nominal value of a share in order to buy it

share quoted ex dividend /ˌʃeə ˌkwəʊtɪd eks ˈdɪvɪdend/, **share quoted ex div** /ˌʃeə ˈkwəʊtɪd eks/ *noun* a share price not including the right to receive the next dividend ○ *The shares went ex dividend yesterday.*

share split /ˈʃeə splɪt/ *noun* the act of dividing shares into smaller denominations

sharing /ˈʃeərɪŋ/ *noun* the act of dividing up

sharp practice /ˌʃɑːp ˈpræktɪs/ *noun* a way of doing business which is not honest, but is not illegal

shelf registration /ˈʃelf ˌredʒɪstreɪʃ(ə)n/ *noun* a registration of a corporation with the SEC some time (up to two years is allowed) before it is offered for sale to the public

shell company /ˈʃel ˌkʌmp(ə)ni/ *noun* a company that has ceased to trade but is still registered, especially one sold to enable the buyer to begin trading without having to set up a new company (NOTE: The US term is **shell corporation**.)

'…shell companies, which can be used to hide investors' cash, figure largely throughout the twentieth century' [*Times*]

shelter /ˈʃeltə/ *noun* a protected place

shop window /ˌʃɒp 'wɪndəʊ/ *noun* a large window in a shop front, where customers can see goods displayed

short /ʃɔːt/ *adjective, adverb* **1.** for a small period of time **2.** not as much as should be ○ *The shipment was three items short.* ○ *My change was £2 short.* □ **when we cashed up we were £10 short** we had £10 less than we should have had

short bill /'ʃɔːt bɪl/ *noun* a bill of exchange payable at short notice

short-change /ˌʃɔːt 'tʃeɪndʒ/ *verb* to give a customer less change than is right, either by mistake or in the hope that it will not be noticed

short credit /ˌʃɔːt 'kredɪt/ *noun* terms which allow the customer only a little time to pay

short-dated bill /ʃɔːt ˌdeɪtɪd 'bɪl/ *noun* a bill which is payable within a few days

short-dated gilts /ʃɔːt ˌdeɪtɪd 'gɪlts/ *plural noun* same as **shorts**

shorten /'ʃɔːt(ə)n/ *verb* to make shorter ○ *to shorten credit terms*

shortfall /'ʃɔːtfɔːl/ *noun* an amount which is missing which would make the total expected sum ○ *We had to borrow money to cover the shortfall between expenditure and revenue.*

short lease /ˌʃɔːt 'liːs/ *noun* a lease which runs for up to two or three years ○ *We have a short lease on our current premises.*

short position /ˌʃɔːt pə'zɪʃ(ə)n/ *noun* a situation where an investor sells short, i.e. sells forward shares which he or she does not own. Compare **long position**

short-range forecast /ˌʃɔːt reɪndʒ 'fɔːkɑːst/ *noun* a forecast which covers a period of a few months

shorts /ʃɔːts/ *plural noun* government stocks which mature in less than five years' time

short-term /ˌʃɔːt 'tɜːm/ *adjective* **1.** for a period of weeks or months ○ *to place money on short-term deposit* ○ *She is employed on a short-term contract.* **2.** for a short period in the future ○ *We need to recruit at once to cover our short-term manpower requirements.*

short-term capital /ˌʃɔːt tɜːm 'kæpɪt(ə)l/ *noun* funds raised for a period of less than 12 months. ◊ **working capital**

short-term forecast /ˌʃɔːt tɜːm 'fɔːkɑːst/ *noun* a forecast which covers a period of a few months

short-term loan /ˌʃɔːt tɜːm 'ləʊn/ *noun* a loan which has to be repaid within a few weeks or some years

short-term security /ˌʃɔːt tɜːm sɪ'kjʊərɪti/ *noun* a security which matures in less than 5 years

shrink /ʃrɪŋk/ *verb* to get smaller ○ *The market has shrunk by 20%.* ○ *The company is having difficulty selling into a shrinking market.* (NOTE: **shrinking – shrank – has shrunk**)

shrinkage /'ʃrɪŋkɪdʒ/ *noun* **1.** the amount by which something gets smaller ○ *to allow for shrinkage* **2.** losses of stock through theft, especially by the shop's own staff (*informal*)

SIB *abbr* Securities and Investments Board

sick pay /'sɪk peɪ/ *noun* pay paid to an employee who is sick, even if he cannot work

sight deposit /'saɪt dɪˌpɒzɪt/ *noun* a bank deposit which can be withdrawn on demand

sight draft /'saɪt drɑːft/ *noun* a bill of exchange which is payable when it is presented

sign /saɪn/ *verb* to write your name in a special way on a document to show that you have written it or approved it ○ *The letter is signed by the managing director.* ○ *Our company cheques are not valid if they have not been signed by the finance director.* ○ *The new recruit was asked to sign the contract of employment.*

signatory /'sɪgnət(ə)ri/ *noun* a person who signs a contract, etc. ○ *You have to get the permission of all the signatories to the agreement if you want to change the terms.*

signature /'sɪgnɪtʃə/ *noun* a person's name written by themselves on a cheque, document or letter ○ *She found a pile of cheques on his desk waiting for signature.* ○ *All our company's cheques need two signatures.* ○ *The contract of employment had the personnel director's signature at the bottom.*

simple /'sɪmpəl/ *adjective* not complicated, not difficult to understand

simple average cost /ˌsɪmpəl 'æv(ə)rɪdʒ kɒst/, **simple average price** /ˌsɪmpəl 'æv(ə)rɪdʒ praɪs/ *noun* the average cost of stock received during a period calculated at the end of the period as the average unit price of each delivery of stock, rather than an average price of each unit delivered as in weighted average price

simple interest /ˌsɪmpəl 'ɪntrəst/ *noun* interest calculated on the capital invested only, and not added to it

single-entry bookkeeping /ˌsɪŋg(ə)l ˌentri 'bʊkiːpɪŋ/ *noun* a method of bookkeeping where payments or sales are noted with only one entry per transaction, usually in the cash book

single-figure inflation /ˌsɪŋg(ə)l ˌfɪgə ɪnˈfleɪʃ(ə)n/ *noun* inflation rising at less than 10% per annum

single premium policy /ˌsɪŋg(ə)l ˌpriːmiəm ˈpɒlɪsi/ *noun* an insurance policy where only one premium is paid rather than regular annual premiums

sink /sɪŋk/ *verb* **1.** to go down suddenly ○ *Prices sank at the news of the closure of the factory.* **2.** to invest money into something ○ *He sank all his savings into a car-hire business.* (NOTE: **sinking – sank – sunk**)

sinking fund /ˈsɪŋkɪŋ fʌnd/ *noun* a fund built up out of amounts of money put aside regularly to meet a future need, such as the repayment of a loan

sinking fund method /ˌsɪŋkɪŋ fʌnd ˈmeθəd/ *noun* a method of providing for depreciation which increases every year by multiplying each previous year's charge by a compound rate of interest

sister company /ˈsɪstə ˌkʌmp(ə)ni/ *noun* another company which is part of the same group

sitting tenant /ˌsɪtɪŋ ˈtenənt/ *noun* a tenant who is occupying a building when the freehold or lease is sold ○ *The block of flats is for sale with four flats vacant and two with sitting tenants.*

skimming /ˈskɪmɪŋ/ *noun* the unethical and usually illegal practice of taking small amounts of money from accounts that belong to other individuals or organisations

sleeping partner /ˌsliːpɪŋ ˈpɑːtnə/ *noun* a partner who has a share in the business but does not work in it

slide /slaɪd/ *verb* to move down steadily ○ *Prices slid after the company reported a loss.* (NOTE: **sliding – slid**)

sliding /ˈslaɪdɪŋ/ *adjective* rising in steps

slip /slɪp/ *noun* a small piece of paper

'…with long-term fundamentals reasonably sound, the question for brokers is when does cheap become cheap enough? The Bangkok and Taipei exchanges offer lower p/e ratios than Jakarta, but if Jakarta p/e ratios slip to the 16–18 range, foreign investors would pay more attention to it' [*Far Eastern Economic Review*]

slow payer /ˌsləʊ ˈpeɪə/ *noun* a person or company that does not pay debts on time ○ *The company is well known as a slow payer.*

slump /slʌmp/ *noun* **1.** a rapid fall ○ *the slump in the value of the pound* ○ *We experienced a slump in sales* or *a slump in profits.* **2.** a period of economic collapse with high unemployment and loss of trade ○ *We are experiencing slump conditions.* ■ *verb* to fall

fast ○ *Profits have slumped.* ○ *The pound slumped on the foreign exchange markets.*

slush fund /ˈslʌʃ fʌnd/ *noun* money kept to one side to give to people to persuade them to do what you want ○ *The government was brought down by the scandal over the slush funds.* ○ *The party was accused of keeping a slush fund to pay foreign businessmen.*

small ads /ˈsmɔːl ædz/ *plural noun* short private advertisements in a newspaper, e.g. selling small items or asking for jobs

small and medium-sized enterprises /ˌsmɔːl ən ˌmiːdiəm ˌsaɪzd ˈentəpraɪzɪz/ *plural noun* organisations that have between 10 and 500 employees and are usually in the start-up or growth stage of development. Abbreviation **SMEs**

small business /ˌsmɔːl ˈbɪznɪs/ *noun* a little company with low turnover and few employees

Small Business Administration /ˌsmɔːl ˈbɪznɪs ədˌmɪnɪstreɪʃ(ə)n/ *noun* *US* a federal agency which provides finance and advice to small businesses. Abbreviation **SBA**

small businessman /ˌsmɔːl ˈbɪznɪsmæn/ *noun* a man who owns a small business

small change /ˌsmɔːl ˈtʃeɪndʒ/ *noun* coins

small claim /ˌsmɔːl ˈkleɪm/ *noun* a claim for less than £5000 in the County Court

small claims court /ˌsmɔːl ˈkleɪmz ˌkɔːt/ *noun* a court which deals with disputes over small amounts of money

small companies rate /ˌsmɔːl ˈkʌmp(ə)niz ˌreɪt/ *noun* a rate of corporation tax charged on profits of small companies

small company /smɔːl ˈkʌmp(ə)ni/ *noun* a company with at least two of the following characteristics: a turnover of less than £2.0m;, fewer than 50 staff, net assets of less than £975,000

SME *abbr* small and medium-sized enterprises

social /ˈsəʊʃ(ə)l/ *adjective* referring to society in general

social security contributions /ˌsəʊʃ(ə)l sɪˈkjʊərɪti kɒntrɪˌbjuːʃ(ə)nz/ *plural noun* regular payments by employees and employers to the National Insurance scheme

society /səˈsaɪəti/ *noun* the way in which the people in a country are organised

soft currency /sɒft ˈkʌrənsi/ *noun* the currency of a country with a weak economy, which is cheap to buy and difficult to exchange for other currencies. Opposite **hard currency**

soft landing /ˌsɒft ˈlændɪŋ/ *noun* a change in economic strategy to counteract inflation, which does not cause unemployment or a fall in the standard of living, and has only minor effects on the bulk of the population

soft loan /ˌsɒft ˈləʊn/ *noun* a loan from a company to an employee or from one government to another at a very low rate of interest or with no interest payable at all

software /ˈsɒftweə/ *noun* computer programs

sole /səʊl/ *adjective* only

sole agency /ˌsəʊl ˈeɪdʒənsi/ *noun* an agreement to be the only person to represent a company or to sell a product in a particular area ○ *He has the sole agency for Ford cars.*

sole agent /ˌsəʊl ˈeɪdʒənt/ *noun* a person who has the sole agency for a company in an area ○ *She is the sole agent for Ford cars in the locality.*

sole distributor /ˌsəʊl dɪˈstrɪbjʊtə/ *noun* a retailer who is the only one in an area who is allowed to sell a product

sole owner /ˌsəʊl ˈəʊnə/ *noun* a person who owns a business on their own, with no partners, and has not formed a company

sole proprietor /səʊl prəˈpraɪətə/, **sole trader** /səʊl ˈtreɪdə/ *noun* a person who runs a business, usually by themselves, but has not registered it as a company

solvency /ˈsɒlv(ə)nsi/ *noun* the state of being able to pay all debts on due date. Opposite **insolvency**

solvency margin /ˌsɒlv(ə)nsi ˈmɑːdʒɪn/ *noun* a business's liquid assets that exceeds the amount required to meet its liabilities

solvency ratio /ˌsɒlv(ə)nsi ˈreɪʃiəʊ/ *noun* a ratio of assets to liabilities, used to measure a company's ability to meet its debts

solvent /ˈsɒlv(ə)nt/ *adjective* having enough money to pay debts ○ *When she bought the company it was barely solvent.*

sort code /ˈsɔːt kəʊd/ *noun* a combination of numbers that identifies a bank branch on official documentation, such as bank statements and cheques. US term **routing number**

source /sɔːs/ *noun* the place where something comes from ○ *What is the source of her income?* ○ *You must declare income from all sources to the tax office.*

source and application of funds statement /ˌsɔːs ən ˌæplɪkeɪʃ(ə)n əv ˈfʌndz ˌsteɪtmənt/, **sources and uses of**

funds statement /ˌsɔːsɪz ən ˌjuːzɪz əv ˈfʌndz ˌsteɪtmənt/ *noun* a statement in a company's annual accounts, showing where new funds came from during the year, and how they were used

source document /sɔːs ˈdɒkjʊˌment/ *noun* a document upon which details of transactions or accounting events are recorded and from which information is extracted to be subsequently entered into the internal accounting system of an organisation, e.g., a sales invoice or credit note

spare /speə/ *adjective* extra, not being used ○ *He has invested his spare capital in a computer shop.*

special deposits /ˌspeʃ(ə)l dɪˈpɒzɪts/ *plural noun* large sums of money which commercial banks have to deposit with the Bank of England

special drawing rights /ˌspeʃ(ə)l ˈdrɔːɪŋ raɪts/ *plural noun* units of account used by the International Monetary Fund, allocated to each member country for use in loans and other international operations. Their value is calculated daily on the weighted values of a group of currencies shown in dollars. Abbreviation **SDRs**

special offer /ˌspeʃ(ə)l ˈɒfə/ *noun* a situation where goods are put on sale at a specially low price ○ *We have a range of men's shirts on special offer.*

special resolution /ˌspeʃ(ə)l ˌrezəˈluːʃ(ə)n/ *noun* a resolution concerning an important matter, such as a change to the company's articles of association which is only valid if it is approved by 75% of the votes cast at a meeting

specie /ˈspiːʃiː/ *noun* money in the form of coins

specification /ˌspesɪfɪˈkeɪʃ(ə)n/ *noun* detailed information about what or who is needed or about a product to be supplied ○ *to detail the specifications of a computer system* □ **the work is not up to specification** *or* **does not meet our specifications** the product is not made in the way which was detailed

specific order costing /spəˌsɪfɪk ˌɔːdə ˈkɒstɪŋ/ *noun* same as **job costing**

specify /ˈspesɪfaɪ/ *verb* to state clearly what is needed ○ *to specify full details of the goods ordered* ○ *Do not include VAT on the invoice unless specified.* ○ *Candidates are asked to specify which of the three posts they are applying for.* (NOTE: **specifies – specifying – specified**)

spend /spend/ *verb* to pay money ○ *They spent all their savings on buying the shop.* ○

The company spends thousands of pounds on research.

spending /'spendɪŋ/ *noun* the act of paying money for goods and services ○ *Both cash spending and credit card spending increase at Christmas.*

spending money /'spendɪŋ ˌmʌni/ *noun* money for ordinary personal expenses

split /splɪt/ *noun* 1. an act of dividing up 2. a lack of agreement ○ *a split in the family shareholders* ■ *adjective* divided into parts

split commission /ˌsplɪt kə'mɪʃ(ə)n/ *noun* a commission which is divided between brokers or agents

split-level investment trust /ˌsplɪt ˌlev(ə)l ɪn'vestmənt ˌtrʌst/ *noun* an investment trust with two categories of shares: income shares which receive income from the investments, but do not benefit from the rise in their capital value, and capital shares, which increase in value as the value of the investments rises, but do not receive any income. Also called **split trust, split-capital trust**

split payment /ˌsplɪt 'peɪmənt/ *noun* a payment which is divided into small units

spot cash /ˌspɒt 'kæʃ/ *noun* cash paid for something bought immediately

spot price /'spɒt praɪs/, **spot rate** /ˌspɒt 'reɪt/ *noun* a current price or rate for something which is delivered immediately. Also called **cash price**

'…the average spot price of Nigerian light crude oil for the month of July was 27.21 dollars per barrel' [*Business Times (Lagos)*]

spread /spred/ *noun* 1. same as **range** 2. the difference between buying and selling prices, i.e. between the bid and offer prices ■ *verb* to space something out over a period of time ○ *to spread payments over several months*

'…dealers said markets were thin, with gaps between trades and wide spreads between bid and ask prices on the currencies' [*Wall Street Journal*]

'…to ensure an average return you should hold a spread of different shares covering a wide cross-section of the market' [*Investors Chronicle*]

spreading /'spredɪŋ/ *noun* an action of spacing income from artistic work such as royalties over a period of time, and not concentrating it in the year in which the money is received

spreadsheet /'spredʃiːt/ *noun* a computer printout showing a series of columns of figures

Square Mile /ˌskweə 'maɪl/ *noun* the City of London, the British financial centre

squeeze /skwiːz/ *noun* government control carried out by reducing the availability of

something ■ *verb* to crush or to press; to make smaller ○ *to squeeze margins* or *profits* or *credit*

'…the real estate boom of the past three years has been based on the availability of easy credit. Today, money is tighter, so property should bear the brunt of the credit squeeze' [*Money Observer*]

SSAPs *abbr* Statements of Standard Accounting Practice

staff incentives /ˌstɑːf ɪn'sentɪvz/ *plural noun* higher pay and better conditions offered to employees to make them work better

staff training /ˌstɑːf 'treɪnɪŋ/ *noun* the process of teaching staff better and more profitable ways of working

stag /stæg/ *noun* a person who buys new issues of shares and sells them immediately to make a profit

stage /steɪdʒ/ *noun* a period, one of several points in a process of development ○ *the different stages of the production process*

staged payments /ˌsteɪdʒd 'peɪməntz/ *plural noun* payments made in stages

stagger /'stægə/ *verb* to arrange holidays or working hours so that they do not all begin and end at the same time ○ *Staggered holidays help the tourist industry.* ○ *We have to stagger the lunch hour so that there is always someone on the switchboard.* ○ *We asked our supplier to stagger deliveries so that the warehouse can cope.*

stagnant /'stægnənt/ *adjective* not active, not increasing ○ *Turnover was stagnant for the first half of the year.* ○ *A stagnant economy is not a good sign.*

stagnate /stæg'neɪt/ *verb* not to increase, not to make progress ○ *The economy is stagnating.* ○ *After six hours the talks were stagnating.*

stagnation /stæg'neɪʃ(ə)n/ *noun* the state of not making any progress, especially in economic matters ○ *The country entered a period of stagnation.*

stake /steɪk/ *noun* an amount of money invested

'…her stake, which she bought at $1.45 per share, is now worth nearly $10 million' [*Times*]

'…other investments include a large stake in a Chicago-based insurance company, as well as interests in tobacco products and hotels' [*Lloyd's List*]

stakeholder /'steɪkhəʊldə/ *noun* a person or body that is involved with a company or organisation either personally or financially and has an interest in ensuring that it is successful (NOTE: A stakeholder may be an employee, customer, supplier, partner, or even the local community within which an organisation operates.)

'…the stakeholder concept is meant to be a new kind of low-cost, flexible personal pension aimed at those who are less well-off. Whether it will really encourage them to put aside money for retirement is a moot point. Ministers said companies would be able to charge no more than 1 per cent a year to qualify for the stakeholder label' [*Financial Times*]

stamp /stæmp/ *noun* a device for making marks on documents; a mark made in this way ○ *The invoice has the stamp 'Received with thanks' on it.* ○ *The customs officer looked at the stamps in her passport.* ■ *verb* **1.** to mark a document with a stamp ○ *to stamp an invoice 'Paid'* ○ *The documents were stamped by the customs officials.* **2.** to put a postage stamp on an envelope or parcel

stamp duty /'stæmp ˌdjuːti/ *noun* a tax on legal documents such as those used e.g. for the sale or purchase of shares or the conveyance of a property to a new owner

stamp pad /'stæmp pæd/ *noun* a soft pad of cloth with ink on which a stamp is pressed, before marking the paper

standard /'stændəd/ *noun* the usual quality or usual conditions which other things are judged against ■ *adjective* normal or usual ○ *a standard model car* ○ *We have a standard charge of £25 for a thirty-minute session.*

standard agreement /ˌstændəd ə'griːmənt/, **standard contract** /ˌstændəd 'kɒntrækt/ *noun* a normal printed contract form

standard cost /ˌstændəd 'kɒst/ *noun* a future cost which is calculated in advance and against which estimates are measured

standard costing /ˌstændəd 'kɒstɪŋ/ *noun* the process of planning costs for the period ahead and, at the end of the period, comparing these figures with actual costs in order to make necessary adjustments in planning

standard direct labour cost /ˌstændəd dɪˌrekt 'leɪbə ˌkɒst/ *noun* the cost of labour calculated to produce a product according to specification, used to measure estimates

standard letter /ˌstændəd 'letə/ *noun* a letter which is sent without change to various correspondents

standard rate /'stændəd reɪt/ *noun* a basic rate of income tax which is paid by most taxpayers

standby credit /'stændbaɪ ˌkredɪt/ *noun* **1.** credit which is available if a company needs it, especially credit guaranteed by a euronote **2.** credit which is available and which can be drawn on if a country needs it, especially credit guaranteed by a lender (a group of banks or the IMF in the case of a member country) and usually in dollars

standing order /ˌstændɪŋ 'ɔːdə/ *noun* an order written by a customer asking a bank to pay money regularly to an account ○ *I pay my subscription by standing order.*

staple commodity /ˌsteɪp(ə)l kə'mɒdɪti/ *noun* a basic food or raw material

start /stɑːt/ *noun* the beginning ■ *verb* to begin to do something □ **to start a business from cold** *or* **from scratch** to begin a new business, with no previous turnover to base it on

starting /'stɑːtɪŋ/ *noun* the act of beginning

starting date /'stɑːtɪŋ deɪt/ *noun* a date on which something starts

starting rate of tax /ˌstɑːtɪŋ reɪt əv 'tæks/ *noun* a tax rate (currently 10%) paid on the first segment of taxable income, before the basic rate applies

starting salary /'stɑːtɪŋ ˌsæləri/ *noun* a salary for an employee when he or she starts work with a company

start-up /'stɑːt ʌp/ *noun* the beginning of a new company or new product ○ *We went into the red for the first time because of the start-up costs of the new subsidiary in the USA.*

start-up financing /'stɑːt ʌp ˌfaɪnænsɪŋ/ *noun* the first stage in financing a new project, which is followed by several rounds of investment capital as the project gets under way (NOTE: The plural is **start-ups**.)

state /steɪt/ *noun* **1.** an independent country **2.** a semi-independent section of a federal country such as the USA □ **as per account stated** the same amount as shown on the account or invoice ■ *verb* to say clearly ○ *The document states that all revenue has to be declared to the tax office.*

'…the unions had argued that public sector pay rates had slipped behind rates applying in state and local government areas' [*Australian Financial Review*]

state bank /steɪt 'bæŋk/ *noun* in the USA, a commercial bank licensed by the authorities of a state, and not necessarily a member of the Federal Reserve system, as opposed to a national bank

state benefits /ˌsteɪt 'benɪfɪts/ *plural noun* payments which are made to someone under a national or private scheme

State Earnings-Related Pension Scheme /ˌsteɪt ˌɜːnɪŋz rɪˌleɪtɪd 'penʃən ˌskiːm/ *noun* a state pension which is additional to the basic retirement pension and is based on average earnings over an employee's career. Abbreviation **SERPS**

statement /ˈsteɪtmənt/ *noun* something said or written which describes or explains something clearly

statement of account /ˌsteɪtmənt əv ə ˈkaʊnt/ *noun* a list of sums due, usually relating to unpaid invoices

statement of affairs /ˌsteɪtmənt əv ə ˈfeəz/ *noun* a financial statement drawn up when a person is insolvent

Statement of Auditing Standards /ˌsteɪtmənt əv ˈɔːdɪtɪŋ ˌstændədz/ *noun* an auditing standard, issued by the Auditing Practices Board, containing prescriptions as to the basic principles and practices which members of the UK accountancy bodies are expected to follow in the course of an audit. Abbreviation **SAS**

statement of cash flows /ˌsteɪtmənt əv ˈkæʃ ˌfləʊz/ *noun* a statement that documents actual receipts and expenditures of cash

statement-of-cash-flows method /ˌsteɪtmənt əv kæʃ fləʊs ˈmeθəd/ *noun* a method of accounting that is based on flows of cash rather than balances on accounts

statement of changes in financial position /ˌsteɪtmənt əv tʃeɪndʒs ɪn faɪˌnænʃəl pəˈzɪʃ(ə)n/ *noun* a financial report of a company's incomes and outflows during a period, usually a year or a quarter

Statement of Financial Accounting Standards /ˌsteɪtmənt əv faɪˌnænʃ(ə)l əˈkaʊntɪŋ ˌstændədz/ *noun* in the United States, a statement detailing the standards to be adopted for the preparation of financial statements. Abbreviation **SFAS**

Statements of Standard Accounting Practice /ˌsteɪtmənts əv ˌstændəd əˈkaʊntɪŋ ˌpræktɪs/ *plural noun* rules laid down by the Accounting Standards Board for the preparation of financial statements. Abbreviation **SSAPs**

state of indebtedness /ˌsteɪt əv ɪnˈdetɪdnəs/ *noun* the fact of being in debt, owing money

state pension /ˌsteɪt ˈpenʃən/ *noun* a pension paid by the state

state retirement pension /steɪt rɪˌtaɪəmənt ˈpenʃən/ *noun* a pension paid by the state to people when they reach retirement age

statistical /stəˈtɪstɪk(ə)l/ *adjective* based on statistics ○ *statistical information* ○ *They took two weeks to provide the statistical analysis of the opinion-poll data.*

statistical discrepancy /stəˌtɪstɪk(ə)l dɪˈskrepənsi/ *noun* the amount by which sets of figures differ

statistician /ˌstætɪˈstɪʃ(ə)n/ *noun* a person who analyses statistics

status /ˈsteɪtəs/ *noun* the importance of someone or something relative to others, especially someone's position in society

status inquiry /ˈsteɪtəs ɪnˌkwaɪəri/ *noun* an act of checking on a customer's credit rating

status quo /ˌsteɪtəs ˈkwəʊ/ *noun* the state of things as they are now ○ *The contract does not alter the status quo.*

statute /ˈstætʃuːt/ *noun* an established written law, especially an Act of Parliament □ **statute book** all laws passed by Parliament which are still in force

statute-barred /ˌstætʃuːt ˈbɑːd/ *adjective* referring to legal action which cannot be pursued because the time limit for it has expired

statute book /ˈstætʃuːt bʊk/ *noun* all laws passed by Parliament which are still in force

statutory /ˈstætʃʊt(ə)ri/ *adjective* fixed by law ○ *There is a statutory period of probation of thirteen weeks.* ○ *Are all the employees aware of their statutory rights?*

statutory auditor /ˌstætʃʊt(ə)ri ˈɔːdɪtə/ *noun* a professional person qualified to carry out an audit required by the Companies Act

statutory books /ˈstætʃʊt(ə)ri bʊks/ *plural noun* company records required by law, e.g. a register of members

statutory instrument /ˌstætʃʊt(ə)ri ˈɪnstrʊmənt/ *noun* an order which has the force of law, made under authority granted to a minister by an Act of Parliament

statutory maternity pay /ˌstætʃʊt(ə)ri məˈtɜːnɪti ˌpeɪ/ *noun* payment made by an employer to an employee who is on maternity leave. Abbreviation **SMP**

statutory regulations /ˌstætʃʊt(ə)ri ˌregjʊˈleɪʃ(ə)nz/ *plural noun* regulations covering financial dealings which are based on Acts of Parliament, such as the Financial Services Act, as opposed to the rules of self-regulatory organisations which are non-statutory

stay of execution /ˌsteɪ əv eksɪˈkjuːʃ(ə)n/ *noun* the temporary stopping of a legal order ○ *The court granted the company a two-week stay of execution.*

step /step/ *noun* a type of action ○ *The first step taken by the new MD was to analyse all the expenses.*

stepped costs /ˌstept ˈkɒsts/ *plural noun* costs which remain fixed up to some level of activity but then rise to a new, higher level once that level of activity is exceeded

sterling /ˈstɜːlɪŋ/ *noun* a standard currency used in the United Kingdom ○ *to quote prices in sterling* or *to quote sterling prices*

'…it is doubtful that British goods will price themselves back into world markets as long as sterling labour costs continue to rise faster than in competitor countries' [*Sunday Times*]

sterling area /ˈstɜːlɪŋ ˌeəriə/ *noun* formerly, an area of the world where the pound sterling was the main trading currency

sterling balances /ˌstɜːlɪŋ ˈbælənsɪz/ *plural noun* a country's trade balances expressed in pounds sterling

sterling crisis /ˈstɜːlɪŋ ˌkraɪsɪs/ *noun* a fall in the exchange rate of the pound sterling

sterling index /ˈstɜːlɪŋ ˌɪndeks/ *noun* an index which shows the current value of sterling against a basket of currencies

stock /stɒk/ *noun* **1.** the available supply of raw materials ○ *large stocks of oil* or *coal* ○ *the country's stocks of butter* or *sugar* **2.** the quantity of goods for sale in a warehouse or retail outlet **3.** shares in a company **4.** investments in a company, represented by shares or fixed interest securities ■ *adjective* usually kept in stock ○ *Butter is a stock item for any good grocer.* ■ *verb* to hold goods for sale in a warehouse or store ○ *The average supermarket stocks more than 4500 lines.*

'US crude oil stocks fell last week by nearly 2.5m barrels' [*Financial Times*]

'…the stock rose to over $20 a share, higher than the $18 bid' [*Fortune*]

stockbroker /ˈstɒkbrəʊkə/ *noun* a person who buys or sells shares for clients

stockbroker's commission /stɒk ˌbrəʊkəz kəˈmɪʃ(ə)n/ *noun* the payment to a broker for a deal carried out on behalf of a client

stockbroking /ˈstɒkbrəʊkɪŋ/ *noun* the business of dealing in shares for clients ○ *a stockbroking firm*

stock certificate /ˈstɒk səˌtɪfɪkət/ *noun* a document proving that someone owns stock in a company

stock code /ˈstɒk kəʊd/ *noun* a set of numbers and letters which refer to an item of stock

stock control /ˈstɒk kənˌtrəʊl/ *noun* the process of making sure that the correct level of stock is maintained, to be able to meet demand while keeping the costs of holding stock to a minimum (NOTE: The US term is **inventory control**.)

stock controller /ˈstɒk kənˌtrəʊlə/ *noun* a person who notes movements of stock

stock depreciation /ˈstɒk dɪpriːʃi ˌeɪʃ(ə)n/ *noun* a reduction in value of stock which is held in a warehouse for some time

stock exchange /ˈstɒk ɪksˌtʃeɪndʒ/ *noun* same as **stock market**

Stock Exchange /ˈstɒk ɪksˌtʃeɪndʒ/ *noun* a place where stocks and shares are bought and sold ○ *He works on the Stock Exchange.* ○ *Shares in the company are traded on the Stock Exchange.*

'…the news was favourably received on the Sydney Stock Exchange, where the shares gained 40 cents to A$9.80' [*Financial Times*]

Stock Exchange listing /ˈstɒk ɪks ˌtʃeɪndʒ ˌlɪstɪŋ/ *noun* the fact of being on the official list of shares which can be bought or sold on the Stock Exchange ○ *The company is planning to obtain a Stock Exchange listing.*

stock figures /ˈstɒk ˌfɪgəz/ *plural noun* details of how many goods are in the warehouse or store

stockholder /ˈstɒkhəʊldə/ *noun* a person who holds shares in a company

stockholding /ˈstɒkhəʊldɪŋ/ *noun* the shares in a company held by someone

stock-in-trade /ˌstɒk ɪn ˈtreɪd/ *noun* goods held by a business for sale

stock ledger /ˈstɒk ˌledʒə/ *noun* a book which records quantities and values of stock

stock level /ˈstɒk ˌlev(ə)l/ *noun* the quantity of goods kept in stock ○ *We try to keep stock levels low during the summer.*

stock market /ˈstɒk ˌmɑːkɪt/ *noun* a place where shares are bought and sold, i.e. a stock exchange ○ *stock market price* or *price on the stock market*

stock market manipulator /ˈstɒk ˌmɑːkɪt məˌnɪpjʊleɪtə/ *noun* a person who tries to influence the price of shares in his or her own favour

stock market valuation /ˌstɒk ˌmɑːkɪt ˌvæljuˈeɪʃ(ə)n/ *noun* a value of a company based on the current market price of its shares

stock option /ˈstɒk ˌɒpʃən/ *noun* a right to buy shares at a cheap price given by a company to its employees

stocks and shares /ˌstɒks ən ˈʃeəz/ *plural noun* shares in ordinary companies

stocktaking /ˈstɒkteɪkɪŋ/, **stocktake** /ˈstɒkteɪk/ *noun* the counting of goods in stock at the end of an accounting period ○ *The warehouse is closed for the annual stocktaking.*

stocktaking sale /ˈstɒkteɪkɪŋ seɪl/ *noun* a sale of goods cheaply to clear a warehouse before stocktaking

stock transfer form /ˌstɒk ˈtrænsfɜː fɔːm/ *noun* a form to be signed by the person transferring shares

stock turn /stɒk ˈtɜːn/, **stock turnround** /stɒk ˈtɜːnraʊnd/, **stock turnover** /ˌstɒk ˈtɜːnəʊvə/ *noun* the total value of stock sold in a year divided by the average value of goods in stock

stock valuation /ˌstɒl væljuˈeɪʃ(ə)n/ *noun* an estimation of the value of stock at the end of an accounting period

stop /stɒp/ *noun* the end of an action ○ *Work came to a stop when the company could not pay the workers' wages.* ○ *The new finance director put a stop to the reps' inflated expense claims.*

stop-loss order /stɒp ˈlɒs ˌɔːdə/ *noun* an instruction to a stockbroker to sell a share if the price falls to an agreed level (NOTE: The US term is **stop order**.)

stoppage /ˈstɒpɪdʒ/ *noun* the act of stopping ○ *stoppage of payments* ○ *Bad weather was responsible for the stoppage of deliveries.* ○ *Deliveries will be late because of stoppages on the production line.*

storage capacity /ˈstɔːrɪdʒ kəˌpæsɪti/ *noun* the space available for storage

store card /ˈstɔː kɑːd/ *noun* a credit card issued by a large department store, which can only be used for purchases in that store

straddle /ˈstræd(ə)l/ *noun* **1.** a spread, the difference between bid and offer price **2.** the act of buying a put option and a call option at the same time

straight line depreciation /ˌstreɪt laɪn dɪˌpriʃiˈeɪʃ(ə)n/ *noun* depreciation calculated by dividing the cost of an asset, less its remaining value, by the number of years it is likely to be used

strategic management accounting /strəˌtiːdʒɪk ˌmænɪdʒmənt əˈkaʊntɪŋ/ *noun* a form of management accounting in which emphasis is placed on information which relates to factors external to the firm, as well as non-financial information and internally generated information

strategy /ˈstrætədʒi/ *noun* a course of action, including the specification of resources required, to achieve specific objective ○ *a marketing strategy* ○ *a financial strategy* ○ *a sales strategy* ○ *a pricing strategy* ○ *What is the strategy of the HR department to deal with long-term manpower requirements?* ○ *Part of the company's strategy to meet its marketing objectives is a major recruitment and retraining programme.* (NOTE: The plural is **strategies**.)

strike /straɪk/ *verb* □ **a deal was struck at £25 a unit** we agreed the price of £25 a unit

strong /strɒŋ/ *adjective* with a lot of force or strength ○ *This Christmas saw a strong demand for mobile phones.* ○ *The company needs a strong chairman.*

'…everybody blames the strong dollar for US trade problems' [*Duns Business Month*]

'…in a world of floating exchange rates the dollar is strong because of capital inflows rather than weak because of the nation's trade deficit' [*Duns Business Month*]

strongbox /ˈstrɒŋbɒks/ *noun* a heavy metal box which cannot be opened easily, in which valuable documents and money can be kept

strong currency /ˌstrɒŋ ˈkʌrənsi/ *noun* a currency which has a high value against other currencies

strong pound /ˌstrɒŋ ˈpaʊnd/ *noun* a pound which is high against other currencies

structure /ˈstrʌktʃə/ *noun* the way in which something is organised ○ *the price structure in the small car market* ○ *the career structure within a corporation* ○ *The paper gives a diagram of the company's organisational structure.* ○ *The company is reorganising its discount structure.*

sub /sʌb/ *noun* wages paid in advance

sub- /sʌb/ *prefix* under or less important

subcontract /ˌsʌbkənˈtrækt/ *verb* (*of a main contractor*) to agree with a company that they will do part of the work for a project ○ *The electrical work has been subcontracted to Smith Ltd.*

subcontractor /ˈsʌbkənˌtræktə/ *noun* a company which has a contract to do work for a main contractor

subject to /ˈsʌbdʒɪkt tuː/ *adjective* depending on

sublease /sʌbˈliːs/ *verb* to lease a leased property from another tenant ○ *They subleased a small office in the centre of town.*

sublessee /sʌbleˈsiː/ *noun* a person or company that takes a property on a sublease

sublessor /sʌbleˈsɔː/ *noun* a tenant who leases a leased property to another tenant

sublet /sʌbˈlet/ *verb* to let a leased property to another tenant ○ *We have sublet part of our office to a financial consultancy.* (NOTE: **subletting – sublet**)

subordinated loan /səˌbɔːdɪnətɪd ˈləʊn/ *noun* a loan which ranks after all other borrowings as regards payment of interest or repayment of capital

subscribe /səbˈskraɪb/ *verb* □ **to sub-scribe for shares**, **to subscribe to a share issue** to apply for shares in a new company

subscription /səbˈskrɪpʃən/ *noun* **1.** money paid in advance for a series of issues of a magazine, for membership of a society or for access to information on a website ○ *Did you remember to pay the subscription to the computer magazine?* ○ *She forgot to renew her club subscription.* **2.** □ **subscription to a new share issue** application to buy shares in a new company □ **the subscription lists close at 10.00 on September 24th** no new applicants will be allowed to subscribe for the share issue after that date

subscription price /səbˈskrɪpʃən praɪs/ *noun* a price at which new shares in an existing company are offered for sale

subsidiary /səbˈsɪdiəri/ *adjective* less important ○ *They agreed to most of the conditions in the contract but queried one or two subsidiary items.* ■ *noun* same as **subsidiary company** ○ *Most of the group profit was contributed by the subsidiaries in the Far East.*

subsidiary account /səbˌsɪdiəri əˈkaʊnt/ *noun* an account for one of the individual people or organisations that jointly hold another account

subsidiary company /səbˌsɪdiəri ˈkʌmp(ə)ni/ *noun* a company which is more than 50% owned by a holding company, and where the holding company controls the board of directors

subsidise /ˈsʌbsɪdaɪz/, **subsidize** *verb* to help by giving money ○ *The government has refused to subsidise the car industry.*

subsidised accommodation /ˌsʌbsɪdaɪzd əˌkɒməˈdeɪʃ(ə)n/ *noun* cheap accommodation which is partly paid for by an employer or a local authority

subsidy /ˈsʌbsɪdi/ *noun* **1.** money given to help something which is not profitable ○ *The industry exists on government subsidies.* ○ *The government has increased its subsidy to the car industry.* **2.** money given by a government to make something cheaper ○ *the subsidy on rail transport* (NOTE: The plural is **subsidies**.)

substantial /səbˈstænʃəl/ *adjective* large or important

subtenancy /sʌbˈtenənsi/ *noun* an agreement to sublet a property

subtenant /sʌbˈtenənt/ *noun* a person or company to which a property has been sublet

subtotal /ˈsʌbˌtəʊt(ə)l/ *noun* the total of one section of a complete set of figures ○ *She added all the subtotals to make a grand total.*

subtract /səbˈtrækt/ *verb* to take away something from a total ○ *The credit note should be subtracted from the figure for total sales.* ○ *If the profits from the Far Eastern operations are subtracted, you will see that the group has not been profitable in the European market.*

subtraction /səbˈtrækʃən/ *noun* an act of taking one number away from another

subvention /səbˈvenʃ(ə)n/ *noun* same as **subsidy**

succeed /səkˈsiːd/ *verb* **1.** to do well, to be profitable ○ *The company has succeeded best in the overseas markets.* ○ *Her business has succeeded more than she had expected.* **2.** to do what was planned ○ *She succeeded in passing her computing test.* ○ *They succeeded in putting their rivals out of business.* **3.** to take over from someone in a post ○ *Mr Smith was succeeded as chairman by Mrs Jones.* □ **to succeed to a property** to become the owner of a property by inheriting it from someone who has died

success /səkˈses/ *noun* **1.** an act of doing something well ○ *The launch of the new model was a great success.* ○ *The company has had great success in the Japanese market.* **2.** an act of doing what was intended ○ *We had no success in trying to sell the lease.* ○ *She has been looking for a job for six months, but with no success.*

sum /sʌm/ *noun* **1.** a quantity of money ○ *A sum of money was stolen from the human resources office.* ○ *He lost large sums on the Stock Exchange.* ○ *She received the sum of £5000 in compensation.* **2.** the total of a series of figures added together ○ *The sum of the various subtotals is £18,752.*

sum at risk /ˌsʌm ət ˈrɪsk/ *noun* an amount of any given item, such as money, stocks, or securities that an investor may lose

sum of digits method /ˌsʌm əv ˈdɪdʒɪts ˌmeθəd/ *noun* a method of depreciating a fixed asset where the cost of the asset less its residual value is multiplied by a fraction based on the number of years of its expected useful life. The fraction changes each year and charges the highest costs to the earliest years.

sum-of-the-year's-digits depreciation /ˌsʌm əv ðə ˌjɪəz ˌdɪdʒɪts dɪˌpriːʃi ˈeɪʃ(ə)n/ *noun* accelerated depreciation, conferring tax advantage by assuming more rapid depreciation when an asset is new

sums chargeable to the reserve
/sʌmz ˌtʃɑːdʒəb(ə)l tə ðə rɪˈzɜːv/ *plural noun* sums which can be debited to a company's reserves

sundry /ˈsʌndri/ *adjective* various

sunk costs /ˌsʌŋk ˈkɒsts/ *plural noun* a cost which has been irreversibly incurred or committed prior to a decision point and which cannot therefore be considered relevant to subsequent decisions

superannuation /ˌsuːpərænjuˈeɪʃ(ə)n/ *noun* a pension paid to someone who is too old or ill to work any more

supervisor /ˈsuːpəvaɪzə/ *noun* a person who supervises ○ *The supervisor was asked to write a report on the workers' performance.*

supplementary benefit /ˌsʌplɪ ˌment(ə)ri ˈbenɪfɪt/ *noun* formerly, payments from the government to people with very low incomes. It was replaced by Income Support.

supplier /səˈplaɪə/ *noun* a person or company that supplies or sells goods or services ○ *We use the same office equipment supplier for all our stationery purchases.* ○ *They are major suppliers of spare parts to the car industry.* Also called **producer**

supply /səˈplaɪ/ *noun* the act of providing something which is needed

supply and demand /səˌplaɪ ən dɪ ˈmɑːnd/ *noun* the amount of a product which is available and the amount which is wanted by customers

supply price /səˈplaɪ praɪs/ *noun* the price at which something is provided

support price /səˈpɔːt praɪs/ *noun* a price in the EU at which a government will buy agricultural produce to stop the price falling

surcharge /ˈsɜːtʃɑːdʒ/ *noun* an extra charge

surety /ˈʃʊərəti/ *noun* **1.** a person who guarantees that someone will do something ○ *to stand surety for someone* **2.** deeds, share certificates, etc., deposited as security for a loan

surplus /ˈsɜːpləs/ *noun* more of something than is needed

'Both imports and exports reached record levels in the latest year. This generated a $371 million trade surplus in June, the seventh consecutive monthly surplus and close to market expectations' [*Dominion (Wellington, New Zealand)*]

surrender /səˈrendə/ *noun* the act of giving up of an insurance policy before the contracted date for maturity

surrender value /səˈrendə ˌvæljuː/ *noun* the money which an insurer will pay if an insurance policy is given up

surtax /ˈsɜːtæks/ *noun* an extra tax on high income

suspend /səˈspend/ *verb* to stop doing something for a time ○ *We have suspended payments while we are waiting for news from our agent.* ○ *Sailings have been suspended until the weather gets better.* ○ *Work on the construction project has been suspended.* ○ *The management decided to suspend negotiations.*

suspense account /səˈspens əˌkaʊnt/ *noun* an account into which payments are put temporarily when the accountant cannot be sure where they should be entered

suspension /səˈspenʃən/ *noun* an act of stopping something for a time ○ *There has been a temporary suspension of payments.* ○ *We are trying to avoid a suspension of deliveries during the strike.*

SVA *abbr* shareholder value analysis

swap /swɒp/ *noun* an exchange of one thing for another

sweetener /ˈswiːt(ə)nə/ *noun* an incentive offered to help persuade somebody to take a particular course of action, a bribe (*informal*)

switch /swɪtʃ/ *verb* **1.** to change from one thing to another ○ *to switch funds from one investment to another* ○ *The job was switched from our British factory to the States.* **2.** to change, especially to change investment money from one type of investment to another

syndicate /ˈsɪndɪkeɪt/ *verb* to arrange for a large loan to be underwritten by several international banks

'…over the past few weeks, companies raising new loans from international banks have been forced to pay more, and an unusually high number of attempts to syndicate loans among banks has failed' [*Financial Times*]

synergy /ˈsɪnədʒi/ *noun* the process of producing greater effects by joining forces than by acting separately ○ *There is considerable synergy between the two companies.*

system /ˈsɪstəm/ *noun* an arrangement or organisation of things which work together ○ *Our accounting system has worked well in spite of the large increase in orders.* ○ *What system is being used for filing data on personnel?*

systems analyst /ˈsɪstəmz ˌænəlɪst/ *noun* a person who specialises in systems analysis

T

T+ *noun* an expression of the number of days allowed for settlement of a transaction

tab /tæb/ *noun* same as **tabulator** (*informal*)

tabulate /'tæbjʊleɪt/ *verb* to set something out in a table

tabulation /ˌtæbjʊ'leɪʃ(ə)n/ *noun* the arrangement of figures in a table

tabulator /'tæbjʊleɪtə/ *noun* a feature on a computer which sets words or figures automatically in columns

T account /'tiː əˌkaʊnt/ *noun* a way of drawing up an account, with a line across the top of the paper and a vertical line down the middle, with the debit and credit entries on either side

take /teɪk/ *noun* **1.** the money received in a shop ○ *Our weekly take is over £5,000.* **2.** a profit from any sale ■ *verb* **1.** to receive or to get □ **the shop takes £2,000 a week** the shop receives £2,000 a week in cash sales □ **she takes home £250 a week** her salary, after deductions for tax etc. is £250 a week **2.** to perform an action **3.** to need a time or a quantity ○ *It took the factory six weeks* or *The factory took six weeks to clear the backlog of orders.* ○ *It will take her all morning to do my letters.* ○ *It took six men and a crane to get the computer into the building.* (NOTE: **taking – took – has taken**)

take away /ˌteɪk ə'weɪ/ *verb* to remove one figure from a total ○ *If you take away the home sales, the total turnover is down.*

take-home pay /'teɪk həʊm ˌpeɪ/ *noun* same as **disposable personal income** ○ *After all the deductions, her take-home pay is only £300 a week.*

take off /ˌteɪk 'ɒf/ *verb* to remove or to deduct something ○ *He took £25 off the price.*

take-out /'teɪk aʊt/ *noun* the act of removing capital which you had originally invested in a new company by selling your shares

take over /ˌteɪk 'əʊvə/ *verb* to start to do something in place of someone else ○ *Miss Black took over from Mr Jones on May 1st.*

takeover /'teɪkəʊvə/ *noun* an act of buying a controlling interest in a business by buying more than 50% of its shares. Compare **acquisition**

'…many takeovers result in the new managers/owners rationalizing the capital of the company through better asset management' [*Duns Business Month*]

takeover bid /'teɪkəʊvə bɪd/ *noun* an offer to buy all or a majority of the shares in a company so as to control it ○ *They made a takeover bid for the company.* ○ *She had to withdraw her takeover bid when she failed to find any backers.* ○ *Share prices rose sharply on the disclosure of the takeover bid.*

Takeover Code /'teɪkˌəʊvə kəʊd/ *noun* a code of practice which regulates how takeovers should take place. It is enforced by the Takeover Panel.

Takeover Panel /ˌteɪkˌəʊvə 'pæn(ə)l/ *noun* a non-statutory body which examines takeovers and applies the Takeover Code. Also called **City Panel on Takeovers and Mergers**

takeover target /'teɪkəʊvə ˌtɑːgɪt/ *noun* a company which is the object of a takeover bid

take up rate /'teɪk ʌp ˌreɪt/ *noun* the percentage of acceptances for a rights issue

takings /'teɪkɪŋz/ *plural noun* the money received in a shop or a business ○ *The week's takings were stolen from the cash desk.*

tally /'tæli/ *noun* a note of things counted or recorded ○ *to keep a tally of stock movements* or *of expenses* ■ *verb* to agree, to be the same ○ *The invoices do not tally.* ○ *The accounts department tried to make the figures tally.*

tally clerk /'tæli klɑːk/ *noun* a person whose job is to note quantities of cargo

tally sheet /'tæli ʃiːt/ *noun* a sheet on which quantities are noted

tangible assets /ˌtændʒɪb(ə)l 'æsets/, **tangible fixed assets** /ˌtændʒɪb(ə)l 'prɒpəti/, **tangible property** *plural noun* assets that are physical, such as buildings, cash and stock. Leases and securities, although not physical in themselves, are classed as tangible assets because the underlying assets are physical.

tangible asset value /ˌtændʒəb(ə)l ˌæset ˈvæljuː/, **tangible net worth** /ˌtændʒəb(ə)l net ˈwɜːθ/ *noun* the value of all the assets of a company less its intangible such as assets goodwill, patents. It is shown as a value per share.

tangible book value /ˌtændʒəb(ə)l bʊk ˈvæljuː/ *noun* the book value of a company after intangible assets, patents, trademarks, and the value of research and development have been subtracted

taper relief /ˌteɪpə rɪˈliːf/ *noun* the relief for capital gains on assets sold after being held for some period of time. The longer the assets have been held, the more relief is given against capital gains.

target /ˈtɑːɡɪt/ *noun* something to aim for
○ *performance targets*

> '...he believes that increased competition could keep inflation below the 2.5 per cent target' [*Investors Chronicle*]

> '...the minister is persuading the oil, gas, electricity and coal industries to target their advertising towards energy efficiency' [*Times*]

target company /ˌtɑːɡɪt ˈkʌmp(ə)ni/ *noun* same as **takeover target**

> '...in a normal leveraged buyout the acquirer raises money by borrowing against the assets of the target company' [*Fortune*]

target cost /ˈtɑːɡɪt kɒst/ *noun* a product cost estimate derived by subtracting a desired profit margin from a competitive market price. This may be less than the planned initial product cost, but will be expected to be achieved by the time the product reaches the mature production stage.

target market /ˈtɑːɡɪt ˌmɑːkɪt/ *noun* the market in which a company is planning to sell its goods

tax /tæks/ *noun* **1.** money taken by the government or by an official body to pay for government services **2.** an amount of money charged by government as part of a person's income or on goods bought □ **to levy** *or* **impose a tax** to make a tax payable ○ *The government has imposed a 15% tax on petrol.* ■ *verb* to make someone pay a tax, to impose a tax on something ○ *Businesses are taxed at 40%.* ○ *Income is taxed at 35%* ○ *Luxury items are heavily taxed.*

tax abatement /ˈtæks əˌbeɪtmənt/ *noun* a reduction of tax

taxable /ˈtæksəb(ə)l/ *adjective* able to be taxed

taxable base /ˌtæksəb(ə)l ˈbeɪs/ *noun* the amount subject to taxation

taxable benefit /ˌtæksəb(ə)l ˈbenɪfɪt/ *noun* a benefit which is included in a person's taxable income and is subject to tax

taxable income /ˌtæksəb(ə)l ˈɪnkʌm/ *noun* income on which a person has to pay tax

taxable items /ˈtæksəb(ə)l ˌaɪtəmz/ *plural noun* items on which a tax has to be paid

taxable matters /ˌtæksəb(ə)l ˈmætəs/ *noun* goods or services that can be taxed

taxable person /ˌtæksəb(ə)l ˈpɜːs(ə)n/ *noun* a person who is registered for VAT, and who charges VAT on goods or services supplied

taxable supply /ˌtæksəb(ə)l səˈplaɪ/ *noun* a supply of goods which are subject to VAT

tax adjustments /ˈtæks əˌdʒʌstmənts/ *plural noun* changes made to tax

tax adviser /ˈtæks ədˌvaɪzə/, **tax consultant** /ˈtæks kənˌsʌltənt/ *noun* a person who gives advice on tax problems

tax allowance /ˈtæks əˌlaʊəns/ *noun* a part of the income which a person is allowed to earn and not pay tax on

tax assessment /ˈtæks əˌsesmənt/ *noun* a calculation by a tax inspector of the amount of tax a person owes

taxation /tækˈseɪʃ(ə)n/ *noun* the act of taxing

tax at source /ˌtæks ət ˈsɔːs/ *verb* to deduct tax from earnings before they are paid to the recipient

tax auditor /ˈtæks ˌɔːdɪtə/ *noun* a government employee who investigates taxpayers' declarations

tax avoidance /ˈtæks əˌvɔɪd(ə)ns/ *noun* the practice of legally trying to pay as little tax as possible

tax bracket /ˈtæks ˌbrækɪt/ *noun* a section of people paying a particular level of income tax

tax code /ˈtæks kəʊd/ *noun* a number given to indicate the amount of tax allowance a person has

tax collector /ˈtæks kəˌlektə/ *noun* a person who collects taxes which are owed

tax concession /ˈtæks kənˌseʃ(ə)n/ *noun* an act of allowing less tax to be paid

tax consultant /ˈtæks kənˌsʌltənt/ *noun* a professional who advises on all aspects of taxation from tax avoidance to estate planning

tax credit /ˈtæks ˌkredɪt/ *noun* **1.** a sum of money which can be offset against tax **2.** the part of a dividend on which the company has already paid tax, so that the shareholder is not taxed on it

tax date /ˈtæks deɪt/ *noun* the date on which a transaction occurs for tax purposes, particularly relevant to invoices on which VAT is charged

tax-deductible /ˌtæks dɪˈdʌktɪb(ə)l/ *adjective* possible to deduct from an income before tax is calculated

tax deposit certificate /tæks dɪˈpɒzɪt səˌtɪfɪkət/ *noun* a certificate showing that a taxpayer has deposited money in advance of a tax payment. The money earns interest while on deposit.

tax dodge /ˈtæks dɒdʒ/ *noun* an illegal method of paying less tax than an individual or company is legally obliged to pay

tax domicile /ˈtæks ˌdɒmɪsaɪl/ *noun* a place that a government levying a tax considers to be a person's home

tax evasion /ˈtæks ɪˌveɪʒ(ə)n/ *noun* the practice of illegally trying not to pay tax

tax-exempt /ˌtæks ɪɡˈzempt/ *adjective* **1.** referring to a person or organisation not required to pay tax **2.** not subject to tax

tax exemption /ˈtæks ɪɡˌzempʃən/ *noun* US **1.** the fact of being free from payment of tax **2.** the part of income which a person is allowed to earn and not pay tax on

tax exemption cut-off /ˌtæks ɪɡ ˌzempʃ(ə)n ˈkʌt ˌɒf/ *noun* a limit on tax exemption because of high income

tax-exempt special savings account /tæks ɪɡˌzempt ˌspeʃ(ə)l ˈseɪvɪŋz əˌkaʊnt/ *noun* a discontinued type of account into which money could be placed to earn interest free of tax, provided it was left untouched for five years. Since 1999 the scheme has gradually been phased out but money in existing TESSAs can be reinvested in ISAs. Abbreviation **TESSA**

tax form /ˈtæks fɔːm/ *noun* a blank form to be filled in with details of income and allowances and sent to the tax office each year

tax-free /ˌtæks ˈfriː/ *adjective* with no tax having to be paid ○ *tax-free goods*

tax harmonisation /ˌtæks hɑːmənaɪ ˈzeɪʃ(ə)n/ *noun* the enactment of taxation laws in different jurisdictions, such as neighbouring countries, provinces, or states of the United States, that are consistent with one another

tax haven /ˈtæks ˌheɪv(ə)n/ *noun* a country or area where taxes are low, encouraging companies to set up their main offices there

tax holiday /ˈtæks ˌhɒlɪdeɪ/ *noun* a period when a new business is exempted from paying tax

tax incentive /ˈtæks ɪnˌsentɪv/ *noun* a tax reduction afforded to people for particular purposes, e.g., sending their children to college

tax inspector /ˈtæks ɪnˌspektə/ *noun* a government employee who investigates taxpayers' declarations

tax law /ˈtæks lɔː/ *noun* the body of laws on taxation, or one such law

tax liability /ˈtæks ˌlaɪəˈbɪlɪti/ *noun* the amount of tax that a person or organisation has to pay

tax loophole /ˈtæks ˌluːphəʊl/ *noun* a legal means of not paying tax

tax loss /ˈtæks lɒs/ *noun* a loss made by a company during an accounting period, for which relief from tax is given

tax loss carry-back /ˌtæks lɒs ˌkæri ˈbæk/ *noun* the reduction of taxes in a previous year by subtraction from income for that year of losses suffered in the current year

tax loss carry-forward /ˌtæks lɒs ˌkæri ˈfɔːwəd/ *noun* the reduction of taxes in a future year by subtraction from income for that year of losses suffered in the current year

tax obligation /ˈtæks ˌɒblɪˈɡeɪʃ(ə)n/ *noun* the amount of tax a person or company owes

tax office /ˈtæks ˌɒfɪs/ *noun* a local office of the Inland Revenue. It does not necessarily deal with the tax affairs of people who live locally.

tax on capital income /ˈtæks ɒn ˌkæpɪt(ə)l ˈɪnkʌm/ *noun* a tax on the income from sales of capital assets

tax payable /ˌtæks ˈpeɪəb(ə)l/ *noun* the amount of tax a person or company has to pay

taxpayer /ˈtækspeɪə/ *noun* a person or company that has to pay tax ○ *basic taxpayer* or *taxpayer at the basic rate* ○ *Corporate taxpayers are being targeted by the government.*

tax planning /ˈtæks ˌplænɪŋ/ *noun* planning how to avoid paying too much tax, by investing in, e.g., tax-exempt savings schemes or offshore trusts

tax point /ˈtæks pɔɪnt/ *noun* the date on which goods or services are supplied, which is the date when VAT becomes is due

tax pressure /ˈtæks ˌpreʃə/ *noun* the financial difficulty that a company may face because of the taxes it must pay

tax rates /'tæks ˌreɪts/ *noun* percentage rates of tax on different bands of taxable income

tax rebate /'tæks ˌriːbeɪt/ *noun* money returned by the Inland Revenue because it was overpaid

tax refund /'tæks ˌriːfʌnd/ *noun* an amount that a government gives back to a taxpayer who has paid more taxes than were due

tax relief /'tæks rɪˌliːf/ *noun* an allowance to pay less tax on some parts of someone's income

tax return /'tæks rɪˌtɜːn/ *noun* a completed tax form, with details of income and allowances

tax revenue /'tæks ˌrevənjuː/ *noun* money that a government receives in taxes

tax schedules /'tæks ˌʃedjuːlz/ *plural noun* a six types of income as classified for tax

tax shelter /'tæks ˌʃeltə/ *noun* a financial arrangement such as a pension scheme where investments can be made without tax

tax system /'tæks ˌsɪstəm/ *noun* the methods used by a government in imposing and collecting taxes

tax threshold /'tæks ˌθreʃhəʊld/ *noun* a point at which another percentage of tax is payable ○ *The government has raised the minimum tax threshold from £4,000 to £4,500.*

tax treaty /'tæks ˌtriːti/ *noun* an international agreement that deals with taxes, especially taxes by several countries on the same individuals

tax year /'tæks ˌjɪə/ *noun* a twelve month period on which taxes are calculated. In the UK this is 6th April to 5th April of the following year.

technical /'teknɪk(ə)l/ *adjective* **1.** referring to a particular machine or process ○ *The document gives all the technical details on the new computer.* **2.** referring to influences inside a market, e.g. volumes traded and forecasts based on market analysis, as opposed to external factors such as oil-price rises, wars, etc,

'…market analysts described the falls in the second half of last week as a technical correction' [*Australian Financial Review*]

'…at the end of the day, it was clear the Fed had not loosened the monetary reins, and Fed Funds forged ahead on the back of technical demand' [*Financial Times*]

technical analysis /ˌteknɪk(ə)l əˈnæləsɪs/ *noun* a study of the price move-

ments and volumes traded on a stock exchange

technical correction /ˌteknɪk(ə)l kəˈrekʃ(ə)n/ *noun* a situation where a share price or a currency moves up or down because it was previously too low or too high

technical decline /ˌteknɪk(ə)l dɪˈklaɪn/ *noun* a fall in share prices because of technical analysis

technical reserves /ˌteknɪk(ə)l rɪˈzɜːvz/ *noun* the assets that an insurance company maintains to meet future claims

teeming and lading /ˌtiːmɪŋ ən ˈleɪdɪŋ/ *noun* an attempt to hide missing funds by delaying the recording of cash receipts in a business's books. US term **lapping**

telegraphic transfer /ˌtelɪgræfɪk ˈtrɑːnsfə/ *noun* a transfer of money from one account to another by telegraph

telephone banking /ˌtelɪfəʊn ˈbæŋkɪŋ/ *noun* a service by which a bank customer can carry out transactions over the phone using a password. It may involve direct contact with a bank representative or may be automated used the phone dial.

teller /'telə/ *noun* a person who takes cash from or pays cash to customers at a bank

tenancy /'tenənsi/ *noun* an agreement by which a tenant can occupy a property

tenant /'tenənt/ *noun* a person or company which rents a house, flat or office to live or work in ○ *The tenant is liable for repairs.*

tender /'tendə/ *noun* an offer to do something for a specific price ○ *a successful tender* ○ *an unsuccessful tender* □ **to put a project out to tender, to ask for** *or* **invite tenders for a project** to ask contractors to give written estimates for a job □ **to put in** *or* **submit a tender** to make an estimate for a job

tenderer /'tendərə/ *noun* a person or company that tenders for work ○ *The company was the successful tenderer for the project.*

tendering /'tendərɪŋ/ *noun* the act of putting forward an estimate of cost ○ *To be successful, you must follow the tendering procedure as laid out in the documents.*

tender offer /'tendə ˌɒfə/ *noun* a method of selling new securities or bonds by asking investors to make offers for them, and accepting the highest offers

10-K /ˌten ˈkeɪ/ *noun* the filing of a US company's annual accounts with the New York Stock Exchange

tenor /'tenə/ *noun* a time before a financial instrument matures or before a bill is payable

10-Q /ˌten ˈkjuː/ *noun* the filing of a US company's quarterly accounts with the New York Stock Exchange

term /tɜːm/ *noun* a period of time when something is legally valid ○ *during his term of office as chairman* ○ *the term of a lease* ○ *We have renewed her contract for a term of six months.* ○ *The term of the loan is fifteen years.*

term account /ˈtɜːm əˌkaʊnt/ *noun* same as **term deposit**

term deposit /ˈtɜːm dɪˌpɒzɪt/ *noun* money invested for a fixed period at a higher rate of interest

terminal bonus /ˌtɜːmɪn(ə)l ˈbəʊnəs/ *noun* a bonus received when an insurance comes to an end

termination clause /ˌtɜːmɪˈneɪʃ(ə)n klɔːz/ *noun* a clause which explains how and when a contract can be terminated

term loan /ˈtɜːm ləʊn/ *noun* a loan for a fixed period of time

terms /tɜːmz/ *plural noun* the conditions or duties which have to be carried out as part of a contract, or the arrangements which have to be agreed before a contract is valid ○ *to negotiate for better terms* ○ *She refused to agree to some of the terms of the contract.* ○ *By* or *Under the terms of the contract, the company is responsible for all damage to the property.*

'…companies have been improving communications, often as part of deals to cut down demarcation and to give everybody the same terms of employment' [*Economist*]

'…the Federal Reserve Board has eased interest rates in the past year, but they are still at historically high levels in real terms' [*Sunday Times*]

term shares /ˈtɜːm ʃeəz/ *plural noun* a type of building society deposit for a fixed period of time at a higher rate of interest

terms of reference /ˌtɜːmz əv ˈref(ə)rəns/ *plural noun* areas which a committee or an inspector can deal with ○ *Under the terms of reference of the committee, it cannot investigate complaints from the public.* ○ *The committee's terms of reference do not cover exports.*

terms of sale /ˌtɜːmz əv ˈseɪl/ *plural noun* the conditions attached to a sale

TESSA *abbr* tax-exempt special savings account

testamentary /testəˈmentəri/ *adjective* referring to a will

testamentary disposition /testəˌmentəri ˌdɪspəˈzɪʃ(ə)n/ *noun* passing of property to people in a will

testate /ˈtesteɪt/ *adjective* having made a will ○ *Did he die testate?*

testator /teˈsteɪtə/ *noun* someone who has made a will

testatrix /teˈsteɪtrɪks/ *noun* a woman who has made a will

third party /ˌθɜːd ˈpɑːti/ *noun* a person other than the two main parties involved in a contract, e.g., in an insurance contract, anyone who is not the insurance company nor the person who is insured

third quarter /ˌθɜːd ˈkwɔːtə/ *noun* a period of three months from July to September

3i *abbr* Investors in Industry

three quarters /ˌθriː ˈkwɔːtəz/ *noun* 75% ○ *Three quarters of the staff are less than thirty years old.*

threshold /ˈθreʃhəʊld/ *noun* the point at which something changes

threshold agreement /ˈθreʃhəʊld əˌɡriːmənt/ *noun* a contract which says that if the cost of living goes up by more than an agreed amount, pay will go up to match it

thrift /θrɪft/ *noun* **1.** a careful attitude towards money, shown by saving it spending wisely **2.** *US* a private local bank, savings and loan association or credit union, which accepts and pays interest on deposits from small investors

'…the thrift, which had grown from $4.7 million in assets in 1980 to 1.5 billion this year, has ended in liquidation' [*Barrons*]

'…some thrifts came to grief on speculative property deals, some in the high-risk junk bond market, others simply by lending too much to too many people' [*Times*]

thrifty /ˈθrɪfti/ *adjective* careful not to spend too much money

throughput accounting /ˌθruːpʊt əˈkaʊntɪŋ/ *noun* a management accounting system which focuses on ways by which the maximum return per unit of bottleneck activity can be achieved

tied financial adviser /taɪd faɪˌnænʃəl ədˈvaɪzə/ *noun* a qualified person, authorised to act by the Personal Investment Authority, who advises private clients on the financial products offered by a single company, as opposed to an independent financial adviser, who only advises on a wide range of products

tighten /ˈtaɪt(ə)n/ *verb* to make something tight, to control something ○ *The accounts department is tightening its control over departmental budgets.*

'…the decision by the government to tighten monetary policy will push the annual inflation rate above the previous high' [*Financial Times*]

tighten up on /ˌtaɪt(ə)n ˈʌp ɒn/ *verb* to control something more strictly ○ *The government is tightening up on tax evasion.* ○ *We must tighten up on the reps' expenses.*

tight money /taɪt ˈmʌni/ *noun* same as **dear money**

tight money policy /taɪt ˈmʌni ˌpɒlɪsi/ *noun* a government policy to restrict money supply

till /tɪl/ *noun* a drawer for keeping cash in a shop

time /taɪm/ *noun* **1.** a period during which something takes place, e.g. one hour, two days or fifty minutes **2.** the number of hours worked **3.** a period before something happens □ **to keep within the time limits** *or* **within the time schedule** to complete work by the time stated

time and method study /ˌtaɪm ən ˈmeθəd ˌstʌdi/ *noun* a process of examining the way in which something is done to see if a cheaper or quicker way can be found

time and motion expert /ˌtaɪm ən ˈməʊʃ(ə)n ˌekspɜːt/ *noun* a person who analyses time and motion studies and suggests changes in the way work is done

time and motion study /ˌtaɪm ən ˈməʊʃ(ə)n ˌstʌdi/ *noun* a study in an office or factory of the time taken to do specific jobs and the movements employees have to make to do them

time deposit /ˈtaɪm dɪˌpɒzɪt/ *noun* a deposit of money for a fixed period, during which it cannot be withdrawn

time-keeping /ˈtaɪm ˌkiːpɪŋ/ *noun* the fact of being on time for work ○ *He was warned for bad time-keeping.*

time limit /ˈtaɪm ˌlɪmɪt/ *noun* the maximum time which can be taken to do something ○ *to set a time limit for acceptance of the offer* ○ *The work was finished within the time limit allowed.* ○ *The time limit on applications to the industrial tribunal is three months.*

time limitation /ˈtaɪm lɪmɪˌteɪʃ(ə)n/ *noun* the restriction of the amount of time available

time rate /ˈtaɪm reɪt/ *noun* a rate for work which is calculated as money per hour or per week, and not money for work completed

timescale /ˈtaɪmskeɪl/ *noun* the time which will be taken to complete work ○ *Our timescale is that all work should be completed by the end of August.* ○ *He is working to a strict timescale.*

time sheet /ˈtaɪm ʃiːt/ *noun* a record of when an employee arrives at and leaves

work, or one which shows how much time a person spends on different jobs each day

time work /ˈtaɪm wɜːk/ *noun* work which is paid for at a rate per hour or per day, not per piece of work completed

tip /tɪp/ *noun* money given to someone who has helped you ○ *The staff are not allowed to accept tips.*

title /ˈtaɪt(ə)l/ *noun* a right to own a property ○ *She has no title to the property.* ○ *He has a good title to the property.*

title deeds /ˈtaɪt(ə)l ˌdiːdz/ *plural noun* a document showing who is the owner of a property

token /ˈtəʊkən/ *noun* something which acts as a sign or symbol

token charge /ˌtəʊkən ˈtʃɑːdʒ/ *noun* a small charge which does not cover the real costs ○ *A token charge is made for heating.*

token payment /ˈtəʊkən ˌpeɪmənt/ *noun* a small payment to show that a payment is being made

token rent /ˌtəʊkən ˈrent/ *noun* a very low rent payment to show that some rent is being asked

toll /təʊl/ *noun* a payment for using a service, usually a bridge or a road ○ *We had to cross a toll bridge to get to the island.* ○ *You have to pay a toll to cross the bridge.*

toll call /ˈtəʊl kɔːl/ *noun US* a long-distance telephone call

toll free /ˌtəʊl ˈfriː/ *adverb, adjective US* without having to pay a charge for a long-distance telephone call ○ *to call someone toll free* ○ *a toll-free number*

top-hat pension /ˌtɒp hæt ˈpenʃən/ *noun* a special extra pension for senior managers

top management /ˌtɒp ˈmænɪdʒmənt/ *noun* the main directors of a company

top up /ˌtɒp ˈʌp/ *verb* **1.** to fill up something which is not full ○ *to top up stocks before the Christmas rush* **2.** to add to something to make it more complete ○ *He topped up his pension contributions to make sure he received the maximum allowable pension when he retired.*

total /ˈtəʊt(ə)l/ *adjective* complete or with everything added together ○ *The total amount owed is now £1000.* ○ *The company has total assets of over £1bn.* ○ *The total cost was much more than expected.* ○ *Total expenditure on publicity is twice that of last year.* ○ *Our total income from exports rose last year.* ■ *verb* to add up to ○ *costs totalling more than £25,000* (NOTE: UK English is **to-**

talling – totalled, but the US spelling is to-taling – totaled.)

total absorption costing /ˌtəʊt(ə)l əb ˌzɔːpʃən ˈkɒstɪŋ/ *noun* a method used by a cost accountant to price goods and services, allocating both direct and indirect costs. Although this method is designed so that all of an organisation's costs are covered, it may result in opportunities for sales being missed because it results in high prices. ◊ **marginal costing**

total assets /ˌtəʊt(ə)l ˈæsets/ *noun* the total net book value of all assets

total asset turnover ratio /ˌtəʊt(ə)l ˌæset ˌtɜːnəʊvə ˈreɪʃiəʊ/ *noun* a measure of the use a business makes of all its assets. It is calculated by dividing sales by total assets.

total invoice value /ˌtəʊt(ə)l ˈɪnvɔɪs ˌvæljuː/ *noun* the total amount on an invoice, including transport, VAT, etc.

total overhead cost variance /ˌtəʊt(ə)l ˌəʊvəhed kɒst ˈveəriəns/ *noun* the difference between the overhead cost absorbed and the actual overhead costs, both fixed and variable

total return /ˌtəʊt(ə)l rɪˈtɜːn/ *noun* the total percentage change in the value of an investment over a specified time period, including capital gains, dividends, and the investment's appreciation or depreciation

tracker fund /ˈtrækə fʌnd/ *noun* a fund which tracks one of the stock market indices, such as the FTSE

track record /ˈtræk ˌrekɔːd/ *noun* the success or failure of a company or salesperson in the past ○ *He has a good track record as a secondhand car salesman.* ○ *The company has no track record in the computer market.* ○ *We are looking for someone with a track record in the computer market.*

trade /treɪd/ *noun* **1.** the business of buying and selling **2.** a particular type of business, or people or companies dealing in the same type of product ○ *He's in the secondhand car trade.* ○ *She's very well known in the clothing trade.* ■ *verb* to buy and sell, to carry on a business ○ *We trade with all the countries of the EU.* ○ *She trades on the Stock Exchange.* ○ *The company has stopped trading.* ○ *The company trades under the name 'Eez-iphitt'.*

'…a sharp setback in foreign trade accounted for most of the winter slowdown. The trade balance sank $17 billion' [*Fortune*]

'…at its last traded price, the bank was capitalized around $1.05 billion' [*South China Morning Post*]

'…with most of the world's oil now traded on spot markets, Opec's official prices are much less significant than they once were' [*Economist*]

'…the London Stock Exchange said that the value of domestic UK equities traded during the year was £1.4066 trillion, more than the capitalization of the entire London market and an increase of 36 per cent compared with previous year's total of £1.037 trillion' [*Times*]

'…trade between Britain and other countries which comprise the Economic Community has risen steadily from 33% of exports to 50% last year' [*Sales & Marketing Management*]

trade agreement /ˈtreɪd əˌɡriːmənt/ *noun* an international agreement between countries over general terms of trade

trade association /ˈtreɪd əsəʊsiˌeɪʃ(ə)n/ *noun* a group which links together companies in the same trade

trade barrier /ˈtreɪd ˌbæriə/ *noun* a limitation imposed by a government on the free exchange of goods between countries. Also called **import restriction** (NOTE: NTBs, safety standards and tariffs are typical trade barriers.)

trade bill /ˈtreɪd bɪl/ *noun* a bill of exchange between two companies who are trading partners. It is issued by one company and endorsed by the other.

trade counter /ˈtreɪd ˌkaʊntə/ *noun* a shop in a factory or warehouse where goods are sold to retailers

trade credit /ˈtreɪd ˌkredɪt/ *noun* a credit offered by one company when trading with another

trade creditors /ˈtreɪd ˌkredɪtəz/ *plural noun* companies which are owed money by a company. The amount owed to trade creditors is shown in the annual accounts.

trade cycle /ˈtreɪd ˌsaɪk(ə)l/ *noun* a period during which trade expands, then slows down, then expands again

trade date /ˈtreɪd deɪt/ *noun* the date on which an enterprise becomes committed to buy a financial asset

trade debt /treɪd det/ *noun* a debt that originates during the normal course of trade

trade deficit /ˈtreɪd ˌdefɪsɪt/ *noun* the difference in value between a country's low exports and higher imports. Also called **balance of payments deficit, trade gap**

trade description /treɪd dɪˈskrɪpʃən/ *noun* a description of a product to attract customers

trade discount /treɪd ˈdɪskaʊnt/ *noun* a reduction in price given to a customer in the same trade

traded options /ˌtreɪdɪd ˈɒpʃənz/ *plural noun* options to buy or sell shares at a specific price on a specific date in the future, which themselves can be bought or sold

trade fair /'treɪd feə/ *noun* a large exhibition and meeting for advertising and selling a specific type of product ○ *There are two trade fairs running in London at the same time – the carpet manufacturers' and the mobile telephones.*

trade gap /'treɪd gæp/ *noun* same as **trade deficit**

trademark /'treɪdmɑːk/, **trade name** /'treɪd neɪm/ *noun* a name, design or symbol which has been registered by the manufacturer and which cannot be used by other manufacturers. It is an intangible asset. ○ *You can't call your beds 'Softn'kumfi' – it is a registered trademark.*

trade mission /'treɪd ˌmɪʃ(ə)n/ *noun* a visit by a group of businesspeople to discuss trade ○ *He led a trade mission to China.*

trade-off /'treɪd ɒf/ *noun* an act of exchanging one thing for another as part of a business deal (NOTE: The plural is **trade-offs**.)

trade price /'treɪd praɪs/ *noun* a special wholesale price paid by a retailer to the manufacturer or wholesaler

trader /'treɪdə/ *noun* a person who does business

trade surplus /'treɪd ˌsɜːpləs/ *noun* the difference in value between a country's high exports and lower imports

> 'Brazil's trade surplus is vulnerable both to a slowdown in the American economy and a pick-up in its own' [*Economist*]

trade terms /'treɪd tɜːmz/ *plural noun* a special discount for people in the same trade

trade-weighted index /treɪd ˌweɪtɪd 'ɪndeks/ *noun* an index of the value of a currency calculated against a basket of currencies

trading /'treɪdɪŋ/ *noun* **1.** the business of buying and selling **2.** an area of a broking house where dealing in securities is carried out by phone, using monitors to display current prices and stock exchange transactions

trading, profit and loss account *noun* an account which details the gross profit or loss made by an organisation for a given period **trading account**, and after adding other income and deducting various expenses, is able to show the profit or loss of the business

trading account /'treɪdɪŋ əˌkaʊnt/ *noun* an account of a company's gross profit

trading area /'treɪdɪŋ ˌeəriə/ *noun* a group of countries which trade with each other

trading company /'treɪdɪŋ ˌkʌmp(ə)ni/ *noun* a company which specialises in buying and selling goods

trading estate /'treɪdɪŋ ɪˌsteɪt/ *noun* an area of land near a town specially for building factories and warehouses

trading financial assets /ˌtreɪdɪŋ faɪ ˌnænʃəl 'æsets/ *noun* financial assets acquired or held in order to produce profit from short term changes in price

trading limit /'treɪdɪŋ ˌlɪmɪt/ *noun* the maximum amount of something which can be traded by a single trader

trading loss /'treɪdɪŋ lɒs/ *noun* a situation where a company's receipts are less than its expenditure

trading partner /'treɪdɪŋ ˌpɑːtnə/ *noun* a company or country which trades with another

trading profit /'treɪdɪŋ ˌprɒfɪt/ *noun* a result where the company' receipts are higher than its expenditure

trading stamp /'treɪdɪŋ stæmp/ *noun* a special stamp given away by a shop, which the customer can collect and exchange later for free goods

trainee /treɪ'niː/ *noun* a person who is learning how to do something ○ *We take five graduates as trainees each year.* ○ *Office staff with leadership potential are selected for courses as trainee managers.* ○ *We employ an additional trainee accountant at peak periods.*

training levy /'treɪnɪŋ ˌlevi/ *noun* a tax to be paid by companies to fund the government's training schemes

training officer /'treɪnɪŋ ˌɒfɪsə/ *noun* a person who deals with the training of staff in a company

tranche /trɑːnʃ/ *noun* one of a series of instalments, used when referring to loans to companies, government securities which are issued over a period of time, or money withdrawn by a country from the IMF ○ *The second tranche of interest on the loan is now due for payment.*

transaction /træn'zækʃən/ *noun* □ **a transaction on the Stock Exchange** a purchase or sale of shares on the Stock Exchange ○ *The paper publishes a daily list of Stock Exchange transactions.*

> '...the Japan Financial Intelligence Office will receive reports on suspected criminal transactions from financial institutions, determine where a probe should be launched and provide information to investigators' [*Nikkei Weekly*]

transaction costs /træn'zækʃən kɒsts/ *noun* incremental costs that are directly attributable to the buying or selling of an asset. Transaction costs include commissions, fees, and direct taxes.

transaction date /trænˈzækʃən deɪt/ *noun* the date on which control of an asset passes from the seller to the buyer

transaction exposure /trænˌzækʃən ɪkˈspəʊʒə/ *noun* the risk that an organisation may suffer the effects of foreign exchange rate changes during the time it takes to arrange the export or import of goods or services. Transaction exposure is present from the time a price is agreed until the payment has been made or received in the domestic currency.

transfer /ˈtrænsfɜː/ *noun* an act of moving an employee to another job in the same organisation ○ *She applied for a transfer to our branch in Scotland.* ■ *verb* to move someone or something to a different place, or to move someone to another job in the same organisation ○ *The accountant was transferred to our Scottish branch.* ○ *He transferred his shares to a family trust.* ○ *She transferred her money to a deposit account.*

transferable /trænsˈfɜːrəb(ə)l/ *adjective* possible to pass to someone else

transfer of property /ˌtrænsfɜː əv ˈprɒpəti/, **transfer of shares** /ˌtrænsfɜː əv ˈʃeəz/ *noun* the act of moving the ownership of property or shares from one person to another

transferor /trænsˈfɜːrə/ *noun* a person who transfers goods or property to another

transferred charge call /trænsˌfɜːd ˈtʃɑːdʒ kɔːl/ *noun* a phone call where the person receiving the call agrees to pay for it

translate /trænsˈleɪt/ *verb* to put something which is said or written in one language into another language ○ *He asked his secretary to translate the letter from the German agent.* ○ *We have had the contract translated from French into Japanese.*

translation /trænsˈleɪʃ(ə)n/ *noun* something which has been translated ○ *She passed the translation of the letter to the accounts department.*

translation exposure /trænsˌleɪʃ(ə)n ɪkˈspəʊʒə/ *noun* the risk that the balance sheet and income statement may be adversely affected by foreign exchange rate changes

traveller's cheques /ˈtræv(ə)ləz tʃeks/ *plural noun* cheques bought by a traveller which can be cashed in a foreign country

travelling expenses /ˈtræv(ə)lɪŋ ek ˌspensɪz/ *plural noun* money spent on travelling and hotels for business purposes

treasurer /ˈtreʒərə/ *noun* **1.** a person who looks after the money or finances of a club or society, etc. **2.** company official responsible

for finding new finance for the company and using its existing financial resources in the best possible way **3.** *US* the main financial officer of a company **4.** (*in Australia*) the finance minister in the government

Treasury /ˈtreʒəri/ *noun* **1.** a government department which deals with the country's finance (NOTE: The term is used in both the UK and the US; in most other countries this department is called the **Ministry of Finance**.) **2.** the department of a company or corporation that deals with all financial matters

Treasury bill /ˈtreʒəri bɪl/ *noun* a short-term financial instrument which does not give any interest and is sold by the government at a discount through the central bank. In the UK, their term varies from three to six months, in the USA, they are for 91 or 182 days, or for 52 weeks. (NOTE: In the USA, they are also called **Treasuries** or **T-bills**.)

treasury management /ˌtreʒəri ˈmænɪdʒmənt/ *noun* an entity's method of dealing of its financial matters, including growing funds for business, maintaining cash flows and currencies, and managing currencies and cash flows

treasury products /ˌtreʒəri ˈprɒdʌkts/ *noun* any financial item produced by a government for sale, such as bonds

Treasury Secretary /ˈtreʒəri ˌsekrət(ə)ri/ *noun US* the member of the US government in charge of finance (NOTE: The equivalent of the **Finance Minister** in most countries, or of the **Chancellor of the Exchequer** in the UK)

trend /trend/ *noun* a general way in which things are developing ○ *a downward trend in investment* ○ *There is a trend away from old-established food stores.* ○ *The report points to inflationary trends in the economy.* ○ *We notice a general trend towards selling to the student market.* ○ *We have noticed an upward trend in sales.*

'…the quality of building design and ease of accessibility will become increasingly important, adding to the trend towards out-of-town office development' [*Lloyd's List*]

trial balance /ˈtraɪəl ˌbæləns/ *noun* the draft calculation of debits and credits to see if they balance

trillion /ˈtrɪljən/ *noun* one million millions (NOTE: In the UK, trillion now has the same meaning as in the USA; formerly in UK English it meant one million million millions, and it is still sometimes used with this meaning; see also the note at **billion**.)

'…if land is assessed at roughly half its current market value, the new tax could yield up to ¥10 trillion annually' [*Far Eastern Economic Review*]

'…behind the decline was a 6.1% fall in exports to ¥47.55 trillion, the second year of falls. Automobiles and steel were among categories showing particularly conspicuous drops' [*Nikkei Weekly*]

'…the London Stock Exchange said that the value of domestic UK equities traded during the year was £1.4066 trillion, more than the capitalization of the entire London market and an increase of 36 per cent compared with previous year's total of £1.037 trillion' [*Times*]

true /truː/ *adjective* correct or accurate

true and fair view /ˌtruː ən feə ˈvjuː/ *noun* a correct statement of a company's financial position as shown in its accounts and confirmed by the auditors

Trueblood Report /ˈtruːblʌb rɪˌpɔːt/ *noun* a report, 'Objectives of Financial Statements', published by the American Institute of Certified Public Accountants in 1971, that recommended a conceptual framework for financial accounting and led to the Statements of Financial Accounting Concepts issued by the Financial Accounting Standards Board in the United States

true copy /ˌtruː ˈkɒpi/ *noun* an exact copy ○ *I certify that this is a true copy.* ○ *It is certified as a true copy.*

trust /trʌst/ *noun* 1. the fact of being confident that something is correct or will work 2. a legal arrangement to pass goods, money or valuables to someone who will look after them well ○ *She left his property in trust for her grandchildren.* 3. the management of money or property for someone ○ *They set up a family trust for their grandchildren.* 4. US a small group of companies which control the supply of a product

trust company /ˈtrʌst ˌkʌmp(ə)ni/ *noun* US an organisation which supervises the financial affairs of private trusts, executes wills, and acts as a bank to a limited number of customers

trust deed /ˈtrʌst diːd/ *noun* a document which sets out the details of a private trust

trustee /trʌˈstiː/ *noun* a person who has charge of money in trust ○ *the trustees of the pension fund*

trustee in bankruptcy /trʌˌstiː ɪn ˈbæŋkrʌptsi/ *noun* a person who is appointed by a court to run the affairs of a bankrupt and pay his or her creditors

trust fund /ˈtrʌst fʌnd/ *noun* assets such as money, securities or property held in trust for someone

turn /tɜːn/ *noun* 1. a movement in a circle, or a change of direction 2. a profit or commission ○ *She makes a turn on everything he sells.*

turnaround /ˈtɜːnəraʊnd/ *noun especially US* same as **turnround**

turn down /ˌtɜːn ˈdaʊn/ *verb* to refuse something ○ *The board turned down the proposal.* ○ *The bank turned down their request for a loan.* ○ *The application for a licence was turned down.* ○ *He turned down the job he was offered.*

turn over /ˌtɜːn ˈəʊvə/ *verb* 1. to have a specific amount of sales ○ *We turn over £2,000 a week.* 2. US to pass something to someone ○ *She turned over the documents to the lawyer.* (NOTE: In this meaning, the usual UK term is **hand over**.)

'…a 100,000 square foot warehouse can turn its inventory over 18 times a year, more than triple a discounter's turnover<S' [*Duns Business Month*]

'…he is turning over his CEO title to one of his teammates, but will remain chairman for a year' [*Duns Business Month*]

turnover /ˈtɜːnəʊvə/ *noun* 1. the amount of sales of goods or services by a company ○ *The company's turnover has increased by 235%.* ○ *We based our calculations on the forecast turnover.* (NOTE: The US term is **sales volume**.) 2. the number of times something is used or sold in a period, usually one year, expressed as a percentage of a total

turnover tax /ˈtɜːnəʊvə tæks/ *noun* same as **sales tax**

turn round /ˌtɜːn ˈraʊnd/ *verb* to make a company change from making a loss to become profitable □ **they turned the company round in less than a year** they made the company profitable in less than a year

turnround /ˈtɜːnraʊnd/ *noun* 1. the value of goods sold during a year divided by the average value of goods held in stock 2. the action of emptying a ship, plane, etc., and getting it ready for another commercial journey 3. the act of making a company profitable again (NOTE: [all senses] The US term is **turnaround**.)

'…the US now accounts for more than half our world-wide sales; it has made a huge contribution to our turnround' [*Duns Business Month*]

two-bin system /ˌtuːbɪn ˈsɪstəm/ *noun* warehousing system, where the first bin contains the current working stock, and the second bin has the backup stock

U

UITF *abbr* Urgent Issues Task Force

ultimate holding company /ˌʌltɪmət ˈhəʊldɪŋ ˌkʌmp(ə)ni/ *noun* the top company in a group consisting of several layers of parent companies and subsidiaries

umbrella organisation /ʌmˈbrelə ˌɔːɡənaɪzeɪʃ(ə)n/ *noun* a large organisation which includes several smaller ones

unaccounted for /ˌʌnəˈkaʊntɪd fɔː/ *adjective* lost without any explanation ○ *Several thousand units are unaccounted for in the stocktaking.*

unadjusted trial balance /ˌʌnədʒʌstɪd ˌtraɪəl ˈbæləns/ *noun* a trial balance that has not yet been adjusted at a period end for items such as closing stock

unappropriated profits /ˌʌnəprəʊprieɪtɪd ˈprɒfɪts/ *noun* profits that have neither been distributed to a company's shareholders as dividends nor set aside as specific reserves

unaudited /ʌnˈɔːdɪtɪd/ *adjective* having not been audited ○ *unaudited accounts*

unauthorised /ʌnˈɔːθəraɪzd/, **unauthorized** *adjective* not permitted ○ *unauthorised access to the company's records* ○ *unauthorised expenditure* ○ *No unauthorised persons are allowed into the laboratory.*

unbalanced /ʌnˈbælənst/ *adjective* referring to a budget which does not balance or which is in deficit

unbanked /ʌnˈbæŋkt/ *adjective* referring to a person who does not have a bank account

uncalled /ʌnˈkɔːld/ *adjective* referring to capital which a company is authorised to raise and has been issued but for which payment has not yet been requested

uncashed /ʌnˈkæʃt/ *adjective* having not been cashed ○ *uncashed cheques*

unconsolidated /ˌʌnkənˈsɒlɪdeɪtɪd/ *noun* not grouped together, as of shares or holdings

unconsolidated subsidiary /ˌʌnkənsɒlɪdeɪtɪd səbˈsɪdiəri/ *noun* a subsidiary that is not included in the consolidated financial statements of the group to which it belongs. An unconsolidated subsidiary would appear on a consolidated balance sheet as an investment.

uncontrollable /ˌʌnkənˈtrəʊləb(ə)l/ *adjective* not possible to control ○ *uncontrollable inflation*

uncontrollable costs /ˌʌnkən ˈtrəʊləb(ə)l kɒsts/ *noun* costs appearing on a management accounting statement that are regarded as not within the control of that particular level of management

uncovered bear /ˌʌnkʌvəd ˈbeə/ *noun* a person who sells stock which he or she does not hold, hoping to be able to buy stock later at a lower price when the debt needs to be settled

uncrossed cheque /ˌʌnkrɒst ˈtʃek/ *noun* a cheque which does not have two lines across it, and can be cashed anywhere (NOTE: They are no longer used in the UK, but are still found in other countries.)

undated /ʌnˈdeɪtɪd/ *adjective* with no date indicated or written ○ *She tried to cash an undated cheque.*

undated bond /ʌnˌdeɪtɪd ˈbɒnd/ *noun* a bond with no maturity date

under- /ʌndə/ *prefix* less important than or lower than

underabsorbed overhead /ˌʌndərəbzɔːbd ˈəʊvəhed/ *noun* an absorbed overhead which ends up by being lower than the actual overhead incurred

underbid /ˌʌndəˈbɪd/ *verb* to bid less than someone (NOTE: **underbidding – underbid**)

underbidder /ˈʌndəbɪdə/ *noun* a person who bids less than the person who buys at an auction

undercapitalised /ˌʌndəˈkæpɪtəlaɪzd/, **undercapitalized** *adjective* without enough capital ○ *The company is severely undercapitalised.*

undercharge /ˌʌndəˈtʃɑːdʒ/ *verb* to ask someone for too little money ○ *She undercharged us by £25.*

underemployed /ˌʌndərɪmˈplɔɪd/ *adjective* with not enough work ○ *The staff is underemployed because of the cutback in production.*

underemployed capital /ˌʌndərɪmplɔɪd ˈkæpɪt(ə)l/ *noun* capital which is not producing enough interest

underlease /ˈʌndəliːs/ *noun* a lease from a tenant to another tenant

underlying inflation /ˌʌndəlaɪɪŋ ɪnˈfleɪʃ(ə)n/ *noun* the rate of inflation that does not take mortgage costs into account

underspend /ˌʌndəˈspend/ *verb* to spend less than you should have spent or were allowed to spend

understandability /ˌʌndəˌstændəˈbɪlɪti/ *noun* when referring to financial information, the quality of being sufficiently clearly expressed as to be understood by anybody with a reasonable knowledge of business

understate /ˌʌndəˈsteɪt/ *verb* to make something seem less than it really is ○ *The company accounts understate the real profit.*

undersubscribed /ˌʌndəsʌbˈskraɪbd/ *adjective* referring to a share issue where applications are not made for all the shares on offer, and part of the issue remains with the underwriters

undertake /ˌʌndəˈteɪk/ *verb* to agree to do something ○ *We asked the research unit to undertake an investigation of the market.* ○ *They have undertaken not to sell into our territory.* (NOTE: **undertaking – undertook – undertaken**)

undertaking /ˈʌndəˌteɪkɪŋ/ *noun* **1.** a business ○ *He is the MD of a large commercial undertaking.* **2.** a promise, especially a legally binding one ○ *They have given us a written undertaking not to sell their products in competition with ours.*

undervaluation /ˌʌndəvæljuˈeɪʃ(ə)n/ *noun* the state of being valued, or the act of valuing something, at less than the true worth

undervalued /ˌʌndəˈvæljuːd/ *adjective* not valued highly enough ○ *The dollar is undervalued on the foreign exchanges.* ○ *The properties are undervalued on the company's balance sheet.*

'…in terms of purchasing power, the dollar is considerably undervalued, while the US trade deficit is declining month by month' [*Financial Weekly*]

underwrite /ˌʌndəˈraɪt/ *verb* **1.** to accept responsibility for something **2.** to insure, to cover a risk ○ *to underwrite an insurance policy* **3.** to agree to pay for costs ○ *The government has underwritten the development*

costs of the project. (NOTE: **underwriting – underwrote – has underwritten**)

'…under the new program, mortgage brokers are allowed to underwrite mortgages and get a much higher fee' [*Forbes Magazine*]

underwriter /ˈʌndəraɪtə/ *noun* a person or company that underwrites a share issue or an insurance

underwriting /ˈʌndəraɪtɪŋ/ *noun* the action of guaranteeing to purchase shares in a new issue if no one purchases them

underwriting fee /ˈʌndəraɪtɪŋ fiː/ *noun* a fee paid by a company to the underwriters for guaranteeing the purchase of new shares in that company

underwriting syndicate /ˈʌndəraɪtɪŋ ˌsɪndɪkət/ *noun* a group of underwriters who insure a large risk

undischarged bankrupt /ˌʌndɪstʃɑːdʒd ˈbæŋkrʌpt/ *noun* a person who has been declared bankrupt and has not been released from that state

undistributable profit /ˌʌndɪstrɪbjuːtəb(ə)l ˈprɒfɪt/ *noun* profit that is not legally available for distribution to shareholders as dividends

undistributable reserves /ˌʌndɪstrɪbjuːtəb(ə)l rɪˈzɜːvz/ *plural noun* same as **capital reserves**

undistributed profit /ˌʌndɪstrɪbjuːtɪd ˈprɒfɪt/ *noun* a profit which has not been distributed as dividends to shareholders

unearned income /ˌʌnɜːnd ˈɪnkʌm/ *noun* same as **investment income**

unemployed /ˌʌnɪmˈplɔɪd/ *adjective* not having any paid work

unemployment /ˌʌnɪmˈplɔɪmənt/ *noun* the state of not having any work

'…tax advantages directed toward small businesses will help create jobs and reduce the unemployment rate' [*Toronto Star*]

unemployment pay /ˌʌnɪmˈplɔɪmənt peɪ/ *noun* money given by the government to someone who is unemployed

unexpired cost /ˌʌnɪkspaɪəd ˈkɒst/ *noun* the net book value, or depreciated historical cost of an asset, not yet charged to the profit and loss account

unfair competition /ˌʌnfeə ˌkɒmpəˈtɪʃ(ə)n/ *noun* the practice of trying to do better than another company by using techniques such as importing foreign goods at very low prices or by wrongly criticising a competitor's products

unfavourable variance /ʌnˌfeɪv(ə)rəb(ə)l ˈveəriəns/ *noun* an adverse variance, one which produces an unexpected loss

unfunded debt /ˌʌnfʌndɪd ˈdet/ *noun* short-term debt requiring repayment within a year from issuance

ungeared /ʌnˈgɪəd/ *adjective* with no borrowings

unguaranteed residual value /ˌgærəntiːd rɪˌzɪdjuəl ˈvæljuː/ *noun* the amount of the residual value of a leased asset whose realisation is not assured

uniform accounting policies /ˌjuːnɪfɔːm əˈkaʊntɪŋ/ *noun* the use of the same accounting policies for all the companies in a group, for the preparation of consolidated financial statements

uniform business rate /ˌjuːnɪfɔːm ˈbɪznɪs reɪt/ *noun* a tax levied on business property which is the same percentage for the whole country. Abbreviation **UBR**

uniformity /ˌjuːnɪˈfɔːmɪti/ *noun* the principle of using common measurements, accounting standards, and methods of presentation across different organisations, to ensure comparability

unincorporated /ˌʌnɪnˈkɔːpəreɪtɪd/ *adjective* referring to a business which has not been made into a company, i.e. which is operating as a partnership or a sole trader

unissued capital /ˌʌnɪʃuːd ˈkæpɪt(ə)l/ *noun* capital which a company is authorised to issue but has not issued as shares

unissued stock /ˌʌnɪʃuːd ˈstɒk/ *noun* capital stock which a company is authorised to issue but has not issued

unit /ˈjuːnɪt/ *noun* **1.** a single product for sale **2.** a single share in a unit trust

unitary taxation /ˌjuːnɪt(ə)ri tæk ˈseɪʃ(ə)n/ *noun* a method of taxing a corporation based on its worldwide income rather than on its income in the country of the tax authority

unit cost /ˈjuːnɪt kɒst/ *noun* the cost of one item, i.e. the total product costs divided by the number of units produced

unitholder /ˈjuːnɪtˌhəʊldə/ *noun* a person who holds units in a unit trust

uniting of interests /ˌjuːnɪtɪŋ əv ˈɪntrəsts/ *noun* the international accounting standards term for merger accounting

unit-linked insurance /ˌjuːnɪt lɪŋkd ɪn ˈʃʊərəns/ *noun* an insurance policy which is linked to the security of units in a unit trust or fund

unit of account /ˌjuːnɪt əv əˈkaʊnt/ *noun* a standard unit used in financial transactions among members of a group, e.g. SDRs in the IMF

unit price /ˈjuːnɪt praɪs/ *noun* the price of one item

units of production method of depreciation /ˌjuːnɪts əv prəˌdʌkʃən ˌmeθəd əv dɪˌpriːʃiˈeɪʃ(ə)n/ *noun* a method of calculating depreciation that determines the cost of an asset over its useful economic life according to the number of units it is expected to produce over that period

unit trust /ˈjuːnɪt trʌst/ *noun* an organisation which takes money from small investors and invests it in stocks and shares for them under a trust deed, the investment being in the form of shares (or units) in the trust (NOTE: The US term is **mutual fund**.)

unlawful /ʌnˈlɔːf(ə)l/ *adjective* against the law, not legal

unlimited /ʌnˈlɪmɪtɪd/ *adjective* with no limits ○ *The bank offered him unlimited credit.*

unlimited company /ʌnˌlɪmɪtɪd ˈkʌmp(ə)ni/ *noun* company where the shareholders have no limit as regards liability

unlimited liability /ʌnˌlɪmɪtɪd ˌlaɪə ˈbɪlɪti/ *noun* a situation where a sole trader or each partner is responsible for all a firm's debts with no limit on the amount each may have to pay

unliquidated claim /ʌnˌlɪkwɪdeɪtɪd ˈkleɪm/ *noun* a claim for unliquidated damages

unlisted company /ʌnˌlɪstɪd ˈkʌmp(ə)ni/ *noun* a company whose shares are not listed on the stock exchange

unlisted securities /ʌnˌlɪstɪd sɪ ˈkjʊərɪtiz/ *plural noun* shares which are not listed on the Stock Exchange

unpaid /ʌnˈpeɪd/ *adjective* not paid

unpaid invoices /ʌnˌpeɪd ˈɪnvɔɪsɪz/ *plural noun* invoices which have not been paid

unprofitable /ʌnˈprɒfɪtəb(ə)l/ *adjective* not profitable

'…the airline has already eliminated a number of unprofitable flights' [*Duns Business Month*]

unquoted company /ʌnˌkwəʊtd ˈkʌmp(ə)ni/ *noun* company whose shares are not listed on the stock exchange

unquoted investments /ʌnˌkwəʊtd ɪn ˈves(t)mənts/ *plural noun* investments which are difficult to value, e.g. shares which have no stock exchange listing or land of which the asset value is difficult to estimate

unquoted shares /ˌʌnkwəʊtɪd ˈʃeəz/ *plural noun* shares which have no Stock Exchange quotation

unrealisable gains /ˌʌnrɪəlaɪzəb(ə)l ˈgeɪnz/ *noun* apparent increases in the value of assets that could not be turned into realised profit

unrealised capital gain /ˌʌnrɪəlaɪzd ˌkæpɪt(ə)l ˈɡeɪn/ *noun* an investment which is showing a profit but has not been sold

unrealised profit/loss /ˌʌnrɪəlaɪzd ˌprɒfɪt ˈlɒs/ *noun* a profit or loss that need not be reported as income, e.g., deriving from the holding of an asset worth more/less than its purchase price, but not yet sold

unredeemed pledge /ˌʌnrɪdiːmd ˈpledʒ/ *noun* a pledge which the borrower has not claimed back because he or she has not paid back the loan

unregistered /ʌnˈredʒɪstəd/ *adjective* referring to a company which has not been registered

unrestricted income funds /ˌʌnrɪstrɪktɪd ˌɪnkʌm ˈfʌndz/ *noun* a charity's funds that are available to its trustees to use for the purposes set out in the charity's governing document

unsecured creditor /ˌʌnsɪkjʊəd ˈkredɪtə/ *noun* a creditor who is owed money, but has no security from the debtor for the debt

unsecured debt /ˌʌnsɪkjʊəd ˈdet/ *noun* a debt which is not guaranteed by a charge on assets or by any collateral

unsecured loan /ˌʌnsɪkjʊəd ˈləʊn/ *noun* a loan made with no security

unsubsidised /ʌnˈsʌbsɪdaɪzd/, **unsubsidized** *adjective* with no subsidy

unused allowances /ʌnˌjuːzd əˈlaʊənss/ *noun* a part of the married couple's allowance or the blind person's allowance which is not used because the recipient does not have enough income, and which can then be passed to their spouse

up /ʌp/ *adverb, preposition* in or to a higher position ○ *The inflation rate is going up steadily.* ○ *Shares were up slightly at the end of the day.* ○ *She worked her way up to become sales director.*

up front /ˌʌp ˈfrʌnt/ *adverb* in advance □ **money up front** payment in advance ○ *They are asking for £100,000 up front before they* will consider the deal. ○ *He had to put money up front before he could clinch the deal.*

upside potential /ˌʌpsaɪd pəˈtenʃəl/ *noun* the possibility for a share to increase in value. Opposite **downside risk**

upturn /ˈʌptɜːn/ *noun* a movement towards higher sales or profits ○ *an upturn in the economy* ○ *an upturn in the market*

Urgent Issues Task Force /ˌɜːdʒənt ˌɪʃuːz ˈtɑːsk ˌfɔːs/ *noun* a committee of the UK Accounting Standards Board that considers major urgent and emerging accounting issues. Its pronouncements are known as UITF Abstracts. Abbreviation **UITF**

usage /ˈjuːsɪdʒ/ *noun* the way in which something is used

usage method /ˈjuːsɪdʒ ˈmeθəd/ *noun* a method of depreciating a machine, by dividing its cost less residual value by the number of units it is expected to produce or the length of time it is expected to be used

use *noun* /juːs/ a way in which something can be used ■ *verb* /juːz/ to take something, e.g. a machine, a company or a process, and work with it ○ *We use airmail for all our overseas correspondence.* ○ *The photocopier is being used all the time.* ○ *They use freelancers for most of their work.*

useful economic life /ˌjuːsf(ə)l ˌiːkənɒmɪk ˈlaɪf/ *noun* the period during which an entity expects to derive economic benefit from using an asset such as a machine and over which it can be depreciated

user /ˈjuːzə/ *noun* a person who uses something

user's guide /ˈjuːzəz ˌɡaɪd/, **user's handbook** /ˈjuːzəz ˌhændbʊk/, **user's manual** /ˈjuːzəz ˌmænjʊəl/ *noun* a book showing someone how to use something

usury /ˈjuːzəri/ *noun* the lending of money at high interest

utilisation /ˌjuːtɪlaɪˈzeɪʃ(ə)n/, **utilization** *noun* the act of making use of something

'…control permits the manufacturer to react to changing conditions on the plant floor and to keep people and machines at a high level of utilization' [*Duns Business Month*]

utilise /ˈjuːtɪlaɪz/, **utilize** *verb* to use something

V

vacant possession /ˌveɪkənt pə ˈzeʃ(ə)n/ *adjective* being able to occupy a property immediately after buying it because it is empty ○ *The property is to be sold with vacant possession.*

valuation /ˌvæljuˈeɪʃ(ə)n/ *noun* an estimate of how much something is worth ○ *to ask for a valuation of a property before making an offer for it*

valuation of a business /ˌvælju ˌeɪʃ(ə)n əv eɪ ˈbɪznɪs/ *noun* the act of estimating the value of a business. This can be done on various bases, such as an assets basis, its break-up value, its value as a going concern, etc.

value /ˈværljuː/ *noun* the amount of money which something is worth ○ *the fall in the value of sterling* ○ *She imported goods to the value of £2500.* ○ *The valuer put the value of the stock at £25,000.* □ **to rise** *or* **fall in value** to be worth more or less ■ *verb* to estimate how much money something is worth ○ *He valued the stock at £25,000.* ○ *We are having the jewellery valued for insurance.*

value-added statement /ˌvæljuː ˌædɪd ˈsteɪtmənt/ *noun* a simplified financial statement that shows how much wealth has been created by a company. A value added statement calculates total output by adding sales, changes in stock, and other incomes, then subtracting depreciation, interest, taxation, dividends, and the amounts paid to suppliers and employees.

value in use /ˌvæljuː ɪn ˈjuːs/ *noun* the present value of the estimated future net cash flows from an object, including the amount expected from its disposal at the end of its useful life. Value in use replaces book value when an asset suffers impairment.

valuer /ˈvæljʊə/ *noun* a person who estimates how much money something is worth

variable /ˈveəriəb(ə)l/ *adjective* changeable

variable costs /ˌveəriəb(ə)l ˈkɒsts/ *plural noun* production costs which increase with the quantity of the product made, e.g. wages or raw materials

variable rate /ˌveəriəb(ə)l ˈreɪt/ *noun* a rate of interest on a loan which is not fixed, but can change with the current bank interest rates. Also called **floating rate**

variance /ˈveəriəns/ *noun* the difference between what was expected and the actual results

variance accounting /ˌveəriəns ə ˈkaʊntɪŋ/ *noun* a method of accounting by means of which planned activities (quantified through budgets and standard costs and revenues) are compared with actual results

VAT declaration /ˈvæt dekləˌreɪʃ(ə)n/ *noun* a statement declaring VAT income to the VAT office

VAT group /ˌviː eɪ ˈtiː gruːp/ *noun* in the United Kingdom, a group of related companies that is treated as one taxpayer for VAT purposes

VAT inspection /ˈvæt ɪnˌspekʃ(ə)n/ *noun* a visit by officials of the Customs and Excise Department to see if a company is correctly reporting its VAT

VAT inspector /ˈvæt ɪnˌspektə/ *noun* a government official who examines VAT returns and checks that VAT is being paid

VAT invoice /ˈvæt ˌɪnvɔɪs/ *noun* an invoice which includes VAT

VAT invoicing /ˈvæt ˌɪnvɔɪsɪŋ/ *noun* the sending of an invoice including VAT

VATman /ˈvætmæn/, **vatman** *noun* a VAT inspector (*informal*)

VAT office /ˈvæt ˌɒfɪs/ *noun* the government office dealing with the collection of VAT in an area

VAT paid /ˌviː eɪ ˈtiː peɪd/ *adjective* with the VAT already paid

VAT receivable /ˌviː eɪ ˌtiː rɪˈsiːvəb(ə)l/ *adjective* with the VAT for an item not yet collected by a taxing authority

VAT registration /ˌviː eɪ ˌtiː ˌredʒɪ ˈstreɪʃ(ə)n/ *noun* the process of listing a company with a European government as eligible for the return of VAT in certain cases

VCT *abbr* venture capital trust

vending /'vendɪŋ/ *noun* selling

vendor /'vendə/ *noun* **1.** a person who sells something, especially a property ○ *the solicitor acting on behalf of the vendor* **2.** a person who sells goods

venture /'ventʃə/ *noun* a commercial deal which involves a risk ○ *They lost money on several import ventures.* ○ *She's started a new venture – a computer shop.*

venture capital /,ventʃə 'kæpɪt(ə)l/ *noun* capital for investment which may easily be lost in risky projects, but can also provide high returns. Also called **risk capital**

venture capital trust /,ventʃə 'kæpɪt(ə)l trʌst/ *noun* a trust which invests in smaller firms which need capital to grow. Abbreviation **VCT**

vertical communication /,vɜːtɪk(ə)l kə,mjuːnɪ'keɪʃ(ə)n/ *noun* communication between senior managers via the middle management to the workforce

vertical equity /,vɜːtɪk(ə)l 'ekwɪti/ *noun* the principle that people with different incomes should pay different rates of tax

vertical form /'vɜːtɪk(ə)l fɔːm/ *noun* one of the two styles of presenting a balance sheet allowed by the Companies Act. Also called **report form**

vertical integration /,vɜːtɪk(ə)l ,ɪntɪ'greɪʃ(ə)n/ *noun* same as **backward integration**

vested interest /,vestɪd 'ɪntrəst/ *noun* a special interest in keeping an existing state of affairs

virement /'vaɪəmənt/ *noun* a transfer of money from one account to another or from one section of a budget to another

visible /'vɪzɪb(ə)l/ *adjective* referring to real products which are imported or exported

visible exports /,vɪzəb(ə)l 'ekspɔːts/ *plural noun* real products which are exported, as opposed to services

visible imports /,vɪzɪb(ə)l 'ɪmpɔːts/ *plural noun* real products which are imported, as opposed to services

visible trade /,vɪzəb(ə)l 'treɪd/ *noun* trade involving visible imports and exports

void /vɔɪd/ *adjective* not legally valid

volume /'vɒljuːm/ *noun* a quantity of items

volume discount /'vɒljuːm ,dɪskaunt/ *noun* the discount given to a customer who buys a large quantity of goods

volume of output /,vɒljuːm əv 'autput/ *noun* the number of items produced

volume variances /,vɒljuːm 'veəriənss/ *noun* differences in costs or revenues compared with budgeted amounts, caused by differences between the actual and budgeted levels of activity

voluntary /'vɒlənt(ə)ri/ *adjective* **1.** done freely without anyone forcing you to act **2.** done without being paid

voluntary liquidation /,vɒlənt(ə)ri ,lɪkwɪ'deɪʃ(ə)n/ *noun* a situation where a company itself decides it must close and sell its assets

voluntary redundancy /,vɒlənt(ə)ri rɪ'dʌndənsi/ *noun* a situation where the employee asks to be made redundant, usually in return for a large payment

voluntary registration /,vɒlənt(ə)ri ,redʒɪ'streɪʃ(ə)n/ *noun* in the United Kingdom, registration for VAT by a trader whose turnover is below the registration threshold. This is usually done in order to reclaim tax on inputs.

vote /vəut/ *noun* the act of marking a paper or holding up your hand, to show your opinion or to show who you want to be elected

voting /'vəutɪŋ/ *noun* the act of making a vote

voting paper /'vəutɪŋ ,peɪpə/ *noun* a paper on which the voter puts a cross to show for whom he or she wants to vote

voucher /'vautʃə/ *noun* **1.** a piece of paper which is given instead of money **2.** a written document from an auditor to show that the accounts are correct or that money has really been paid

W

wage /weɪdʒ/ *noun* the money paid to an employee in return for work done, especially when it is paid weekly and in cash ○ *She is earning a good wage* or *good wages for a young person.* (NOTE: The plural **wages** is more usual when referring to the money earned, but **wage** is used before other nouns.)

'European economies are being held back by rigid labor markets and wage structures' [*Duns Business Month*]

'…real wages have been held down dramatically: they have risen at an annual rate of only 1% in the last two years' [*Sunday Times*]

wage adjustments /weɪdʒ əˈdʒʌstmənts/ *plural noun* changes made to wages

wage claim /weɪdʒ kleɪm/ *noun* an act of asking for an increase in wages

wage-earner /weɪdʒ ˌɜːnə/ *noun* a person who earns a wage

wage indexation /weɪdʒ ˌɪndekseɪʃ(ə)n/ *noun* the linking of increases to the percentage rise in the cost of living

wage scale /weɪdʒ skeɪl/ *noun* same as **pay scale**

wages costs /weɪdʒɪz kɒsts/ *noun* the costs of paying employees' salaries. Along with other costs such as pension contributions and salaries, these costs typically form the largest single cost item for a business.

wages payable account /ˌweɪdʒɪz ˌpeɪəb(ə)l əˈkaʊnt/ *noun* an account showing gross wages and employer's National Insurance contributions paid during some period

wages policy /weɪdʒɪz ˌpɒlɪsi/ *noun* a government policy on what percentage increases should be paid to workers

wall safe /wɔːl seɪf/ *noun* a safe installed in a wall

warehouse /weəhaʊs/ *noun* a large building where goods are stored

warehouse capacity /weəhaʊs kəˌpæsɪti/ *noun* the space available in a warehouse

warrant /wɒrənt/ *noun* an official document which allows someone to do something ■ *verb* to guarantee ○ *All the spare parts are warranted.*

'…the rights issue will grant shareholders free warrants to subscribe for further new shares' [*Financial Times*]

warrantee /ˌwɒrənˈtiː/ *noun* a person who is given a warranty

warrantor /ˌwɒrənˈtɔː/ *noun* a person who gives a warranty

warranty /wɒrənti/ *noun* **1.** a legal document which promises that a machine will work properly or that an item is of good quality ○ *The car is sold with a twelve-month warranty.* ○ *The warranty covers spare parts but not labour costs.* **2.** a promise in a contract **3.** a statement made by an insured person which declares that the facts stated by him are true

wasting asset /ˌweɪstɪŋ ˈæsɪt/ *noun* an asset which becomes gradually less valuable as time goes by, e.g. a short lease on a property

watchdog /wɒtʃdɒg/ *noun* an independent person or organisation whose task is to police a particular industry, ensuring that member companies do not act illegally

WDA *abbr* **1.** writing-down allowance **2.** written-down allowance

WDV *abbr* written down value

wealth tax /welθ tæks/ *noun* a tax on money, property or investments owned by a person

wear and tear /ˌweər ən ˈteə/ *noun* the deterioration of a tangible fixed asset as a result of normal use. This is recognised for accounting purposes by depreciation.

weight /weɪt/ *noun* a measurement of how heavy something is ■ *verb* to give an extra value to a factor

weighted average /ˌweɪtɪd ˈæv(ə)rɪdʒ/ *noun* an average which is calculated taking several factors into account, giving some more value than others

weighted average cost /ˌweɪtɪd ˈæv(ə)rɪdʒ kɒst/, **weighted average price** /ˌweɪtɪd ˈæv(ə)rɪdʒ praɪs/ *noun* the average price per unit of stock delivered in a period calculated either at the end of the period ('periodic weighted average') or each time a new delivery is received ('cumulative weighted average')

weighted index /ˌweɪtɪd ˈɪndeks/ *noun* an index where some important items are given more value than less important ones

weighting /ˈweɪtɪŋ/ *noun* an additional salary or wages paid to compensate for living in an expensive part of the country ○ *The salary is £15,000 plus London weighting.*

Wheat Report /ˈwiːt rɪˌpɔːt/ *noun* a report produced by a committee in 1972 that set out to examine the principles and methods of accounting in the United States. Its publication led to the establishment of the FASB.

white knight /waɪt ˈnaɪt/ *noun* a person or company which rescues a firm in financial difficulties, especially one which saves a firm from being taken over by an unacceptable purchaser

White Paper /waɪt ˈpeɪpə/ *noun* a report issued by the UK government as a statement of government policy on a particular problem. Compare **Green Paper**

whole-life insurance /ˌhəʊl ˈlaɪf ɪnˌʃʊərəns/, **whole-life policy** /ˌhəʊl ˈlaɪf ˌpɒlɪsi/ *noun* an insurance policy where the insured person pays a fixed premium each year and the insurance company pays a sum when he or she dies. Also called **whole-of-life assurance**

wholesale /ˈhəʊlseɪl/ *adjective, adverb* referring to the business of buying goods from manufacturers and selling them in large quantities to traders (retailers) who then sell in smaller quantities to the general public ○ *I persuaded him to give us a wholesale discount.* □ **he buys wholesale and sells retail** he buys goods in bulk at a wholesale discount and then sells in small quantities to the public

wholesale banking /ˌhəʊlseɪl ˈbæŋkɪŋ/ *noun* banking services between merchant banks and other financial institutions, as opposed to retail banking

wholesale dealer /ˈhəʊlseɪl ˌdiːlə/ *noun* a person who buys in bulk from manufacturers and sells to retailers

wholesale price /ˈhəʊlseɪl praɪs/ *noun* the price charged to customers who buy goods in large quantities in order to resell them in smaller quantities to others

wholesale price index /ˌhəʊlseɪl ˈpraɪs ˌɪndeks/ *noun* an index showing the rises and falls of prices of manufactured goods as they leave the factory

wholesaler /ˈhəʊlseɪlə/ *noun* a person who buys goods in bulk from manufacturers and sells them to retailers

wholly-owned subsidiary /ˌhəʊlli əʊnd səbˈsɪdjəri/ *noun* a subsidiary which belongs completely to the parent company

will /wɪl/ *noun* a legal document where someone says what should happen to his or her property when he or she dies ○ *He wrote his will in 1984.* ○ *According to her will, all her property is left to her children.*

windfall profit /ˌwɪndfɔːl ˈprɒfɪt/ *noun* a sudden profit which is not expected

windfall profits tax /ˈwɪndfɔːl ˌprɒfɪts tæks/, **windfall tax** /ˈwɪndfɔːl tæks/ *noun* a tax on companies that have made large profits because of circumstances outside their usual trading activities. A windfall tax was imposed on the privatised utility companies in 1997.

winding up /ˈwaɪndɪŋ ˈʌp/ *noun* liquidation, the act of closing a company and selling its assets

winding up petition /ˌwaɪndɪŋ ʌp pəˈtɪʃ(ə)n/ *noun* an application to a court for an order that a company be put into liquidation

window dressing /ˈwɪndəʊ ˌdresɪŋ/ *noun* **1.** the practice of putting goods on display in a shop window, so that they attract customers **2.** the practice of putting on a display to make a business seem better or more profitable or more efficient than it really is

window envelope /ˌwɪndəʊ ˈenvələʊp/ *noun* an envelope with a hole covered with film so that the address on the letter inside can be seen

window of opportunity /ˌwɪndəʊ əv ɒpəˈtjuːnɪti/ *noun* a short period which allows an action to take place

window shopping /ˈwɪndəʊ ˌʃɒpɪŋ/ *noun* the practice of looking at goods in shop windows, without buying anything

wind up /ˌwaɪnd ˈʌp/ *verb* to end a meeting, or to close down a business or organisation and sell its assets ○ *She wound up the meeting with a vote of thanks to the committee.*

WIP *abbr* work in progress

withdraw /wɪðˈdrɔː/ *verb* **1.** to take money out of an account ○ *to withdraw money from the bank or from your account* ○ *You can withdraw up to £50 from any cash machine by using your card.* **2.** to take back an offer ○ *When he found out more about the candidate, the HR manager withdrew the offer of a job.*

○ *When the employees went on strike, the company withdrew its revised pay offer.* (NOTE: **withdrawing – withdrew**)

withdrawal /wɪð'drɔːəl/ *noun* the act of removing money from an account ○ *to give seven days' notice of withdrawal* ○ *Withdrawals from bank accounts reached a peak in the week before Christmas.*

withholding tax /wɪð'həʊldɪŋ ˌtæks/ *noun US* a tax which removes money from interest or dividends before they are paid to the investor, usually applied to non-resident investors

with profits /wɪθ 'prɒfɪts/ *adverb* referring to an insurance policy which guarantees the policyholder a share in the profits of the fund in which the premiums are invested

work /wɜːk/ *noun* **1.** things done using the hands or brain **2.** a job, something done to earn money ○ *It is not the work itself that the employees are complaining about* ○ *He goes to work by bus.* ○ *She never gets home from work before 8 p.m.* ○ *His work involves a lot of travelling.* ○ *He is still looking for work.* ○ *She has been out of work for six months.*

'…the quality of the work environment demanded by employers and employees alike' [*Lloyd's List*]

workforce /'wɜːkfɔːs/ *noun* the total number of employees in an organisation, industry or country

working capital /'wɜːkɪŋ ˌkæpɪt(ə)l/ *noun* capital in the form of cash, stocks and debtors but not creditors, used by a company in its day-to-day operations. Also called **circulating capital, floating capital, net current assets**

working conditions /'wɜːkɪŋ kən ˌdɪʃ(ə)nz/ *plural noun* the general state of the place where people work, e.g. whether it is hot, noisy, dark or dangerous

working partner /'wɜːkɪŋ ˌpɑːtnə/ *noun* a partner who works in a partnership

work in progress /ˌwɜːk ɪn 'prəʊgres/ *noun* the value of goods being manufactured which are not complete at the end of an accounting period ○ *Our current assets are made up of stock, goodwill and work in progress.* Abbreviation **WIP** (NOTE: The US term is **work in process**.)

'…the control of materials from purchased parts through work in progress to finished goods provides manufacturers with an opportunity to reduce the amount of money tied up in materials' [*Duns Business Month*]

work out /ˌwɜːk 'aʊt/ *verb* to calculate ○ *He worked out the costs on the back of an envelope.* ○ *He worked out the discount at 15%.* ○ *She worked out the discount on her calculator.*

work permit /'wɜːk ˌpɜːmɪt/ *noun* an official document which allows someone who is not a citizen to work in a country

works /wɜːks/ *noun* a factory ○ *There is a small engineering works in the same street as our office.* ○ *The steel works is expanding.* (NOTE: takes a singular or plural verb)

works committee /'wɜːks kəˌmɪti/, **works council** /'wɜːks ˌkaʊnsəl/ *noun* a committee of employees and management which discusses the organisation of work in a factory

workstation /'wɜːkˌsteɪʃ(ə)n/ *noun* a desk, usually with a computer terminal, printer, telephone and other office items at which an employee in an office works

World Bank /wɜːld 'bæŋk/ *noun* a central bank, controlled by the United Nations, whose funds come from the member states of the UN and which lends money to member states

World Wide Web /ˌwɜːld ˌwaɪd 'web/ *noun* an information system on the Internet that allows documents to be linked to one another by hypertext links and accommodates websites and makes them accessible. Also called **web**

worthless /'wɜːθləs/ *adjective* having no value ○ *The cheque is worthless if it is not signed.*

write down /ˌraɪt 'daʊn/ *verb* to note an asset at a lower value than previously ○ *written down value* ○ *The car is written down in the company's books.* □ **closing written-down value, opening written-down value** the written-down value of an asset at the end or the beginning of an accounting period

write off /ˌraɪt 'ɒf/ *verb* to cancel a debt, or to remove an asset from the accounts as having no value ○ *We had to write off £20,000 in bad debts.*

'$30 million from usual company borrowings will either be amortized or written off in one sum' [*Australian Financial Review*]

write-off /'raɪt ɒf/ *noun* the total loss or cancellation of a bad debt, or the removal of an asset's value from a company's accounts ○ *to allow for write-offs in the yearly accounts*

writing-down allowance /ˌraɪtɪŋ daʊn ə'laʊəns/ *noun* a form of capital allowance giving tax relief to companies acquiring fixed assets which are written down on a year-by-year basis

written-down allowance /ˌrɪt(ə)n daʊn ə'laʊəns/ *noun* an allowance which can be claimed on capital expenditure by a business or self-employed person in the years after the purchase was made. In the first year, the first year allowance (FYA) applies. Abbreviation **WDA**

written-down value /ˌrɪt(ə)n daʊn ˈvæljuː/ *noun* a value of an asset in a company's accounts after it has been written down or recorded at a lower value than previously

written resolution /ˌrɪt(ə)n ˌrezəˈluːʃ(ə)n/ *noun* a decision to be reached by postal vote of the members of a UK private company equivalent to a resolution at a meeting

XYZ

xa *abbr* ex-all

year /jɪə/ *noun* a period of twelve months

year end /ˌjɪə ˈend/ *noun* the end of the financial year, when a company's accounts are prepared ○ *The accounts department has started work on the year-end accounts.*

year-end closing /ˌjɪə end ˈkləʊzɪŋ/ *noun* the financial statements issued at the end of a company's fiscal (tax) year

yearly /ˈjɪəli/ *adjective* happening once a year ○ *We make a yearly payment of £1000.* ○ *His yearly insurance premium has risen to £250.* ○ *For the past few years she has had a yearly pay rise of 10%.*

year of assessment /ˌjɪə əv əˈsesmənt/ *noun* a twelve-month period on which income tax is calculated. In the UK it is April 6th to April 5th of the following year.

year to date /ˌjɪə tə ˈdeɪt/ *noun* the period between the beginning of a calendar or financial year and the present time. A variety of financial information, such as a company's profits, losses, or sales, may be displayed in this way. Abbreviation **YTD**

Yellow Pages /ˌjeləʊ ˈpeɪdʒɪz/ *trademark* a section of a telephone directory printed on yellow paper which lists businesses under various headings such as computer shops or newsagents

yen /jen/ *noun* a unit of currency used in Japan (NOTE: It is usually written as ¥ before a figure: **¥2,700** (say two thousand seven hundred yen).)

yield /jiːld/ *noun* the money produced as a return on an investment, shown as a percentage of the money invested

'…if you wish to cut your risks you should go for shares with yields higher than average' [*Investors Chronicle*]

YTD *abbr* year to date

zero /ˈzɪərəʊ/ *noun* nought, the number 0 ○ *The code for international calls is zero zero (00).*

zero-based budgeting /ˌzɪərəʊ beɪst ˈbʌdʒɪtɪŋ/ *noun* a method of budgeting which requires each cost element to be specifically justified, as though the activities to which the budget relates were being undertaken for the first time. Without approval, the budget allowance is zero.

zero-coupon bond /ˌzɪərəʊ ˈkuːpɒn bɒnd/ *noun* a bond which carries no interest, but which is issued at a discount and so provides a capital gain when it is redeemed at face value

zero inflation /ˌzɪərəʊ ɪnˈfleɪʃ(ə)n/ *noun* inflation at 0%

zero-rated /ˌzɪərəʊ ˈreɪtɪd/ *adjective* referring to an item which has a VAT rate of 0%

zero-rating /ˈzɪərəʊ ˌreɪtɪŋ/ *noun* the rating of a product or service at 0% VAT

Supplement

ACCOUNTING ORGANISATIONS

United Kingdom

Association of Chartered Certified Accountants (ACCA)
64 Finnieston Square
Glasgow
United Kingdom
G3 8DT
T: 00 44 (0)141 582 2000
F: 00 44 (0)141 582 2222

British Accounting Association (BAA)
c/o Sheffield University Management School
9 Mappin Street
Sheffield
S1 4DT
T: 00 44 (0)114 222 3462
F: 00 44 (0)114 222 3348
www.shef.ac.uk/~baa/

Chartered Institute of Management Accountants (CIMA)
26 Chapter Street
London
SW1P 4NP
T: 00 44 (0)20 8849 2251
F: 00 44 (0)20 8849 2450

Institute of Chartered Accountants in England and Wales (ICAEW)
Chartered Accountants' Hall
PO Box 433
London
EC2P 2BJ
T: 00 44 (0)20 7920 8100
F: 00 44 (0)20 7920 0547

Institute of Chartered Accountants in Ireland
CA House
87/89 Pembroke Hall
Dublin 4
T: 00 353 1637 7200
F: 00 353 1668 0842

Institute of Chartered Accountants of Scotland
CA House
21 Haymarket Yards
Edinburgh
EH12 5BH
T: 00 44 (0)131 347 0100
F: 00 44 (0)131 347 0105
Institute of Financial Accountants
Burford house

44 London Road
Sevenoaks
Kent
TN13 1AS
T: 00 44 (0)1732 458080
F: 00 44 (0)1732 455848
www.accountingweb.co.uk/ifa/journal/index.html

International

American Accounting Association (AAA)
5717 Bessie Drive
Sarasota, FL 34233-2399
USA
T: 00 1 (941) 921-7747
F: 00 1 (941) 923-4093
www.aaahq.org/index.cfm

Association of Chartered Accountants in the United States (ACAUS)
341 Lafayette Street
Suite 4246
New York, NY 10012-2417
USA
T: 00 1 (212) 334-2078

Australian Accounting Standards Board (AASB)
PO Box 204
Collins St West
VIC 8007
Australia
T: 00 61 (3) 9617 7600
T: 00 61 (3) 9617 7608
www.aasb.com.au/

Institute of Chartered Accountants of New Zealand (ICANZ)
Level 2, Cigna House
40 Mercer Street
PO Box 11 342
Wellington 6034
New Zealand
T: 00 64 4 474 7840
F: 00 64 4 473 6303

National Society of Accountants (NSA)
1010 North Fairfax Street
Alexandria, VA 22314
USA
T: 00 1 703 549 6400
F: 00 1 703 549 2984

Specimen Co Ltd

Profit and Loss Account for the Year to 31 December 2004

	£000	£000
* Turnover		9,758
* Cost of sales		6,840
* Gross profit		2,918
* Distribution costs	585	
* Administrative expenses	407	
		992
		1,926
* Other operating income		322
		2,248
* Income from shares in group companies	200	
* Income from other fixed asset investments	75	
* Other interest receivable and similar income	36	
		311
		2,559
* Amounts written off investments	27	
* Interest payable and similar charges	26	
		53
Profit on ordinary activities before taxation		2,506
* Tax on profit on ordinary activities		916
* Profit on ordinary activities after taxation		1,590
* Extraordinary income	153	
* Extraordinary charges	44	
* Extraordinary profit	109	
* Tax on extraordinary profit	45	
		64
* Profit for the financial year		1,654
Transfers to Reserves	400	
Dividends Paid and Proposed	750	
		1,150
Retained profit for the financial year		504

About the Profit and Loss Account

While two vertical and horizontal formats are permissible, most UK companies use the vertical format illustrated. The horizontal profit and loss account format may be summarised as follows:

	£		£
Cost of sales	X	Sales	X
Gross profit	X		
	X		X
Expenses	X	Gross profit	X
	X		X

In Germany and Italy only the vertical format is allowed.

According to the UK Companies Act a company must show all the items marked with * on the face of the profit and loss account. It must also disclose the value of certain items in the notes to the profit and loss account, such as:

a) interest owed on bank and other loans
b) rental income
c) costs of hire of plant and machinery
d) amounts paid to auditors
e) turnover for each class of business and country in which sales are made
f) number of employees and costs of employment

Specimen Co Ltd

Balance Sheet for the Year to 31 December 2004

	£000	£000	£000
* FIXED ASSETS			
* Intangible assets			
Development costs	1,255		
Goodwill	850		
		2,105	
* Tangible assets			
Land and buildings	4,758		
Plant and machinery	2,833		
Fixtures and fittings	1,575		9,166
* Investments		730	
			12,001
* CURRENT ASSETS			
* Stocks	975		
* Debtors	2,888		
* Cash at bank	994		
		4,857	
* CREDITORS: AMOUNTS FALLING DUE WITHIN ONE YEAR			
Bank loans	76		
Trade creditors	3,297		
Accruals	20		
		3,393	
* NET CURRENT ASSETS			1,464
* TOTAL ASSETS LESS CURRENT LIABILITIES			13,465
* CREDITORS: AMOUNTS FALLING DUE AFTER MORE THAN ONE YEAR			
Debenture loans		1,875	
Finance leases		866	
Bank and other loans		124	
			2,865
* PROVISIONS FOR LIABILITIES AND CHARGES			
Taxation including deferred taxation	33		
Other provisions	557		
			590
			10,010
* CAPITAL AND RESERVES			
* Called-up share capital		5,000	
" Share premium account		500	
" Revaluation reserve		1,158	
• Other reserves		262	
			6,920
• PROFIT AND LOSS ACCOUNT			3,090
			10.010

About the Balance Sheet

While vertical and horizontal balance sheets are permissible, most UK companies prefer the vertical format as illustrated. The conventional form of horizontal balance sheet can be summarised as follows:

	£		£
Capital brought forward	X	Fixed Assets	X
Profit for the year	X		
Capital at year end	X		
	X		
Long term liabilities	X		
Current liabilities	X	Current Assets	X
	X		X

In Germany and Italy only the horizontal format is allowed.

The UK Companies Act requires companies to show all the items marked with * in the example on the face of the balance sheet; the other items can be shown either on the balance sheet or in the notes to the accounts. In addition, the law requires companies to show the value of certain items in separate notes to the balance sheet, such as details of fixed assets purchased and sold during the year.

The notes to the published accounts almost always begin with a description of the accounting policies used by the company in the accounts, e.g. the depreciation policy. In the UK most accounts are prepared on a historical cost basis but this is not compulsory and other bases, such as current cost or historical cost modified by revaluation of certain assets, are also allowed.

Specimen Co Ltd

Statement of Source and Application of Funds

For the year to 31 December 2004

	£000	£000
Source of Funds		
Profit before tax		2,615
Adjustment for items not involving the movement of funds:		
Depreciation	772	
Profit on the sale of fixed assets	(12)	
Provision for bad debts	3	
Development expenditure	45	
		808
Total generated from operations		3,423
Funds from other sources		
Issue of shares	250	
Sale of fixed assets	75	
Dividends received	240	
		565
		3,988
Application of funds		
Dividends paid	550	
Taxation paid	777	
Purchase of fixed assets	1,437	
		2,764
Increase in working capital		1,224
Increase in stock	82	
Decrease in debtors	82	
Decrease in creditors	545	
		383
Decrease in bank overdraft	297	
Increase in cash balances	544	
		841
		1,224

Specimen Co Ltd

Cash Flow Statement for the year to 31 December 2004

	£000	£000
Operating activities		
Cash received from customers		8,804
Interest and dividends received		276
Cash paid to suppliers		(3,642)
Cash paid to and on behalf of employees		(1,789)
Interest paid		(26)
Net cashflow from operations		3,423
Corporation tax paid		(777)
Investing activities		
Purchase of investments	(866)	
New fixed assets acquired	(1,437)	
Sale of fixed assets	75	
Net cashflow from investing activities		(2,228)
Financing activities		
New share capital	250	
Repayment on finance leases	(65)	
Dividends paid	(550)	
Net cashflow from financing activities		(365)
Net cash inflow		53

Specimen Co Ltd

Statement of Value Added for the Year to 31 December 2004

	£000	£000
Turnover		9,758
Bought-in materials and services		5.233
Value Added		4.525
Applied the following way:		
To pay employees' wages, pensions and other benefits		1,827
To pay providers of capital		
Interest on loans	26	
Dividends to shareholders	750	
		776
To pay government		
Corporation tax payable		961
To provide for maintenance and expansion of assets		
Depreciation	772	
Retained Profits	189	
		961
		4,525

About the Value Added Statement

Value added statements are not required by UK law or the SSAPs and are
rarely found in company annual reports. However, many people consider
them very useful indicators of a company's operational efficiency and it is
possible that they will become more widely reported in future.

'Value added' means the difference between the total value of output and the
total cost of materials and services used in production. The value added
statement shows how this added value is applied: to pay works and
managers, taxes and dividends, to maintain operating capacity (i.e.
depreciation) and the amount added to reserves.